HAWAII PONO
A SOCIAL HISTORY

LAWRENCE H. FUCHS

HAWAII PONO: A
SOCIAL HISTORY

HARCOURT, BRACE & WORLD, INC.   NEW YORK

To Natalie

CONTENTS

❂

PART THREE

THE DYNAMICS OF DEMOCRACY
1900–1960

One of the major purposes of this book is to celebrate Hawaii. *Hawaii Pono* signifies that Hawaii is worthy of praise, since *"pono"* means right or excellent. Hawaii is no longer an experiment in race relations or colonial administration. In the Islands, peoples of many races and cultures, largely only two or three generations from illiterate, peasant life, present the world's best example of dynamic social democracy.

This book originated in 1951 with research on the territorial policies of the United States government. Hawaii frequently came to my attention in subsequent research on ethnic and religious factors in American politics. In 1958, a senior grant in American governmental processes was awarded by the Social Science Research Council for the study of ethnic tensions and accommodation in Island politics. Early in the research, it became evident that neither contemporary ethnic tensions nor Island politics could be properly understood without probing into the political, economic, and social history of modern Hawaii. Because of the liberal terms of the S.S.R.C. grant and the co-operation of librarians, scholars, and other citizens of Hawaii, the scope of the study was therefore expanded.

While this volume results from the collaboration of many people and the researches of dozens of scholars, it is also a highly personal and subjective work. It is hoped that my observations on immigrant acculturation, political control, and social change will be of value to social scientists, and that this interpretation of the evolution of Hawaii will ring true to thousands of sensitive and perceptive Islanders. But it should be emphasized that this book is an *interpretation*—not a definitive history. It is not expected that others will perceive the essential and significant events in the evolution of Hawaii exactly as I do.

This volume is not a series of photographs, but, rather, a large mural, portraying the major actors and actresses of twentieth-century Hawaii. An attempt has been made to picture them as they saw themselves and each other. But, unavoidably, something of the painter has been put on the canvas too. If others say, as indeed they must, that here Fuchs has left out an important part of the picture or there he has overdrawn his characters, it is because no two individuals will perceive or emphasize historical events in the same way.

Personal as this book is, I have tried not to judge individuals or groups, but to understand them. Still, many readers may infer criticism from my words, because history, dealing with real people and events, like a painting, inevitably judges what it depicts. It troubles me to realize that some individuals may be hurt because words they spoke or things they did many years ago are related in these pages. But a man who vigorously opposed labor unions in the 1920's or who was a Communist in the 1930's should not be judged by the standards of the 1960's.

Understanding, not disparagement, is my aim. Admittedly, deep understanding often leads to love, and in trying to empathize with Hawaii's peoples by visiting and living with them in the plantation camps, villages, and cities, there developed an abiding love for them which I hope is revealed in *Hawaii Pono*.

Waltham, Massachusetts
May 1961

LAWRENCE H. FUCHS
Dean of Faculty
Brandeis University

abura-mushi: female "cockroach"

ahupuaas: a large land division

alii: Hawaiian chief

aloha: greeting, love

barrio: Philippine village

buraku: local group within the Japanese village

chori, chorinbo: the eta

furyoshonin: nisei poolhall bum

hanai: adopted

haole: foreigner; more especially, white man or Caucasian

hapa: part or half

hukilau: a net fishing party

hula: dance

ilis: division of ahupuaas, often run as plantations

imua: forward

issei: Japanese immigrant to the U.S., ineligible for citizenship

kahuna: a general name for a professional person under the ancient Hawaiian feudal system

kalaimoku: king's chief councillor

kamaaina: born in Hawaii or having lived there many years

kanaka: man, people in general

kapu: taboo, prohibited, keep out

kibei: American citizen of Japanese parents who was educated primarily in Japan

kokua: help

kuhina nui: Prime Minister

kuleanas: homesites

kumiai: groups in Hawaii organized for paternalistic and co-operative purposes by the Japanese immigrants

lanai: porch

luau: feast

luna: overseer or foreman

makaainana: commoner

malihini: newcomer

malo: loin cloth

mauka: toward the mountains

moku: a large parcel of land given by the king to a high chief

mura: Japanese village

mus: secret organizations

nana i ka ili: Hawaiian campaign slogan meaning "look for the skin"

nisei: American citizens of issei parents

on: obligation

pake: Hawaiian slang for Chinese

pauhana: *pau* = finished; *hana* = work; quitting time

pilikia: trouble

poi: Hawaiian staple made by pounding taro root and mixing with water

pono: righteous or excellent

punalua: the premissionary custom of sharing mates

samurai: military class in Japanese feudal system

sansei: American citizen of nisei parents

tao: common man

tapa: material made by beating bark of the mulberry tree and staining with dyes

taro: plant with starchy edible root

turnuhans: Filipino barrio associations, co-operatives

tutus: grandmothers

wahine: woman, wife

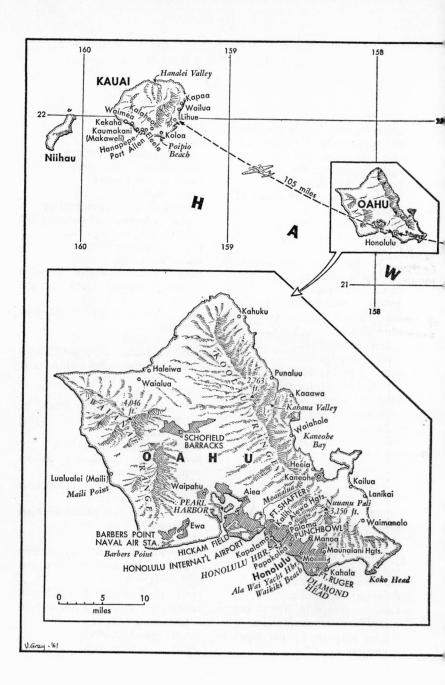

KAUAI

Hanalei Valley

Niihau

Waimea
Kalaheo
Kekaha
Kaumakani
(Makaweli)
Hanapepe
Port Allen
Eleele

Kapaa
Wailua
Lihue
Koloa
Poipio
Beach

105 miles

OAHU

Honolulu

H

A

W

OAHU

Kahuku

Haleiwa
Waialua

Punaluu

2,763
ft.

Kaaawa

Kahana Valley

4,046
ft.

SCHOFIELD
BARRACKS

Waiahole

Kaneohe
Bay

Lualualei (Maili)
Maili Point

Waipahu

Heeia
Kaneohe

Kailua

Aiea

Lanikai

PEARL
HARBOR

Moanalua

FT. SHAFTER
Nuuanu Pali
3,150 ft.

Kalihi
Alewa Hgts.

Ewa

Palama
PUNCHBOWL

Waimanalo

BARBERS POINT
NAVAL AIR STA.
Barbers Point

HICKAM FIELD

HONOLULU INTERNAT'L AIRPORT

Kapalama
HONOLULU HBR.
Papakolea

Manoa

Maunalani Hgts.

Honolulu
Ala Wai Yacht Hbr.
Waikiki Beach

Moiliili

FT. RUGER

Kahala
Koko Head

DIAMOND
HEAD

0   5   10
miles

V.Gray - '61

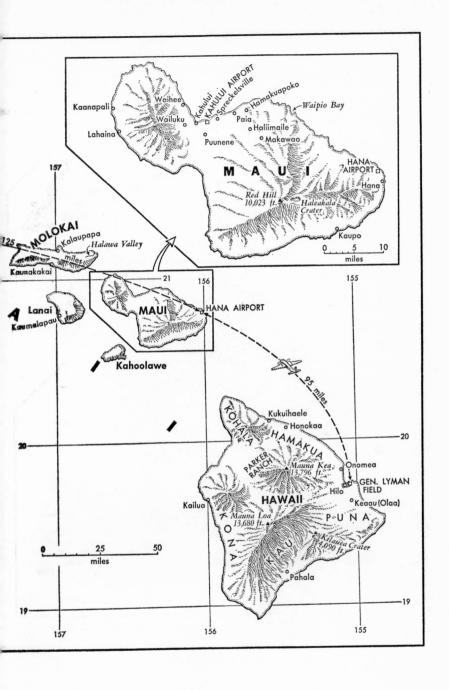

KAANAPALI
Waihee
Wailuku
Kahului
KAHULUI AIRPORT
Spreckelsville
Hamakuapoko
Waipio Bay
Lahaina
Paia
Haliimaile
Puunene
Makawao
HANA
AIRPORT
Hana
MAUI
Red Hill
10,023 ft.
Haleakala
Crater
Kaupo
0   5   10
miles

157
MOLOKAI
125
Kalaupapa
Halawa Valley
miles
Kaunakakai

Lanai
Kaumalapau

Kahoolawe

21   156
MAUI   HANA AIRPORT

155

95 miles

Kukuihaele
KOHALA
Honokaa
HAMAKUA
PARKER
RANCH
Mauna Kea
13,796 ft.
Onomea
20
GEN. LYMAN
FIELD
Hilo
Kailua
HAWAII
Keaau (Olaa)
Mauna Loa
13,680 ft.
PUNA
KONA
KAU
Kilauea Crater
4,090 ft.
0   25   50
miles
Pahala

157   156   155

20

19   19

A KINGDOM PASSES

The word *pilikia* (trouble) was on the lips of hundreds of Hawaiians on the evening of January 16, 1893, as they peeked from behind doors and around corners, watching American sailors arrogantly parade two light cannon through the virtually empty streets of Honolulu. By prearrangement with a small group of resident Americans, and with the full support of the American Minister to the Independent Kingdom of Hawaii, the visiting bluejackets were quartered in the vacant building known as Arion Hall, directly across the street from the government building and only a short distance from the palace.

Queen Liliuokalani protested the landing, but the American occupation of Hawaii was beyond her control. Early the next afternoon, the local revolutionaries seized the government building, demanded the Queen's abdication, and declared martial law. The United States government, through its Minister, gave immediate diplomatic recognition to the rebel group, which then proclaimed the abrogation of the monarchy, forced the resignation of the sorrowful but dignified Queen, and launched the American flag where the Hawaiian pennant had flown.

The rebel leaders believed they had wrested political power from an extravagant and autocratic native government. But to the overwhelming majority of Hawaiians, from the Queen to the commoner in the taro patch, a black cloud had descended over the Islands; their birthright had been stolen.

American control over the life of the Islands had been extensive for many years. In 1778, Hawaii had been discovered by the English explorer Captain James Cook, and after more than a thousand years of little change, the life of the Islands was altered radically within a few decades. Capitalism replaced feudalism, and oligarchy supplanted monarchy. As the influence of the *haoles*—Caucasians of North European origin, mostly American—continued to permeate Island life, demoralization and disease reduced the Hawaiian people from a vibrant 300,000 to little more than 40,000, and many of these were only partly Hawaiian.

Hawaii was probably the last of the Pacific Islands to be settled by Polynesians. Scholars guess that the time of the final migration from Tahiti was about A.D. 750. Powerful oarsmen navigated the Pacific, bringing to the eight major islands of the Hawaiian chain the culture of central and eastern Polynesia. Their outriggers slipped into the bays and inlets of Hawaii, where they saw on each of the four largest islands volcanic mountains jutting sharply toward the sky, deeply corrugated on the windward side and sloping gently to the leeward. Clouds probably hovered, as they nearly always do, over the tops of the mountains, and trade winds cooled the open places exposed to the subtropical sun.

Hawaiians of royal or chieftain rank were often huge, in some instances well over six feet tall and weighing more than 300 pounds; commoners were not so large. Most Hawaiians, apparently robust, healthy, and loving the outdoor life, reaped the harvests of the soil and sea. More than 2,000 miles from the nearest sizable body of land, on islands roughly the same total size as the State of New Jersey, they developed, within a larger feudalistic framework, their own systems of communal sex, family relationships, and property rights. They farmed, fished, prayed, and fought together in ignorance of the Western world.

Pilikia there was, but it was *pilikia* of their own making or, they believed, of the gods'. Wars, sanctioned by feudal chiefs and priests, periodically filled the gullies with blood. Tidal waves devoured whole villages; volcanic eruptions poured molten lava down the hillsides, covering once fertile soil with black rock in a destructive rush to the sea. And in the months of December, January, and February, when the trade winds stopped, oppressively hot and heavy rainfalls came from the south, damaging the taro, bananas, and breadfruit.

Despite the recklessness of man and nature, the population of Hawaii was relatively stable before the arrival of Cook. That intrepid and indefatigable explorer stumbled upon Hawaii while searching for a route to Britain via Alaska. Cook, welcomed as the long-departed god Lono, and his men were treated to repasts of pig, fish, and fruit by Hawaiian men and to sexual refreshment by native girls. In return, the Hawaiians were introduced to venereal disease, firearms, and the idea of trade for profit.

The social system that the haoles found in Hawaii was feudal but not primitive. Though the Hawaiians had neither a written language nor iron implements, they were not Stone Age men. Each major island had its king, and below him were three major classes: the *alii,* the highest-ranking chiefs, who were in turn divided into several grades; the *kahunas,* who, after years of apprenticeship and study, qualified as advisers to the *alii,* serving as professional prophets, seers, historians, teachers, priests, astronomers, medical practitioners, sorcerers, and skilled workers; and the *makaainana,* the commoners, who made up the bulk of the population. There were the slaves, too, marked from birth for a life of debasement. Hundreds of religious *kapus,* or taboos, were enforced by the priests to keep the commoners in their place. The complex religion, closely interwoven with occupational and recreational life in the Islands, revolved around four main gods and many lesser ones.

Hawaiian economic life depended on a fairly complex division of labor. Special skills were required for the manufacture of outrigger canoes and the preparation of *tapa,* the material made by beating the bark of the mulberry tree into a paper-like fabric which was stained with vegetable dye to be worn as clothing or used as bedcovers. Some men were bird catchers, collecting feathers for the chiefs' cloaks and helmets. An adz maker sharpened the stones used for building and fighting. Other workers thatched roofs. Each island began to specialize in a skill. Oahu was reputed to make excellent *tapa;* Maui, superior canoes and paddles. The Kona Coast of Hawaii, the big island to the southeast, supplied dried fish.

There was considerable diversity of agriculture in the Islands. The starchy root of the *taro* plant which was pounded and mixed with water to form the gelatinous Hawaiian staple *poi,* grew on the wettest slopes of the mountains; bananas were grown where there was less moisture.

Polynesian ingenuity appeared in the Hawaiian system of irrigation, used especially in the production of *taro.* The system was praised by the English explorer George Vancouver as surpassing anything of the kind he had ever seen. Yams, sugar cane, and breadfruit were commonly grown and eaten. The Hawaiians also ate a variety of fish, domestic goose, owl, and wild birds. For meat—though the commoners did not get much of it—the Islanders relied on small dogs and pigs.

Even Hawaiian science had made some progress. Astronomers could recognize more than 120 stars; the local botanists and geologists had named and classified forty-three types of trees and fifty-seven varieties of rock; and the medical *kahunas* used more than 300 herbs of known value.

The *kapus* gave the social system great stability, perpetuating the control of the kings, chiefs, and priests. But the family relationships, living conditions, and religious practices resulting from adherence to many *kapus* shocked early Western visitors. Chiefs might have four or more separate buildings on a house lot, while a dozen or more commoners lived in an unventilated hut with the pigs and dogs. The word of a chief could send hundreds of commoners to their slaughter, or the command of a priest could single out men and women for human sacrifice. Abortions and even infanticide were common. Incest between brothers and sisters of royal blood was encouraged. Sex was enjoyed without sin or shame. Constancy between mates was not governed by a *kapu*. Duty was owed to a kinship group larger than the immediate family unit, and husbands and wives could separate easily and without formality. The commoners shared sex as they shared water and produce. They worked and lived in close and friendly co-operation.

The religious, family, and property systems of feudal Hawaii and feudal Europe were different, but there were many parallels between the two. Military service under the Hawaiian kings was like the service owed by medieval knights to their lords, an obligation of the *alii* and not of the commoners, and all land was held by the chiefs on a condition of obedience and payment of taxes to their kings. Taxes depended entirely on the will of the monarchs, and payments were often made in pigs, *tapa,* dogs, fishlines, and nets. It is unlikely that the commoners were able to keep more than one third of their produce for themselves, because the *makaainana,* too, were expected to make presents to the chiefs.

The kings owned all the land and property and held power of life and death over their people. They subdivided land and gave it to many chiefs. The important chiefs held large estates, called *ahupuaas,* which usually extended from the shore to the mountains and were similar to the large estates of the nobility in England and on the Continent. These were carved into *ilis,* which were run by lesser chiefs, who served almost as plantation proprietors, cultivating the land with their own retainers or hiring it out as did the gentlemen farmers of Europe. These chiefs in turn provided small plots for the commoners to use, promising them a certain amount of protection in return for their labor. The small plot where the individual family grew its yams, *taro,* and sweet potatoes corresponded to a European peasant's holding.

In the years following Cook's discovery, warring kings, aided by haole weapons and advisers, fought for control of the Islands. The massive Kamehameha I subdued all claimants to the throne of the Big Island, Hawaii, his own island, and then sailed his legions to successful invasions of Maui, which controlled Kahoolawe (now uninhabited, but then farmed by Hawaiians), of Lanai, Molokai, and then Oahu, where he drove the warriors of the local king up the Nuuanu Valley and over the cliff. Insatiable, he headed for Kauai with a large force but returned exhausted and depleted, due, said Kamehameha, to a storm at sea; Kauaians insist that he was repulsed by the courage of their islanders, and even to this day, skulls are plucked from the "invasion" beaches to prove the point. Finally, in 1810, the King of Kauai was persuaded to place his lands on Kauai and Niihau under Kamehameha.

Through skillful use of patronage and force, Kamehameha cemented his power. He picked a chief counselor, the *kalaimoku,* to help him govern, and appointed governors for the several islands. He gave patronage in the form of land to the major chiefs, usually members of his family, his followers, or descendants of the original group that had pledged their allegiance to him. These huge sections of land, called *mokus,* were then divided into the customary *ahupuaas.*

Despite the unification of the Islands, the period of Kamehameha's rule was, for the Hawaiian people, one of disintegration, owing to decimation from war, the infiltration of Western commercial practices, the avarice of the chiefs and priests, the spread of haole diseases, and, perhaps most important, the breakdown of the Hawaiian religion. When the first boatload of New England Congregationalist missionaries arrived in 1820, only one year after the death of the Islands' first great king, they found a Hawaii quite different from the idyl that Cook had stumbled upon forty-two years earlier.

. . .

On the windward coast of Oahu, in the village of Punaluu, visitors to Hawaii in the 1950's sometimes met a strikingly handsome man, about five feet eleven, whose bronzed and muscular figure was clothed about his loins with the traditional Hawaiian *malo,* this one made of red cloth. David Kaapuu, except for his coconut hat and big cigar, was the prototype of the Hawaiian aborigine described in early literature. Vigorous, alert, industrious, full of humor, and hospitable, this philosopher prince of Punaluu brought to life images of the strong men who swam nearly naked to greet the earliest whalers and trading vessels. He was trying desperately to be faithful to the old ways and said, more with sorrow than bitterness, that he had been destroyed even before he was born.

Although the chiefs were generally bigger and healthier than the commoners, chroniclers from 1778 to 1810 were unanimous in stressing the energy and productivity of the Hawaiian villagers. Cook and Vancouver emphasized the strength, intelligence, and cleanliness of the Hawaiian people who farmed, fished, and enjoyed athletic games and dances. But by the 1820's and '30's, commentators invariably complained of the laziness of the Hawaiians, their apathy and bad health. By the time of the arrival of the missionaries, the demoralization of the natives and the destruction of their culture was well under way.

There are today residual pockets of Hawaiiana on Niihau, in the Halowa Valley on Molokai, at Hana and Kaupo on East Maui, and in the Kau and Kona sections of the Big Island, where Hawaiians speak menacingly of *kapus* and the vengeance of ghostly priests who still punish their violators. Even in Honolulu there are Hawaiians who knowingly whisper of ghosts who stalk *their* land, now wrongfully occupied by others. But many Hawaiians, for reasons not entirely clear, stopped believing in the *kapus* toward the end of Kamehameha's reign. Perhaps some of the *kapus* had been broken by the King's favorite chieftains and warriors during the grand conquest. Many *kapus* were undoubtedly violated by hundreds of sailors, merchants, and traders. Hawaiians, finding the priests unable to punish the visitors, probably began to doubt the power of the religious *kahunas.* Women, including royalty, began to break the rules. By 1910, the chiefs themselves, imitating the foreigners, were violating the *kapus.* The few hundred white residents in the Islands had impressed on the educated leaders and rulers of Hawaii the ineffectiveness of the taboos, and, observing the superiority of haole cannon over Hawaiian clubs, of haole ships over native canoes, the Hawaiian *alii* began to doubt the power of their ancient gods.

Kamehameha, recognizing the weakness of his heir presumptive, Liholiho, designated one of his wives, the huge Kaahumanu, as prime minister, or *kuhina-nui*. She was a powerful woman who had undoubtedly already ignored some of the *kapus* imposed on her sex. Soon after her husband's death, she ate at the same table with the new King, publicly breaking another *kapu*. Kaahumanu, who was later converted to Christianity, persuaded Liholiho to abandon the *kapus* officially in 1819, just before the first missionaries were to embark from Massachusetts.

The rules of conduct that the Reverend Hiram Bingham and his Congregational brothers and sisters came to promote in Hawaii could hardly have been more different from the mores they replaced. The Hawaiians believed life was to be lived here and now; the men from colder climes insisted that life on earth was merely preparation for everlasting life beyond. Even in this life, the Hawaiian was not usually trying to prove his virtue, or improve his status; to the New England missionaries, life was a continuous struggle for moral and material self-improvement to receive God's grace. To the Hawaiian, the sharing of food, hut, and woman came naturally; the New Englanders maintained a stern sense of privacy concerning property and person. Sex to the Polynesians was pure joy; to these haoles, a grim and burdensome necessity. Children born in or out of wedlock received the affection of the Hawaiians; to Bingham and his friends, bastards were conceived in sin.

The process of decay, however, preceded the arrival of the churchmen. The *kapus* had been abolished, the idols destroyed, and the authority of the priests was in question. Christianity rushed in to fill the void. The missionaries proclaimed the new religion without major opposition. Their success was assured by the strong support of Kaahumanu, who gradually took over control from Liholiho.

The one crucial element of the Hawaiian social system that the missionaries did not immediately challenge was the authority of the regent, the king, and the high chiefs. Hawaiian rulers felt secure in their control of the government and leaned increasingly on the haoles, both missionaries and merchants. At least eleven white men were in the service of Kamehameha I, two of them as key advisers, and one as governor of the island of Hawaii. Liholiho also grew dependent on the haoles, using them as carpenters, bricklayers, and as skilled workers needed to build over thirty sloops and schooners. These men were often given tracts of land and treated as chiefs. Kamehameha III, who ruled for twenty-five years beginning in 1825, continued to encourage haoles in trade and government service with huge gifts of land and other perquisites. He increasingly relied on the missionaries for advice, promoting their religion, language, and educational methods.

The new religion of Hawaii was suitable for the new economics of the Islands. The smaller, ostensibly monogamous family relationship, eliminating confusion of progeny, facilitated the accumulation of property. The enforcement of haole codes against stealing protected it.

Although Christianity reinforced and promoted the accumulation of property, the missionaries were motivated by spiritual goals. Not so the shipwrecked sailors, European and American merchants and shrewd Yankee traders who came, and often stayed, for lust and profit. The spread of the profit motive was a chief cause of the destruction of the Hawaiian. During the first contact on Kauai, the Englishmen were given between sixty and eighty pigs, a few fowl, potatoes, and taro by the gleeful and jabbering natives, who received, in exchange, some nails and a few pieces of iron. What was an exchange of gifts to the Hawaiians was a shrewd and profitable trade to the sailors. To cheat the Hawaiians was hardly a sin, since they were considered savages, as Cook's landing parties on the Big Island clearly indicated by removing the wooden fences around the temples for firewood. Later, off the Kona Coast, the Hawaiians made away with a small English boat. This seemed pure thievery to Cook, and he attempted to get the boat back by landing with a small armed force in a vain effort to capture the high chief who had been his friend. His men shot into a crowd of natives, and Cook was bludgeoned to death with clubs. His second-in-command retaliated with cannon, setting a village on fire and killing many Hawaiians.

The hospitality of the Islanders to haole visitors remained fundamentally unweakened. European and American traders soon found Hawaii a place for happy refreshment, an oasis on long voyages, where they took on pork, fresh vegetables, firewood, and water, and Hawaiian men, as crew for the China trade. The chiefs rushed to trade with the haoles for fancy clothes, ornaments, and weapons. In their rapacity they invented new kinds of taxes to impose on the commoners, claimed the rights to everything on the soil, took fishing grounds and

fruit trees, and often worked the commoners to death by driving them
into the wet upland regions to cut sandalwood for shipment to Canton,
where the odorous, slow-burning wood was in heavy demand.

The lot of the commoner became increasingly wretched and insecure.
But even the *makaainanas* learned to become shrewd traders, and
during the peak of the sandalwood period, commoners were caught
cheating the sailing vessels by supplying sea water where fresh water
was promised. The women sold themselves for a yard of cloth or
a white shirt where formerly they gave their bodies freely. Even gods
and graven images were sold for a few rusty nails.

When the sandalwood was exhausted, the whalers came in the
1830's and '40's, breaking down the native culture still further.
Diminishing labor and agricultural resources went into producing
commodities for sale to the visitors, taking from produce ordinarily
consumed by the natives; and the tastes of the chiefs for foreign goods
resulted in heavier taxes. Hundreds of Hawaiian boys went sailing with
the big ships and were alienated from ancient ways. Derelict haole
seamen roamed the streets of Honolulu, Lahaina, and other ports,
encouraging a swift trade in alcohol and sex. By the end of the third
decade of the nineteenth century, the old social ties and group self-
respect were virtually demolished. The *kapus* were gone, and the
authority of the chiefs was threatened as the invading haoles gained in
power and prestige.

On Punchbowl Street in Honolulu, at the site of the first religious
meeting held by the Protestant Boston missionaries to Hawaii on April
25, 1820, there stands Kawaiahao, the first organized church in the
Islands. On many midweek afternoons in the meeting rooms near this
massive coral-stone Congregational church, dozens of Hawaiian *tutus*
(grandmothers) meet for special services or social activities. Here sit
the wives and daughters of former mayors and territorial legislators,
the granddaughters and great-granddaughters of royalty. Paradoxically,
most of the *grandes dames* of Kawaiahao devotedly follow the teachings
of the early missionaries while bitterly rejecting the teachers. They
gossip to each other rapidly in Hawaiian about recipes, scandals, the
"good old days," and invariably about those terrible "sugar-missionaries" who stole the land and despoiled the Hawaiian people. Many
haole leaders of the nearby mission society would be shocked to hear
from the lips of these wrinkled but stately Hawaiians the resentment

they bear against the missionaries. When haole and Hawaiian Congregationalist leaders meet, there are the usual pleasantries and reminiscences, and, on the part of the Caucasians, the good feeling that comes from what they perceive as their tradition of benefaction and friendship toward the Hawaiian people. Were the truth known, self-satisfaction would often give way to incredulity.

So thickly veiled is the hostility which some older Hawaiians feel toward the missionaries, that missionary descendants and their supporters rarely consider it necessary to defend their record to the Hawaiians, unaware that many Hawaiians pounce on every bit of information and misinformation that reveals the alleged greed and duplicity of the "sugar-missionaries."

The Cousins Society, descendants of the missionaries and the pillars of the Central Union Church, the elite Congregational church of Hawaii, are proud of the missionary record. Missionaries set up the first printing press west of the Rockies, developed the Hawaiian alphabet, established schools throughout the Islands, printed textbooks, translated the Bible into Hawaiian, and promoted constitutional government under the Kingdom. By 1832, only twelve years after their arrival, 53,000 pupils were studying under their supervision; by 1846, 80 per cent of the people could read. Missionaries brought Christianity to the Islands on a mass-production basis, the peak years of 1839–41 resulting in the admission of more than 20,000 Hawaiians to the church. In Hilo, the windward coastal city on the Big Island, the Reverend Titus Coan admitted 5,244 new members in one year alone, sprinkling Hawaiians with a whisk broom which had been dipped in a basin of water. Today, the Congregationalists constitute the largest Protestant denomination in the Islands, with more than 100 churches, of which more than sixty are Hawaiian with Hawaiian pastors.

The missionary record is obviously complex. The pollyanna view that ascribes only generous motives to the New England churchmen and their immediate descendants is not the whole truth. However, the conspiratorial interpretation—as illustrated in a prolix manuscript written by a staunch follower of Queen Liliuokalani which denies that the missionaries had a single decent impulse—is patently incorrect.

The missionaries did have a tremendous impact, and by speeding the process of social change, they contributed to the psychological demoralization of the Hawaiians. The Hawaiian language, dance, and art were degraded. The land, property, political, and religious systems

were under constant attack. But other factors contributed more powerfully to the decline of the Hawaiians. Between Cook's visit and the
arrival of the first missionary band from New England, disease, war,
and famine had taken nearly half the population. Syphilis and gonor-
rhea, colds and pneumonia added to the rising tide of disease and death,
and what was probably a cholera epidemic around 1805 touched almost every family. Even without the missionaries, it is unthinkable
that Hawaiian culture and people could have withstood the sudden
impact of Western civilization. Indeed, the missionaries often helped
arrest some of the decay. Until the arrival of nine missionary doctors
forty-two years after Cook's discovery, the natives were without
protection against the new diseases. The Western doctors commented
on the huge number of deaths in infancy and the amazing vulnerability
of the natives to such simple ailments as diarrhea, teething, and colds.
Powerful-looking, robust Hawaiians would succumb as easily to measles
as to cholera. When an epidemic of measles struck in the fall of 1848,
hundreds—perhaps thousands—burning with fever, are supposed to
have rushed to the sea to die. Smallpox came later, in 1853, ravaging
the population and killing more than 10,000 in three years.

Nearly every commentator on Hawaii during the mid-nineteenth
century noted widespread drunkenness and other forms of psychological
retreat. For many, drink helped relieve the trauma of social change.
In extreme cases—and there appear to have been a great many—
Hawaiians lost the will to live. Natives were known to make an appointment with death, saying that they would die on Thursday, and on
Thursday they died. Disease undermined the pride of the Hawaiians,
and this loss of pride further weakened their psychological resistance
to virulent viruses and bacteria.

In the last half of the nineteenth century, smallpox hit four more
times, and cholera struck again in 1895. The catalogue of miserable
diseases formerly unknown to the Hawaiian now included such childhood ailments as mumps, influenza, and whooping cough, as well as
such horrors as bubonic plague. From a relatively stable prehaole population of about 300,000 in 1778, the natives were reduced to 57,000 by
1866. It would be an overstatement to argue, as a Yale anthropologist
did in 1889, that the Hawaiians died because they lacked the will to live,
but it is clear that within thirty years after Cook's arrival, indifference
and apathy had overtaken the Hawaiian people, to be replaced not
many years later by overwhelming despair.

One factor in the growing despondency of the Hawaiians was the ascending power of the haoles. Only about one fourth of the men who held cabinet power under the monarchy had any Hawaiian blood. From Kamehameha I's appointment of the haole sailor John Young as governor of the Big Island to the nomination of the Reverend William Richards and, later, Dr. Gerrit P. Judd, both missionaries, as personal advisers to the King, the government came increasingly into the hands of Caucasians. The haoles' goal, in addition to promoting Western civilization, was to secure their own position in the Islands, which first meant limiting the arbitrary power of the king. Their efforts bore fruit in 1839 when Kamehameha III promulgated a declaration of rights and laws protecting religious freedom, and again one year later with the establishment of a constitutional monarchy with a hereditary House of Nobles and an elective House of Commons. The newly created office of prime minister—really an extension of the old office of *kuhina-nui,* which had been filled with such effectiveness by Queen Kaahumanu until her death in 1832—became the chief center of haole power. Judd, who came to Hawaii in 1828 as a medical missionary, held that post between 1842 and 1854, presiding over sweeping haole reforms, including an American trade treaty in 1842 and the Great Mahele in 1848.

Probably no single event so drastically changed the social system of Hawaii as the Great Mahele, resulting from the decision of Kamehameha III to permit land to be purchased by private persons. Actually, the Great Mahele was the culmination of a series of changes in land tenure which dated from the decision of Kamehameha I to allow the heirs of lesser chiefs to inherit land instead of having land go to the head chief when one of the lower chiefs died. Europeans and Americans continued to ask for land on which to build warehouses, stores, and homes. Many land grants were made by the kings in return for services, and once in possession, haoles treated the soil they held as they would have back home—leasing, buying, selling, and accepting it in payment of debts.

Kamehameha III originally upheld the ancient theory that all land belonged ultimately to the King. Between 1836 and 1839, however, the Hawaiian government was forced to sign a number of treaties with foreign nations which in some cases stipulated the special land rights of foreigners living in Hawaii. Then in 1841, the King issued a proclamation making it possible for foreigners to obtain leases for

lands on which they were living but for which they had no written
title. This proclamation, still based on the assumption that all the soil
belonged to the King, acknowledged merely that Kamehameha III
did not have the right to dispossess foreigners at his pleasure. But
the plan failed because foreigners wanted fee-simple titles and not
leases that might ultimately be canceled. The haoles pressed for more
and more land, evoking protests in Hawaiian newspapers from natives
who claimed that the white men signed an oath of allegiance to the
King only to trick him into yielding coveted real estate. In 1845, Dr.
Judd proposed to the legislature that a commission be set up to issue
awards to all those holding valid land claims. He wanted a law permitting the sale of land to Hawaiian subjects, including haoles. The
new legislature went even further, passing legislation permitting the
leasing of lands to subjects and aliens for periods up to fifty years. A
land commission was constituted to confirm the validity of land-use
claims. And in 1846, the government offered land for sale at a dollar
an acre in the Manoa Valley of Oahu and the Makawao district on
Maui. But the haoles realized that the land system could not be changed
without clearing the titles of kings and chiefs, and a special committee
was set up to perform this task. Completing their work in March 1848,
the committee listed the lands to be retained by the King and those to
be kept by the chiefs, each giving up their claim to the other's land.
Complicated divisions, which plague land lawyers to this day,
ensued. Many chiefs failed to present their claims to the land commission within the fixed period of time, thereby forfeiting their rights
until laws were passed to permit their heirs to secure title to the land
ascribed to them by the Mahele committee. On March 8, 1848, the
King divided his own land into two parts, one part, called crown land,
to be his own private property, and the other larger part designated
as government land, to be controlled by the legislature and its agents.
In December, four years after the legislature had approved the original
plan for land settlement, the haole Chief Justice, William Lee, presented a program to permit commoners to claim lands that their ancestors had cultivated throughout the centuries. Finally an act of
July 1850 permitted aliens to purchase land in fee simple.

The feudal land system was abolished, but the concentration of
land ownership continued. Approximately 250 chiefs became fee-
simple owners of more than one third of the land. Another slice,
again more than one third, went to the government, and nearly one third

was kept as crown land by the King. Of 4,000,000 acres, less than 30,000 went to the common people of Hawaii. By 1886, two thirds of the government land sold had gone to the haoles, and much of the land that the chiefs and commoners were awarded had come into haole hands, too. Even the royal lands began to slip away from the crown through leases and sale to private corporations.

The commercial production of sugar accelerated the haole quest for private land. With private ownership now possible, capital could be invested with security, and the road was clear for the rise of the sugar industry. The haoles did not find it difficult to obtain land from the natives, both *makaainana* and *alii*. Chief Justice Lee told the Hawaiians that they could secure their lands and work on them or sit still and die, but the idea of private property was alien to the commoners, and to many of them land reform meant the hoarding of land by foreigners for private gain.

In feudal days, the Hawaiian was free to move about on the land except during periods of *kapu* or on certain lands that were permanently forbidden to him. Land was to be used, not owned. By 1936, only a little more than 6 per cent of the original *kuleana* lands—some 28,000 acres of house and garden plots given by the Land Commission to 11,-000 commoners—were in the possession of Hawaiians or part-Hawaiians. Few Hawaiians had any idea of the value of property, and Hawaiians of today lament the one-sided "deals" which they assume were put over on their ancestors. Hawaiian stories concerning land deals have reached legendary proportions. A Hawaiian schoolteacher speaks of her grandmother selling half of what is now the Waialae Golf Course for a jug of wine. In the beautiful Kahana Valley, disgruntled Hawaiians retell the story of the deception of a haole woman who loaned money to natives to attend a Mormon convention in Utah in return for extensive verdant property. Others remember that their families gave away half of Niihau under the influence of rum and haole duplicity. Trickery there undoubtedly was, but most of the commoners lost their land because they valued other things more. Gradually, the chiefs and their families sold their lands, too. Beset by bad management, debts, and mortgages, the native owners gradually saw their land gravitate into the control of one of the large land estates managed by haoles.

After the Mahele, foreigners eagerly purchased government lands at moderate prices. Even some of the missionaries found land speculation compatible with spreading the Gospel. One bought and sold forty-seven parcels in his lifetime, and another engaged in thirty land transactions. The ten who did the most land business averaged twenty-two parcels. By 1852, sixteen of the forty-six members of the Congregational mission possessed land titles, averaging 493 acres per man, some of which had come as gifts from chiefs or the King.

The second generation of missionary families was even more active in land speculation. The Reverend William C. Shipman, who died in 1861, bought and sold a number of parcels, but his son—much more the businessman than the missionary—acquired cheaply huge holdings from the trustees of the estate of King Lunalilo, who died in 1874. Despite the provision in Lunalilo's will that the income from his vast lands and estate be used to found and support a home for aged Hawaiians, 2,000 acres of his land were sold cheaply after being appraised at no more than what one small residential lot would bring today. The younger Shipman bought adjacent lands, and by the time of Hawaii's annexation to the United States in 1898, owned the land as the Olaa Sugar Plantation on the Big Island.

Two major fears dominated the thinking of American haoles during the 1830's and '40's. The first was the fear of irresponsible native government which would fail to protect private property and the other privileges of foreigners. That concern was substantially alleviated by the constitution of 1840 and the Great Mahele.

Americans were also afraid of the growing influence of the French and British governments, who were constantly intriguing to gain more than a foothold in the Islands. Two English ships visited Hawaii in 1836, and under threat of fire, Kamehameha III signed a treaty ceding the Islands to Great Britain. Fortunately for the Americans, London repudiated the cession. French ships came in 1839 and 1842, forcing an unfavorable treaty on the Kingdom during the first visit. In Honolulu, Americans close to the King urged him to seek international recognition of Hawaiian independence to forestall further intimidation. In Washington, Secretary of State Daniel Webster agreed to sign a treaty recognizing the Kingdom and to send a consul to Honolulu to represent the United States. At the same time, President John Tyler pronounced the American claim to a paramount interest in Hawaii, and proclaimed that the United States would not permit any other nation to seek undue control over the Kingdom or any exclusive rights in commercial matters. These views, when presented in London and Paris, were received as an extension to the Hawaiian Islands of the Monroe Doctrine. Despite this warning, the French naval commander for the Pacific returned in August 1849, landed troops, and occupied public buildings for five days. Washington again repeated the Tyler Doctrine, insisting that it would not permit interference with the sovereignty of Hawaii; it feared that Great Britain might abrogate its agreement with France not to interfere with the independence of the Kingdom. The French government, however, repudiated its admiral, as the British had done theirs thirteen years earlier, both nations slowly realizing that the only practical alternatives for Hawaii were independence or American control. Americans in the Islands, with increased influence in the government, persuaded the Hawaiian legislature to grant emergency powers to the King to conclude the cession of Hawaii to the United States should the French persist in arbitrary demands. Terms of annexation were negotiated, but conversations on the subject were terminated with the death of Kamehameha III in 1854. His successor was opposed to annexation, and the idea was temporarily abandoned. Nevertheless, American interests in Hawaii were clearly in the ascendant. The British, who had constituted the dominant foreign influence prior to 1830, and the French, who had been moving extensively throughout the South Pacific, now assumed subordinate roles in Honolulu.

The British and French Foreign Offices watched with dismay the fast-growing commercial ties between Hawaii and the United States, but there appeared to be nothing they could do. The Reverend Richard Armstrong observed that the mercantile business of the town was almost entirely in the hands of Americans; between 1847 and 1850, the number of retail stores in Honolulu grew from thirty-two to seventy-five. Armstrong's mission colleague and financial agent of the Board of Missions, S. M. Castle, helped establish the mercantile house of Castle & Cooke, destined to become one of the most influential American concerns in the Islands. In 1863, the American Minister in Honolulu wrote the State Department that not less than four fifths of Hawaii's foreign commerce was American. The whaling industry, primarily an American business, had boomed soon after the signing of the 1842 treaty, and four years later, nearly 600 whaling ships a year were reported in Hawaiian ports. For every European vessel, there were ten American ships, a ratio that was to continue during the peak of whale fishing over the next twelve years.

Whaling collapsed after the Civil War, but a new industry emerged to bring wealth to the haoles of the Kingdom and promote closer connections with the mainland. Although sugar cane grew wild in Hawaii long before the haoles came, no native had dreamed of shipping the sweet brown crystals to the tables of New York, Chicago, and San Francisco. Pressure for the Great Mahele now came from sugar planters as much as from any other group; they wished security on border rights and land ownership, some dimly perceiving markets on the mainland once capital could safely be invested in sugar lands. Between 1837 and 1847, sugar production increased more than 100 per cent. By 1860, after the Great Mahele and the passage of the Masters' and Servants' Act (1850), which established a Hawaiian Board of Immigration to import laborers to work on the plantations, more than 3,000,000 pounds of sugar were produced annually in Hawaii. From then until annexation, when nearly two thirds of the workers of Hawaii labored on sugar plantations, sugar was king in the Islands. Other crops were grown in Hawaii, even for export; during the California Gold Rush, potatoes, onions, pumpkins, oranges, molasses, and coffee were shipped to the West Coast. A flour mill was completed in 1855, and a small volume of wheat was exported for several years. The production of rice expanded steadily until 1862, a big year for sugar. Still, sugar had unusual advantages over these other crops. The only mainland competition came from certain sections of the American South, for sugar is a plantation crop, and cannot easily be developed where the small independent freehold system prevails. In Hawaii, vast tracts could be leased from government lands or purchased from the chiefs, while labor, much cheaper and more docile than on the mainland, reduced labor costs to balance the increased cost of transportation across the ocean.

Only one serious obstacle blocked the ambitions of Island planters for fabulous mainland markets—the American tariff on sugar. Between 1848 and 1876, when a reciprocity treaty between the Kingdom and the United States was signed, Island planters tried to persuade Washington to remove the tariff on sugar. Opposition from Louisiana sugar planters tabled one treaty in the Senate in 1857. Ten years later, the American Minister to Honolulu negotiated another reciprocity treaty, advising Washington that it would help in the "quiet absorption" of the Islands into the United States. As they had in the past, Hawaiian planters received help from politicians in California, the major market for Island sugar. But reciprocity was again defeated in the Senate, despite President Andrew Johnson's argument that the Islands must not be allowed to pass under foreign control. Southern senators were joined by others who feared that the reciprocity principle, giving special privileges to Hawaii, would endanger other treaties which included the so-called "most-favored-nation clause."

In Hawaii, royalists were afraid that the failure of reciprocity might lead to local demands for American annexation. An American secret agent sent to the Islands by Secretary of State William H. Seward reported growing annexation sentiment, writing that all that was needed for revolution was assurance from the United States that it would back annexation. In February 1873, the Honolulu newspaper the *Pacific Commercial Advertiser* commented, "There is unquestionably a large party, respectable in point of wealth and position, that is now openly and earnestly advocating . . . the annexation of these islands to the United States of America." Hawaiian planters were thirsting for an open American market, and American indifference made them reckless. They sent a drumfire of rumors to friends on the mainland alleging growing British influence in the Islands and had them circulate a report in Washington concerning an alleged movement to import Hindus as plantation labor under British supervision. There was also talk of selling Hawaiian sugar in the free-trade ports of Australia.

To tempt Washington, the proannexation haoles suggested that the Kingdom lease Pearl Harbor to the United States for future development as a naval base, in exchange for reciprocity. Native mass meetings protested the Pearl Harbor idea, and anti-American sentiment among Hawaiians soared. With the death of King Lunalilo (the sixth Hawaiian king after five Kamehamehas), American haoles swung their influence behind High Chief Kalakaua and against Queen Emma, wife of Kamehameha IV and warm supporter of closer ties with Britain. The election of Kalakaua as king by the legislature resulted in popular demonstrations for Emma. Local haoles pointedly warned Washington again against the rise of English influence. In exchange for American support, Kalakaua, who had previously shown pronounced anti-American tendencies, probably promised to back reciprocity. Popular resentment against him was so high that soon after the election he was forced to ask for 150 American marines to protect his crown. The Americans were in a position to extract at least one favor in return and presented the King with a petition for reciprocity signed by virtually every planter and important merchant in Hawaii. Haole advisers watched approvingly from Honolulu while Kalakaua visited the United States to throw his ample bulk and jolly nature behind the reciprocity drive.

The newly proposed treaty was exceedingly favorable to the United States. The list of Hawaiian products to be admitted to the United States free was considerably narrowed (after all, sugar was the important thing), and the American list included just about everything exported by the United States. More important, the treaty forbade the Hawaiian government to give any territorial, commercial, or political preferences to any other power. Most significant in the long run was the provision transferring Pearl Habor to the United States Navy. But even with these favorable terms, the treaty had rough going in Congress; some West Coast refiners opposed reciprocity because they feared the competition of unrefined high-grade Hawaiian sugar. Foreign policy requirements won out, however. Although Hawaii was already shipping 24,000,000 pounds of sugar each year to the United States, as compared with only a little more than 1,000,000 pounds to all other nations combined, the fear of incipient foreign domination of the Islands was stressed in congressional debates and in the favorable majority report of the House Ways and Means Committee. What if the British colonies were to pull off a similar agreement and wean Hawaii away from America, argued the mainland allies of reciprocity.

The effects of reciprocity were tremendous. The volume of sugar exported to the United States increased sharply in the 1880's. Sugar reached out everywhere, surging into rice lands, coffee lands, *taro* patches, and small Hawaiian *kuleanas*. In 1875, there were twenty plantations; five years later there were sixty-three. Closing his books in 1876, the head of C. Brewer & Company, Ltd., one of the major growing sugar agencies, wrote, "So ends the year 1876, praise God." Praise God, indeed! Praise Kalakaua. Praise the British bogeyman. Praise Yankee inventiveness and drive.

The two most significant results of the expansion of the sugar industry were the increasing political and financial influence of a small number of haoles and the importation of thousands of Oriental peasants to work on the plantations. In some ways, life in Hawaii soon resembled that of the post-Civil War South, with a small and powerful oligarchy in control of economic and social perquisites, and large masses of dark-skinned laborers whose direct contact with Caucasians was limited to working under haole overseers in the field.

At the top of this power structure were the men who ran the great sugar agencies. Earlier, the plantations had been in sharp competition with each other, functioning independently in their financial and marketing operations. As late as 1860, the Hawaiian planters usually arranged for the transportation and sale of their sugar individually through ship captains and corresponded directly with suppliers for the purchase of tools and equipment. This system was obviously inefficient. Plantation managers were busy with administrative and technical problems and not necessarily expert in floating loans, buying supplies, keeping books, marketing produce, or recruiting labor. The agency system, later consisting of the so-called "Big Five" factors, was the answer. General merchants in Honolulu were looking for invest-ments after the decline of the whaling industry, and in 1863, C. Brewer & Co., Ltd. became agents for three sugar plantations, assum-ing financial, purchasing, and marketing responsibilities. Its example was followed by firms known today as Castle & Cook Ltd., American Factors Ltd., Alexander & Baldwin, Ltd., and Theo. H. Davies & Com-pany Ltd. Only one of the Big Five did not begin as a Honolulu store; Alexander & Baldwin started as a plantation-development corporation on Maui and subsequently branched out into mercantile enterprises.

During the expansion of the late 1870's, badly managed plantations faced with bankruptcy were forced to turn stock over to the factors in exchange for loans. The agencies advanced their activities and profits, in many cases taking over the actual management and ownership of the plantations. By 1867, Castle & Cooke was serving as an agent for four sugar companies, one of which had been founded on the Big Island in 1863. Thirty years after annexation, the Big Five handled almost 90 per cent of the sugar tonnage shipped from Hawaii.

The second generation of missionaries, including the Alexanders, Baldwins, Cookes, Hitchcocks, Rices, and Wilcoxes, constituted an inner elite within the oligarchy, but there was room for mainland haoles, too, and opportunities existed for the enterprising *malihini* (new-comer) who was sufficiently good-looking and intelligent to marry into a missionary family. As a notable example, Joseph Ballard Atherton, a bookkeeper for Castle & Cooke, was taken into the firm in 1865, after becoming Cooke's son-in-law. The *malihinis* did not have to be American to prosper; to be haole was enough.

Coming from Liverpool, England, for example, a Welshman named Theophilus Harris Davies took over a bankrupt merchandising house in 1867 to satisfy its creditors. When the sugar boom hit Hawaii, Davies was ready to finance or assist with the organization of twenty-two plantations on Hawaii, Maui, and Kauai. As the sugar economy grew, it brought forth a variety of enterprises to service it. There was a constant need to repair the early milling machinery, which was then manufactured and shipped from Boston. Davies helped finance the incorporation of the Honolulu Iron Works Company in 1875 and became its first president. The Iron Works soon began the actual manufacture in Hawaii of mills and other machinery needed by the plantations. The haole manager, Alexander Young, branched off into businesses of his own, becoming a wealthy and powerful man in a short time.

There was a need for construction, too. A youthful cabinetmaker, Christopher Lewers, who had come to Honolulu from Dublin in 1850 to seek a brother missing in the Pacific, stayed to open a lumber yard on Fort Street, founding the company which was taken over by a new partnership immediately following the Reciprocity Treaty and is known today as Lewers & Cooke, Ltd., Hawaii's largest construction firm. The key figures were a haole bookkeeper named Joshua G. Dickson (a cousin of Lewers) and Charles Montague Cooke, who realized that the expansion of sugar would result in heavy demands for construction.

The growth of sugar stimulated banking and transportation as well as construction. Hawaii's most important banker, Charles Reed Bishop, a young man on his way to Oregon to seek his fortune in 1846, stopped at Honolulu after rounding Cape Horn. He was captivated by the magic of the Islands and remained to work in the finance department of the Kingdom, to invest in sugar, and to become Collector of Customs. In 1850, he married the beautiful Hawaiian princess Bernice Pauahi Paki, descendant of Kamehameha and the largest landholder in Hawaii. He joined another haole to open Hawaii's first bank eight years later, concentrating at first on financing the whale-oil and whale-bone trade. After reciprocity, Bishop's banking business grew at a rapid rate, catering to the needs of the sugar industry.

Another Horatio Alger story centers around the success of a stranded sailor named Benjamin Dillingham. Stopping in Honolulu in 1865, he was thrown from a horse; while he recovered in the Seamen's Hospital from a broken leg, his ship sailed. He was a handsome and intelligent mariner, and Emma Louise Smith, a daughter of a missionary, came to read to him. He married her in 1869 and went into business with Alfred Castle's help. With an enterprising haole named James Campbell and several other men, he began to acquire rural lands. Recognizing that land development depended upon fast, cheap transportation, he obtained from King Kalakaua an exclusive franchise to build and operate a railroad. A dynamic entrepreneur, he pushed the establishment of sugar plantations in the areas on Oahu opened by the railroad, built a shipping terminal, filled in swamps, and built wharves and warehouses for shipping sugar and handling coal and general cargo.

Also enterprising was Captain William Matson, who sailed the *Emma Claudina* into Hilo Bay in May 1882, to begin the Matson Navigation Company. Matson bet on steam over sail, and with the removal of the tariff through reciprocity, he put one ship after another on the Hawaii-mainland run, carrying tropical fruits and, mainly, sugar. Financed and controlled by West Coast mainland interests as well as by leading haole firms in Honolulu, Matson has been carrying Island sugar to the mainland ever since.

Sugar was the hub of the Hawaiian economy. And the success of sugar depended on two things: a market on the mainland with no tariff and cheap servile labor to work in the fields. To the natives, who did not like the discipline of regular hours, it was incomprehensible why any man should have to work from dawn to dusk week after week performing backbreaking labor for someone else when the fish were plentiful in the sea and the coconut dropped from the tree. A mainland visitor, commenting on the attitude of Hawaiian workers, noted that "if the overseer leaves for a moment, down they squat . . . and the longest-winded fellow commences upon a yarn . . . that keeps the others upon a broad grin . . . as soon as he comes in sight, [they] seize their spades and commence laboring with an assiduity that baffles description, and perhaps all the while not strain a muscle."

The quest for cheap labor never ceased and led to the organization in 1850 of the Royal Hawaiian Agricultural Society to recruit outside labor. From 1852, when 293 Chinese were brought to Hawaii, until 1930, approximately 400,000 men, women, and children were transported to the plantations of Hawaii. Plantation agents poked into the far corners of the world, recruiting in Canton, Mongolia, Korea, Japan, Puerto Rico, the Madeiras, the Azores, Portugal, Spain, Italy, Poland, Austria, Germany, Norway, Russia, Siberia, Micronesia, Polynesia, Melanesia, and, later, the Philippines. Prior to annexation, about 45,-000 Chinese, 15,000 Japanese, 13,000 Portuguese, 1,400 Germans, 600 Scandinavians, and 400 Galicians were recruited. The Chinese were mainly peasants from Canton; the Japanese, mostly from southwest Japan, were mainly peasants who had small plots of their own or tenant farmers who won marginal existence from the land. The vast majority of the laborers, including the Portuguese, could not read or write in any language; but illiteracy was rated by the planters as an asset, contributing to docility. Nearly all of the immigrants considered themselves temporary residents, bound to the terms of their contract and anxious to save some money and return home. A minority stayed on, either working for the plantations or drifting to Honolulu and Hilo, but taking no part in the continuing struggle between haoles and natives for governmental control of the Kingdom.

After the Great Mahele, the expansion of haole investments in land, sugar, and other enterprises was followed by haole demands for even greater political influence, because the continued importation of labor and a favorable reciprocity treaty with the United States depended upon the approval of the government in Honolulu. There were two potential major threats to those investments. The first was the British and French attempts at infiltration, provoking an American proannexation movement in the early 1850's, just before the issuance of the Tyler Doctrine. The second was the alleged irresponsibility and extravagance of native officials. As early as 1847, the Reverend Richard Armstrong asserted that the white population would not permit itself to be governed by natives only, prophetically adding that perhaps the history of Hawaii would repeat that of recently annexed Texas.

The earliest American settlers correctly realized that they could not gain influence in government unless the powers of the King were limited. They wanted a responsible and economic government and full protection of property rights. In 1840, the spokesmen for the hundred American haoles in Honolulu were influential in establishing Hawaii's first constitution, authorizing an elective House of Representatives. In 1850, its membership was increased from seven to twenty-four, and elections in that year brought haole control of the lower house. Two years later, the King and the legislature approved a revision of the constitution, providing for an annual legislative session, expanded power for the lower house, and election by universal manhood suffrage, a democratic reform that was to plague the haoles in later years. It was one thing to limit the power of the King; it was quite another to enfranchise the commoners. Thirty years later, the haoles of Honolulu discovered that their ancestors had pushed democracy too far. But in 1852, the 2,000 haole residents of Honolulu seemed content with universal suffrage. Even nine years later, many haoles opposed the successful effort of Kamehameha V to impose a new constitution which again restricted voting to property holders. Until the death of that autocratic monarch in 1872, the haoles appear to have been more afraid of autocracy than of democracy.

Four high chiefs appeared equally entitled to succeed Kamehameha V to the throne. One of them, Prince Lunalilo, aware that he was extremely popular, issued a proclamation calling for a mass vote. He was elected by a large majority. The new King was friendly to the Americans and appointed Charles Reed Bishop as Premier for the fourteen months of his reign, but the precedent of electing the king posed a potential threat to haole influence should a popular and eloquent aspirant to the throne care to exploit the natives' growing anti-Americanism. That threat was to materialize only a few years after Lunalilo's death.

Lunalilo persuaded the legislature to abolish property qualifications for voting in the new constitution of 1874, but retained other autocratic powers reinstituted by his predecessor. His successor, Kalakaua, at first co-operated with the Americans, supporting various projects, including reciprocity, and appointing officials acceptable to the haole community. But Kalakaua disliked foreigners and wanted very much to win the applause of Hawaiians, many of whom opposed the Reciprocity Treaty with its Pearl Harbor provision.

The natives still had great pride in their Hawaiian heritage and bitterly resented the haughtiness of some haole spokesmen. Their resentment of haoles had been deepening for some time. It was encouraged by the attitude of men like the Reverend Hiram Bingham, who described the Hawaiians as barbaric and naked savages, and by the members of the House Foreign Affairs Committee of the United States Congress, who boasted in 1842 that the natives had been converted from "the lowest debasement of idolatry to the blessing of the Christian gospel. . . ." The first two American Ministers were similarly arrogant. The first, George Brown, ended his initial meeting with the King in a tirade on the evils of alcohol, and later, when a fellow American was convicted of rape, Brown, alleging the absence of Hawaiian jurisdiction, created such an uproar that the Kingdom forced his recall. The second Minister also behaved like an overlord. Anthony Ten Eyck wrote to the State Department that nothing but brute force could prompt honesty and efficiency by native rulers. He, too, had trouble with criminal cases, demanding that the trials of Americans in both civil and criminal cases be held before a Caucasian jury chosen by representatives of the United States. At one point Ten Eyck threatened the Hawaiian Foreign Minister, R. C. Wyllie, with forcible annexation by the United States unless certain concessions were made.

The Yankees believed that temperance was a mark of morality in government. Choosing religion over profits, the Royal Hawaiian Agricultural Society in 1851 voted down a proposal to develop distilleries. Kalakaua, they soon found, was hardly an ascetic, and his taste for good wine and his extravagant ambitions led to unjustifiable accusations of licentiousness. Whatever his virtues, Kalakaua was not a prudent king. To help his people most, Kalakaua should have chosen a course between demagoguery and pliancy; he would have found sympathetic and progressive haoles to aid him. But his personal vanity and animosity toward the haoles obscured his judgment. Puritan haoles also believed in thrift and were shocked by the King's elaborate coronation, for which he introduced new silver coins the San Francisco Mint struck at the behest of Claus Spreckels, the California sugar giant. This caused a mild inflation and much unhappiness among the haoles on Honolulu's Merchant Street where the local captains of industry were located.

Also frightening to the Americans of Honolulu was Kalakaua's growing racism. He planned a Polynesian empire and seemed to be saying that Polynesia should be kept for the Polynesians, with Hawaii as the ruling island group. The haole newspaper the *Gazette* replied haughtily to these ambitions by asserting that the white race was destined to rule the Pacific Islands and that any political advantages that Hawaii might claim over Polynesian areas were the results of Caucasian efforts.

When Walter Murray Gibson, an antihaole American, was elected to the legislature in 1878, the King saw his opportunity to gain popularity among the natives. Gibson had been preaching hatred of the white man in his own Hawaiian-language newspaper since 1873. The third partner in the alliance against the local haole leaders was Claus Spreckels. Gibson rallied the natives behind the King in return for power and prestige; Spreckels supplied the money in return for government favors; and the King entrenched his power. Kalakaua even dared to appoint as premier a flamboyant Italian named Celso Caesar Moreno, a darling of the natives but an anathema to the haoles who forced his dismissal within five days by persuading the European and American Ministers not to acknowledge his appointment.

Kalakaua and the foreigners continued to jockey for power, and between 1876 and 1887, no cabinet remained in office more than two years. When Gibson was re-elected to the legislature in 1882 by a huge majority over monolithic haole opposition, Kalakaua made him Premier. The Gibson ministry immediately went into action, and a bill was passed making it possible for natives to purchase liquor legally at retail stores or saloons, a privilege heretofore reserved for haoles. Gibson had the legislature pass a law conveying the Wailuku crown lands on Maui to Spreckels, though the planters correctly feared that this outsider aspired to become the biggest sugar producer in the Islands. In 1882, the legislature passed a subsidy for the Oceanic Steam Ship Company, a Spreckels line, and the California financial magnate continued efforts to gain control over the Hawaiian National Bank. To Kalakaua, who was trying to avoid taxes, Spreckels gave a large loan, putting the government further in debt. Gibson played the spoils system to the hilt, discharging from office competent men who were sympathetic to the haoles. He even had a bill passed to suppress secret societies (allegedly directed against local Chinese groups), with the idea of preventing revolutionary activity.

A haole opposition group, well organized by the end of 1885, was nevertheless unable to halt the formation of a new Gibson ministry in 1886 and the passage of a bill creating for Kalakaua a military staff modeled after the German system. It was appalled at the $150,000 appropriation for the purchase of a royal yacht, the expenditure of $15,000 for a birthday party for Kalakaua, and a new law licensing the sale of opium. Haoles charged that the King sold opium licenses for exorbitant amounts, pocketing thousands of dollars for himself. In one case, it was charged that a Chinese paid $75,000 to the King, only to be told that the cabinet would not give him a license. Another threat to the haoles was Kalakaua's encouragement of Gibson's Hale Naua

(Temple of Science) Society, established to promote the revival of some pre-Christian Hawaiian customs.

A voluntary secret society called the Hawaiian League, organized by prominent haoles, gained the co-operation of the Honolulu Rifles, an all-haole rifle company supposedly in the King's service. The rebel group included the best and most efficient soldiers in the Kingdom. Interested businessmen gave money to outfit and arm this newly organized unit, which many members of the League joined. Soon there were three haole rifle clubs, a fourth made up of Portuguese immigrants, and a German company.

When Gibson's newspaper, the *Advertiser,* denounced the haoles as interlopers and defied them to win a fair election, it rapidly became clear that haole rifles were more effective than native votes. Faced with an ultimatum, Gibson resigned on June 28, 1887. Two days later, the haoles held a mass meeting of more than 2,500 people, nearly all Caucasians. Kalakaua acceded to all haole demands, even granting a new constitution, which made the King subordinate in theory as well as in fact to the propertied haoles of Honolulu.

The new constitution provided for election to the House of Nobles by those who possessed a specified income or amount of property. In addition, it gave the legislature the power to override the King's theretofore absolute veto by a two-thirds vote. Constitutions since 1854 had limited the franchise to Hawaiian subjects, but now haoles of substance who did not wish to become subjects of the crown in order to vote could retain their foreign citizenship and their influence in the government. Japanese were barred from voting, in clear violation of the Hawaiian-Japanese Treaty of 1871, which provided that Japanese subjects in Hawaii should enjoy the same privileges as subjects of other nations. Chinese were also kept from the polls, although individual Chinese had become wealthy merchants, and a number possessed Hawaiian citizenship. The House of Nobles was thus converted from an instrument of the King to the legislative voice of the haoles. The House of Representatives was reduced in size, now being equal to the upper chamber, and cabinet members were made *ex officio* members of the legislature, enabling the cabinet and upper house to constitute a majority. In effect, the popular branch could be outvoted by the propertied branch. The goal of universal suffrage, brought to the Islands by the Americans, had been abandoned.

Natives held protest meetings, and counterrevolution was in the air.

One intrigue, led by part-Hawaiian Robert Wilcox, sought to dethrone the King in favor of his younger sister, Princess Liliuokalani, and to form a new constitution. The haole leaders learned of the plot and asked the American Minister to retain a U.S. warship at Honolulu. Marines landed and quelled the revolt with little trouble.

The growing tensions between the natives and the haoles were manifest in the emergence of two political parties. The main haole group, the Reform Party, was opposed by the natives and a few haoles in a new organization, unimaginatively called the National Reform Party, which campaigned for a revision of the constitution.

The government remained in control of a haole clique until the death of the King. Few natives earned the income ($600) or possessed sufficient unincumbered property (worth $3,000) to establish their voting rights. Queen Liliuokalani came to the throne determined that she would rule the Kingdom in her own right, and she appointed Hawaiians and part-Hawaiians to key posts. On January 14, 1893, after her supporters drove a Reform ministry from power and secured passage of legislation licensing both a lottery and the opium traffic, the Queen attempted to promulgate a new constitution, restoring the crown's control over the House of Nobles and limiting the suffrage to actual subjects. She reasoned that the constitution of 1887 had been forced on Kalakaua by bayonet, and that it was her right and duty to go back to the prebayonet constitution. The Supreme Court of Hawaii upheld the Queen's contention, but once again American rifles proved more effective than Hawaiian votes or legal decisions. The Queen was threatened and forced to announce officially that hereafter she would not arbitrarily try to modify the constitution.

Haole plans for revolution had been developing for some time despite the Queen's attempt to meet the demands of her opponents. Sugar planters were restless because the McKinley Tariff of 1890 gave American producers a bounty of two cents a pound and, more importantly, eliminated the duty on all imported sugar, wiping out Hawaii's advantage under the Reciprocity Treaty. But the key revolutionaries were mostly professional men and businessmen of the city rather than planters. A number of planters feared that the destruction of the monarchy would lead to annexation and the elimination of the contract-labor system. The merchant and professional classes had already forced the government to restrict Chinese immigration. Two divergent views had emerged within the haole aristocracy—one insisting that everything be subordinated to the demands of sugar, and the other fearing the importation of masses of Orientals.

The vast majority of haoles nevertheless welcomed revolution. Four fifths of the property of the Islands was owned by whites, who could, under the current constitution, cast but 4,015 votes; only their control over the House of Nobles sustained haole influence in the government. It seemed to them far better to have the thing done with once and for all—to end the monarchy.

A Honolulu publisher, Lorrin Thurston, was the leading conspirator. He furnished the State Department with an explicit statement of plans to uncrown the Queen and collaborated with the American Minister, John Stevens, who wrote home that Hawaii would either become a part of American civilization or be absorbed someday by Asia. President Benjamin Harrison's administration responded by telling the Commander of the American Pacific Squadron that the United States would be happy to annex Hawaii.

The Committee of Safety, which was to spearhead the revolution, was led by Thurston, advised by Stevens, and dignified through the support of one of the great names in Hawaiian history, Sanford Ballard Dole. The tall, athletic, bearded Dole was to become the first and only president of the Hawaiian postrevolutionary Republic, as well as the first postannexation governor of Hawaii. He represented the best of the haole missionary tradition in Hawaii. His parents had come to the Islands in 1840, leaving their home in Maine to serve the Congregational church by administering the Punahou School for the children of haoles. Dole was genuinely interested in the Hawaiians, whose language he spoke fluently, and had devoted much of his law practice to defending their interests. He had attacked the contract-labor system anonymously in his newspaper, the *Punch Bowl,* opposing that aspect of the system which permitted the transfer of a laborer from one employer to another without the laborer's consent. He believed that Chinese workers should have a chance for homesteads and citizenship, and later, after the large-scale importation of Japanese, he was anxious to set up homesteads for independent farmers from the mainland. But Dole wanted a constitution that would protect haole rights and privileges. He endorsed the bayonet constitution imposed on Kalakaua, and after the downfall of Liliuokalani, Dole, as a widely respected associate justice of the Hawaiian Supreme Court, accepted the invitation of the Committee of Safety to head the Provisional Government.

The early life of the revolutionary government was shaky. A new American President, Democrat Grover Cleveland, repudiated the actions of his predecessor and other American officials in supporting the revolution. Cleveland's personal investigator, ex-Congressman John L. Blount, of Georgia, amassed volumes of evidence to prove that the revolution was accomplished by force, with American compliance, against the wishes of the vast majority of Hawaiians. Cleveland demanded the restoration of the Queen, but Dole refused. The American government withdrew its pressure, and in 1894, Dole was elected President of the new Republic of Hawaii.

Before the Republic was established, a group of haoles in Honolulu had tried desperately to persuade the Cleveland administration to annex Hawaii. They had hoped for a favorable report from Blount, and Thurston wrote, "As a Southerner, he is thoroughly familiar with the difficulties attendant upon government with an ignorant majority in the electorate, and will thoroughly appreciate the situation upon this point." The newspaper publisher urged Dole to convince the Cleveland administration of the impossibility of a plebiscite with its certain adverse popular vote. But Blount was plainly disillusioned by haole tactics in Honolulu. He realized that the haoles hoped to win him over with good food, wine, and fine cigars. Thurston told Dole to round up some common Hawaiians to appear before the investigator to request annexation. That could be done, the dynamic newspaper editor said, if they were made to realize that the only alternative was the Provisional Government, and if their expenses were paid. But Blount disappointed the haoles. He did not appreciate the argument that the natives were incapable of knowing what was good for them. He observed that the Hawaiian Patriotic League, opposing the annexation and in favor of monarchy, enlisted the bulk of native Hawaiian voters. He also noticed that some natives were forced to sign annexation petitions out of fear for their jobs as government employees or workers on sugar plantations. Concluding that the Provisional Government could only rest on military force, he successfully counseled Cleveland against an annexation treaty.

It then remained for the Provisional Government to call a constitutional convention to establish the Republic. To be elected to the convention it was necessary to promise to support the Provisional Government and to oppose any attempt to re-establish the monarchy. A royalist mass meeting of about 2,500 persons denounced the plan, but military rather than popular rule prevailed. One haole leader urged the creation of "an uncommonly strong central government with very large powers in the hands of a few." Under the new constitution, voters had to meet varying property and income qualifications. Few Hawaiians, under these provisions, were able either to sit in the legislature or to vote for representatives to the upper house, appropriately called the Senate. President Dole was encouraged by the well-known mainland professor John W. Burgess, who agreed that government should be "placed in the hands of the Teutons." The constitution came into effect without a popular referendum, and the oligarchy legitimized its power. Happiest of the haoles, perhaps, were a majority of the sugar planters, who feared that revolution would lead to annexation and the end of cheap labor. To crown their joy, the U.S. Congress passed the Wilson-Gorham Tariff in 1894, abolishing the domestic sugar bounty on the mainland, restoring the duty on foreign sugar, and leaving the Hawaiian Reciprocity Treaty intact. The United States, despite official misgivings over the revolution, gave prompt recognition to the new government.

But the sugar interests were not dominant in the new government. Dole and his cabinet, comprised to a large extent of the descendants of missionaries, represented the merchant-professional groups of Honolulu. The missionary strain in the Republic was obvious. Probably as many as 70 per cent of the key officers in the new government were related to missionaries; the Minister of Finance, the Attorney General, the Chief Justice, the Minister to Washington, the head of the Land Survey Office, and the Mayor of Honolulu were all descendants of churchmen and churchwomen.

Their main concern, aside from maintaining control, was to Americanize the Islands. The Masters' and Servants' Act was made less harsh. New legislation was enacted which allowed entrance to immigrants who had at least $50 and could prove that they were able to support themselves. A land act, passed in 1895, limited the amount of public land that could be sold in a single parcel to 1,000 acres and stipulated that general leases on public lands be restricted to not more than twenty-one years. The act also provided means by which persons desiring small holdings could acquire them from public lands. Education received increased attention under the Republic. A law passed in 1896 made attendance compulsory at either private or public school for all children between six and fifteen years of age.

As receptive as they were to certain reforms, the leaders of the Republic did not believe in political democracy. "The common people were not intrusted with rule," wrote the Reverend Sereno E. Bishop in the missionary magazine the *Friend,* "because in their childishness and general incapacity, they were totally unfit for such rule." Bishop believed that the affairs of the people of Hawaii could only be directed by the few, for the many did not have the intelligence and character to serve as governors: "The mass of the native people are destitute of such qualifications. They are babes in character and intellect. . . ." His was the dominant opinion. The Republic was to be governed by an oligarchy.

Nearly seventy years later, at a small parent-teacher meeting in the rural schoolhouse in the village of Kaaawa, a haole speaker from the mainland talked about racial *aloha* in Hawaii. Hawaiians, haoles, Japanese, and Koreans exchanged guarded but friendly opinions. Two members of the group remained silent—a part-Hawaiian, haole-looking man, well over seventy, and his aged but beautiful Hawaiian wife. Suddenly he blurted out a deeply felt tirade against the haoles and the missionaries who ran the Republic. He told in vivid detail how, as a boy of seven, policemen ransacked his house, looking for ammunition alleged to have been hidden by his royalist father. To him, seventy years later, the Republic was a police state, and he remained a royalist.

The counterrevolution, he remembered, was planned for January 7, 1895, by friends of the Queen, heartened by the Cleveland administration's withdrawal of an American warship from Honolulu Harbor. With the consent of the Queen, arms had been hidden, a constitution written, and a list of officers planned. But the story of revolt leaked out, and on the night of January 6, the police, in search of hidden arms, stumbled upon an armed band of revolutionaries at Waikiki Beach. After an exchange of shots, the rebels fled to the mountains, where, in a few days, they were dispersed or captured; the abortive revolt was at an end. A member of a prominent haole family had been fatally wounded, and leaders in the Dole government urged harsh measures against the revolutionaries. On January 7, the country was placed under martial law, and the Honolulu jail was crowded with suspects. Some Hawaiians believe to this day that some captured revolutionaries were tortured. Nine days later, after all royalist leaders had been arrested, the Queen was taken into custody at her residence and imprisoned in Iolani Palace. Eight days after her imprisonment, the Queen swore allegiance to the Republic, recognized the end of the monarchy, and promised not to aid attempts to restore it. In return for urging all former subjects to support the new government, she expressed the hope that clemency would be granted the revolutionaries. She was not entirely disappointed. Of the 190 prisoners placed on trial, several received death sentences which were commuted, and all prisoners were released and pardoned by 1896. Although Liliuokalani was fined and imprisoned in the palace, the fine was never collected and she was given a conditional release in September. But the counter-revolution was effectively smashed. Without the Queen's leadership, her supporters were broken.

Their power was secure, yet the leaders of the Republic were plagued by an unusual paradox. Although the planters needed more laborers, and Japan was the logical source, the Japanese in Hawaii were growing in numbers and, from the point of view of the Americanizers, were indigestible. A compromise was struck between the planters, anxious for laborers from any source, and the Americanizers in Honolulu, who wanted to bring in Europeans and mainland haoles rather than Orientals. For every hundred Chinese or Japanese immigrants imported, the planters promised to bring in ten Europeans or Americans. The plantations would pay for the transportation of the men, and the government would foot the bill for the women and children. But the planters found it difficult to fill the 10 per cent quota for non-Orientals. The price for white labor was too high. Between the beginning of 1895 and the end of 1896, nearly 10,000 peasants came from southern Japan to work in the fields. The next year, the government at Honolulu refused to allow three successive shiploads of Japanese immigrants to enter the country. The dilemma persisted. Sugar needed laborers, but the Japanese were an alien, unassimilable force tied to a strange foreign power. In 1896, the Caucasians, excluding the Portuguese, constituted less than 7 per cent of the population, but the struggle for long-term political control seemed far away, and in the meantime huge profits might be made if enough laborers could be found to work in the sugar fields. At the time of annexation, therefore, more than half of the population of Hawaii was of Japanese origin.

To many, the one logical answer to the Oriental "peril" seemed to be annexation. With the election of Republican President William Mc-Kinley, the supporters of annexation in Honolulu and Washington worked with renewed vigor. Many planters opposed the drive, believing it would end the large-scale importation of cheap labor. A few sugar men were more frightened by the alleged threat of Oriental absorption, but the real annexation leadership again came from the merchant and professional groups in town. The Honolulu *Star* insisted that it was "the white race against the yellow . . . nothing but annexation can save the Islands."

Only a few years before, the annexationists had threatened that Hawaii would become another Singapore or Hong Kong—a British Crown Colony. Now they warned against annexation by Japan. These prophecies found receptive ears among the alarmist imperialists of the Mc-Kinley administration. Foremost among them was Under Secretary of the Navy Theodore Roosevelt, who gave secret instructions to the commanding officer of the U.S. Navy in Honolulu to seize the Islands and proclaim a protectorate at the first sign of aggression from Japan. Actually, Tokyo made no plans to take over the Islands, and when annexation was finally accomplished, and assurances were made by Washington concerning the proper protection of Japanese treaty rights, Japan acquiesced in the American decision. The annexation treaty could not muster a two-thirds vote in the Senate, but the Senate Foreign Relations Committee circumvented the treaty procedures by favorably reporting a joint resolution of annexation, needing only a majority of one in each House, which it obtained in July of 1898. Annexation was accomplished—the fruit of approximately seventy-five years of expanding American influence in Hawaii.

What were the major characteristics of the new society in Hawaii? In most respects, Polynesian Hawaii had been remade in the image of the West. Monogamy had replaced plural marriage. Private ownership took the place of communal property. Christianity was widely followed. A constitutional system had been substituted for the autocratic monarchy. Western dress, music, and recreational habits were the vogue. At least that was the picture of *one* Hawaii at the turn of the century—the Hawaii of Honolulu, where the haoles dominated. On the plantations, however, Oriental influences could be seen everywhere. The languages spoken, the games played, the gods worshiped, and the attitudes toward family, property, and authority were all predominantly Oriental. A third Hawaii existed in the Islands—the Hawaii of the Hawaiians, found in the more remote Hawaiian villages, where some natives prayed fervently to Madam Pele, the Goddess of Fire, to shake loose molten lava from the mountains and wash foreign customs into the sea.

The social structure of Hawaii was a curious amalgam of a tropical European colony and a New England settlement. In Hawaii, as in the European colonies, there was virtually no middle class. Oriental immigrants comprised almost 75 per cent of the population. There were many Chinese merchants and peddlers and a sprinkling of Japanese trade workers in town; but none of them could vote, few held land, and there was no social mixing with the upper-class haoles. The vast number of Japanese and Chinese on the plantations were treated by their overseers, even after the end of the Masters' and Servants' Act, with impersonal harshness. On the top were the haoles, only slightly more than 5 per cent of the population, controlling politics, land, enterprise, and labor. Some haoles joined Hawaiians and Portuguese in buffer occupations, between the oligarchy and the laborers. They served as clerks, foremen, semiskilled and skilled laborers, overseers, and even plantation managers. There was no middle class in the American sense of small independent landholders or small businessmen. Prestige, power, and status were firmly in the possession of a small haole elite.

In one important respect, Hawaii was more like New England than a European colony. The New England drive for education had been transplanted to Hawaiian soil long before annexation. The missionaries and their descendants, even after becoming established as merchants and planters, believed in "uplifting the people." Next to religion, education—in those days closely tied to Christian goals—was prized. As on the New England frontier and later in the Middle West, the missionaries built schoolhouses soon after churches. In 1840, a system of public education was established, making attendance compulsory to the age of fourteen. By 1880, native Hawaiians and part-Hawaiians comprised 92 per cent of the pupils enrolled in the public schools. In the 1880's and '90's, the Portuguese, Chinese, and Japanese began sending their children to public and private schools. Although the decade of the 1890's was one of progress in education, much of it failed to reach the plantations. Even though one of the earliest progressive educators, Henry S. Townsend, was the principal of one of the larger private schools and Inspector General of all public schools in Hawaii, few schools were available for plantation children. In the year of revolution, 1892, only 353 Chinese and sixty Japanese boys and girls attended public school throughout the Islands. But universal public education, open to all—indeed, compulsory for all—was the goal even under the oligarchy. The leading haoles, in their zeal for education, had placed a Trojan horse within the oligarchical system.

In one fundamental respect Hawaii was unique—neither like anything in America nor like any other plantation colony. Miscegenation and intermarriage were not only widespread, but accepted, and, in some cases, approved. Perhaps as many as thirty of the early white residents married Hawaiian women of chiefly rank. The existence of the mission depended, in its earliest days, on the good will of native chiefs and royalty, and haoles could not oppose marriages favored by Hawaiian leaders. Important haole names—Bishop, Wilcox, Shipman, Campbell, and others—were joined in marriage to Hawaiians. By 1853, two thirds of the foreign men living outside Honolulu—mainly haoles— were married to part-Hawaiian or Hawaiian women. Even in Honolulu, nearly two of every ten had married nonhaoles. But the practice was not limited to the haoles. By 1900, more than 300 legal ceremonies and hundreds more not recognized by law had joined Chinese men and Hawaiian women. Even in this period, when many haoles expressed a deep hostility toward the Chinese who were leaving the plantations and competing for jobs in town, these marriages were not openly opposed. Perhaps the haoles' own tradition of miscegenation kept them from attacking the marriages—legal and otherwise—of Chinese men and Hawaiian women.

This was Hawaii at the time of annexation. Contradictions abounded. A handful of haoles, intolerant of opposition, ran the Islands, but discontent was openly expressed in uncensored native newspapers. The oligarchy, self-consciously Caucasian, made few open appeals to racial prejudice. The small group, sharply limiting the suffrage to maintain political control, nevertheless helped foster education. The small aristocracy, reaping the benefits of a plantation system, with its ruthlessness, was constantly torn between the desire for power and profit and the evangelism of both the Congregational church and the American dream of freedom and opportunity for all. Even before annexation, the seeds of conflict had been sown in the very nature of the Island oligarchy.

Annexation introduced other problems for the oligarchy. The leaders of Hawaii knew that they would now come under American immigration laws. Unlimited immigration from any source was a thing of the past; contract labor could never be renewed. And the Organic Act, by which Congress insisted that Hawaii re-establish universal manhood suffrage, opened the door to expanding nonhaole influence. Haoles from Honolulu pleaded to be permitted to retain their system of restricted suffrage, arguing, as the Reverend Bishop had earlier, that the Hawaiians were, like children, not to be trusted with the vote. But Congress was adamant; an American territory, it insisted, must maintain the voting privilege for all. Hawaii was to be a part of the Union on American terms.

For the next four decades, the oligarchy lived with and managed its contradictions with success. Hawaii was a plantation society with no significant middle class, only one effective political party, and sharp limitations on opportunity. Thus it remained for the next forty years, until the cumulative impact of public education, universal suffrage, and World War II transformed its social structure.

PART ONE

❋

Ways of Life

1900 – 1941

In Hawaii, it was not so much income or occupation or education which determined one's friends, voting affiliation, or prospects for power and prestige. In the forty years following annexation, the peoples of Hawaii thought of themselves, not primarily as doctors, lawyers, druggists, or field hands—or even as Americans—but as haoles, Hawaiians, Portuguese, Chinese, Japanese, and Filipinos.

Of course, there were important differences within each ethnic group, differences in the day-to-day living habits between a Japanese farmer and a Japanese plantation laborer, or between a Chinese merchant in Honolulu and a Chinese rice farmer on Kauai, or between a haole carpenter and the descendant of a well-to-do missionary family. There were obvious differences in personality within groups, differences formed in parental or childhood relationships. But the fears, joys, hopes, and needs of the vast majority of Hawaii's people in the decades that followed annexation were determined mainly by their ethnic identity.

Each ethnic group, because of its historical antecedents and the nature of its adaptation to Hawaii, developed a distinctive way of life. The experiences of most individuals within each group were strikingly similar. Through those experiences, group goals in Hawaii were forged, and by the mid-1930's the ways of life of Hawaii's peoples were governed in large measure by the central goals of each group.

For the kamaaina *haoles, the goal was to control; for the Hawaiians, to recapture the past; for the Portuguese, to be considered haole; for the Chinese, to win economic independence; for the Japanese, to be accepted; for the Filipinos, to return to their home in the Philippines.*

Chapter One

BORN TO RULE

To the people of Hawaii in 1900, the haoles—approximately 5 per cent of the population of the Islands—constituted an elite group of Caucasians, nearly all of them of American or British stock. A small group of missionary descendants, their relatives by marriage, and a few business associates comprised the haole inner core; their dominant purpose was the control of Hawaii. They governed the Islands in a leisurely but conscientious fashion, primarily from the offices of the major sugar agencies. They lived in stately mansions surrounded by royal palms in the hills of Honolulu, or in large sprawling houses set on manicured lawns in rural areas.

On Kauai, two families dominated, the Rices and the Wilcoxes; on Maui, the Baldwin family ruled. On their respective islands, these families decided who "belonged" and who did not. The third generation, most of whom were born before the turn of the century, included eight Rice and six Wilcox children living near Lihue. Three young Baldwins —of the fourth generation—lived at Spreckelsville. As youngsters, they were educated by governesses and tutors in rambling rococo homes near the plantations their families controlled. Other children, close to the inner circle, were invited to join them for schooling and parties. One private tutor lived first on the Rice property and later with the Wilcoxes, where he gave instruction to the children of both families.

Trips to Honolulu were by inter-island steamer over rough seas that frightened the girls but delighted the boys. For the Rices, there were occasional visits with their friends the Robinsons, of English descent, who lived in the tradition of British squires on the west side of the island. As adolescents, they went off for schooling at Punahou, which, to the missionary families of Hawaii, probably meant even more than Harvard to the Brahmins of Back Bay Boston.

Punahou was not just a school. It was *the* school. It did not matter so much where one went to college after Punahou, although the Baldwins showed a preference for Yale. The boys, knowing that one day they would assume responsibility for the plantations, ranches, and businesses of Hawaii, placed little emphasis on higher education. Few of them cared about art, literature, or music, and scarcely any of the missionary sons chose professional careers. After all, doctors, lawyers, teachers, and musicians could easily be hired.

The boys were expected to work their way up the ladder of business and plantation control as quickly as possible. This meant joining the right clubs as well as learning the technical end of sugar, cattle, or finance. On Maui, for example, they joined the Maui Chamber of Commerce, the Maui County Fair and Racing Association, and the Maui Country Club. For their convenience and comfort on visits to Honolulu, they joined the Pacific Club, the Oahu Country Club, the Hawaii Polo and Racing Club, and perhaps a few others.

The young men were expected to marry someone from a family with a missionary background or from a haole family closely allied with the inner group. It was a serious mistake to become involved with a common Hawaiian woman, as a few of the boys found out. One of them, after a youthful escapade with a Hawaiian commoner, married a full-blooded lady of chiefly birth, a widow with two daughters who was accepted by haole society because of her good bloodlines.

The girls, if they married at all, were expected to choose only haoles of their own class. To improve their prospects, they were frequently sent off to the best Eastern schools; Wellesley and Mount Holyoke were favorites. As women of gentle breeding, they were not expected to pursue careers, though there were exceptions. When Mabel Wilcox announced in 1902 that she wanted to be a nurse, her mother extracted a promise that she would give up the idea until the age of twenty-five. But she stuck it out, studied at Johns Hopkins, and ultimately returned to Kauai as the first public-health nurse on the island.

A love of travel was shared by many of the missionary haoles. Trips to the mainland and Europe were frequent, but when away from home, members of the inner group stayed at the same hotels and clubs, ate at the same restaurants, and talked mostly to each other. The extreme insularity of the rural elite and their families was a topic of gossip even among their cousins in Honolulu. It is no wonder that in 1959 two fourth-generation sisters of one missionary family on the island of Hawaii, when asked to part with some of their land for the family's economic gain, protested that the sale might bring strange people to live within only three and a half miles of their own home.[1]

The life of the elite in Honolulu—where the Athertons, Castles, Cookes, and Dillinghams held sway—was just as gracious as on the outer islands, and much gayer. There were ministers of foreign nations and high-ranking Navy officers to entertain. Parties were given at Moanalua, five miles from the center of the city. One newspaperman said in 1893 that he had seen more people in evening dress in Hawaii than in any part of the United States. Guests came to soirees in the hills by special trains, run just to accommodate them. For many years after annexation, the city had a charming opera house, where professional plays and concerts were given, and society pages of the haole newspapers described handsome carriages containing ladies swathed in expensive capes and jewels arriving before its lighted door.

One man, who recalls working for missionary descendant Samuel Damon on a ranch near Honolulu at the turn of the century, reported that in the afternoon, Damon would bring his supervisors in for tea and gossip. The palms swayed in the breeze as the haole ranchmen, on the fringe of the inner circle, repeated stock-worn haole aphorisms. "If those Chinamen don't stop hanging themselves on the plantation, there won't be many more of them." "But there are plenty of Japanese coming in now." "Too many, they'll be crowding us in town soon." "What we need is some more good tough Scotch managers." And so it went— the endless round of conversation about Oriental laborers, Scotch managers, Hawaiian *wahines,* boat and horse races, and polo. The next day they might all go to Moanalua (in later years to Kapiolani) to watch a polo match. Perhaps the Rice brothers had come in with the Kauai cowboys, or perhaps Frank Baldwin, who led the Maui team until 1934, had brought his three sons from Maui to challenge the Oahu ponies and players.[2]

The members of the inner group believed in certain absolute truths. The most important was that they were destined to rule Hawaii. They saw themselves as generous, benevolent, and wise, loving the Islands more than outsiders could know, and they assumed there was no question but that they knew what was best for Hawaii. If they were determined to control the enterprise, politics, and labor of Hawaii, it was not for themselves, but for the good of the Islands. The elite belonged in Hawaii, and Hawaii belonged to it. Oh yes, Hawaii belonged to the Hawaiians, too; but it was clear in the minds of the *kamaaina* elite that the Hawaiians—lovable, shiftless, and improvident—could not govern the Islands. Progress in Hawaii was due to the haole missionaries, their descendants and friends; there could be no mistake about that. Their haole underlings acquiesced in these attitudes and in the way of life prescribed for them.

The men and women who ruled Hawaii for four decades after annexation grew up in families that not only assumed the right to rule, but also assumed that wealth and power brought certain obligations. The haole missionary families especially felt a sense of community obligation through private charity. If there was little justice in Hawaii at the turn of the century, there was much charity. This sentiment, best known in Hawaii by the word paternalism, had two major sources. The first was the missionary conscience. The second was the receptivity of the Hawaiians. The missionary conscience produced a considerable uneasiness among many haoles in their relationships with Hawaiians. A common sense of obligation to the natives stemmed from a knowledge that no matter how strong the missionaries' self-conception as the natural custodians of the Islands, they were intruders in the eyes of many Hawaiians.

The Hawaiians had been used to a system of paternalism. They could understand the idea of the many working for the few, and they could also understand and expect the few to dispense charity among the many. In some respects, leading haoles replaced the chiefs. Dozens of recorded stories tell of important haoles passing out money to native workers at celebrations or on holidays; other stories, verified many times, tell of haole concern for individual Hawaiian families.

Private charity was by no means the only manifestation of missionary concern. Great sums were spent to further religious education and to support the Protestant churches. Many trusts and foundations, named after missionary families—the Athertons, Castles, Cookes, Wilcoxes—were set up early in the century. Hospitals, the Y.M.C.A., and the Y.W.C.A. were favorite targets of missionary generosity. The Wilcoxes engaged in many philanthropies on Kauai, and in 1906, Albert S. Wilcox founded the Kauikeolani Children's Hospital in Honolulu. On Maui, the Baldwins founded the Alexander Settlement House to provide social services and organized recreation.

A number of nonmissionary members of the oligarchy also caught the spirit. Charles R. Bishop established and endowed the Bishop Museum in Honolulu in 1889 and made generous contributions to the Kamehameha Schools (founded under conditions of his wife's will for the education of children in Hawaii), the public-library system, the Salvation Army, the Kapiolani Maternity Home, Queen's Hospital, and the leper settlement at Kalaupapa. The agency known as H. Hackfeld & Company (later renamed American Factors), although under German direction, was early infected with the spirit of paternalism. In 1899, to signal the success of their first half-century of business in Hawaii, its officers sent $1,000 to each of thirteen charitable organizations in Honolulu, including the Hawaiian Relief Society, the German Benevolence Society, the British Benevolent Society, the Ladies Portuguese Charitable Association, the Chinese Hospital, and the Japanese Benevolent Society.

Throughout this century, leading haoles have been proud of their record in public health and public education, although comparisons with conditions in advanced states on the mainland did not always justify self-congratulation. Visiting mainland experts invariably found much to criticize in sanitation and educational facilities. In 1929, a professor from Yale gave Honolulu a low score in public health and sanitation, and various federal surveys on education found Hawaii lagging. Haole leaders usually reacted to criticism by asserting that the outsiders did not understand conditions in the Islands.[3]

The elite was similarly defensive with respect to criticisms of plantation management in Hawaii. It extended paternalism to the plantations, and, in its opinion, did more to uplift the workers than any reasonable estimate would deem necessary. In the first place, they were paid more than they could possibly have made in their homelands. Furthermore, the workers were provided with an elaborate system of perquisites, including, in many cases, better housing, health facilities, and cultural opportunities than existed back home. To the elite, the complaints of workers were often unfathomable. Certainly life was better in Hawaii than it had been in Japan, China, or the Philippines. Working and living conditions in the Islands were superior to those in Fiji, the British West Indies, and Puerto Rico, where natives and immigrants were also plantation workers. In the view of the haole elite, the laborers of Hawaii were also better off than the workers in migratory farm-labor camps on the mainland and in the sweatshops and slums of the big mainland cities. Compared to these models, Hawaii was a workers' paradise.

Following the end of contract labor, paternalism was stepped up on many of the plantations. In 1901, the Ewa plantation spent $5,000 for benevolent and religious purposes among the laborers, and a smaller plantation spent $2,000 in the same way.[4] Managers and owners nodded in agreement when a visiting mainland official asserted that year that workers in Hawaii were much better off than the laborers in Puerto Rico and Cuba.[5] Another visitor noted approvingly in 1910 that less than 10 per cent of the sugar property in the Territory of Hawaii was subjected to absentee control. He concluded that the conditions of plantation workers in the Islands were probably better than in any other tropical country in the world where "colored" people worked.[6]

For several years, some of the plantations had provided hot water and free fuel. Public baths were available on the larger plantations. On a few there were even libraries for haole and Hawaiian employees. One plantation in 1905 conducted a day nursery for Japanese children while their mothers worked.[7] By 1915, all of the larger plantations provided hospitals and medical attention for employees. In many cases a small monthly deduction from each worker's salary covered these costs, but on a few plantations medical care was given free. All of the European immigrants imported to Hawaii by the Island government were entitled, according to the terms of their contract, to medical and hospital treatment without charge.

Actually, the extent of paternalism varied greatly from plantation to plantation. Those plantations run by the missionary agencies, Castle & Cooke and Alexander & Baldwin, tended to be the most liberal.[8] There was also a noticeable tendency for paternalism to come to life as a result of plantation strikes, or when laborers were leaving the plantations in large numbers, or in response to criticism from the mainland.

The defensiveness of the haoles against outside criticism of plantation conditions was sometimes accompanied by feelings of uneasiness that paternalism was not working out just right in the plantation camps. That mood was manifest in the *Planters' Monthly* during the 1880's, when the Chinese were leaving the plantations in great numbers. It also appeared in the pages of the missionary magazine the *Friend*. In September 1909, when many members of the elite were advocating stern repressive measures against the Japanese workers who had recently gone on strike, an article in this magazine urged the plantation owners to let the Japanese own their own houses and have schools to train their children. But most of the haole leaders usually agreed that every possible charity on the plantations was being given.[9]

Outsiders often failed to understand paternalism. For example, what was paternalism to the oligarchy was labled fascism by a mainland representative of the National Labor Relations Board in 1937.[10] Of course, paternalism meant the right to control as well as the obligation to serve—a father not only serves his family, but he controls it, too. As one defender of the sugar agencies explained after paternalism on the plantations had ended: "Just why a father's care should be regarded as reprehensible has not been explained."[11]

In actuality, the relationship of the haole elite to the Oriental immigrants hardly resembled that of parents to children. Whereas the haole leaders knew Hawaiians as individuals, they rarely met the Orientals as anything but laborers or servants. Even in 1959, a haole lady who had grown up among the landed aristocracy of the Kona Coast admitted that it was difficult to think of the Japanese as anything but servants.[12] In 1910, a haole leader said that the "Asiatics" in Hawaii had no more impact on the institutions and customs of the Islands than did "the cattle of the ranges."[13] Five years later, a representative of the federal government observed that the haole leaders thought of the Japanese, Chinese, and Koreans "primarily as instruments of production."[14]

As cattle on the ranges or instruments of production, the Orientals did not merit special coddling. When many plague deaths occurred in Honolulu's Chinatown district in 1899, where more than half of the people were Japanese, the Board of Health burned a large portion of the district. The scanty precautions taken to keep the blaze from getting out of control were inadequate, and the raging fire destroyed the homes, possessions, and businesses of more than 4,000 Orientals. When the plague infiltrated a haole neighborhood, the Board protected nearby buildings with heatproof screens, boarded the windows, and removed goods to safe places before firing the area; and when a well-known haole woman became ill with the plague and died, the Board decided not to remove her to the house where dead Orientals were kept, because it would have been unsuitable. Nor would it have been appropriate to put the family in a quarantine camp with the Asians who had been exposed.[15]

The haole elite's attitude toward the Orientals, while nearly always uniformly negative, passed through two distinct phases. During the last decades of the nineteenth century and into the second decade of this century, the elite generally agreed that the Oriental was inferior to the white man and should be kept in a subordinate status. This "natural inferiority" excused for some the naval custom of flogging for disorder or insubordination through the nineteenth century, even after the Bureau of Immigration prohibited whipping in 1868. In the early days it also excused the selling of labor contracts.

The idea of the natural inferiority of Asians was a corollary of the theory of Caucasian racial supremacy. Darwin's influence had reached Hawaii, and its leading Anglo-Saxons were confident that the racial ideas of historian John Fiske and sociologist John W. Burgess had been proven correct. It did not matter that their logic was circuitous and self-validating; to wit, Anglo-Saxons ruled in the colonies, and hence were entitled to rule. What mattered was that there was a respectable body of professional opinion to justify the Caucasians' belief in their own biological and moral supremacy.

Although the theory of racial supremacy was probably believed by many haoles in Honolulu, for complex reasons unique to the Islands it never received legislative recognition, as in many mainland areas. Caucasian superiority could not be flaunted in the faces of Hawaiians, who after annexation had an overwhelming majority of the votes. Indeed, the haoles had in part built their power on the Hawaiian tradition of racial *aloha*. Haoles had accepted Hawaiian favors and Hawaiian daughters in marriage when, under the Kingdom, it was politically expedient; and the outward assertion of haole racial supremacy would have been insulting to *hapa*-haole families.

In addition to Hawaiian votes and the tradition of Hawaiian-haole miscegenation, another factor inhibited the outward expression of racial supremacy. Until 1907, haole planters were dependent upon Tokyo for immigrant labor. At the turn of the century, the planters could not say, as California had said, "We do not want Japs." Criticism of the Orientals, which appeared from time to time in the haole newspapers of Honolulu, was mild compared to the virulent attacks in editorials and articles in the San Francisco *Chronicle*. Racism was thus kept mainly a private affair, even in that era when it was justified openly on mainland college campuses.

It was not until the 1920's that the haole view of the natural inferiority of Orientals gave way to more ambivalent attitudes. As Japanese invaded the economic and political life of the Islands, the haole elite was no longer certain that the Oriental was naturally inferior to the Caucasian. Haole managers and supervisors often complained that the Japanese were capable of working and studying much more diligently than Caucasians. In 1925, a haole psychologist who was friendly with a number of the leading families wrote a book arguing that the Japanese had a *superior* racial endowment, and further warned that "There is going on a ceaseless racial struggle for dominance that no number of platitudes about brotherly love will obviate; and . . . this struggle for dominance is by no means weighed on equal terms." The Japanese were more fit for the struggle, he argued, because Japan had been isolated over a long period of time, was a small country, did not spend its energies in religious and political wars, and lacked humanitarian traditions.[16] However faulty the reasoning, many leading haoles agreed that stern measures might be needed to curb the unfair "racial superiority" of the Japanese.

There was also a substantial minority of leading haoles who accepted neither the inferiority nor the superiority theory. During the 1920's and '30's, this group pushed uplift programs for the Orientals. Realistically facing the permanency of a large Oriental population in the Islands, they aimed to haolify, or Americanize, it. Even this minority within the elite was not always agreed on what Americanization meant. But there was general consensus that at the very least it did mean going to Christian churches, playing American sports, and eating apple pie; there was nearly complete accord that it did not mean labor unions, political action, and criticism of the social order in the Islands.

Politically, the Orientals were inarticulate until well into the twentieth century, but they did present serious problems to the haole elite in governing Hawaii. In fact, the controversy within the oligarchy over the importation of Oriental immigrants was the most divisive issue confronting the haoles in the late nineteenth and early twentieth centuries. Those who were most directly connected with sugar constantly reached for cheap immigrant labor. Many merchants and professional men in town did not agree with that policy. It was this group that forced the Hawaiian government to restrict Chinese immigration in 1886, and that brought about the annexation of the Islands to the United States, setting up, through the Organic Act, a fundamental constitution for Hawaii that forbade the further importation of contract labor and canceled all contracts made subsequent to annexation.

The Americanizers frequently stressed their fear of a rising "yellow menace" in Honolulu and the need for a substantial Caucasian labor population. They were cheered by the Third Report of the U.S. Commissioner of Labor in 1906, which urged the plantations to open home sites for white settlements, but the planters continued to rely almost entirely upon Japan for their labor supply. After the United States government signed a Gentlemen's Agreement with Japan cutting off Japanese immigration to the United States in return for relaxation of West Coast anti-Japanese legislation, the planters were again forced to search for European workers. Between 1907 aand 1913, they had only sporadic success and, to the discomfort of the Americanizers, relied increasingly on Filipino labor to fill their quest for thousands of cheap and tractable workers.

After Oriental immigration had been reduced to a trickle, the haole planters began to agree with the elite in Honolulu on the need to halt the "yellow peril." Earlier disagreements on the alleged dangers of Japanese immigration gave way to near unanimous feeling, the uplifters excepted, against the Japanese. A high point of hostility was reached in the early 1920's when the haoles adopted a strong program against Japanese schools, press, and labor leaders. And with few exceptions, the leading haole citizens of Hawaii, in their newspapers, testimony before congressional committees in Washington, and private conversations, revealed their fear and distrust of the Japanese population through the 1930's. There persisted among the haole elite a nagging, unpleasant feeling that the Japanese had somehow not responded correctly to paternalism. They had been, to put it frankly from their point of view, ungrateful.

Between annexation and 1940, the proportion of haoles in Hawaii grew from 5 to 25 per cent, but in the census year 1920, it was still under 9 per cent. Sharp haole gains in population were not registered until the 1920's and '30's. Despite the urgings of the Americanizers, relatively few European laborers (not counting Portuguese) had been brought to the Islands: 600 Scandinavians in 1881; approximately 1400 Germans between 1881 and 1885; 400 Galicians (really Poles from Austria) between 1897 and 1898; and 2,400 Russians, mostly between 1909 and 1912, arrived in the Islands under the auspices of the plantations.

About 12,000 Portuguese were imported between 1878 and 1887, and an additional 6,000 arrived with nearly 8,000 Spanish laborers between 1906 and 1913.[17] The Portuguese, while often privileged through haole beneficence, generally were not considered as haoles by the inner group or anyone else. They were assigned a special role in the Hawaiian social order as buffers between the Orientals and the haoles.

The Scandinavians, most of the Germans, the Galicians, and the Russians were imported as laborers. In each case, the planters were disappointed. The Europeans were expensive to import and support; they demanded and received preferential treatment over the Orientals, and hundreds of them emigrated from the Islands after a short time. Soon after the Scandinavians arrived, they began to complain about plantation conditions. Many had been artisans and factory workmen in Norway and Sweden, and they likened their plantation contracts to slavery. Most of them left the plantations as soon as they were able.[18] The Galicians were even more troublesome. In 1898, they created disturbances at Waipahu and at the Pioneer Mill, near Lahaina, and seventy Poles marched from Waipahu to Honolulu to protest over-work and brutal *lunas* (overseers). Although the judge released twenty-two minors from their contracts, sixty-five of the adult laborers were jailed when they refused to return to work.[19]

Spurred by the Reciprocity Treaty of 1876 and dissatisfaction with the Scandinavians, the planters looked to Germany as a new source of labor in the 1880's. The principal importer was the German agency H. Hackfeld & Co. Hackfeld, controlled by the Isenberg family, had added seven new plantations between 1876 and 1881. German laborers adjusted well at the Lihue plantation on Kauai, where the Isenbergs lived and German culture flourished until World War I. At Lihue efforts were made to give the Germans a community life similar to that left behind in northwest Germany, but on other planta-tions the Germans, like other Europeans, had trouble adjusting to Oriental labor conditions. There were strikes at two different plantations on Kauai in 1883. At Koloa especially, they complained of abuse by the overseers, most of whom were Hawaiian.[20]

Dissatisfied haole immigrants did not long remain field hands. They either left Hawaii, migrated to Honolulu or Hilo, or moved into supervisory positions on the plantations. As plantation operations grew more complex, new supervisory jobs were created. The lesser haoles were invariably given preference in filling these positions.

By 1901, a government official from the mainland, after visiting fifty-four of the fifty-five sugar plantations, wrote that all white plantation employees were more or less favored, with relatively good living and working conditions. The larger plantations provided a club for white employees, which included billiard and reading rooms, and encouraged their Caucasian workers to play polo and tennis.[21] Five years later, another visitor wrote: "White employees on the plantation are usually well paid and seldom overworked . . . so far as the purely physical conditions of employment are concerned, the lot of the white plantation worker in Hawaii is a very pleasant one." A white mechanic, after leaving the plantations, was reported as saying in 1905, "The white mechanics on the plantation have an easy job. I never did a real day's work myself . . . we get used to sitting around and seeing Japanese work, and so get lazy."[22]

By 1911, the vast majority of white employees were paid salaries on an annual basis.[23] A decade later, a spokesman for the plantations told a congressional committee, "You cannot get a man with white blood in him to go into the harvesting fields. It is most arduous work. Cane grows very thickly, there is hardly a breath of air in the dense growth of cane, and most of the varieties of cane are covered with a fuzz which gets on one's body and it is very uncomfortable and disagreeable . . . for the harder kinds of work you cannot get white people to go into those fields at all."[24]

Occupational stratification was determined primarily on ethnic lines. The best jobs went to the haoles of American, English, or Scotch origin except on the German plantations, where Germans were favored. Next came the Hawaiians, Portuguese, Chinese, Japanese, and Filipinos, in that order. Even T. G. S. Walker, an extremely liberal manager during the 1930's, who gained the reputation of being a "Japanee lover" and "Filipino lover," assumed that nonhaoles could not be promoted past minor supervisory positions.

The Scotch played a unique role in the plantation hierarchy. In the nineteenth century, Theophilus H. Davies, a Welshman, imported many Scots to run his Honolulu agency and its plantations. A large number of the first Scots were dirt plowmen brought over to handle mule teams; but they were Caucasian, literate, and thought to be great economizers and drivers of men. Hence, by the turn of the century, Scotch managers and supervisors were numerous. By 1905, almost two out of every five plantation managers were of Scotch descent,[25] and the reputation of the Scotch for hard work and frugality became legendary among members of the elite. The head of the Bishop Bank, missionary son Samuel Damon, sent recruiters to Scotland in 1912 to hire clerks and tellers.[26] Upward mobility for the Scotchman was common. One of Damon's recruits who married the sister of a member of the inner elite and subsequently became a treasurer of American Factors, encouraged his brother after World War II to come to Hawaii. The newcomer rose from field *luna* to section *luna,* with 2,000 acres under his jurisdiction, then to head *luna* on another plantation, assistant manager, and manager within a period of ten years.[27]

Not only was occupational status based upon ethnic identity, but haoles on the plantations received preferential treatment and higher wages for the same work performed by others. On thirty-eight sugar plantations in 1901, Scotch blacksmiths averaged $4.16 a day, part-Hawaiians $2.94, Portuguese $2.37, and Japanese $1.50. On the same plantations, mainland haole carpenters were getting $3.67 a day, Scotch carpenters $2.90, part-Hawaiians $1.73, Portuguese $1.54, and Japanese $1.09. Pay differentials by ethnic origin were consistently applied, whether to chief engineers or to laborers in the field. For example, in 1910 the base-pay rate for Caucasian field hands was increased from $22 to $24 per month following an increase from $18 to $20 a month for Orientals. As late as 1915, Scotch and American overseers were being paid 75 per cent more than their Portuguese counterparts.[28]

Better wages for equal work and upward mobility for the *malihini* haole were also prevalent in Honolulu during the first four decades of the twentieth century. From 1900—when mainland haole carpenters with Oahu's steam railroad made one and a half times as much as Hawaiian carpenters, twice as much as Portuguese, and more than two and a half times as much as Japanese carpenters—until 1940—when major haole firms invariably recruited managerial personnel from the mainland rather than upgrade Oriental assistants—the lesser haoles of Honolulu were encouraged to consider themselves members of a privileged class.[29] In 1905, an official from Washington said that the skilled Caucasian laborers in Honolulu, with their fine homes and servants, were as privileged as the skilled haoles on the plantations, with their gardens and stables. He pointed out that the white people in the city form a sort of caste, and they "strive to maintain the dignity of their position." Never was a white worker seen carrying a dinner pail in Honolulu, and the wives of carpenters and painters, he said, often kept a Japanese servant. Bricklayers, plasterers, and carpenters were seldom seen mowing the grass or gardening, and Oriental yard-men became an institution in Hawaii. Of course there were unskilled Caucasian laborers—teamsters, watchmen, and clerks—just as there were gang and field bosses and lower-paid operators on the plantations and in the mills; but by 1905 most of these jobs were held by Portuguese or part-Hawaiians, not haoles.[30]

The Germans and the Scandinavians who remained in Hawaii, as well as the Scotch, moved easily into the haole classification. As time went by, to be haole meant to be Caucasian of North European or American—as distinguished from Portuguese or Spanish—origin. As early as 1889, there were eight taxpaying German corporations, twelve taxpaying German firms, and 518 German taxpayers. The Board of Education of the Kingdom even contributed to the support of German schools in the 1880's and '90's. But with American entry into World War I, German plantation control ended, nearly all German businessmen left the Islands, and Germans in minor positions were dismissed at the slightest excuse. The remaining Germans were only a small fraction of the haole population.

The one large group of Caucasians not considered haole by most haoles, Hawaiians, and Orientals was the Portuguese. Perhaps they were not accepted as haoles because of their swarthy skin or perhaps because approximately three quarters of the Portuguese immigrants had been illiterate peasants. Most of the Portuguese came from the Madeiras or the Azores, and were welcomed by the planters and Americanizers. Their children quickly filled crucial economic and political posts.[31] But the Portuguese were favored as "whites" and Europeans, not as haoles. To encourage the reproduction of Germans and Portuguese, the Lihue plantation, for many years after annexation, gave a present of $5 to the mother at the birth of a child.[32] The haoles liked the Portuguese for many reasons: their votes added substantially to the strength of the Republican party; they easily accepted authority; and they came to Hawaii to stay and not "to make a pile and go back home." By 1906, the first group of Portuguese had settled into Hawaii and had their own language school, four newspapers, and two welfare societies. The writer of an article in the haole paper the *Pacific Commercial Advertiser* exclaimed, "As plantation laborers, Portuguese are admitted by all to be the best of all the nationalities that have been hired here and the cheapest." Contrasts between the Chinese and the Portuguese were drawn frequently. The Portuguese were not only white and Christian, but they seemed content to take the jobs assigned to them; the second-generation Chinese were possessed with a demonic drive for education and were, as critical haoles often pointed out, unwilling to do manual labor.[33] Comparisons with the Japanese, too, showed the Europeans at a good advantage from the haole point of view. The Portuguese were often stereotyped as open and truthful, the men from Japan as secretive and sneaky. The haoles would joke about the propensity of the Portuguese for talk and repeat the cliché, "Telephone, telegraph, teleportuguese," but at least everyone knew what they were up to.

In Hawaii, the inner haole elite determined policy, the Scotch managed, and the Portuguese supervised. The Portuguese formed the *luna* class of the Islands. In the beginning, they were available for field occupations, but they were rarely asked to do the heavy work. A Hawaiian sugar-plantation official admitted in 1923 that the Portuguese, while physically as strong as the Japanese, were not asked to do the heavy work of harvesting.[34] Although seven out of ten of the gainfully employed male Portuguese were classified as laborers at annexation, only three out of ten were so categorized by 1930.

The Portuguese laborers did not disappoint the haole planters as much as the Scandinavians and Galicians, but some Portuguese disliked remaining field hands. During the 1920's and '30's, a considerable number of Portuguese went into commerce or became skilled laborers in the cities, although the proportion of Chinese entering these fields was greater. As Europeans, the Portuguese were eligible for naturalization and were favored by homesteading laws. By 1930, about 45 per cent of all Portuguese in Hawaii were in Honolulu, engaging in a wide range of occupations and living mainly on the slopes of Punchbowl and the upper portions of the Kalihi Valley.

The vast majority of Portuguese entered the *luna* class either as supervisors or as skilled and semiskilled workers. They acted as day-to-day buffers between the haoles and Oriental laborers. The job of head overseer, to say nothing of manager, did not go to the Portuguese; in 1901 not a single Portuguese had become even a head overseer's assistant, although there were eight Germans and four Scotchmen in that position.[35] But there were almost three times as many Portuguese *lunas* in the field as any other ethnic group. By 1915, no Portuguese had yet been appointed head overseer, although the Portuguese had continued to dominate the *luna* and assistant *luna* categories despite the fact that there were ten times as many Japanese as Portuguese laborers on the plantations. The Portuguese were always paid more for the same work than their Oriental counterparts, although the gap between these rates was not as great as the differential that separated them from the haoles. For example, in 1915, 132 Portuguese overseers averaged $2.24 a day, while eighty-one Americans were paid $3.82 and seventeen Japanese received $1.86.[36]

The wage gap between haole and Portuguese was symbolic. No matter how hard the Portuguese might try and no matter how much they might be favored over the Orientals, they were not usually accepted as haoles. Non-acceptance by the Hawaiians and haoles constantly forced the Portuguese to show their superiority over the Orientals. Time after time, Portuguese insisted they were haole. "We were the first white men to come to the Islands," a Portuguese restaurant-keeper erroneously put it in 1958.[37]

Pieced together, the Portuguese self-portrait was something like this: We came with our families (unlike the Orientals) to settle down and stay, to build Hawaii, not just to make money and run away. We worked the land hard and kept our homes well. Our wives stayed at home where they belonged (unlike the Orientals). We loved the outdoors and animals and pets. We had no crazy ideas about becoming lawyers, doctors, or engineers, but were willing to work with the great and good men who settled Hawaii and made it what it is today. We saved our money and were open and honest with others (unlike the Orientals). We were devout Catholics and instilled in our children respect for the social order. We did not become troublemakers (unlike the Orientals).

The Portuguese self-portrait often accorded with the facts. A visit in the 1950's to the hilltop homes of hearty Portuguese ranchers on Kauai or the Big Island was a delightful experience. There was humor a haole visitor could understand. There was good talk, ample food, and there were comfortable living quarters. But there was also, except among the more successful politicians, businessmen, and ranchers, much bitterness.

In 1940, the Portuguese had neither won the coveted goal of being accepted as haole nor been able to maintain occupational and social distance between themselves and the Orientals. In fact, they were slipping behind the Chinese and Japanese in income and occupational prestige. The self-portrait of the Portuguese family bent on making their children productive and conforming members of the social order was all too devastatingly true. A survey in 1910 showed that of all the groups in Hawaii, the Portuguese spent the least amount of their income on education.[38] They had come from the Madeiras and Azores with no tradition of respect for education or intellectual achievement. In Hawaii they were encouraged to believe that their role as *lunas* over the Orientals was permanent. The social order in Hawaii, like the social order back home, would not change, thought the Portuguese. When it did change, they felt profoundly deceived. Their anger erupted, not against the haoles, but against those who had refused to accept the terms of the social order as the Portuguese had done.

The growing competition and success of second- and third-generation Orientals during the 1920's and '30's reinforced the widespread Portuguese need to demonstrate their "haoleness."[39] Whereas the Hawaiians were often called *"kanakas"* by other groups in the Islands, some Portuguese labeled them "black *kanakas*." When the Chinese, and to a lesser extent the Japanese, gave signs of displacing the Portuguese in politics as well as in the trades and skilled occupations during the 1930's, the Portuguese leaned increasingly on a racial explanation for the success of the Orientals. "Japanese businessmen," recalled a contractor from Kauai, "are not like us white men. They won't give the other fellow a fair share."[40]

Beginning in 1910, a large number of Portuguese females solved the problem of identity by marrying haole men; between 1912 and 1934, more than 20 per cent of the Portuguese women who married chose haole husbands. During the same period, only two out of every hundred Portuguese males married haole girls. A substantial number of Portuguese girls married part-Hawaiians, too, thus moving farther away from haole identity. But well over 50 per cent of the women and 70 per cent of the men married within their own group, thus perpetuating the problem of the Portuguese—nonacceptance as haoles.[41]

Other Caucasians, however, continued to improve their status, and by 1935, haoles, comprising about one fifth of the population of the Islands, constituted less than 1 per cent of the agricultural labor force and filled more than 40 per cent of the professional services.[42] Business or corporation law, rather than professional leadership, provided the best entry to the inner haole elite. There were not enough sons and sons-in-law to fill all the top spots, and the policy leaders of Hawaii were constantly looking for congenial and ambitious newcomers. Of course, marrying the right women would speed entrance into the charmed circle, as lawyers Walter Frear and Arthur G. Smith discovered.

The leaders preferred home-grown haoles rather than college-educated mainlanders. For example, Alan S. Davis, whose father was English and whose mother came from Ireland, and who was one day to become president and chairman of the board of C. Brewer & Co., was graduated from Honolulu High School around 1906. He was taken under the wing of E. D. Tenney, whose sister had married George P. Castle, and who was a major figure in the sugar industry. After a year, he was made production manager of the Waipahu Pineapple Cannery; then he became an executive of the Hawaiian Trust Company, where he remained for twenty-five years. Befriended later by Clarence C. Cooke and Frank C. Atherton, two of the top haole leaders of the 1920's and '30's, he became president of Hawaiian Tuna Packers and of C. Brewer & Co.

Upward mobility was not difficult for the bright mainland haole, but the *malihini* found it virtually impossible to crack the inner group except through marriage. It was possible to make money by taking stock in sugar or other growth companies, but money alone was no passport to status, prestige, or power in Hawaii. One of the first *malihini* manager-executives to rise to a high policy position in Hawaii was Leslie A. Hicks, who eventually became president and later chairman of the board of the Hawaiian Electric Company. Hicks's father was a rigger who was born in Massachusetts and had made carriages in northern Maine. After losing his business through the dereliction of his partner, the father traveled on to Maryland, Montana, and California as a railroad builder and gold miner, and in 1908 he wound up in Hawaii. Young Hicks went to Punahou for one year and became a rod-and-chain man for the Territorial Survey Office at the age of fifteen. He went back to school a few years later and pushed through the University of Hawaii, although he had had no high-school education. His destiny changed when he married the daughter of a man named Frank E. Blake, from Newburyport, Massachusetts, who had become an accountant and then manager for the new Hawaiian Electric Company. Hicks joined the company and was promoted to production engineer in 1925. His success in designing electric plants prompted Richard A. Cooke, then the company's president, to move Hicks up to the position of treasurer. He was made manager of the corporation in 1937 and later became president.[43]

Although it was possible for individuals from the managerial haole class to rise to positions of considerable influence, they were still thought of as "hired men" by members of the *kamaaina* elite. Occupational mobility did not lead to social acceptance. A bright business executive or lawyer not related by blood or marriage to the inner elite might be awarded a position of power in politics or corporation management but still be denied the sweet taste of full membership in the elite. The two groups—policy makers and managers—met frequently on Merchant Street and even occasionally for a game of golf, but black-tie affairs at the Dillinghams' or Castles' might be closed to the lesser haoles. At Punahou, the children of the *kamaaina* elite kept their distance from their future employees.

In the rural plantation areas, the distinctions between the two groups were in some ways less sharp, in others more distinct. The now middle-aged sons and daughters of the supervisory group recall how, when young, they were permitted to play with the Rice children on Kauai or the Baldwins on Maui; but they also remember that they were instructed to go home if a *kamaaina* cousin appeared for play, and that they were warned as adolescents not to date members of Hawaii's important families.[44]

These subtle social distinctions, while keenly felt by many in the managerial group, went largely unnoticed by Hawaii's vast nonhaole population. They could see that most managerial children went to Punahou, and, indeed, a majority of white children prior to 1920 were in private schools. Policy differences within the haole group on such issues as immigration were apparent to the better-informed nonhaoles, but class differences were not clearly discernible. To them, all of the haoles shared membership in a privileged class.

Nowhere was the haole sense of privilege and power clearer to the others than on the plantations. Every living and working arrangement on the sugar and, later, the pineapple plantations was calculated to make haoles as a class feel superior. In almost every instance, plantation officials encouraged segregation of haoles from nonhaoles. Even into the late 1930's, when many occupational status taboos had been broken, haole social life was restricted. On a plantation on Molokai, the only Orientals present at haole dinners or cocktail parties came as the spouses of haoles from outside communities. On the big Lanai pineapple plantation, nonhaole schoolteachers were explicitly excluded from the haole social circle.[45]

Social distance was important in maintaining the plantation system of power. The king, after all, goes among his people, but does not invite them to tea. The great social gulf between the manager and the others was made apparent by his standard of living. The manager was king. He lived in a superb house, usually on the highest hill in the area. His court consisted of other haoles—assistant managers, section *lunas,* bookkeepers, and engineers. Even on the smallest plantations, his house was a mansion, and he was surrounded by servants. In some cases he paid house servants out of his own munificent salary, but the gardeners and handymen came with the job. By 1910, many managers were making $1,000 a month in addition to extensive perquisites, a fantastic sum in Hawaii, where the field hands were getting less than seventy-five cents a day. By 1938, when, by mainland standards, workers' wages were still low, some plantation managers were making $18,000 a year, plus extras.[46]

No wonder the manager felt like a monarch. His every word was followed with excitement by the plantation community and even in the small villages beyond. He might speak graciously at the sixth- or eighth-grade commencement of the village school and give out prizes on behalf of the plantation; he might ungraciously fire and punish employees according to his whims. It was up to him whether gambling and drinking would be sanctioned or prostitutes permitted to visit the camps. It was his decision whether movies would be shown or primitive recreational facilities be built. His word determined whether workers could leave the camps for weekends in Hilo or Honolulu. On at least one plantation in the 1930's, the manager's dress was copied by his supervisors and assistants. When the manager changed from high-topped field boots to low shoes, field boots went out of style. When he switched from one brand of whisky to another, the storekeeper noticed that the latter brand was more in demand.[47]

There were so few outside checks on the power of managers that many were easily corrupted. One of them expressed it, many years after his retirement, by saying that so much power with no checks "makes one feel close to God." This was not the closeness to God that the first haole missionaries had hoped to promote; the managers felt a sense of grandeur, of superiority, and immunity from criticism. In some cases, there were checks on the abuse of power, but they were exceptions rather than the rule. Old-timers on Kauai recall that Gaylord P. Wilcox was always strict with his managers and supervisers, forbidding the manhandling of workers at Grove Farm, near Lihue.[48] Others remember that in the late nineteenth and early twentieth centuries workers were abused much more fiercely at Kekaha, Lihue, and Koloa, which were in German hands, than at the Wilcox plantation. After annexation, leading planters realized that free laborers could not be abused as were the contract laborers, and they sometimes tried to restrain an overzealous manager. One leading official of the Hawaiian Sugar Planters' Association wrote a manager in 1905, admonishing, "In times past we got too much in the habit of treating the Japanese and Chinese as if they were more animals than men. We cannot do this now . . . so, while you must not give way to loafers for a moment, it would be well to be firm in a more kindly manner than was the custom ten years ago." Later, in the 1920's and '30's the Oahu managers were checked by public opinion in Honolulu. The swashbuckling, devil-may-care type of manager of the old days had gone out of fashion.[49]

The plantation manager, because of his unique power, has become a legendary figure in Hawaii. The cruelest manager in the recollection of elderly *kamaaina* haoles was the Prussian W. E. Anton Cropp, who managed at Koloa for the decade immediately preceding annexation. Cropp kept a small jail, more of a dungeon than a prison, to which he would banish recalcitrant Oriental workers for an indefinite stay. Cropp was replaced at the end of contract labor by an Irish mule skinner named Pat McLane, who was no less colorful. McLane's reputation as manager from 1900 to 1906 rested on his unorthodoxy. He was the first manager to compete for labor by increasing wages. Also he was probably the first manager to pay extra wages for faster work. But H. Broomfield Brown, on Lanai, was perhaps the most colorful manager of all. During Brown's tenure as manager in the 1930's, no domestic animals or pets were allowed on the island. Brown watched every activity on the plantation from a telescope in his house on the top of a hill. Because there was little vegetation at that time, he could plainly see the village below and, beyond that, sections of the pineapple fields. He spotted workers loafing on the job and rode into the fields to give them a tongue-lashing. If he caught anyone dropping candy wrappings or other trash in the village, he personally inflicted a strong reprimand. When the inter-island boat docked at the harbor at Kaumalapau, Brown, impeccably dressed, would inspect each debarkee to keep out gamblers, salesmen, and prostitutes.[50]

Nowhere were the managers more important than on the island of Hawaii. Remote from Honolulu supervision or from missionary-family influence on Kauai and Maui, the Big Island's managers ran the government and economy of the county to a considerable extent, as well as their own plantations. On Hawaii, more than any place else, power was irresponsible. On the Hamakua Coast, Scotch managers were feared more than respected, even into the 1920's. A former haole supervisor remembers head *luna* John Cullen, at Kohala, complaining in the early 1920's that softness was beginning to destroy the manager's control over his workers. Cullen longed for the days of the black whip, before social workers and school teachers began to interfere with the manager's authority. Cullen, who subsequently killed himself, one day raced his horse through the hedge and beautiful flower garden of a Japanese worker's house. He pounded on the door, shouting "Where's Toshi?" After receiving a nervous wifely answer that Toshi was sick, he raced through another portion of the hedge. Many on the Big Island recall Manager George C. Watt, of the North Kohala plantation, during the mid-1920's. His haole friends remember him as a wonderful father and husband, but when he went out in the morning on his big sorrel horse, with his whip in hand, he became an unfriendly and ruthless manager. Every morning Watt would call each of the first five workers he met a "son of a bitch." One day, he gave his customary greeting to a Portuguese tractor driver whose mother had died only ten days before. The boy picked up a stone and threw it at Watt. He missed, grabbed the rein of Watt's horse, reached for a small stick, and smashed the manager on the arm, breaking the club. A haole assistant manager, who saw this episode, watched the Scotchman ride away, leaving the Portuguese boy in tears. Later, Watt secretly apologized, explaining to his assistant that he was merely exercising his authority and had no intention of insulting anyone's mother. A Filipino businessman who was formerly a plantation worker remembers Watt as a tyrant. Watt once confided to a friend that he was not hired to carry on a program of economic and social reform. His job was to produce sugar at low cost. In his own words, "We are the victims of the system."[51]

What happened on the plantations depended largely on the manager. He could be kind, intelligent, and sensitive or brutal and stupid. During the late 1920's and early '30's, it became apparent that the plantations could no longer afford the latter type, for it was becoming difficult to keep laborers on the plantations. The rehabilitation of plantation housing, the planning of recreational facilities, and other changes under the "modern manager" became the order of the day. The shift in emphasis was exemplified by the difference between two generations of Scotts, managers at the Aiea plantation. The father, John, is remembered by old-timers as being as tough and mean as any manager. The son, Alvah, began by denying he was a reformer who would pamper his men, but he ultimately adopted extensive welfare methods.[52]

The shift in emphasis during the 1930's did not mean that managers were to be spendthrift. Some managers, such as Alvah Scott and T. G. S. Walker, of the Kahuku plantation on Oahu, gained reputations as high-cost managers, and were ultimately fired. Walker was probably the most revolutionary manager in Hawaiian plantation history. He hired a brilliant young doctor, H. T. Rothwell, to build a new hospital at Kahuku, which was eventually recognized by the National Association of Physicians and Surgeons. Alexander & Baldwin officials remember Walker's complaints during the early 1930's that the haoles in Honolulu did not have enough faith in their Oriental employees. He constantly preached mutual trust. In 1935, he helped his workers put in a nine-hole golf course and tennis courts at the plantation, which created something of a sensation in managerial circles, since tennis was supposed to be a haole game. In 1938, he prevailed upon the A. & B. directors to spend $100,000 on housing improvements.

The lesser haole managerial and business groups in town and the haole skilled workers were never as certain of their privileges as the haoles on the plantations. From the 1880's on, they complained of competition from the Orientals. The haoles in town had to guard their privileges zealously, especially during the 1920's and '30's, as a large new class of haoles arrived in Hawaii—mainly Honolulu—from the mainland, and as Orientals fought for education and better jobs in the city. The haole population of Hawaii more than doubled between 1920 and 1930, a much larger increase than for the Islands as a whole. The new haoles were largely absorbed by the growing manufacturing and mechanical, transportation, public-service, and trade industries of the Islands. Hawaii needed clerks, managers, foremen, craftsmen, and professionals.

Just as control was the integrating objective of the elite, the desire to maintain privilege was the major purpose of the lesser haoles. The immigrant haoles did not have to go through a period of apprenticeship. They were, after all, literate and largely skilled. Most of them settled in Honolulu. By 1930, 74.2 per cent of the haoles lived in Honolulu and Hilo, and 7.7 per cent in the rural part of Oahu. The censuses in 1920 and 1930 showed the haoles to be living in self-segregated high-prestige districts—the upper Nuuanu Valley, Manoa Valley, Waikiki, Kahala, Alewa Heights, Pacific Heights, Makiki Heights, and Maunalani. The newer haoles, many of them coming from the South and more from the West Coast, were more actively anti-Oriental than the *kamaaina* elite, and racial tensions increased in Honolulu, where a middle class was emerging during the 1920's and '30's owing to the rise of the Orientals in town and migrations of haoles from the mainland. Haoles increasingly resented paying for the growing educational requirements of the nonhaole population. One sociologist found "marked racial prejudice . . . in the middle class" during the 1920's.[53] In the 1930's, another observed that "the intensive competition within the city constituted a threat to the stability of race relations in the Islands."[54]

Racial tensions between *malihini* haoles, including servicemen, were highest during the 1930's, first at the time of the famous Ala Moana case and later as relations between Tokyo and Washington brought the two nations closer to war. In the Ala Moana or Massie rape case of 1931–32, Mrs. Massie, the wife of a naval officer, alleged that five local youths of dark skin had attacked and raped her in Ala Moana Park. The young men—two Japanese, two Hawaiians, and a Chinese-Hawaiian—were not convicted; the racially mixed Honolulu jury could not agree on a verdict. Although Mrs. Massie's testimony was confused and vague, and the Pinkerton Detective Agency subsequently vindicated a judgment of acquittal in every respect in a private report to the Governor of Hawaii, a large segment of the *malihini* haole population was persuaded that haole womanhood had been viciously despoiled. Many newer haoles applauded when Mrs. Massie's husband, mother, and two young sailors kidnaped and murdered one of the young Hawaiians while the youths were waiting for a new trial. Lieutenant Massie and his accomplices were convicted, but under pressure from the U.S. Navy, Governor Lawrence Judd commuted their sentences within an hour after conviction.[55]

Another factor encouraging racial tension was the growth of the military population in the Islands during the 1920's and '30's. In 1920, there were less than 4,000 military personnel in the Islands, but twenty years later, nearly 60 per cent of the employed males of Caucasian ancestry in Hawaii were members of the armed services. Military personnel usually were not integrated into Island life, but mainland racial attitudes undoubtedly affected local haoles.[56] Ironically, the Hawaiian tradition of miscegenation made a similar impact on the American boys. The latter, homesick and bored with the routine of military life, were often encouraged by Hawaiian mothers and grandmothers to make a close acquaintance with girls of darker complexion. During 1926–27, 62 per cent of the haole servicemen stationed in the Islands who marched to the altar married nonhaole women.[57] The newer civilian haoles also frequently married Portuguese or part-Hawaiian or Hawaiian females. Between 1912 and 1934, approximately 45 per cent of all haole men marrying picked nonhaole brides. Approximately 10 per cent of the haole females during the same period married nonhaole men, tending to favor Caucasian-Hawaiians.[58] Intermarriage was so extensive that by 1930 nearly one fourth of the civilian "other Caucasian" (the term used by the census takers for haoles) children had some Portuguese, Spanish, or Puerto Rican ancestry.

The newer haoles were not "born to rule" as were the members of the *kamaaina* haole elite, but most of them quickly took their places in the ethnic-social class system of the Islands, a position distinctly above the other ethnic groups with respect to educational and occupational opportunity. Intermarriage blurred the distinctness somewhat, but, for the most part, the haoles, including the lesser haoles, remained a privileged group apart.

Chapter Two

PILIKIA AND ALOHA

The essential purpose of the haole elite for four decades after annexation was to control Hawaii; the major aim of the lesser haoles was to promote and maintain their privileged position. Most Hawaiians were motivated by a dominant and inclusive purpose—to recapture the past.

The present and the future appeared devastatingly bleak to the Hawaiians, who continued to decline in numbers due to social disorganization, psychological demoralization, susceptibility to disease, and intermarriage. Until 1920, it appeared that the Hawaiian people were headed for extinction. The pure Hawaiian population had decreased from nearly 70,000 in 1853 to 24,000 by 1920. The number of part-Hawaiians—mainly Chinese-Hawaiians or haole-Hawaiians—had been growing steadily, and after 1920 increased even more rapidly; but in the seventy years from 1850 to 1920 the number of persons with Hawaiian blood living in the Islands was cut almost in half.[1]

The decline continued even after infanticide had been stopped and abortions had been sharply curtailed. In every census year the pure Hawaiians led all others in infant mortality and deaths from tuberculosis. In 1924, for example, among pure Hawaiians there were 291 deaths of children under one year of age for every 1,000 births, compared to thirty-three deaths among haole babies.

The physical decline of the Hawaiians was matched by their inability to adjust to many aspects of haole civilization. Although the Hawaiians' dominant response to the new and hostile environment of the Islands was withdrawal into the past, the present confronted them everywhere. Continuity with past habits concerning sex and property relationships encouraged an extraordinarily high rate of crime against property and sex, as determined by haole laws. Continuity was not the only explanation of what was viewed by others as antisocial behavior, however. The Hawaiians, more than any other group in the Islands, found it difficult to adjust to the highly competitive haole social order. As a result, they were often found in the crowded and substandard living conditions that encouraged crime.

But economic opportunity as well as social degradation existed in Honolulu, and between 1896 and 1920, while the total Hawaiian population veered sharply downward, the number of Hawaiians living in Honolulu actually increased. By 1920, more than half of the part-Hawaiians and 36 per cent of the pure Hawaiians in the Islands lived in Honolulu, as compared with only 33 per cent of the population as a whole. The Hawaiians, for the most part, crowded into tenements which ill suited their traditional way of life. In 1910, an investigation of living conditions among the Polynesians in Honolulu found people in Papakolea, a heavily populated Hawaiian area near Punchbowl, living in shelters made of packing boxes and old lumber gathered from rubbish heaps. In many cases several families lived together in two or three rooms, and the children's diet was insufficient. The death rate among pure Hawaiians in Honolulu was double that on the outer islands. As late as 1936, most Hawaiians in the area used outdoor stoves for cooking, made from large empty oil cans cut at the top and down one side and placed against a wall.[2]

A few families, related to chiefs or royalty, and usually *hapa*-haole, owned handsome properties in Honolulu and lived in high fashion. Others did well in law or insurance and were able to compete with haoles on their own terms, and because the Hawaiians constituted the largest voting group, a disproportionate number were found in semi-political occupations. For example, in 1930 there were 138 pure Hawaiian policemen, eighty Caucasian-Hawaiians and twenty-two of Asian-Hawaiian stock, compared with only twenty-three haoles, fifteen Japanese, and six Chinese. Because of their interest and influence in politics, there were more judges, lawyers, and teachers who were Hawaiian and part-Hawaiian than of any other group. But the vast majority of Hawaiians in Honolulu played lesser occupational roles. They avoided retail trades and the professions other than law. In 1930, there was not a single pure Hawaiian physician or surgeon in the Islands, and fewer part-Hawaiian medical men or dentists than were found in any other major ethnic group with the exception of the Filipinos, whose work was limited almost entirely to the plantations. Throughout the postannexation era, many Hawaiians worked as laborers and were especially active as stevedores and teamsters. Others went into the communications, manufacturing, and mechanical industries. They displayed relatively little occupational mobility, while other groups moved out of the unskilled and semiskilled labor classes during the 1920's and '30's.

Many Hawaiian migrants to the cities came from sugar plantations, for the vast majority of Hawaiians could not accustom themselves to plantation life. Whereas in 1882, one of every four employees of the sugar plantations was Hawaiian or part-Hawaiian, the proportion dropped to three of every hundred shortly after annexation; by 1932, only one of every hundred employees on the plantations was of Hawaiian ancestry. Very few of those remained field laborers, and during the 1920's and '30's the Hawaiians were well represented in the *luna,* clerical, and skilled-laborer groups.[3]

A small number of Hawaiians left the plantations for work on cattle ranches, where they had greater freedom of movement, a more carefree, happy-go-lucky existence. They liked the more fraternal and personal relationships between employer and employee. Nearly all of Hawaii's cattle ranches were family operated, with no more than two full-time hired hands. The Hawaiian cowboy became a popular and romantic figure, and even on the larger ranches these Hawaiian cowboys appeared to have made a successful adjustment. The work was not as monotonous as on the plantations, there were few Orientals to crowd them, and the cowboys were left pretty much on their own. Ranch paternalism was in many respects no different from the paternalism of the *alii.* On the bigger ranches, mostly owned and run by haoles, the managers handled personal problems for the workers, helped them out of scrapes, paid their debts, and even provided housing, medical assistance, and low prices on rice, *poi,* and meat.

The ranch was closer in many ways to ancient Hawaii than the city or the plantation. But it was in the rural villages and more especially in the out-of-the-way subsistence communities that Hawaiians could be most like their ancestors. Throughout the postannexation period, large numbers of Hawaiians lived in the rural areas of Kohala and Kona on the Big Island, and the Koolauloa district on the windward coast of Oahu. Other Hawaiian enclaves could be found in Hana on the east coast of Maui, and on the island of Molokai. In 1930, there were still seventeen remote districts, geographically unsuitable for industrial agriculture, in which Hawaiians constituted more than 50 per cent of the population. Andrew Lind in his brilliant sociological study, *An Island Community*, wrote of scores of smaller valleys in isolated districts throughout the Islands, each of which provided a haven for a few Hawaiian families. "The old fish and poi economy, with its accompaniment of tutelary deities, tabus, religion and magic, still persists in modified form within many of these isolated communities. A small plot of *taro* and access to the sea and the mountains are apparently all that is required for the satisfaction of their material wants." There, the ancient system of child adoption or exchange, the medical practices of the *kahunas,* such as their use of herbs and vegetable compounds, and even variants of the old Polynesian system of polygamy continued well into the twentieth century.[4]

Outside of these subsistence communities, the Hawaiians could recapture the older civilization only in fancy, not in fact. Everywhere the new economy imposed new demands. It became increasingly apparent that the Hawaiian could compete neither with the haole nor with the Oriental. Steadily, the land slipped out of Hawaiian hands. The number of Hawaiians owning real estate remained approximately the same between 1900 and 1930, while the proportion of Portuguese doubled and that of Chinese increased fivefold.[5]

The inability of the Hawaiians to adjust to the city or to hold onto their lands led Hawaiian leaders such as Prince Jonah Kuhio and John Wise to push a resolution through the territorial legislature in 1919 requesting Congress to provide public lands for the purpose of rehabilitating the Hawaiian people. Congress established the Hawaiian Homes Commission in 1920, which set aside public lands at nominal rentals on long-term leases for persons with at least one half Hawaiian blood. At first, only lands on Molokai and three small districts on Hawaii were designated; later, sections on Oahu, Maui, and Kauai came under the jurisdiction of the Commission. As a mainland congressman put it, "The purpose of this bill is to permit people of Hawaiian blood to again get possession of land in Hawaii." As the Act was amended, Hawaiians could apply for land for residential homesteads and then borrow money from the Commission's Home-Loan Fund to erect houses or purchase livestock and farm equipment or for the general development of the land.

Despite the high hopes of its sponsors, many factors reduced the effectiveness of the rehabilitation program. Only a small fraction of the

200,000 acres of land set aside under the Act was suitable for agriculture. Many Hawaiians resented being told that they could live on wasteland. In 1931, a territorial investigative committee reported that the relationship between homesteaders and the commissioners was strained. The Hawaiians incurred many debts by purchasing on the installment plan, and the Commission found it necessary to regulate such buying. A legislative committee found six years later that housing conditions were often poor and unsanitary and that homestead economics were unsteady because the homesteaders were deeply in debt for luxuries while often lacking necessities. On Molokai, at the original and largest homestead settlement, Hawaiian farming suffered. High winds, dust, pests, lack of water, and high transportation costs proved troublesome. Land and weather conditions were such that it may have been extremely difficult to grow anything but pineapple, a crop that cannot be raised profitably on small plots. The Molokai settlers might have gone under were it not for the introduction of pineapple. By 1933, over 4,000 acres were devoted to pineapple, with only 240 acres planted in other crops. The Hawaiians leased their own leased land to major pineapple companies, thus entirely defeating the original purpose of the rehabilitation program. The pineapple companies hired Filipinos to work on the Hawaiian land and turned monthly checks over to the homesteaders.[6]

This system often encouraged idleness among the Hawaiians at Molokai, a condition also found at Papakolea, the Hawaiian Homes area in Honolulu, where no farms were possible. There, the lands, taken over by the Commission in 1934, supported approximately 100 families. The homesteaders, according to one investigator in 1936, did not appear to understand the system of private land ownership and seemed unwilling to do anything to protect themselves against the onslaughts of haole and Oriental competition.[7]

The rehabilitation idea did not produce a Hawaiian renaissance. It was, after all, too much to ask. The haole religion, family structure, sex mores, land system, property relationships, art, and handicrafts were fundamentally different from what was known in ancient Hawaii. The Hawaiian Homes Commission Act represented one more, perhaps the major, futile Hawaiian effort to recapture the past.

The Hawaiians had as much difficulty accumulating capital as they did holding on to the land. They did not believe in saving for a rainy day, nor did they stress education. Thrift was a haole concept, stemming from a society based on private property. Average deposits in savings banks were consistently lower than for all other ethnic groups. Indeed, the per-capita savings for Hawaiians and part-Hawaiians plummeted sharply during the depression of the 1930's, while other groups held their own. By 1934, more than 10 per cent of the Hawaiian or part-Hawaiian men between the ages of twenty and fifty-four were on relief, triple the proportion of Japanese and almost ten times that of Filipinos. When economic adversity hit the Hawaiians, despondency spread among the people advertised on the tourist posters as gay, devil-may-care Polynesians.[8]

The haole civilization emphasized competition, individual planning, and material success; Hawaiian culture stressed co-operation and day-to-day living. At first the Hawaiians, especially the *alii,* weakened their own moral and social order by reaching for the comforts, power, and prestige they thought would flow from the winning of foreign goods and skills. Having undermined their own cultural foundations, they were still sufficiently affected by them to be unable to compete successfully with the haoles. The ingenious pioneer sociologist of Hawaii, Romanzo Adams, told of a successful Hawaiian businessman who was not well liked by his people and who related that when he urged his men to work hard they thought he was grasping. Adams explained that a Hawaiian storekeeper could not coldly refuse credit to a needy neighbor merely because payment was not probable. The tradition of sharing among hungry and needy friends was too deeply ingrained to sacrifice on the altar of the haole goal "to get ahead."[9]

Increasingly, as frustrations accumulated, most Hawaiians, rightly or wrongly, believed that they had not chosen the haole way of life—it had been forced upon them. They were driven off their own lands and obliged to accept an alien social system. Although the Orientals came to make money, and they always had the choice, at least in theory, of going back home, the Islands were home to the Polynesians. There was no place else to go, and steadily, through no fault of their own, they became, in many important respects, strangers in their own land.

The tourist posters continued to portray the Hawaiian with sparkling eyes and teeth and a jolly air. It is true that a large proportion of entertainers in the Islands were Hawaiian or part-Hawaiian. Everywhere, in towns and in the rural areas, Hawaiians could be found strumming ukuleles, putting on a gay show at *luaus,* or entertaining each other with uproariously funny and often lusty tales. The Hawaiians were musical, of course, and they possessed a remarkable sense of the incongruous. But some private Hawaiian humor was close to tragedy. What could be more incongruous than the history of Hawaiian-haole relations? For many Hawaiians, music and humor were undoubtedly links with the past, and the past loomed increasingly important and glorious, although distant, in their minds' eyes.

Outside of Waikiki, the face of the Hawaiian during the 1920's and '30's was often apathetic rather than animated. Apathy, a condition noticed by nineteenth-century travelers to Hawaii, signaled a grudging acquiescence in the new system. Whether the surface emotion was apathy or gaiety, quite often the deeper feeling was despair. There developed a fatalistic recognition that the Hawaiians were a dying people and that the Hawaiian way of life was dying with them.

A Hawaiian self-stereotype pictured the native as more generous, more trusting, and more existential than the haole or the Oriental. Each aspect of the Hawaiian self-image could be traced in part to fundamental differences between Hawaiian social organization and ethics and the haole success ethos.

The Hawaiians spoke of generosity as "Hawaiian *aloha*," something that could not be commercialized. *Aloha* was given freely, not to make money or to influence votes. One Hawaiian, admired by his fellow Polynesians on the island of Kauai, spoke repeatedly of "Hawaiian heart." It was Hawaiian heart that encouraged the *hanai* pattern of child adoption in the rural areas as late as the 1930's. A *hanai* child was given away by its true parents as a mark of love or respect for the recipient foster parents, who sometimes gave more attention to the *hanai* child than to their own. *Hanai* also means "to feed," and the people were proud that Hawaiian *aloha* prompted them to welcome visitors with copious amounts of food as soon as they arrived.[10]

The Hawaiian repudiation of or inability to understand the haole drive for success also led to the self-stereotype of Hawaiian trust. The Hawaiian, interviewers were told many times, was easily fooled because he believed what others said. As a leader on Oahu put it, "The Hawaiians were not double faced." Another spokesman asserted, "The Hawaiians have no idea what a white lie is." The haoles and Orientals, being acquisitive, were said to trick the Hawaiians. During the 1930's, stories multiplied concerning the alienation of land through chicanery.[11]

To succeed—whatever that meant—seemed the haole and Oriental goal. As the Hawaiians saw it, the out-groups planned and saved to get ahead, wasting each precious day to achieve a distant goal. With a sense of superiority, a well-known Hawaiian entertainer pointed out that she likes to do what she feels like doing at the moment. She and other Hawaiians stress the importance of following one's mood rather than the "shoulds" and "oughts" of life and of being totally absorbed in each experience. "Sometimes," she said, "I have to be Hawaiian and not haole."[12]

Left with memories that became legends, many Hawaiians withdrew further into an unreal past in which fact and fiction were often blurred. King Kalakaua was recalled as a sterling hero, a man of impeccable virtue and huge generosity. Queen Liliuokalani became an unblemished saint. Genealogy, formerly the basis for the claims of chiefs to positions of leadership, continued to receive emphasis even after it failed to perform this function. In the late 1930's, a Hawaiian clerk, whose father had once been appointed by Kalakaua as superintendent of the Oahu Tramway System, paid a visit to the Archives, where he traced his genealogy back to the year 1090. Others, unable or unwilling to follow the trail to the Archives, nonetheless elaborated on their genealogies at length.[13]

Beginning in 1902, a secret organization known as the Order of Kamehameha was formed with the object of preserving and perpetuating the ancient customs and traditions of Hawaii. The first meeting, held at the home of Prince Jonah Kuhio, was attended by many of the leading Hawaiians and Caucasian-Hawaiians of Oahu. Secrecy was stressed, the *alii* wore special capes, and the symbols of the organization represented Kamehameha's efforts to unify the Kingdom.[14] Later, in 1918, increasing concern among Hawaiian leaders over the disappearance of the old ways led to the formation of two additional organizations. One, the Hawaiian Civic Club, was founded by the Prince, then the Delegate to Congress, to help preserve Hawaiian culture and to assist with the social welfare of Hawaiians. The other, an aristocratic group, the Hale o Na Alii (House of Chiefs), was founded by his sister-in-law, Princess Abigail Kawananakoa, for the same general purpose. These groups and others provided a focus for Hawaiian introspection, for the never-ending Hawaiian quest to recapture the past.

The Hawaiians had come from a caste society and were not prepared to deal with an increasingly dynamic and competitive social order. Most Hawaiians, rather than strive to better their positions, accepted their role in the stratified system of postannexation Hawaii. Later, when social changes undermined the structure, the Hawaiians were unable to grapple with the new order.

Hawaiians traditionally depended upon the paternalism of chiefs and royalty. In 1859, a law was passed establishing a hospital for sick and destitute Hawaiians, but the hospital succeeded only when the King, with the help of Queen Emma, personally solicited funds to sustain it, thus beginning Queen's Hospital. Aged and enfeebled Hawaiians were provided for through the action of King Lunalilo, who, in his will, left funds to build the Lunalilo Home in 1887. Later, the Kapiolani Maternity Home was established through the generosity of Queen Kapiolani and her nephews. The maternity home and the Kapiolani Home for Leper Girls became the absorbing interest of the Queen after the death of her husband, Kalakaua. Queen Liliuokalani, the last of the Hawaiian monarchs, set aside her land to take care of orphaned and destitute Hawaiian children. The trustrees received permission from the courts to use the income to place children in foster homes or, in the case of a half-orphan, to enable the parent to maintain a home for the child.

With royalty gone and the surviving *alii* diminished in wealth and importance, many Hawaiians looked increasingly to haole and *hapa-haole* philanthropy. In some cases, haole families did take the place of feudal chiefs. The Baldwins and the Shipmans, like the feudal chiefs of old, took care of "their Hawaiians." Alfred W. Carter, who was a trustee of the Parker estate, became known as the "Lord of Kohala," a leader to whom Hawaiians could come for practical aid and psychological comfort. Complete paternalism existed on the tiny island of Niihau, where the Robinson family, owners of the island, ministered to some 200 Hawaiians and part-Hawaiians who worked on the Robinson ranch.

One favorite of Princess Bernice Pauahi Bishop, a part-Hawaiian who would have been adopted by the Bishops if his mother had permitted it and who would eventually have inherited the Bishop money and land, exemplified the Hawaiian dependence on haole chiefs. On many important decisions during his adult life, the part-Hawaiian would go to his haole boss, head of a major Island company, to find out what to do. When Mr. Bishop died, the part-Hawaiian was asked to carry the ashes to the burial place of the Princess, who had been his benefactress and had loved him deeply. His employer could not give him permission to go to the ceremony, although he undoubtedly wanted to, because the part-Hawaiian was needed for special work during the June pineapple season. The worker related to a friend that because the boss had been good to him, he would listen to his haole chief. Later, the employer discharged his obligation as chief when he paid his retainer's expensive hospital bills.[15]

Paternalism discouraged self-help, as was shown in the management of the Kamehameha Schools. Created under the will of Mrs. Bishop, the schools were supported by income from Bishop estate lands. Although the will did not specify that only children of Hawaiian ancestry could be admitted to the schools, preference has always been given to Hawaiians. But of the first trustees picked to manage the estate and the schools, not one was of Hawaiian blood. Rather, the four trustees— Samuel Damon, William Owen Smith, Charles M. Cooke, and Charles M. Hyde—were missionary descendants of wealth and power. A Congregational minister who was a strong advocate of what the second principal called "Christian industrial education" was picked to be the first principal of the Kamehameha School for Boys in 1887 (the girls' school was not begun until seven years later).[16] Future haole trustees such as Alfred W. Carter, Albert F. Judd, and George M. Collins, sustained that educational concept. The Schools, while recruiting well-trained teachers, did not provide a substantial liberal-arts curriculum or encourage students to aspire to higher education. Life at the Schools during the first four decades of this century was highly regimented. Especially until 1930, the boys' school emphasized vocational training and military drilling and the girls' concentrated on training future mothers and homemakers.

Paternalism, whether Hawaiian or haole, was aimed not at encouraging independence, but at promoting adjustment of the Hawaiians to their role in a stratified society and alleviation of the more serious aspects of social disorganization. As disorganization—crime, infant mortality, disease, broken homes, absenteeism at school—continued, and as life became increasingly competitive, the dependence of Hawaiians on others grew, leading to still lower self-respect and increased disorganization, and thus completing the cycle of despair. The Hawaiian assumption of a natural hierarchy of leadership further inhibited self-help. It was not only the haoles who believed that the Hawaiians were unfit to manage their own affairs. Few Hawaiian protests were heard as haoles assumed the role of spokesmen for them by becoming trustees of the important Hawaiian estates.

Acceptance of paternalism was one expression of continuity with the past. Religiosity and class divisions were others. In ancient Hawaii, religion permeated every aspect of life. The new religion was not so closely intertwined with daily life, but it remained intensely personal for the Hawaiians. Haole visitors to Hawaiian churches observed the deep personal relationship that the natives seemed to feel toward their God and the overwhelming faith expressed in Him. The new religion, although it had done so much to undermine the old social order, actually provided emotional relief to Hawaiians who were upset by changing circumstances. It must have seemed to many that only a miracle could save the Hawaiians, and only the gods or God could make miracles.

Church membership among the Hawaiians was unusually high. The Congregational church of the early missionaries remained a favorite, but large numbers of natives were won over to Catholicism and, later, to the Church of the Latter-day Saints. Missionaries for the last two religious groups were especially successful in rural areas, where, to many Hawaiians, they seemed more earthy and practical than the ascetic Congregationalists.[17] Revivalist sects also flourished among the Hawaiians, as they do on the mainland among depressed and despairing peoples. Within the churches, the hymns and responses were in Hawaiian. It was mainly the music, the rousing, militant hymns and soft, rolling tributes to God, that evoked deep-rooted group feelings and memories.

Because the Hawaiians of old had lived in a caste society, when the first Hawaiian Congregational church, Kawaiahao, became crowded, with commoners and chiefs, another church, Kaumakapili, was founded to accommodate the commoners. Far into the twentieth century, Hawaiians with strong blood lines expected the descendants of commoners to know their place. Descendants of the chiefs formed social cliques, and even at the Kamehameha Schools, girls of meager origin were sometimes slighted because of their *makaainana* ancestry. Among ordinary people, there persisted the belief that descendants of commoners should not try to overcome their heritage. One native story told of a Hawaiian asking another who had a bucket of crabs in his hands, "Why don't you put a cover on the bucket before the crabs escape?" The answer came with assurance, "No, they won't escape. As soon as one fellow gets to the top, the others pull him down."[18]

Whereas internal jealousy among the descendants of commoners was primarily the result of bad adjustment to the new social order, friction among the children of the chiefs was in part ancient Hawaiian practice. Quarrels among the chiefs of old, sometimes leading to wars, had been common. In twentieth-century Hawaii, the leading matriarchs and patriarchs of the small remaining Hawaiian elite were not nearly as unified as the haole elite. Bitter quarrels festered for two or three generations. Jonah Kuhio's sister-in-law gossiped freely about the Prince behind his back. Quarrels centered around such issues as: "Who was really the most loyal and faithful retainer of the Queen?" "Who really owned the most land on Maui?" "Who had the best blood lines?" These chiefly disputes did not erupt into bloodshed as in the past, but they carried on a tradition that was centuries old.

American politics, based upon universal suffrage and competition between political factions, was one of the major by-products of haole civilization, yet participation in Island politics paradoxically linked the natives to the past. In an atmosphere sometimes heavy with puritanism, politics provided welcome respite for Hawaiians. No political speech could begin unless preceded by entertainment, and many Hawaiians looked upon political campaigns as opportunities to break into song and hula. The Hawaiians, as the largest voting group in the Islands, loved the pageantry aimed at recalling the past that aspiring politicians consistently presented. They enjoyed the excitement and occasional mystery of politics. For years after annexation, opposing politicians would gravely charge each other with belonging to secret organizations such as the Shriners or Masons, darkly intimating to their Hawaiian audiences that these fraternal organizations were like the groups of native *mus* of old, who were alleged to be marauders roaming the countryside in search of some marked and doomed Hawaiian. Legend told how a *mu,* whose main task as public executioner was to procure victims for sacrifice, could cause a man to disappear from the face of the earth forever when a chief marked that man for elimination.[19]

Politics linked the natives to the old order also by giving them a chance to choose between the chiefs. Even where the purchasing of votes was widespread, many Hawaiians would accept bribes only from the leaders they had already chosen. The bulk of the Hawaiians followed Prince Kuhio, as the living *alii nui,* the highest living chief, into the Republican party. Jonah's brother, David, who never forgave the haoles for dethroning the Queen, became one of the leaders of the Democratic party in Hawaii. Each leader had his retainers, to whom he would promise patronage and other benefits, and the retainers had their followers. The passing of money to Hawaiians at election time some-

times represented the discharge of the leader's obligation to his followers.

Another and perhaps more important factor leading to widespread
Hawaiian participation in politics was a sense of power. Unquestionably, politics provided the one aspect of life under the haoles in which
Hawaiians retained this sense. The feeling was realistically based on
the fact that the Hawaiians and part-Hawaiians constituted an absolute
majority of the registered voters in the Islands for the first quarter of
the twentieth century and the largest single voting group until 1940.

They could not take their power too seriously, however. Twice before, revolutions at the point of haole bayonets had overturned the
power of Hawaiian voting majorities. Few Hawaiians dreamed of control, but many relished the power that enabled them to extract patronage, services, and even cash payments from the haoles who did control.
Some dimly perceived that politics along racial lines might restore the
Islands to native control. Widely used among Hawaiian candidates was
the slogan *"Nana i ka ili"* (Look for the skin). But "Look for the
skin" was not a useful slogan for Hawaiian nationalists after Orientals
began to vote. Indeed, a large number of natives were always willing
to join the haoles to defend against the alleged potential "Oriental
menace."

At first, the Hawaiians derived satisfaction from small individual
benefits, failing to understand the use of group power in American
politics. Anxious to express their resentment against opponents of the
Queen, they made successful politicians out of loyalist heroes. One of
these, for example, who was alleged to have killed a prominent haole
during the counterrevolution under the Republic, finding himself poor
and out of a job on the Big Island and owning little more than the *malo*
around his waist, went into politics and became a successful and important figure in Big Island politics.[20]

It was the vision of certain key Hawaiian politicians to use the vote
of the natives as a group to bring about major reforms in their behalf.
That reason, among others, was why Jonah Kuhio joined the Republicans, the controlling party in both Honolulu and Washington. His
greatest achievement was the Hawaiian Homes Commission. Although
in many respects Hawaiian homesteading proved to be a failure, it
continued throughout the territorial era to be a symbol of Hawaiian
political power. Other Hawaiian politicians thought increasingly in

terms of exercising power for the good of the group. Young William Richardson, whose grandfather had been an aide to Liliuokalani, and who was later to become chairman of the Democratic Oahu County Committee, recalled long-time Mayor John H. Wilson, son of the Queen's Marshal, telling him in the late 1920's, "Look, Bill, you've got to do things for the Hawaiian people; you've got to work for them. Politics is the way to do it."[21]

The ability of Hawaiians to control politics was inhibited by their ambivalent feelings toward the haoles. On the one hand, the haoles were the bearers of prestige. The Hawaiians had been tremendously impressed by the show and novelty of early haole ships and dress, and Captain Cook was thought to have been the great god Lono, whose light skin was admired by the natives. The Hawaiians learned to respect haole technology, especially their weapons and ships. Later, they came to think of the haole religion as superior. After annexation, it was the haoles who provided employment for the natives as policemen, firemen, park keepers, janitors in public buildings, laborers on public works, and workers on ranches, plantations, and in industry. The Hawaiians looked to the haoles for protection from the Orientals. As competition drove the Hawaiians from such trades as carpentry, many tried to associate themselves with the haoles rather than the Orientals. But on the other hand, most Hawaiians and even leading *hapa*-haoles retained bitter feelings toward the Americans for dethroning the Queen and, perhaps even more important, for alienating the land.

Jonah Kuhio himself was perhaps the best individual illustration of Hawaiian ambivalence toward the haoles. Jonah, in the dress of a stylish haole businessman, sipping his wine at the Pacific Club, could hardly be distinguished from the gentlemen of Merchant Street whose hospitality he enjoyed. For nearly twenty years a delegate to Congress, he was as anti-Oriental as any of the leading Americanizers of Honolulu. He once argued that Hawaiians could not work on the plantations because, like Americans, they were superior to Orientals.[22] Yet he felt deep hatred for the haoles and great love for a mythical ancient Hawaiian past. In a moment of extreme frankness, he blurted out to a congressional committee, "Your civilized nation insisted on bringing in liquor because of your commercial greediness; insisted that the Hawaiian government admit liquor into the Hawaiian Islands. Our kings had prohibited these things, but right could not prevail against might."[23]

What especially gnawed the "Hawaiian heart" was that the haoles believed they were actually right. To many Hawaiians, the haoles, through
disease, demoralization, economic attrition, and intermarriage were
systematically destroying the natives. There could be no "right" in that.
Yet, as the *hapa*-haole daughter of a Hawaiian judge under Kalakaua
put it many years later, "We have been deceived. The haoles kept us
in the dark to cover their sins, pretending they were righteous."[24] She
shared these feelings only with her closest Hawaiian friends, otherwise
going about her business, mingling in haole society, practicing deception
in retaliation. Many Hawaiians, whether of chiefly or common origin,
became accomplished deceivers in their relationships with haoles. Feeling that the ultimate destiny of the Hawaiian people was hopelessly
predetermined, recognizing, perhaps incorrectly, that their own prestige,
comfort, and immediate security depended upon haole largesse, they
kept their deepest hostilities to themselves. A sensitive haole observer
remarked after systematic study that many Hawaiians simply withdrew
from contact with haoles.[25] Another of Hawaii's able sociologists,
Bernhard L. Hormann, wrote, "Of the various ancestral groups found
in Hawaii . . . the Hawaiians in some respects stand out most from
the rest of the community. . . . There is among some Hawaiians the
feeling of bitterness, which causes them to withdraw." By withdrawing, many Hawaiians kept the haoles from learning how they
really felt. But high-society *hapa*-haoles in town could not withdraw.
They could only veil their true feelings. One of these, a daughter of
one of the last princes—a secret guarded from even her closest haole
friends—overstated it this way on the eve of statehood: "Every
Hawaiian holds in his bosom a longing for the monarchy and a deep
distrust of the haoles, but our cause is hopeless. What can we do?"[26]

The response of many Hawaiians was the displacement of their deep
hostility toward haoles against the Orientals, openly blaming them—
especially the Japanese, following annexation—for their frustrations.
During the 1880's and '90's, Hawaiians helped haoles write land laws
discriminating against the Chinese, and the literature of that period
abounds with statements of fierce hatred on the part of both groups
against Chinese immigrants. Later, the much more numerous Japanese
replaced the Chinese as an object of Hawaiian enmity. The so-called
"Japanese menace," looming increasingly large in the 1920's and
'30's, was viewed as an immediate economic and an ultimate political

threat. Common were the complaints that the Japanese were driving
the Hawaiians from such trades as carpentry and fishing. Soon, it was
feared, the Japanese would outnumber Hawaiian voices in politics.
An almost hysterical fear of the Japanese once led Jonah Kuhio to
suggest that perhaps immigrants from Japan had refrained from voting
as a result of instructions from Tokyo to bide their time in taking over
the Islands. "The Japanese think and act, not as members of an
American community, but collectively as Japanese," he asserted in
1919.[27] Many remember the feelings of consternation and shock in
the Hawaiian community when two Japanese were elected to the territorial legislature in 1930. The handwriting was on the wall.[28]

There were hundreds, perhaps thousands, of exceptions to the waves
of anti-Japanese sentiment which periodically swept the Hawaiian
community during the first four decades of this century. Close friendships existed between Japanese and Hawaiians in town and country,
even an occasional marriage took place, but for the most part the
Hawaiians only feared but did not know the Japanese.

The Hawaiians dreamt of the past, and sometimes intensely disliked
the haoles and Orientals, yet they continued their traditions of sex and
marriage without discrimination of race, color, or creed. Their attitude
toward miscegenation was unique in America. On the mainland, haoles
who might criticize discrimination in economics or politics would be
horrified at widespread interracial marriage. On the whole, Hawaiians,
who in the late nineteenth century disenfranchised the Chinese, and
who, in subsequent years, would happily have disenfranchised the
Japanese, did not take their prejudices to bed with them. Sex, if not
private, was personal, and the one haole taboo which never was accepted was the prohibition against interracial marriage. A racist congressman from California and Jonah Kuhio, at a time when both men
were stridently anti-Japanese, carried on a colloquy in Washington
which revealed the uniqueness of the Hawaiian point of view:

Mr. [John E.] Raker: I am asking has there been any inter-marrying
of the people of Hawaii and the Chinese?
Mr. Kalanianaole [Kuhio]: There has been some, yes.
Mr. Raker: Are you in favor of that inter-marriage or against it?
Mr. Kalanianaole: I have no opinion to give on that.
Mr. Raker: If you brought the Chinese over to Hawaii, would you be
opposed to their marriage with Hawaiians?

Mr. Kalanianaole: That is their business. . . . That is the business of
the individual whether he wants to marry a Japanese or Chinese or
anybody else.[29]

The Hawaiians, Prince Kuhio might have pointed out, had even
married Caucasians. They had married the haoles because the Hawaiians, unlike many Caucasians, held no belief in the racial superiority
of any group. They married them also because, in ancient Hawaii, the
haole system of monogamy would have been viewed as selfish, indeed
primitive. The Hawaiian family system permitted each man or woman
to choose freely several mates, who became *punalua* to each other.
Kamehameha had given some of his early advisers Hawaiian women
of chiefly rank for wives, recognizing them as chiefs, too; and commoners had welcomed haole men as husbands, beginning the Hawaiian
tradition of interracial marriage. When the Chinese and, later, the
haole servicemen and Filipinos came in without women, these newcomers found Hawaiian mates, although the Hawaiian *punalua* system
had largely been abandoned. There were twice as many pure Hawaiians
as part-Hawaiians in 1910; only twenty years later, there were more
mixed bloods than full Hawaiians. Between 1920 and 1940, more
than 40 per cent of Hawaiian grooms and 50 per cent of Hawaiian
brides married outside their group; during these same years approximately four out of every ten part-Hawaiian males and six of ten part-
Hawaiian females also out married. The part-Hawaiian became the
fastest growing group in the Islands just as the pure Hawaiians rapidly
approached extinction.[30]

This new ethnic category became a breed apart, although the overwhelming majority of them identified primarily with their Hawaiian
heritage. A daughter of a Filipino-Hawaiian now recalls watching her
part-Hawaiian mother sprinkling the house with salt and water to ward
off evil spirits after a funeral. Another part-Hawaiian remembers that
his family would not eat eels because the eel had been an ancient
protector for that family.[31]

The economic status of the part-Hawaiians varied. Some were in-
heritors of considerable wealth, stemming from the business enterprise
of a haole grandfather or from lands belonging to a Hawaiian grandmother. A small number of *hapa*-haoles assumed positions of power
and/or prestige in politics or haole business. The Asian-Hawaiians,
nearly all of whom were part Chinese until 1940, produced a remark-

able number of successful politicians and small businessmen. In the years before World War II, there even began to emerge a distinctive Chinese-Hawaiian in-group feeling that they had somehow captured the best of Chinese business acumen and ambition along with legendary Hawaiian affability.[32]

As part-Hawaiians and Hawaiians continued to intermarry with others, two important things happened. First, elements of the Hawaiian heritage diffused through the population. It was largely through the part-Hawaiian that the Hawaiian tradition of *aloha* was carried. In addition to miscegenation, the tradition ordained that, despite group animosities, Hawaiians treat individuals with friendliness and generosity. Hawaiians who complained of Oriental economic competition could easily give affection to an adopted Chinese child. Hawaiians who resented the overthrow of the monarchy by American haoles might welcome and feed a *malihini* haole stranger for weeks at a time. *Aloha* was not just an advertising man's gimmick. Nor did it mean only sexual hospitality. It was and is an authentic Polynesian tradition which rubbed off on the Islands' newcomers as the years went by. The second major result of widespread Hawaiian miscegenation was that part-Hawaiians, through their contact with haole and Oriental cultures, began to compete more successfully in the new social order. But the latter development did not begin with force until after World War II. For the Hawaiian and part-Hawaiian, the first four decades after annexation were too often filled with frustration and an impossible effort to recapture the past.

Chapter Three

SUCCESS, *PAKE* STYLE

A visitor from China, arriving in the Islands in 1930, shook his head in disbelief and wrote: "Here in the Islands is an interesting experiment . . . the unassimilable immigrant stock becoming full-fledged American citizens and contributing to the development of the community in which they were born and where they plan to spend their lives."[1] Actually, the experiment was over. The Chinese, more than any other immigrant group, had already acquired those characteristics which foreign observers think of as "typically American." Among second-generation Chinese, the English language, Christian religion, and American business and political methods had been energetically adopted.

The results would have amazed representatives of the Hawaiian Board of Immigration under the Republic who had written only thirty years before: "A Chinaman is unprogressive. He remains a Chinaman as long as he lives, and wherever he lives; he retains his Chinese dress; his habits; his methods; his religion; his hopes; aspirations and desires. He looks upon foreign methods, appliances, and civilization with scorn as inferior to his own. . . ."[2] The transformation from the pig-tailed foreigner described by the Hawaii Board of Immigration to the full-fledged American of the 1930's represented the most successful adjustment of an immigrant group to life in Hawaii.

In 1823, the first Chinese peddler appeared in the streets of Honolulu. During the next two decades, a scattering of his countrymen, by-passing closer islands, followed his route to Hawaii. By the middle of the century, a few Chinese were active in the sugar industry, particularly at Onomea on the Big Island. Most of the Chinese merchants lived in Honolulu, and the 1853 census reported 124 Chinese men and no Chinese women living in town. Two years earlier, approximately 180 Chinese had been brought in from China under special contract by the haole sugar planters, who had just begun an extensive search for cheap labor. An additional 195 field workers, who had been engaged for five years at $3 a month plus passage, food, clothing, and housing, arrived in January 1852. Altogether, approximately 46,000 Chinese were brought to Hawaii prior to annexation. Early planter enthusiasm for the puzzling but hard-working Chinese turned to disappointment as the workers saved their money to leave the plantations at the expiration of their contracts. The Kingdom's Chinese Exclusion Act, passed in 1886, prohibited their further importation after 1888; but exemptions under the law permitted an additional 15,000 to be recruited and brought to the Islands in the 1890's.[3]

The Chinese served under the Masters' and Servants' Act of 1850, which meant that if a worker left his master, he was obliged to return to work and serve for an additional period up to twice the time of his absence, provided that the additional term did not go one year over the contract period. In the beginning, this meant a man could be forced to serve for eleven years, since contracts were permitted to extend to a decade. Later, most contracts were for five or three years. If a laborer violated work rules, the planter could apply to any district justice to have the man jailed or sentenced to hard labor until he agreed to serve according to the contract.

The Hawaiian Board of Immigration represented the humanitarian inclinations of Americanizers in Honolulu who, while not wanting the Orientals to be brought to Hawaii at all, pestered the planters to ameliorate hard plantation conditions. In 1880, the Board set rudimentary sanitary standards for the plantation camps, and it periodically liberalized the Masters' & Servants' Act. After 1872, for example, a laborer could not be made to work beyond the period of his contract to pay off his debt to the planter; he was permitted to commute his contract by paying the employer the correct proportion of the amount advanced for his transportation expenses. And in 1882, legislation was passed prohibiting the extension of a worker's term due to desertion.

The planters, in the early days, while finding fault with the Chinese, as they were later to do with all immigrant groups, were satisfied that their labor problem had been solved. Prince Liholiho represented the planter view when he observed of the Chinese in 1855, "With all their faults and a considerable disposition to hang themselves, they have been found very useful . . . some of our largest sugar and coffee plantations are now chiefly dependent on them. . . ."[4]

Despite the early satisfaction of the planters and the sporadic humanitarianism of the Board of Immigration, a large proportion of the Chinese appear to have been miserable under plantation life. The promise of good food, housing, and the possibility of making what seemed easy money was false; they were thrown into crowded, unsanitary work camps under rough and sometimes brutal strange-speaking *lunas*. The gap between the idyllic picture drawn by scheming recruiting agents (Chinese as well as others) and the realities of plantation life was often cruelly wide.

The behavior of others was sometimes offensive to the Chinese. Not only did the natives eat fish and *poi* with their fingers, but the Portuguese, too, sometimes ate with their hands; the Japanese sometimes walked around in the nude, and Japanese men and women even bathed together. But this puzzling behavior was not nearly so distressing as the actions of the *lunas*. The naval custom of flogging for disorder or insubordination continued even after it was prohibited by the Board of Immigration in 1868.[5] Again in 1885, the Board issued a circular prohibiting beatings and ill treatment of laborers, citing a case in which a Chinese field hand was nearly beaten to death by an overseer. The attitude of far too many managers was, "The Board has made their rule. Let them enforce it."[6] On one plantation, a German supervisor kicked Chinese workers who did not move fast enough to suit him. At another plantation, the Secretary of the Board of Immigration wrote in 1897, "The treatment of sick laborers on the plantation is such that it practically amounts to cruelty." He explained that a room about eighteen by twelve feet was used as a hospital, but that the workers called it "jail." The room, he said, "was in filthy condition. These sick men had to leave their quarters early in the morning . . . to go to the hospital, remaining there all day until the evening whistle blows when they are allowed to return to their quarters." At one camp, fourteen men were found sleeping in a room fifteen by twenty feet; in another, sixteen by twenty feet, twenty men were housed. Managers docked the workers' pay without reason. Although the set monthly wage on one plantation was, for the Chinese, $11, "there were very few that received over six or seven dollars." Sometimes the working day was stretched beyond what the contract specified. "I do not know what particular time is kept on the plantation," wrote the Secretary of the Board of Immigration, "but . . . the mill clock is one of a kind that moves quickly or slowly, as required."[7]

Even under the best of managers and *lunas,* work in the cane fields must have been much more difficult that most Chinese had anticipated. After a predawn bowl of rice, the coolies hiked to the fields. There, far from home and loved ones, unable to complain to the foreign-speaking boss, they performed arduous tasks such as stripping stalks in what may have seemed like a sugar cane jungle. A casing of dead leaves had to be ripped from every stalk to let the sun and air penetrate the cane. No breeze came through the thick cane, and fine dust from the stalks crept into the eyes and nose. The hairs which fringed each cane joint were prickly, and they scratched and burned the workers' skin in the process of threshing and pulling off the useless leaves.[8]

There were few outlets for Chinese protest. A haole visitor from the Board of Immigration might seem sympathetic, but the visitor was here today and gone tomorrow, and there was little he could do to inhibit the repressive *lunas.* The Chinese Consul usually turned a deaf ear to the complaints of his laboring countrymen. Officials from China were conservative men, representing authoritarian governments, who were willing to co-operate with the most reactionary forces in the Islands. They could, and often did, frighten the workers by threatening to report "antisocial" behavior back home, where such an opinion would bring disgrace to their families. One Consul, Yong Wei Pin, obliged many of his countrymen to purchase, for the then huge sum of $5.25, a certificate stating that the holder was a good man and not a member of any secret society against the Chinese government. The Chinese believed that such a paper would protect their relatives in China from criticism or worse. According to a petition sent to the American Secretary of State, John Hay, Yong Wei Pin caused the arrest and suicide in China of the mother of one recalcitrant Chinese worker.[9]

Where verbal protests usually failed, direct action by Chinese workers sometimes brought relief from oppressive conditions. At Kohala, in August 1891, approximately 300 Chinese rioted against a recruiter who had persuaded them to deduct one third of their monthly wages for protection. They were brutally dispersed by a posse, but the deduction was subsequently held unconstitutional by the Hawaiian courts.[10] A riot against the cruel head *luna* of the Lihue plantation in April 1897 resulted in his discharge, but not until one Chinese had been killed and fifteen deported.[11] Two years later, about 130 Chinese marched from their plantation at Spreckelsville to Wailuku on Maui to demand successfully that hot meals be served in camp. But strikes and riots did not always result in desired action.[12] In October 1899, a riot at the Waianae plantation was repulsed by a posse that injured seventeen Chinese. Four ringleaders were sentenced to eighteen months in prison, and the protest was crushed.[13]

The most common Chinese response to plantation life was neither protest nor riot; it was to leave the plantation just as quickly as possible. The Chinese constituted 50 per cent of the employees on the plantations in 1882; they were less than 10 per cent by 1902. From nearly 6,000 Chinese plantation laborers in 1886, their numbers fell to less than 4,000 in 1902, a few less than 1,500 in 1922, and 706 in 1932. On the eve of statehood, only 302 Americans of Chinese descent remained on Hawaii's sugar plantations. At first, the Chinese, who traditionally valued land, calling it "living property," frequently tried rice farming.[14] Some of the Chinese immigrants married Hawaiian women and settled down to *taro* planting to satisfy the appetites of *poi*-eating Polynesians. A few Chinese *taro* farmers prospered, but the *taro* industry was largely replaced by rice, partly because of the decreasing native population. Not much work was needed to put *taro* land into proper condition for rice growing. In some areas, the temperature, rainfall, and topography were perfect. The Chinese sought Hawaiians who would lease or sell land cheaply. In addition to the primary market for rice in Honolulu, there was a great demand from California, especially following the Reciprocity Treaty of 1876, which admitted rice as well as sugar to the United States duty free. Traditional co-operative farming practices plus Chinese zeal to succeed encouraged the growth of the industry. In 1899, there were 504 rice farms covering an area of almost 10,000 acres and annually producing rice valued at more than $1,500,000.[15]

Rising costs, competition from California, the end of Chinese immigration, and especially the pressure of the sugar industry to obtain land forced the decline of the Chinese rice-farming industry after 1910. With the virtual disappearance of rice farming, the Chinese immigrants in Hawaii gave up their dream of staying close to the land. Whereas almost 12 per cent of the Chinese males in Hawaii were engaged in farming in 1890, less than 2 per cent were still on the farms in 1940.[16] The farmers from the *taro* and rice valleys followed those Chinese who had left the plantations to go directly to Honolulu and Hilo or the other villages and towns of the major islands. They went to the cities to become laundrymen, tailors, dressmakers, cooks, bakers, waiters, and servants; and many started their own businesses as peddlers, store-keepers, and café owners. As early as 1889, the Chinese practically monopolized the restaurant business, the butchering of pork, and cake peddling. The Chinese rapidly became the most urban group in Hawaii. On the eve of annexation, they made up approximately one quarter of the population of Honolulu, and forty years later, just prior to the attack on Pearl Harbor, more than eight out of every ten Americans of Chinese ancestry lived in the capital.[17]

Objectively, living conditions in Honolulu were in some respects worse than on the plantation. The Chinese lived packed in tumble-down shacks within a narrow Chinatown district adjacent to the harbor. At the turn of the century, Honolulu health inspectors reported that garbage collections in Chinatown were virtually nonexistent, the water supply dangerous, the treatment of the sick hopelessly inferior. Sun-light never reached some of the shacks, which were cesspools of filth and disease. As many as six persons occupied one tiny room. The Chinese crowded the streets outside their apartments and their tin-shops, shoeshops, tailorshops, and bakeries. In this narrow district there were more than 4,000 immigrants, nearly half the Chinese population in all of Honolulu.

The seeming self-segregation of the Chinese encouraged haole and Hawaiian attacks during the 1870–1900 period. It was in the latter part of that period that the term *"pake"* acquired a negative meaning.[18] *Pake* had already been used as a synonym for Chinese in Hawaii. Actually, in China, the word *pak-ye,* meaning uncle, was used as a term of respect when a child addressed an elder. Perhaps the early Chinese men who married Hawaiian women encouraged their children to use the term when showing respect to age. Used to being mocked by others on the plantation, the Chinese now also suffered indignities in town. Many migrated back to China during the 1890's, rejecting both town and plantation and fulfilling their original desire to return home.

Why did the Chinese leave the plantations if they worked just as hard and long and were more vulnerable to disease in the city? The answer was that they sought protection by grouping together in their own community, and they sought economic opportunity afforded by urban life. In the city, paradoxically, one could be more of an individual and more Chinese at the same time. Banished were the *lunas,* whose whims seemed to govern almost every decision affecting the laborers' lives. Present in the city was the opportunity to join other Chinese in forming clan and family associations and, indeed, to develop a national Chinese group consciousness.[19] Benevolent and charitable associations emerged to care for the aged and sick. The city, despite its wretchedness, seemed to say, "Here you can be American *and* Chinese." In the city, too, one could make a little money. Many services that the haoles needed—servants, carpenters' helpers, fishermen—the Chinese were anxious to provide.

There were three phases of adjustment for the Chinese in Hawaii during the period prior to World War II. The plantation phase was marked by psychological isolation from Hawaii, by internal tensions between the clan and dialect groups, and by feeble attempts to keep the religion and values of Chinese village life from disappearing. In the first phase the village was uppermost in their minds. Someday the plantation would be behind them, and they would return triumphant to the friends and relatives who now seemed so distant.

The second phase was marked by migrations to the cities and the realization that Hawaii was not just a stopping place. The decision to stay, or, more often, the barely conscious recognition that one would never be able to go home, raised troublesome questions for the Chinese: Who am I? What do I want? Who can help me? How can I protect myself against the enmity of others? Trying to answer these questions, the Chinese formed clan societies, instituted benevolent organizations, and published small newspapers. The attacks from the outside at first intensified the class, clan, and *Punti-Hakka* tensions among the Chinese. A *Punti* man might respond to hostility against the Chinese by proclaiming that the *Hakka* were really to blame for the troubles of the Chinese. But as time passed, it became apparent that these distinctions —so important to the Chinese—were completely lost on outsiders. Similarly, the success of a young Chinese student at high school or the business success of an elder reflected credit, insofar as the haoles and Hawaiians were concerned, not on a particular district or family, but on the Chinese as a whole.

As the Chinese improved their economic situation, moved from Chinatown, adopted Christianity, and as Hawaiian-haole animosity shifted to the Japanese, internal divisions gave way to growing unity. The Chinese *in* Hawaii became the Chinese *of* Hawaii, markedly different from their relatives back in China, but, in their own way, at least as nationalistic. The third phase saw the emergence of second- and third-generation leaders, educated in American schools and exercising the franchise, as spokesmen for group needs, claims, and goals of the Chinese-Americans of Hawaii.

The China left behind was not yet a nation, and the central loyalty of the immigrants was to their clan or kinship group. Although the vast majority came from the Kwangtung province in southern China, they spoke many dialects. The major division was between the *Punti,* who comprised about three quarters of the immigrants, and the *Hakka.* The *Hakka* had originally come to Kwangtung province from the north. They settled in the highlands above *Punti* villages, and for a period of almost a thousand years the two groups viewed each other with mutual hostility. The *Hakka* thought of themselves as courageous and ingenious, and considered the *Punti* lazy and stupid. The *Punti* viewed the *Hakka* as intruders whose foreign ways were to be scorned. On one thing they agreed: *Punti* and *Hakka* do not mix. As long as the immigrants to Hawaii believed they would someday return to China, even when they lived side by side in the plantation barracks or in the closely packed hives of Chinatown, they maintained the ancient rivalry between *Punti* and *Hakka.*[20]

In the first phase of adjustment there were no Hawaii-oriented group goals. The immigrants, some with zeal and others halfheartedly, tried in small ways to resurrect the life of their villages. Differences between the Chinese were commonly settled by the village headmen, as was the custom back home.[21] In times of economic distress or illness, a small Taoist shrine was often erected. Children were discouraged from attending haole schools, where they might be drawn away from the customs of their forefathers. In 1878, only eighty-five Chinese children were recorded as having attended public school, although nearly 6,000 Chinese had been born in the Islands.[22] A small proportion of the men lost their Chinese identification altogether. These Chinese soon became familiar with Hawaiian foods and island customs and began to speak a new dialect, later known in Hawaii as "pidgin," enabling them to communicate with their native spouses and part-Hawaiian children.[23] But the vast majority of Chinese men either returned to China for their brides or remained single until they died. Most of the immigrants gave little thought to Hawaii, for they still longed for small villages at home.

When hundreds of Chinese began to admit to themselves that they would never see their villages again, the Chinese in Hawaii entered their second phase of adjustment. The decision to stay evoked the hostility of the Hawaiians and haoles. The Chinese had been imported as temporary plantation laborers; they were not wanted as permanent residents of Honolulu, Hilo, and other towns. Under attack, the Chinese family societies, villagers' clubs, and district associations, already formed in the first phase of adjustment, became even more important to the Chinese.[24] Between 1882 and 1909, when the attacks on the Chinese were still frequent, at least sixteen mutual-aid associations were formed on Oahu, open to membership on a clan, village, or district basis. Other groups sprang up on the outer islands. On rural Hawaii, for example, there appeared the Chee Ying Society of Hamakua and the Hung Wo Society of Kohala. On Maui there emerged the Fuk Sin Tong, in Wailuku, among many others. By 1910, there were over seventy-five such groups spread throughout the Islands.[25]

Chinese-language newspapers were organized, five appearing between 1886 and 1901. Four met the common fate of most immigrant weeklies: they disappeared quickly. But one, the *New China Daily Press,* established in 1900, survived. The publishing of newspapers and the formation of benevolent and social organizations produced group leaders for the Chinese; editors and organization officials gained prestige and power within the Chinese community. But new tensions and disagreements emerged as leaders, self-appointed or elected, argued not only over the future of the Chinese in Hawaii, but over the future of China itself.

The concept of China as one nation took hold during the second adjustment phase of the Chinese in Hawaii. When Dr. Sun Yat-sen came to the Islands in 1910, he founded branches of the Chinese revolutionary organization, Tung Ming Hui (later changed to Kuomintang), in Hilo and on the island of Maui. The major opposition to the Kuomintang, which contributed over a quarter of a million dollars in gold in support of the revolutionary movement, came from the Chinese Reform Society, formed as a branch of the Bo Wung Wui in Honolulu in 1900. After the death of the emperor in 1908, its name was changed to the Imperial Constitutionalist party, and later, after the republic was established, to the Chinese Constitutionalist party. Other political organizations, known as Hoong Moon, existed throughout Hawaii, with the goal of overthrowing the Ching dynasty and bringing back the Mings.[26]

In some cases, the newspapers, clubs, and political organizations formed in the second adjustment phase intensified the tensions and divisions among the Chinese. Resigned to their fate in Hawaii, vast numbers of aliens clung to everything Chinese and, paradoxically, held tenaciously to the prejudices of the village or the clan or the *Punti* or the *Hakka.* Others, a minority among the aliens and a large majority among the second generation, dealt instead with the problem of being accepted as Chinese-Americans.

Those who stressed acceptance placed a premium on learning the English language and supporting the Christian churches. In 1885, they subscribed $2,000 to build a new hall for the Chinese Y.M.C.A. They also began to think of organizing the Chinese community as a whole. In 1882, they formed the United Chinese Society to represent the Chinese community to other ethnic groups and the government. Later, it was supplemented by the Chinese Chamber of Commerce, formed in 1912, as many Chinese in Hawaii entered the third phase of adjustment to American ways in the Islands.

Whereas denial of a group future for the Chinese in Hawaii characterized the first phase of adjustment, and questioning and doubt marked the second, growing confidence and unity symbolized the third. Most Chinese born in Hawaii adopted Christianity, were given haole first names, played haole sports, and wore haole clothes, yet they took a renewed interest in Chinese culture.[27] The fresh interest in things Chinese was partly the result of the increased number of Chinese families and partly due to the birth of the Chinese republic, which increased the national consciousness of overseas Chinese. The Chinese language schools, instead of disappearing, grew in number and force throughout the Chinese community. The supporters of the Chinese Constitutional Monarchy party established a school in 1911, and another school was founded with the aid of Sun Yat-sen himself. By 1929, there were thirteen Chinese schools in Hawaii, and five years later, there were twenty such schools, attended by 40 per cent of the Chinese students who were also attending regular schools.[28] In the beginning, the language schools were conceived of as a way to retard the rapid Americanization of Chinese children. In the 1920's, the attitude changed. The schools were thought of as bridges between generations and as aids to economic and cultural advancement. The second generation saw the schools as a way to perpetuate Oriental culture among their American children.

New clubs and organizations were formed in the third phase of adjustment. One of the first of these was the Chinese Students' Alliance, organized in 1904 with the object of promoting greater unity among the Chinese and encouraging higher education. The new clubs emphasized the business, cultural, and political interests of the Chinese of Hawaii. Romanzo Adams, writing in 1929, observed that the high-school graduates who had been ready to forget their Chinese ancestry ten or twenty years before were now capitalizing on their race for what seemed to him to be mainly business purposes.[29] Some of the new organizations formed in the 1920's and even the '30's, like the Yin Fu Society, established in 1921, primarily for *Hakka*-speaking Chinese, were village or clan clubs, but the major tendency now was to form inclusive organizations, open to all Chinese. Trade organizations such as the Chinese Butchers' Association (1935); educational groups such as the Chinese University Club (1919); and sports organizations such as the Hawaii Chinese Aero Club (1936) were born.[30]

The growing proportion of young Chinese women promoted group unity. As the ratio of Chinese women to men rose, the Chinese tended toward increased endogamy. That so large a number of Chinese failed to take Hawaiian wives was a result primarily of the importance of ancestor worship in the Chinese religions. Whether the background was in Taoism, Confucianism, or, in some cases, Buddhism, the purpose of a Chinese marriage was to provide for the continued worship of family ancestors. If there had been a normal sex ratio to begin with, it is extremely doubtful that many Chinese would have succumbed to the charm of Hawaiian women. With normal sex ratios in the second generation, the Chinese of Hawaii showed a marked preference for their own people. Whereas 41.7 per cent of the Chinese men married outside of their group between 1912 and 1916, the proportion went down to 24.8 per cent between 1920 and 1930.[31]

In the third phase of adjustment, the political interest of the Chinese turned from China to Hawaii. During the 1920's, the first generation maintained a lively interest in Kuomintang politics. The 1927 split of the Kuomintang regime between Chiang Kai-shek and the Wuhan government was mirrored in Honolulu. The *Liberty News* spoke for the Wuhan government, while a new newspaper, the *United Chinese News,* appeared in 1928 to uphold the policies of Chiang and the Nanking regime. While the elders haggled over events in China, the second and third generations focused on politics at home, which for them meant Hawaii. In January 1925, the Hawaii Chinese Civic Association was formed to promote the civic and political welfare of American citizens of Chinese ancestry. It became the first inclusive Chinese pressure group in Hawaii. Under the leadership of Dr. Dai Yen Chang, it was successful in obtaining territorial exemption from taxation for the Chinese Y.M.C.A. and in killing nuisance bills aimed at Chinese merchants; it unsuccessfully fought the establishment of the English Standard school system, which, in effect, segregated a majority of Oriental students from haole children.[32]

Politics provided an opportunity for status and influence as the number of Chinese citizens grew. The Chinese were only 4.3 per cent of the registered voters in 1920, but that figure doubled by 1930. The voting power of the second generation was an important spur to group consciousness. Earlier, a number of Chinese-Hawaiians had been elected to territorial or county positions, usually receiving strong support from the small number of Chinese who voted. The best known of these was William H. Heen, appointed in 1917 as circuit court judge, a position previously held only by haoles or Hawaiians; in 1919 he was elected city and county attorney in Honolulu. Heen, whose Chinese father had been a mess boy on an American warship and who, after jumping ship, married a Hawaiian girl, became a hero to both the Chinese and the Hawaiians. He remembered years later that the Chinese took special pride in his political successes during the 1920's and '30's.[33] The Honolulu Board of Supervisors and the territorial House of Representatives in 1927 seated their first Chinese members, and Heen was elected to the territorial Senate in 1929. When Yew Char ran for re-election to the territorial House as a Democrat from Oahu's fifth district, he won overwhelming support in the heavily Chinese twenty-fifth precinct.

Chinese interest and power in politics quickened during the 1930's. The issues of the *Hawaii Chinese Journal,* first published in 1937, were full of praise for Chinese candidates. In a word, the attitude was: "We have arrived as citizens, and as Chinese-Americans we ought to state frankly our claims and hopes, be proud of and back our candidates." One of these candidates was Hiram L. Fong, later to be elected to the U.S. Senate. Fong, whose father was an immigrant laborer, grew up in the slums of Kalihi in Honolulu, and after putting himself through

Harvard Law School, he entered territorial politics. He served as a deputy city and county attorney between 1935 and 1939, and won election to the House of Representatives in 1938. Fong, illustrative of the politics of the third phase, was self-consciously but unashamedly Chinese.

The third phase of adjustment, no less than the second, was full of paradoxes. As Chinese group consciousness, solidarity, and goals developed, the Chinese abandoned many Oriental traditions. Oriental religions waned, and the Chinese Catholic Club, reflecting the strong pull of Catholicism for the Chinese, became one of the most impressive religious groups in the Islands. As the Chinese of Hawaii wandered from Taoism and other Eastern religions, they also left the ghetto of Chinatown. In most American cities, the Chinese were segregated in one or two less desirable areas, but by 1920, less than half of the Chinese in Honolulu were found in such ghettos, and in ten years the proportion fell below one third. During the period of growing Chinese unity in the 1920's and '30's, dispersion increased at a rapid pace. In 1930, all but three of twenty-four residential areas examined by University of Hawaii sociologist Clarence Glick reported the presence of at least 200 Chinese. By 1939, Chinese professional and business men had successfully penetrated some of the best residential areas in the heights of Honolulu, theretofore reserved for the haoles.[34]

Throughout the second and third phases of adjustment, growing group consciousness led to the development of Chinese group goals. The essential goal of any immigrant group depends upon the values of the old culture and the opportunities in the new. For the Chinese, the overriding goal became success based on economic independence and occupational prestige within the social order.[35] In short, the Chinese adopted for their central goal the dominant ethos of American civilization: success. The goal was well suited to both the Chinese value system and the opportunities existing in Hawaii.

A combination of Chinese thrift, diligence, and family solidarity enabled many of them to gain economic independence in an expanding Hawaiian economy. The Chinese emphasis on education and scholarship combined with compulsory education laws in the Islands helped promote occupational prestige.

The Chinese had been familiar with a competitive commercial economy for thousands of years. In the old country they were often forced to extreme thrift and hard work in order to survive. Chinese culture emphasized the value of property in bringing prestige to its owner. Romanzo Adams explained, " . . . the Chinese scheme of life is one in which the acquisition and possession of property is important. They are more interested in earning in order to save, saving in order to invest, investing in order to secure profit, holding, spending and giving in order to enhance prestige. Attention is directed more steadily and consistently toward economic success and consequently they know much more about the business situation and are superior in their business technique."[36]

Since they were what one Chinese anthropologist has called "situation-centered," they did not think of changing Hawaii, but, rather, of adjusting to the dominant patterns of life in the Islands.[37] Large numbers of migrants from the plantations and others who came directly to the towns as free immigrants from China quickly perceived that although they could not own or produce the wealth of the Islands, they could serve those who did. Far better to provide services for the haoles in Honolulu and Hilo or the plantation workers in the villages than to work under the direct control of the Scotch or Portuguese boss. Families and clans helped each other, exploiting their contacts not only in Hawaii, but in China as well. The Chinese created markets by importing from Hong Kong such items as cuttlefish, dried fish, oranges, dates, and nuts, and by 1889, 60 per cent of the licenses issued to retail merchants and 20 per cent of those given to wholesale merchants in Hawaii went to Chinese.[38]

The immigrants who came to Hawaii had a vision of improving their status in the villages back home. For those who decided to stay, the objective of status enhancement was simply shifted to Hawaii.[39] The Chinese recognized, both in their own subculture and in the outside haole community, that the merchant in Hawaii was held in high esteem. Successful second- and third-generation Chinese, with smiles on their faces, related the story of the immigrant Chinese peddler carrying twenty pounds of fish in a sack over his shoulder who tried to impress the Hawaiians by saying, "Me merchant, me merchant." The Chinese also knew that there was money in business, and that money in this American territory could purchase education and prestige. A popular ditty at the turn of the century went, "Chinee, Chinaman, sitting on a fence, try to make a dollar out of fifteen cents."[40]

Throughout the three phases of Chinese adjustment to Hawaii, the family remained of crucial importance. Emphasis on the welfare of

the family above that of any individual aided many Chinese commercial ventures. All members of the family, even small children,
were expected to make some contribution to the family business.
Young children carried packages for customers or unloaded goods;
their older brothers and sisters served as clerks or cashiers. Money
that ordinarily went to outside help was thus put back into the business.
The emphasis on maintaining the good name of the family and respect
for the family's ancestors also reinforced the drive for family success in
business.[41]

Fortunately for the Chinese, their group cohesiveness and goals
developed at a time when the Hawaiian economy was expanding and
new jobs were being created. While the number of gainfully employed
agricultural workers in Hawaii remained the same between 1900 and
1920, there were three times as many jobs in the manufacturing and
mechanical industries and twice as many positions in transportation,
communications, trade, and clerical services by 1920 as had been
available twenty years earlier.[42] The Chinese, through hard work and
family unity, brilliantly exploited new opportunities. Of course there
was opposition from some competing haoles, but nearly all of the
major haole anti-Oriental hostility after 1910 was directed against
the much more numerous and, from the haole point of view, troublesome Japanese.

There were dozens of bankruptcies and failures, owing in part to
terrific internal competition, but the Chinese were singularly mobile
among all the larger nonhaole groups in the relatively restricted social
order of pre-Pearl Harbor Hawaii, and a large number of them climbed
the ladder of success. Agreeing with Calvin Coolidge that the business
of America is business, a surprising number of first-generation Chinese
re-enacted the Horatio Alger story. A typical pioneer was Chun Hoon,
who arrived in Hawaii at the age of fourteen in 1889 and started in
business by peddling baskets of fresh produce carried on a long pole
over his shoulders. Somehow he saved enough money to start a grocery
store and later expanded into a wholesale food-and-vegetable business
known as Chun Hoon, Ltd. There followed a successful supermarket,
pharmacy, and general-merchandise store. Another success story was
that of C. Q. Yee Hop, who arrived in Hawaii in 1887 at the age of
eighteen with only a few cents in his pocket. Peddling and saving gave
him enough cash to buy land on the Big Island, where he intended to
raise cattle for his butcher shop. Ingeniously, he used the *koa* and *ohia*

trees on his property to establish the Hawaiian Hardwood Company. Successful in that enterprise, in 1932 he organized the American Brewing Company, Ltd., producer of Royal Beer. Although by 1939, the Chinese constituted only a little more than 7 per cent of the population of the Islands, fifty-six of the 275 manufacturing establishments in Hawaii were owned by Chinese, thirty-two of whom were American citizens.[43]

As many Chinese found business profitable, they began to accumulate personal property and, later, savings. Profits went back into business or into new businesses, and the number of Chinese owning assessed personal property and the total value of Chinese personal property went up rapidly.[44] As time went by, an increasing number of Chinese could afford to open savings accounts, build their deposits, and purchase real property. Whereas twice as many Portuguese as Chinese had savings accounts in 1911, the proportion was even by 1920, and ten years later the Chinese had substantially passed the Portuguese. More importantly, the average deposit made by the Chinese practically tripled between 1920 and 1930, while average Portuguese deposits went up only a fraction more than 20 per cent. The pattern was similar with respect to real estate. In their early years, the Chinese could not afford to buy land. In 1911, more than six times as many Hawaiians and part-Hawaiians as Chinese owned real estate; twenty years later, the ratio was less than three to two. During the same period, the per-capita assessed value of real estate held by the Chinese grew from $41 to $570, more than 1,000 per cent; the figures for the part-Hawaiians for the same years were $290 and $468.[45]

Chinese business was not big business. Big business was firmly in the grip of the haole elite, which was more concerned about competition from mainland invaders than Chinese tradesmen, small manufacturers, and wholesalers. Although not stridently hostile to Chinese business, the *kamaaina* elite extended little help. To achieve economic independence, Chinese businessmen had to create markets where none had existed, pool their own resources for capital, and work unusually hard and long, continually postponing present pleasures for future gratifications. Many Chinese, who believed that the great Chinatown fire at the turn of the century was instigated by the haoles to destroy their small enterprises, would not have trusted haole help had it been available. But for the most part, the haole banks were too conservative to aid in the expansion of Chinese business. In 1916, the Chinese started their own small bank, the Chinese-American Bank, followed in 1922 by the Liberty Bank of Honolulu, which began with the then large sum of $200,000 in capital. The Chinese-American Bank closed in 1933, and was replaced by the American Security Bank two years later, which also began with $200,000. The Honolulu Trust Company, also formed by Chinese, was organized in 1921 with $100,000. These small beginnings led in the 1940's and '50's to a substantial complex of Chinese financial institutions. In the beginning, they gave Chinese-owned fresh-fruit-and-produce markets, restaurants, small factories, and village stores a much-needed boost. The availability of larger amounts of capital also encouraged second-generation Chinese businessmen to incorporate. Most of the early businesses had been partnerships, and as late as 1935, almost half the partnerships on the island of Oahu were Chinese.[46]

The Chinese of Hawaii strove for economic independence. Very few of them, even in the second generation, entered the large haole firms. The reluctance to become a small cog in a big industrial wheel stemmed not just from haole discrimination, but from a decided preference on the part of the Chinese for their own family enterprises. After the plantation experience, they wanted to be their own bosses. A 1936 study of Chinese white-collar workers in forty-nine large haole businesses showed that only two of those employed by the six major industrial plants and six by the five large sugar factors were paid more than $2,500 a year. Not a single Chinese-American engaged by the sugar agencies made more than $4,000 a year. The Chinese climb up the economic ladder of Hawaii during the 1920's and '30's was clearly a do-it-yourself project.[47]

If the Chinese strove for business success, it was not because there was any inherent virtue in business activity. Business success meant money, and money meant education, status, and, at the end of the rainbow, physical comfort. Business preoccupied the Chinese from day to day, but it was education for their sons and daughters they dreamed about. One of the most important aims of the old Chinese village was to produce scholars who might compete successfully in civil-service examinations and become officials. Indeed, for centuries, scholarship was an important criterion for membership in the Chinese upper class.[48]

The Chinese of Hawaii followed the ancient tradition of respect for education and intellectual merit. A survey made at a Honolulu settlement house in 1910 showed that the Chinese spent three times as much on education in proportion to their income as did the haoles. One of Hawaii's most successful Chinese businessmen, the son of an illiterate cook, remembers how families pooled their resources to help the oldest son go to school. The students carefully budgeted their money, sometimes going hungry to make ends meet. Usually they attended both the English and the Chinese schools, and after school hours many found part-time work or assisted the family business. To sacrifice for education became an obsession in the Chinese community, and the strong motivation of the Chinese children to please their parents resulted in excellent performance at school. In the public and private secondary schools, Chinese children consistently won a disproportionate number of honors.[49]

Opportunities for education in Hawaii were far greater than they had been in China. The Chinese could choose among free public schools and private schools such as Iolani, founded by the Episcopal church, or Catholic St. Louis College. Their zeal for education continued beyond the age for compulsory school attendance, and by 1920, the proportion of Chinese children sixteen and seventeen years of age attending school was larger than for the haoles. In 1930, nearly eight out of every ten Chinese in the sixteen to seventeen age range were in school, compared with four out of ten for the other groups in the Territory. The vast majority of these students, nearly 80 per cent, came from homes where either father or mother had been born in China.[50]

Education brought status in Hawaii just as it had in China. A surprising number of Chinese pushed beyond high school to college and even to graduate and professional schools. To achieve a professional status would not only mean economic independence, but would bring honor to the family.

In 1900, there were only twelve teachers of Chinese ancestry in the Islands. Thirty years later, there were 191. Even more astounding was the growing proportion of Chinese physicians and dentists. Teacher training was possible in Hawaii at the University, but a medical or dental education required a trip to the mainland, preceded by scrimping and saving, and, especially for doctors, an extended period of education when sisters might go without lipstick and fathers without a second bowl of rice. By 1940, there were thirty medical doctors and twenty-six dentists of Chinese ancestry in the Territory.[51]

Increased education during the 1920's led a large number of second-generation Chinese into white-collar occupations as well as the professions. Between 1920 and 1940, the percentage of Chinese professional workers leaped from 1.5 to 5.7, while the proportion of clerical workers rose from 11.5 to 28.7 per cent. If occupational prestige was the sole measure of status, the Chinese could congratulate themselves that they had arrived. Over the course of two generations, from 1890, when 87 per cent of the Chinese gainfully employed worked as unskilled plantation laborers, servants, or small farmers, to 1940, when six out of every ten Chinese-Americans were in the preferred professional, proprietary, clerical, or skilled occupations, the Chinese had doggedly followed the American success trail.[52]

In pursuing the American success ethos, the Chinese gave the haole elite little cause for concern prior to World War II. The Chinese accepted the social order as it existed without trying to reform it. During the 1930's, they produced not one single labor leader, radical intellectual, or left-wing politician. The Chinese, true to their ancient culture, rarely criticized authority.[53] Although their fathers and grandfathers despised plantation life, the Chinese were hardly affected by the Japanese and Filipino struggle to improve plantation conditions.[54] Finding it sound policy to stand aside in the incipient struggle for the control of Hawaii, Chinese newspapers rarely criticized the elite as did Japanese journals. The Chinese of Hawaii became known for their ability to get along with all groups. For the most part, the Chinese failed to share the rising hostility of Hawaiians, haoles, and Portuguese for the Japanese. Chinese affability in part derived from the fact that the Japanese increasingly patronized Chinese businesses and professions and were a factor in the growing success of Chinese politicians. Probably the major reason for Chinese acceptance of the Japanese was the former's acceptance of Hawaii as it was. The huge Japanese population, no less than the *kamaaina* haoles, seemed a permanent feature in the Island social system. The Chinese were determined to succeed within that system. Hostility against others filled no psychological, economic, or political need for them.

The only break in the Chinese attitude came during the Sino-Japanese War, during the late 1930's. As long as the fighting was confined to North China, the Chinese-Americans of Hawaii were not deeply concerned. After Canton fell, the *United Chinese News* and other Chinese papers began to harp on Japanese atrocity stories. Approximately 45 per cent of the Chinese schoolchildren were attending

Chinese language schools in 1937, and their schools encouraged boycotts of Japanese goods. Rumors spread which made some Japanese afraid to go to Chinese restaurants for fear that ground glass might be put in the food. But according to one student of Chinese-Japanese relations during the war, there was little boycotting, and the adult Chinese, although less conciliatory than the Japanese, were remarkably free of resentment against the local Japanese population.[55]

For the most part, the Chinese were too busy to agitate either for or against anyone or anything. Early in their sojourn in America, they caught a vision of success, a vision that became a goal relentlessly pursued. The early plantation manager who complained, "The Chinese is never satisfied, no matter how well off he is," should properly have directed his complaint against Andrew Carnegie or Henry Ford. The Chinese of Hawaii became quintessentially American, conservative in politics, enterprising in business, conspicuous in consumption, and, above all, "successful."

Chapter Four

PRIDE AND PLACE

When King Kalakaua arrived in Tokyo during his 1881 world tour, he remembered his promise to the haole planters of Hawaii. He would urge the Japanese government to let its peasants emigrate to the Kingdom to work in the expanding sugar fields. Kalakaua secretly disliked the haoles, but he loved power and was keenly aware that it was haole influence which put Hawaii's crown on his head. His 1881 mission failed in Tokyo, but three years later he sent his great friend, Major Curtis Iaukea, to repropose Japanese immigration to Hawaii. The Chinese, who were soon to be shut off by the Kingdom's Exclusion Act, increasingly competed with Hawaiians in town; the Portuguese were too expensive and not available in the quantities desired. Japan, with its millions of subsistence farmers, held promise of a ceaseless source of hard-working, uncomplaining, and inexpensive labor. But Iaukea, too, failed to win agreement in Tokyo to Kalakaua's proposal.

Then the relentless forces of nature came to the aid of frantic haole planters. One bad season in southern Japan was followed by another, and by 1886, starvation was widespread among the peasants. When the planters of Hawaii promised free medical care, high wages, housing, and perquisites, the Japanese government agreed to permit its citizens to emigrate to Hawaii as contract laborers. Into Japanese villages went the recruiting agents, telling of the beauty of Hawaii, the endless summer, and the abundance of money. In the southern islands of Honshu and Kyushu and, a few years later, even far to the south in Okinawa, word was passed of the land of plenty. After the government gave its permission in 1886, thousands of Japanese peasants applied to emigrate.

There were three distinctive periods of Japanese immigration to

Hawaii. Of the 180,000 who eventually made the difficult journey, about one seventh (mostly men) came between 1886 and 1897; most of the men and nearly half of the women arrived between 1898 and 1907 in a second group; and approximately two sevenths (mostly women and children) came between 1908 and 1924, after the Gentlemen's Agreement had effectively stopped large-scale Japanese migrations. In the beginning, the immigrants had no intention of remaining in Hawaii. To work hard to accumulate 3,000 yen and return triumphant to the village was the goal of the vast majority. More than half of the immigrants did eventually go home; the others remained, and after 1896 they constituted the largest single ethnic group in the Islands.

Each immigrant group brought to America its own belief systems and customs. Hawaii's Japanese imported the peasant culture of southern Japan. It was a co-operative culture, characterized by reciprocal obligation between members of the family, the village, and the nation, but it was authoritarian, too. In Japanese society there was an inviolable hierarchical order. Morality consisted primarily in keeping the distinctions clear, in knowing one's place and in not violating the natural order of things. Religion, sex relations, family organization, economic and political relationships were all based on the system of reciprocal obligation among unequals. There was no natural right to a better life or to revolution.[1]

The Japanese village, called *mura,* was composed of fifteen to twenty local hamlets, called *buraku.* In every *buraku* there were about twenty households, each governed by a master, who lived with his wife, his unmarried children, and often parents or servants or the eldest son and his family. Within the family, the father was a virtual dictator, making nearly all important group decisions. The status of the individual was determined by the prestige of the family, and the typical Japanese placed his family above everything else.[2]

Because Shintoism, the Japanese folk religion, and Buddhism were both based largely on ancestor worship, filial piety was a major governing principle in Japanese family life. The Japanese son worshiped his family ancestors and the imperial ancestors of Japan. The dead became gods, acquiring supernatural power, and their happiness depended upon the respectful service given them by the living, just as the happiness of the living depended upon the fulfillment of pious duties to the dead. Following Shinto doctrine, every event in the living world, including every human action, was controlled by the dead. To neglect the dead or cause them shame by bad conduct was the supreme crime. To treat the elders of the family—those who would soon join the ancestors—without proper respect was almost as shameful. From the cult of ancestor worship followed the rule of seniority in each household; all must obey the master, the females must obey the males, and the younger members were subject to their elders. There are Japanese-Americans in Hawaii today who remember that at mealtime the eldest boy was served first, the second son next, and so on. The family, in the words of Lafcadio Hearn, one of the foremost Western interpreters of Japan, "was a despotism . . . in its extreme form, the paternal power controlled everything, the right to marry or to keep the wife or husband already espoused, the right to one's own children, the right to hold property, the right to hold office, the right to choose or follow an occupation."[3]

From Buddhism and Shintoism, with their emphasis on ancestor worship and filial piety, flowed four dominant Japanese characteristics which distinguished the *issei* (first generation) and their sons and daughters from the other groups of Hawaii: first, a deep sense of obligation to family, village, and country—the Japanese concept of *on*; second, face, or profound apprehension concerning the opinions of others respecting the fulfillment of one's obligations; third, self-restraint or self-control preventing disgrace to one's family; and fourth, a fierce pride in things Japanese.

These four characteristics manifested themselves in a variety of ways in Hawaii. In Japan, the peasant carried a heavy burden of *on,* or obligation. He was deeply indebted to his parents and, depending on place and circumstance, to the feudal lord, the shogun, and the Emperor. *On* to parents or the Emperor was usually limitless. To receive love or kindness without feeling a profound sense of *on* would be impossible. In Hawaii, the Japanese sense of obligation was modified by circumstances and time but showed up on the plantations, where even *nisei* (second-generation) insisted upon giving handsome gifts to their plantation managers for the slightest favor. One former manager recalls that he found it difficult to send even a Christmas card to his Japanese workmen because in return they would send him chickens or boxes of cigars, things they could ill afford. *On* appeared on the Kona Coast, too, where Japanese coffee growers who did not help in the building of community bridges or roads were disgraced. *On* to the new adopted country, the United States, compelled patriotism among many Japanese of

Hawaii during both World Wars. But most of all, *on* in Hawaii in the early days meant diligently sending money home to one's parents or village and accepting parental mate selection.

The very idea of *on* implied fulfillment of one's duties. Knowing one's place and keeping one's station in life often demanded self-control and self-restraint. The impulse to marry a beautiful girl outside the village, the desire to snap back at an older brother, the urge to improve one's position, made possible by the disintegration of feudalism and the growth of industrialization in Japan, all had to be suppressed. Self-restraint in Hawaii could mean many things. It could be a Japanese mother who, in the throes of labor pains, puzzles the haole doctor with her stone-faced silence; it could be a young nisei who, having fallen in love with a haole girl, buries his innermost thoughts; it could be a plantation worker who, insulted by his overseer, carries his resentments to his silent bed; it could be a tongue-tied *mama-san*, too embarrassed to bargain with a merchant; it could be plantation workers "humbly beseeching" their employers to consider a request for higher pay; it could be the refusal of young *sansei* (third-generation) politicians to attack an issei elder statesman, despite their dislike for him and his policies; or it could be, and was and is, the refusal of these same politicians to pack a party slate with too many Japanese lest they be criticized for not knowing their place.

Self-restraint, which was closely related to *on,* was also tied to the Japanese concept of face. The very self-restraint that those hostile to the Japanese immigrants labeled as deviousness, secretiveness, and insincerity stemmed partly from the desire of the Japanese in the Islands to receive the approval of others. If bad pronunciation would be laughed at by others and bring disgrace to the family, why say anything at all? If revelation of hostile feelings or family troubles would bring shame, it was much better to keep quiet. Social workers in Hawaii found that even the Japanese children showed extreme reserve, hiding their thoughts and feelings.[4] In a strange and hostile environment, most Japanese constantly feared that they would do the wrong thing and disgrace their family's name. Ruth Benedict has written of the Japanese fear of failure.[5] In Hawaii, this could be seen among members of a young nisei baseball team who had gone down in defeat or in students on report-card day—both might bury their tearful faces so that none might see their shame. In Japan, failure to live up to *on* or to know one's station brought dishonor to the family. In Hawaii, failure to succeed on competitive haole terms also made the heart heavy.

Closely tied to the notion of face was Japanese pride. The performance of *on,* the proper display of self-restraint, and success that won the approval of outsiders were sources of intense pride in the Japanese household. All immigrant groups are more or less ethnocentric, but Japanese feelings of superiority and exclusiveness stemmed from the religion of ancestor worship itself. The sun goddess was regarded as the most important first ancestor of the Japanese ruling family, and all of the people of Japan looked upon themselves as descended from the early deities. To cut oneself off from Japan or things Japanese meant severance from one's divine origin.

In Hawaii, great emphasis was placed on building Japanese language schools. The Japanese started their schools in 1896, long before many of them thought of remaining in Hawaii, to prepare the children for life in Japan.[6] It was important to Japanese parents that their American-born children be taught filial piety, patience, courtesy, cooperation, self-reliance, obligation, and the other virtues that were thought of as distinctly Japanese.[7] The inculcation of Japanese values was believed to be so important that the schools flourished long after the dream of eventual return to Japan was abandoned. By 1937, more than eight of every ten eligible Japanese children were enrolled in Japanese language schools.[8]

Japanese pride and exclusiveness meant much more to Hawaii than a springing up of Buddhist temples, Shinto shrines, and language schools. It meant great stability and continuity in social organization. Even before the large-scale coming of picture brides between 1910 and 1920, there were relatively few Japanese arrests and convictions, juvenile delinquency was low, and the proportion of Japanese receiving charitable aid was smaller than for any other group.[9] Japanese pride was also revealed in their attitude toward intermarriage. It might be bad to marry outside the village or prefecture, but to marry a non-Japanese brought misery and shame to the household. The attitude toward intermarriage was slowly modified as second- and third-generation Japanese became integrated in Hawaii's interracial society, but even in recent decades, the Japanese have revealed less inclination than other groups to marry outsiders. A now prominent Chinese businessman remembers that in 1940 a Japanese broker came to him and said, "Mr. X, if you break up the marriage between my son and a Chinese girl, I'll do anything for you for the rest of my life." The boy married his girl anyway, and somehow the old man adjusted to the mores of racial *aloha,* as many in his generation were forced to do.[10] But the persistence of extreme forms of Japanese exclusiveness even after World War II is strong testimony to Japanese pride. A minority of them refused to believe the news of Japan's surrender in 1946, and later felt personally shamed and humiliated by Japan's defeat.[11] As late as 1960 a local psychiatrist reported extreme cases of Japanese hostility toward other groups in personal relationships.[12]

Relative Japanese solidarity did not prevent the continuation of old intragroup conflicts or the birth of new ones. Indeed, status differences that meant little in the old country loomed large in the first phase of immigrant adjustment. Of the four major classes in Japan—*samurai,* farmers, artisans, and merchants—only the farmers came to Hawaii in large numbers. The major cleavage among them in Hawaii was between the Okinawans and the Naichi. The Naichi, from the four main islands of Japan, but mostly from Honshu, considered themselves superior to the Okinawans, whose island was approximately 275 miles from the southern tip of the Japanese mainland.[13] In some ways the Okinawans were culturally closer to the Chinese than to the Naichi, Okinawa having been incorporated into the Japanese empire only about twenty years before the large migrations to Hawaii. Throughout the 1920's and '30's, approximately 15 per cent of the Japanese in Hawaii were of Okinawan origin. Many of them brought to Hawaii resentment of Japanese domination, and had the double problem of adjusting to Naichi as well as American culture. Coming from the conquering group and being more numerous, the Naichi, struggling for acceptance in Hawaii, tended to emphasize their alleged superiority over the Okinawans. Today, college graduates of Okinawan extraction can still remember the tauntings they received as little girls and boys from other Japanese children.[14]

The Okinawans were looked down upon by the Naichi but they were not despised as were the *eta.* In Japan, the *eta* were outside the three classes of commoners (farmers, artisans, and merchants) and were scarcely thought of as human beings. Japanese writers even denied that the *chōri,* as the *eta* were often called, belonged to the Japanese race. The origin of the *eta* is still a mystery, but one interpretation holds that with the introduction of Buddhism came the idea of the transmigration of souls and the sacredness of animal life. Those occupations that dealt with the killing of animals became unclean; people who performed such jobs, the *chōri*—later colloquially called *chorinbo* in Hawaii—were segregated, as were their children and their children's children thereafter. Tribes of these outcasts held a monopoly over certain occupations, to which they were legally confined. Most of the *eta* became tanners and leather dressers, but many were well diggers, garden sweepers, strawworkers, or sandalmakers, according to local privileges. Another group was employed officially as executioners; another as night watchmen; a third as grave makers. They lived in separate settlements and could not enter any shop or house outside these settlements, and between even the lowest of the commoners and the *eta* there was an impassable barrier. In Hawaii, the *eta* frequently passed into the general Japanese population, but there are many in Hawaii today who recall the horror of parents and grandparents at the thought of *eta* and other Japanese children mixing in the language and public schools.[15]

Other cleavages were between villages and prefectures, but they were not nearly as important for the Japanese as for the Chinese, because Japan had long since reached nationhood. Among the issei, these old cleavages were sometimes intensified during the first adjustment phase. Later, new tensions emerged to take their place, tensions born of a society that stressed achievement, mobility, and freedom of choice.

Like the Chinese and the Portuguese before them, the Japanese immigrants came to work on the plantations. Between 1882 and 1902, the number of Japanese employed by Hawaii's sugar plantations leaped from fifteen to 31,029. For many Japanese, the plantation was a great disappointment. As they approached their new homes, they saw hot red-brown earth, unshaded by trees, and acres and acres of cane to be stripped and cut by hand. Home became the plantation village, perhaps a collection of long shacks divided into rooms ten feet square. Two couples often crowded into these or similar rooms and shared a kitchen and homemade stove, constructed of old cans, rocks, and clay, which used dry cane for fuel. Settled in their shacks, husband and wife prayed for the birth of sons, who, after their parents' lives had ended, would perform the many rites giving their elders a better chance for eternal life.[16]

Most of the immigrants came without their women, hoping to save enough to return home at the expiration of their contracts. They scrimped and saved as much as possible, eating sparsely, mending and remending their clothes, and depriving themselves of even the slightest pleasures. Insofar as possible, they reproduced their home environment on the plantation. They improvised crude hot baths, where men and women could soak together at the end of the day's work in the field. Small shrines were erected, and food was provided for the parents, grandparents, and other deceased family members, represented in the room by pictures of miniature gravestones. They celebrated the Emperor's birthday and other holidays and were overjoyed by Japanese military successes against the Russians.

Attempts to reproduce village life on the plantation could not possibly succeed. Japanese men without their families frequently were unhappy. Many had been demoralized by the exploitation of private immigrant companies, and difficulties in adjusting to plantation life often brought forth petty jealousies and disputes, without a village headman to settle them.[17] Personal disappointments and internal frictions were intensified by the ill treatment handed out by the more brutal plantation *lunas*. The black snake whip was often used to drive the Japanese to work harder, for the penal contract-labor system, which lasted until annexation, was, in effect, forced labor. As long as the penal clause was operational, laborers could escape harsh plantation conditions only through suicide or desertion. In the 1890's, special plantation police were used to ferret out and arrest deserters; passbooks were employed to keep the workers from moving from one plantation to another. In 1898, the Hawaiian Board of Immigration admitted that one cause of the high rate of Japanese desertions was the inhuman practices of some plantation *lunas*.[18]

The Japanese did not always take maltreatment silently. While anxious to accept their place and discharge their *on,* their strong pride made them rebel against what they perceived to be insults to their country and people. From the spring of 1890 through the fall of 1899, the major newspapers of Honolulu reported at least thirty plantation disturbances caused by Japanese workers, and there were undoubtedly dozens of unreported altercations between individual *lunas* and workmen. When a *luna* named Schimmelpfennig beat a Japanese laborer at Koloa in January 1894, a mob of Japanese workers chased him through the streets and then refused to work until the case had been laid before the Japanese Consul.[19] Earlier, 250 Japanese left their plantation at Kukuihaele, on the Big Island, in protest against a *luna* who shot and wounded a Japanese field hand.[20] From Kahuku, on windward Oahu, 120 Japanese marched to Honolulu to express their dissatisfaction with an overbearing *luna*.[21] When the haole *luna* Charles K. Fardin docked a worker's wages at Paia, a group of Japanese field hands roughed him up, and four of the ringleaders were arrested.[22] A strike broke out in November 1897 at Ewa, on Oahu, after a Japanese worker's arm was broken when he was pushed down by a tough *luna*. The Japanese march to Honolulu was turned back, and the leading strikers at Ewa were arrested, locked up, and fined $3 each.[23]

Many of the riots or near riots were caused by conflicts within the immigrant group. At Ewa, four Japanese beat a man who broke an agreement not to outdo others on the job.[24] On Maui, a large mob killed their own Japanese interpreter.[25] And at Heeia, on windward Oahu, six Japanese were arrested after they broke windows of the house of a worker who would not join them in a contemplated demonstration.[26]

Although demonstrations of discontent prior to annexation were sporadic and rarely dealt with such issues as wages and working hours, annexation ended contract labor, and the pent-up frustrations and resentments of Japanese workers immediately resulted in a march of several hundred of them from Oahu plantations to Honolulu. For a few days after the Organic Act took effect, practically all plantation work had to be suspended. The demonstrations did not constitute a real strike, since no demands were made. They were more of a celebration for what the workers believed would be their newly granted freedom.[27]

The planters did take steps to improve workers' morale following annexation. A Hawaiian Sugar Planters' Association official warned that the Japanese would no longer stand for being treated inhumanly "when they themselves are an extremely polite race."[28] But the tradition of forced labor continued in practice, if not in law. The black snake whip was still seen and felt: *lunas* still cursed in their foreign tongue; workers who caused trouble were still thrown out of plantation houses; and fines were frequently levied to punish workers for bad behavior. At one small plantation in 1905, the fine for trespass was 50 cents, for insubordination or neglect of duty $1.[29]

But workers were now free to leave the plantations if they could find work elsewhere in Hawaii or manage the fare to the mainland or back to Japan. The planters devised a new contract system in hopes of damming the flow of workers from the plantations. A long-term contract was offered which made the worker a share cropper living in a plantation labor camp, receiving a minimum wage, and, pending the harvest of his crop, a bonus from the plantation. The plantation financed the croppers' tools, fertilizer, and irrigation. Even before annexation, certain plantation managers had experimented with profit-sharing companies consisting of small groups of Japanese, Chinese, and Portuguese. After annexation, long- and short-term contracts were widely used; by 1929, nearly half of the workers employed by the sugar plantations were either long- or short-term contractors.[30]

There was little mechanization on the plantations during the first decade of the twentieth century. Field operations consisted of plowing, preparing the land, ditching fields on the irrigated plantations, planting, fertilizing, cultivating—mostly with a hoe—stripping the dead leaves from the lower cane stalks, cutting, and loading. These last two operations were usually done on a piece or contract basis and, because they were so onerous, were more highly paid than the other field jobs. A worker's day in the field usually lasted ten hours, beginning at daylight and ending at four o'clock in the afternoon. A day in the sugar mill lasted twelve hours, but mill jobs were preferred. In the mill, out of the hot sun, workers might learn to do machine-shop work or carpentry and improve their position on the plantations.[31]

Work camps were segregated according to race. Although the poorest houses during this period were assigned to the Japanese, many of the issei probably preferred segregation, so that they could maintain their Japanese customs. Traveling from camp to camp and observing the separateness of the Japanese, a representative of the Department of Labor in Washington commented in 1905 that it would be impossible to "expect an assimilation from this population, even from their descendants . . . the two nationalities [haole and Japanese] . . . are separated from one another by every possible bar . . . they differ widely in their experience of political institutions. They differ radically in their spiritual ideals and religious beliefs. They differ wholly in their moral and social conventions, in their philosophy of life, and their habit of thought. They therefore live apart, each maintaining separate and distinct its conventions and ideals."[32]

While many of the Japanese undoubtedly preferred their ghetto communities to social integration, they really had no choice in the matter and undoubtedly resented the stamp of inferiority that went with segregation. The planters encouraged separateness to keep the racial groups apart, each in its own place in the plantation class system.

The work was hard; plantation management was cold and impersonal; and the Japanese were the low group on the plantation totem pole. This meant that despite the influx of Japanese labor, the number of Japanese *lunas* actually decreased between 1900 and 1905, while the number of Portuguese and Hawaiian overseers went up.[33] It also meant that the Japanese received less pay than anyone else for the same work. The average monthly salary of haole *lunas* in the field went from $87.54 in 1902 to $96.03 in 1910, while the pay of the Japanese *lunas* remained essentially the same, changing only from $31.52 to $31.95. For the same work, the Chinese received $5 more and the Portuguese $10 more than their Japanese counterparts.[34]

Living conditions did not improve much after annexation. Between 1902 and 1905, wages for field workers dropped much more sharply than food prices, and during the next five years wages barely kept ahead of prices. By 1909, the real earnings of Japanese workers were actually less than they had been immediately after annexation.[35] The workers did not know it, but profits during that decade were quite high. Even the plantation stores, which were supposed to be selling to the Japanese and others at cost, reported high net profits while wages were still going down. The immigrants were aware that their own general living costs had gone up because of increased family size and the need for language schools, churches, and other community services.[36] By 1909, the Japanese laborers had to provide for 5,000 more women than in 1904; there were 20,000 children, fifty-nine churches and missions with sixty-one ministers and preachers, and sixty-eight schools with a teaching force of eighty. They were still sending money home, although each *yen* meant less since the cost of living in Japan had risen sharply between 1904 and 1909.[37]

In their periodic outbursts against rising costs and *luna* oppression, the workers could count on little help from the Japanese Consul General, who, as the local representative of the Divine Emperor, carried great prestige. He was anxious to keep the immigrants under his control. To forestall the organization of local labor organizations, he formed the Central Japanese League, with the ostensible purpose of negotiating benefits for plantation employees.[38] Minor strikes and walkouts continued despite the Consul General's efforts, and he fell out with leading officials of the League, who argued for more militant action. Until the major strike of 1909, however, the walkouts and protests were not co-ordinated. Class rights were not asserted, but the workers frequently demonstrated against individual acts of injustice. An outraged worker would sacrifice as much as a month's wage to secure the discharge of a brutal overseer. Others struck for an additional water pipe for their camp; still others demonstrated against a haole overseer charged with improper relations with female field workers.[39] A sizable demonstration, involving 2,000 men, took place at Waialua, on Oahu, in December 1904, when the men complained because their wages for cutting and loading cane, which had been dropped in 1903, failed to rise although the 1904 price of sugar had gone up three cents a pound. To show their good faith, the Japanese waited until the cane was ground and on the tracks before they called out the mill hands. The workers at Waialua had other complaints. A hospital nurse was accused of accepting presents from patients; there was a complaint against a preacher who was sent out by the Mission Board and paid by the plantation; there were demands for better water tanks, water supplies, water closets, repair of leaky roofs and replacement of broken windows in houses. When the Japanese asked that they be paid when called out at night to put out cane fires, the manager, who knew his workers, said he was surprised that the Japanese would ask for pay, that this was the kind of thing any man should do for another. Immediately, the laborers voted to cancel that demand, saying that they would be willing to turn out to put out fires "no matter what time or place, without any pay." The manager was pleased that the strikers expressed good will toward the plantation and that they eschewed violence; he met many of their minor requests for repairs but did not budge on the wage demand.[40]

Between 1905 and 1910, subtle changes took place within the Japanese community. Because the standard of living in Japan was rising so quickly, it became more difficult for workers to return home. The Gentlemen's Agreement of 1907, which ended sizable immigration from Japan, also made many of the immigrants think twice about going home and cutting themselves off forever from the Islands. An increasing number of Japanese realized that their future was in Hawaii, and many began to send for picture brides.[41]

A new type of leader was emerging among the issei, more self-assertive, more articulate, indeed, more Americanized. It was "undemocratic and un-American," some of them complained, to force workers who planned to become American citizens—the young nisei—to live under plantation conditions. Pay the workers well, they claimed, and "Hawaii will have, not in a very distant future, a thriving and contented middle class—the realization of the high ideal of American-

ism."[42] These leaders spoke a new language. They attacked discrimination, asking in one pamphlet why a Japanese worker was paid less than
others for the same kind and amount of work. "Is it not the color of his
skin or hair, or the language he speaks . . . ?" they queried.[43]

Among the new leaders were men with education—teachers, clerks,
and newspapermen. Some had gone to the mainland and had been
exposed to trade-union ideas. One of them, Motoyuki Negoro, who had
studied law at the University of California, wrote a treatise on the working conditions of Japanese laborers which was published by Yasutaro
Soga in the Japanese paper *Nippu Jiji*. On December 1, 1908, Soga,
aided by Honolulu merchants, hotelkeepers, and others, founded the
Higher Wages Association, the first plantation trade-union movement
organized in Hawaii. Eighteen days later, the Association presented its
demands to the Hawaiian Sugar Planters' Association, which immediately rejected them. A Japanese labor strike began in May and lasted
only two weeks before foundering on internal dissension and finally
dissolving in the face of trenchant planter opposition. The new leadership of this strike was mild, however, by American trade-union standards. With customary Japanese restraint, the workers at the Oahu Sugar
Company petitioned their manager:

> Dear Sir: We have the pleasure to express our keen appreciation of your
> past kindness and favor, and it is particularly pleasing to recollect that we
> have taken part in the development of the Oahu Sugar Company. . . . It
> shall be our fondest and most cherished hope to continue to help the
> development and progress of your plantation . . . we look back upon the
> past with pleasure and pride, and look forward with hope and enthusiasm.
> . . . Therefore it has become our painful burden to hereby respectfully
> present to you our request for reasonable increase of wages.[44]

There was less Japanese hostility toward management than there was
dissension among the Japanese themselves. The more conservative issei
opposed the strike and held the view expressed in six major Japanese-
language newspapers that the action of the agitators was detrimental to
the good reputation of the Japanese who resided under the protection
of the United States, "with which nation our Empire is on most friendly
terms." The *Hawaii Shimpo* called the strikers thugs and blackmailers.
But the *Nippu* retaliated by labeling the conservatives traitors, pigs,
spies, and dogs. The conservatives, who identified with Japan, received

support from the Consul General, who issued a proclamation urging the laborers to return to work. Many of the merchants and priests also encouraged the strikers to return to their jobs, and the Japanese Merchant Association passed a resolution claiming that the strike would generally upset the economic condition of the Japanese.[45] The crisis that comes to every immigrant group as they enter their second adjustment phase had arrived. The Japanese, as had the Chinese before them, found it their turn to ask: Who are we? What do we believe and what do we want? And what does the future hold for us?

After the 1909 strike, the planters realized they would have to make concessions to improve labor morale. Elderly Japanese today remember that brutality on the plantations was cut down after the strike. A new stepped-up bonus system was introduced in 1911, giving employees who worked an average of twenty days each month a share of plantation profits at the close of the season, based upon the price of sugar in New York City. In some years the bonus was substantial, as in 1915, when the bonus paid laborers equaled 20 per cent of their annual earnings.[46] The planters extended their system of perquisites, and by 1915, all large plantations were providing hospitals and medical care for their employees. The contract system was further developed by providing for three classes of contracts. First was the simple contract that provided for piece work rather than time work. The second gave a gang of laborers a certain area of planted cane, a small advance, and, at the completion of the harvesting, an agreed-upon sum for each ton of cane raised. The third was a form of tenancy by which the laborer rented a small piece of land, produced as an independent landholder, and sold his cane to the plantation at a contract price. But the lowest-paid Japanese was still getting only $18 a month after the strike, hardly enough to live on, according to the U.S. Commissioner of Labor, since food for a man and wife cost $14 a month.[47]

Mechanization was slow in coming to the plantations, and the various plantation tasks—seeding, weeding, irrigating, cutting, bundling, and loading—were still done by hand. A common sight was a small Japanese man picking up a large bundle of cane longer than he was tall, placing it on his shoulders, walking up a plank no more than a foot wide, and dumping it on the railroad car.

The work was hard, but the discriminations which assaulted Japanese pride were probably resented more than the physical labor. The aliens were marked as ineligible for naturalization, and rarely were they or their sons invited to share responsibilities or encouraged to learn American ways. The small indignities of plantation life produced a constant pressure to leave the plantation for town, and between 1902 and 1922, the Japanese plantation population dropped from 31,000 to 17,000. This decrease occurred despite a large increase in total population, which resulted mainly from the summoning of families from Japan. Between 1908 and 1924, more than 62,000 immigrants arrived from Japan, almost half of them women and slightly more than 5,000 of them children.[48] The number of skilled Japanese employees on the plantations reached its peak in 1909, but in the years immediately following, the skilled and semiskilled employees, trained on the plantations, found more freedom and more money in town.[49]

Little did the Japanese workers know that at the Arlington Textile Mill in Lawrence, Massachusetts, in 1912, an immigrant laborer, subject to industrial accidents and cooped up indoors, made a scant $4.30 a week. Out of this sum, he and his 7,000 fellow workers had to pay room, board, carfare, and other expenses unknown to the plantation worker. Here, too, the Irishman, Pole, or Italian was often lost in the impersonality of big-city life. Little did the workers of Hawaii know of migratory work camps for Mexican laborers in the southwestern United States, where working conditions were much worse than those in the Islands. To an outside observer, the Japanese appeared to be making slow but steady progress—moving off the plantations, sending their children to school, and even accumulating a small share of Hawaii's wealth. Each year throughout the 1900's and '20's they sent more than a million dollars back to Japan.[50]

If the Japanese on the plantations were ignorant of misery elsewhere and failed to count their blessings, they did see discrimination in Hawaii. They saw the big house of the haole manager on the hill, the favoritism given to haoles and others, and the daily slights and hurts against their own people.

Another major strike was attempted in 1920, this time with the cooperation of Filipino laborers. When the strike failed, and as Filipinos arrived to glut the labor market, the leaders of Hawaii sought to crush the spirit of the Japanese, whom planter spokesmen considered definitely unassimilable and hostile to Hawaii's ways of life. After the failure of the 1920 strike, life on the plantations for the more rebellious of the Japanese workers became unbearable. Strike leaders were blacklisted; participants in the strike were kept from advancing to better plantation jobs; the Japanese generally were scorned by the others; and in Honolulu a concerted effort was made to destroy the Japanese-language press and schools and the remnants of the Japanese labor movement. Filipino laborers were imported by the thousands to keep wages low on the plantations. As had the Chinese before them, an increasing number of Japanese discovered that town and village life not only meant more freedom but more money, and from 1921 on, the Japanese no longer constituted the most numerous group on the plantations.

Many of those who remained behind adjusted happily to the plantation life of the 1920's and early '30's. The issei could not vote, so it did not matter that the managers sharply limited political activity on the plantations. The village stores and traveling salesmen sufficed to satisfy material wants, and an occasional traveling movie, a holiday or wedding celebration, and a friendly talk after work filled their need for friendship and relaxation. Plantation life required little initiative, since the plantation corporation provided worship and recreation facilities, shops, auto-service stations, housing, and medical services. The Japanese worker had little or no responsibility for building or repairing his home, maintaining roads and bridges, improving the schools; these were administered from Honolulu. Nor was he responsible for contributing to public affairs generally. The plantation communities remained unincorporated, with no mayors or elective councils. The manager, appointed by the board of directors of the corporation, made the decisions. The Japanese viewed the gifts they continued to give their supervisors as "moral obligations and pledges of good will." The older remaining Japanese made their peace with the system and accepted the limitations on their social and occupational ambitions.[51]

Basic working conditions did not improve much in the 1920's, but the long-term cultivation contract, used extensively by the Japanese, freed many of them from day-to-day *luna* control. In the late 1920's, the company divided plantations into fields varying in size from fifty to 280 acres and let contracts to cultivate each field to individuals, who, with the company's help, organized a cultivating gang to weed, irrigate, and fertilize the fields, bringing the cane to the harvesting point. Advance payments of $1 a day, with a bonus of $2.30 if a man worked more than twenty-three days, were made on the contract, since the cane required from eighteen to twenty months before harvesting. A final settlement was made when the cane was cut and weighed at the mill. The workers were paid for the amount of clean cane delivered at the price stipulated in the contract.[52]

The regular rhythm of plantation work and the paternalistic system which took care of basic needs actually filled some of the older Japanese with gratitude, and among those who adjusted to plantation life, accepting its ground rules and limitations, a sizable number achieved small success.[53] By 1930, there were 357 Japanese clerks on the plantations, compared with thirty-six Chinese, thirty Hawaiians, and thirteen Portuguese. The Japanese also constituted the core of the plantations' skilled-labor class, numbering 804, compared with 316 Portuguese and 266 Filipinos. The Japanese were even second to the Portuguese in providing *lunas* for the plantations, and ninty-six Japanese had reached some kind of semiprofessional or professional position.[54]

Many of the younger Japanese did not want to adjust to plantation life, despite the moderate success of some of those who acquiesced in the system. As former plantation children now remember, it was not the unpainted houses without screens or the insufficient and unpalatable drinking water nor the plantation whippings, which few recall, that caused them to hate the plantations.[55] One of them, now an active lawyer on the island of Kauai, thinks that what wounded him most was seeing the older Japanese exploited because of their self-restraint, lack of knowledge, or inability to communicate. Others say they feel exhausted even now as they recall the futility of plantation life. One of the first state legislators tells how his father came to work on a plantation at the age of thirty-five and died at fifty-one with nothing to show for his years of labor.[56] In 1940, a nisei wrote that he assumed that he would live on a plantation all his life and would die there; there was no way out. "You can't go very high up and get big money unless your skin is white. You can work here all your life and yet a haole who doesn't know a thing about the work can be ahead of you in no time."[57] Frustration drove many younger Japanese from the plantations even when opportunities were not apparent elsewhere.

In 1900, the Japanese constituted only 15.7 per cent of the population of Honolulu. Ten years later, they made up 30 per cent of the city's total; 24,000 of them were concentrated in ghetto-like sections in Palama, along River Street, and in such outlying areas as Kalihi, Pawaa, and Moiliili. Even into the 1930's, there were still approx-

imately twenty-five Japanese camps throughout the city.[58] A stranger
from Hiroshima would have felt at home in Moiliili in the 1920's.
There he could have found Buddhist temples, language schools,
and Japanese stores. His friends could direct him to Shinto shrines,
tea houses, and baths. Into the cities poured the Japanese, competing with haole merchants and skilled laborers, the Hawaiian
fishermen and dockworkers, and the Chinese storekeepers and tradesmen. Between 1920 and 1930, the proportion of Japanese retail
dealers and skilled and semiskilled workers leaped forward.[59] There
were more Japanese machinists, painters, glazers, varnishers, carpenters, and fishermen than there were of any other group. The Chinese
had created markets among their own people for specialty foods and
novelties; the Japanese did the same. They also set up stores in the
plantation villages and small towns of the outer islands.[60] Although
there were only 237 Japanese retail dealers in 1896, by 1930 there
were 1,835. Many believed shopkeeping to be one of the easiest
steppingstones to economic security, and by 1930, the Japanese were
operating 49 per cent of the retail stores of Hawaii. Because store
hours were long and hard and the competition was cutthroat, wives
and daughters were sent out to haole homes as domestic servants and
nurses to supplement meager store profits. As late as 1935, the Japanese provided 56 per cent of the domestic servants in the Islands.[61]

A few of the issei became moderately wealthly entrepreneurs. There
was Masutaro Kunihisa, whose son, "Peanuts," later won fame as a
star shortstop for Punahou and as a state senator. Unhappy with his
salary of $12.50 a month as a plantation carpenter, Kunihisa, with his
wife and ten children, had opened a little store in nearby Wahiawa
for plantation laborers in 1919. He named his store "Castner's," after
an American Army officer who had been involved in building the
Army's Schofield Barracks. Castner's grew from a tiny sundries shop to
a large five-and-dime store, and later to a chain of low-priced department stores. There was also a young plantation laborer named Edward
N. Yamasaki on the island of Maui, who could not understand the
willingness of his fellow Japanese to put up with so little in a land of
plenty. He had tried truck farming and cannery work, and after a
trip to the mainland started a service station with a Portuguese friend
named Melim in 1924, an operation that grew into the largest chain
of gas stations in Hawaii. To the west, on the island of Kauai, *papa-
san* Kikuji Kimata encouraged his son to put his money into land.

The father made a few dollars fixing canoes for Hawaiians and doing other odd jobs. Willingly, he and the son took payment in land, and by the 1930's, young Kiyoshi Kimata had become a major landholder near Eleele, on Kauai.[62]

But these cases were exceptions, and a much smaller proportion of Japanese than Chinese went into business. A smaller percentage of those had more than meager success. Japanese businessmen sat around the Japanese Chamber of Commerce in downtown Honolulu during the 1930's lamenting their relative lack of business achievement. Always comparing themselves to the Chinese, they wondered why the *pakes* made money so easily. Frequently they answered their own question by exclaiming that the Chinese knew how to stick together; the Japanese were too competitive, too individualistic. Actually, Japanese family solidarity was considerable. Factors peculiar to the Japanese social structure and to the economic conditions of Hawaii during the 1920's and '30's were more responsible for their relative lack of business success. In Japan, however rich a rice merchant might be, he would have ranked below the carpenters, potters, fishermen, or small farmers in the neighborhood, some of whom might be employed by his own family. The business of money-making had even been held in contempt by the superior classes, and to profit by the purchase and resale of labor's produce was regarded as dishonorable. Well might the merchants of Honolulu have been surprised that there were so many Japanese manufacturers and storekeepers in Hawaii. Japanese comparisons with the Chinese were not fair to themselves. The Chinese had moved to town when opportunities were greater; the Japanese when opposition from haoles, Portuguese, and Chinese was severe. The Chinese realized more quickly that they would stay in Hawaii; the Japanese held on much longer to the dream of returning home. In addition, the Japanese concept of *on* held them back in American economic competition. They resisted the American custom of borrowing and buying on credit. To build up inventories without paying cash, a practical necessity in storekeeping, sometimes seemed dishonorable.[63]

Most of the Japanese who left the plantations, at least up until the 1920's, would have preferred to own or share small farms, but land seemed even more scarce in the Islands than back home. Many of the relatively fertile valleys that were available soon became crowded with Japanese farmers, but in an economy that seemed destined for large-scale plantation agriculture, the life of the small farmer was very hard.

Nonetheless, many of them stuck it out, and of the 5,955 farms in the Islands in 1930, nearly 70 per cent were operated by Japanese owners or tenants. They were small farms, constituting only 2 per cent of the farm land in the Territory, and only 619 were actually owned by the operators. The Japanese who grew up on such farms remember happily their fathers' love for the soil, whether in far-off Hanalei Valley on Kauai or over the Pali from Honolulu in the valleys of Kaneohe.[64]

On Hawaii, substantial groups of independent farmers concentrated in the volcano area and on the hot, dry Kona Coast to the leeward. No harder challenge could be presented to the rugged, almost indomitable Japanese farmers than the Kona district, where they went from the plantations to eke out a living from the barren lava soil by growing coffee on farms of only a few acres. The land they tilled, with its rocky lava soil, their shacks, and the coffee trees planted right up to the door-steps were owned by big haole corporations or Kona landholders. Among the 1,000 families in Kona by the mid-1930's, more than 90 per cent of whom were Japanese, some 800 breadwinners were coffee farmers. The economics of Kona had always been precarious, and occasionally desperate but for the farmers and their families, at least until the mid-1930's, Kona was as similar to the southern villages of Kumamoto prefecture in Japan as one could come in Hawaii. Groups called *kumiai,* corresponding to the *buraku* of Japan, were organized for fraternal and co-operative ventures. Members aided one another at times of grief, marriage, and in building houses. There were eight language schools in Kona, and most of the teachers were natives of Japan. Three Buddhist priests from Japan ministered to the religious needs of the community. But under the pressure of American individualism, the *kumiai* eventually disintegrated, and in the 1930's the Japanese ways crumbled, much to the distress of die-hard issei parents.

Yet the parents themselves were sometimes partly responsible. In Japan, the farmer knew he would die a farmer, and he expected his boy to grow up a farmer and his daughter to marry a hard-working farmer boy. In Kona, he carried in his bosom the American faith in education and the hope that his children would be able to struggle above the immigrant-farmer class. It was possible to see, even in the restricted environment of Kona that in Hawaii a man could rise by great indi-vidual effort, and that there were riches to be had if the efforts were successful. Incentive to succeed gripped the Japanese farmer as it did the Japanese shopkeeper, and just as it had captured the Chinese of Hawaii. Anthropologist John Embree has related how incentive even played a part in the Japanese funerals of Kona. "Each through competition tries to outshine his neighbors," he wrote a year before Pearl Harbor.[65] In Japan, only a rich landowner could afford to have a picture taken of a parent's funeral. In Kona, however, it was a rare funeral that had no local photographer in attendance.

If success was measured by refrigerators, radios, and rich diets, the Japanese were becoming more successful in the 1920's than could ever have been possible in Japan. But success in these terms did not obsess the Japanese—they were dominated instead by the desire to be accepted. The elite wanted control; the Portuguese longed to be haole; the Hawaiians dreamed of recapturing the past; the Chinese sought economic independence; but the Japanese wanted more than anything to be accepted for what they were—immigrants from Japan in Hawaii.

The 1920's were a time of deep internal division among those Japanese who had decided to make Hawaii their home. The goal was clear: it was acceptance. But their strategies were in dispute. There were those like Fred Makino, editor and publisher of the *Hawaii Hochi,* who said: Support the labor movement and strike for higher wages, fight for rights through politics, use the courts when necessary, and you will win respect as a Japanese-American. Others counseled: Be grateful, restrained, obedient, and you will be granted respect as an American of humble immigrant parents. While the Reverend Takie Okumura and others led the movement to comply with laws restricting the Japanese language schools, Makino struggled against him, until the U.S. Supreme Court decided in 1927 that the statutes were unconstitutional. When a Japanese youth, Myles Yutaka Fukunaga, alleged to have kidnaped for ransom and killed the son of a Caucasian business leader, was being convicted by public opinion, Makino defied prominent Honoluluans and called for a fair trial.

Only the issei who rejected Hawaii altogether did not care what the other groups thought. For them, Japan was more than a homeland. It was the center of their moral, cultural, and spiritual life. Often, to the distress of their children, they refused to learn even a little bit of English or to dress "haole" for a visit to school. For the Japanese-centered issei of the 1920's and '30's, the behavior of the second generation appeared scandalous and sometimes even sacrilegious. The *furyoshonin,* the nisei pool-hall bum, could never have happened in

Honshu. The *abura-mushi*, the female "cockroach," who "played around" with the boys, even haoles, had no counterpart in the rural Japan that they knew. For these issei, it was better to ignore Hawaii as much as possible. When possible, they sent their children back to Japan for an education, and this group became the *kibei* of Hawaii, born in the Islands but Japanese educated, and in some cases more Japanese than their parents.[66]

Most of the issei and the first group of the second generation adopted a conservative strategy in their quest for acceptance. Conscious of place and face, they tried to adjust to the social structure, seeking acceptance within it. Change from the Japanese authority system, where everyone must know and keep his place, to the social structure of Hawaii required no fundamental revision of attitudes. It was well into the second generation, and in some cases the third, before most Japanese discovered the American ideal of equal opportunity for all and realized that the Hawaiian social order did not conform to it. Nisei and sansei in the late 1950's repeatedly told interviewers that their fathers and mothers expressed little hostility toward the social system. They may have recalled with bitterness the unfriendliness or meanness of a plantation boss, but their judgment was against the individual and not the system.

This group increasingly looked for leadership to that small number of nisei born in the Islands near the turn of the century who had been fortunate and able enough to establish links with haoles and other outsiders. Foremost among these was Wilfred Tsukiyama, later to become the first Chief Justice of the Supreme Court of the State of Hawaii. "Tsuki," educated at the University of Chicago Law School, became an active Republican in 1924. He recalls that he idealized Abraham Lincoln and studied the principles of the Republican party before joining. Party principles aside, Tsukiyama was thoroughly inculcated with the Japanese virtues of obligation, self-restraint, and face. He was ever-courteous, grateful, and humble, willing to accept life as it existed, and hoping for recognition on its terms. In 1929, he became the first Japanese to be appointed to an important post when he was made deputy attorney for the city and county of Honolulu. Four years later, he was made city and county attorney, in which position he served until the breakdown of Japanese-American relations in 1940. Then, characteristically, Tsukiyama withdrew from public life to private law practice, believing it would be indelicate for a Japanese to come to the fore at such a time. Later, Tsukiyama was accused by a new generation of Japanese politicians of having sold out to the Caucasians. Why, they asked, did he resign from a Selective Service board under haole pressure at the start of the war? Why hadn't he asserted Japanese interests over the years? To accuse Tsukiyama was, in a sense, absurd. His entire generation might well have been indicted. Tsukiyama, true to his Japanese heritage, had bowed to authority and tried honestly and vigorously to represent his people within Hawaii's authoritarian political system. If he lacked reforming zeal, so did his entire generation, with only a few exceptions.

Tsukiyama was the lion of his group, but there were others. Steere Noda, the son of an Ewa plantation worker, was, in 1911, the first graduate of a Japanese high school in Honolulu, five years before Tsukiyama received his diploma. While he was mastering his Japanese lessons, Noda became a star baseball player at Mid Pacific Institute, and following graduation, he won a job with the Internal Revenue Service, and later a position as district court clerk and interpreter. He studied law and was licensed to practice in the district courts of the Territory. Like Tsukiyama's, Noda's clients were almost entirely drawn from the issei or his own group, the early second-generation Japanese. After a defeat for the Board of Supervisors in Honolulu, he intended to run again in 1942, but Pearl Harbor smashed his political hopes, as it broke the spirit of the older Japanese. Like Tsukiyama, Noda withdrew from public life. He had been willing to represent his Japanese clients in the district courts in the 1930's, and he would have been happy to represent them in politics in the '40's if there had been no war, but, proud of his Japanese ancestry, he believed that he and other Japanese should know their place in Hawaii. Later, he was to complain that some younger nisei and sansei were too pushy and arrogant.[67]

Tsukiyama's mild success in the 1920's boosted the morale of the Japanese. Until his appointment to office, the Japanese had resigned themselves to being excluded from the politics and government of Hawaii. One of today's younger, more militant politicians remembers that the political talk in his parents' living room invariably centered on Tsukiyama, a Japanese to be proud of. "Tsukiyama, he's all right," the boy's uncle would say. "He's in there," remarked an older cousin. "Yes, he's up there with the haoles." The desire to be accepted was strong, and Tsukiyama and others like him symbolized the possibility of acceptance.[68]

A tiny group among the issei and many more among the second-generation Japanese challenged the Tsukiyama approach to adjustment in Hawaii. They wanted to be accepted and respected as Japanese in Hawaii no less than the majority, but unlike the others, they believed that respect would have to be won by struggle against the powerful men of Hawaii, rather than through deference to them. Whereas Tsukiyama and most of his generation stressed place, a sense of the fitness of things, a few of the issei, fiercely proud of their Japanese heritage, fought to overcome the system that accorded them an inferior place. For the nisei, it was not so much a matter of Japanese pride as it was American rights. It was inevitable that with the increasing Americanization and acculturation of the nisei would come a more radical approach to this problem.

The overwhelming majority of the nisei had been educated or were being educated in Hawaii's public schools. McKinley High School, from 1910 to 1920 Oahu's only public high school, was already being called "Tokyo High." Through their textbooks at school and the ideas of schoolteachers imported from the mainland, they were introduced to some of the most dynamic and revolutionary political and social ideals of human history—the ideals expressed in the Declaration of Independence. Implicit in the Declaration were two basic concepts that stirred the Japanese: that all men are created equal in the sight of God and are entitled to an equal opportunity to make the most of their talents; and that when the existing social order is inimical to equal opportunity, the system should be overturned. The *kamaaina* elite and its representatives, who spoke constantly of Americanizing the Japanese, meant that the nisei should speak good English, wear American clothes, play baseball, eat hot dogs, and become dutiful Christians—acculturation, but not to the dominant political and social ideologies of America embodied in the Declaration of Independence. There was the paradox. To hold to American social ideals was to believe in equal opportunity. Following the American political process meant claiming rights to opportunity through group action. These were the characteristics that distinguished the American system but were alien to the Orient.

It was not only the textbooks and mainland-educated schoolteachers that were responsible for the increased acculturation and Americanization of the children of the second generation. In the American pattern, young Japanese boys and girls organized and joined numerous clubs and associations, according to their interests. In rural Japan, the extended family had been the crucial social group; not so in Hawaii. Even in the rural areas, occupational, religious, and fellowship groups such as the Boy Scouts, the Y.'s, sports and recreation clubs, adult groups, school organizations, and discussion groups were formed. Slowly but steadily, the nisei were learning that in America it was possible to get things done through group initiative. The impact of the schools was tremendous in turning the second generation toward an approach to acceptance through group demands rather than individual deference. Small group autonomy, which had been looked down upon in Japan because it upset the control of the village headman or mayor, may have been un-Japanese, but it was thoroughly American.[69]

Recognizing the ever-increasing Japanese acculturation and Americanization, the major Japanese newspapers of the 1920's knew they would have to keep pace with second-generation opinion. They continued throughout this period not only to reflect, but also to influence, the development of group goals as they consistently urged their readers to focus on Hawaii, not Japan. All ten major Japanese newspapers agreed on the policy of permanent residence and pushed for Americanization of the second generation. Practically all endorsed the language schools, claiming there was no inconsistency between their maintenance and Americanization.[70] The *Nippu Jiji,* although it was more conservative than the *Hawaii Hochi,* urged the Japanese people not to send their money back to Japan, but to invest it in the Territory or save it for their children; in a later editorial, it criticized the first generation for not being able to understand their own children and for not attempting to know the haoles better. The *Nippu* had been the most militant Japanese newspaper during the 1909 strike, but after its editor was jailed for his alleged leadership in that strike, the editorial policy became more cautious.[71]

The *Hawaii Mainichi,* even more than the *Nippu,* followed a conservative line, appealing especially to the issei of Hilo. Its second-generation readers were also repulsed by the radical approach and worked sedulously for acceptance as Americans within the prevailing authority system of Hawaii. They counseled each other to win acceptance by being friendly, courteous, and grateful to the men who ran Hawaii. By devotion to the Japanese principles of *on* and self-restraint, the conservatives hoped to win acceptance from others.

But the forces of social change in Hawaii which were later to transform the social structure were working against the conservative ap-

proach. Respect for authority, based on filial piety, was under constant
assault by the system of money wages which made children and wives
relatively independent of the family heads, and by the system of education which encouraged individual initiative and choice.[72] Whereas only
slightly more than a quarter of the children in the public schools were of
Japanese ancestry in 1910, the proportion doubled within the next ten
years.[73] The brighter, more ambitious of these schoolchildren recognized that the democracy preached in the schools was in many
ways foreign to Hawaii. To win acceptance through traditional Japanese displays of gratitude and co-operation seemed absurd. As Americans, they had to organize and to press their claims as a group.
Many followed the arguments of the *Hochi,* by the late 1920's the most
influential of Hawaii's Japanese-language newspapers. More enthusiastic about the 1920 strike than the *Nippu,* the *Hochi* talked less about
promoting harmony between labor and capital and was more militant
during the language-school controversy, supporting litigation against
the Territory's antilanguage-school laws. The *Hochi* passed the *Nippu*
in circulation in 1928, and when its publisher and editor, Fred Makino,
floated a $100,000 bond issue to make improvements in his plant, he
found ready subscribers among the Japanese, although the bonds were
regarded more as donations than loans.[74] Makino attacked the oligarchy
daily and urged the young Japanese to free themselves from all ties that
bound them to Japan. In an editorial entitled "The Nordic Caste
System," the *Hochi* blasted segregation of haoles and Orientals in
churches, the Y.M.C.A., schools, and business establishments, and
called for more social contacts between the two groups.[75] Makino
argued in the July 1927 issue that the key concepts of Americanism are
justice and a square deal. To be really American meant exercising
freedom and independence, not bowing down in humility or kowtowing
to superiors. The *Hochi* warned against the inferiority complex characteristic of many of the second generation, who accepted the domination
of the haoles and were too sensitive to slights, too willing to withdraw
from the battle. As it was expressed editorially in the *Hochi:* " . . . when
the young Japanese are able to look their white brothers squarely in the
eye and tell them to 'get out of the way,' they will find out whether
there is any race discrimination that can hinder them or keep them from
success!"[76]

   To the conservatives, the outraged haole reaction to the militant
ideas expressed by the *Hochi* and radical Japanese leaders was proof

enough that the activists were on the wrong side. Supported by the *Nippu,* the conservatives had successfully stalled legislation against the foreign-language schools in 1919 after revising textbooks to make the schools more congenial to the wishes of the haole community. Some outsiders had written off Japanese patriotism during the war as a covert attempt to take over. Anti-Japanese Governor Lucius E. Pinkham even tried to exclude Americans of Japanese ancestry in the 1915–16 National Guard recruiting campaign, although Selective Service later made it possible for them to join. The Japanese purchase of savings stamps and bonds during the war in an amount far beyond expectations brought from a prominent *hapa*-haole territorial senator a comment that "the Japanese are very shrewd and seem to know the value of these stamps."[77] The conservatives took to heart the urgings of a haole missionary to Japan, Sidney Gulick, who had written in 1915 that "Japanese are always and everywhere Japanese, loyal to their emperor for generations untold. American and Asiatic civilizations are based on postulates fundamentally different and antagonistic. The two civilizations cannot be assimilated," he maintained, unless "the propaganda and practice of vital Christianity" can make the Japanese assimilable.[78] When the 1920 strike roused the fierce antagonism of the *kamaaina* elite against the Japanese, the conservatives were more convinced than ever that the militants were on the wrong track. After the strike, restrictive bills were sped through the legislature to punish the Japanese for their affronts. The Honolulu *Star Bulletin* of March 27, 1920, intoned: "In our opinion this [hostile] feeling toward the Japanese has been engendered almost entirely by their temperamental characteristics, their insincerity . . . as evidenced by their conduct of the present strike on this island. . . . Studying deeper into the cause of the feeling entertained against the Japanese we have their insularity, their failure to enter into community life and become a part of it, their herding together and aloofness from their occidental neighbors."

Was segregation primarily self-imposed, or was it forced on the Japanese? This was the question that Senator William H. King, of Utah, asked after his 1918 visit to the Islands. He told a group of haole visitors from Honolulu that many of the Japanese he saw seemed to be Americanized, but they were not given the opportunity to participate in civic life. King pointed out that they were isolated and "not welcome as American citizens. . . ." The Japanese he talked to "manifested the deepest attachment to our institutions and to our form of govern-

ment."[79] His visitors probably thought that the Senator did not understand how insincere and deceptive the Japanese were, and, perhaps
even more important, King did not have to live with them. In Hawaii,
the Japanese were numerous and, unless checked, would someday
control the Islands.

In a speech before the Honolulu Rotary Club in October 1921,
Vernon S. McClatchy, chief anti-Japanese spokesman from California,
warned the Rotarians against Japanese economic and political as-
cendancy in Hawaii.[80] When alien Japanese applied for citizenship,
the so-called Americanizers warned against a rush of applications
which would lead to the time not far distant "when Hawaii will have a
Japanese voting population sufficient in numbers to control legislation
and control politics."[81] If the Japanese did not exercise their franchise,
argued some haole leaders, it was merely a trick, under instructions
from Tokyo, an attempt to lull the haoles into a false sense of security.
Walter Dillingham, perhaps the most powerful man in Hawaii during
the 1920's, put it this way to a Congressional committee:

> Supposing, for the sake of an example, that the Japanese on one of her
> mandated islands in the Pacific should develop the island by bringing in a
> great number of American citizens, and finally they had a situation where
> 110,000 red blooded American citizens were on the island where there
> were 18,000 pure blooded Japanese. How would I feel having a college
> classmate visit me, to usher him from the boat to the house, kick off sandals
> and toss a kimona and say, "This is my home. My wife and I came here
> from America fifteen years ago, and we have made our home here and
> have entered into the spirit of the life. I want you to meet my boy." In
> comes a fine, upstanding boy, fifteen years of age. I say, "He is going to the
> University of Japan. He reads, writes, and speaks Japanese better than he
> does English, and if we ever have a rumpus with Uncle Sam that boy is
> true blue; he is going to fight for the Empire."
> Now just imagine pointing with pride to your son and saying that, and
> you realize what you're asking of the Japanese in Hawaii.[82]

In case the committee failed to get Dillingham's point, a spokesman
for the Hawaiian Sugar Planters' Association added that it would be
impossible to assimilate the Japanese of Hawaii, yes, even the second
generation.[83]

The *kamaaina* elite realized that group autonomy for the Japanese
of Hawaii would eventually destroy the system of authority based on
elite control which had been nurtured so carefully over three gen-

erations. To counter the Japanese threat, it attempted to persuade Congress to import Chinese immigrants to work on the plantations. In addition to fighting the naturalization movement after World War I, restricting the foreign-language schools, and blacklisting the leaders of the 1920 strike, it had passed a law in 1921 that made it a misdemeanor to publish anything designed to create distrust between peoples of different races or between citizens and aliens. Although never applied and probably unconstitutional, the legislation did inhibit the more conservative Japanese newspapers. Later, Governor Lawrence Judd went even further and denounced the alien press. The foreign-language press existed only through the kindness and tolerance of the United States government, he pointed out, and aliens were violating their hospitality by attacking Hawaii's social system. If the Japanese wanted racial harmony, Judd warned, they ought to behave.[84] *Kamaaina* haole fears received scholarly support in a book written by a University of Hawaii psychologist in 1925 who argued that the Japanese, "aggressive and unscrupulous in pursuing an advantage," would someday, at the right moment, take over the Territory.[85]

Under the weight of ostracism and repression, the internal Japanese debate over strategies for acceptance continued. The American Citizens of Japanese Ancestry, formed shortly after World War I to promote Americanism, was followed by the missionary-founded student organization New Americans, under the leadership of the Reverend Takie Okumura. Okumura maintained that it was a mistake to push Buddhism on the second generation; Buddhism, which was alien to America, was a handicap to the assimilation of the Japanese.[86] Okumura had visited Japanese communities throughout the Territory in 1920 to urge his fellow Japanese to pledge their loyalties to the United States. To him this meant acquiescing in the social system of Hawaii and encouraging the young people to remain on the plantations. His group published a newspaper during the late 1920's and early '30's and ran an annual workshop conference to train leaders. The New American movement received support from the *Nippu Jiji*, which ran an annual contest for essays on Americanism. "American citizens of Japanese ancestry must exercise their political rights as impartially as possible," wrote one prize winner in 1927.[87] "If we expect to be true Americans in spite of our ancestry, we must be Americans in every way . . . we must associate with Americans and adopt their ideals, customs and traditions . . ." wrote another student a year later.[88]

While the conservatives blamed the militant and aggressive Japanese for the hostility of the haoles and others, those who were skeptical of the New Americans maintained that haole respect could not be won without a fight. They pointed to continued discrimination despite the growing use of the Japanese Nationality Law of December 1, 1924, which made it possible for the Americans of Japanese ancestry, or A.J.A.'s, as they were often called, to throw off their Japanese citizenship. They pointed out that if the Japanese happened "to vote for the same candidate, they are accused of having voted in a racial block, and, on the other hand, if they happened to stagger their votes, they are spoken of as lacking in cooperative spirit. . . ."[89]

The conflict over strategy became more important as an increasing number of nisei registered to vote. The Japanese constituted less than 3 per cent of the registered voters of the Islands in 1920; they made up nearly 8 per cent six years later; and by 1936, one out of four registered voters in Hawaii was of Japanese ancestry, thereby constituting the largest voting group in the Islands. Perceptive haole politicians had attempted to organize this vote as far back as 1917, when Lawrence Judd met with fifteen A.J.A.'s and asked them to join the Republican party. Hawaii's two top Democrats, John Wilson and Lincoln Mc-Candless, tried to persuade some of the same young Japanese leaders to join the Democrats. One of those who attended both meetings recalled many years later that all but one of the boys "felt it was better to be with the dominant party," and, therefore, to join the Republicans.[90] A few A.J.A.'s were active in election campaigns in the repressive early 1920's. Foremost among them was businessman Takaichi Miya-moto, who campaigned for McCandless in his bid for the delegateship in 1922, and who became the first president of the Japanese Democratic Workers' Club. The vast majority of the Japanese who were active in politics, however, were Republicans. In the late 1920's, Dr. Harry Kurisaki was the first Japanese to be elected to the Republican County Committee and the G.O.P. Central Committee. During the same decade, five unsuccessful attempts were made by Japanese candidates—all Republicans—to win seats in the territorial House. Finally, in 1930, Noboru Miyake was elected to the Board of Supervisors on Kauai; and on the Big Island, Tasaku Oka won the House seat from East Hawaii.

It made practical sense to be a Republican. The Republicans furnished cars, set up rallies on the plantations, and made good campaign contributions. The Democrats were frozen out, often not even permitted to appear on plantation property. The Republicans were in control nationally, and this meant that the territorial administration would be Republican. The Republican *kamaaina* elite were all too often in a position to make or break a struggling young business or professional man. In 1928, Dr. Kurisaki, encouraged by Fred Lowrey, head of the Honolulu Chamber of Commerce, ran for the House, explicitly seeking Japanese help. Kurisaki went to Tokuji Onodera, of the Japanese Chamber of Commerce, to solicit issei support, but Onodera refused, saying that if the Japanese took an interest in politics as a group, they would antagonize the haole community. This conservative view was rejected by the friends of Andy Yamashiro, elected from the fifth district on Oahu to the territorial House in 1930 with strong Japanese support, including the help of his father, a successful businessman who organized many issei to campaign for Andy. In the 1930's, dozens of A.J.A.'s entered active politics, but most of them still found it prudent to join the Republican party. Twenty-four A.J.A.'s ran for office in 1936; nine were elected, but only one, George Watase, a member of the Kauai Board of Supervisors, was a Democrat. Two years later, twenty-two Japanese ran for office. Sixteen of these were Republicans; four, non-partisans; and two, Democrats. Again Watase was the only Democrat to be elected. In 1940, the last prewar election saw twenty-nine Japanese candidates enter the primaries, only four of whom were Democrats. Among the thirteen elected, Watase again was the only Democratic representative.[91]

Ironically, leading Republicans constantly raised the scare of Japanese block voting during the 1930's, although the vast majority of active politicians among the A.J.A.'s were Republicans and even in those districts where the Japanese had a clear majority of the vote, Japanese candidates were rarely elected. The compulsion for acceptance was so great that it inhibited Japanese group voting in many cases. The Japanese preferred not to flex their political muscles as immigrant groups had done on the mainland. In Hawaii, it was too dangerous. The haoles might, in retaliation, impose a commission form of government, stripping the citizens of the franchise altogether.

The conservative strategy dominated before the war, although it did not succeed in winning acceptance for the Japanese. No matter how they tried to please, the more powerful groups in Hawaii kept up a constant barrage of criticism. The Sino-Japanese War found a vast majority of Hawaiians, haoles, and Chinese sympathizing with China against Japan, and the motion-picture column of the *Nippu Jiji* reported that young nisei Americans were miserable after watching newsreel pictures of Japanese planes bombing Chinese cities. "Go back to Japan, where you came from, you *daikon* eater" was a sentiment now openly, if rarely, expressed on the playing fields of Hawaii.[92]

The Japanese ways of the issei and the *kibei* made it difficult for the nisei to win acceptance, especially in a time of growing tensions between the United States and Japanese governments. Leaders in the haole community viewed with contempt the reception the Japanese of Hilo gave two visiting battleships from Japan in October 1939 and the early efforts of the Japanese community to raise money for the Japanese side in the Sino-Japanese War.[93]

Despite their difficulties in winning acceptance, individual economic or professional success became fairly common. By 1930, four out of every ten Japanese had bank accounts in Hawaii; 106 were dentists, eighty-three physicians or surgeons, seventy-five teachers, and twenty-two lawyers or judges. The Japanese could be proud that their crime and juvenile-delinquency rates were the lowest in the Territory. A few Japanese owned real estate, and a handful amassed sizable amounts of capital. But there was a great uneasiness in the Japanese community of Hawaii through the 1930's, as international events continued to frustrate their drive for acceptance.

On the eve of Pearl Harbor, the Japanese were regarded with increased suspicion and distrust by many outsiders. The bombs that descended on Hickam Field on the morning of December 7, 1941, brought the Japanese of Hawaii face to face with their greatest ordeal. The war was to be for them a period of darkness and tragedy; it was also to be their time of glory.

Chapter Five

STRANGERS AND AFRAID

A Filipino visitor from Manila and his haole writer friend sat waiting on a rough sandy beach near the Seaview Inn on Molokai. Out of the morning mist hanging over the bay appeared a fisherman dressed in an open khaki shirt, rough tattered pants, and heavy boots. The tide was low, and the heavy-shouldered, bald, and bronzed fisherman could be seen walking on the ocean floor a quarter of a mile away. As he approached, he quickened his pace, sloshing through the quiet sea. "Juan, my countryman, my countryman," he called out in his native Visayan dialect to the wiry, thin-lipped Filipino visitor on the beach. Dripping-wet and grinning from ear to ear, the fisherman embraced his friend. Then, sheepishly, with a shy smile, the middle-aged fisherman presented his guest from Manila with his morning's catch—squid from the waters off Molokai. To the Filipino fisherman in Hawaii, the visitor from Manila was a symbol of home.[1]

The story of this Visayan is the story of countless Filipinos in Hawaii prior to statehood. The episode above took place in 1959, a quarter of a century after the fisherman had arrived in the Islands to work as a strikebreaker during the 1924 Filipino strike. Illiterate, pliable, and used to backbreaking labor, the fisherman, with big hands, broad shoulders, and a friendly heart, worked as hard as he could to save money to return to his *barrio* in the central Philippines. He lived frugally in his barracks, and in three and a half years, his heart aching for sight of his family, he saved enough American dollars to return to the *barrio*. There he lived for two years on his savings. Then, in 1930, with bold dreams, he came back to the golden islands of Hawaii, hoping to amass a small fortune and return home again, where he would become famous as the peasant who made good in Hawaii. He did not take into account the depressed agricultural wages of the 1930's or his own increasing needs and expenses; this time when he came home, his relatives and friends would expect great things—enough money to buy land, to marry, and to be generous to those close to him. The days passed, then months and years, and the dream of returning home triumphant, while never abandoned, faded. The Visayan enjoyed his fishing and liked his neighbors on the friendly island of Molokai, but what he loved—his family, *barrio,* and country—was far away. While he was gone, both wonderful and tragic events had occurred in the Philippines. A brother was killed during the Japanese occupation; a nephew was celebrated as a war hero; his sister married and bore children, one named after him. The Philippines became an independent state and a member of the United Nations.

With the passage of the Organic Act, the planters of Hawaii looked longingly across the Pacific to the Philippines as a major source of cheap labor. They had hurriedly imported 40,000 Japanese immigrants during the two years between annexation and the passage of the Organic Act. Hasty efforts were made to bring in others. In late December 1900, a group of Puerto Ricans, the first of 3,000 to be recruited from that island, arrived, and a few hundred Negroes were imported from the mainland. Then in 1904, several thousand Koreans came to help fill the void created by the suspension of Japanese immigration during the Russo-Japanese war.[2] But always, the Philippines were on the minds of the planters. As close as Japan, China, Korea, and closer than Puerto Rico and Portugal, the Philippine archipelago, crowded with subsistence peasants, seemed a natural source of labor. There were obvious advantages other than proximity. The Filipinos were nationals, and no foreign country could bar their entry to Hawaii. The planters were pleased also that in Manila they would be dealing with American officials.

As Japanese left for the mainland in increasing numbers in 1904 and 1905, the sugar factors of Honolulu voiced demands for cheap Filipino labor. When Japan voluntarily restricted emigration to Hawaii through the Gentlemen's Agreement in 1907, and when the Japanese laborers on Oahu staged their 1909 strike, the Philippines again looked attractive to the planters. Hawaii's Board of Immigration, in some respects an arm of the Hawaiian Sugar Planters' Association, agreed that the Philippines might be the best source for permanent labor. So successful were the recruiting agents, that between 1910 and 1932

more than 100,000 Filipino men came to work in the cane and pineapple fields of Hawaii.[3]

In many respects, the economic patterns in which the Filipino
laborers found themselves in Hawaii were similar to what they had
known back home. The majority of the immigrants came from the
peasant areas of Ilocos Norte and Ilocos Sur, where they worked as
tenants or laborers on the estates of the *caciques,* those Filipino landholders who had been granted special rights by Spanish governors during the more than 300 years of Spanish rule between the discovery of
the Philippine Islands by Magellan in 1521 and American conquest in
the Spanish-American War. The *tao,* or common man who worked
the land, was usually debt-ridden and often reduced to abject poverty.
To own land became the goal of hundreds of thousands of peasants,
who did anything—even to the point of enslaving themselves—to
earn the right to the soil beneath their feet. The peasants lived in
barrios—close-set villages that had as few as ten or as many as a
hundred houses—and perquisites, less generous than those given on the
sugar plantations of Hawaii, were provided for the workers on the
larger estates and plantations.[4]

Physically, the Hawaiian Islands were reminiscent of the homeland,
although everything was on a smaller scale than in the Philippines. At
home, there were more than 7,000 islands, divided into three major
parts: Luzon, in the extreme north, Mindanao, in the extreme south,
and Visaya, in the middle. The mountains were taller, volcanoes and
their eruptions more numerous, windstorms and typhoons more
threatening, the sun hotter, and the rain wetter.[5]

But there were differences as well as similarities between life in
Hawaii and what the immigrants had known in the Philippines. The
most important difference was the lack of women and children in
Hawaii. Kinship patterns had been extremely important in the archipelago, where the individual household was merely a subunit of a larger
family group. But of the 52,672 Filipinos in Hawaii in 1930, nine out
of ten were males. Although 40 per cent of the adult Filipino men were
reported to be married, nearly three fourths of them had left their wives
in the Philippines.[6] Because they were without their families, and because they dreamed of financial success and a heroic return home, the
single men, living a barracks-like existence on the plantations, felt little
need for a permanent social organization. Thus, the Filipino *barrio*
associations, called *turnuhans,* in which Filipino laborers worked to-

gether to plow, plant, harvest, husk, and build houses, and through which mutual assistance was given at baptisms, weddings, and burials, were not repeated in Hawaii, as the Japanese and Chinese associations had been. Although their plantation work might resemble work in the *barrio,* and the physical landscape might be reminiscent of the Philippines, the Filipino without his family could not feel at home.

The Filipinos did not bring their wives because they were determined to accumulate money and return home as quickly as possible. In some instances, recruiting agents for the Hawaiian Sugar Planters' Association encouraged the laborers to transport their women with them to Hawaii, but the ambitious Filipino accurately reasoned that his wife would cost as much to feed and transport as himself without substantially increasing the family's income. No, it was better for her to remain in the *barrio* with the family. A manual for Filipino laborers, published by the Association in 1930 in Ilocano and Visayan dialects, recorded a typical laborer telling his wife, "You better stay home, Maria, and take good care of our six. . . ." The husband promised to love his wife and urged her to be pure in heart. She cautioned him against sharp characters who might steal his money. They embraced and said tearful farewells.[7]

There was not much better than an even chance that the departing husband would ever see his Maria again. He might return to the *barrio,* or he might send for her at a later date, but he might also go to California or live out his days in Hawaii. Between 1922 and 1930, only 48 per cent of these Filipino men who arrived in the Territory returned to the Philippines.[8] Yet the desire to go home became the major obsession of the Filipinos in Hawaii. To speak of the *barrio* in loving terms brought tears to the eyes of the toughest Filipino field worker; but attachment to the *barrios* did not deter growing nationalism among the immigrants in Hawaii. Filipino nationalism had developed in the previous century under Spanish rule, and national revolutions had broken out during the Filipino-Spanish War of 1896–98, one of them leading to a short-lived Filipino republic. Improved communication and transportation under American rule, advancements in educational opportunities, and common cultural developments in art, music, literature, and sports greatly accelerated nationalist feeling in the period of Filipino migrations to Hawaii. During the long Spanish rule, only a handful of privileged Filipinos were permitted to go to school. The recruiting policies of the Hawaiian Sugar Planters' Association aimed at bringing the least-educated Filipino peasants to Hawaii, and dozens, perhaps hundreds, of laborers pretended to be illiterate to pass the planters' major test.

The joy in Filipino hearts at the passage of the Duffy-Tydings Act of 1934, which granted the Philippine Islands eventual independence, was matched by the poignant anguish of immigrants in Hawaii, who began to realize that they might never return home. To no other ethnic group in Hawaii did fate deal so many bad cards. Every circumstance conspired to deepen the Filipinos' sense of longing for the homeland and to intensify their sense of inferiority in Hawaii. Unlike the other immigrant groups, the Filipinos were nationals without a country. They were Americans but did not have the full rights of American citizens. They were Filipinos, but the Philippines were ruled by the United States. Moreover, the Filipino arrival in Hawaii coincided with narrowing economic opportunities, especially during the depression of the 1930's, and like each new ethnic group, the Filipinos were given the lowest plantation jobs. Unlike the others, they found it difficult to leave the plantations for the cities. For a great many of those who remained, a feeling of failure ensued. With less family life, greater illiteracy, fewer economic opportunities, and eyes fixed on a homeland not yet independent or in a position to protect them, thousands of Filipinos were overwhelmed by frustration.

Two patterns of difficulties that normally confront immigrant groups in the initial phase of adjustment troubled the Filipinos, too. First was the pattern of hostility shown toward any new group by older immigrant groups, and second was the sharpening of old-country tensions and internal cleavages because of frustrations and disappointments in the new social situation.

The Filipinos were immediately resented by the Japanese. On the plantations and in the poorer sections of the cities, the issei considered the Filipinos uncouth. The boisterous, fun-loving, and seemingly irresponsible Filipinos, without families, were especially disturbing to Japanese fathers and mothers. Their language was so strange that the two groups often failed to understand each other. The Filipinos were Catholics, but unlike the haole or Oriental Catholics, they did not seem to be burdened with their religion. They gambled and fought over women, and even on the Christian Sundays they might be found at a cockfight or in an improvised pool hall. Special phrases of derision were cast at Filipino children, such as one which accused them of throwing knives. Reinforcing the scornful Japanese attitude was their nagging fear that Filipinos would glut the labor market and reduce the economic opportunities for Japanese laborers. As early as 1909, the *Hawaii Shimpo* excoriated the Filipino workers. In the late 1920's and early '30's, the *Hawaii Hochi* and the *Nippu Jiji* warned against the Filipinization of Hawaii, maintaining that the Filipinos reduced American standards, using, in fact, the very argument that had been hurled against the Japanese by haoles.[9]

The major internal conflict in the Filipino community was between two important dialect groups. The people of the Philippines had been infused over the centuries with Malayan, Indonesian, Chinese, and Spanish blood, and intermixture was so widespread that nothing close to a pure subtype developed among the Filipino people. Because of the vast distances between inhabited islands, several dialect groups, with distinctive socio-cultural characteristics, had developed instead. Among these, the most important to Hawaii were the Ilocano and the Visayan. By the twentieth century, the Visayan was the largest group in the Philippines, subsuming several subdialect groups, and the earliest recruiting by the Hawaiian Sugar Planters' Association in the Philippines was done in the central islands among this group. Later, agents recruited among the Ilocanos in the northern sections of Luzon, one of the poorer and more crowded portions of the archipelago, where land was strictly limited and controlled by the landlords. These peasants responded to the call of quick money; in Hawaii it might be possible to accumulate wealth and raise one's social standing. Even when the planters discontinued paying the fare of laborers in 1925, thousands of Ilocanos paid their own passage, some mortgaging what little they had to go to Hawaii.[10] By 1930, more than 90 per cent of the Filipinos in Hawaii were Ilocanos from one of the most isolated parts of the archipelago. The Tagalog, the dialect group with the highest social prestige in the Philippines, supplied few immigrants to Hawaii. In the Hawaiian Filipino community, the Visayan took the place of the Tagalog as the upper status group. Not as literate, sophisticated, Western, or urban as the Tagalog, the Visayan still displayed these qualities in much greater degree than their Ilocano cousins from the North.[11] The Visayans usually blamed the Ilocanos for the low status of the Filipinos in Hawaii. They were accused of uncleanliness and of being savages. The Ilocanos often countered with accusations of Visayan laziness, extravagance, and unreliability, charges substantiated by impartial observers and even occasionally by the Visayans themselves. The Ilocanos, sometimes called the Scotchmen of the Philippine Islands, tended to be thriftier and more hard-working than their southern brothers. A survey in the late 1930's showed that their families averaged nearly twice the savings and a fraction of the indebtedness of Visayan households.[12] But with high hopes, low skills (close to half were illiterate), and many disappointments, the Ilocanos were easy prey to exploitation. Among the Chinese and Japanese, there had been extortionists, gangsters, gambling rings, and prostitution in the first immigrant phase. Similar practices plagued the Filipinos. Even unscrupulous Filipinos, posing as recruiting agents, were known to have taken money from would-be immigrants as payment for fare, only to leave them stranded in Manila.[13]

The petty jealousies which the Chinese and Japanese thought unique to their own groups were repeated among the Filipinos. The Filipinos asked themselves why the other groups were so united: Why do the Japanese get ahead? How is it the Chinese are successful? Where are our leaders? Why don't we trust each other? Why do we fight among ourselves? These queries were ceaselessly posed but never satisfactorily answered. In the late 1950's, Filipinos told interviewers that the trouble with the Filipinos was that they had a low opinion of themselves, that they did not trust each other and would exploit other Filipinos; in business, they would rather trade with the Japanese or Chinese. The story so frequently told by Hawaiians, Chinese, Japanese, and Portuguese—that individuals who succeeded were scorned by their countrymen through petty jealousies and spite—was told time and again by the Filipinos, as though it happened only to them.

Would-be Filipino labor leaders denounced each other almost as often as they attacked the bosses. Representatives from Manila, allegedly sent to help the Filipino workers, often came to exploit them instead. The most notorious of these was Cayetano Ligot. Sent as a labor commissioner by the Resident General in Manila in the 1920's, Ligot is now believed by some Filipinos to have been allied with the Hawaiian Sugar Planters' Association. Filipinos still jokingly speak of the "mistake Ligot," when things over which they seem to have no control go wrong.[14]

The misery and loneliness that made the Filipinos vulnerable to crooked businessmen and gamblers also brought forth the religious movement known as the Filipino Federation of America. The Federation began in 1927, a time of aimlessness and isolation for thousands of Filipinos. From the island of Cebu came Hilario Moncade y Caminos, claiming that he would deliver the Filipinos of Hawaii as the chosen people. Changing his name to Hilario Camino Moncado, he promised that the Filipinos would lead the Malayan people everywhere back to former glories. The General, as he was later to call himself, wore expensive clothes, traveled everywhere by clipper, opened large offices in Los Angeles, and married an international glamour girl. He proclaimed himself the Messiah, and urged that the first duty of the members of the Federation was to work for the freedom of the Philippines. Paying exorbitant fees to join the organization and high annual dues, thousands of Filipinos in Hawaii supported Moncado but received nothing in return. Other messianic cults also did well among the Filipinos, although none of them approached the size and power of the Federation.[15]

The vast majority of the Filipinos who remained in Hawaii stayed on the plantations. They were given the most difficult and menial jobs; planting, fertilizing, weeding, cultivating, watering, and harvesting the cane or pineapple. They did repair work on buildings, roads, and ditches, and sometimes they worked as yard men or servants for haole managers or their assistants. Boys as young as ten could be found stripping and hoeing cane or doing special jobs, such as catching hostile bugs in a pop bottle for twenty-five cents a day. Working and living conditions were at least as tolerable as they had been under the *caciques,* but they fell far short of the immigrants' hopes. The foreign *lunas* were often cruel. One successful small businessman remembers a Portuguese *luna,* in cowboy hat and leggings, grabbing his father at a slight provocation and kicking him in the backside. Another Filipino, now a labor leader, recalls conditions at Camp Three at Waialua in the early 1920's. He remembers a tiny house, crowded with wooden beds, set into the mountains at the end of the plantation road; single men were jammed in the dwelling. Heavy rains came through the leaky roof into the windowless shack. At four o'clock in the morning, after a fitful night, they would hear the raucous voice of the policeman calling, "Hey, Filipino, get up!" At night, his father sometimes sat on the edge of his bed crying, with his head buried in his hands, lamenting his inability to save enough cash to go home.[16]

In 1922, a resident missionary admitted in the *Friend* that "much of the labor unrest on the plantations is due to treatment meted out to the workers by ignorant, stupid, obstinate immoral lunas."[17] Nine years later, a representative of the U.S. Department of Labor complained that there were still too many unpainted houses, without screens, badly in need of repairs and improved sanitary conveniences. In some camps, he said, the water supply was "insufficient for proper sanitation and is not palatable for drinking."[18]

The Hawaiian Sugar Planters' Association had made sporadic efforts to improve plantation housing facilities and other perquisites, but in the memory of many Filipinos, their group was the last to benefit from such improvements.[19] The Filipinos, living in a segregated camp, had the least-desirable locations as well as inferior jobs. They were the first to be fired, the last to be promoted, and, when advanced to a semiskilled or skilled position, they were paid less than any other group for the same job.

During the 1920's, while the Japanese and Chinese were moving to the cities for better jobs and more pay, few Filipinos joined them. In 1930, more than 90 per cent of the gainfully employed male Filipinos were still unskilled laborers. More than four fifths of these worked on the sugar and pineapple plantations, constituting the bulk of the agricultural workers in the Islands. During the 1930's, unemployment became a reality in Hawaii for the first time as total employment remained relatively stable while thousands were added to the employable population each year. No group in the Islands was hit harder than the Filipinos by the economic slump.[20] Cutbacks on the plantations now forced workers to the cities, and between 1930 and 1940, the proportion of Filipinos living in Honolulu and Hilo went from 11 per cent to 17.2 per cent.[21] A new class of Filipino drifters congregated in slum neighborhoods around King and Liliha Streets in Honolulu. These were despairing men, alienated from the soil, preyed upon by crooks and religious cultists. On the plantations, and even in the slums on North King Street, there were occasional intensely gay fiestas, celebrations of weddings or holidays; these helped a little to relieve the tedium and even the misery of day-to-day frustrations. Spontaneously humorous, friendly, and generous, the Filipinos were despondent, too.

The reasons for Filipino despondency were not hard to find. Illiteracy was one. Unlike the Chinese and Japanese, the Filipinos did not possess a strong tradition of respect for education and intellectual achievement. In 1930, three out of every ten Filipinos, including the children, were illiterate. Of the Filipinos sixty-five years old or older, 70 per cent were illiterate, and even among the youngest and strongest Filipinos—those fifteen to nineteen—nearly one out of four could not read or write any language. How could the Filipinos in town compete, even for the toughest jobs, when as late as 1930 more than 50 per cent of them were unable to speak English? There were as yet no Filipino physicians or dentists and only three teachers in the Territory of Hawaii.

Filipino children had a poor attendance record at school—only 24.2 per cent of the eligible sixteen- and seventeen-year-olds attended school in 1930, compared with 54 per cent of the eligible Japanese, 68 per cent of the Koreans, and 77 per cent of the Chinese children. A Filipino boy in high school in the 1920's was a rarity. It was cause for great celebration when the first one finally was graduated from McKinley High school in 1924.[22]

The low ratio of females to males continued to be the greatest source of trouble. The 1930 census showed one Filipino woman for every four marriageable men, and five years later, there were 29,413 single Filipino males in the Territory, compared with 366 single females, a fantastic imbalance, which made prostitution and a certain amount of homosexuality and violence over sex inevitable. Prostitutes were systematically imported to the plantations to service the men in the barracks. But even without sexual relations, a great premium was put on female companionship, and groups of women prepared elaborate food in the men's barracks for parties and then stayed to entertain them.[23] In the Philippines, romantic marriage had been discouraged, and a boy's parents usually took the intiative in selecting the girl. In Hawaii, the Filipinos' unusual sex ratio made such parental control impossible. Romantic marriages cutting across ethnic lines were commonly accepted, and during the 1920's one out of every four Filipino grooms married outside of his group. In the next decade, 37.5 per cent of the new Filipino husbands married non-Filipino *wahines,* mostly Hawaiians and part-Hawaiians.[24]

This widespread intermarriage and the large number of single Filipino men inhibited the development of family control and a stable social life. Filipino men demanded faithfulness from Hawaiian wives, who found it difficult to understand the tremendous value their husbands placed on marital fidelity. Easygoing Hawaiian mothers objected when strong-willed Filipino fathers tried to beat discipline into their children.

The low morale of the Filipinos was not relieved by the hostility and insensitivity of others. The whitewash that Labor Commissioner Ligot gave to plantation conditions only increased Filipino frustrations. Another official from the Philippines, a young man named Francisco Varona, did prod the Hawaiian Sugar Planters' Association into making improvements, but his stay in the Islands was short, and Varona could have no fundamental impact on economic conditions in Hawaii or on the day-to-day unfriendliness of the Japanese and the disdain of the haoles. When the Governor General of the Philippines sent his aide-de-camp, C.R.A. Duckworth, to Honolulu to investigate the treatment of the Filipinos, Duckworth concluded that the Filipino "is given something better than a square deal . . . all that is needed is the will to serve and the will to save." Duckworth assured the Governor General that complaints of ill-treatment stemmed only from malcontents and drifters in Honolulu—"labor agitators," he called them. The vast majority of the workers, he wrote, had confidence in Ligot. Since Duckworth had gathered his information from the Hawaiian Sugar Planters' Association, his conclusions reinforced the growing Filipino opinion that Manila did not really care what happened to them.[25]

There was no stability in organization or leadership in the Filipino community. Between 1921 and 1936, sixteen Filipino social organizations appeared in Honolulu, with an average life of five years. Clubs and newspapers boomed suddenly and died just as abruptly.[26] Since the Filipinos had not yet made the decision to remain in Hawaii, the more permanent type of civic association, encouraging civic participation and group claims, had not yet appeared. And, as their readers preferred, the newspapers were preoccupied with events in the Philippines.

The 1930 census showed that of the 45,000 adult Filipinos in Hawaii, a paltry few were eligible to participate in Island politics. In the territorial election of 1934, there were only 102 registered Filipino voters, of whom eighty-eight balloted. Throughout the 1930's, the bulk of Filipinos probably remained indifferent to the governance of Hawaii.

On the eve of Pearl Harbor, those Filipinos still remaining in Hawaii were, in their own eyes, the least successful immigrants. Approximately half had left the Territory, two thirds to return to the Philippines and the remainder to go to California. The Filipinos in Hawaii were plagued by failure: they had failed to make enough money to return home, and they had failed to establish successful community life in Hawaii. Their love for their homeland had grown more intense with distance and time. Their disappointments in Hawaii conspired to make them glorify even more the richness and beauty of life in the *barrios*. In twenty years, the Filipinos in Hawaii had not become the Filipinos *of* Hawaii, and it was not until after World War II that they emerged from the first difficult phase of immigrant adjustment in which their major purpose had been simply to return home.

PART TWO

The Web of Oligarchy

1900–1941

In Hawaii, the socially superior—the kamaaina *haole* elite—also governed. The elite constituted an oligarchy which ruled in the broadest sense. It controlled not only the formal points of the political process, but labor and wealth in the Islands as well.

Oligarchies are not necessarily more oppressive than democracies. Majority opinion encouraged the conviction of John Scopes in Tennessee and Sacco and Vanzetti in Massachusetts. Majority opinion in the United States supported Attorney General A. Mitchell Palmer in his crusade against radical thinking during World War I. Immigrant groups have often been treated with scorn and even violence—the Catholics on the East Coast in the mid-nineteenth century, the Chinese in California at the turn of the century, and Jews and Negroes in many communities throughout our history. Even by American, rather than colonial, standards, the oligarchy in Hawaii was more beneficent and charitable than were controlling groups in most rural areas on the mainland or many captains of industry and finance in Chicago, New York, and Pittsburgh. If most of the men who ran Hawaii during the 1920's and '30's believed in the racial supremacy of Caucasians and opposed labor unions, they were not different from the vast majority of their counterparts on the mainland.

In some respects, Hawaii's oligarchy was different. No community of comparable size on the mainland was controlled so completely by so few individuals for so long. Rarely were political, economic, and social controls simultaneously enforced as in Hawaii. Rarely were controls so personal, and rarely were they as immune from such counterforces as Eugene Debs's socialism, Woodrow Wilson's New Freedom, and Franklin D. Roosevelt's New Deal as in Hawaii. For forty years, Hawaii's oligarchy skillfully and meticulously spun its web of control over the Islands' politics, labor, land, and economic institutions, without fundamental challenge.

Chapter Six

STRATEGY FOR CONTROL

A representative of the Hawaiian Sugar Planters' Association looked across the table in a committee hearing room in the U.S. House of Representatives, and warned, "I do not think that there is any contest as to who shall dominate; the white race, the white people, the Americans in Hawaii are going to dominate and will continue to dominate—there is no question about it." Royal M. Mead, sitting in his hard-backed witness chair, suggested that it might be wise if his previous remarks did not go into the record. Although the committee chairman agreed, he or his clerk failed to expunge Mead's candid assertion from the record of the 1920 House subcommittee hearings on the Hawaiian labor situation.[1]

The oligarchy had spun a web of control over every major aspect of Island life. To dominate, in its view, was not a lustful, greedy ambition. The goal was not just power; nor was it wealth or prestige. It was achievement of a way of life in which the ruling haole elite, through its ingenuity, dedication, and charity, had made Hawaii a veritable paradise on earth.

"To think of Hawaii in an economic sense is to think of sugar," wrote a University of Hawaii professor in 1926. "That industry is ruled by a financial oligarchy around which is built the business and social structure of the Islands."[2] A professional journalist in 1912, a special investigator from Washington in 1932, and a Ph.D. candidate from Yale in 1935 agreed.[3] Each was struck by the extraordinary unity of the haole elite and its remarkable power in Island life. A small group of men, drawn together through business interests, intermarriage, school associations, and personal friendships sustained on the polo fields of Hawaii, at the Pacific Club, and on broad sheltered *lanais,* controlled the Territory's government in its important respects.

There were three key points of control in Island politics: the delegate to Congress, the territorial governor, and the territorial legislature. It was Congress that established Hawaii's Organic Act and that could alter Hawaii's internal government or the Islands' relationship with the rest of the Union. Congress set trade policies—including the tariff on foreign sugar—without which the Islands' sugar industry and the wealth of the oligarchy would fail. Congress determined the nation's immigration policy, deciding the terms and the extent of immigration to Hawaii from the Orient and the Philippines. Congress also authorized improvement of harbors and, later, military installations in the Territory. It was thus a matter of vital importance to the oligarchy to control Hawaii's delegate to Congress and to make friends with other influential congressmen, especially those who served on the Insular Affairs Sub-Committee of both houses.

The Islands' governor, under Hawaii's Organic Act, was more powerful than any state governor. Appointed by the President for a four-year term, he was not impeachable and could, if he chose, remain largely unresponsive to public opinion. Hundreds of appointments, usually made in the states by local governments or under the influence of state legislators, were his to designate. He was empowered to suspend the writ of habeas corpus and to place any part of the Territory under martial law. The governor's fiscal powers were much greater than those of the President of the United States in relation to Congress. He possessed a veto over items in appropriations bills and was given the authority to extend legislative sessions if appropriations bills he desired were not passed. Functions usually administered locally in the states were assigned to his jurisdiction by the Organic Act. Education, welfare, safety, sanitation, health, highways, and public works were highly centralized under his control.[4]

To keep the web of oligarchy unbroken, it was also necessary to control the territorial legislature, the body that determined land policies, voted taxes, spent the oligarchy's money, granted franchises, and regulated the press, schools, and other aspects of Island life.

The oligarchy's success in maintaining control at all three crucial points between annexation and Pearl Harbor was phenomenal. At nearly all times during the four decades of elite rule, the governor and a substantial number of the legislators were men who had held admin-

istrative or policy positions in the major sugar agencies or their subsidiaries. Gubernatorial appointees to the boards of Tax Equalization,
Tax Appraisal, Immigration, Public Lands, and the tax appeal courts
were frequently men prominent in the great agricultural corporations
of Hawaii. A scholar, soon to be welcomed to the inner council of the
oligarchy, wrote in 1935 that the governors, legislators, and other important government officials since 1900 "have been to a large degree
determined by and considerate of the sugar leaders."⁵ One-party control of the legislature—the Democrats failed to elect even a third of the
legislators during the entire period—assured legislative policies friendly
to the oligarchy. Between 1910 and 1940, more than 80 per cent of the
legislators elected to the territorial House and Senate were Republican.
Even more important, the oligarchy could count on friendly governors,
whether appointed by Republican or Democratic Presidents, throughout the forty-year period, and, except for a brief aberration between
1900 and 1902, the territorial delegate to Congress, even when he was
a Democrat, worked hard to protect the major interests of Hawaii's
sugar industry.

That the financial leaders of Hawaii were able to maintain control of
the Islands' political life, although hopelessly outnumbered, was due in
part to their extraordinary political skill. The Republic had been established by force and was ruled by limiting the franchise of Hawaiians
and part-Hawaiians, who in 1894 comprised only 18 per cent of the
registered voters. Three years later, many of them were back on the
voting rolls, but the haoles, with the help of alien and citizen Portuguese, still held a clear majority of votes, although they comprised less
than 22 per cent of Hawaii's population.⁶

Annexation, so ardently desired by the haole merchant and professional class of Honolulu, abruptly overturned the Republic's system
of limited suffrage with the passing of the Organic Act. Overnight, the
Hawaiians who had been loyal to the Queen were enfranchised again
and had a clear majority of the votes. Congress did not impose universal
manhood suffrage without opposition from Merchant Street. While the
Organic Act was being debated in Congress, a defender of the elite
view wrote in the Boston *Herald* that the responsible leaders of Hawaii
were agreed that "no one should be allowed to vote for the men who
are to pass laws governing the Islands unless they possess a small property qualification, say of 100 dollars." The Americans in Hawaii, he
argued, "do not want to be swamped by Asiatics. It will not do to have

the men who have built up the country . . . at the mercy of a herd of Orientals, who have no interest in it except to make the most they can out of it in the easiest possible way. . . ." But the Orientals had no votes in Hawaii. The Hawaiians did, but they could not be trusted with the franchise, wrote the Boston reporter. "Kanakas are children . . . they vote whichever way, not their best, but their last friend says . . . a Kanaka's word on any transaction is good for nothing. . . ." The Honolulu *Pacific Commercial Advertiser,* the oligarchy's major journal of opinion, observed that the Boston man knew what he was talking about when he expressed the fear of right-thinking men in Hawaii that the aborigines would restore the monarchy and drive out the Caucasians.[7]

It was difficult for haole leaders to believe that Congress would punish them through the abolition of the property qualification for voting. The haole semiweekly the *Hawaiian Gazette* complained that Congress, by striking out the property clause in the name of Americanism, was showing a preference for "the native and . . . hater of things American. . . ."[8] In another editorial, the *Gazette* warned that the aborigines and their natural allies will "restore the throne of Hawaii." Antioligarchy papers, run by former loyalists, praised the Organic Act's liberal suffrage provision.[9] Even the *Evening Bulletin,* edited by Wallace Rider Farrington, a recently arrived haole conservative from Maine, lauded the bill for its protection of the rights of American citizens against the "oligarchical rules laid down by the present ruling faction. . . ."[10]

After the bill was passed, many haole leaders were troubled by the thought of *kanaka* control. The editor of the *Hawaiian Gazette* warned the natives not to stand apart from the haoles and form their own party. "If color is to rule any sub-division of American territory," he wrote, "the color will be white."[11] The *Pacific Commercial Advertiser,* violently opposed to a Hawaiian block vote, accused the *kanaka* papers and Farrington's *Evening Bulletin* of inciting the Hawaiians to throw out the haoles.

The warning fell on deaf Hawaiian ears. The bayonet constitution forced on Kalakaua probably still angered most Hawaiians, and former royalist leaders organized the Home Rule party in defiance of haole Republicans and Democrats, to restore the Islands to *kanaka* control under the liberal suffrage policies imposed by Congress. The Home Rule party was born in a drill shed at Honolulu on June 6, 1900, only a few weeks before the Islands were to become a territory of the United

States. Representatives of two Hawaiian societies, the nationalist Hui
Aloha Haina (love of country) and the Pi Ki, an opposition group
which had supported the Provisional Government, pledged mutual
loyalty and devotion to the cause of the natives. Queen Liliuokalani
addressed their convention and brought tears to Hawaiian eyes when
she told them that the monarchy had ended but that there was much
good work to be done for the people.

The Home Rule platform called for liberal labor policies but protective measures against Japanese labor. It requested homesteads for
the Hawaiian people and warned against restrictions on native voting.
It included a plank favoring a large appropriation for damages caused
by the burning of Chinatown during the great bubonic plague epidemic.
Its candidate for delegate, royalist Robert Wilcox, who had led the
counterrevolutionary forces to re-establish Liliuokalani on the throne,
reminded the Hawaiian voters—who formed more than two thirds of
the electorate—of alleged haole infamies. In retaliation, the *Advertiser*
made daily attacks on Wilcox, and the Bank of Hawaii and Castle &
Cooke placed large notices in the paper urging support of a Republican
ticket.

Wilcox, in a special election, ran brilliantly in Hawaiian districts,
although opposed by two popular Hawaiians, Democrat David Kawananakoa and Republican part-Hawaiian Samuel Parker. He won
again against the same two candidates a few months later, although
their combined vote topped his tally. The Home Rulers won nine of
thirteen seats in the territorial Senate and elected fourteen representatives to the House, compared with nine Republicans and four Democrats. Haole attacks against Wilcox were carried to Congress, to which
the territorial Republican Central Committee sent a representative to
protest against seating the delegate-elect, charging that he was anti-
American, a bigamist, and a friend of Emilio Aguinaldo, the Filipino
rebel. Wilcox was seated and quickly alarmed haole leaders by intro-
ducing a bill to extend the general land laws of the United States to
the Territory, the regulations for homesteading to be administered by
the Secretary of the Interior. Governor Dole, the former President of
the Republic who had been appointed by President McKinley to be
Hawaii's first governor, dispatched a representative to the Republican
Congress to argue against Wilcox.[12]

No less frightening were the actions of the Home Rule legislature in
Honolulu. Strongly antihaole, the Home Rulers carried on many of

their legislative meetings in Hawaiian, although the Organic Act had stipulated that all sessions of the legislature were to be conducted in English. They refused to read Dole's message until the fifth day of their first session, and tried to take the power of appointment away from Dole by sending up their own list of names for approval by the Governor. One bill was introduced to pardon all inhabitants of local prisons, another to pay local youths who were going to the mainland for education, still another to do away with compulsory vaccinations, and another, vetoed by Dole, to license *kahunas* as physicians. A Republican representative moved to ask for bids for printing the House journals, arguing that the service provided by the printing firm then used was poor and that accepting bids might lead to better service. The Home Rulers answered that if the Republicans were in the majority, they would give the printing to their friends and not to the lowest bidder.[13] So frightened were some haoles that in an editorial in the *Advertiser* it was suggested that Negroes be imported for plantation labor because they would make good Republicans under haole leadership, thus taking the government control away from the irresponsible *kanakas*.[14]

Cool heads rejected the *Advertiser*'s proposal and planned instead to implement the American political maxim "If you can't lick 'em, join 'em." While the missionary journal the *Friend* warned against the slogan "Hawaii for the Hawaiians," a small group of missionary descendants, representing the haole elite, carefully laid plans to capture the delegateship and the territorial legislature.[15] They recognized that the Hawaiians, with more than two thirds of the vote, would continue to choose a predominantly native legislature. In 1901, the Hawaiians constituted 73 per cent of the legislature, much more than under the monarchy. The aim would not be to keep Hawaiians out of the government, but to make them serve the policies of the oligarchy.

The first step in the plan of the *kamaaina* elite, according to the late Governor and Delegate Samuel Wilder King, was a clandestine meeting in the stately Pacific Club between Henry P. Baldwin, missionary descendant and powerful plantation owner from Maui, and Prince Jonah Kuhio Kalanianaole. The haoles needed a man who could beat Wilcox, someone who could rally Hawaiian chiefs to the Republican cause, and who, out of interest for himself and his people, would make a deal to restore control to haole hands. Kuhio was their man. Until two in the morning, Baldwin, who spoke fluent Hawaiian, played on Kuhio's substantial vanity. He probably spoke of important meetings in Washington and of the great good Kuhio could do for his people. Perhaps he reminded Kuhio that there was no turning back—the monarchy could not be restored—and if the Hawaiians did not produce responsible leadership, the haoles might encourage Washington to take direct control over the Territory. Wilcox was irresponsible, Baldwin must have pointed out, and made the worst possible impression in Washington. Besides, Kuhio had only to look around to realize that the Hawaiians should join the haoles to protect themselves against the rising Oriental tide. There would come a day, Kuhio was probably warned, when the Japanese, who already outnumbered Hawaiians and haoles combined, would inundate the politics of the Islands, and Kuhio had best be prepared. It is not difficult to imagine Kuhio, in unusual solemnity, puffing on his big cigar, sipping his favorite after-dinner liqueur, and listening as Baldwin outlined the benefits and responsibilities of the delegateship.

The man who listened to these arguments, according to King, did not have to be reminded of his royal obligations to his people. Born at Koloa, Kauai, in 1871, he was the second son of the high chief of Kauai, D. Kahalepouli, and the Princess Kekaulike. According to Hawaiian custom, Prince Jonah and his older brother, David, became the *hanai,* or adopted sons, of their aunt, Queen Kapiolani, and the boys soon learned to call King Kalakaua "Papa." Kalakaua's sister, Liliuokalani, later named them heirs to the throne and gave them the title "Prince." Kuhio was twenty-two when the monarchy was overthrown, and at twenty-four he helped assist the revolt against the Republic in an effort to restore the Queen. But the Prince was captured, thrown in jail, and stripped of potential power. Perhaps he remembered these things as he listened to Baldwin's proposal that he run as Republican candidate for delegate against Wilcox. He undoubtedly knew that the haoles were trying to use him for their purposes, but his shrewdness was matched by his conceit. He would join the haoles, but not to serve them. Rather, he would use them for the benefit of the Hawaiian people. He would force them to give the Hawaiians jobs and land. He would see that Hawaiians were appointed to key government posts. Someday he might even be governor. Yes, Baldwin was partly right, the monarchy was over, haole financial control was great, the Republican party ruled in Washington and controlled patronage, and Wilcox was irresponsible. A bargain was struck. Royalist and missionary agreed to a political alliance which would substantially govern Hawaii for the next several decades.[16]

The choice of Kuhio was superb from the oligarchy point of view. Although he always asked more for the Hawaiian people than the oligarchy was willing to give, he conscientiously pushed probusiness policies in Washington and made a wonderful spokesman in the national capital, where his convivial manner and regal bearing won him many friends. More importantly, Kuhio, as heir to the throne of Hawaii, possessed a powerful following in the Islands. He excelled in all sports, and was the last of Hawaii's *alii* to be taught the intricate holds of the *hakoko,* a form of wrestling similar to jujitsu. He was known to have been a favorite of the Queen, who sent him to Washington with her attorney to lobby for her interests in Congress when she was imprisoned in her home, Washington Place, under the Republic. He married a favorite, Elizabeth Kahanu, daughter of the chief of Maui. The popular Prince was able to persuade many former chiefs and Hawaiian leaders to run for office on the Republican ticket. So well liked was Kuhio that he was elected delegate ten times before his death in 1922.

The haoles were delighted to give a Hawaiian the delegateship in return for the destruction of the Home Rule party and clear-cut control over the legislature. Kuhio and the Republicans swept Wilcox and the Home Rulers out of power in the 1902 election. The Prince was clearly the haoles' candidate. He won whopping pluralities in haole precincts like the second in the fourth district on Oahu—then three-quarters haole—where he received 87.3 per cent of the votes cast for delegate. Wilcox and the Home Rulers still won majorities in Hawaiian precincts that were not under the influence of the major haole "chiefs." In a remote Hawaiian district on the Big Island, 95 per cent native, the Prince could not muster 30 per cent of the vote. But on the Kona Coast, where haole and Hawaiian chiefs joined forces to back Kuhio in the almost entirely Hawaiian fifth precinct of the second district, the voting pattern was reversed. In the most Hawaiian district on Maui, almost 100 per cent *kanaka,* Kuhio won a majority because of the influence of Henry P. Baldwin and his Hawaiian retainers. The Hawaiians on Niihau in the employ of the Robinson family also voted heavily for the Prince. But in the remote Hawaiian districts of Oahu, Wilcox won pluralities.[17]

Throughout the Territory as a whole, the Home Rulers undoubtedly won a majority of the Hawaiian votes. But a minority of Hawaiians, combined with the near-monolithic strength of haoles and Portuguese, was enough to change the balance of power and to keep it in favor of the G.O.P. for the next several years. Kuhio brought into the Republican fold such able Hawaiian leaders as John Wise, John Lane, Stephen Desha, and William C. Achi, each with a record of loyalty to the Queen and his own important following.

Henceforth the politics of the natives would be personal, and not partisan. It would, to some extent, be based on an old feudal principle. The chief, in this case the aspirant candidate, promised to take care of his followers, either through money, jobs, or individual services. In return, the followers supported the leaders at the polls. In those districts where the natives were relatively free from the economic influences of the new Hawaii, royalist sentiment was strong, and Hawaiian leaders not obligated to the haoles could bring in strong pluralities for Home Rule and, later, for Democratic candidates. But often party labels meant nothing, as was shown in 1904, when Kuhio won nine out of ten votes for delegate on the Republican ticket in the overwhelmingly Hawaiian first precinct of Niihau, while the haole candidate for the Senate from the same district did not receive a single vote, and Home Ruler L. Nakapaaahu, a candidate for the territorial Senate, won even more votes than the Prince.

To a large extent, Island politics was native politics. The Hawaiians and part-Hawaiians had a clear majority of voters through the 1922 election, and more than any other group until 1938. In every election, Hawaiians and part-Hawaiians comprised more than half of the candidates for office. The Hawaiian voter turnout was always substantially higher than that for other groups, including the haoles.[18] One calculation for 1930 shows that there were more Hawaiians and part-Hawaiians registered than were eligible to vote. Nine out of ten of those who registered showed up at the polls.[19]

Hawaiian political enthusiasm was enhanced by the colorful qualities of election campaigns and the pecuniary rewards often proffered by candidates. Both factors were advantageous to the Republicans, who had the money to pay for votes as well as to hire musicians, singers, and hula dancers. Samuel Wilder King, a part-Hawaiian friend of the haole inner elite, recalled that in the early days many of the Hawaiian secondary political leaders drank greedily at the Republican trough. His recollections were confirmed in 1959 in interviews with many older Hawaiian politicians.

Outright bribery was probably less important than promises of jobs in winning native support for Republican candidates. According to old-timers who were part of the inner circle of Hawaiian and haole leaders in the Republican party, key jobs on some ranches and most plantations could not be held without dedicated service in the Republican cause. Government jobs also bound thousands of Hawaiians to the G.O.P. A political scientist discovered that in 1927 Hawaiians held 46 per cent of the appointive executive positions, 55 per cent of the clerical and other government jobs in the Territory, and more than half of the judgeships and elective offices.[20] Certain categories of government service, such as local law enforcement, were virtually turned over to the Hawaiians by the oligarchy. An investigation of law enforcement in Hawaii in 1932 found the field highly influenced by "*kanaka* politics." Three years later, another study showed that Hawaiians, then less than 15 per cent of the population, held almost a third of the public-service jobs in the Islands.[21]

The haole-Hawaiian alliance that brought success to the oligarchy through the Republican party was under constant strain. Like most political marriages, it was based on mutual selfishness. But in this case there had been a long history of bitter struggle, even bloodshed, between the allies. Two revolutions and one counterrevolution had left hatred and suspicion which could not be obliterated by political expediency. As long as Kuhio lived, the tensions between the two factions were razor sharp. Each tried to use the other for its own purposes. In some respects, mutual benefits were won, but clearly the oligarchy was more successful in manipulating Hawaiian votes for its purposes than were Kuhio and his followers in using the oligarchy to restore the Hawaiian people to their former dignity.

Kuhio tried his best to represent the sugar planters and Honolulu business interests in Washington despite his hatred of them. "Cupid," as this roly-poly, jovial Prince was often called, never forgot his days as a prisoner of the Republic, but he strove to live up to his part of the bargain as delegate, to win economic benefits for Hawaii in Congress. He corresponded extensively with the Honolulu Chamber of Commerce and other business interests on such matters as the development of Pearl Harbor and Honolulu Harbor, lighthouses, mail delivery to Hawaii, franchises, and tariff protection. After his arrival in the capital, he received a long memorandum from the president of the Chamber of Commerce outlining legislation that the Chamber desired. In a letter to Merchant Street, Kuhio promised to try his best to implement its programs, and, soon after, he introduced legislation embracing many of the Chamber's proposals.

The Prince wrote oligarchy Governor George Carter in August 1904 that he would like to have a secretary to assist him in his work in Washington. He would like, said Kuhio, "a man who would be acceptable to the business organizations, and who, serving also as their special representative, would work harmoniously with me to secure the results which we all in common desire."[22] It was mutually agreed that George B. McClellan would fill the bill. Kuhio was naïvely pleased when the Merchants Association and the Chamber suggested paying part of McClellan's salary, a logical move, since Merchant Street was in touch with the Delegate's secretary constantly and received confidential reports from him on the Prince's behavior. In 1905, Cupid wrote the president of the Chamber praising McClellan and suggesting that "the commercial body take definite steps to retain his services as my secretary...."[23]

Financial pressure plagued Kuhio throughout his life and often made him vulnerable to haole influence, although there is no evidence that he ever succumbed in any fundamental way. His correspondence shows that he was tormented by creditors, and at one point he fell forty months behind in his dues to the cherished Order of Kamehameha. In November 1913, a Paris hotel tried repeatedly to collect a bill for $61.20, and in the following year, the Prince was forced to borrow money on his life insurance to keep creditors from embarrassing him in public.[24]

But it was not personal financial difficulty that caused Kuhio to work to protect the major economic interests of Hawaii. He not only believed in the haole economy; he lived it. He enjoyed good food, wine, and cigars, travel, expensive clothes, and fine home furnishings. He knew that it was sugar and, to a lesser extent, pineapple that had brought these things to Hawaii. He also knew that Hawaii's major industry was dependent on tariff protection. With the election of a Democratic President and Congress in 1912, Kuhio was bombarded with warnings from Hawaii's financial interests to watch out for attempted tariff reform. The Prince met with the new President on April 7, 1913, to argue against Democratic plans for free sugar.[25] Individual companies were in communication with Cupid, too. The Hawaiian Trust Company, the Hawaiian Pineapple Company, and the major sugar factors peppered him with suggestions and warnings.[26] Because

congressmen had faith that Kuhio would not support legislation detrimental to the people of Hawaii, he was extremely useful in advocating
the haole businessmen's point of view. One of the last services he performed in Congress was to introduce bills granting favored franchises
to electric and power companies in various communities on Oahu, the
Big Island, Maui, and Kauai. Another was to propose legislation extending the franchise of the Hawaiian Rapid Transit and Land Company. The perpetual franchise called for in this bill was customary in
Hawaii, where, more than in any other part of the United States, the
business of government was business. Alfred L. Castle, missionary descendant and secretary and a director of Hawaiian Rapid Transit,
joined Kuhio in pushing the bill before congressional committees.
Congressmen suspected that the bill was unusually greedy and might
prove harmful to the riding public, but when one of them asked whether
or not the bill had the backing of the people in Hawaii, Kuhio assured
them of its popular support.[27]

Because he tried earnestly to represent the business interests of the
Islands in Congress, Kuhio resented it when the Hawaiian Sugar Planters' Association set up their own office in Washington, staffed by a
lobbyist and assistants. In early 1904, the Prince wrote to the president
of the group that he had tried to be a good agent for the business community, and it would be unwise to undercut him by placing a lobbyist
in the capital to represent Hawaii.[28] But the sugar planters trusted
neither Kuhio's ability nor his motives, and in some respects their chief
lobbyist became Hawaii's most important representative in Washington. Kuhio was further angered when the Chamber of Commerce set up
its lobby in the capital, and its representative, George McClellan, the
Prince's former secretary, went around Washington acting like a delegate. Kuhio notified the president of the Chamber that he would not
work with McClellan. McClellan retaliated in a letter warning that
Kuhio's political prospects in 1920 depended upon the Prince's acquiescence in McClellan's role as spokesman for Hawaii in Washington.
Kuhio sometimes wondered if he really was Hawaii's delegate.[29] One
Island magnate, Walter Dillingham, later kept his own paid representative in Washington. There are friends of Dillingham in Honolulu today
who believe that he made his fortune by cultivating and entertaining
every President, Vice-President, Secretary of State, and key senator in
the United States Congress for more than forty years prior to statehood.[30] Dillingham won huge contracts for dredging Pearl Harbor and

for construction work in various parts of Honolulu by dealing directly with government agencies.

Kuhio tried to serve Merchant Street in Washington, thinking he would gradually take over the Republican party for the Hawaiian people where, in his view, it really mattered—in Honolulu. He wanted *quid pro quo* for his services in the capital. Writing in December 1903, he urged Republican leaders in Honolulu to give the Queen a pension, because "it would get the natives to believe that only through the Republican Party can such benefits be got." Kuhio won the pension for Liliuokalani, but complained constantly that he was not being consulted by the haole leaders in Honolulu with respect to patronage. The appointment of George Robert Carter as governor on November 23, 1903, by Theodore Roosevelt was a shock to the Prince, who again had not been consulted. Carter had been a director of C. Brewer & Company, organizer and manager of the Hawaiian Trust Company, a director of the Hawaiian Fertilizer Company, and oligarchy spokesman as Secretary of Hawaii in 1902. His appointment was a slap in the face to Kuhio's nationalist followers, who expected that the Prince would be able to advance the claims of *kanakas* in Washington. Kuhio wrote a haole leader that he had promised the Hawaiians in his campaign that the only way they could win benefits would be to elect a Republican delegate; and now the Republican administration was treating him as they had Home Ruler Wilcox.[31]

A Hawaiian follower wrote Cupid early in 1904 that Carter and other Republican leaders in Honolulu were trying to discredit the Prince, and Kuhio was so discouraged that he thought of resigning as delegate.[32] A fellow member of the Kamehameha Lodge urged him to implement his desire to capture the sheriff's office and other local offices from the haoles through a county home-rule bill, which would break up the centralized power of the oligarchy in Honolulu. Home rule, or county government, became the early focus of Kuhio's plan to advance the power of the Hawaiians. A letter from his close friend Curtis P. Iaukea, in January 1903, complained that Governor Dole had set up an executive council of haoles which centralized government in Honolulu to the detriment of Hawaiians. "I shall not rest," wrote Iaukea, "until we see the day when the power shall be vested in the hands of the people and not a vestige of the past left by which those who overthrew the monarchy can have a thread to hang on and maintain themselves in power [*sic*]. . . ."[33]

Major sugar factors such as Castle & Cooke and C. Brewer openly campaigned against county home rule. The *Pacific Commercial Advertiser* forcefully attacked any plan which assumed that Hawaiians were fit for self-government. Iaukea, complaining that the Republicans won the 1903 election by fraudulent methods, asked the Prince, "Must the people's will be sidetracked because a few businessmen, who have long enjoyed the political control of this country under a centralized government, stand in the way of American and popular institutions?" Control over local affairs was crucial to the Hawaiians, argued Iaukea, who even suggested that Hawaiians work with the Home Rulers and Democrats in local matters.[34]

Kuhio agreed and appointed Iaukea his first secretary without pay, although the government provided a $100 secretarial allowance for the Delegate. Iaukea refused to take a salary, saying he wanted to serve the Prince just as he had served the Queen. "Time honored custom and birth have endowed myself with privileges to enter royal presence at any and all times. Its doors can never be closed to me whilst mine must ever be at an alii's command. . . . As long as an alii lives there will be found faithful retainers . . . ready to do what native custom and usage have ordained and established. . . ."[35] At first, Kuhio and his friend met strong haole opposition in Honolulu in trying to establish local government at the county level. Kuhio shrewdly bargained with key haole leaders on the outer islands, including Charles Rice, grandson of one of the first missionaries, who was fast becoming the political boss on Kauai. Rice saw that county government meant more power for him as well as for the natives of Kauai, and successfully supported the Prince in his efforts.[36] Kuhio encouraged his followers to make county rule the major issue of the 1904 campaign, and, under political pressure, Governor Carter appointed a commission to draft a new county act to submit to the 1905 legislature. Five counties were constituted—one each for Oahu, Maui and Kauai, and two on the Big Island—although Carter refused to consider a proposal to permit counties to levy and collect taxes. New county offices were created, including sheriff, clerk, auditor, attorney, treasurer, and supervisor, to sit as county councils for the local governments. Over the years, the responsibilities of the counties have changed, but their major functions have always been police, fire protection, water supplies, road construction, sewage systems, rubbish collection and disposal, and construction and maintenance of certain public buildings, parks, and playgrounds. Although the major responsibilities of government—education, taxation, and assessment—remained centralized in Honolulu, Kuhio's first major victory was won. Hundreds of new political jobs were created, to be filled primarily by Hawaiians.

Patronage absorbed more and more of Kuhio's time, but his political compromises with the haoles frequently turned his closest Hawaiian followers against him. When Governor Carter fired the territorial Treasurer, A. N. Kepoikai, the deposed officeholder wrote Kuhio that Carter was purging Hawaiians, refusing to let them hold positions of honor and trust. Kuhio assuaged the aggrieved Kepoikai with a judgeship on Maui, but later, when his appointment was not renewed, Kepoikai told the Prince that his heart was heavy because Cupid had abandoned his Hawaiian friends.[37] In the spring of 1904, when Kuhio decided to accept as his secretary a representative from the haole merchant interests instead of his long-time retainer, Iaukea, the Hawaiian servant turned bitterly against him and ran as his opponent in the contest for delegate in 1904.[38]

Kuhio was realistic in recognizing that the haoles were willing for him to be delegate because he served their interests in smashing the Home Rulers and establishing a Republican legislature. He wrote his dear friend John Lane, who had also been imprisoned under the Republic, that the oligarchy believed that he, Kuhio, would never hurt the interests of the Territory and that if it put a haole up to head the Republican ticket, it would be "taking chances of losing everything from its delegate down. . . ."[39] Lane wrote that the oligarchy was taking advantage of Kuhio and implied that they were too often getting the best of him. He charged that Carter's recommendation not to pay the legislature for extra sessions was wrong because "our own people who are not financially provided for would be compelled to give up the Legislature to those who can afford the expenses of being in town and we would be harmed and the power would be in the hands of those against us, pilikia. . . ."[40] Kuhio agreed that "it has been and is their stated policy to down every and all Hawaiians, and it is up to us Hawaiians to force ourselves ahead. . . ."[41] Several months later, Kuhio again confided that the administration was against him and secretly against all Hawaiians. Their attitude, he wrote, is "we don't want no Niggers." Still, he told Lane, the only way for the Hawaiians to recapture Hawaii was to gain control of the Republican party "and furthermore to keep on sending me to Congress not only to the next session, but to the one after. . . ." The Hawaiian Home Rulers and Democrats should join him in the Republican party, he asserted, and eventually they would have enough power to dictate the choice of a native Hawaiian as governor. "The name Republican Party will alone be a blind, and at the same time we Hawaiians can . . . carry on our intentions without any fear of the race question ever being brought up and thrown in our face."[42]

Another oligarchy representative, Walter Francis Frear, followed Carter in the governorship. Frear, married to the daughter of haole entrepreneur Benjamin Dillingham, had been a Supreme Court justice under the Republic, and between 1900 and 1907 was the first chief justice of the territorial Supreme Court. A director and official of many banking, sugar, railroad, and pineapple companies in Hawaii, he was a haole elite representative par excellence. Hawaiians close to Kuhio became more desperate for the future of their people as haole control in Honolulu tightened and the Prince was continually bypassed both in Washington and the Islands by Republican leaders. Part-Hawaiian legislator and former royalist Henry Lincoln Holstein wrote the Prince that he wished "we were back to the old days again. If only the tabu were removed and people were not killed for crossing a high chief's shadow. There was more contentment and satisfaction then, while now the rub is on and we all have to keep our eyes peeled for some white son-of-a-gun or some Home Rule crank hav'nt [*sic*] a knife up his sleeve ready to lay us out for the sake of office."[43] Another part-Hawaiian legislator who was loyal to Kuhio, W. J. Coelho, wrote that something must be done to check the haole move to destroy the *kanakas*. He accused the planters of playing a double game, and called them "missionary hypocrites." Echoing the desperate sentiments of many Hawaiians, he wrote that "our cup is bitter, but let's fight it to the bitter end."[44]

With home rule partially restored, Hawaiian leaders concentrated on the land issue. In the belief that the land had been stolen, Kuhio sought to have the government administer the land laws in favor of the Hawaiians rather than the sugar plantations. So important to the Hawaiians was the land issue that Kuhio sent a long indictment of Governor Frear, dated December 2, 1911, to the Secretary of the Interior, charging the Governor with failing to administer the homestead laws and working only in the interests of the sugar plantations. The essence of the attack on Frear was that because of "his close affiliation with the corporate interests of the Islands, induced and existing largely through matrimonial and social ties . . . his administration is conducted along lines calculated to favor and promote the still further concentration of land, wealth, and power into the hands of a few individuals, operating in most instances under corporate forms." Frear, in short, had failed to withdraw public lands under cane cultivation for homestead purposes. He had co-operated with plantation management in opposing associations of homesteaders. There were other charges, many going into great detail. Walter L. Fisher, the Interior Secretary, went to Honolulu to investigate. At the hearings, Kuhio charged that "the vital trouble is that the people who control the industrial life of Hawaii have been so blinded by long continued prosperity and the habit of controlling everything from their own standpoint that they, themselves, do not realize how deadly that policy is to the ultimate welfare of the Territory."[45]

So unhappy were Kuhio and his friends with Republican appointments that they speculated on the possibility of amending the Organic Act to permit the governor to come from the mainland instead of requiring him to be a citizen of the Territory. Kuhio's part-Hawaiian friend W. K. Kinney pointed out that "federal officials, even though they were strangers, treat the Hawaiians better than did the Territorial officials, *kamaainas* though they be, and you yourself told me you believe the Hawaiians were ready for a Governor from the Mainland, believing that they would get a squarer deal from them than they ever got from George Carter or Frear and further than they are likely to get from anyone in the same bunch. . . ."[46] The planters were opposed to having a Hawaiian appointed and knew that Kuhio coveted the governorship for himself. He was determined to block Frear's reappointment, and hoped privately to replace him, although in correspondence he agreed with Kinney that it would be good for him to get away from the "claim of the planters that after all is said and done, you want to get a Hawaiian in the Governor's chair. . . ." It was better, argued Kinney, not "to go into an election purely on racial lines," but to get someone who would do the right thing on the land question. Kinney warned, "You certainly can never count on any sincere and genuine support by the planters again."[47] Later, Kinney thought Kuhio was toying with the idea of backing his secretary, McClellan, to replace Frear and cautioned against helping someone who was merely an agent of the planters. "You have aroused the expectations of the common people [on the land question] so that they have at least some reason to believe that you really and truly are out for a fight on a broad issue."[48] John Lane worked tirelessly to have Kuhio replace Frear, but the Prince, in a letter to the Secretary of the Interior, pulled himself out of the race in an effort to speed Frear's dismissal.[49]

At the 1912 Republican territorial convention, Kuhio's friends charged that financial coercion was applied against Hawaiian delegates who did not agree with oligarchy policies. The Hawaiians pleaded for a secret ballot, and were supported by Judge Sanford B. Dole, former territorial governor, who characteristically acknowledged that his conscience "would not tolerate the thought of anything of the sort mentioned here today as being carried out." One part-Hawaiian friend of the Prince complained that two delegates, one from Maui, the other from the Big Island, both holding government positions, told him they voted for Kuhio on the secret ballot but against him on the roll call. Another man was alleged to have cried out, "Gentlemen, I am a poor man with a large family, but I do not care if I lose my job tomorrow. I vote for Prince Kuhio."[50] Frear's campaign for reappointment was strongly supported by the sugar agencies, although it was opposed by a newer Republican element, led by Wallace Farrington, which hoped for more liberal policies.

As editor and publisher of the *Evening Bulletin,* Hawaii's second most-important newspaper, Farrington frequently took issue with the *Advertiser,* which consistently attacked Kuhio and the Hawaiians as irresponsible. The *Advertiser* backed Frear, but Farrington supported Kuhio when he pushed unsuccessfully for a new governor.

With Frear's reappointment, some Hawaiian leaders speculated about leaving the party. In July 1912, Kinney wrote the Prince that he ought to quit the Republicans and support those who aid homesteading.[51] Kuhio hoped that a Republican would be elected President and would appoint him governor in 1913, but when Woodrow Wilson won, he looked forward to the designation of a Democrat who might be more sympathetic to his views than Carter or Frear had been. His confidant, John Lane, hoped Wilson would appoint Lincoln L. McCandless, Hawaii's leading haole Democrat and vigorous foe of the many oligarchy leaders, because McCandless would recognize Hawaiians in appointments. After all, remarked Lane, there would only be the small matter of party affiliation dividing McCandless and Kuhio.[52]

But Kuhio's hopes that a Democratic appointee would administer the land laws more liberally than his predecessor were dashed with the appointment of Lucius E. Pinkham, who, although nominally a Democrat, had been president of the territorial Board of Health under Carter and Frear between 1904 and 1908, and later was a recruiting agent for the Hawaiian Sugar Planters' Association in the Philippines. The Prince wrote the Governor-elect asking for his views on homesteading, and received what he termed a "distinctly disappointing" reply.[53]

Another issue that strained the alliance between the Prince and Merchant Street was immigration. Kuhio and his friends opposed the so-called "Dillingham Bill," to empower corporations to recruit immigrants without the assistance of the territorial government. The planters were anxious to increase Filipino immigration. Kuhio and his followers warned against a large "Asiatic population" and repeatedly urged homesteading by haole immigrants from the mainland. A large middle class was what Hawaii needed, Kuhio maintained. A docile labor class would serve only the interests of a handful of planters and their associates in Honolulu. If Asians kept coming in, he said, self-government would someday be taken from Hawaii, and its population would be treated as were the Indians on reservations of the mainland.[54]

The bitter factional fight over patronage, land, and immigration led the oligarchy to attempt to depose Kuhio as delegate in 1914, despite the fact that the Prince had won smashing victories in the two previous elections. It was a risk for Merchant Street, but Kuhio had become too troublesome. An all-out effort was made to stop Kuhio from winning renomination in the Republican primary election, and considerable resources and energy were thrown into the fight in an attempt to replace Kuhio with Charles Rice, of Kauai. Kuhio's friends were frightened. Legislator H. L. Holstein wrote to the Prince's new secretary, Hawaiian John Desha, that the Hawaiian people were not alerted to the danger; they did not realize that the fight between Rice and Kuhio was a fight between "corporation and the people . . . the haole against the Hawaiian . . . the influential against the weak." Every haole paper from Kauai to Hawaii was against the Prince, according to Holstein, who maintained that "we can beat . . . the enemy if the 9000 Hawaiians only have some pride of race in them."[55] Cupid was pleased when McCandless, running in the Democratic primary, told a Hawaiian audience that he would be happy if they voted for Kuhio in the Republican primary.[56] Encouraged, Holstein wrote that he now thought that Kuhio would defeat Rice, because "the Hawaiians have . . . risen in their glory in manhood and pride of their own . . . the Democrats will pull so strongly for Cupid that the primaries may elect him . . . if the Hawaiians of all parties will keep that as a will to be carried to completion, and to vote solid for Cupid, regardless of party lines, Rice will be snowed under and McCandless will stay at home."[57] Kuhio beat Rice in the primary, and the natives and part-Hawaiians responded to his campaign in the fall as they never had before. Holstein wrote, "Hawaiians are now inoculated . . . with love for native hearth and pride of race."[58] The Prince won by a two-to-one margin over Mc-Candless and George Carter, the former governor, who ran under Theodore Roosevelt's Progressive label.

The strain on the alliance continued until Kuhio's death. He remained nominally a Republican, but he was bitter toward his allies. McCandless increased his vote over Kuhio in Hawaiian districts in 1916 and 1918, and wherever the Hawaiians were not under the influence of powerful local haole *alii,* they gave the Democratic candidate for delegate about as many votes as the Prince received. But not all of Kuhio's friends deserted him. Many natives worked hard for Cupid, who dedicated himself to opening up land for Hawaiians by amending the Islands' land laws. Haole leaders continued to support him in his campaigns, although they bypassed him whenever possible. Distasteful as he was, he was more acceptable than the haole agitator McCandless, who ominously denounced the sugar tariff.

Before the Prince died, he joined with Merchant Street in pushing through Congress his largest accomplishment in the twenty-year political alliance. This was the so-called "Hawaiian Rehabilitation Bill" of 1920. The Prince, influenced by his friend John Wise, became obsessed with the idea of returning the Hawaiian people to the land. This could only be done, he believed, by setting aside special lands for Hawaiian homesteading at practically no cost. A key member of the oligarchy recalled in 1959 that the sugar leaders "were not the least bit interested in Hawaiian rehabilitation," but decided to support Kuhio and the Hawaiian homesteading plan in return for his support of other amendments to the Organic Act.

In order to obtain Merchant Street approval of his plan for Hawaiian homesteads, the Prince agreed to remove highly cultivated sugar lands from the existing homestead laws. He was persuaded that the money received from the sugar agencies for leasing those lands to the plantations would pay for the Hawaiian Homes Commission and its operations. A second change requested by the agencies concerned the 1,000-acre restriction. The plantations had been evading the provision in the Organic Act that limited corporations' ownership to 1,000 acres. The sugar agencies created partnerships or corporations to get around the law but were aware that they might be beaten in a court fight if this circumvention were properly attacked. One of the major plantation lawyers, a missionary descendant, observed that he would get a fat fee if forced to go to court on the issue, but he was certain to lose. Now was the time to eliminate the 1,000-acre restriction, the planters reasoned.[59]

Other land provisions were put into the omnibus bill to make homesteading more difficult for Orientals. Another amendment, endorsed by both Kuhio and Merchant Street, forbade aliens to work on federal projects, thus reserving good jobs for native Hawaiians and keeping Japanese aliens on the plantations, where the agencies wanted them. The new Democratic Governor, Charles J. McCarthy, appointed by Wilson to succeed Pinkham, seemed as willing to go along with the oligarchy on most issues as his predecessor had been. He appointed Charles Rice and Alfred Castle to go to Washington to help the Prince lobby for the bill. There, in a nine-room suite at the New Willard Hotel, senators and members of the House of Representatives were entertained by visitors from the Islands.

The Hawaiian Rehabilitation Bill passed without serious opposition. In it was something for every important group in the Republican coalition. The merchant and professional groups in town were pleased that the Japanese would be kept from federal jobs and would find it difficult to win homesteads. The planters were especially happy with the repeal of the 1,000-acre provision. Kuhio and his friends sincerely believed that the rehabilitation of the Hawaiian people had begun.

Two *kamaaina* islanders, one a member of the oligarchy and the other a Hawaiian politician, recall that Merchant Street land lawyers supervised the drafting of the act that specified which lands were to be made available to the Hawaiian Homes Commission. "Good cane lands were omitted," the *kamaaina* haole remembered years later. "Only rotten lands were left for us," bitterly recalled the Hawaiian in a sharp overstatement.[60] Nearly forty years later, the executive director of the Hawaiian Homes Commission would report that most of the lands set aside for rehabilitation of the native Hawaiians were in extremely remote areas or in various forest-reserve sections unsuitable for actual settlement. Only 2 per cent of the lands set aside could "be properly developed at reasonable cost."[61] Undoubtedly, the bill was more of a triumph for the planters than for Kuhio, but he probably never realized it.

The Prince's dream of becoming governor was thwarted again in 1920 following the election of Warren G. Harding as President, and soon after, Kuhio carried his disappointment to the grave. The friendly, joyful poker games with powerful congressmen at his hotel quarters on K Street would be no more.

The new Governor, Wallace R. Farrington, despite his early aberrations, was an orthodox conservative Republican except on educational matters. He frequently made liberal statements on racial tolerance and education and, indeed, encouraged many nonhaoles in advancing their education; on land and labor questions, however, he consistently acted in the oligarchy's interest. Like his predecessors, he sincerely believed that the business of government in the Islands was business, and that to serve sugar and pineapple was, in large measure, to serve Hawaii.

The oligarchy was not threatened by Kuhio's death. Throughout the 1920's, the Republicans controlled the governorship and held overwhelming majorities in the territorial legislature. In 1923, all fifteen members of the Senate were elected on the G.O.P. ticket, and twenty-nine of thirty House seats were won by Republicans. But the oligarchy did temporarily lose the delegateship. Kuhio's mantle could not be transferred to part-Hawaiian John Wise, who was thought by Hawaiians to be "in" with the haoles. In 1922, William P. ("Billy") Jarrett, a popular part-Hawaiian, defeated Wise, and in 1924, he beat Philip Rice, a missionary descendant from Kauai. In Congress, Jarrett could do little harm to the oligarchy; he was but a lonely and inconsequential Democratic delegate from the remotest portion of the United States amidst a sea of Republicans, whose key members on the Interior Affairs committees dealt directly with haole representatives in the capital. Jarrett's elections were disturbing, nonetheless. It would not do to have a crucial pressure point represented by the "wrong" man.

A part-Hawaiian elected official sat on the porch of Miss Ella Paris's boardinghouse in a small village on the Kona Coast. Although he was a Republican, he chuckled as he thought of Billy Jarrett's successful bid for re-election. Billy was a good fellow, and the politician surmised that Jarrett deserved to win as he had in the Big Island. Suddenly, he heard a sputtering motor, and a fancy car driven by Royal Mead, of the Hawaiian Sugar Planters' Association, came to a stop in a swirl of dust at the porch.

"What happened on Hawaii?" Mead wanted to know. "What's wrong with the Big Island voters? Can't they do their share to elect a Republican delegate? Why do the Hawaiians bite the hand that feeds them?" Hawaiian voting had gone heavily against Rice and in Jarrett's favor in the 1922 election. In the overwhelmingly Hawaiian (98.5 per cent) first precinct of the first district, Jarrett received 91 per cent of the vote, and in the twelfth precinct of the second district (95.6 per cent Hawaiian), more than three out of four electors picked Jarrett. Still, Mead said, Republican senatorial candidate Ernest Akina and Republican House candidate Norman Lyman did very well, winning easily in these same precincts. The local Republican was blunt in his reply: "Some Hawaiians might have voted for the Prince out of love and respect for his royal lineage; but to expect them to vote for a Rice against Billy Jarrett was asking too much."

"What about those Japanese voters in West Hawaii? Why were they voting Democratic?" Mead asked. The reply was again sharp. The plantation camps, the official said, were infested with vermin, and, what was worse, the attitudes of the haole managers and *lunas* were vile. The Baldwins had made some improvements on Maui, but the managers in Hawaii were irresponsible, and the Republican party would pay a high price for its failure to curb them.[62]

From his questioning, Mead learned two lessons. First, the Republicans should find another Hawaiian to run for delegate; second, they should exercise greater control over the growing plantation vote. Their new candidate was Victor K. Houston, whose mother had come from an important Hawaiian family. Houston was more of a mainlander than an Islander, but he was in Hawaii in 1926, serving in the Navy at Pearl Harbor with the rank of commander. He was amiable, intelligent, friendly to business, and, of course, part-Hawaiian. Houston won by a small margin in 1926, and Jarrett's pluralities went down in all heavily Hawaiian precincts except the eleventh on Kauai.

For several years, Houston served as delegate in the Kuhio tradition. He kept in touch with many Hawaiian and part-Hawaiian leaders and tried to serve their interests. He wanted better lands for the Hawaiian

Homes Commission, although he was unable to do anything about it. He opposed the large-scale importation of Filipino laborers, although he muted his views in the face of planter opposition. He was also in favor of statehood, as Kuhio had been before him, recognizing that Hawaiians would have more to say about the government of the Islands if state officers were popularly elected. But in other matters, he tried his best to represent the dominant business interests of Hawaii. He was in constant communication with the executive head of the Hawaiian Sugar Planters' Association, receiving, among other information, the latest stock and dividend statistics on major corporations.[63] In 1929, he told a meeting of the Honolulu Chamber of Commerce that he wanted to represent its wishes in Washington.[64] Protection for sugar and pineapple was his main concern, but he took time to put in a good word with the Collector of Revenue to relieve the Hawaii Polo and Racing Club from taxation at the request of Walter Dillingham, founder of the club.[65]

The percentage vote in Japanese plantation districts was much greater for Houston in 1926 than it had been for Rice two years earlier. New methods had been found to turn the increasing Japanese vote in the first and second districts on Hawaii, the fifth on Oahu, and the sixth on Kauai into a Republican asset. The proportion of registered voters of Japanese ancestry in Hawaii had leaped from 2.5 per cent in 1920 to 7.6 per cent in 1926. Four years later, it would double, and by 1936 would rise to 24.9 per cent. On the eve of Pearl Harbor, three out of every ten voters in the Islands were Americans of Japanese descent. From 1926 to 1940, the oligarchy was concerned at least as much with controlling the Japanese vote as with influencing Hawaiian electors. By 1940, there were twice as many Japanese as haole voters, and political control on the plantations was imperative.[66]

Laws under the Republic had excluded all Oriental immigrants from political participation, although they constituted three quarters of the population of voting age. Only a handful of Chinese who had been citizens of the Republic of Hawaii were granted American citizenship after Hawaii was annexed. Although no Japanese were registered to vote in 1905, some haole leaders were already concerned that the Islands might someday fall under the control of the Japanese. Still, the threat was remote, and most haoles feared economic, more than political, competition.

There were three possible approaches for the oligarchy to the problem of the Japanese vote. The first was to recruit Japanese leaders for the Republican party, giving them positions of influence, encouraging them to run for office, and distributing patronage among them. The second was to limit the size of the Japanese vote through legislation and intimidation. The third was to control the vote through economic pressure. Only the last two methods were tried. No courses in citizenship were offered on the plantations. Those Japanese who were citizens were often forced to great lengths to prove their citizenship in order to register. Nisei were frequently obliged to get sworn statements from midwives or others who had knowledge of their birth in Hawaii. By 1920, probably fewer than one third of all Japanese eligible to vote had registered.[67] Senator William H. King, of Utah, concluded from his observations in Hawaii that the Japanese were not encouraged to go into politics. Indeed, they were pushed aside by others. Henry A. Baldwin, son of Henry P., of Maui, told a congressional committee that the Japanese did not seem interested in the political and civic affairs of his country. Perhaps, he suggested, they were under instructions from Tokyo not to register to avoid the impression that they were trying to assume political control of the Islands.[68] Senator Frank Lee Willis, of Ohio, asked witness Walter Dillingham why he thought it was that so few Japanese voted. The Honolulu industrialist could not say, but Prince Jonah Kuhio commented that they probably would not take part in government unless their Japanese rulers gave permission.[69]

In the early 1920's the oligarchy did everything that reasonably could be done to dishearten the Japanese. They were kept out of federal and territorial jobs. They were discouraged from opening homesteads. Their language schools were curtailed and their newspapers regulated. The *Advertiser* and the *Star Bulletin* referred repeatedly to the "Japanese problem." One section of the Press Regulation Bill actually provided that any pamphlet, bulletin, or printed matter in a foreign language dealing with politics would have to be submitted in translation to the Attorney General for clearance, along with the names of the persons, residences, and businesses of the authors. Any language other than English or Hawaiian was deemed a foreign language, but the bill was aimed primarily at the Japanese. It is doubtful if the authors of the Press Regulation Bill ever intended that it should be applied. It was meant to intimidate the Japanese, to curtail their labor and political activity, to postpone the day when thousands of nisei and sansei would march to the polls.

Comparable repressive measures were passed on the mainland. In New York State, a 1921 law conditioned the right to vote upon literacy in the English language. But on the mainland, immigrant political leaders were being developed under the tutelage of older bosses, and immigrants were active in political life. In Hawaii, on the other hand, Oriental aliens were not eligible for citizenship, and their sons and daughters who were eligible were discouraged from exercising their rights. As late as 1933, at a meeting of the Taxpayers League in Honolulu, composed almost entirely of extremist haoles, a modification of the Organic Act that would restrict the franchise on a racial basis was overwhelmingly endorsed.[70]

A few alarmists among the *kamaaina* elite leaders were so frightened of the potential Japanese vote that they frequently discussed the possibility of a commission form of government for Hawaii, composed largely of military or naval men appointed by the President. That would be better, thought many of them, than submitting to Japanese pluralities under self-government.[71] When a United States senator asked Governor McCarthy in 1922 if he thought Hawaii would be better off under a commission form of government, McCarthy answered that he and the other leaders of Hawaii would be the first to ask Congress for such a form in order to "maintain Americanism in Hawaii" if it appeared that the Japanese were taking over. The Senator wondered if the Japanese would know that such action was directed at them. "Let them think so; what do we care," replied McCarthy.[72] Part-Hawaiian John Wise and haole Robert Shingle, who was married to a wealthy part-Hawaiian, were frightened. What would happen to Hawaiians under a commission government? The Japanese threat was not that imminent, the majority of the haole leaders agreed. They could take care of things. Hawaii would remain American with a little help from Congress.[73] Senator James Phlelan, of California, approved and introduced a constitutional amendment to deny citizenship to anyone born in the United States whose parents were not eligible for citizenship.

Haole leaders correctly predicted that they would be able to influence the growing Japanese vote on the plantations. Their methods were not very subtle, but they were effective. A part-Hawaiian political leader, later a judge and a key figure in the modern Republican party, remembers how plantation managers provided an audience for friendly candidates,[74] but kept the opposition from the plantation premises, which invariably meant that Japanese workers never saw a Demo-

crat unless he sneaked into their camp or unless they ventured out
to hear him in a public park or school ground. In the late 1920's, the
plantation managers themselves became active in politics, many of
them serving as campaign managers. They picked a number of key
workers, gave them time off from their jobs, and taught them to recruit
votes. In the 1930 election on Kauai, the manager of the McBryde
plantation served as Republican campaign manager for the West Side.
In East Kauai, a pineapple cannery executive ran the G.O.P. campaign.
Frequently, managers called in *lunas* shortly before election and explained which candidates were to be supported. *Lunas* were assigned
to stand at the polls and hand copies of the approved slate to voters.
A worker with Democratic inclinations lived in fear. His home was a
shack owned by someone else. He lived on credit from the plantation
store. If he quit his job, he would be blacklisted. A Japanese Democrat
who ran for the Board of Supervisors in the 1928 election remembers
a secret midnight visit to the camp at Makaweli to visit a friend. They
hid behind the hibiscus on hands and knees as the Japanese aspirant
to the Board slipped twenty-five cards announcing his candidacy to his
cohort. Another friend, a plantation storekeeper, refused the cards,
saying that he would lose his job if they were found in his possession.
One man, later a member of the territorial Senate, recalls that his
manager picked him to become a campaign worker. He wanted to
demur, but defiance of the boss's wishes would jeopardize his future
on the plantation. The most popular method of checking what went on
inside the voting booth was to hang a pencil from the railing directly
over the Republican side of the ballot. If the loop around the railing
shifted, instructions were being disobeyed.[75]
   The oligarchy had succeeded in winning Japanese votes. In the
most Japanese district on Maui between 1928 and 1940, the Republican
vote for delegate was never less than 72 per cent of the ballots cast. In
the two most Japanese precincts of the Big Island during the same
period, the G.O.P. vote was invariably between 70 and 80 per cent.
In the 1936 election, the Democratic candidate for delegate received
less than 10 per cent in both Japanese precincts.
   An increasing number of nisei electors, however, lived in Honolulu
and other towns where relative anonimity permitted genuine political
choice and gave Democratic candidates a chance among the Japanese.
In the most Japanese precinct of Kauai's sixth district, Lincoln Mc-
Candless won small pluralities in 1930, 1932, and 1936, as did Demo-

cratic candidate David Trask in 1938. But there, the Democrats were helped by a substantial number of Hawaiian votes; probably no more than one out of two nisei voters sided with them. Throughout the late 1920's and during the '30's, most of the heavily Japanese districts on the outer islands were nearly as solidly Republican as the silk-stocking haole precincts in Honolulu. In the two most Japanese precincts on Oahu, Democratic pluralities were recorded only twice in the six elections between 1928 and 1940. Not once did a Democratic candidate win a plurality in the rural ninth precinct of the fifth district.[76]

In Honolulu, the Japanese were, nevertheless, generally more outspoken than they were on the plantations. A Japanese intellectual addressing a group of his countrymen, most of them businessmen, in downtown Honolulu on January 13, 1921, warned that "the complete solution of the Japanese question will never be reached until American-born Japanese exert their influence in political circles."[77] The *Hawaii Hochi* incessantly attacked what it called the "czars of industry."[78] The *Hawaii Asahi,* of Hilo, scorned the monopolized industries of the Territory and joined the *Hochi* in urging nisei political participation in an effort to defeat the oligarchy.[79] In 1930, the *Hochi* backed McCandless for delegate against Houston, arguing that the Democrats were for all the people, with special privileges to none. More home rule, even statehood, maintained the *Hochi,* would make Hawaii flourish.[80] The *Yoyen Jiho* in Koloa, Kauai, and the *Kwasan* of Hilo, blasted Merchant Street.[81] So strong were the Japanese papers in their criticisms that the secretary-treasurer of the Hawaiian Sugar Planters' Association warned Delegate Houston in December 1927 that he should "take it as a cardinal principle that Japanese newspapers are biased and wrong." Nonetheless, key members of the oligarchy were mailed translations of the Japanese newspapers by the Association, with allegations of their "insidious influence."[82]

But their influence was bound to grow. Because of mass Hawaiian defections and with the help of Japanese votes, Lincoln McCandless was elected delegate in 1932. Although McCandless was, in many respects, as anti-Japanese as the oligarchy, he recognized the political importance of encouraging nisei voters to be Democrats. More important than McCandless was the influence of the Democratic Mayor of Honolulu, part-Hawaiian John Wilson. Wilson even suggested that new Japanese voters could form the basis of a rejuvenated Democratic party.[83] He pushed the appointment of Japanese citizens as postmasters and urged party leaders to give them recognition in other ways. Still, nearly all Japanese candidates for office, reared in the older patterns of Hawaii, were Republicans, and few were elected. The largest number chosen was four, in 1932. And an astonishingly small proportion of Japanese citizens was appointed to public office. Although citizens of Japanese descent constituted more than a quarter of the voters in 1930, only 1.6 per cent of them held appointive positions in the territorial government. Ten years later, when nearly a third of the voters were Japanese, only 2.9 per cent were in appointive jobs.[84]

Despite the dire prophecies of haole leaders, the Japanese did less bloc voting than immigrant groups on the mainland in comparable phases of acculturation. One study, made by a University of Hawaii professor in 1938, showed less Japanese "plunking" (ethnic bloc voting) than among other groups.[85] In the contest for a House seat in 1932, voters in the nearly half-Japanese first precinct of the third district failed to support George Yamayoshi, a Democrat, who ran behind six Republicans and only slightly ahead of a Chinese Democrat. Two years later, George Watase, running on the Democratic ticket, and Benjamin Tashiro, a Republican, did very well in the most Japanese precinct on Kauai, and in 1936, Andy Yamashiro and George Neguchi, Democrat and Republican respectively, did well in the most Japanese precinct of Oahu's fifth district. Neguchi led the ticket there again in 1938, and Japanese candidates for the legislature ran well in Japanese precincts two years later.[86] In spite of these Japanese victories, the statistics show less plunking than might have been expected. Japanese self-restraint plus the Japanese concern for the opinion of others probably modified the tendency of immigrant groups to vote for their own kind, and contributed further to the ability of the oligarchy to maintain control of the key elective offices of the Islands through the 1930's.

Chapter Seven

NO NEW DEAL FOR HAWAII

The skillful juggling of the haole-Hawaiian alliance and the influence of the plantation vote enabled the oligarchy to maintain its control for nearly four decades, despite the imposition of universal citizen suffrage by Congress in the Organic Act. Helping sustain the oligarchy during difficult periods was the weakness of the Democratic party of Hawaii—a weakness stemming from two sources. The Democratic leaders of Hawaii, with one or two exceptions, did not own the wealth of the Islands and could not support their drive for votes with economic rewards. The party was also beset by chronic personal factionalism, and in the 1930's by ethnic cleavages as well. These weaknesses prevented the Democrats in Hawaii from taking advantage of the two great opportunities presented by the elections of Woodrow Wilson in 1912, and Franklin D. Roosevelt in 1932. Primarily because of Democratic frailties in the Islands, neither the New Freedom nor the New Deal was transported to Hawaii.

A small Democratic party was formed immediately after annexation by mainland haoles from the Southern and border states, Irish visitors from the Northeast, and a few Bryan Democrats from the Middle West. They were *malihinis,* and they were almost all "hired men," without sufficient economic resources to support their cause. The party was organized on Kauai in 1902 by a young accountant, a head bookkeeper at the McBryde plantation, and a storekeeper at the Kapaa plantation. One of them recalls that the Home Rule party was far more successful among the Hawaiians than were the Democrats. At Hanapepe, for example, Democratic leaders counted on twenty-eight votes in a certain precinct but received only five after Home Ruler John Bush, a part-Hawaiian speaking for Wilcox, attacked all haoles, Democrats and

Republicans alike, and urged support for the Home Rulers along racial lines. The Home Rulers faded after their defeats in 1904, 1906, and 1908, although the Home Rule and Democratic candidates together still outpolled Kuhio in the 1908 election.[1]

The Kuhio-oligarchy alliance combined with Republican control in Washington kept the Democrats from becoming a critical challenge to the oligarchy until 1912. That year, the election of Woodrow Wilson to the Presidency assured the appointment of a Democratic governor. In addition, a substantial portion of Home Rule support had been transferred to Democratic candidates for the territorial legislature. The proportion of Democrats in both houses increased from 9 to 38 per cent. Returns from certain precincts showed large numbers of Portuguese voting Democratic, and in the Chinese fifteenth precinct of the fifth district on Oahu, Democratic candidates for the House and Senate ran far ahead of the Republicans. Among those elected to the legislature were Delbert E. Metzger, one of the founders of the Democratic party in Hawaii, who was later appointed by Roosevelt to a federal judgeship, and Curtis P. Iaukea, former retainer of Prince Kuhio, who broke with him in 1904. Important oligarchy spokesmen, among them George F. Renton and Alfred Castle, were beaten. The Republicans, led by such men as missionary descendants George P. Cooke and Clarence Cooke in the House and Charles Rice and Henry A. Baldwin in the Senate, still had a majority, but the surprising Democratic victory in the Islands cheered the little band of haole Democratic leaders.

Far more important was the election of a national Democratic administration. The Democratic Territorial Committee promptly endorsed Lincoln L. McCandless for appointment as governor. Successful in the well-digging business, McCandless was one of the few Democrats who could afford the territorial campaign. Although he ran unsuccessfully for delegate against Kuhio in 1908, 1910, and 1912, in his last election, he did receive slightly more than 45 per cent of the votes cast for the two men, enough to give the Prince and the oligarchy a scare. McCandless was elected to the legislature as a Republican in 1904, but soon collided with Governor Carter over land policies. Specifically, McCandless was outraged when Carter exchanged 48,000 acres of land on Lanai owned by the territorial government for two lots in Honolulu held by William G. Erwin. McCandless went to court, charging that the Governor lacked authority to exchange more than 1,000 acres of land, but the case was thrown out by the territorial Supreme Court on the grounds that a citizen could not appeal unless he personally was involved to the extent of $5,000.

Clearly Lincoln McCandless was the number-one candidate for governor in 1912, but there were other candidates, too. Many of the newly-elected Democratic territorial legislators resented McCandless's primacy in the party, which they considered merely the result of his relative wealth. Metzger, a progressive, visited Washington to push his own appointment. At least two other Democrats made the long trek to the capital to lobby for themselves.[2] The Secretary of the Interior, Franklin K. Lane, charged by President Wilson with finding a new governor, was uncertain as to whom the Democrats in Honolulu really wanted. Republican leaders shrewdly began a campaign of vilification against McCandless, charging him with immoral character. Hoping to exploit the puritanical attitudes of Wilson and Lane, one of them wrote the Secretary of the Interior claiming that McCandless kept a number of Hawaiian *wahines*.[3] Other letters against McCandless followed. An affidavit from what one of his friends called "a woman of the worst character" was secured and sent to Secretary Lane.[4] When the Ministerial Union of Honolulu wrote Lane charging Democrat Mc-Candless with immorality, that was enough for the Secretary of the Interior. McCandless had been stopped.

The President of the United States was probably disgusted with Hawaii. Its Democrats were confused, and their leading candidate was allegedly immoral. The Republicans were united, the pillars of "right" society. Concerned with much more important affairs on the mainland, President Wilson delayed an entire year before making his appointment. When it came, Democratic leaders in Honolulu were shocked. The new Governor, Lucius E. Pinkham, had been recommended by a Democratic congressman from California to whom Wilson was obligated. Pinkham was alleged to have been a Democrat on the mainland, but in Hawaii he had worked for and with the Republican oligarchy. In making his recommendation, Secretary of the Interior Lane leaned heavily on Republican advice from Farrington and oligarchy lawyer Frank Thompson.[5] On Oahu, Pinkham had worked for Benjamin Dillingham as a bookkeeper at the Oahu Railroad and Land Company and as manager of the Pacific Hardware Company. Retired from business, he was appointed by Governor Carter to be president of the territorial Board of Health in 1904, in which position he served four years.

He was next sent by the Hawaiian Sugar Planters' Association to the Philippines to recruit laborers. When his job there was finished, Pinkham, in semiretirement, traveled extensively in America, Europe, and Asia. Then, at the age of sixty-three, after having been away from the Islands for five years, President Wilson appointed him to the governorship.

Pinkham's appointment was welcomed on Merchant Street. He had shown the right attitudes toward labor and Hawaii's nonhaole groups. When Japanese doctors assigned by the Board of Health to the Aiea plantation to care for laborers sent complaints to the Board, Pinkham attacked them furiously as aggressive profit seekers in a letter to the Japanese Consul.[6] Later, as governor, he reacted to complaints from workers on the plantations by turning them over to the Hawaiian Sugar Planters' Association. His opinion was that it would pay the Association to increase paternalism in order to keep evil conditions from becoming too publicized. "I think it is wise to keep the matter of unemployment and the indigent as free from public notoriety as possible . . ." he wrote, and encouraged the sugar planters to make a small contribution to the associated charities.[7]

On matters concerning Maui, Pinkham was deferential to Henry A. Baldwin, and in 1916, the Democratic Governor decided not to call a special session of the legislature in order to permit Baldwin to make a trip to the mainland.[8] With respect to Kauai, he sought the advice of Republican Senator Charles Rice. Who did Rice want for the Liquor Commission? Pinkham wanted to know early in 1915.[9] At another point, Rice, irritated that Pinkham had not made the right appointment, queried, "What were your reasons for not appointing Miss Elsie Wilcox to this position? She being recommended to you as the best one for the position by the two Senators from Kauai."[10] On Hawaii, the so-called Democratic Governor took advice from Republican plantation heads such as John M. Ross, the manager of the Hakalau plantation, who, less than eight months after Pinkham's appointment, wrote the Governor that his administration was excellent.[11]

The Democrats in the Islands were less pleased with the new territorial administration. Part-Hawaiian John Wilson, probably the most popular Democrat in the Islands, complained that Pinkham would not listen to recommendations from any of the leading Democrats in the Territory in making appointments. An orthodox Republican who opposed liberal homesteading was appointed president of the Board of

Agriculture and Forestry, and Pinkham nominated three Republicans for circuit judgeships without consulting the Democrats. Within six months after his appointment, the chairman of the Democratic Territorial Committee claimed that the vast majority of Pinkham's appointments were Republicans and that he was unaware of Pinkham's having consulted with any Democrats with respect to major appointments. By May 1914, Democratic leaders were calling Pinkham "our Republican Governor."[12] Leading Democrats drew up an impeachment which they sent to President Wilson in July, charging that Pinkham had not appointed a single Wilson Democrat to office. It was also claimed that under Pinkham's administration, the tax assessments on sugar plantations had been reduced $25,000,000 below the previous year's figure, while the value of land had actually gone up.[13] Under the assessment system permitted by Pinkham, plantation managers told the assessors just how much they would be able to pay. Their position in 1914 was that there had to be a drop in assessments because of the reduction in the sugar tariff. The territorial Treasurer, after a certain amount of bargaining, accepted the basic assessments turned in by the managers.

Pinkham was publicly denounced by the Democratic Territorial Committee chairman. But Woodrow Wilson was too busy to listen to the pleas of Hawaii's Democrats. Pinkham served his four-year term, during which the Democrats received a smashing defeat in the election for the territorial House of Representatives in 1916 and in the election for both houses two years later. Despite efforts in the Democratic newspaper, the *New Freedom,* to appeal to Hawaiian and Portuguese voters, the party was demoralized.[14] Its leaders still hoped in 1918 that McCandless, who openly attacked the sugar planters, would win enough Hawaiian votes to beat Kuhio in the election for delegate. But the Prince was a Hawaiian, after all, and McCandless was a haole who spoke only faltering Hawaiian. The Republicans spent money liberally to defeat him, one report alleging that 600 workers were paid $10 each on Election Day to round up votes.[15]

President Wilson's second appointment, Charles J. McCarthy, gave the Democrats of Hawaii only slightly more comfort than had Pinkham. McCarthy at least was a Democrat and had been a supporter of Queen Liliuokalani. He had been elected as a Democrat to the office of city treasurer in Honolulu in 1912, and had been known to complain against the land and assessment policies of the oligarchy. Kuhio approved of the appointment, and hopes rose that important policies would be changed in Hawaii.

McCarthy appointed Delbert Metzger territorial treasurer and stood by him in his enforcement of the insurance laws against the factors and the von Hamm-Young Company, Ltd., the biggest insurance agency in the Islands. Strict licensing and rigid reporting were insisted upon despite oligarchy resistance. Metzger also prepared an elaborate formula for re-evaluating land, which raised assessments by approximately $40,000,000.[16] In other matters, McCarthy was more pliable and acquiesced in what Democrat John Wilson called "the system" on Merchant Street. Not a wealthy man, McCarthy had engaged in various business enterprises but was unable to succeed in any of them. Born a poor Irish boy from Boston and San Francisco, he was flattered by associations with the missionary *kamaaina* descendants in the Islands. When Governor McCarthy visited Maui, he stayed at the mansion of Henry Baldwin, who sent him a steady barrage of Republican advice on the stationery of the Maui Agricultural Company. It was no surprise to insiders that McCarthy approved of Baldwin's copartnership with Angus MacPhee to develop government lands on Kahoolawe. McCarthy wrote the *kamaaina* Yale man that he knew Baldwin would not use the lands for selfish purposes, but would work in the public interest.[17]

McCarthy shared the racial prejudices of the age. He was strongly anti-Japanese and agreed that haole planters should press Congress for the importation of Chinese immigrants to the Territory to offset the growing insolence of the Japanese workers. He appointed Walter Dillingham, the most powerful of the haole leaders, as chairman of a labor committee to go to Washington in 1921 to urge the permissive legislation. Dillingham reminded McCarthy that it was important to keep their reasons for the legislation private. For his part, Dillingham said, he would keep the whole labor situation in Hawaii out of the papers in Washington. Later, when the Governor gave his own testimony before congressional committees, he was as strongly anti-Japanese as any of the representatives of the plantations.[18] McCarthy's choice for chairman of the committee to visit Washington to press for changes in the land laws to make them more favorable to the sugar planters was Charles Rice, whom he backed in pushing provisions to restrict Japanese homesteading and prohibit the employment of Japanese aliens on federal projects.

Annoyed by Metzger's policies and anxious to have a bona fide Republican appointed governor following the election of Harding, the oligarchy prevailed upon McCarthy to resign before the expiration of his term. His reward was a high-paying job as Washington representative of the Honolulu Chamber of Commerce, in which position he served two years. Later, McCarthy was employed by Dillingham as general manager of the Hawaiian Dredging Company.

The Republicans were again in control in Washington, and the Democrats had failed to cut through the web of oligarchy in their first big opportunity. Hundreds of Hawaiian, Portuguese, and Japanese precinct workers had been thoroughly demoralized by the appointments of Pinkham and McCarthy. The lists of workers for every precinct in the fifth district of Oahu, the strongest Democratic district in the Territory, showed that there were not more than a half-dozen haole names out of several hundred.[19] Yet the haole Democrats in Washington had appointed *malihini* haoles to the governorship who seemed as out of sympathy with rank-and-file Democrats as the Republicans had been. With the exception of the election of the popular part-Hawaiian Billy Jarrett as delegate in 1922 and 1924, the oligarchy held solid control over all crucial political pressure points until 1932. Jarrett's death in 1927 destroyed Democratic hopes for recapturing the delegateship. Two years later, the Democratic candidate for delegate, Bertram G. Rivenburgh, was swamped by Houston, who received more than 70 per cent of the vote. The legislature in the late 1920's was more than 90 per cent Republican, and Republican Governors Wallace Farrington and Lawrence Judd, the latter a missionary descendant appointed by Herbert Hoover after working for two of the major sugar factors, followed by instinct and conviction the major policies of the haole elite.

Governor Judd set the tone for his administration in his first inaugural address by paying tribute to the sugar industry and by promising an economical administration which would enable business to prosper. Poor people, he said, should not be exempt from property taxes, since they might then become insensitive to the costs of government.[20]

In 1932, a second great opportunity was presented to the Democrats of the Islands. Hawaii followed the national Democratic landslide by electing McCandless over Houston as delegate and by increasing Democratic strength in the territorial legislature from 7 to 31 per cent. The most important triumph took place in Washington, however, where Franklin D. Roosevelt promised a New Deal for all Americans.

But the Democrats in the Islands found themselves unable to capitalize on Roosevelt's election, a situation compounded by the confusion which followed the Ala Moana or Massie rape case. Late one balmy September night in 1931, after an evening of partying and drinking, Mrs. Massie, the pretty, dark-haired wife of a young Navy lieutenant, was accosted and attacked by five dark-skinned youths in Ala Moana Park, near Waikiki. A jury which represented the multi-ethnic population of the Islands could not agree on a verdict for her alleged assailants. A private report from the Pinkerton Detective Agency to Governor Judd showed subsequently that the woman's story was full of contradictions and that in the opinion of the consultants, an acquittal was absolutely justified. But the United States Navy believed differently. The Commandant of the Fourteenth Naval District sent scorching wires to the Secretary of the Navy denouncing the administration of justice in Hawaii. Mixed-blood juries, he said, were not capable of giving justice to a white person. The police department, he pointed out, was honeycombed with Hawaiians and was not able to cope with hoodlums. Alarmed, the Secretary of the Navy wanted to know if the fleet should be dispatched to Honolulu.[21] But the naval officer husband did not wait for battleships. He and his mother-in-law kidnaped one of the accused youths, took him to the officer's house, and shot him. With the help of two enlisted men, they threw his body over a high cliff into the Pacific Ocean. This time, a new Honolulu jury convicted the accused. The Navy was furious: dark-skinned rapists were allowed to get away while the white American lieutenant and his mother-in-law went to prison. Public opinion on the mainland, stirred by the Hearst newspapers, turned against Hawaii and scorned its racial *aloha*. Under great pressure, Governor Judd defended Hawaii but also urged the death penalty for rape and mandatory sterilization for all other sex criminals. Houston was under even greater pressure in Washington, where the Navy League bombarded President Hoover, who was then desperately worried about unemployment, with demands to do something to punish Hawaii. Congress was inflamed because no one had yet been punished for the alleged rape, and Houston, seeking to avoid greater damage to Hawaii, asked the President to pardon the Lieutenant and his mother-in-law.[22] Governor Judd was instructed by Washington to commute their sentences within one day of their conviction. The Navy had been mollified, but Hawaii was under a cloud.

Hoover appointed Seth Richardson, a Washington attorney with a distinguished record of government service, to investigate the enforcement of justice in Hawaii. Richardson found some shortcomings in the administration of justice in Hawaii, comparable to those found in mainland cities, but, unlike key Navy officials, he was not alarmed. There was no doubt in the mind of naval leaders about what should be done. Admiral Yates Sterling, Jr., the Naval Commandant, denounced Hawaii's racial melting pot as producing people of low moral character. Hawaii, he said, should have a commission form of government.[23] Moreover, Sterling pointed out, the Japanese were disloyal, and in the event of a war between Japan and the United States, there would be a race war in Hawaii. The reports sent by the Navy in Honolulu to the department in Washington were hysterical. They described dark gangs of prowlers, lusting after white women, Japanese annoyances directed at Navy personnel, and riots caused by fighting between natives and Orientals against whites. These fantastic exaggerations built a strong Navy pressure in Washington to strip Hawaii of its territorial form of government and to place it under military rule.

In the winter of 1932, shortly after Roosevelt's election, Republican Senator Hiram Bingham of Connecticut introduced legislation to put Hawaii under the Navy Department and give it a commission form of government. Supported by the Hearst newspapers, the bill gained considerable headway in Washington, but was opposed by the oligarchy. The haole elite, certain of its control over the legislature, confident of its ability to influence the appointment of a governor by Roosevelt, and fearing mainland military officers much more than local Democrats, fought the Bingham Bill. The *Hawaii Hochi* correctly pointed out that for years the oligarchy had used the threat of a commission form of government to frighten Hawaiians and Japanese into compliance with its views. Now, said the *Hochi,* its chickens had come home to roost.[24] Houston struggled in Congress to defend Hawaii, and inserted many items in the *Congressional Record* explaining the Islands' position. Walter Dillingham told his agent in Washington to persuade Senator Bingham to withdraw the bill.[25] But the pressure against Hawaii was tremendous. Houston's mail included indignant letters referring to the Ala Moana case and asking Congress to defend the honor of American womanhood. Admiral William D. Pratt, Chief of Naval Operations in the Pacific, warned that American men would not stand for violation of their women. If the law fails, a man is justified in taking it into his own hands, the Admiral insisted.

It was in this atmosphere that Roosevelt, among his many pressing duties, had to make a decision concerning the future of Hawaii. Just as Wilson had done, he asked his Secretary of the Interior to look into the situation and make a recommendation. Interior Secretary Harold Ickes was anxious to break up the "sugar trust" in Hawaii, but he was doubtful that there was a Democrat in the Islands qualified for the job, especially after the turmoil caused by the Ala Maona case. At Ickes's request and with Roosevelt's support, Representative John E. Rankin of Mississippi introduced a bill amending the Organic Act to permit the President to appoint a mainlander as governor. For once, the oligarchy and local Honolulu Democrats were in agreement; they did not want a mainland man, in or out of uniform, to run Hawaii. Richard Cooke, whose brother George was president of the Senate, went to Washington to try to achieve the miracle of another Pinkham or McCarthy.[26] Dillingham, in Washington to get public-works contracts for his dredging company, did not hesitate to make his recommendation to fellow Harvard graduate Roosevelt.[27] The favorite candidate of the Republicans was the Territory's Chief Justice, James L. Coke.[28] McCandless, naturally enough, believed he was entitled to the appointment, but the Democrats in the legislature again opposed him.[29] He at long last had been elected delegate in 1932, partly because Houston was blamed for the release of Lieutenant Massie and his accomplices. This time, all but two of the Democratic legislators signed a petition in support of the popular Mayor of Honolulu, John Wilson. Wilson had powerful backing from James Farley, Roosevelt's Postmaster General and chairman of the Democratic National Committee. Farley had promised Wilson before the election that Roosevelt would deal only with the duly accredited Democratic organization in the Territory, whereupon Wilson came out for Roosevelt prior to the Chicago Democratic convention.[30] What counted with Farley was that Wilson had persuaded the Hawaii delegation to the Chicago Democratic convention to support Roosevelt, whereas others, two of whom were also self-designated candidates for the gubernatorial post, had wanted an uninstructed delegation. Roosevelt had begun corresponding with Wilson as early as January 1929, correctly judging, probably on the advice of Farley, that Wilson was the most influential Democrat in the Islands.

But Wilson was loyal to the candidacy of McCandless until the President and Farley made it clear that they would not risk losing the delegateship for the party in a special election by naming McCandless as governor. The President explained that many congressmen had been turned down for jobs on just that principle. It was at that point that Wilson, who had been a delegate to Democratic conventions six times, mayor of Honolulu three terms, and a Democratic committeeman for over twenty years, entered the race for the governorship. There were other candidates. Secretary of State Cordell Hull and Senator Kenneth McKellar, both from Tennessee, pushed fellow Tennessean Ingram M. Stainback, who had come to Hawaii to practice law in 1912 and served as territorial attorney general under Pinkham.

McCandless's letters to his brother, James, showed that he still desperately wanted the nomination, and when he was turned down, he focused his wrath on John Wilson, whom he blamed for standing in his way.[31] After his private campaign failed, McCandless wrote Farley complaining of Roosevelt's failure to reward the Democrats of Hawaii.[32] On June 12, he met with the Democratic political boss to nominate Dr. Rufus H. Hagood for governor. Farley promised to discuss it with the President, but months went by with no action from the White House.[33] Hagood, who had been McCandless's campaign manager in 1932, wrote his friend, serving as delegate in Washington, of the story that John Wilson was being backed by the Japanese community.[34] The rumors, probably sped by Hagood and McCandless, prompted a secret Department of Justice investigation of Wilson's alleged "Japanese backing."[35] McCandless's enmity toward Wilson grew when he received a letter from Delbert Metzger explaining that Wilson's friends had approached him with proposals to have Wilson become governor and then run for delegate in the fall to make way for Metzger's appointment as governor. "This is just dirty *kanaka* politics and spells nothing but treachery," wrote the usually tolerant Metzger, stirring the latent racism in McCandless.[36] Despite Farley's efforts, Wilson's campaign sputtered in the face of strong oligarchy opposition, McCandless's growing enmity, and the implacable racism of the U.S. Navy.

Supporting Hagood, McCandless begged Louis Howe, the President's closest adviser, to persuade Roosevelt to make an appointment soon. He pointed out that the Republicans had controlled the legislature for thirty-three years. "Mr. Howe, I plead with you to let us have a Democratic administration. We have had enough of Republican rule. . . ." The date was September 1, 1933, almost half a year after Roosevelt's inauguration, and not one Democrat could be appointed in the territorial departments of Public Works, Education, Public Lands, Health, Treasury, or the Attorney General's office until a new governor was in charge. The Democrats were starved for patronage, and Mc-Candless urged Howe to follow the recommendations of the Democratic Territorial Central Committee.[37] But Roosevelt was dilatory. He was waiting for the Rankin bill, which was still stumbling in Congress, and he was annoyed because Farley and Ickes and the Democrats in Hawaii could not get together on a candidate.

The break between Wilson and McCandless was complete. Wilson's friend wrote that McCandless represented the "selfish, double crossing haoles and carpetbaggers. . . ."[38] Wilson had written that Metzger's intentions were probably all right, and that he was a little better than McCandless and the rest of the haole Democrats in the Territory.[39] Honolulu's jaunty Mayor felt justified in bucking the recommendation of the Central Committee because of Roosevelt's unwillingness to appoint the seventy-four-year-old McCandless. He was encouraged by widespread support among the precinct clubs throughout the Territory and could not understand why McCandless would oppose him once the old man's chances were gone. Wilson wrote, "It looks to me that it has boiled down to a racial issue. I do not know of another reason that Linc has or any of our other haole Democrats from the South, have against me."[40] A part-Hawaiian friend of Wilson denounced Mc-Candless for saying that it was a mistake to appoint a Hawaiian as governor. He wondered how Linc would dare raise such a question, charging that McCandless had spent a lifetime "debauching Hawaiian women. . . ."[41] McCandless's remarks against Hawaiians were especially surprising since he had won heavily in Hawaiian districts in the 1932 campaign by exploiting Houston's advocacy of a pardon for the naval officer convicted of murdering the local boy in the Ala Moana case.

The campaign of mutual recrimination angered Ickes. Finally, on January 8, 1934, Wilson, encouraged by Farley, visited the Secretary of the Interior. Ickes accused Democratic leaders in Hawaii of being selfish. He said he would prefer to find someone who was not connected with politics or big business, or perhaps a mainlander who would be free from control by the Big Five. The people of Hawaii would be better off if the Rankin bill were allowed to pass, he pointed out.[42]

Two new names were presented to Ickes for consideration. One, Oren E. Long, Superintendent of Public Instruction, had been mentioned by some of Ickes's relatives. The other, Joseph Boyd Poindexter, had served as a U.S. district court judge in Hawaii between 1917 and 1924. Poindexter, an Oregonian, then settled down in the Islands to practice law. It was Poindexter who finally received the appointment, fully one year after Roosevelt had assumed office. Unlike Pinkham, Poindexter was a legitimate Democrat. He filled fourteen of the twenty-three major appointive posts with Democrats, including such key slots as public works commissioner, treasurer, tax commissioner, and Public Welfare Department head. But Poindexter was suited by neither temperament nor conviction to lead the New Deal revolution in Hawaii. Seemingly insensitive to the growing political importance of the nisei, he made no efforts to bring them into his administration. He made no policy proposals to break the oligarchy's hold on Hawaii. He had not protested when Richard A. Cooke was appointed the first civil works administrator in the Territory or when Cooke acted to reduce pay and increase work hours for Civil Works Administration employees on the grounds that high wages would disrupt the wage scale of Hawaii's agricultural industries, a position overruled in Washington and leading to Cooke's resignation. Other key Republican leaders received important federal appointments from the New Deal administration, apparently with Poindexter's endorsement. With no fundamental roots in the Democratic party of Hawaii, Poindexter was more concerned with an efficient and economical administration than with building a political organization. For eight months, Poindexter failed to appoint anyone to his cabinet and kept some 2,000 Republicans on the payroll, to the dismay of patronage-hungry Democrats. On the outer islands, Republicans continued to control patronage although a Democrat sat in Iolani Palace.

Poindexter probably had more sympathy for labor and nonhaoles than any of his predecessors. He helped provide housing for Filipino strikers at a grove on Molokai near the village of Kaunakakai during the 1937 strike on Maui. He did not believe in the strike, however, and, with the support of President Manuel Quezon, of the Philippines, he urged the strikers to go back to work and talk things over with their employers.[43] Neither he nor the President who had appointed him was seriously interested in transforming Hawaii's power structure. When

Roosevelt visited Hawaii in July 1934, he expressed an interest in deep-sea fishing and seeing some Hawaiians. He enjoyed a *hukilau* (group net-fishing) at beautiful Kahana Bay on windward Oahu, stopped to say hello to David Kaapuu, a vigorous advocate of old Hawaiian ways, and ate and drank his way through a series of receptions and luncheons given by the Army and Navy and Harvard graduates in the Islands.[44] He held no conversations with grass-roots political leaders, and his social schedule was so heavy that he was obliged to cancel projected visits to a sugar plantation and a pineapple cannery.

The Japanese and Chinese of Hawaii had hoped Roosevelt would take a special interest in them. The *Nippu Jiji* published a special forty-four-page edition attempting to portray the situation of the Japanese in Hawaii. The *Liberty News,* the largest Chinese newspaper, did the same for the Chinese community. The Waipahu Japanese Civic Club asked for an opportunity to meet Roosevelt and give him a gift to demonstrate that they were "eager in the desire to bring up good American citizens in our community."[45] But among the approximately 200 guests invited to the Governor's reception for Roosevelt on July 26, there were not more than three or four of Japanese origin and a similar number of Chinese descent. This was at a time when the president of the graduating class and the editor of the newspaper at McKinley High School were both nisei. When thirty-one guests sat down for dinner at Washington Place, not a single Japanese, Chinese, or Portuguese citizen was present; only one Hawaiian, the Speaker of the House, had been invited.[46]

Neglected by Washington, disappointed by the choice of a new governor and divided by factionalism, the Democratic party of Hawaii fell apart once again. The new factionalism was not just personal. One group, led by John Wilson, wanted to build the party through an alliance of liberal haoles, Hawaiians, and Japanese leaders. Wilson wanted a multiracial party; he himself was a multiracial man. His father, who was Irish, Scotch, Hawaiian, and Tahitian, had been the marshal of the Kingdom under Queen Liliuokalani, and his mother had been one of the Queen's favorite ladies in waiting. Married to the beloved Hawaiian hula dancer, Aunt Jennie Wilson, he felt a deep kinship with the natives of the Islands. But unlike many of them, he was not anti-Japanese. Indeed, he befriended many young nisei, recognizing that the future success of the party would, in large measure, depend on them. Wilson complained to Farley in the spring of 1937 that Poindexter was

not giving enough attention to the various racial groups in the Islands
in distributing patronage. He pointed out that the Republicans had
never failed to appoint at least one or two Hawaiians and Portuguese to
the territorial judiciary, and it was disgraceful that the Democrats
seemed more exclusive than the G.O.P. in their appointments.[47] Delbert E. Metzger, then a federal district court judge, had written Farley
earlier that it was important to appeal to all groups and races, that they
must have "impartial and just consideration, according to number and
usefulness. The Democratic Party must have many friends among
the Japanese and Portuguese as well as the Hawaiians, else it had as
well close shop."[48] A liberal haole urged Farley to support Wilson's
nominees even if they were Japanese. They are American citizens, he
added, and are increasingly important.[49] One of them, George Watase,
requesting reappointment to the Liquor Commission, pointed out that
there were about 2,000 Japanese votes on Kauai and that it "takes a
lot of guts from my kind to come out publicly and stand up for the
Democratic Party...."[50]

Poindexter was largely indifferent to the effort to build a multiracial
party, and a number of key haole leaders were opposed to Wilson's
open multiracial approach. Federal District Judge Ingram Stainback,
influential in Washington, was regarded with suspicion by Hawaiians
in the party. After Stainback had urged a haole appointment coveted by
Wilson's friend William C. Achi, the Hawaiian wrote, "It is alright for
these haoles to play that kind of game . . . the haoles are united in this
respect and they get all they can while the getting is good."[51] Mc-
Candless moved increasingly into the camp of haoles and Portuguese who did not trust the Hawaiians and, especially, the Japanese.
He listened to his friend Manuel DeMello warn against too many Japanese appointments and correctly guessed that there was growing sentiment against him among nonhaoles in the party.[52]

McCandless' record as delegate to Congress between 1932 and
1934 deepened Democratic factionalism. In Congress, as all other
delegates had before him, he co-operated with the sugar interests to
protect the major industry of the Islands. Knowing that under free
competition Hawaii's sugar plantations would fail, McCandless fought
the Democratic Jones-Costigan Bill, which sharply limited Hawaiian
sugar production, and supported legislation that would permit Filipinos to go to the Territory as laborers but not to the mainland. Mc-
Candless, in his old age, had become conservative. He had built

extensive business holdings throughout the Islands, including the McCandless Construction Company, and complained to his brother in 1933 that Japanese truck drivers were getting too much money.[53] Wages on the sugar plantations were high enough, he thought, and the sugar tariff was indispensable to the economy of Hawaii.[54]

The Democratic party, never strong, fell on evil days in 1934 and 1935, at a time when Democrats throughout the mainland were triumphant. Wilson fought McCandless for nomination as delegate in a no-holds-barred primary election campaign in 1934. The Honolulu mayor sought and received the support of small Japanese Democratic groups, but McCandless was backed by the sugar interests, including Charles Rice and his powerful machine on Kauai.[55] Wilson received a plurality of votes in Honolulu, but McCandless won the nomination with victories on the outer islands. McCandless had joined the oligarchy to win on Maui and Kauai, wrote Wilson.[56]

The bitter fight smashed the Democratic party of Hawaii for the next twenty years. The Democrats lost three seats in the House of Representatives as McCandless went down to defeat in the contest for delegate; by 1939, they had lost an additional five, and only two of thirty members of the House belonged to the party of Jefferson and Jackson. McCandless was beaten in the election by part-Hawaiian Samuel Wilder King, whose father had been Minister of Justice under the Republic and whose conservative inclinations had made him a suitable representative of the Old Guard. Two years later, with McCandless dead, Republican King defeated Democratic candidate Bertram G. Rivenburgh, winning more than two thirds of the votes cast, while Democrat Franklin Roosevelt went on to a landslide victory on the mainland. The struggling Democrats on the Big Island, Maui, and Kauai were torn by personal differences—left in the wake of the great McCandless-Wilson battle—which went unattended by ministrations from Washington or Governor Poindexter.

Never had the weaknesses of the Democrats and the strengths of the Republicans of Hawaii been more fully demonstrated than they were in the 1934 election. McCandless charged that Wilson's opposition to him was responsible for the Democratic debacle.[57] The *New Freedom,* born twenty years before as an idealistic, progressive paper, devoted its last issues before expiring in 1935 to accusations against John Wilson for wrecking the party.[58]

Later, McCandless agreed that perhaps the Republicans were responsible for his defeat. He charged that sugar-plantation employees had been coerced to vote for King and that the Republican candidate had spent far more in his campaign than was permitted by the federal Corrupt Practices Act of 1925. King, he asserted, had filed false statements of campaign contributions and expenditures. Democrats had pushed the slogan "*Páa ka waha hóohana ka peni*" (shut your mouth and use your pencil), but plantation districts showed strong pluralities for King. Democrats testified that they were obliged to sneak into plantations when *lunas* were sleeping. Campaign workers explained that the laborers were afraid to vote Democratic and that managers instructed them on how to vote immediately before they entered the booths. The evidence submitted revealed the overwhelming probability that much more had been spent on King's behalf than the law permitted. When John Waterhouse, president of the Hawaiian Sugar Planters' Association, was asked if he knew of large contributions made to the Republican Central Committee, he declined to answer on the grounds of self-incrimination. John Russell, of Theo. H. Davies; Richard A. Cooke, of C. Brewer; and Frank C. Atherton, of Castle & Cooke, all refused on the grounds of self-incrimination to tell how much money they had given to the campaign in behalf of their companies. Despite the evidence, King, as is usual in such contests, was permitted to keep his seat. McCandless returned to Hawaii, a broken old man, his dream of the governorship now crushed, as, indeed, was the Democratic party of Hawaii.[59]

Despite the weaknesses of the Democrats, Republican control in Hawaii was not monolithic. The oligarchy dominated the crucial political pressure points in the Islands, but there was and could be no party line with respect to county government. In fact, the oligarchy maintained control over critical points partly because the Rices on Kauai, the Baldwins on Maui, the landlords of West Hawaii, and the managers of East Hawaii were permitted to run their own *kuleanas* as they saw fit. On each of the outer islands, government was highly personal and thoroughly Republican. Nowhere was this truer than on the island of Maui. There, Henry P. Baldwin and, later, his son, Henry A., ruled almost as completely as the chiefs of old. Because of the diligence of missionary son Henry P., who bought land cheaply from Hawaiians and Chinese, the Baldwins owned and managed the largest sugar plantation in the Islands. The Hawaiian Commercial & Sugar

Company was the economy of Maui. The *Maui News,* the island's only newspaper, was published by the Baldwins. The policies of churches and schools were largely decided by them. Probably nowhere in Hawaii, if anywhere in the world, was there so little democracy amid so much charity as on Maui. In their way, the Baldwins were extremely generous, especially devoted to charities sponsored by Christian churches. It was also their way to run the affairs of the island with a firm hand.

Henry P. Baldwin preferred not to hold public office. He was content merely to exercise power. To him, Governor Carter wrote on December 12, 1904, "Instinctively I turn to you for information on everything that happens in Maui."[60] Baldwin told the Governor to get some money to Maui to build roads where the Home Rulers were strong in order to win them over to the Republicans. If money was spent the right way, he urged, the Hawaiians, who were ready to jump to the party that did the most for them, would go Republican.[61] As clearly as anyone else, he recognized that Hawaiian votes would have to be curbed or managed if the oligarchy was to maintain control. It was almost impossible to win in an open contest against the Home Rulers, he complained, because of their appeal to Hawaiians along racial lines. It was important to control the Board of Registration on Maui, he pointed out, writing, "There are a great many of the 'barefoot kanakas' here on Maui that should not be allowed to vote, strictly speaking. The Board of Registration in the past, has been very lenient, allowing them to register if they could write their names, whereas the law requires them to be able to read and write intelligently."[62] Baldwin and his successors left nothing to chance, and in the years that followed, his work for Republican control was justified. Between 1909 and 1941, the Republicans, under the direction of the Baldwin family, completely dominated the Maui Board of Supervisors and its chairman. Of the 160 county officers elected during that period, only one was a Democrat.

Unlike his father, Henry A. (Harry) Baldwin enjoyed holding office. He was elected to the territorial Senate six times and to the delegateship in the special 1922 election following Kuhio's death. Each new governor learned to work through Baldwin in making appointments on Maui. When Farrington took office, for example, he was notified by the chairman of the Republican Territorial Central Committee that all Maui appointments were to be okayed by Baldwin for the Committee.[63] Baldwin's influence extended beyond Maui's shores. In 1922, the

hopes and fears of the oligarchy rested on his candidacy for the delegateship. Kuhio had died with no obvious Hawaiian successor, and the
Maui planter agreed to run in the special election against Lincoln
McCandless, who had already lost six times to the Prince. To help
promote victory, two part-Hawaiian Democrats were thrown into the
contest. Well financed, they toured the Islands, attacking McCandless
and praising Baldwin. The vote went heavily for Baldwin. A haole
friend remembers sitting with Baldwin's brother-in-law, Harold Waterhouse Rice, as precinct returns came in for Maui. Happy to see the
large Baldwin vote, Rice allegedly boasted that defectors would be
punished.[64]

After his election, Baldwin was more powerful than ever. When the
manager of the Kuhuku plantation resigned, Baldwin told Governor
Farrington to appoint him as the Territorial government sugar expert,
and the Governor was happy to comply.[65] The Maui high chief influenced Farrington on the disposition of government lands and continued to exercise power over gubernatorial appointments on Maui
throughout the 1920's and '30's.[66]

Probably no member of the oligarchy enjoyed power more than
Charles Rice, of Kauai. Like Baldwin, Rice, of missionary descent, was
frequently elected to the territorial legislature. He served in the House
between 1905 and 1911, and in the Senate between 1913 and 1936.
Rice ran what was probably the most efficient political machine in the
Territory. Partly because of temperament and partly because he was not
heavily invested in the sugar industry of Hawaii, Rice was occasionally
cantankerous in dealing with Merchant Street. It was not until he was
made manager of all American Factors plantations on Kauai in 1914
that the Honolulu oligarchy could count on Rice's sustained interest
in sugar. Even then, what mattered most was his power on Kauai. Much
less of a team man than Baldwin, he built a vast cattle business and
acquired the important Ford, Goodyear, and Shell Oil agencies for the
Islands, partly to remain financially independent of the sugar interests.

Rice's power sense had been inherited from his father, William Hyde
Rice, a missionary son turned rancher and sugar planter. The elder
Rice had served eleven years in the legislature under the monarchy and
the Republic. For the Rice family, politics was not an obligation; it was
a joy. With the advent of county government, Charles Rice had his
brother, William, appointed high sheriff of Kauai. Under Billy Rice
was a deputy sheriff for each of the five districts set up under the County

Home Rule Act, and five or six policemen under each deputy. It was through this political machine that Charles Rice ran Kauai. Favors were bestowed on friends, punishments meted out to enemies.

Rice generously used the carrot at least as much as he employed the stick. He systematically encouraged young Portuguese, Hawaiians, and even Chinese to run for office under his sponsorship. It did not matter as much to Rice as it did to Baldwin or others that they run as Republicans. Republican or Democrat, their main responsibility was to be loyal to Rice and Kauai. With his backing, a candidate could count on the enthusiastic support of the police.[67]

With respect to appointments for Kauai, Hawaii's governors listened to Rice. Governor Carter left it up to the Rice brothers to change election district lines on the Garden Island as they felt necessary.[68] Governor Frear wanted Charles Rice to tell him whom to appoint as chairman of inspectors of elections in the various precincts and districts.[69] Rice never hesitated to tell any of Hawaii's chief executives who should serve on the Liquor Commission, Board of Education, or other territorial agencies that included representatives from his island.[70]

When Charles Rice was made general manager for the American Factors plantations on Kauai, his power was considerably enhanced. Old-timers remember that it was impossible to get a supervisory job without his approval. When John Wilson asked fellow-Democrat Mc-Candless why he had recommended a certain appointment at Hana-pepe, the Delegate admitted frankly that Charles Rice wanted it.[71] Rice discovered that the election of a Democrat in Washington or even of a Democratic delegate to Congress did not cramp his style on Kauai. Rather, it was his friends in the oligarchy who gave him trouble. When Merchant Street failed to support him as chairman of the Senate Ways and Means Committee in the territorial legislature in 1936 because he demanded certain appropriations for Kauai, Rice sold property in Lihue to enable the mainland firm of Kress and a Japanese merchant to open two department stores in competition with American Factors' Lihue store. Prior to Rice's retaliation, it was virtually impossible for anyone to lease land in Lihue to compete with the Amfac outlet.

Economic revenge was not enough for Rice. He mailed a $1,000 check to support Roosevelt's candidacy in 1936. Correctly assaying F.D.R.'s bright prospects, he declared himself a Democrat, supported Roosevelt openly, and subsequently served as a delegate from Hawaii to three national Democratic conventions. Believing, also correctly, that the Democrats would be in power in Washington for a long period of time, Rice established his claim for Hawaii's share of patronage. He also predicted to confidants that Hawaii's nonhaole population would someday revolt against the Republicans and the plantations and stated that he did not want to be identified with the symbols of the past.[72]

Secretly, he made a personal loan to a radical labor leader who later became a powerful figure in the Islands. In 1938, he met quietly with members of the infant longshoremen's union, after which they worked hard for him in the 1938 Republican primary election to back a long-time Portuguese political follower, Clem Gomes, against missionary cousin Elsie Wilcox, for the Senate seat for Kauai. Miss Wilcox, Rice remembered, had opposed him in his fight to retain the chairmanship of the Ways and Means Committee two years earlier. Several of Rice's Portuguese and Oriental supporters were encouraged to switch parties with him. In 1938, Rice backed John B. Fernandes, who had joined the Republican party only three years before when he ran as a Democrat against plantation manager Lindsay A. Faye for Kauai's Senate seat. Despite strong efforts, Faye could not control his Portuguese *lunas* on Election Day. At Faye's plantation at Kekaha, the vote was one-sidedly Republican, but in the Portuguese precincts at Kapaa and Kalaheo the *bacalhaos* (codfish), as Faye had called them, put Rice's man over the top.

Unlike Baldwin, Rice confined his charity to politics. His greatest boasts concerned what he had done for Kauai. Fire stations, roads, and other benefits for the island paid for by the Territory remain as monuments to his great personal power.

Local politics on the Big Island was considerably more complicated than on either Maui or Kauai. On the Kona Coast of West Hawaii, the landed gentry—the Greenwells, Hinds, and Ackermans—ruled. In East Hawaii, the managers of the plantations and, later, William C. ("Doc") Hill, a haole businessman, dominated. In Kona, even more than on Maui, the gentry assumed its right to govern. The first of the Kona Greenwells, a British rancher, Henry M. Greenwell, accused of beating a Chinese cook to death in 1853, was acquitted by a jury of twelve Englishmen under the theory that *kanakas* could not be trusted to judge a white man.[73] After annexation, it was not always possible to control the votes of Hawaiians, but the haole *alii* of Kona, through their ownership of land, and aided by the Kuhio-haole alliance, were never shaken. With the advent of a coffee economy for the growing Japanese population of West Hawaii, Kona politics more than ever was land-poor politics. The two largest coffee mills of the area, one owned by American Factors and the other by the Hind family, were also the two biggest distributors of groceries and the major banking and insurance institutions of West Hawaii. The coffee mills made a profit from the groceries they sold, the loans they extended, and from the coffee they husked, grated, and distributed. The growers, happy to be off the plantations and away from the personal control of *lunas,* submitted to the domination of the mills and the families who leased the land of Kona. Many growers sneaked coffee, produced on their own mortgaged farm and promised to one mill, over to another mill in order to obtain cash for the family's immediate needs.[74]

The instruments of control were simple. Keep the farmers submerged in debt and threaten to take away their leased land. Leases were short and grocery costs were high. Economic survival in isolated Kona was far more important to the Japanese farmers than territorial politics. It made bad sense to oppose the haole landowners of Kona. The elite would run things the way it wanted anyway, just as it always had. After the death of the Home Rule party, there simply was no political opposition in Kona.

In East Hawaii, the picture was quite different. There, the managers not only managed, but, to some extent, owned the wealth. The height of their power was reached during the 1920's, when John T. Moir, John Ross, and others owned the controlling interest in the Bank of Hilo, the First Trust Company, the Hawaiian Insurance and Guaranty Company, a local transportation company, and other businesses. Many firms they did not control outright, such as the Hilo Electric Light Company, they influenced substantially.

A Hilo businessman remembers the cloudy morning in 1919 when managers Moir and Jim Henderson walked into his store and issued an ultimatum giving him six months to close up and get out. The tradition of managerial control in East Hawaii went back to the 1880's, when C. C. Kennedy, the manager of the Waiakea mill, and John Scott, manager of the Hilo Sugar Company, ruled the roost. Their principal protégé was Moir, a large, whiskered man, who was the closest thing to a political boss in East Hawaii before the advent of Doc Hill. As on Kauai, the police constituted the local political machine, and Sheriff

Samuel K. Pua worked with Moir and his friends to reward the faithful and punish the deviant.

Because of the absence of a powerful missionary family, the politics of East Hawaii were relatively fluid, and because of its distance from Honolulu, the influence of Merchant Street was indirect. In 1915, the Democrats actually won a majority on the county's Board of Supervisors, something that was impossible on Kauai or Maui. In only two elections between 1905 and 1941 did the Democrats fail to win at least one seat on the Board. After the Democratic upset in 1915, however, Republicans closed ranks, and not a single Democrat was elected in 1917 and 1919. In addition, popular Democratic politicians, among them Portuguese Charles Silva and Hawaiian James Kealoha, later to become Hawaii's first lieutenant governor under statehood, were persuaded to switch parties. One lifelong Democrat remembers two attempts by Republican agents to bribe him to come over through the promise of many clients for his law business. It was so much easier to be a Republican in East Hawaii.

In the late 1920's and early '30's, the manager-owners of East Hawaii began to die, leaving their wealth to sons and daughters who were divorced from the plantations, and the management of the plantations to men who had no roots or wealth in East Hawaii. Into this situation came William C. Hill. Born in rural poverty in the hills of North Carolina, as a boy Hill had moved with his family to Moscow, Idaho, in 1892. There, facing stark poverty, Hill quit school at twelve and ran away. He dug ditches, carried hod, watched cattle on trains to Chicago, picked fruit in Oregon, and worked as a day laborer on the Barbary Coast in San Francisco. There he signed on a freighter headed for Hawaii. In Hilo port, he jumped ship at the age of sixteen without a nickel in his dungares. A Hawaiian family fed and took care of Hill for five or six days before he got a job crushing ice in a drugstore in Hilo. Then, while wandering through a Chinese store, Hill took his first step on the path toward wealth and power in Hawaii. He bought four dozen pairs of eyeglasses at eighty cents apiece on credit. Into the plantation camps he trudged and cajoled and wheedled issei laborers, through a youthful Japanese helper, into buying his glasses at $4 a pair. Soon he learned to speak rudimentary Japanese. He filled his suitcase with jewelry and watches and chains, as well as glasses, because he knew that many issei wanted to own a watch and chain on their arrival back home in Japan. Shortly after World War I, Hill had saved enough money to go into his own jewelry business in Hilo. There he continued to make friends, and in 1928, he ran for the territorial House of Representatives. In the first election, the machine did not support Hill, and he was obliged to sneak into the plantations to reach his Japanese friends. In 1932, he ran for the Senate on the same ticket with plantation manager James Campsie and fared badly in the Japanese precincts on the Kona Coast, but well everywhere else. Hill was still bitter toward the sugar interests for their opposition to his jewelry store in Hilo, and they refused to accept him as a part of the team, beating him in his quest for re-election in the 1934 Republican primary. Outside politics, Hill was building substantial business interests, and in 1938, when he bought the Pacific Bottling Company, Hill made peace with the sugar planters. Already, Democrats on the Big Island were complaining that Hill controlled appointments through Democratic Governor Poindexter.[75] Hill was fast building his own political machine, based not on control of the police, but on an expanding network of economic interests.[76]

On Oahu, local politics was more competitive than anywhere else. A Democrat, part-Hawaiian Joseph J. Fern, was elected mayor in the first mayoralty election of 1908, only ten years after annexation. Six times more before Pearl Harbor, the Democratic candidate was elected mayor of the city and county of Honolulu, and twice the Democrats won a majority on the Board of Supervisors. As Democrat Louis Cain told Senator Arthur H. Vandenberg, of Michigan, in a letter in the fall of 1934, people in Honolulu have the right to vote freely.[77] It was in Honolulu that opposition newspapers repeatedly emerged. Some were of the old Hawaiian type, vestigial supporters of royalty. Others were the *malihini* haole papers, among them the *New Freedom*. And there were also the foreign-language papers, such as the *Hawaii Hochi* and *Nippu Jiji*. These papers, and there were dozens, did not have large circulations, but they were read and followed.

The web of oligarchy was not airtight; especially in Honolulu, dissent was possible. Who got a new library, parks, or roads did not matter so much. What counted was control over the crucial pressure points of Island politics—the delegate, the governor, and the territorial legislature—and in these, the oligarchy, because of the Kuhio–Merchant Street alliance, control over the plantation vote, and the weaknesses of the territorial Democratic party, was remarkably successful.

NO CONCESSIONS
WHATSOEVER

To the planters of Hawaii, the labor problem was clear-cut: to get enough workers, to get them cheaply, and to keep them on the plantations. "The experience of sugar growing the world over goes to prove that cheap labor, which means in plain words servile labor, must be employed in order to render this enterprise successful."[1] So spoke the *Planters Monthly,* organ for the sugar planters of Hawaii, in 1882, and within the next two years, the government of Hawaii spent nearly half a million dollars recruiting and transporting laborers to the Islands to meet the voracious demands created by the Reciprocity Treaty with the United States.

The planters had tried Hawaiian labor without success, although every legal effort had been made to keep the workers on the plantations. In 1841, a law was passed authorizing the collection of fines or the withholding of wages for procrastination or inefficiency. Nine years later, a new statute provided that "no native subject of the King may leave the Islands without express permission given on proved necessity."[2] In addition, each plantation made its own rules to keep the wandering, fun-loving *kanakas* hard at work in the fields. At Waihee, it was specified that no laborer could leave the plantation without permission; nor could he raise his hand in an aggressive manner or incite others to acts of insubordination. At Kohala, no card playing was permitted, and laborers were requested to attend church every Sunday and prayer meeting every Friday morning. Workers could not leave the plantation by day or night without consent of the manager or *luna.*[3]

Contract labor was legalized under the Masters' and Servants' Act of 1850. Boys from the ages of ten to twenty and girls from ten to eighteen could be apprenticed by their parents to a planter, and adults could contract themselves as indentured servants. Even more important to the future of Hawaii's sugar industry was the provision for the importation of contract labor for terms up to ten years. Under this statute thousands of Orientals, first Chinese and then Japanese, were recruited and transported to the Islands. Contracts were bought and sold, and workers were thrown into jail for breaking plantation rules. Contrary to law, flogging for disobedience was a common practice. In the planters' defense, a mainland scholar, writing in 1903, found that the horrors of the "coolie" trade as practiced in other countries were not matched in Hawaii, and she found the contract system to be "the only practical method of securing labor in a country so remote from the source of supply...."[4]

Suddenly, through annexation, the U.S. Congress halted contract labor. The penal contract, Congress decided, was foreign to the American spirit, as were Hawaii's property qualifications for suffrage. Most planters, anticipating the restrictions imposed by Congress, had opposed annexation. The representatives sent from Honolulu to Washington to negotiate annexation in 1893 were instructed to ask for the continuation of Hawaii's immigration policies.[5] But in 1898, the year of annexation, America's Chinese Exclusion Act of 1882 was extended to Hawaii. Under the Organic Act, the further importation of contract labor was forbidden and all existing contracts canceled after annexation day. A major source of supply—China—had been cut off, and a principal method of labor control had been abolished.

The planters ingeniously discovered other supply bases, and within the first ten years of territorial government, patterns of planter control were established. The first was to recruit laborers who were ignorant, illiterate, if possible, and docile—workers who would be satisfied to remain on the plantations. When it was suggested that American Negroes be imported to fill Hawaii's labor needs, a correspondent wrote the *Pacific Commercial Advertiser* that "the time has been when a Negro could be ordered and even driven; but that time has passed . . . a Negro will not submit to a scolding or cursing while in the discharge of his plantation duties, and prides himself upon a freedom to 'talk back' when abused by his employer. This would most likely displease a luna, whose charge had been the management of a set of Chinese who never dared venture a reply...."[6] To help control workers, a law, carried over from the penal code of 1869, provided that a police officer might arrest without warrant any person whom the officer suspected of intending to commit an offense.[7] The *Advertiser* warned that the remedy for those Japanese who were not obligated to stay on the plantations under their contracts was to "enforce the vagrancy law without giving the coolie much benefit of the doubt."[8]

Co-operation could be won only through intimidation, thought most planters. Offer the "coolie" a compromise, warned an *Advertiser* editorial, "and he regards it as a sign of fear; yield to his demands and he thinks he is the master and makes new demands; use the strong hand and he recognizes the power to which, from immemorial times, he has abjectly bowed. There is one word which holds the lower classes of every nation in check and that is Authority."[9] The *Advertiser*'s advice reflected the dominant mood of plantation management and represented the response of managers and *lunas* to the petty annoyances and walkouts of Japanese workers that followed annexation. The U.S. Commissioner of Labor reported in 1902 that although it was against the law to handle laborers brutally, many beatings were still administered.[10]

When Puerto Rican citizens complained in the San Juan *News* of ill treatment at the Koloa plantation on Kauai, the acting U.S. Secretary of the Interior asked Governor Dole to investigate. After a delay of more than six months, Hawaii's acting Governor, Henry E. Cooper, requested a report from W. O. Smith, the secretary of the Hawaiian Sugar Planters' Association, gratuitously adding that "I feel confident that there has been no such ill treatment as is alleged by the complainants."[11] Smith, in turn, passed the request on to the manager of the plantation from which the complaints had come, but not before telling Cooper that he was certain that labor agitation came from restless and disaffected Puerto Ricans in Honolulu rather than from the plantation itself. Manager McLane not only denied all charges of ill-treatment, but submitted an extraordinarily literate statement signed by the ten allegedly disaffected Puerto Ricans, who retracted their accusations of cruel and unfair treatment. Such charges were misleading, they now asserted, and were made at the behest of radical countrymen who had persuaded them to sign the letter to the San Juan *News*. They told investigators that the workers were well and happy and pointed out that the manager had been especially good to them. In the meantime, the High Sheriff of the Territory of Hawaii received a letter from an assistant officer assuring him that any Puerto Ricans who had quit one plantation job were refused employment by other plantations.[12]

Plantation intimidation was backed by police co-operation. When 1,700 Japanese refused to work at the Pioneer Sugar Company at Lahaina, Maui, in 1905, the Maui police dispersed the mob, killing one Japanese laborer and wounding two others.[13]

Also contributing to the control of immigrant labor were two attachés from the Japanese consulate, who assisted plantation management and the police in the Lahaina strike. The sugar merchants usually received help from the representatives of the Chinese, Japanese, and, later, Filipino governments in quelling disturbances on the plantations. After all, the consulates were only fulfilling the obligations of friendly countries. It was far better, the planters agreed, to have conservative government officials represent the laborers than to have agitators in their midst. Soon after annexation, the Japanese Consul General organized the Central Japanese League, expressly for the purpose of representing his countrymen in labor disputes, which he hoped could be prevented from growing into strikes. He placed posters throughout the Islands in English and Japanese, urging his countrymen not to leave Hawaii for the mainland, but to honor their nation by remaining on the plantations.[14]

Because hundreds of Japanese were able to find jobs in towns and even to ship to the mainland, new methods of control were devised. In March 1903, a resolution was passed by the Executive Committee of the Republican Territorial Central Committee, which said that Asiatic labor should not be employed on public works in the Territory, because the workers were needed on the plantations. Within a few months, this resolution was voted into law. Business firms in Honolulu were discouraged from hiring Japanese. Employing 400 men between them, the two major companies manufacturing and repairing sugar-mill machinery refused to hire Asians.[15]

But many Japanese, lured by dreams of big money and driven from Hawaii by plantation conditions, continued to leave for the West Coast. In 1902, more than 1,000 left Hawaii for the mainland. Two years later, 6,000 left, and in 1905, over 10,000 departures were listed.[16] Hawaii's plantations found it difficult to compete with the advertisements of the Great Northern and Western Railroad. After warning Delegate Kuhio to fight any immigration law that would impose educational qualifications on immigrants coming to Hawaii, Governor Carter suggested in 1904 that it might be a good idea to have such legislation to keep laborers from leaving the Territory for the mainland.[17] A year

later, a law was passed by the Territory's legislature fixing a high
license fee for agents recruiting labor to work outside the Territory and
punishing by fine anyone who worked without a license.[18]

It was not until 1917 that Congress legislated against Japanese going
to the mainland from Hawaii. Long before then, planters had begun to
look for labor sources other than Japan. They recognized that to control labor it was not enough to have a surplus. The surplus should be
made up of many different nationalities, since any one country might
be cut off, as was Japan through the Gentlemen's Agreement in 1907.
Just as important, a variety of nationalities could be aligned against
each other. "Keep a variety of laborers . . ." urged the manager of the
McKee Sugar Company in 1895, "and thus prevent any concerted action in case of strikes, for there are few, if any, cases of Japs, Chinese,
and Portuguese entering into a strike as a unity."[19]

The Japanese had once been welcomed as a way of stopping the
Chinese threat, just as the Chinese had been welcomed to replace the
recalcitrant Hawaiians. Now Puerto Ricans, Koreans, Spanish, Rus-
sians, and Filipinos would be used to keep the Japanese in their place.
After a Japanese strike at Waipahu on Oahu, in 1906, the *Pacific
Commercial Advertiser* complained:

A more obstreperous and unruly lot of Japanese than Waipahu is cursed
with, are not to be found in these Islands. . . . The Japanese Consul, once
all-powerful among laborers of his race in Hawaii, meets insults and threats
on every hand. . . . To discharge every Jap and put on newly-imported
laborers of another race would be a most impressive object lesson to the
little brown men on all the plantations. . . . It would subdue their dangerous
faith in their own indispensability. So long as they think they have things
in their own hands, they will be cocky and unreasonable. . . . Ten or fifteen
thousand Portuguese and Molokans in the fields would make a vast difference in the temper of the Japanese.[20]

A year earlier, the territorial legislature had told the Board of
Immigration to secure rates with transportation companies for the
importation of laborers from southern Europe, but planters found
white laborers far more expensive than Orientals, and the European
ventures of the Hawaiian Sugar Planters' Association waned.

The planters, annexation notwithstanding, had visions of renewing
the importation of Chinese workers. Every gubernatorial report between 1901 and 1905 urged a modification of the Chinese Exclusion

Act. As Governor Carter wrote in 1904, "It would be of great advantage to the agricultural interests of these Islands . . . if there could be a modification of the Chinese Exclusion Act, permitting the immigration to these Islands of a limited number of Chinese agricultural laborers, such laborers to be restricted to agricultural labor and domestic service and strictly prohibited from engaging in mechanical and mercantile pursuits."[21] Under America's immigration laws, the Chinese would be trapped in Hawaii, frozen in their jobs on the plantations, and, unlike the Japanese, not permitted to go to the West Coast. A mainland official observed that the admission of Chinese peasants was thought by the plantation interests to be "the best practical way of escape from the present evils of Japanese competition and economic domination."[22] Lucius Pinkham, before he was governor of Hawaii, was appointed chairman of a commission, paid by the sugar planters of Hawaii, to investigate the feasibility of changing the Chinese Exclusion Act.

Many haole merchants, professional men, and artisans still opposed the large-scale importation of Chinese. Closer to their point of view than to that of the sugar interests, the *Pacific Commercial Advertiser* pleaded for European immigrants, not Asians.[23] The Americanization of Hawaii was the immediate and passionate aim of these groups, not the importation of more Orientals. They agreed with the haoles in wanting to restrict the Orientals to the plantations, and to keep them out of the towns, where they competed with haole tradesmen and skilled and semiskilled workers. Bills were introduced in the legislature in 1905 to regulate trades such as blacksmithing, carpentry, electrical work, and harness making in which much higher license fees were stipulated for aliens than for citizens. Other bills were introduced but not passed: a measure providing for stringent tenement-house and building regulations, intended to raise rental fees for Chinese and Japanese in Honolulu; a law forbidding the purchase of materials and supplies by the Territory from an alien; and another obliging alien merchants selling spirits, working as boatmen, or running pool halls, bowling alleys, or livery stables to pay double license fees.[24]

Efforts to harass the Japanese in town and render them obedient on the plantations did not succeed as well as the planters had hoped. Many methods for controlling labor had been used—maintaining a surplus, playing race against race, keeping aliens out of the city, restricting government jobs, prohibiting laborers' movement to the mainland, working through foreign consuls and police officials, and intimidation—but despite them all, spontaneous labor movements did emerge.

Sporadic protest movements on the plantations went unnoticed by mainland unions and unaided by the infant haole craft unions in Honolulu. West Coast unions fought annexation; the American Federation of Labor and the Knights of Labor protested against this potential threat to their members. The unions were afraid that Orientals would migrate from Hawaii to the mainland and that factories might move to Hawaii to exploit the cheap labor.[25] Following annexation, haole artisans in Honolulu tried, with sporadic success, to organize the boilermakers, electrical workers, machinists, plumbers, blacksmiths, longshoremen, and others.[26] In 1903, the skilled and some unskilled Caucasian workers in Hilo, approximately half of whom were Portuguese, formed the Federation of Allied Trades to check the spreading Oriental competition,[27] but any effort to organize labor for collective-bargaining purposes met with strenuous disapproval and opposition from Hawaii's employers, and by 1907 the craft unions in Honolulu had almost disappeared.[28]

Hawaii's first industrial union, the Higher Wages Association, was formed in 1908, by a small group of Japanese in Honolulu who decided that their countrymen could never win higher wages and benefits on the plantations through unco-ordinated, intermittent strikes. Encouraged by the Gentlemen's Agreement, which dammed the flow of Japanese strikebreakers, the Association called Hawaii's first major strike in May 1909 against some of the larger Oahu sugar plantations. Strike leaders protested wage-rate differentials, which paid Caucasians a third more than Oriental field hands for the same work. Also offensive to the planters was their request that workers be granted an acre of good land and a decent cottage to "give Hawaii a middle class of substantial citizens."[29]

The angry planters retaliated by paying strikebreakers, mostly Hawaiians and Portuguese, double wages, or $1.50 a day.[30] The Hawaiian Sugar Planters' Association refused to consider a wage increase or to meet any of the workers' grievances while the strike was on. Their policy—not to recognize any union as a legitimate bargaining instrument—was to be followed for the next quarter of a century. The 1909 strike dragged on for nearly a month, and its leaders, editor Yasutaro Soga and two staff members from the *Nippu Jiji* and Fred Makino, then a drugstore proprietor, were arrested on charges of conspiring to impoverish a plantation by calling a strike. On August 22, they were found guilty, fined $300 each and sentenced to ten months in jail.[31] As Governor McCarthy described it some years later: "The planters, through their attorney in Hawaii, steamrolled those Japanese—the leaders—put them out of business, and they put some of the leaders of this strike in jail. . . ." The strike was thoroughly smashed.[32]

After that, wages were increased, working conditions on the plantations improved, and the bonus system was instituted to improve worker incentive. But managers, mindful of the need to punish the Japanese for their impudence, replaced many Japanese overseers and mechanics with Caucasians and Hawaiians.[33]

Plantation paternalism expanded between 1909 and 1919—new houses, better sewage and water systems, and expanded medical services. Still, a Woodrow Wilson progressive from the mainland, journalist Ray Stannard Baker, called the conditions of the sugar workers "serfdom." He quoted a plantation official as saying that although Japanese nisei were entitled to homesteads as much as any other citizens, "the problem with us is to interpret the law so none of them can get in." When Baker asked one of the big planters on Maui if he thought the coming generation of Japanese would make intelligent citizens, he was told, "Oh, yes, they'll make intelligent citizens, alright, but not plantation laborers—and that's what we want."[34]

In 1915, the legislature passed a Workmen's Compensation Act, which a representative from the Labor Department in Washington described as more satisfactory for management than for the workers. He concluded that the employees of large business enterprises, except some transportation companies, had probably been better cared for under the old system of private compensation for medical and surgical expenses. The new Act provided surgical, medical, and hospital benefits for the first fourteen days, but not to exceed $50, and allowed for only 60 per cent of wages during the period of temporary total disability. In case of death or permanent disability, the law did not define the rights of workers. The Act did, however, provide for employees of many small enterprises theretofore neglected.[35]

The 1909 strike had been broken in part by the failure of racial groups to co-operate. Seven years later, a strike was called by the International Longshoremen's Association's small local, composed mostly of Hawaiians and Filipinos, but including some Japanese, at the McCabe, Hamilton and Renny docks. This time it was the Japanese who served as strikebreakers. One Japanese contractor boasted inaccurately that no Japanese stevedore would join the strike, but "we will rely on the fair-mindedness and sincerity of the shipping companies. . . ."[36] When thirty-eight Japanese longshoremen did join the union, 150 Japanese strikebreakers were recruited. Other strikes in Honolulu in the postwar period were also defeated. Four hundred workers at the Honolulu Iron Works walked out in 1919 in sympathy with struck workers at another company whose leader had been discharged, given a steamer ticket, and told to leave the Islands immediately.[37]

Japanese leaders in Honolulu tried again to form a union of plantation workers in August 1917, under the ungainly title of the Plantation Laborers Wage Increase Investigation Association. Although its petition was turned down by the Hawaiian Sugar Planters' Association, in the following year groups from five Hamakua plantations on the Big Island organized their own higher-wages campaign. Other grass-roots movements for higher wages built up among the Japanese across the Islands. Although largely spontaneous, they were often encouraged by Japanese newspapers and businessmen.

In October 1919, seventy-five delegates from the Japanese Young Men's Association on Hawaii met at Hilo to call for an eight-hour day, overtime pay, increased wages, and an end to the bonus system. At Waialua, the Young Men's Buddhist Association asked for improved working conditions and better wages. A few days later, the Japanese Association of Hawaii, organized by Dr. Genshi Negoro, held a mass meeting in Honolulu, attended by Japanese school leaders, newspapermen, and contractors, and also by Pablo Manlapit and two Filipino laborers.

Manlapit, elected acting president of the newly formed Filipino Federation of Labor, visited his countrymen on the plantations of Oahu and sent delegates to Maui and Kauai to organize Filipinos there. The Filipino Federation of Labor, beset by quarrels among the leaders, was slowed slightly when Manlapit and his friends were arrested for holding a meeting on a government road at Waimanalo on October 29. But the eloquent Filipino agitator was released and left for the Big Island to carry on his campaign with the aid of young Japanese leaders there.[38]

Japanese unions were formed at more than a dozen plantations throughout the Islands during the following month. On Oahu, young leaders visited camps at night with lanterns and held secret meetings. About seventy workers met at Koloa on Kauai, to form a federation of Japanese laborers there; a Maui federation was organized at a temple school at Wailuku; and on December 1, on the Big Island, the Japanese Young Men's Association of Hawaii changed its name to the Hawaii Federation of Labor. Later in that month, the various island-wide federations that had been formed by plantation groups combined into the territory-wide Federation of Japanese Labor.

A committee representing the Federation at all the plantations on the Big Island now sent its first petition to the Hawaiian Sugar Planters' Association asking for a wage increase from seventy-two cents to $1.25 per day and substantial modifications of the bonus system, including the right of laborers to claim their bonuses in a court of justice. They demanded an eight-hour day, overtime pay for work on Sundays and legal holidays, and leave with pay for women laborers for two weeks before and six weeks after the delivery of their babies. In support of their position, the workers presented the results of their investigation of the prices of forty-five commodities, including food and clothing, showing an average price increase of 115 per cent between 1916 and 1919, while wages remained the same.[39]

The Association completely rejected the Federation's demands, pointing out that in 1919, an excellent year for sugar, the lowest-paid unskilled day laborer could earn $37.40 a month if he worked for his bonus to the limit. He had, in addition, a free house, fuel, and medical attention. "We do not deem it necessary," asserted the sugar officials, "to give consideration to the other remarks ... which are more or less repetitive of the agitators who are interested in starting trouble either from personal motives or because of the financial profit which they expect to derive from the contributions made by laborers." Dividends were not as high as claimed, said the Association. For example, in 1918, the sugar planters complained that they paid only 8.18 per cent interest on capital value, considered to be a low rate of interest in Hawaii, although payments were higher the following year.[40]

On January 3, Manlapit wrote the Federation of Japanese Labor that the Filipino group would strike on January 19, and asked his Japanese brothers to join in, "shoulder to shoulder."[41] There were mass meetings and fund-raising campaigns throughout the Islands, and on the 19th, more than 3,000 Filipino workers struck at Aiea, Waipahu, Ewa, and Kahuku, all on Oahu. The *Hawaii Shimpo* begged Japanese laborers to support the Filipinos, saying that "their problem is your problem. . . ."[42] The Japanese Federation had not yet decided to strike. The next day, a Filipino mob at Waipahu, harrying Japanese workers on their way to the field, was driven off by the manager and police. Within twenty-four hours, the Japanese at Waipahu decided on an indefinite layoff, the policy advocated by Federation officials. On January 22, the same officials ordered a general layoff on Oahu and sent an appeal for support to the outer islands.

The *Hawaii Hochi* asked, not for a layoff, but for a sympathy strike to show the Filipinos that the Japanese were reliable.[43] The *Hawaii Choho* warned the Japanese workers that between the Filipinos and themselves "there are no barriers of nationality, race, or color." On January 24, Oahu plantations were idle, and two days later, the Japanese Federation called for a general strike to begin on February 1.

The reaction of the business community was immediate and hostile. "By its action in calling a general strike of the sugar plantation laborers of Hawaii," said the *Pacific Commercial Advertiser,* "the Japanese Labor Federation has forced the issue on a question that has been looming larger and constantly larger during the past month. Is Hawaii to be an American territory or is it to be an Oriental province?" The *Advertiser* denounced Japanese Buddhist priests, newspaper agitators, and other "subjects of the Mikado" who had disturbed peaceful plantation relations. The workers should be locked out, and Japanese merchants in Honolulu supporting the strikers with their contributions should be boycotted. "What we face now is an attempt on the part of an alien race to cripple our principal industry and to gain dominance of the American territory of Hawaii," warned the *Advertiser.*[44] The *Nippu Jiji* immediately complained that the haole papers were distorting the issue. The strike was neither racial nor political; it was economic.[45]

Workers on the outer islands had not yet struck, perhaps because they feared police retaliation, which was always greater there than on Oahu. The *Advertiser,* in an editorial entitled "Not a Strike, but a Conspiracy," called for a lockout of all Japanese and Filipinos on Maui, Kauai, and Hawaii plantations.[46] John Waterhouse, President of the H.S.P.A., wrote that "the action taken by the Japanese Federation of Labor is, as we see it, an anti-American movement designed to obtain control of the sugar business of the Hawaiian Islands." The laborers would not strike, he said, since they were satisfied with plantation conditions but were afraid of the Japanese Federation.[47] On February 6, the *Advertiser* printed the names of fifty Japanese businessmen and white-collar workers who were supporting the strike, urging that these men be punished for their activities. On February 8, it called for the destruction of the Japanese press, asserting that it was "dangerous to the peace and prosperity of Hawaii." The foreign-language press "will always be dangerous. The only thing to do is to scotch it. Putting a muzzle on it isn't enough. That would be like muzzling a mad dog. It should be exterminated." The foreign-language-school system should be eliminated too: ". . . there is little reason to believe that it can be sufficiently controlled to render it safe."[48]

Then, suddenly, a quarrel erupted between Manlapit and leaders of the Japanese Federation. One of the Japanese officials remembers that Manlapit wanted not just gifts of rice for the workers, but more money for the Filipino Federation of Labor. Although he told his countrymen to go back to work, on Oahu plantations they refused. A Filipino Protestant minister, N. C. Dizon, disagreeing with Manlapit, complained that "the Filipino leaders have deserted their people. . . ."[49] The Federation continued to care for Filipino strikers in town when they trooped in from Aiea and Ewa. In another complete about-face, Manlapit announced on February 10 that the planters had tried to bribe him to attack the Japanese and call his workers back to the camps.[50] He would continue the strike, although he remained erratic in his statements to the press.

Manlapit's motives are not yet clear. When he had urged the Japanese in January to go out on strike with him, the Federation had delayed, asking the Filipinos again and again without success to postpone their strike. The Filipinos had placed great hopes in the Japanese, and Filipino workers suffered intensely during those few weeks in January before the Japanese laborers were called out. When the Japanese struck, Manlapit appeared mollified. Then came the sudden order calling off the Filipino strike, followed by the February bombshell: charges of bribery against the Hawaiian Sugar Planters' Association by the Filipino leader in the *Hawaii Hochi*.

When the *Advertiser* featured a story carrying Manlapit's charges against the Japanese Federation of Labor for its attempt to take over the Islands for Japan, the *Hochi* on the same day repeated the Filipino's allegations of planter perfidy. Manlapit said that he had been invited to an attorney's home and asked what he would do if $25,000 were placed on the table before him. Manlapit asked for $50,000, aware, he told the *Hochi*'s publisher, that a dictaphone and stenographer were in the next room. The planters' representative, lawyer Frank Thompson, gave Manlapit $500 to go to the mainland on the *Matsonia*. "If you don't leave Honolulu as we command we will have you arrested and put in jail," said Thompson, according to Manlapit, who said also that he had been warned by the haole lawyer to leave Honolulu before he was assassinated by Filipinos.

Thompson's side of the story appeared in the Honolulu *Star Bulletin* and the *Advertiser* two days later: Manlapit had complained bitterly against the Japanese for failing to deliver promised financial support and offered to call off the strike for $50,000. "I told him that I had no authority to offer anybody any money and that if I had he couldn't get a five cent piece out of me if he called the strike off that very minute," said Thompson. The lawyer did warn the Filipino that his countrymen might "sew you up in a bag," and offered Manlapit fare out of his own bank account to leave the Territory. At a second meeting, at the Hotel Moana, according to Thompson, Manlapit had asked for and received $500 so that he and his family could get a new start in California. The next morning, the money was returned, and Manlapit telphoned that he had made up his mind not to go, but as a good American citizen to stay and help break the Japanese Federation of Labor.

In mid-February, despite the delays of the Japanese and Manlapit's fluctuations, a large majority of Oahu's 5,871 Japanese workers and 2,625 Filipino laborers were on strike. The Hawaiian Sugar Planters' Association's retaliation was stepped up. Workers were forced to meet on government roads or in railroad stations. Mass evictions were ordered; a total of 12,000 persons were evicted, more than one third of whom were children. At Waialua, the manager gave Japanese workers three days to go back to work or be evicted from their homes for good. Hawaiian and Portuguese strikebreakers were brought to the camps at $4 a day, and Chinese and Koreans at $3. Orders were given, applauded in the *Advertiser,* not to enroll strikers' children in the Honolulu schools. Influenza, beginning in certain camps in January, spread throughout the Islands, and by mid-February it was estimated that of the 5,000 refugees in Honolulu, 1,200 were ill with the flu. In the refugee camp near Waialua, forty-three persons died within ten days.[51]

Some space for refugees was found in temples and churches, but it was not enough. The Board of Health forced groups to leave at least two temporary shelters. When refugees were evicted from the old *sake* brewery in Honolulu, Federation officials retorted, "Drive them anywhere if you please. Which is more sanitary, to have them sleep here or on the streets or in the parks?" At the Haleiwa camp, where twenty workers or members of their families had the flu, the manager cut off the water supply and locked the toilets, the *Nippu Jiji* said.[52]

The *Star Bulletin* and the *Advertiser* kept up their anti-Oriental attacks. Buddhism was a sinister influence behind the plantation strike, the *Star Bulletin* said.[53] Agreeing with the *Advertiser,* it complained about the "priests of Asiatic paganism," who were in an unholy alliance with foreign-language schoolteachers and Japanese editors "to control the industrialism of Hawaii. . . ." Hawaii must remain "in the hands of Anglo-Saxons whose brains and means have made the Territory what it is."[54] The *Advertiser* reported that confirmation of the racial character of the crisis had appeared in an editorial in the *Nippu Jiji,* which admitted that the strike had "taken on a color of internationalism."[55] It omitted the *Nippu's* refutation of the allegation. The *Advertiser* also quoted strike leader Takashi Tsutsumi as saying that the Japanese government was back of the strikers and that a Japanese cruiser would come to take them home but it did not print his denial of the story. Tsutsumi had written: "I am not an advocate of narrow Japanese imperial principles. But I am a staunch believer in democracy . . . under stars and stripes, Hawaii is a free country. It is because laborers are held fast by out-of-date Japanese principles, we have started this labor movement in order to enable them to display American spirit. . . ." Tsutsumi promised that the union movement in Hawaii would not adopt the violent policies of the Industrial Workers of the World.[56]

Actually, the Japanese strike leaders in 1920 were much more American in their outlook than their predecessors in the 1909 strike. There had been no male immigration to Hawaii for thirteen years, and it was the younger Japanese, educated in American schools, who largely provided leadership for the strike on the plantation level. The Consul General again took the conservative view. Like a predecessor in 1909, he tried to persuade the strikers to go back to work and settle their disputes amicably.

The 1909 strike had been 100 per cent Japanese. This one began with a walkout of Filipinos, who were joined by reluctant Japanese a few months later, and ended with 500 Filipinos still striking. Yet in

1920, much more than in the previous strike, planters attacked the laborers as being racially and nationalistically motivated. The Filipino union actually was undemocratically led by self-appointed agitators. Unlike the Japanese Federation, its units were not self-governing locals. Still, there was almost nothing hostile to the Filipinos in either of the major haole newspapers or in the statements of the Hawaiian Sugar Planters' Association. These newcomers were pictured as tools of the dangerous and sneaky Japanese. Given the difficulties in Filipino leadership and the efforts to arouse anti-Japanese sentiment among them, it is all the more surprising that so many Filipino workers— approximately 20 per cent of the force on Oahu—remained on strike to the unhappy end.

Health conditions in Honolulu, made worse by the presence of 5,000 refugees, alarmed Curtis Iaukea, who was acting as governor while Governor McCarthy was in Washington lobbying for changes in the Organic Act to permit the importation of Chinese laborers to Hawaii. Iaukea refused to side with the sugar planters. He reported pressure for him to petition the United States government to use military forces against the strikers. He replied to an attack in the *Advertiser* and the *Star Bulletin:* "It is a matter of history that armed forces of the United States were used to over-awe the Hawaiians at the time of the overthrow of the monarchy, and there seems to be a desire to repeat this measure of intimidation." Although Iaukea wrote a letter to Manlapit on February 7 asking him to call off the strike because 2,000 Filipinos in Honolulu without housing created a public-health menace, he consistently refused to follow the planters' line of attack. He agreed that the Japanese were keeping order and wrote to Governor McCarthy that the American press was the voice of the planters: "I am convinced that the racial issue has been deliberately emphasized to cloud the economic issue."[57]

While the strike was on, Governor McCarthy and representatives of the territorial legislature were in Washington co-operating with Delegate Kuhio for passage of the Hawaiian Rehabilitation Bill. They testified before the Senate Subcommittee on Immigration, urging a provision in the bill to prohibit the employment of aliens on federal projects. A part-Hawaiian representative complained that the Japanese were taking the best jobs from the natives. They pointed out that an alien Chinese was given a contract for the General Army Hospital and that hundreds of Japanese were used in the construction of Fort

Ruger, Fort Shafter, Schofield Barracks, and the drydock at Pearl Harbor.[58] The alien provision was slipped into the Rehabilitation Bill, but it was only one small step in the strategy of the planters to create such a large labor surplus that Hawaii would never again be confronted with a strike.

Neither the acting Governor's efforts to have the strike leaders call the workers back nor his desire to blunt the propaganda of the haole planters succeeded. It appeared that the walkout would continue indefinitely, when the Reverend Albert W. Palmer, of Honolulu's haole-elite Central Union Church, offered in a Sunday-morning sermon a new plan for ending the dispute. He contradicted the planters' assertion that the Oriental was inherently un-American. "One of the most disheartening things that I know of in Hawaii is the oft repeated formula: 'That may all be very well on the mainland, but you couldn't have it here, conditions are different. We have the Orientals to deal with.' . . . Isn't it about time that we wake up to the fact that we are part of America . . . ?" Palmer urged the strikers to go back to work and requested the Hawaiian Sugar Planters' Association to recognize the right of Oriental laborers to bargain collectively through a labor union. Iaukea praised the plan, but the *Star Bulletin,* with the first indication of the planters' reply, after praising Palmer's fairness, pointed out that the minister did not understand that the leaders of the present strike "must be utterly defeated and entirely discredited." Farrington argued in the *Star Bulletin* that Oriental laborers were not prepared for collective bargaining. If Palmer's plan were to be put into effect, "the foreign language schoolteachers and the priests on the plantations would, without a doubt, seize control of the laborers and of the collective bargaining machine." The newspaper reminded Hawaii's most important minister that the Islands' industry did not need the machinery of communism or bolshevism, but recognition of the fraternity of mankind and "of the fundamental principles of constructive Christianity."[59]

Palmer defended his plan in a letter to the paper. The Oriental who gives to the Red Cross and purchases Liberty Bonds would be capable of organizing a labor union, which is, after all, "typically an Anglo-Saxon organization." He pointed out that Japanese agitators could not control under his plan because no one race would be permitted to have a majority on any committee, and if labor negotiations failed, impartial arbitration by American citizens was provided for.[60] But the planters were not to be deflected by Palmer or Iaukea, who publicly doubted that there was any Japanese conspiracy to wrest control of the plantations from their present owners. The *Star Bulletin* ominously warned strikers that the sugar planters would never permit the conspiracy to Japanize Hawaii to succeed. "The sugar planters are definitely on record, pledged to break the strike, no matter how long it takes, no matter how much it costs. . . ."[61]

The most militant of Hawaii's Japanese newspapers, the *Hochi* and the *Choho,* also attacked the Palmer plan, which they viewed as unconditional surrender. But the Japanese Medical Society, Christian Ministers Association, Bankers Club, Chamber of Commerce, and two of the three largest Japanese newspapers, the *Nippu Jiji* and *Hawaii Shimpo,* applauded it. At first, many leaders of the Federation resisted the minister's idea, claiming that the plantation committees, having no relation to each other, would be under the control of plantation managers. But the pressure was great for Japanese leaders to accept the plan as a basis for negotiation. The *Nippu Jiji,* through editor Soga, urged Federation leaders not to repudiate the plan too quickly. On February 27, Palmer met with Federation officials, who agreed to support the plan and go back to work.

A turning point in the strike had been reached. Sensing the weakness of the workers, John Waterhouse, acting for the Sugar Planters' Association, declined to consider the Palmer plan and refused to discuss it with Federation officials. He clung to the planter reasoning that the strikers were determined to take over the sugar industry for Toyko.[62] For the next month, the strikers were under tremendous pressure. On March 18, there remained 400 flu patients among the striking Japanese in Hawaii. Six had died two days before.[63] Federation officials and Fred Makino began to quarrel over tactics.[64] Money was running low, and the haole newspapers kept up their drumfire of criticism against Japanese nationalism. In an editorial almost two columns wide, the *Star Bulletin* argued that the Japanese were inherently deceitful and incapable of co-operating with other racial groups.[65] The *Nippu* replied that the Japanese could not easily join hands with Chinese and Koreans, who frequently treated them as enemies, or with the Portuguese and Spanish, who were praised so fulsomely by the *Star Bulletin* and who received preferential treatment as laborers. Filipinos were the only group, it maintained, willing to co-operate.[66]

In March and April, police activity was stepped up against the strikers, and, in desperation, the striking laborers physically and

verbally attacked Japanese who returned to work. Stories and rumors
of kidnapings by Japanese against Japanese appeared in the *Advertiser*.
Early in March, a Japanese Federation member was indicted by a
grand jury for allegedly kidnaping a conservative nisei at Waialua.[67]
On April 3, the *Advertiser* printed on the first page a picture of two
conservative Japanese, anxious to go to work, who were allegedly
beaten by workers for the Japanese Federation of Labor. Soon
after another issei returned to work, his house at Waialua was burned
while he slept. The secretary of the Hawaiian Sugar Planters' Association, Royal Mead, in a startling admission, pointed out that the
older Japanese strikers wanted to go back to work, but that it was the
younger element—"those born here in American citizenship—who are
the most radical among the agitators." The *Nippu* counseled against
violence on March 5, but two days later, the *Advertiser* reported that a
Japanese laborer who had returned to work at Waimanalo was kidnaped by representatives of the Japanese Federation and later stabbed
one of his assailants in desperation.[68] The conservative *Hilo Kwazan*,
which had consistently opposed the strike, angered by Japanese violence against Japanese and distressed by the miserable condition of
wives and children of strikers, urged the workers to sever all connection
with the Federation.[69]

Federation officials called a meeting for April 20 of leaders from the
major islands to discuss the next step. The conference endorsed a
change of name from the Japanese Federation of Labor to the Hawaiian
Federation of Labor, prompting the *Advertiser*'s comment that "one
can't make a skunk cabbage smell like a rose by changing its name."
The delegates urged representatives of all races to join the Federation
and resolved to expel any member "tainted with Communism, radical-
ism, or anarchism."[70] The *Nippu*, now losing enthusiasm for the strike,
advised the Federation to think of the public interest and to realize
that some of the merchants who had supported the strike "are feeling
uneasy." The delegates nevertheless voted unanimously against unconditional surrender, boasting unrealistically that 5,000 plantation
workers, including 1,400 Filipinos and 300 other non-Japanese, would
remain out.[71] In a last-ditch move to prove its Americanism, the
Federation voted to apply for affiliation with the American Federation
of Labor. The *Advertiser* warned the local A.F. of L. that the Japanese
would infiltrate other labor organizations if the cane-field and mill
workers were accepted as an affiliate. "Do you want a little brown man

as a conductor on your car, to give you the signals and dictate to you?"[72] Haole labor will not go for that, promised the *Advertiser*. Heeding the haole paper's warnings, the national organization turned down the Federation's application.

The planters, whose 1920 crop had been insured for nearly $20,000,000, successfully fought a war of attrition against the strikers. Now, in May and June, they stepped up their campaign through judicial and police harassment. Already the plantations were producing 75 per cent of their normal output of sugar with the help of Hawaiian strikebreakers—"the mainstay of the plantations in the harvesting fields"—and others, including Portuguese, Chinese, Koreans, and Puerto Ricans.[73] But the planters did not like paying strikebreakers' wages and were anxious to end the walkout. Criminal prosecutions were started against a number of strike leaders and Japanese newspapermen. The first, against Pablo Manlapit for embezzlement, was not completed, but it frightened Manlapit. A true bill was presented against Yasutaro Soga for publishing libel in the first degree. Nine others were arrested for conspiracy to imprison and for kidnaping, but they were released without being prosecuted. Four were charged with assault with a dangerous weapon, and two of them were convicted. A year after the strike ended, twenty-one of the strike leaders on the Big Island were rounded up and charged with conspiring to commit the felony of inflicting bodily injury through dynamiting the house of a conservative issei at the Olaa plantation. Fifteen of the Japanese arrested in connection with the case were convicted and sentenced to not less than four years apiece. They were released after serving three years and one month in the territorial penitentiary.

One hundred and sixty-five days after the Filipino walkout, Hawaii's 1920 strike had been broken. With leaders under constant harassment, the strikers of Oahu were demoralized. The strike terminated at the end of June, and by the end of July, a majority of the strikers were back at work. "No concessions whatsoever, either direct or implied, were made," boasted John Waterhouse, who regretted that "we still have with us, however, the Japanese newspapers and Japanese and Filipino agitators whose main excuse for existence seems to be to create trouble. I doubt, however, that they care for a repetition of the lessons taught them this year."[74]

Full of shame, the bedraggled and defeated Japanese strike leaders were allowed to deliver their surrender in person to Waterhouse. Humiliated, they issued a statement acknowledging, "Today, John Waterhouse, representing the capitalists, shook hands with the representatives of labor. . . ." The controversy had been settled by the "magnanimity of the capitalists." Although their defeat was absolute, they tried desperately to save face by claiming at mass meetings in Aala Park, Waipahu, and Waialua that they had at least forced the president of the Hawaiian Sugar Planters' Association to meet them in person.[75] Plantation managers posted notices announcing that no new employees, including strikebreakers, would be fired to make a place for returning strikers, who would have to take available jobs and move into the houses assigned to them. Complaints would not be tolerated; those who complained would be fired.

It had been a year Hawaii would not soon forget. In the twelve months preceding July 1, 1,088 persons had died of influenza and another 416 of pneumonia, although most of these fatalities would probably have occurred had there been no strike. Many Japanese who had been connected with the strike were blacklisted. Strikers were told to return to work in the spirit of *aloha,* but thousands of them tried to find new jobs in town, and hundreds left for the mainland. In 1919, there had been 24,791 Japanese sugar workers in the Territory of Hawaii. By 1924, only 12,781 remained. On the plantations, following the strike, new wage and bonus schedules cut the differentials between races. The minimum wage rate was increased 50 per cent, and contract rates and wages of semiskilled employees rose. More than a million dollars was spent between 1921 and 1924 on extensive improvements in plantation and housing water systems. Paternalism, it was hoped, would pacify the laborers' demands for collective bargaining.

Chapter Nine

MERCHANT STREET VERSUS THE VOICE OF LABOR

The planters were determined not to face a repetition of the 1920 strike. They had tried without success to interest Congress in amendments to the Chinese Exclusion Act to permit the importation of Chinese laborers to the Territory. In April 1921, they decided it was time to try again. Outgoing Governor McCarthy, soon to become representative of the Chamber of Commerce, received a visit from Henry A. Baldwin and E. Faxton Bishop, now president of the Hawaiian Sugar Planters' Association, who proposed that he call a meeting to discuss the problem of Hawaii's labor shortage. At their suggestion, McCarthy summoned representatives of the two major newspapers, Jonah Kuhio, Speaker of the House Henry Lincoln (Linc) Holstein, and territorial Senate President Charles F. Chillingworth. Walter Dillingham represented transportation interests, Bishop the sugar planters, Albert Horner the pineapple industry, and William H. McInerny the retailers.

The group agreed that Hawaii needed a new labor supply and that China was the only potential source. Bishop drafted a resolution to be introduced in the legislature which authorized the governor to appoint a special commission to assist the congressional delegate in obtaining early relief for Hawaii's alleged labor shortage. The membership of the commission was: Walter Dillingham, as chairman, Charles Chillingworth, and Albert Horner.[1]

The resolution called for a proclamation by the President of the United States of a labor emergency in Hawaii and asked that the Secretary of Labor be empowered to admit to Hawaii for a period of five years aliens who would otherwise be inadmissible. The immigrants would be limited to agricultural and domestic work and would not be permitted to go to the mainland. Their number was not to exceed 20 per cent of the total population of the Territory.

A precedent was found in a law passed by the Republic in 1897 which provided that no Chinese except clergymen, teachers, merchants, and a few other special categories of persons who had previously lived in Hawaii be permitted to enter the Islands except for domestic service or agricultural labor in rice mills or in sugar plantations or mills. The intent of the commissioners was plain. By glutting the labor market, thousands of Japanese would be forced to return to Japan.

The Commission arrived in Washington on May 18, but the resolution was not introduced until June 20. Hearings were begun the following day before the House Committee on Immigration and Naturalization. Dillingham told the congressmen that field laborers in Hawaii were becoming restless and independent. Horner admitted that the success of sugar depended on cheap labor. He also explained that sugar and pineapple are to Hawaii what textiles are to New England; the entire economy pivots around the success of sugar.[2]

Governor Farrington, who also made the trip to Washington, acknowledged, perhaps inadvertently, that the planters had tried to break the strike with the co-operation of the Japanese Consul General and others representing the government of Japan, but that the workers had gotten out of hand.[3] Delegate Kuhio admitted that the planters always consulted the Consul General during labor troubles to seek his help in handling the Japanese, but now the workers were unmanageable. Royal Mead, speaking as a private individual, denied that there was any such thing as unemployment in Hawaii. "There are no idle men except men who wish to be idle." He explained that it had been the experience in the Islands that "the higher the basic wage is, the lower the turnout and less efficiency you will have."[4] Dillingham agreed. Representing his Hawaiian constituents, John Wise, territorial Senator who came from Hawaii to testify, complained that the federal government permitted its contractors to hire aliens and paid them $5 or $6 a day. "I am a Hawaiian who loves his country," boasted Wise, "and who loves it so deeply that he fought against the annexation of Hawaii to the United States and was only convinced that it would be the proper thing to go under the United States government after long and serious consideration of the matter, rather than to go under Japan."[5]

The commissioners not too skillfully presented dozens of similarly

worded communications from citizens of the Territory—haoles in
nearly every case, and many of them Dillingham's employees. A typical
letter, from John A. Hughes, a builder of cars for Dillingham's railroad,
repeated that it was contrary to nature's laws for white men to toil at
hard work "under an equatorial sun."[6] L. M. Whitehouse, an engineer
for the city and county of Honolulu, wrote: "The ideal laborer for this
situation is one who is thoroughly imbued with the idea that his mission
on earth is to wield a hoe and a cane knife and to cultivate the soil."[7]
Whitehouse explained that the haoles needed house servants as well as
laborers. Hawaii must go to China for labor, he said, because the only
laborers who succeed in Hawaii are those from the tropics.[8]

Dillingham was the planters' major spokesman for the resolution.
On August 13, the Honolulu industrialist opened his testimony before
the Senate Committee on Immigration by arguing that the importation
of Chinese "coolies" was necessary to prevent the eventual control of
the Islands by the Japanese.[9] When he was asked why white laborers
would not migrate to Hawaii from the mainland, he gave the standard
reply: "When you are asked to go out in the sun and go into the cane
brake, away from the tropical breeze, you are subjecting the white men
to something that the good Lord did not create him to do. If He had,
the people of the world, I think would have had a white pigment of the
skin, and not variegated colors."[10]

Dillingham, assisted by Royal Mead, painted a frightening picture of
the "Japanese menace." But the senators were not sufficiently frightened to take the quick action demanded, and besides, it was extremely
hot even for Washington, and senators were anxious to get away. Hearings were held for two days, and the Committee adjourned. Horner and
Chillingworth left for Hawaii on October 11, but Dillingham remained
until early November. They had spent nearly $21,000 of the money
appropriated by the territorial legislature for lobbying.[11]

The summer meetings in Washington had not been as successful
as Dillingham had hoped. The Senate Committee seemed indifferent,
occasionally bored. Three members of the House Committee had been
sympathetic to the arguments presented by the commissioners, but two
others were openly hostile and a third critical. A California congressman wondered how it would be possible to force a Chinese immigrant
to go home after the specified period of five years called for in the
resolution if he had married an American citizen. John Wise thought

there would be no trouble, because the Chinese would come to the Islands with the idea of going back in five years.

Mr. [John E.] Raker: Suppose he refused to go; how are you going to get him home?

Mr. Wise: Then we take him home.

Mr. Raker: By force?

Mr. Wise: By force if necessary.

Mr. Raker: If to that union there should be born a child, could you tear him away from that child, born in that country, tear him away by force and send him home, would you? Do you want that kind of law to be passed by Congress, to become effective in the Hawaiian Islands?

Mr. Wise: Yes, I do want it.[12]

Representative James W. Taylor, of Tennessee, was curious about the emphasis Hawaii's haoles gave to the inability of white men to work in Island heat. When he asked Dillingham what the average summer temperature was in Hawaii, the Islands' leading industrialist replied that he did not know. Apparently aware of a trap, Dillingham explained that although the temperature might not be as high as it was in many places on the mainland, the heat was of a different kind, intolerable for white workers.

For the most part, the congressmen on the Committee were as anti-Oriental as the proponents of the resolution. But that did not necessarily help the cause of the commissioners. Indeed, many congressmen could not understand why the haoles desired to import Chinese, since the latter were, in their view, just as bad as the Japanese.

The commissioners also met greater opposition from organized labor than they had anticipated. Representatives of the A.F. of L. and George W. Wright, a machinist who had become editor of the English-language section of *Hawaii Hochi* and was now president of the Honolulu Central Labor Council, argued that there was no actual shortage of labor in the Territory, but that men were being driven off the plantations by evil labor conditions. The Central Labor Council was a voluntary grouping of organizations qualified to be affiliated with the A.F. of L., and included representatives of Hawaii's small unions—the teamsters, boilermakers, barbers, carpenters, electrical workers, machinists, painters, plasterers, plumbers, sailors, hod carriers, and others. These unions, with a combined membership of only about

1,200, had had an off-and-on, hand-to-mouth existence since annexation, and they were unable to win recognition from the employers of
Hawaii for collective-bargaining purposes.

According to Wright, he had received visits from Dillingham, Chillingworth, Horner, Bishop, and other representatives of the sugar plantations, who tried to persuade him and the Central Labor Council
to support the resolution calling for the importation of Chinese laborers.
Wright complained that the oligarchy leaders had given information
to the newspapers suggesting that such support had been won. Actually,
he charged, they had tried to bribe him and the Council by promising
to recognize organized labor in Hawaii and to arrange for collective
bargaining if the labor group would endorse the proposal for immigration. When the Labor Council refused, the business spokesmen, according to Wright, threatened never to agree to collective bargaining.[13]

Wright argued that the 1920 strike was purely economic and that
it was ridiculous to charge the Japanese with attempting to control
Hawaii's industry. He admitted that he was afraid that the importation
of Chinese laborers would push still more Japanese into competition
with his workers in town, and he did not want additional thousands
of cheap laborers competing for jobs in Hawaii.[14]

His testimony, replete with facts and figures, was probably dis-
counted by the House Committee after he admitted that he and the
treasurer of the Central Labor Union, Wilmot Chilton, had considered
raising money from the Japanese Chamber of Commerce to finance
their trip to Washington. Chilton explained that the Chamber was
afraid to give them money because of retaliation from the Honolulu
Chamber of Commerce but did encourage the Labor Council representatives to solicit Japanese shopkeepers as individuals. He said he
decided against visiting any Japanese stores, but he refused to tell the
Committee the names of contributors who had financed his and Wright's
trip to Washington, because, he said, they would be punished.[15]

The commissioners returned home uncertain as to the fate of their
proposal, but Dillingham went back to Washington early the next year
to take care of his own business interests and to lay the groundwork
for a return visit by the Commission. Governor Farrington agreed with
Dillingham in February that it would be wise to insert in the immigration resolution a provision calling for the employment of a certain percentage of citizens in Hawaii's sugar mills. Yes, wrote Farrington, that
would be helpful to Henry A. Baldwin in Hawaiian districts in his cam-

paign for the delegateship following Kuhio's death.[16] Dillingham's letters from the Racquet Club in Washington, where he was drawing $20 per diem as chairman of the Emergency Labor Commission, revealed how closely he identified the public interest in the Territory with the development of his own industrial empire. Writing in March, he told Governor Farrington of a trip to New York, where, it developed, he was awarded a section of a large contract to build an oil-storage plant at Pearl Harbor. Also there was a good prospect of an additional drilling at Kahului, and Dillingham hoped the Governor would act promptly in pushing the project so that Dillingham could make best use of the dredges available. Oh, yes, he reminded the Governor, there was no need to apologize for bringing up the matter of an additional $3,000 in salary for the Governor. Dillingham promised to go to work on it right away. In April and June, Dillingham gave a series of dinners at the Racquet Club for congressmen to meet Henry A. Baldwin, the new delegate. Throughout the spring, he expanded his business contacts in Washington, New York, Maine, and Boston, visited with justices of the Supreme Court and high federal officials, and clearly established himself in the eyes of important officials as Hawaii's most important industrialist.[17]

On June 7, more than a year after the Commission had arrived in Washington, the hearings were resumed before the Senate Committee. The representative of the A.F. of L., Edgar Wallace, opposed the resolution. He argued that the way to correct the labor shortage in Hawaii was to raise wages.[18] Delegate-elect Baldwin returned to the theme of the Japanese menace. The labor strike in 1920 was run by priests and schoolteachers, he told the Committee, and, moreover, the Japanese did not assimilate with Americans.[19]

Again the hearings were adjourned. Dillingham wired a confidential coded cable to Farrington on June 19 urging the Governor to put pressure on his friend President Harding and emphasizing the need to keep the Territory under American control. "Cannot place too much stress on danger of losing American control through preponderance in numbers of Japanese . . ." he cabled. To get action, Dillingham believed it might be necessary to have Harding send a commission to the Territory to investigate the "Japanese menace."[20]

The House Committee on Immigration and Naturalization finally submitted in 1923 a report favoring by merely one vote the planter-sponsored legislation. The report, opposed by the Committee's powerful chairman, accepted the thesis that American control was threatened by a shortage of common field labor in Hawaii and that the Japanese had it within their power to control the agriculture of the Territory for racial or nationalistic purposes. However, the feeling of urgency which had been developed in the early months of the Commission's visit waned, and a combination of powerful mainland beet-sugar interests, the influence of the A.F. of L., and racial antagonism toward the Chinese defeated the attempt to import cheap Chinese labor.

George Wright returned to Hawaii determined to organize a territory-wide interracial labor union. An industrial union was necessary, he argued. The craft- and trade-union movement could never develop in Hawaii along traditional lines because the vast majority of Hawaii's workers were common field laborers.[21] Officially, the union was called the United Workers of Hawaii, but it was generally known as the "One Big Union." In January 1922, bylaws and a constitution were endorsed at a special meeting of workers in Honolulu, and Wright submitted articles of incorporation to oligarchy Attorney General Harry Irwin. The preamble to the constitution urged the development of class con-sciousness and solidarity among workers regardless of racial back-ground.[22] At a mass meeting at Aala Park, a bulletin was distributed pledging the union's assistance in securing better wages and living conditions for all workers in Hawaii. It proposed to establish a fund for the benefit and relief of union members, to support the movement for a labor temple, to conduct open forums for the discussion of im-portant questions, to establish a labor periodical, and to maintain free reading rooms and gathering places for its members.

The Attorney General passed on to Governor Farrington the decision concerning the articles of incorporation, and the Governor immediately wrote Dillingham in Washington for his opinion.[23] Should the charter for the One Big Union be approved? asked Farrington. Dillingham's reply arrived on March 7; he said that it would be a mistake to grant the charter. To the public, the Governor explained that he could not legalize an organization that would be "in my estimation clearly and dangerously un-American." Behind the group of American citizens requesting the charter, he asserted, was "a dictatorial group of aliens."[24] Wright denounced the Governor's attitude, but there was little the One Big Union could do in the face of implacable oligarchy opposition. Hawaii's first major effort to establish an interracial union had been blocked.

To suppress strikes, the territorial legislature enacted laws against "criminal syndicalism, anarchistic publications, and picketing" between 1919 and 1923. Under the first law, anyone who advocated violence or sabotage as a means for dealing with an industrial dispute could be imprisoned for ten years. Under the press-control statute, any publication that restrained persons "from freely engaging in lawful business or employment" could be silenced. The picketing bill prohibited peaceful picketing of all kinds. A trespass law, more effective than the others, passed in 1925, forbade anyone from entering "improved or cultivated lands of another if forbidden to do so" by posted notices. No legislative angle was overlooked by the owners and managers of Hawaii's wealth in their campaign against plantation unionism.[25]

Neither silencing the One Big Union nor further legislation solved what the planters called their "labor shortage." But there was no legal barrier to migrations from the Philippines, and the Hawaiian Sugar Planters' Association stepped up its recruiting activity in those islands. Filipino workers, largely unmarried and illiterate laborers from the North, rapidly replaced the Japanese as the majority group on the plantations. Moving among the new workers was Pablo Manlapit, anxious for revenge against the haole oligarchy who had twice thrown him in jail and had made it difficult for him to practice law in the Islands. Manlapit went from plantation to plantation between 1920 and 1924 organizing the Filipino Higher Wage Movement and encouraging unrest among the workers.[26]

Filipino complaints of poor working conditions and low pay filtered through to Washington, and Governor General Leonard Wood of the Philippines appointed a special investigator to visit Hawaii and make a report. Cayetano Ligot issued what he called an "authoritative statement relative to Filipino laborers in Hawaii," which blamed the workers themselves for their troubles. The Filipinos were too unstable, he said, and had fallen prey to a class of gamblers and collectors who sneaked into the plantations to disrupt their work habits. Management was trying its best, reported Ligot, to provide wholesome working conditions and decent wages for the Filipino laborers. He urged the Filipinos to give their services wholeheartedly on the plantations to bring honor to the Filipino people.[27]

Manlapit was not to be denied. In April 1924, one month after Ligot's report was made, he called a strike of Filipino workers on one plantation after another. He demanded a minimum wage of $2 a day and the reduction of the working day to eight hours. The Hawaiian Sugar Planters' Association President answered that an increase in wages would endanger Hawaii's sugar industry, which was now committed to large expenses for welfare work and a major recruiting program in the Philippines.[28] The walkout, which involved twenty-three of forty-five plantations, lasted eight months.

By June, approximately 3,000 (Manlapit claimed 12,000) laborers were out, 25 per cent of all those employed in the plantations. But the strike was doomed from the start. Fresh supplies of Ilocano laborers poured into the Islands to work as strikebreakers; strikers were evicted from their houses and forced to set up temporary camps in outlying districts, where their morale was quickly broken; leaders and sympathizers were arrested and thrown in jail.

After its experience in the 1920 strike, the Association worked efficiently with government authorities to break the Filipino strike in 1924. Jack Butler, the executive head of the Hawaiian Sugar Planters' Association, explained the Association's spy system to Governor Farrington. Wright, the "labor agitator," was trailed so that the Association would have a report on each meeting he attended. The confidential dossier on Wright showed, for example, that on January 13, 1922, he and Manlapit made friends with a haole storekeeper and bookkeeper at Waipahu who helped them in their travels to the plantations to secure signatures on a petition for higher wages. Butler assured Farrington that the Association had a complete account of Wright's daily activities.[29] Smaller spy systems were developed throughout the Islands. Sheriff William Rice boasted to Governor Farrington two days before the outbreak of violence at Makaweli that he had men posted in every camp to learn in advance what the strikers were scheming.[30]

Planter spokesmen were adept at employing bribes as well as threats. A Filipino high-school senior, after writing an essay on the strike that was favorable to the workers, was called before Jack Butler, who told him that the Association would subsidize the boy's education at the mainland university of his choice if he would keep quiet.[31] Bribes and threats could not entirely prevent outbreaks of violence. On Kauai, the police quickly broke up most strike meetings. But violence occurred at the Makaweli plantation when strikers armed themselves with guns, cane knives, rocks, and clubs and captured two Filipino strikebreakers. Sheriff Rice led a posse to the camp of the evicted strikers on the banks of a small river just above Hanapepe village to release the two prisoners.

When the strikers resisted, a riot ensued, lasting several days; sixteen Filipinos and four policemen were killed and many others wounded. At the Sheriff's request, Governor Farrington sent the National Guard to Kauai. Six officers and eighty-five men from various rifle companies and two machine-gun squads went to the island and remained for eighteen days. There they helped arrest 101 of the 133 rioters; seventy-six were brought to trial, and sixty were given four-year jail sentences.[32] Manlapit was indicted for subornation of perjury and given a prison sentence of two to ten years. One Filipino woman, then a nurse at the immigration station, states that several witnesses testified falsely against Manlapit. They said they had been promised $10,000 each and a ticket back to the Philippines to testify against him. Instead, they were given their tickets and promissory notes for $100 each when they arrived in Manila.[33] According to the *Hawaii Hochi,* Manlapit had been "railroaded into prison . . . a victim of framed up evidence, perjured testimony, racial prejudice, and class hatred."[34] True or not, Manlapit was paroled shortly after his sentencing in 1924 on condition that he leave the Territory.

In many cases, Ilocanos had been used as strikebreakers against Visayans, intensifying the bitterness between the two groups. Whatever confidence had existed in Ligot was now completely shaken. The Filipinos' brief protest against Hawaii's wage and labor system had cost them money and self-respect and shattered their spirit.

The sugar planters now further extended paternalistic programs. New clubhouses, athletic facilities, and even radio programs were begun, although some planters protested that it was a mistake to "mollycoddle" Hawaii's laborers.[35] Letters were sent to the Philippines encouraging additional emigration. The laborers kept coming, but not all of them were accepted. The Hawaiian Sugar Planters' Association decided that there must be no more Manlapits, and 100 of 600 Filipino laborers who had come on their own in September 1928 were sent back because they were literate and therefore unsuitable for plantation labor.[36]

The planters usually took the position that it was wrong to treat the Filipinos as aliens and thereby prevent their free emigration from the Philippines, but they did urge a tariff on Filipino sugar. In March 1929, Baldwin wrote Delegate Houston that he must not permit the legislature to cut off Filipino migration to Hawaii; Puerto Ricans would be too expensive. Mainland organizations and California legislators agitated for Filipino exclusion, but Farrington and Houston were ready to ask for an exemption for Hawaii should such a law be passed.[37] Complaints of Filipino unemployment and indigence in Hawaii received circulation in Manila, and the Filipino government temporarily suspended the Association's recruiting license early in 1930, announcing another investigation of living conditions in the Territory. Within a few months, the license was restored, owing partly to Ligot's reports praising plantation conditions.

Houston suggested that one way to deal with unemployment was to reduce the working day from twelve to eight hours.[38] But his suggestion was not adopted, and unemployment continued to grow. In March 1932, nearly 1,000 Filipinos held a mass meeting in Aala Park, where Ligot admonished them to be more diplomatic and to behave more courteously if they wanted help from the Association.[39] With the appointment of New Deal Governor General Frank Murphy to the Philippines, Ligot was recalled. After two months of investigation, Murphy's representative, Jose Figueras, demanded better treatment of labor and asked that Filipinos be appointed as camp bosses, interpreters, and social workers, and that Pablo Manlapit, now back in Hawaii, be recognized as a labor leader for collective-bargaining purposes. So annoyed were the agencies that Governor Lawrence Judd, a Republican holdover in the Islands, asked Murphy to recall Figueras because the Filipino's conduct was prejudicial to the Territory.[40]

Between 1922 and 1935, labor-union activity in the Islands gradually disintegrated. The haole labor movement virtually ceased to exist. There remained only a few A.F. of L. locals, without contracts and with probably less than 1,000 members. The Japanese unions folded one by one, and after 1925, the Filipino union existed only on paper.

Only after the passage of the National Labor Relations Act in 1935, and especially after its legality was upheld in 1937, were the benefits of trade-unionism felt by the unskilled and semiskilled workers of Hawaii.[41] As late as 1937, the Territory had no minimum-wage law, no legislation protecting women in industry, and no adequate child-labor law.[42] Most employers in Hawaii were willing to adjust to certain welfare programs, but they were determined to fight unionization. A new employers' group, the Industrial Association of Hawaii, was organized in 1936 to answer the Wagner Act and to fight mainland labor-union organizers.[43] An N.L.R.B. examiner concluded in 1937 that Castle & Cooke had violated the federal law by firing longshoremen who sought collective bargaining; he found that workers were not permitted to make disparaging remarks against their employers, and that the police department and Army Intelligence co-operated with the Industrial Association, managed by former Governor Judd, now an attorney for Castle & Cooke.[44]

Despite opposition, a longshoremen's union was established at Hilo in late 1935 by Harry Kamoku, a seaman turned longshoreman. In the same year, the organization of longshoremen in Honolulu was begun. At the two ports on Kauai, longshoremen organized and struck in 1937. At the same time, the bartenders and brewery workers began organizing in Honolulu. Helping the longshoremen from time to time was a small group of seamen who were veterans of the 1934 West Coast maritime strike. Among them was the powerfully built Jack Hall, then less than twenty-five years old, who dropped off his ship several times beginning in 1935 to help spread unionism in Honolulu.

In April 1937, Hawaii's last racial plantation strike took place at Puunene on Maui, when several hundred members of the Filipino organization, Vibora Luviminda, left the fields and refused to work until their wage demands were met. Hall and other haole unionists had urged the organization's leader, Antonio Fagel, in vain to make Vibora Luviminda a multiracial union associated with the American labor movement. By the time the strike ended, 3,000 workers were involved. Fagel and nine other Filipinos were arrested on the charge of kidnaping a nonstriker. As usual, the Hawaiian Sugar Planters' Association had the co-operation of Hawaii's Governor, this time Democrat Joseph B. Poindexter, who urged the workers to go back to their jobs.

Between 1935 and 1939, Hawaii saw its first labor newspaper, the *Voice of Labor,* run by a succession of seamen, obtaining whatever support they could from left-wing maritime workers who came through the Islands. The little paper fired steadily at the Hawaiian Sugar Planters' Association, the Chamber of Commerce, and even the New Deal administration in Washington. For a while, it published in each weekly edition reports of the earnings of big companies, among them the Honolulu Rapid Transit Company and the Matson Navigation Company. But its two main themes were class consciousness and interracial solidarity. The pages of the newspaper were filled with repetitious exortations to Hawaii's workers: "Know your class and be loyal to it . . . class collaboration ends in fascism. Fascism ends in war. Down with both!"[45]

Hall emrged in 1938 as the most energetic and powerful union organizer in Hawaii. Although Edward Berman, a student and salesman turned organizer who edited the *Voice of Labor* for a time, was named Congress of Industrial Organizations regional director for the Territory in October 1937, Hall crowded Berman. In May 1938, a month after being named editor of the *Voice of Labor,* Hall assisted Berman and Jack Kawano, who headed the new forty-five-member I.L.W.U. longshore unit, in organizing and directing a strike against the Inter-Island Steamship Company.

On August 1, a group of stevedores marched to the docks at Hilo to protest the arrival of a ship run by eighty-four armed strikebreakers. The ship belonged to the Inter-Island Steamship Company, established in 1883 by a consolidation of two competing lines, which enjoyed a monopoly of interisland traffic in Hawaii. The company owned Hawaiian Airlines, formed in 1929, and three floating dry docks and the Kona Inn at Kailua. Interlocked with the Matson Navigation Company, which held the largest block of Inter-Island stock, many of its key directors and officers were also officials of Matson and Castle & Cooke, a minority stockholder in the Matson firm. The longshoremen insisted on picketing despite the warnings of police, who lined up on the docks with tommy guns, bayonets, and tear gas, ready to break up the demonstration. After tear gas and fire hoses failed to stop the strikers from advancing toward the warehouse, one of the Sheriff's men fired buckshot and bird shot into the crowd of strikers armed only with clubs. At least fifty strikers were wounded in the exchange which followed, and twenty-five went to the hospital. Thereafter known in Island labor circles as the "Hilo massacre," the incident on the docks helped to build labor solidarity in Hawaii. The strike was broken and demands for higher wages and a closed shop were defeated, but the striking unions, including both A.F. of L. and C.I.O. locals, remained intact.[46]

Hall and Berman were not the only aspiring union leaders. Jack Kawano, a dependable, devoted organizer on the waterfront, built a local following of longshoremen. Bartender Arthur Rutledge organized over a thousand hotel and restaurant employees. But Hall already showed signs of becoming the most powerful of the new labor leaders. With little help from the local I.L.W.U., he saw that organized labor could be a political force in Hawaii, especially if the plantations were unionized. Several months after the Inter-Island strike, he made his headquarters at Hanapepe on Kauai, near the McBryde plantation. There and at other plantations he worked systematically for the next two years to organize the United Cannery Agricultural Packing and Allied Workers of America (C.I.O.), and on October 24, 1940, this union won its first N.L.R.B. election at McBryde.

Hall also played politics on Kauai, organizing in August 1938 the first successful labor-in-politics movement in the history of the Islands, the Progressive League of Kauai. With its aid, a small businessman of Portuguese descent, William B. Fernandes, beat an oligarchy representative, Lindsay Faye, by a narrow margin in a 1938 contest for a senatorial seat, and two years later, the League helped another Portuguese businessman, Clem Gomes, in his victory over Elsie Wilcox in the Republican primary contest for senator.

C.I.O representatives were not without competition from the A.F. of L. A Hawaiian Islands Federation of Labor was organized in May 1937, to include longshoremen, laundry and cannery workers, plumbers, boilermakers, and even plantation and mill workers. Some pineapple workers from Molokai and plantation laborers from Maui joined, but the Federation was largely a paper organization, and many of its unions were extremely short-lived. It disintegrated after seven months, although a number of the affiliated unions continued. A.F. of L. members from the building and metal trades kept coming from the mainland to the Islands as war workers, and on the eve of Pearl Harbor, the A.F. of L. actually had at least three times as many members as the C.I.O. But the industrial union had two great advantages: It had successfully organized the waterfronts through the I.L.W.U., and had begun, under Hall's leadership, to organize the plantations. Berman had worked hard in directing C.I.O. longshoremen and seamen during the strike, but, hurt by criticism he received for loss of the strike and ambitious to become a labor lawyer, he left for the mainland; Hall's competition was gone. Had the war been postponed just a few months, a major drive for organization of the plantations on the outer islands would have begun, spearheaded by a nucleus of longshoremen on all islands except Maui. The I.L.W.U., under Hall's constant prodding, was ready to move into the plantations when the war intervened, postponing until 1944 both Hall's official appointment by the I.L.W.U. and further organizational work on the plantations.[47]

Union membership grew from 500 to approximately 10,000 between 1935 and 1941. No longer would mainland haole officials write as one did in 1930 that "labor organizations in the Hawaiian Islands are few in number, small in membership, and, with the exception of the Barber's Union, have no agreements with the employers."[48] Hawaii, because of federal labor legislation and the toughness of local longshoremen and *malihini* sailor organizers, was now ready for large-scale unionization.

Success on the docks was crowned in January 1941 when the I.L.W.U., after filing a petition with the National Labor Relations Board claiming to represent a majority of the longshore employees of Castle & Cooke Terminals, Ltd., won an election majority by better than three to one. On June 12, 1941, the first written contract in Hawaii's longshore history was signed, ending the six-year struggle for a contract between waterfront employers and the I.L.W.U. For the first time in Hawaii's history, a large employer had signed a union agreement, and this was followed by contracts with other stevedoring firms in Honolulu and Hilo and at two smaller ports on the island of Kauai.[49]

Chapter Ten

CO-OPERATION—
NOT COMPETITION

Jim Dole, Hawaii's pineapple pioneer, was a fine human being and one of the shrewdest businessmen in the Islands, but he was not a team player. Herein lies the explanation for the rise and fall of James D. Dole, who in 1901 organized the Hawaiian Pineapple Company to can the luscious fruit that he had proved could be grown in the red dusty soil not suited to sugar cane. The *kamaaina* elite admired the *malihini* Dole for his Christian humanitarianism and business acumen, but its members were periodically troubled by Dole's inability to accept the "co-operative" nature of the Hawaiian economy. It was no great surprise to them when, as president of Hawaiian Pineapple, Dole announced to his board of directors in June 1931 that he had received an offer from the Isthmian Steamship Line to carry pineapple to the mainland at lower rates than could be secured from the Matson Navigation Company, theretofore the Islands' only shipper of pineapple. The lower rates would save the stockholders a considerable amount of money, Dole explained, at a time when the company was hard-pressed. The price of pineapple soared in 1929, and many small planters leased land to the company to grow pineapple. Now, in 1931, the second year of depression on the mainland, it was impossible to market the crop planted two years before. Thousands of tons of pineapple were left in the fields to rot, and the company, which only two years before had earned net profits of more than 25 per cent on capital stock, would soon face bankruptcy.

The directors of Hawaiian Pineapple were aware of these facts, but Dole's solution was unacceptable. Why, they asked, did he insist on being such a complete individualist? They had grudgingly accepted Dole's decision to buy large amounts of cement for construction purposes from the Orient rather than from the mainland in order to save money, but his latest proposal went too far. These were probably the thoughts of Directors Frank C. Atherton and Alexander Budge, president and secretary-treasurer respectively of Castle & Cooke, agent and substantial owner of the Matson Navigation Company. Dole, it seemed, ignored the intricacies of Hawaii's economy. In the long run, the success of pineapple depended on the success of sugar, which in turn could only succeed if the industry was united to press its claims in Congress and in the mainland market. If shipping costs were too high, it would be wiser to talk to Matson officials than to run to the nearest competitor. For his own and the company's sake, Hawaiian Pineapple's chief executive was advised to forget the Isthmian offer.[1]

Dole refused, and in little more than a year he was ousted as the effective head of the pineapple company he had created. In San Francisco, Castle & Cooke officials joined officers of the Matson Navigation Company in discussions on the fate of Hawaiian Pineapple and its president. Dole soon found that banks in San Francisco as well as those in Honolulu were unable to renew his loans. In October 1932, Hawaiian Pineapple was reorganized to avoid catastrophe, and Dole was replaced as general manager by Atherton Richards, a former treasurer of Castle & Cooke and director of the Ewa and Waialua plantations. The man whose name was synonymous with Hawaii's pineapple industry was kept on as president, but only after he had been taught an important lesson: co-operation, not competition, is the keynote of Hawaii's economy.

Co-operation was indeed the keynote—co-operation in the ownership, financing, and managing of sugar; co-operation in banking, in transportation, and in the control of land; co-operation, too, in keeping out pernicious and competitive mainland interests and in restricting cutthroat un-American Oriental enterprise.

Co-operation was especially useful in maintaining control of the sugar industry. Before the turn of the century the major factors, having assumed control of the Territory's most important and productive industry, recognized that mainland interests could destroy them unless they worked together. East Coast sugar financiers representing planter interests in Cuba would bury Hawaii's industry by eliminating the tariff. The beet-sugar growers of the South and Midwest would cut off Hawaii's labor supply by abolishing its peculiar immigration regulations. The sugar trust on the East Coast and the Claus Spreckels interests on the West Coast, dwarfing the Hawaiian factors in size and power, could control the market and force the price of Island sugar down. Competition among plantations and agencies was a luxury the Hawaiian sugar industry could not afford.

The agencies eliminated the enervating competition of the nineteenth century, which had forced many independent sugar plantations into bankruptcy. The agencies purchased large amounts of stock in the plantations they represented, gaining more and more control over their policies. The factors financed the plantations, kept their books, paid their taxes, arranged for shipping, recruited labor, provided engineers, chemists, and agriculturalists, and created the Hawaiian Sugar Planters' Association. The Association, with offices within a hundred yards of the buildings occupied by the agencies, became Hawaii's best example of economic co-operation. "It is true that . . . to attempt to lure away workers from one plantation to another by offers of higher wages would be regarded [by the Association] as the limit of low conduct," wrote a friend of Hawaii's sugar industry.[2] Through the Association it was possible to unify labor policies and to speak with a single voice in research and in lobbying in Island and congressional politics. In two crucial matters—the organization of a West Coast refinery in 1905 and the assumption of control over H. Hackfeld & Company in 1918—the Association proved the value of co-operation to its member agencies. In 1905, Hawaiian planters found themselves at the mercy of West Coast refiners, especially Spreckels. Hawaii's only small refinery, at Aiea, was unable to handle more than a small fraction of the total volume of Hawaii's raw sugar, and in a move to increase their refining capacity, the Association in 1905 bought a controlling interest in the Crockett Refinery in California. Crockett, which had been built first as a flour mill and then used as a beet mill, had been abandoned by its leasee, a major East Coast refiner. After its purchase, Hawaiian producers could ship directly to their own refinery, assured that "California and Hawaiian Sugar" would reach mainland tables.

Between 1906 and 1914, co-operation increasingly meant centralization. Large plantations were combined into still larger plantations. There were fewer sugar factors, but these few became stronger than ever. Local transportation by land and water became more centralized and more directly tied to the sugar producers.[3]

When World War I came, the factors were well prepared to take advantage of an offer made by United States Attorney General Mitchell

Palmer, who had frozen the holdings of one of the Big Five, the German-owned agency, H. Hackfeld & Company. Why not form a company, Palmer suggested, to purchase the assets of Hackfeld from the U.S. Alien Properties Administration? Representatives of *kamaaina* missionary families, the Athertons, Cookes, and Wilcoxes—now plantation owners and managers—agreed with Palmer and organized American Factors, Inc., chose the officers of the new corporation, and happily paid the United States government $7,000,000 for Hackfeld's assets. Later, Hackfeld lost a suit for $12,000,000, in which it charged that its fellow Association members had conspired to drive it from Hawaii.[4]

Under the Association's leadership, called by one student "a curious blend of scientific openmindedness and business furtiveness," Hawaii's sugar industry became even more concentrated.[5] By 1915, sugar constituted about 90 per cent of the value of Hawaiian agricultural production, and more than 20 per cent of the Territory's population was on plantation payrolls. Between 1901 and 1915, the sugar crop had practically doubled. All but three of the forty-seven incorporated sugar plantations in the Islands belonged to the Association, whose assets were raised by a tonnage tax on the sugar produced by its members. Its recruiters combed the Philippines for laborers; its scientists directed a large experiment station to conduct field and mill tests; its statisticians and economists compiled figures and supervised marketing arrangements. Traveling auditors and engineers constantly inspected, advised, and directed mill and field operations. While nearly 10,000 firms and individuals were shareholders in Hawaii's sugar companies and most plantation stocks were quoted and dealt with on the Honolulu Stock Exchange, the forty-four corporation members of the Association, forty-three of which operated mills, were controlled by no more than a dozen men who met regularly for lunch at the Pacific Club or golf at the Oahu Country Club.[6]

The Big Five agencies were not content to confine themselves to the sugar business. They early took steps to gain control of transportation, and by 1911, the U.S. Commissioner of Labor reported that local transportation by land and water and "steamship lines to the mainland are more closely allied than ever with sugar factors and planters."[7] With transportation under control, the factors branched into the hotel business and then systematically acquired considerable control of the big utilities, principal banks, insurance agencies, other financial institutions, and many small wholesale and retail businesses. As early as 1905, $8 out of every $11.50 invested in the mechanical and manufacturing industries in Hawaii were tied to sugar.[8]

Only five years after annexation, the Inter-Island Steamship Company eliminated its sole competitor, the Wilder Steamship Company. For twenty years the firms had rivaled each other, but in 1905, the two companies amalgamated under the control of Inter-Island, which, along with another firm—the Young Bros. Barge Service —enjoyed a monopoly of interisland ocean transportation for the next forty-five years. Control of shipping to the West Coast was more difficult to obtain, but not beyond the grasp of Hawaii's sugar entrepreneurs. For a number of years following annexation, Hawaii's sugar men opposed the congressional statute that forbade transportation of produce or people between two American ports in ships of foreign registry.[9] Rather than fight mainland shipping interests, Hawaii's businessmen decided to join them. In 1909, local sugar men financed Captain William Matson, of the Matson Navigation Company, in having local ships transport Hawaii's sugar to the mainland and thus abide by the law dealing with American port-to-port calls while keeping transportation revenues in the Territory. The business interests of Hawaii were now patriotic supporters of the law they once opposed, a law that helped to kill foreign competition and encouraged Matson's monopoly position. Favored by the agencies, Matson took over or drove out its competitors, and by the early 1930's, when it absorbed the Los Angeles Steamship Company and the Oceanic Steamship Company, it completely dominated the Hawaii–West Coast shipping scene. By 1935, Matson, represented by the sugar agency Castle & Cooke, had a fleet of fifty ships and was primarily owned by Hawaiian capital.[10] One year later, the officials of Castle & Cooke, perhaps recognizing more clearly than anyone else that commercial enterprise in the Islands was completely dependent upon reliable shipping, bought out the Matson terminals in Honolulu and formed Honolulu Stevedores, Ltd., changed in 1940 to Castle & Cooke Terminals, Ltd.

Land transportation was also highly concentrated. By 1910, there were three major railroads in Hawaii, each running without competition. The Dillinghams controlled the Oahu Railway and Land Company, American Factors and Alexander & Baldwin controlled the Hilo Railroad, and the Baldwin family owned the only railroad on Maui.[11]

Also centralized were the banking and trust institutions of Hawaii.

Under the direction of Charles Reed Bishop and Samuel M. Damon, Hawaii's first bank, Bishop & Company, was virtually the Islands' only bank until the Bank of Hawaii, Ltd., was opened in 1897. These two continued to grow under the direction of men closely connected with the ownership and management of Hawaii's sugar plantations. Vice-president of the Bank of Hawaii was Joseph B. Atherton, president of Castle & Cooke, the new bank's first depositor. The bank continued to grow, and in 1922 it successfully absorbed the twenty-one-year-old First Bank of Hilo, the first bank to have been established on the Big Island.[12] According to the Democratic newspaper the *New Freedom,* the two big banks joined forces to destroy the Peoples Bank of Hilo by seeing to it that the Territory made no deposits in the competing bank and by refusing to cash the Peoples Bank's checks.[13] In 1930, the Bank of Hawaii absorbed the Bank of Maui, eliminating a competitor on that island.

The Bishop First National Bank of Honolulu, as it was called after 1929, when it consolidated four Island banks, continued to grow. The Bishop Company, Ltd., was incorporated to hold the capital stock of the consolidation as well as that of Baldwin Bank of Maui. When the corporation changed its name to Bishop National Bank of Hawaii in 1933, the Maui bank became a branch. Competition between the two institutions was virtually nil, and in 1918 there was considerable agitation for a merger between them. But opposition from depositors halted the merger. So extensive was the two banks' control of capital that Chinese and Japanese merchants were obliged to start their own small banking institutions in the 1920's and '30's.

The major trust companies of Hawaii, instead of competing with the banks, as on the mainland, were set up by the two major Island banks and prohibited from conducting banking services. The first of these institutions was the Hawaiian Trust & Investment Company, Ltd., incorporated in 1898 as an outgrowth of the Hawaiian Safe Deposit & Investment Company, which had given birth to the Bank of Hawaii a year earlier. The Hawaiian Trust Company, as it was called after 1901, rapidly developed into the Islands' major trust institution. A second firm, the Bishop Trust Company, Ltd., was formed six years after annexation and in the course of time gobbled up other Island trusts, among them the Guardian Trust Company, Ltd., and Henry Waterhouse Trust Company, Ltd. Unable by law to provide banking services, the trust companies performed functions not usually exercised by similar firms on the mainland, including handling real estate, stock-brokerage, property management, and insurance. They also engaged in more traditional activities as executor, administrator, trustee, guardian, tax consultant, and general and special agent for a wide variety of corporate, partnership, and individual businesses. Co-operation in controlling the banking and trust facilities of the Islands became accepted as an inevitable consequence of Hawaii's centralized economy.

Such concentration was, of course, as much a cause as it was a result of centralization. Wholesale and retail merchants in competition with the big agencies often found it difficult to get bank loans. A nisei store-keeper, discontent with his relatively good salary of $50 a month at a plantation store, started a small store of his own at Waimea on Kauai, in 1926. He had only his brother's and his own savings for the venture, since it was three and a half years before any bank would give him a cent. Private stores operating on the plantations had to buy a good part of their goods from the wholesale departments of plantation agencies in Honolulu.[14] Distributors who tried to compete with these wholesale departments were often the victims of strong pressure to get out of business and stay out. When an ambitious Filipino imported cigars from the Philippines in the 1930's and tried to peddle them to local retailers, he discovered that three of the major factors, also importing cigars from the Philippines, withdrew credit from retailers who purchased cigars from him.[15] By 1935, over 90 per cent of the small retail stores in the Islands purchased their supplies through one or another of the sugar factors, the major suppliers being Theo. H. Davies and American Factors. In rural nonplantation areas, small farmers were inevitably under their control because of chronic debts to the agencies through the local stores.[16] There was virtually no competition among the salesmen for the big distributors. The proprietors of some retail stores never saw a sales manager. Salesmen came in, dumped their supplies, and made no effort to sell service, price, or anything else. Because certain brand-name products were imported to the Islands without competition, two generations of Islanders grew up believing that Carnation was the only evaporated milk, Libby or Del Monte (depending on which factor serviced the store) the only producers of canned vegetables and fruits, and Love's (a *kamaaina* firm) the only bakers of bread.[17]

There was only one major department store in Hawaii, the Liberty House. Begun in 1850 by Captain Henry Hackfeld and soon after bought out by the German Ehlers family, B. F. Ehlers and Company, as it was then called, became a major asset of the sugar agency H. Hack-feld & Company. When Hackfeld was transformed to American Factors during World War I, the department store continued as a subsidiary of the agency and was called the Liberty House. Wrote the *New Freedom* in 1923, "You can start a department store in Honolulu if you want to, but as soon as its business begins to approach that of the Liberty House, for God's sake look out; the Matson Navigation Company will leave your freight on the wharf at San Francisco 'by mistake' and you won't be able to buy a balloon in the mainland market."[18] The Liberty House continued as the only important department store in Honolulu, with the exception of Kress, which had purchased a choice lot in downtown Honolulu by subterfuge in the early 1930's, until 1941, when Sears Roebuck, after a secret investigation, decided to build a small store to break the Liberty House's virtual monopoly on retail department-store trade. Even Sears, with its wealth and power, worked behind the scenes, hiring two real-estate men to buy house lots in small parcels in what was then suburban Honolulu. After the news was out, according to a mainland Sears official, veiled threats were received from American Factors that Matson would not ship Sears products. Only a threat from Sears President, General Leonard Wood, that he would buy his own ship and the suspicion on Merchant Street that the store in the country would fail prevented retaliation by Matson.[19]

Not every new business enterprise was controlled by the Big Five. By 1915, the Japanese controlled the fisheries of Hawaii and were influential in the quarry and stonecutting industry, contracting, and other small businesses. There were tiny loopholes in the oligarchy's financial web, but it frequently took perseverance and ingenuity to find them.[20]

Pineapple, Hawaii's second most-important industry prior to World War II, had been started by Dole when he began to grow pineapple in the Wahiawa area of Oahu as a homesteader in 1900. Dole discovered that pineapple grew well on his sixty-acre farm, and foreseeing a year-round market for canned pineapple, he induced other farmers in the area to raise the fruit, too. In 1901, he formed the Hawaiian Pineapple Company, and two years later, in a cannery converted from a barn, approximately 1,800 cases of the "golden fruit" were packed. Before long it became clear that the rapidly growing pineapple industry was headed for corporate control.[21]

Following a mainland business slump in 1907, the pineapple packers

—including two major mainland firms—established the Pineapple Growers Association of Hawaii to co-ordinate advertising, research, and, to some extent, marketing. The growers imposed a quota system to control their production and assure continued earnings. While the industry had certain features of a monopoly, it did have to compete with other fruits, and during the 1930 depression, the canneries also found themselves in sharp competition with each other.[22] In 1922, Hawaiian Pineapple bought the island of Lanai for a little more than a million dollars, and the two other large packers, Libby, McNeill & Libby and the California Packing Corporation, opened sizable plantations on Molokai and Maui. But the trend toward consolidation continued in the 1930's. In 1920, there were thirteen companies with eleven canneries. Ten years later, when the production of pineapple was much greater, there were only nine companies and eight canneries. One cannery, Dole's Hawaiian Pineapple Company, now under the effective control of Castle & Cooke, produced 40 per cent of the combined pineapple and juice output in the Territory and had over a third of the world's market.[23] On labor and immigration policies, the Pineapple Growers Association of Hawaii worked closely with the Hawaiian Sugar Planters' Association. In the beginning, the canneries and pineapple plantations drew surplus labor from the sugar fields. Later, the sugar association was paid a fixed annual fee to help recruit labor for the pineapple industry.

During the 1920's and '30's, the control of Hawaii's corporations was tightened through a vast network of interlocking directorates. The same individuals appeared repeatedly as directors of sugar corporations or banks that were theoretically in competition with each other. One or more representatives of outstanding *kamaaina* families of the Territory were active on the boards of thirty-eight of the forty corporations listed on the Honolulu Stock Exchange in 1928. One family was represented on eighteen, another on ten. Five families had members on five or more boards of directors. Of the seven plantations managed by Alexander & Baldwin, Hawaii's second largest agency, five were managed by descendants of the original Alexander and Baldwin families. By 1935, exactly one third of the directors and officers of the forty-five sugar plantations and factors in Hawaii were direct descendants of or related by marriage to the original missionary families of the Islands.[24] Through direct representation, social contacts, and intermarriage they had a hand in running practically every major corporation in the

Islands. For example, Frank Atherton, president of Castle & Cooke and the Home Insurance Company, was also a vice-president of American Factors, the Hawaiian Trust Company, and the Territorial Hotel Company, and a director of the Hawaiian Pineapple Company, the Inter-Island Steamship Company, and the Bank of Hawaii. Because he was the son of Juliette M. Cooke, he was a cousin to various members of that family, including Clarence H. Cooke, the president of the Bank of Hawaii, and Richard A. Cooke, chairman of the board at C. Brewer. Richard Cooke was also the copresident of the Hawaiian Electric Company, a director of American Factors, and an officer of six other major corporations. His brother Clarence kept him in touch with affairs at Hawaiian Electric, where he was vice-president. Another brother, T. A. Cooke, was vice-president of the Bank of Hawaii. Walter F. Dillingham, whose mother was a missionary descendant, was at least as influential as Frank Atherton and Richard Cooke. He built his own financial empire through the Oahu Railroad and Land Company and the Hawaiian Dredging Company and was welcomed as a director of American Factors, vice-president of the Honolulu Rapid Transit Company and the Bishop Trust, and as director of three other corporations.[25]

The threads of influence crisscrossed many times, but certain clusters of financial and industrial power could be distinguished. The Dillinghams, with their great building and transportation programs, were tied to the Baldwins through mutual interest in the Bishop Bank and Bishop Trust. The Athertons, powerful in the Castle & Cooke combine, worked closely with the Cookes in the development of the Bank of Hawaii, the Mutual Telephone Company, and the Hawaiian Electric Company. But these divisions were not always clear. The Waterhouses, especially through John, who was related by marriage to the Alexanders and the Baldwins, were also influential in the development of Atherton and Cooke interests. At the same time that John Waterhouse was president of the Bishop National Bank, he was also a codirector of the Hawaiian Trust Company and vice-president of the Mutual Telephone Company. United by school ties, marriage, and by their enemies, Hawaii's financial and industrial leaders rarely allowed personal differences to interfere with their co-operative management and control of the wealth of the Islands.

The most vexatious problem of Hawaii's oligarchy was land. It would little profit the haole elite to control the directorships of Ha-

waii's important corporations if its members could not also control
the land on which Island sugar was grown. Two conditions made this
control difficult. In the first place, only 7.5 per cent of the total area of
Hawaii is suited to agriculture, compared with 73 per cent for Iowa and
30 per cent for the United Kingdom.[26] In the second place, the plantations were obliged to lease a large proportion of that land from the
territorial government and nonsugar interests, and had to fight continuous pressure to put such lands to different use. Despite these obstacles, however, most of the agricultural lands in the Islands gradually
came under the control of the plantations, either through outright
ownership or long-term leases. After the Great Mahele, large landholdings rapidly went to the haoles. By 1890, three of four landowners were Hawaiian, but three of four acres belonging to private
owners were held by haoles or their corporations.[27]

Land often fell into haole hands quite easily. They recognized the
value of land ownership, while the Hawaiians did not. In order to get
revenue from government lands under the monarchy, long-term leases
for large tracts at a small rental fee were frequently given. There was
no provision for a sliding scale of payment when the value of land
and its products increased. In 1905, one large plantation, under a
long-term lease at a very low rental, paid an average rent of two cents
an acre. Chinese farmers leasing small tracts of rice land at the same
time often paid as much as $50 an acre.[28] Because of government
policies friendly to the oligarchy—under the monarchy, Republic,
and the Territory—valuable tracts were often acquired for virtually
nothing. From the time the great Hawaiian king Kamehameha
I gave John Parker, of Newton, Massachusetts, what has since
become the Parker Ranch—one of the largest in the world—as thanks
for his advice and friendship, to the reign of King Kalakaua, when the
monarch issued a royal patent to Benjamin Dillingham for eleven acres
in downtown Honolulu to build a railway, Hawaiian kings, *alii,* and
even commoners readily sold or gave their land away.

Annexation made more complex the task of controlling Hawaii's
croplands, just as it threatened the oligarchy's control of politics and
labor. This was primarily because the Hawaiians, fully enfranchised
through the Organic Act and believing that the land had been stolen
from them, kept up constant pressure through their political leaders to
recapture Hawaii's land for themselves; it was also because of pressure
from the haole Americanizers, constantly urging a liberal homestead

policy, even to the immediate detriment of the plantations, to encourage the immigration of Caucasians to the Islands.

The Americanizers had their way for a brief moment under the Republic when a land act was passed in 1895 that put a limit of 1,000 acres on the amount of public land that could be sold in a single parcel, and general leases on public lands were limited to a term of not more than twenty-one years. The act also provided five methods by which persons desiring small holdings might acquire them from public-land areas, which now included the crown lands formerly in the personal possession of the monarchy. These homestead provisions were continued under the Organic Act, which further attacked large landholdings by limiting the amount of land that corporations could acquire in fee simple (outright ownership) to 1,000 acres. This provision was easily circumvented by forming illegal partnerships, but when part-Hawaiian Delegate Robert Wilcox introduced a bill in Congress in 1901 to extend the general land laws of the United States to the Territory of Hawaii, with the rules and regulations for homesteading to be governed by the Secretary of the Interior, the oligarchy was alarmed. Under these provisions, nearly 800,000 homesteads on more than 100,000,000 acres of land in the United States had been established in forty-two years. The basic principle was that the head of any family or any single person over twenty-one years of age who was a citizen or who had declared his intention of becoming one had the right to purchase 160 acres at $1.25 per acre after residing on and improving the land for six months. Such a radical policy would destroy the system of land control patiently built under the monarchy. As the representative of the Commissioner of Labor in Honolulu put it in 1905, easy homesteading would threaten the large plantation interests, which "are at work to create an unconscious sentiment among a large and important section of the white population adverse to diversified agriculture and increases in small free holds." He explained that the homestead laws were administered in such a way as to "make it very difficult for persons without influence to obtain homesteads or freeholds."[29]

Under the administration of Governors Dole and Carter, land policies of the Territory were consistently friendly to the sugar interests. Governor Frear once explained that Carter had "little or no faith in homesteading."[30] By 1909, half of the privately owned land of Hawaii was controlled by haole corporations, one sixth by individual haoles, another sixth by the haole directors of the Bishop estate, and the remaining sixth by individual part-Hawaiians, Hawaiians, and Asians.[31] Homesteading by American standards had been a gross failure. During the fifteen years under the Land Act of 1895, about 90,000 acres of public lands passed through homestead forms, but so far as real homesteading was concerned, "a large portion of that might as well have been cast into the ocean."[32] The reason was twofold. A substantial portion, perhaps a majority, of homestead lands were not worked as small farms, but were leased to corporations. Even when the homesteader or small farmer tried to make a go of it, he usually was under the thumb of a nearby plantation. Controls over transportation and marketing were so complete that the individual farmer who fell in disfavor with the plantation manager could easily be driven out. The major obstacle to successful homesteading, however, was in the administration of Hawaii's land laws. Governor Frear, at least as much as his two predecessors, shared the planters' desire to keep the best croplands for sugar.[33]

After investigating Hawaii's land situation, Congressman William C. Houston, of Tennessee, a senior member of the Committee on the Territories in the House of Representatives, proposed changes in the homesteading provisions of the Organic Act to encourage more homesteading. One suggestion, passed into law in April 1908, made obligatory the limiting of the term of any lease on agricultural land so that it "may at any time during the term of the lease . . . be withdrawn from operation thereof for homesteading or public purposes. . . ." In 1909, the Territory passed a law to penalize homesteaders who did not act in good faith. Too many had been straw buyers for plantations or had intended to make a killing by leasing homestead lands to corporations. The new measure forbade individuals from applying for more than one homestead and prohibited husbands and wives from taking separate homesteads. Also, the amount of public land that could be sold or exchanged by the Territory in a single transaction was limited to prevent a repetition of the Lanai trade, in which Governor Carter gave away the island of Lanai for two lots in Honolulu. In the following year, Congress adopted a radical change in the Organic Act, making it possible for twenty-five or more persons qualified for homesteading to apply for public lands, even developed agricultural lands, and obliging the Commission of Public Lands to open such areas for homestead purposes. This new provision would have frightened the oligarchy more than it did had not the planters thus far been successful in controlling the administration of land laws and in diverting homestead lands for plantation use. The new law was worrisome nonetheless. Since all new leases and lease renewals would now contain a withdrawal clause canceling the lease if developed sugar land was wanted for homesteading purposes, the planters were aware that leased public land could readily be taken from them by the "wrong" governor and land commissioner.[34]

The planters were divided with respect to the strategy that should be used to counter the new law. One group, whose spokesman was George H. Fairchild, territorial senator and for sixteen years the manager of the Makee Sugar Company, lobbied a proposal through the territorial legislature amending the Organic Act to change a ten-month-old 1910 provision which gave leased public land back to the government to be made available for homesteaders on the expiration of the lease. The Fairchild Bill would withdraw developed lands—lands used for agricultural purposes—from the provisions of the 1910 amendment. The revenues derived from rentals on such lands would be turned over for the support of public schools, the new College of Hawaii, and the promotion of homesteading. The new provision, thought some, would make it much more difficult for homesteaders to get a toehold on plantation land. Another group of planters believed they could live with the 1910 changes just as they had with previous homestead statutes. After all, in the sixty years since the Great Mahele, all but 36,000 of the 213,000 acres of new cane lands had gone over to corporations or private individuals. Some of the haole elite believed that perhaps much of the remaining 36,000 acres could be taken by fake homesteaders despite provisions in the law designed to prevent such frauds. Perhaps the demand for homesteads had also been exaggerated. After all, in 1911, a year of considerable prosperity, only 172 homesteads were approved under the 1910 amendment. As Delegate Kuhio pointed out, too often it pays best for a homesteader to sell out at a good figure to the plantations and leave the country. In many cases where homesteads had been carved out of valuable cane lands, the land had already been sold to the plantation which formerly leased it. A few speculators profited, and the Territory lost the rental of the land formerly leased to the plantations.[35]

There were thousands of acres of undeveloped land the planters would have been happy to see homesteaded. Because they were undeveloped, they required extensive government assistance, which the taxpayers of Hawaii, primarily the men who ran the sugar agencies, were not willing to give. "It is true," wrote one observer, "that in general, sugar planters feared the effect of colonies of homesteaders. If such colonies were successful, they would eventually compete with the plantations for labor and land. If they were unsuccessful they would form an element difficult for small communities to absorb."[36]

The Fairchild proposal did not get through Congress, because of the indifference or disapproval of the planters and the strenuous opposition of Prince Kuhio, who believed it was just another scheme to defraud the Hawaiians. By 1916, the planters who had opposed the Fairchild Bill could congratulate themselves. It was then reported that 62 per cent of all products from homestead lands were sugar cane or pineapple. The liberal 1910 provision which made it possible for any citizen, whether he knew anything about farming or not, to draw lots for his homestead helped encourage the speculators still further, but the small farmer who tried to grow his own crops remained largely dependent on the nearby plantation, looking to it to buy his crop and advance his seed, fertilizer, and store supplies.[37]

Only vigorous administration of the homestead laws against the planter interests could return the Hawaiians to the land and bring in a new class of independent haole farmers, Prince Kuhio realized, and he openly attacked Governor Frear in a complaint to the Secretary of the Interior in October 1911, arguing against Frear's reappointment because of his alleged maladministration of Hawaii's homestead laws. Specifically, he charged Frear with selling in fee simple certain areas within territorial leased land to a plantation, and making it extremely difficult to reclaim the entire area for the public at the expiration of the lease. He accused him also of leasing land to a plantation without protecting nearby homesteads in the use of water.[38] Frear did nothing, Kuhio said, to encourage homesteading or to prevent the plantations from pushing homesteaders off the land. He pointed out that during four years of Frear's administration, not one of the 34,000 acres of public land under cane cultivation had been withdrawn for homestead purposes. The land thrown open, with only one exception, was unwanted by the plantations. Homesteaders, he wrote, were refused fair terms by the plantations for the grinding of cane. In one case, the Hutchinson Sugar Company, a Brewer plantation, refused altogether to deal with a group of homesteaders.[39]

Frear was reappointed anyway, and in the seven years that followed, under his administration and that of Pinkham and McCarthy, little progress was made in homesteading, and the plantations extended their control over the public lands of Hawaii. There were homesteaders, to be sure. About 3,000 persons had secured small holdings by 1919, although several hundred subsequently left the land. Among them were 1,113 Hawaiians, 524 Anglo-Saxons, 938 Portuguese and Spanish, 164 Japanese, and seventy Chinese.[40] But more and more homestead land was in sugar and pineapple, and the "independent producers" were increasingly coming under the control of the nearest plantations. Still, there were features of Hawaii's land laws that the planters wanted changed. The 1,000-acre limitation on corporations in the Organic Act had been violated easily enough, but it would be better not to have the limitation on the books. The 1910 amendment providing for a withdrawal clause in all new plantation leases could be dangerous under an unfriendly governor. It would be much better if long-term leases could be obtained without the threat of land being recalled.[41]

The opportunity for the plantations to tighten Hawaii's land laws in their own interest came through the Hawaiian Rehabilitation Act, which created the Hawaiian Homes Commission. Kuhio realized that it was virtually impossible to build a haole middle class in Hawaii. He now concentrated on winning special homestead privileges for the Hawaiian people. To win oligarchy support for opening up public lands on terms especially favorable to Hawaiians or part-Hawaiians, the Delegate agreed to lobby against the 1,000-acre provision and the 1910 clause making mandatory the withdrawal of cultivated sugar lands under lease from the Territory upon the application of twenty-five or more citizens. An omnibus law was drawn up eliminating the 1,000-acre clause and providing that the Commissioner of Land, with the approval of the governor and at least two thirds of the members of the legislature, might omit the withdrawal provision from the lease of any lands suitable for the cultivation of sugar cane.

The provisions favorable to the planters were obscured by the active discussion of the Hawaiian Homes Commission idea. The first resolution passed by the territorial legislature in 1919 requested Congress to set aside certain crown lands—meaning public lands—for the special benefit of the Hawaiian people. A lobbying commission, representing interests friendly to the planters, was appointed to steer the bill through Congress. The commissioners pointed out that in the Great Mahele the commoners did not receive their just share of the lands of the Kingdom. They recalled that with the overthrow of the monarchy, the crown lands, which Kuhio alleged had been set aside as a trust for the common people, were taken over by the Republic, depriving the natives of their rights. On this ground and on the evidence that the Hawaiian race was dying, Kuhio and his supporters justified special treatment for the Hawaiians in the Territory's homestead policies. It was true, of course, that the common people were entitled to approximately one third of the land following the Great Mahele and that only 28,000 acres had been awarded to them because large numbers of the natives had failed to file their claims with the Board of Commissioners. It was also true that under the monarchy, the crown lands belonged to the king and not to the government, and that under Hawaiian tradition the lands of the crown could be used by the people. Under the monarchy, the land could not be alienated to corporations or haole purchasers unless it passed through Hawaiian hands first. Article 95 of the constitution of the Republic had altered that, declaring that crown land was the property of the government, free and clear from any trust for the Hawaiian people.

Whatever the wisdom or the constitutionality of the Hawaiian Rehabilitation Act, many congressmen were impressed with the injustice that had been done Hawaiians over the years. Under the Republic, large areas of crown lands were disposed of by the government, and had it not been for long-term leases made during the reign of King Kalakaua, even more land would have been alienated. The lands set aside under the Hawaiian Rehabilitation Act to be leased for ninety-nine years at a nominal rental to those of at least one-half Hawaiian blood were principally crown lands which Kalakaua had leased thirty years before. Not an acre of sugar land was to be touched, and for the first five years, which were to be experimental, only certain lands on the island of Molokai could be used. The only strong opposition to the act came from a representative of the Parker Ranch, who, although he also argued against the measure on constitutional and moral grounds, was clearly afraid that 53,000 acres of the Parker Ranch, on which leases would expire in seven years, would be taken up by the Hawaiian Homes Commission.[42] The act passed. The Hawaiians won a great symbolic victory; the planters were assured of control of the cane lands of Hawaii.

The homesteaders on Molokai grew alfalfa, tomatoes, and other vegetables, but found it difficult to ship their produce and sell it in Honolulu. When the California Packing Corporation and Libby, Mc-

Neill and Libby asked permission to lease lands from homesteaders to grow pineapple, the Hawaiian Homes Commission agreed. The homestead philosophy—to encourage independent farming and return the Hawaiians to the soil—was defeated. In some years, however, Hawaiian homesteaders were paid several thousand dollars merely for the use of their lands by the big corporations. Despite the failure of homesteading on Molokai, political pressure in favor of the symbol, the Hawaiian Rehabilitation Act, was so great that amendments to the law in 1923, 1928, 1934, and 1935 put additional acreage on Maui, Kauai, and Oahu under the control of the Hawaiian Homes Commission. By 1935, a total of 203,582 acres were administered by the Commission, but only a small fraction of the land was used for diversified independent farming. At Hoolehua on Molokai, the largest single area for homesteading, comprising more than 5,000 acres and settled by more than 1,000 Hawaiians, was diverted almost entirely to the cultivation of pineapple under contract to large plantations.[43]

The oligarchy was content. By a master stroke it had satisfied the political pressures of the Hawaiians, although more than half of the land administered by the Hawaiian Homes Commission was leased to corporations or individuals and only a small fraction was turned over to Hawaiians for homestead purposes. It was easy to be sympathetic with the rehabilitation movement under the terms worked out with Kuhio. As the Prince's friend Charles B. Dwight wrote to Delegate Houston in 1927, "The big interests now in their hearts are not sympathetic with the rehabilitation movement," but they went along with it because highly cultivated sugar lands were no longer available for homesteading.[44]

The concentration of land under the control of big estates and corporations continued. The 1930 census showed that Hawaii had 5,955 farm units. Only 633 of these were owned, managed, or leased by haoles, compared with 510 by Hawaiians, 4,191 by Japanese, and 335 by Chinese. The haoles, nevertheless, either through corporations or individuals, controlled 2,579,733 acres, more than sixteen times the acreage controlled by Hawaiians or part-Hawaiians, more than forty-five times Japanese-Americans' holdings, and more than 140 times the amount of land held by Hawaii's Chinese citizens.[45]

For forty years, Hawaii's oligarchy was able to conserve and expand its hold on the wealth of the Islands. Dividends of the major corporations were kept high, and taxes were low to keep wealth from being drained off into the public sector. Prior to and immediately following annexation, many speculative plantations failed, but most of those under the control of Hawaii's major factors began a tradition of fantastically high dividends that was rarely interrupted in the thirty years that followed. Statistics published by the Hawaiian Sugar Planters' Association and the Honolulu Stock Exchange showed strong profits year after year for nearly all of the plantations and Hawaii's major nonagricultural corporations. It was not unusual for the plantations to average more than 10 per cent in dividends on capitalization in any given year.[46] Only the Honokaa Sugar Company and the Olaa Sugar Company on the Big Island were in chronic difficulty in the 1930's. During one nine-year period, the Baldwins' Hawaiian Commercial and Sugar Company paid annual dividends of 16 per cent or more, and in 1920, the year of the great strike, it paid 40 per cent in dividends to investors. At Kekaha, on leased land obtained virtually as a gift under the monarchy, such dividends were common. In 1911, 45 per cent was paid on face value of capital; in 1916, 40 per cent; 1917, 36 per cent; 1920, 49 per cent; and 1921, 60 per cent. Consistently high dividends were paid by Wailuku Sugar, Oahu Sugar, and others. Corporations not devoted to sugar, such as the Hawaiian Pineapple Company, Mutual Telephone, and the Oahu Railway and Land Company, also consistently announced handsome dividends. Even during the depression of the 1930's, the dividend record of Hawaii's major corporations remained extraordinarily good by mainland standards.

The tax structure during most of the period was highly favorable to the owners and controllers of Hawaii's wealth. Income taxes were limited sharply and were not graduated. Property taxes, set and administered by the territorial government, invariably favored those who possessed property. Taxation was spread throughout the population whenever possible, through school, road, poll, and excise taxes. If the controllers of Hawaii believed in the trickle-down theory of wealth, they did not believe that much should trickle through the hands of the government.

PART THREE

The Dynamics of Democracy

1900-1960

Because of Hawaii's insularity and the thoroughness of oligarchy control, social changes that swept the mainland prior to World War II rarely affected the Islands. But the bombs that burst on Pearl Harbor shattered the old ways of life in Hawaii. The potentials for change already existed in Hawaii's public-school system and the guarantee by Congress of the right of every American citizen to vote. Social change was encouraged by federal labor legislation favoring collective bargaining. But war gave the greatest impetus to change. The schools were crucibles of democracy; World War II was its catalyst.

Drastic change came rapidly to many aspects of life following the war. Within a few years the nearly monolithic control of one political party gave way to vigorous two-party competition. Where there had been virtually no labor unions, a powerful, aggressive union emerged. Hawaii's economic dependence on industrial agriculture was broken. The 1950's became a period of ferment, of creative and dynamic change. Democracy erupted, with its tensions and strains, but with opportunities, too.

Chapter Eleven

SEEDS OF DEMOCRACY

George C. Watt was always at home to his countryman James C. Campsie. The two powerful Scotch managers, Watt from Kohala and Campsie from Pahala, settled in Watt's parlor with drinks in hand to discuss one of their favorite topics, the dangers of education in Hawaii. Watt pounded the table and exclaimed, "Every penny we spend educating these kids beyond the sixth grade is wasted!" "An understatement," replied Campsie. "Public education beyond the fourth grade is not only a waste, it is a menace. We spend to educate them and they will destroy us."[1] The logic of Hawaii's system of education was beyond the understanding of Campsie and Watt. They did understand that the owners of wealth could not encourage American education and perpetuate a docile plantation labor class at the same time.

The missionaries' zeal for education had been unbounded. Education to serve God was their primary goal. Within a year, the first missionaries developed a Hawaiian alphabet and, in 1822, produced the first textbook in Hawaiian, containing the alphabet and reading lessons. Four years later, there were 400 native teachers, and by 1830, one third of the population was enrolled in schools. In 1831, a high school to train boys of exceptional promise was founded on Maui under missionary sponsorship.[2]

The missionary leaders and their immediate descendants—especially the women—insisted that education was a good thing, not just for the elite, but for everyone. Education, they believed, would make better Christians and citizens of the children of the commonest Hawaiians and Orientals. In 1840, the King's haole advisers passed the first public-school laws, imposing compulsory attendance through the age of fourteen. Five years later, a system of public education was adopted with the appointment of an American to be minister of instruction to the King's cabinet. The schools were placed on a tax-supported basis, and English was soon introduced as the language of instruction. With ten English schools in 1854, the public schools of Hawaii increasingly used that language, and before the close of the century, all textbooks and lessons, except in the most remote rural schools, were in English. At first, Hawaiians or part-Hawaiians constituted nearly the entire public-school population. With the influx of Portuguese families and Oriental laborers, the public schools became the meeting ground for all races of the Islands except the haoles. Whereas Hawaiians and part-Hawaiians made up 92 per cent of the student population of more than 7,000 in 1880, the proportion was reduced to 67 per cent twelve years later. The number of Chinese students increased from eighty-five to 353, the Portuguese from fifty-five to 2,253, and in 1892, there were sixty young Japanese pupils in the public schools of Hawaii.

The children of royalty and missionaries could not, however, be expected to go to common mission schools, and in 1839, a school for royal children was founded in Honolulu by the Reverend Amos Starr Cooke and his wife. In 1841, Punahou was established by the Reverend Daniel Dole for missionary children. There, the children of the favored haoles in Hawaii received a superior education through high school from well-trained mainland teachers. Other private schools, supported in part by the government treasury, were established under denominational auspices. For half a century, these schools carried the burden of secondary education. With Congregational backing, vocational training was given to Hawaiians at the high school at Lahainaluna on Maui and the Hilo Boarding School on Hawaii. In Honolulu, the Catholics established the St. Louis schools, and the Episcopalians founded Iolani for boys and St. Andrews Priory for girls.

Under the Republic, considerable progress was made in secular education. While strong efforts were made to control other phases of life, educators were invited from the mainland to liberalize Hawaii's public schools. The Republic's constitution forebade the use of public money to aid any denominational schools. Higher education was aided by the establishment in 1895 of Honolulu High School, the first public secondary school. The growth of the school system was stimulated by the fact that it provided jobs for Hawaiians and thereby reduced political pressure. Of the 400 teachers employed in the public schools in 1905, 148 were of Hawaiian blood.[3]

The most startling educational achievement, however, was the appointment of Henry S. Townsend to be inspector general of Hawaii's schools in 1896. Townsend had taken courses at the School of Pedagogy—now a part of New York University—where he was saturated with the new philosophy of progressive education. He sent copies of his own paper, called the *Progressive Educator,* to all the teachers in the Islands and inaugurated an Island-wide teachers' association. During the summers he organized special teachers' institutes, and brought illustrious champions of the progressive movement from the mainland to instruct Island teachers in the new ways. Among the distinguished speakers were Colonel Francis W. Parker, internationally famous educator from the University of Chicago, and Columbia University's great high priest of progressive education, John Dewey. At the institutes, the teachers talked about the need for local teacher training, and Townsend persuaded the officials of the Republic to create Hawaii's Normal School to develop home-grown teachers. They also discussed the desirability of abolishing tuition fees at public schools, making education truly universal; and in 1899, the year of Dewey's visit, the Republic did away with all tuition charges. A committee of haole leaders appointed to aid Congress in drafting the Organic Act could boast that "the school system and its methods are peculiarly American. . . . There are few countries in which education is so universal as in Hawaii. . . ."[4]

Townsend made many powerful enemies in the Islands. His constant prating about democracy in the classrooms, the development of student initiative, and the need for more higher education marked him as a radical. Even on the mainland his views were twenty-five to thirty years ahead of his time. In Hawaii, they would "subvert" not merely educational traditions, but an entire way of life. Townsend was denied appointment as superintendent of public instruction under the Organic Act, and departed for the mainland, but he left behind in America's colonial outpost the seeds of educational liberalism which would one day destroy Hawaii's oligarchy.

At the time of annexation, there were actually five school systems in Hawaii. In addition to 140 public schools, there were fifty-five private schools. Only one of these, a missionary-sponsored institution, was a Japanese-language school. Later, the Koreans, Chinese, and Japanese started dozens of such schools to bridge the gap between generations and civilizations. In addition to the industrial schools at Lahaina and Hilo, in 1887 the Kamehameha Schools for boys and girls were founded to give vocational training to children of Hawaiian blood. Catholic St. Louis schools were open to anyone, and Iolani, first established only for Hawaiians, was soon merged with St. Albans, an Episcopal school for haoles, and thereafter was available to qualified Oriental children who could afford the tuition or who fell heir to Episcopal charity. Another school was started by missionary descendants, Mr. and Mrs. Francis W. Damon, who took a number of Chinese boys into their home with the aim of giving them a Christian education.[5]

Punahou stood alone. More than any other institution in the Islands, it perpetuated Hawaii's elite class in the face of the Territory's expanding public-education system. Richly endowed with handsome buildings, excellent teaching facilities, and a campus that many mainland colleges could envy, Punahou was established as a symbol of educational excellence as well as elite status. When twenty-six Chinese boys applied in 1896, the trustees of Punahou, unwilling to adopt an extreme racist policy, were pleased to point to a new rule that no pupil could be admitted who was "incapable of using the English language as a medium of instruction," and quick to argue the advantages of the new free high school established in Honolulu only the year before. Punahou would remain exclusive, but never again exclusively haole. A few Orientals—though only a token—would be admitted; Punahou, established to teach loyalty to God, to inculcate citizenship and community leadership, and to prepare youngsters for college, had not altogether lost its missionary spirit.[6]

Theoretically, the oligarchy could have controlled education as rigidly as it controlled politics and labor. The entire public-school system was centralized in Honolulu and run by a superintendent and six school commissioners appointed by the governor. There was always a minority among the haole elite who argued for limitations that would, for example, end compulsory attendance at ten or twelve or would require teachers to be screened for their ideological fitness, but the missionary spirit of education for all prevailed.

During the first two decades following annexation, the powerful men of the haole community had more important things than education to concern them, and often the "do-gooders," sometimes women missionary descendants, were appointed school commissioners. For the most part, education was left to the commissioners and professional educators. Encouraging the oligarchy's neglect of the schools was the fact that teachers did not cost much. At the turn of the century, salaries ranged from $180 for a rural assistant teacher to $1,200 to $2,400 for a principal in Honolulu. In a large country school a teacher might make $510 to $720 a year, or about half of what a plantation manager earned in a month.[7]

The Americanizers were delighted also to encourage the importation of haole teachers from the mainland. To be sure, the teachers lived apart from the Oriental and Hawaiian communities and, indeed, never really entered haole society. But they did bring what were thought to be those "peculiar" American virtues of fair play and self-reliance to the classroom. Americanism to the teachers meant much more than preaching eternal virtues of good conduct. Patriotism, yes, but patriotism in America carries a revolutionary message: *freedom and equality*. When, in 1906, the Department of Public Instruction asked teachers to suggest quotations for children to memorize and recite in public-school patriotic exercises, recommendations included Joseph Trumbell's "Never shall the sons of Columbia be slaves, while the earth bears a plant, or the sea rolls its waves," Patrick Henry's "I know not what course others may take, but as for me, give me liberty, or give me death," and Abraham Lincoln's ". . . our fathers brought forth on this continent a new nation, conceived in liberty, and dedicated to the proposition that all men are created equal."[8]

Six years later, a mainland reporter visiting the schools was deeply moved as he heard 700 elementary-school pupils at Kaiulani School, in Honolulu, including Chinese, Hawaiians, Japanese, and Koreans, reciting the Gettysburg Address. The journalist was puzzled. Everywhere else in the Islands—outside of the schools—he found restrictions, even repression. Among the owners and managers of wealth in Hawaii, he discovered sharply hostile feelings toward the Orientals and disdain for the Hawaiians. In the schools, however, he met dozens of teachers who, living almost in another world, were confident that the nonhaole residents of the Territory would some day make excellent American citizens. He marveled at one teacher who had been in the schools for twenty-nine years, nurturing each spark of individuality and creativity in her students. The writer was even more astounded to find that Hawaii's newest private school, Mill's Mid-Pacific Institute (later known only as Mid-Pacific Institute), begun by Francis W. Damon, was led by a principal imbued with progressive ideas.[9] At Mid-Pacific, an attempt was made to bring students of all races together in boarding

school and to encourage democracy in education. Because it was subsidized by members of the Damon, Wilcox, and Atherton families—all
missionary descendants—the fees were relatively low, and many ambitious Chinese and Japanese youngsters enrolled.[10]

Oriental families were quick to exploit every educational advantage,
public or private, and during the first eleven years of territorial government, the number of pupils in both public and private schools increased
from 15,537 to 26,122. Japanese enrollment jumped from 1,352 to
7,607 and constituted nearly 30 per cent of the population of Hawaii's
schools. The Chinese nearly trebled their school enrollment between
1900 and 1911, with almost 3,000 pupils entered in public schools.
Haole, Portuguese, and Hawaiian enrollments increased only slightly.
The schools of Hawaii, especially the public schools, were becoming
increasingly Oriental. Only the haoles, among all the races of Hawaii,
showed a majority in the private schools.[11]

The Oriental quest for education was unceasing. Despite the growth
of the schools, there were never enough of them, especially in the rural
areas, to meet the demand of the Orientals. On March 6, 1912, a mass
meeting of citizens from Hanapepe, Eleele, and some of the camps on
the Makaweli plantation was held at Eleele Hall which urged authorities to provide a much-needed school in that area or to increase the size
of the Hanapepe school, which was simply not large enough for all the
students who wanted to attend. In rural areas, haole plantation managers and their associates looked on such demonstrations with disfavor.
The schools were encouraging unrest, and the teachers had too much
freedom. When the second son in a Japanese family living on the west
coast of Hawaii wanted to go to the new high school at Hilo, on the
other side of the Big Island, the father's boss refused to allow it—one
son in a family going to high school was enough.[12] Earlier, in the remote
Kau section of Hawaii, the officials of the Pahala plantation accused
the local principal and his wife, who had been stirring the students and
their families with radical ideas, of drunkenness, bad manners, and
practicing medicine illegally. The school superintendent investigated
and discovered the charges to be unfounded. The plantation was simply
trying to get rid of the principal, who would not do its bidding.[13]

The managers of the plantations and industries, as distinguished from
their owners, and especially the missionary do-gooders deplored the
foolishness of Hawaii's teachers and schools. When Episcopal Bishop
H. P. Restarick sent a circular letter to the plantation managers and

other large employers of labor in the Islands asking their opinions of Hawaii's industrial schools, he received forty-four answers, unanimously blasting the disquieting effects of education generally. The schools cost too much, kept the students too long, and taught them the wrong things. It was the last alleged failing that most agitated the employers of labor. The Normal School, led by Edgar Wood, who had been chosen by the wild-eyed radical Townsend back in 1897, was filling young teachers with crazy so-called "progressive" ideas. Many employers suggested that manual training rather than nature and social studies be taught in the public schools. One man asked for agricultural training in the public schools, "as these islands are a purely agricultural region." "There is no shame in manual labor," wrote another, so why do the educators try to make politicians, clerks, and stenographers out of their charges? Such "gentlemanly persuits" should be discouraged. Simplify the curriculum, advised another. A boy with ambitions to become something more than a laborer "should attend public schools until he has a fair knowledge of how to read a newspaper intelligently in English, to write a legible hand, and to do common arithmetic up to decimal fractions," wrote a prominent employer. After that he should learn a trade. "It does look nowadays as if teachers wanted to educate all and sundry for the higher positions of life . . ." commented a plantation manager who complained against the stirring up of Orientals. Another employer probably came close to expressing true feelings of many when he said, "I do not believe in the compulsory education of alien children. . . ."[14]

The key leaders of the oligarchy were not indifferent to the pleas of the managers, but, for the most part, they refused to act on them. Late one night in 1913, Henry P. Baldwin, the virtual lord of Maui, put the issue squarely to a select group of Hawaii's haole advisers and leading educators. It was within their power, Baldwin said, to stop the expansion of schools on Maui, to model the island after the British colonial system by putting the brakes on education. The discussion continued long into the night in what one of the educators described as one of the most thrilling experiences of his life. Finally, the weary Baldwin, perhaps the most powerful man in the Territory, insisted that Maui must eventually become a first-rate American community. This meant, above all else, education.[15]

Baldwin's wife, herself a missionary descendant, was probably influential in his decision. On Maui, she sponsored the Baldwin House, at Lahaina, which had a kindergarten, night-school classes, a circulating library, a language school, and a high school—all conducted without fees. In Wailuku, she aided in the organization of the Maui Aid Association, which established a series of evening schools among plantation laborers called "American Citizenship Evening Schools." By 1920, there were fourteen such groups, with an enrollment of about 350 boys, predominantly Japanese.[16]

The missionary drive had not yet run its course. The Y.M.C.A. had four educational centers for night school and had begun free kindergartens, used mostly by Orientals. Married to a missionary granddaughter, Governor Frear, who would probably keep the Orientals from owning land and voting if he could, praised his commissioner of education for extending school facilities and increasing teachers' salaries.[17] In 1917, the missionary journal the *Friend* printed a dialogue between the Sugar Grower and the Christian Educator, in which the sugar grower came out second best. Laborers get unnecessary ideas from education, argued the loser. It will make them better citizens, rebutted the "true Christian."[18] In the same year, the legislature reaffirmed the school law of 1896, which insisted on the attendance of all children from six to fifteen in either public or private schools. Appropriate exceptions were made for students who were taught by a competent tutor—used only by wealthly haole families—or for children of not less than fourteen years who were suitably employed under the direction of a parent or guardian.

What Hawaii called "higher education" was aided with the establishment of high schools at Hilo in 1905, Maui in 1913 (following the fateful discussion at Baldwin's house on the future of Maui), and Kauai in 1914. A public college of mechanical and agricultural arts was begun in 1907 as a typically restricted agricultural college, but it was enlarged in 1912 to become the University of Hawaii, with a new College of Arts and Sciences as well as the old college, now called the College of Applied Sciences.

These achievements were remarkable only because Hawaii in many respects resembled a colonial area. A special committee consisting of Wallace R. Farrington, Edgar Wood, and N. W. Bowen, a schoolteacher, reported in 1911 that, compared with progressive states on the mainland, there were too few teachers for pupils in the Islands, and salaries were distressingly low, buildings overcrowded, and the per-capita cost of education was meager. The criticisms of a mainland team of investigators under the direction of the Federal Commissioner of Education in 1920 were even sharper and more detailed. The major premise behind the investigation was that education should "enlarge individuality" and provide "a wider range of thought and action" for Hawaii's people. While saluting the need for agricultural education in Hawaii, the report asked for greater room at the top. Students in the Islands, as elsewhere, should be encouraged to develop an interest in teaching, law, medicine, research, and languages.[19]

The commissioners were impressed by the children, finding them "universally better behaved, cleaner, neater in their appearance, more attentive to work, more amenable to suggestions from their teachers . . ." than in any states they had visited, but they complained that not enough was being done by the community to educate them. The average per-capita expenditure in mainland cities and states of comparable size was considerably higher. For Honolulu, the Territory would have to increase expenditures by one third to bring it up to the average of forty-seven other cities in the United States with populations between 100,000 and 300,000. Honolulu spent more on the police and streets (as a result of politics) than many other cities, but far less on schools. Teachers were underpaid, and there were not enough of them. In some elementary schools there were classes of fifty or sixty children. The superintendent of schools received an annual salary of only $5,700, and the commissioners of education were not paid at all. Not enough was spent on upkeep or maintenance either, according to the commissioners. The average expenditure for that purpose in the Territory was far less per pupil than on the mainland. In Hawaii, equipment such as wastebaskets, brooms, dustpans, and chalk were frequently provided by teachers out of their own salary. At one school, the teachers provided ink rather than use the poor-quality ink supplied by the Department of Public Instruction. More adequate assembly halls were needed. So were pianos in the larger schools, playgrounds, and slide collections. Why, the investigators wanted to know, did not Hawaii follow progressive rural communities on the mainland in providing transportation at public expense for students living at a distance from the schools? The investigators also recommended the inauguration of public kindergartens, something unheard of in the Islands.[20]

Going beyond their mandate to investigate the schools, the 1920 federal commissioners complained that Hawaii's unique system of taxation was not adequate to support a first-class American public-school system. Limited income taxes were earmarked for other purposes. Real-property assessments were amazingly low. Honolulu's real-property tax was considerably below the median for forty-seven mainland cities compared with it, although the city and county of Honolulu ranked far above most other cities in taxable wealth.

Despite the complaints of managers against the new high schools on the outer islands, the observers from the mainland called for an expansion of secondary schools. They recommended an increase in high-school facilities and an enrichment of the curriculum to offer more than private schools could give in secondary education. They praised teachers at McKinley High School and insisted that salaries were too low; in all the high schools in the Territory, only one teacher was paid more than $2,200 a year. The library and courses in the social sciences and American history were praised, but the Commissioners criticized the fact that the "principals' offices in both McKinley and Hilo were so small, so inconvenient and so ill-supplied with decent office furniture as almost to be an affront to the dignity of the men who were forced to occupy them."[21] The report said there should be junior high schools to help prepare every child in the Territory for a high-school education—only three pupils out of every hundred were then in public high schools. After the eighth grade, twenty per cent of all high-school students failed, and another 20 per cent left school voluntarily. More importantly, high schools were inaccessible to hundreds, perhaps thousands, of ambitious youngsters who wanted to attend them. It was impossible for children from West Hawaii to commute to Hilo, and it was almost as difficult for young boys and girls from remote rural areas on Kauai, Maui, and Oahu to attend Lihue High, Hamakuapoko, or McKinley.

The federal investigators recommended also that only high-school graduates be admitted to the Territory's Normal School and that the training period be extended to two years. Eighth-grade graduates were then admitted for a four-year course, and high-school graduates were given one year of training. The University should be expanded, and high-school students should be made more familiar with its opportunities.[22]

The basic trouble was that leading haoles did not care about the public high schools. All but a handful of haole children attended private schools, a situation that seemed un-American to the mainland visitors.

Punahou and the Honolulu Military Academy had only a small number of nonhaoles.[23] Mid-Pacific, which was liberal, and Iolani, which was conservative, were largely Chinese and Japanese, but they were not public schools, where the races of Hawaii mixed together.

The 1920 federal survey had a tremendous impact on the schools of Hawaii. Many of its major recommendations were adopted. Five new high schools were added within the next ten years, and the high-school enrollment doubled. There had been no junior high schools before; fifteen were now created, and by December 1930, there were nearly 10,000 students in them. Training and salary standards at the territorial Normal School were raised under a new mainland educator, Benjamin C. Wist, who replaced Wood in 1921. The median salary at the Normal School went from $1,560 in 1920 to $2,640 five years later, and in 1929, the Teachers College was organized as a part of the University of Hawaii. Free transportation to rural schools was not provided, but bus lines were established in various parts of the Territory, operating at the expense of the counties or plantations. Federal interference in local education had clearly been beneficial.[24]

Many haoles seized upon two recommendations made by the federal investigators. The first was a proposal to do away with foreign-language schools, and the second was a suggestion for grouping students according to their ability to speak, read, and write the English language.[25] Large numbers of haoles opposed private language schools and observed their tremendous growth in Hawaii with alarm. Many public-school teachers were against the foreign-language schools, partly because of postwar xenophobia which affected the Islands as well as the mainland, but also because the foreign schools usurped time that the students might give to their regular studies. The Hongwanji, the most important of five Buddhist sects in Hawaii, operated sixty churches, thirty Young Buddhist Associations, forty Women's Buddhist Associations, thirty-three Sunday schools, and forty-four Japanese-language schools with 155 teachers and an enrollment of 7,100 children. Altogether, there were approximately 185 language schools, 489 foreign-language teachers, and 22,146 youngsters enrolled in Japanese schools.[26] The federal committee had heard pleas also from the Daughters of the American Revolution in Honolulu for the abolition of all foreign-language schools, implying that one language was good enough for any American. The Chamber of Commerce urged that the schools be put under the supervision of public authorities, and the Advertising Club of Hawaii called for their gradual elimination.

Before the federal survey in 1919, legislation had been introduced in the Territory to regulate the language schools. The bill was defeated through the intervention of Secretary of State Robert Lansing, who had wired the Governor of California to prevent anti-Japanese legislation while President Wilson was in France negotiating a peace treaty. In Hawaii, legislators showed restraint in deference to the President's negotiations, although the Japanese Consul General reportedly was in favor of the bill.[27] A bill was finally passed in 1920 regulating, but not destroying, the schools.[28] The law was not strictly applied (it was later declared unconstitutional), and during the next decade, the number of Oriental-language schools actually grew to 199, with ten Korean, fourteen Chinese, and 175 Japanese institutions. Enrollment practically doubled; by 1931, there were nearly 40,000 Oriental youngsters attending language schools daily after regular-school hours.[29]

The suggestion made in the federal survey to segregate pupils in the public schools according to their ability to use English correctly reminded old-timers of the effort made toward the close of the century to establish separate public schools for children of Chinese ancestry. In both instances, the argument that Oriental children speaking pidgin English in the classroom would retard the progress of others reinforced the desire of some haoles and Hawaiians to segregate Asian youngsters in schools of their own.[30] A Washington official observed in 1905 that many haole parents in Hawaii wanted to segregate students in the public schools according to race because of their fear that Asian students would make the haoles more Oriental than American.[31] The issue lay dormant until the 1920 strike, which stirred many haoles of Hawaii to a high level of hostility toward the Orientals. This, combined with a new influx of *malihini* haoles from the West and South with deep racist feelings of their own, brought renewed demands for segregated public schools. Punahou was too expensive and, besides, it was reaching the limits of its capacity. Prior to 1920, most Caucasian children had gone to private schools. Now that was impossible. New haole students from the mainland complained of the antagonism of Orientals in the public schools, which were now more than 60 per cent Japanese and Chinese. Their parents, horrified at being in a minority status for the first time, angrily protested slurs against their children by dark-skinned youngsters who could not even speak English properly. The *kamaaina* elite did not appreciate, these parents maintained, what other haoles had to put up with. The children of well-to-do families had tutors or went to private schools; the others could not.[32]

The pressure for school segregation mounted, but in Hawaii segregation by race was a practical impossibility. Intermarriage was too extensive. Could there be separate schools just for haoles? In 1920, there were only 1,222 haoles among the 41,350 youngsters in the public schools; it would be frightfully expensive to maintain separate establishments from first grade through high school just for them. Aside from the expense, Hawaiians and Portuguese, constituting an overwhelming majority of voters, would never permit such a system. Paradoxically, a few of Hawaii's most distinguished *kamaaina* families had intermarried. Would the children of a Shipman or a Wilcox be denied entrance to a public school because they were part Hawaiian? Impossible! Why not have one set of schools for haoles, Hawaiians, and Portuguese and another establishment for the others, it was suggested; but administration of such a system in Hawaii was impossible. Between 1920 and 1924, when agitation for a segregated school system was greatest, thirty-three haole grooms married Asian-Hawaiians; fourteen picked Chinese girls; thirteen, Japanese; four, Filipinos; and two, Koreans. Would their children have gone to haole schools or been shunted off to the Oriental schools? During the same years, sixty-eight Caucasian-Hawaiians married Asian-Hawaiian women; eight, Chinese; and three, Japanese. One hundred and five Filipino men married Hawaiian women, seventy-two chose Portuguese, and twenty-two picked haole girls. The Chinese made life even more complicated for those who would segregate the schools by race. During the same four years, forty-seven and twenty-nine Chinese men married Hawaiians and Caucasian-Hawaiians respectively. But it was the Hawaiians who made life especially troublesome for the racists. Better than one out of every ten Asian-Hawaiian women married haole men, and more than 25 per cent of the Asian-Hawaiian women were wed by Caucasian-Hawaiian males. The interracial complexities of Hawaii would have confounded any attempt to segregate the schools by race.[33]

Patiently, the officials of the Department of Public Instruction explained to parents that they could not and would not segregate students by race. However, many school officials did look with favor on segregation according to the ability of students to use English correctly. Discussion within the Department of Public Instruction on the merits of the idea was intense. Arthur L. Dean, president of the University of Hawaii, attacked the English Standard system as undemocratic. Others, including Oren E. Long, later to serve as Hawaii's superintendent of schools, governor of the Territory, and U.S. senator, were concerned about the spread of pidgin English and believed that the English Standard system would break down language barriers between the races, in the long run improving racial amity in Hawaii.[34]

In 1924, the Department set up its first English Standard grammar school, Lincoln School, in Honolulu. Others were created throughout the Islands during the 1920's and '30's. It was the job of the commissioners of Public Instruction—posts always held by haoles—to approve petitions to establish English Standard schools.[35] Each local school administered the English Standard examination to determine which children were qualified to enter.

In 1930, haole parents, unhappy with the overwhelmingly Japanese student body at McKinley, forced the Department to open Honolulu's English Standard Roosevelt High School. The principal at McKinley complained that racism was behind the maneuver. "The fear of language contamination," he wrote, "can hardly be the real reason behind the demand for the English standard high school," since haole parents at McKinley, as far as he could make out, had not complained about the language situation there.[36]

The English Standard system did tend, especially in its early years, to segregate Hawaii's public-school students along racial lines. But most of its supporters in the Department probably were not motivated by racism, though there may have been instances of discrimination in the administration of tests, particularly on the outer islands, where school officials were under the thumb of dominant haole interests. One of Hawaii's best-known nisei, later to hold a high post in the territorial government, believes that there was flagrant discrimination on Kauai during the late 1920's and early '30's. He did not pass the English Standard test, although he remembers that his English was as good as it is today, and it is excellent. Most of Hawaii's school administrators and teachers encouraged Oriental children to enter the English Standard school.[37] Rightly or wrongly, they deplored pidgin English and accepted the English Standard school system, not to keep the Oriental youngsters down, but to improve their English and to "protect the good speech habits of a minority of the pupils."[38]

The effects of the dual school system were complex. Clearly, it tended to segregate by race. On Oahu, a haole boy destined for a public-school education would be expected to go to Lincoln Grammar School and later to Thomas Jefferson or Robert Louis Stevenson Junior High and finally to Roosevelt High School. The chances were overwhelming that a Japanese child from the same neighborhood would go to different schools for the entire twelve-year period. In Lincoln Grammar's first year, 572 of the students were haole, with only nineteen Japanese and twenty-seven Chinese. Two years later, there were 683 haole students and only twenty-eight Japanese and thirty Chinese. During the same years, there were 126 and 123 part-Hawaiians, mainly haole-Hawaiians, in the school. From 1925 through 1932, Oriental children never comprised more than 7 per cent of the school population at Lincoln, a quota comparable to that at Punahou. In the mid-1930's, the proportion gradually went up, and by 1939, while an overwhelming majority of students were haole, *hapa*-haole, or Portuguese, the Chinese, Japanese, and Korean pupils constituted nearly 17 per cent of the enrollment.

At Lincoln Junior High the pattern was the same. In its first two years, 1928 and 1929, the Orientals constituted less than 10 per cent of the enrollment. Ten years later, a little more than 20 per cent of the students at Stevenson were of Chinese, Japanese, or Korean descent. The trend was similar at Roosevelt High School between 1930 and 1937. During those seven years, the haole population doubled, but the number of Chinese students increased fivefold and the Japanese nearly six times. By 1929, there were 129 Chinese, fifty-four Japanese, and twenty-one Korean pupils at Roosevelt, or nearly 20 per cent of the student body.

The percentage of Orientals at other English Standard schools on Oahu varied slightly. At Kapalama, located in a nonhaole area, only 6 per cent of the students were of Asian ancestry in 1929. By 1937, the proportion was more than 16 per cent. After 1933, at Kapalama, probably the least exclusive of the English Standard schools, there were about as many part-Hawaiians as haoles in attendance. At the large Aliiolani School, the ratio of Orientals to haoles was somewhat higher than at other English Standard schools. At Jefferson, located near more-haole neighborhoods, it was less. There, even as late as 1937, only 6 per cent of the students were of Oriental origin.

The English Standard schools on Maui and Kauai were almost exclusively haole, part-Hawaiian, and Portuguese at the outset, even in heavily Oriental areas. At Lihue Grammar School in 1925, there were only three Japanese students and no Chinese or Koreans in a student population of seventy-one. At Kaimoa Grammar School at Spreckels-ville on Maui, there were two Chinese and one Japanese. By 1939, both schools had substantial Oriental populations. At Riverside, the English Standard school at Hilo, there was considerable racial integration from the first. After 1928, part-Hawaiians usually outnumbered haole students, and the Oriental proportion went up steadily until 1937, when it almost matched the haole population, with seventy-two students to seventy-nine.[39]

To many of Hawaii's most ardent democrats, the English Standard school system was evil. It emphasized social distinctions between the races. Haoles looked down on students from regular schools. Hawaiian and Oriental children, especially from tougher neighborhoods, accused nonhaole boys at Standard schools of being sissies. To belong to the gang, it was necessary to speak pidgin. Since nearly all haoles went to English Standard or private schools, thousands of Hawaii's children went through the public schools without ever having close contact with Caucasian youngsters. The dual system also helped to perpetuate class distinctions. Students at the English Standard schools usually dressed in better clothes and had more spending money. Inevitably, the Standard schools became the prestige schools, not just for the students, but for teachers as well. Newer and better equipment was given Standard schools. Teaching assignments to them were rewards, the best teachers gravitating to them, where they were needed least.[40]

Not every Oriental opposed the system, and each year saw an increasing number of them admitted. Many of the nonhaole leaders of modern Hawaii who were fortunate enough to attend English Standard schools view them in retrospect as having provided a bridge between classes and races. There they met and learned to know haoles in classrooms and extracurricular activities, and, perhaps more important, haole children met and grew to understand them. The girls especially, attempting to live up to their parents' hopes for them, managed to win admission to the English Standard schools. The boys, frequently blocked by their peer groups from mastering what was accepted as standard English, found the going much rougher when and if they reached the University of Hawaii or mainland universities. Today in Hawaii, it is not unusual to find nisei or sansei wives of professional men who are more fluent in English than their husbands.

On the eve of Pearl Harbor, slightly more than 21 per cent of the students in Hawaii's English Standard schools were of Chinese, Japanese, or Korean descent, the Chinese pupils slightly outnumbering the Americans of Japanese ancestry (A.J.A.'s). After the Japanese attack on Pearl Harbor, nearly 2,000 haole students were withdrawn from the public schools of Hawaii, and many were sent to the mainland for schooling. By 1947, when the Department of Public Instruction decided to abandon the English Standard system, there were more Japanese than haole students in English Standard schools, and the haole children, for whom the schools were designed, constituted less than a quarter of the student population. The integration of Hawaii's schools, which had been predicted by the more idealistic supporters of the English Standard program, had been accomplished.

During the life of the system, only a small minority of Hawaii's children—less than 7 per cent of the public-school enrollment in December 1941—attended English Standard schools. A majority of pupils were still enrolled in the regular public schools, and it was these schools that experienced a great burst of growth in the 1920's following the critical federal survey. It was here that progressive pedagogy took hold. It was these schools that came under sharp attack in the late 1920's and early '30's from leading members of Hawaii's oligarchy, and it was primarily these schools that proved to be Hawaii's crucibles of democracy.

Aside from the controversy over the English Standard schools, three distinct attitudes toward Hawaii's public schools crystalized during the 1920's. The first, whose foremost spokesman was Governor Farrington, was that expanded educational opportunities were compatible with development of Hawaii's basic industries. Nonhaoles should go to school, even the University, to become better citizens and to contribute more to Hawaii's peculiar economy, Farrington believed. A second view, growing in popularity within Hawaii's oligarchy, held that education in Hawaii had to be curtailed, despite criticisms of the 1920 federal survey, for education would destroy an economy based on the utilization of masses of ignorant laborers. A third position, whose principal advocate was McKinley High School principal Miles Cary, urged education to liberate talent and creativity, with the hope of someday transforming the social structure of Hawaii.

Governor Farrington's position was simple. He told his Superintendent of Instruction, Vaughn MacCaughey, that he would work for the expansion of high schools but that the Superintendent and his department should be friendly to industry and should instruct the children in the dignity of manual labor.[41] The sugar interests were wrong in thinking that education would be bad for the Territory, Farrington told his friends and subordinates. In a speech to the second annual convention of the Hawaiian Education Association, he argued that the schools could educate toward the land as well as away from it. Teachers could encourage children to respond favorably to flowers, plants, vegetables, and other growing things if they tried. Even college graduates might be of value to Hawaii's agricultural industry.[42] As publisher of the Honolulu *Star Bulletin,* Farrington publicized Territory-wide contests to reward the agricultural and gardening abilities of Hawaii's children. He was delighted with the school slogan at Kapaa, on Kauai: "Every Kapaa school student an agriculturalist." In 1923, he wrote his Superintendent suggesting the creation of a domestic-service department in the public schools to encourage more Filipinos to become domestic servants.[43] Two years later, he wrote his new Superintendent, Will C. Crawford, complaining that not enough money and too few teachers were being used to promote agriculture. He advised Crawford to remember that agriculture was the source of prosperity in the Territory.[44] In a 1927 address to the Hawaiian Education Association, he proudly asserted that in the previous year more than 10,000 students from the public schools had found vacation employment on Hawaii's sugar plantations and in pineapple canneries.[45] When a social worker told a session of the New Americans Conference, "You cannot force the Oriental youth with a high school education to go back to the plantation—he will not do it," Farrington replied the next day that no one was trying to drive the Orientals back to the plantations, but in Hawaii there should be opportunities available so they would want to remain in agriculture.[46]

Farrington did his best to implement the recommendations of the federal survey. He agreed that it was deplorable that Hawaii had a smaller public-high-school enrollment in proportion to its total public-school enrollment than any state or territory, including Puerto Rico and the Canal Zone. During his administration, five new high schools were added, many intermediate or junior high schools were started throughout the Territory, and the most progressive educational methods employed anywhere in the United States were permitted to enter Hawaii's classrooms.

Farrington supported these developments in the face of mounting criticism from some of the most powerful men in Hawaii. A joint committee of the Hawaiian Sugar Planters' Association and the Chamber of Commerce was formed in 1923 to check the budget of the Department of Public Instruction, requesting explanations for items the committee members thought unnecessary or unwise. John Hind, president of the Association for 1925, revealed in his annual address the deepening resentment of most of Hawaii's sugar planters toward the schools and teachers. Hind attacked the "visionary high-brows" who believed that all Hawaii's children could be educated for "the top rung." This "mistaken idealism" should end, warned Hind, and education should be "looked upon more in the light of a business matter. . . ." The Department of Public Instruction was spending entirely too much money. The taxpayers should be relieved of responsibility for educating Hawaii's youngsters in the public schools "after the pupil has mastered the sixth grade, or possibly the eighth grade, in a modified form."[47] Those familiar with the Hind family on the Big Island were not surprised. Six years before, John Hind's brother, Robert, a leading territorial senator, had fought plans for building a new school until he was forced to submit to political pressure.[48] When John Hind asked that high-school students pay tuition, he was only repeating what plantation managers and owners of the Big Island had been saying for years. But when Frank C. Atherton, missionary descendant and scion of one of Honolulu's most charitable families, criticized the public schools in his address as president of the Hawaiian Sugar Planters' Association the following year, many teachers and school officials were shocked. The curriculum was bad, complained Atherton. "It does not fit our young people to earn a competent living. . . ."[49] English literature would not make Hawaii's boys better mill supervisors, nor would foreign languages help prepare girls for motherhood, he criticized. In 1929, a special committee of the Honolulu Chamber of Commerce criticized the tendency among teachers to think of high schools as preparatory institutions for college. The high schools should not be a "center of intellectual, moral and social activity in the community." They should be highly selective institutions, accepting only the highly qualified, and sending few of them to higher education.[50]

During the 1920's, the schools and teachers were occasionally defended by the Democratic party's perennial candidate for delegate, Lincoln McCandless, whose wife had served as a commissioner for the

Department of Public Instruction. McCandless made education in Hawaii a compaign issue in 1922, stating his views in the Democratic party organ, the *New Freedom,* and in the Japanese newspapers *Hawaii Hochi* and *Nippu Jiji.*[51] But it was Farrington's determination to implement the recommendations of the 1920 survey and his support of three excellent superintendents of public instruction, combined with the still-active proeducation missionary tradition of Hawaii and the ability and determination of an unusual group of teachers, that enabled the public schools to prosper.

The teachers of the 1920's and '30's were the godparents of modern Hawaii. Although Hawaii undoubtedly had many indifferent and inadequate teachers, probably no community in the world was blessed with so devoted a group of educators as were the Islands during those two decades. Teachers from the mainland frequently brought an extra measure of devotion to their tasks. Socially isolated from the Islands' haole elite, they mutually reinforced their antagonism toward the oligarchy's philosophy of education. One teacher, later to achieve a high post in Hawaii's school system, recalls that in the early 1920's, about three quarters of the mainland teachers resented the plantation system. They had read and heard about plantations in the South and associated the plantation system in Hawaii with slavery. Many teachers resented the emphasis on private schools, the lack of respect shown teachers by Hawaii's men of power and wealth, and the meager school budgets they received despite support from Farrington and his superintendents. The more spirited mainlanders particularly despised the efforts made to control them in the rural schools.

Because of these factors and because a large number of mainlanders only came to Hawaii for a short stay, there was great turnover in Hawaii's teaching force. Between 1910 and 1920, nearly two thirds of the 1,785 teachers who entered the public-school system of the Islands dropped out.[52] Those who remained were unusually devoted to their students. They were precisely the kind of teacher who took to heart the official advice of the Department of Public Instruction to nourish every spark of creativity in each child no matter how crudely he speaks or how slow his ways. In many instances they welcomed the opportunity to work with Hawaii's polyglot children and took a real interest in the students' varied cultural backgrounds.[53]

The 1920 survey reported that nine of ten of Hawaii's teachers were women. As late as 1920, haole mainlanders and part-Hawaiians comprised the bulk of the teachers. In the elementary schools that year, 40 per cent of the teachers were haole, 25 per cent Hawaiian or part-Hawaiian, and 12 per cent Portuguese. With the expansion of the Normal School under its dynamic principal Benjamin Wist, the proportion of Hawaii-trained and Oriental teachers rose each year. To become a teacher was the overriding passion of many of Hawaii's brightest children. Teaching was, after all, the only profession that could be won without an expensive mainland education. To many Oriental children it was also the noblest of professions. When the junior and senior high-school students of Hawaii were asked in 1922 what they hoped would be their life's work, 42.8 per cent of the girls replied that they wanted to be teachers. Throughout the 1920's, Japanese students comprised approximately one third and Chinese about one fourth of the enrollment at the Normal School.[54] In 1900, there had only been twelve teachers of Chinese descent in the schools of Hawaii, a scant 2 per cent of the total, but by 1930, 20 per cent of Hawaii's 2,807 teachers were of Chinese ancestry.[55] To many of these men and women, teaching was more than a job; it was a dedication.

Even more than their dedication, it was what they taught and the way that some of them taught that stirred the imaginations of Hawaii's children. Teachers anywhere teach much more than the three R's. They transmit the dominant characteristics of a culture as well. In Hawaii, where the parent generation was still predominantly alien, the teachers were the principal transmitters of American civilization. The way of life they taught was different not only from the old-country ways practiced in the home, but also in sharp contrast with the social system of Hawaii. Because Hawaii's public-school students were predominantly dark-skinned and slant-eyed, the teachers concentrated more than usual on American history and government, free enterprise, and the meaning of democracy. Hawaii's elementary and high-school curricula were loaded with patriotism. The Gettysburg Address, with its emphasis on government by the people, was as popular in the grammar schools during the 1920's as it had been in 1912. In 1928, a teacher from Oklahoma was deeply moved at his first assembly recitation as little nisei boys seriously recalled "our Pilgrim forefathers." Another teacher on Kauai, who did not dare say that he believed labor unions would be good for Hawaii, enthusiastically and openly taught the Declaration of Independence and the Bill of Rights. The heroes of this culture, who filled their young minds with bold dreams, were unlike anything the children had known in Hawaii: George Washington, who led a revolution against colonial government; Thomas Jefferson, who believed that all men were created equal; Abraham Lincoln, who thought that the American government was of, by, and for the people; Andrew Carnegie, immigrant boy who became a multimillionaire; Henry Ford, a humble haole lad now a great industrialist; Daniel Boone and the other American pioneers who conquered the wilderness and who, as one could do in America through hard work and ability, overcame difficulties to achieve success. America was individualistic, competitive, full of opportunity and reward. It was, in short, everything their homes and Hawaii were not.[56]

These aspects of American culture were actively preached in the schools of Hawaii, and teachers and their books often exemplified them. The home-grown instructors, often coming from plantation backgrounds, had *chosen* to become teachers, as the instructors from the mainland had *chosen* to make their home in Hawaii. Freedom was the keynote of this culture. When a teacher asked his young charges what they wanted to be when they grew up, he implied that there was a *choice*. With their first taste of American political history, students learned that American voters *chose* between two great political parties. In the romantic novels they read as teen-agers, they quickly learned that mates were *chosen* in this country by the young people themselves, not by the parents.

Because Hawaii's Department of Public Instruction and some of its most influential teachers were imbued with the educational philosophy of John Dewey, Hawaii's schools emphasized freedom and democracy as much as, or more than, schools on the mainland during the 1920's. The *Hawaiian Educational Review,* the teachers' official organ, preached progressivism. "Subject matter is a mere incidental only," it editorialized in 1920. "Teaching subject matter is the least important thing we do. . . ."[57] In no place more than Hawaii did American schools depart from the traditional European view that the school is only an institution where subjects are to be learned and mastered. The American school is a socializing institution, wrote Hawaii's most influential teacher, Miles Cary, in which students should be encouraged to become creative and individualistic.[58] The director of the newly created Division of Research of the Department, Ross B. Wiley, wrote, "The school must do what it can to develop in its pupils the ability to stand on their own feet and solve their own problems as they arise. They must be able to think for themselves." Hawaii's schools, Wiley said, were committed to the ideals of democracy, and "each class should be, so far as it is possible, a democratic social group."[59]

In 1927, the Department created the Kawananakoa Experimental School to put into practice student-centered education from the first through the eighth grades. Just outside Chinatown, the school catered mainly to Oriental children. In it, classes were organized on the basis of self-government, and children were given responsibilities as class officers. In the eighth grade, youngsters studied in detail the governments of the Territory and the city and county of Honolulu. Progressive pedagogy was also advanced by teachers and principals at the Robello School and the Kahului School and even at such plantation schools as Hanamaulu, Pahala, and Olaa.[60] Ironically, the Department, more centralized than any school system in America, could push progressive ideas from Honolulu in rural communities where the local population was indifferent or opposed. Regularly, this message went out: "Teach individual initiative and responsibility." The teachers were even asked to examine themselves to ascertain that their own attitudes were democratic and progressive.[61]

Materials on the methods developed and practiced in the Kawananakoa School were sent to teachers at all schools just as soon as they were available. Under Wist, the Normal School trained its teachers in the philosophy and practices of progressive education. It co-operated with the Division of Research in organizing curriculum study groups throughout the Territory, and by 1930, it had brought more than 30 per cent of all teachers into such groups. Emphasis was placed on the so-called "activity curriculum," in which students worked together on practical projects. This aspect of the progressive program was favorably received by many plantation managers. At Pahala School, for example, students did agricultural work during school hours. Another group, studying Japan, planted a rice patch. Children at the Kaahumanu School in Honolulu constructed a miniature sugar-plantation village and a pineapple field, and girls at Kawananakoa made furniture, linen curtains, and rugs.

Aside from the learn-by-doing aspect of the progressive movement, there was little the educators said or did that appealed to the powerful haole elite of Hawaii. As criticism mounted, the Department of Public Instruction defended its program in a bulletin entitled *Progressive Education and the Public Schools of Hawaii*. The world, including Hawaii, was changing, argued the educators, and children must develop "the ability to stand on their own feet, to solve new problems as they arise. They must be able to think for themselves." This meant, continued the officials of the Department, that "democracy in the school and in the classroom is a condition necessary to true education."[62]

In no other institution in the Islands was this philosophy carried to greater length than at McKinley High School in Honolulu. There, Miles Cary, with his deep faith in children and contagious enthusiasm for democracy, influenced thousands of graduates during his tenure as principal between 1924 and 1948. Cary had been born in the little town of Orting, Washington; he had come to Hawaii to teach history at McKinley in 1921. Two years later, he was transferred to Maui, as principal of Maui High School, but he returned to McKinley the following year and remained until 1948 except for a short period during World War II when he served as a volunteer worker in a Japanese relocation center in Arizona.

Cary aimed at stimulating initiative among and creating opportunity for his charges. In extracurricular work he encouraged student government, even inviting Governors Farrington and Judd to attend the inauguration of elected student officers and other student functions.[63] Under his administration there were more than sixty extracurricular clubs and organizations, including the Debate Club and the Citizenship Club. The Social Studies Department recognized that student government was a laboratory for teaching citizenship, and there were fourteen standing committees to give students the opportunity to take initiative in self-government. These included a student court of justice, with a sheriff, deputies, commissioners, judge, and board of examiners, which had jurisdiction over such matters as disorder in the halls and the destruction and misuse of school property. The three class presidents, as well as the captains and managers of each major team, served with the principal and coaches on the Athletic Council to determine school athletic policy.[64] The students also published a newspaper, which gave them further opportunity for self-expression. By 1929, half of the students in the school belonged to one or more of its clubs.

Cary pressed also for a progressive curriculum. In 1920, when McKinley was both a junior and senior high school, three basic programs were offered: college entrance, general, and business. At that time, only the students in the college prep and general programs were given what was called "sociology" in their ninth and tenth years, English history in the eleventh, and United States history in the senior year. In 1922, the curriculum was opened to require all students to take a one-year civics course as freshmen and a year of American history in later grades. The following year, the McKinley curriculum was divided into six sections: classical, scientific, commercial, home economics, manual training, and agricultural; and a large number of electives were introduced for all students, including world history, economics, parliamentary law, and social problems. Following Cary's assumption of the principalship, many majors were introduced in 1924 and 1925—languages, mathematics, social sciences, social service, science, art, music, and journalism. A new course called "American problems" was now required of all students in the twelfth grade, as was a year of United States history and government in earlier grades.[65] He agreed with School Superintendent Will Crawford's policy of offering eight foreign languages as electives in the public schools, including Hawaiian, Chinese, Japanese, and Korean.[66]

Progressive education to Cary did not mean vocational training. By 1929, there was only one strictly vocational course at McKinley—cafeteria management—and it had an enrollment of only eight.

In 1928, Cary introduced a major reform, the so-called "core curriculum of English and social studies." The objectives were twofold: first, to center the teaching of English around real social problems; and second, to encourage democratic participation by students as they learned. Despite persistent opposition to the core program as a "radical idea," it was adopted at other high schools. Whether it achieved Cary's objectives remained a matter of dispute among teachers as well as parents until it was finally abandoned in 1961.

For the most part, Cary's teachers were co-operative. Education, wrote one of them, should make students believe in themselves. Others, when asked by Cary about the purposes of education in high school, stressed the importance of leadership. The words that appeared repeatedly were "self-reliance," "individuality," "initiative," "leadership," and "citizenship." "We cannot and should not expect our work to be purely vocational. If too vocational, we fail to teach the essentials which make for a dynamic personality," pointed out one teacher in answering critics among the owners and managers of Hawaii's wealth. Dynamic, not docile, personalities were the objective.[67]

But not all of the teachers agreed with Cary. Late in his career, when criticism mounted against Japan, some teachers were troubled by his sanguine attitude toward the Japanese in Hawaii. When he criticized one of the teachers by listing as a "significant limitation" on her rating sheet that she "becomes alarmed if her students do not think the way she does," the teacher went to higher authorities to complain of Cary's pro-Japanese tendencies. Specifically, she had been cross with a student who said that Japan's activities during the 1930's were similar to those of the United States in developing the Monroe Doctrine. Cary was forced to apologize to the teacher and to remove the critical rating.[68]

In the meantime, Cary's philosophy had done its work. The students drank deeply of democracy at McKinley. Despite the fact that a large proportion of them held jobs during the school day—nearly 15 per cent of them were employed for an average of twenty-four hours a week in 1930—they became enthusiastic about student government, joined the clubs, and started numerous projects on their own.[69] The 1928 McKinley catalogue stressed that the most important characteristic of an educated person is his self-dependence, and two years later, the boys of McKinley, aware that school authorities could not persuade the legislature to budget for their desired swimming pool, organized work parties to build their own.

The catalogue also claimed that "a person is educated who is open minded in his thinking and his attitude towards each new situation which he meets in life." Taking the message to heart, interclass debates covered controversial subjects, including the dangerous topic for 1929 "Resolved: the young people of Hawaii should seek their life work elsewhere."[70] Probably no other subject interested the boys of McKinley as much as their future. In this they were no different from boys at other schools. When asked in 1922 what they hoped to do in the future, 15 per cent wanted to become professional men, 50 per cent skilled workers, 5 per cent agriculturalists (farmers), and only .5 per cent laborers.[71] The planters were right in accusing education of turning their heads. In 1929, sociologist Romanzo Adams concluded that high-school students in Hawaii considered plantation employment to be a mark of inferiority. Adams surveyed the seventh- and eighth-grade boys of seventeen plantation schools, where the influence of plantation management was greatest and opportunities for choosing among occupations minimal. Even in these schools, 8 per cent of the youngsters wanted to be engineers, 11 per cent doctors, lawyers, or teachers, 8 per cent farmers, 12 per cent businessmen, and only 1.7 per cent laborers. At the high schools, a smaller proportion aspired to be laborers. At Kauai High School, well over 60 per cent Japanese and less than 5 per cent haole at the time, half of the students wanted to become professional men and another 20 per cent businessmen. At Maui High, about two thirds Japanese and 10 per cent haole, a somewhat higher proportion wanted to enter the commercial world, but their sights were still set high. At the new Kona Waena High School on the Big Island, where fifty-one of sixty students were of Japanese origin, nearly a third of the total wanted to become farmers, but even here, well over one quarter of the students picked a professional goal.

The drive to succeed was extraordinary. Although probably not more than half of the students in the primary grades at plantation schools eventually went to high school, 88 per cent of those surveyed by Adams said they expected to reach the upper grades. Of the 181 who did not intend to go to high school, two thirds gave as their reason financial problems and the need to help their parents by working. Of the boys in four rural senior high schools and two rural junior high schools, nearly 65 per cent—an absurdly unrealistic proportion—said they intended to go to college. One boy, hoping to become a teacher, wrote, "When my father came from Japan, he was handicapped in his work. I intend to go to school to get an education to lead a better life and live up to the ideals of an American." Another boy commented, "One summer I was awakened to the fact that the plantation was not treating the laborers right. This condition had been existing ever since I was born, but I remained ignorant of it. . . ." The youngster could not understand why his issei father worked so willingly for the plantation when the plantation did so little for him. This boy, destined to complete high school and the University of Hawaii, said, "I went back to school with the determination that I would fight for my people."[72] Plantation conditions, Adams pointed out in a warning to the haole elite, were not acceptable to the boys with a high-school education. They knew that if discharged as a *luna* from one plantation, they could not get a job on another. They also knew that there was no room at the top.

The American dream of room at the top captivated the Oriental teen-agers. When 1,000 children in several Japanese-language schools were asked "When your parents return to Japan, will you stay in Hawaii or go to Japan with your parents?" half of them between the ages of twelve and fifteen replied that they would remain in the Territory.[73] At McKinley, students were encouraged to dream. There, the gap between reality and the vision of success was less than at the rural schools. Between 1910 and 1920, seventy-six graduates of McKinley High School went to college, almost twice the number from the other four high schools combined. This was still much less impressive than the 236 graduates sent to higher education from the much smaller Punahou, but the tradition of higher education for the sons and, to a lesser extent, daughters of Hawaii's immigrants had been established even before Cary's tenure at McKinley. Half of the McKinley graduates attending college were at the University of Hawaii, but ten had been accepted by the University of California, three by Stanford, three by the University of Michigan, and one by Yale. When 394 recently graduated seniors from McKinley were asked in 1928 to tell what they were doing, 105 reported that they were at the University of Hawaii, eighty-three at the territorial Normal School, eleven at mainland universities, and one at a university in Japan. Forty-nine others were taking advanced courses not leading to a degree. Well over half of McKinley's graduates of 1928 were doing graduate work of some kind. The percentage was even higher for the boys alone. Only seventeen were salesmen or salesgirls; four were mechanics; seventeen, carpenters; and one was a truck driver. Not a single graduate was working on a plantation.[74]

McKinley High School became a symbol. To some, it was "Tokyo High," where the children of Hawaii's immigrants were filled with crazy ideas unsuited to Island life. To thousands of schoolchildren on Oahu, it was a symbol of hope. To mainland educators such as William H. Kilpatrick and John Dewey, it was a monument to the progressive idea. A visitor from the Frick Foundation in Pittsburgh remarked in 1931, "Outside of the United States on the continent, the best thing surveyed educationally was the McKinley High School at Honolulu. . . ." An official from the Department of the Interior was also favorably impressed after a visit to the high school in the same year.[75]

McKinley's impact was enormous. Through the 1920's, more than half of the high-school students in the Territory attended it. Until the advent of the English Standard Roosevelt High School in 1930, McKinley was truly cosmopolitan. Among its 1929 student body of 2,339, nearly one of ten students was haole. Orientals comprised the majority; 43 per cent were of Japanese ancestry and 20 per cent of Chinese parentage.[76] Eleven per cent of the student body were Hawaiian or part-Hawaiian, and 4 per cent were Portuguese. The high schools on the outer islands had an even smaller proportion of haoles and were over 50 per cent nisei and sansei.[77]

McKinley was the leading school and Cary the most significant educator in Hawaii during the 1920's and '30's, but private Mid-Pacific Institute and its headmaster, Dr. John Hopwood, ran a close second. Under liberal Congregational auspices and, in later years, classified as nondenominational, Mid-Pacific had no racial quotas and was heavily Oriental. Many Oriental families, especially Chinese, reasoned that their children would have a better chance of getting into college if they attended a private school than if they graduated from McKinley. Many Chinese and Hawaiians went to Catholic St. Louis, although it was predominantly Portuguese. Iolani was heavily Japanese, but it often accepted applicants because they were Episcopalians or had an alumnus relative. At Mid-Pacific, talent was favored and encouraged. Hopwood constantly stressed the need to develop leaders in the student body. He spoke to the graduating class annually, explaining that he intended to make leaders of Mid-Pacific students. He fought a continuing battle with *kamaaina* oligarchy families, who wanted to turn Mid-Pacific into a vocational institution. One important labor leader in the new Hawaii recalled a hot debate in a Mid-Pacific class in 1924 over the police action against strikers at Hanapepe. At Mid-Pacific, too, freedom was encouraged and dreams stimulated. Its graduates, as well as those from McKinley, were putting the plantation behind them.[78]

But it was the growth of public secondary-school enrollment that was especially disturbing to many key leaders of the oligarchy. With fifteen junior and nine senior high schools by 1930, Hawaii's high-school population had jumped from 4,719 to 19,700 within ten years. As long as there was a huge labor surplus, the influence of the schools in drawing young people away from plantation work was frowned on but not regarded as critical. In the late 1920's, however, the leaders of industry became sharply hostile to the policies of the educators. In 1928, the Department of Public Instruction, anticipating further attacks, ruled that, beginning in 1930, 20 per cent of all junior-high-school graduates should automatically be denied permission to enter high school. The decision, to the chagrin of the educators and the disappointment of the planters, had the primary effect of swelling private secondary-school enrollment, rather than interesting Hawaii's youngsters in plantation jobs. Japanese pressure for a public-school education never let up, and while the 20 per cent rule was in effect between 1930 and 1936, the public high-school attendance of Japanese pupils actually increased by 43 per cent, compared with 26 per cent for all others.[79]

Especially upsetting to haole taxpayers was the fact that it was the Orientals, and particularly the Japanese, who used the public schools, while the haoles paid the bills. Although they constituted less than 10 per cent of the public-school population in 1929, the haoles were paying 74 per cent of the taxes.[80] In effect, the wealthy haoles of Hawaii were supporting two school systems: an elaborate private establishment and the regular public-school system. In 1928, the regents of the University voted to establish a system of tuition fees, but their decision was vetoed by Governor Farrington in one of his last acts in defense of Hawaii's educational system before completing his second term in office.

Education in Hawaii became as important to Merchant Street as labor and politics. The progressive educators had talked of education for citizenship or creative action, but in practice that meant a surplus of professional and white-collar workers. Leaders of the Islands' elite began to realize that they could not keep importing labor, but would have to develop laborers and field *lunas* among their own citizens. They listened increasingly to the persuasive young *malihini* principal of Kamehameha Schools, Frank E. Midkiff, who believed that two of three male high-school graduates could be induced to work as field laborers on the plantations if they were grouped together in desirable quarters, encouraged to have a wholesome social life, and promoted as soon as they exhibited merit.[81] Late in 1929, Midkiff wrote Frank Atherton, again president of the Hawaiian Sugar Planters' Association, urging him to appoint a continuing committee of businessmen and educators to work out methods for "directing thousands of our Hawaiian-born children into happy service in connection with our basic industries."[82] After all, Midkiff reasoned, children educated at the expense of Hawaii's corporations should do their part to produce the wealth of the Territory.

Governor Lawrence Judd, Farrington's successor, had already decided to appoint a committee to survey Hawaii's educational program and bring it more in line with Hawaii's industrial needs. Determined to please the critics of Hawaii's schools, Judd wrote Richard Cooke, president of C. Brewer, for advice on how to proceed. There should be two committees, answered Cooke, one of businessmen and one of educators. The former should decide the amount of money the Territory could afford to spend on education, and the latter should then recommend how that amount should be spent.[83] Judd decided on a large advisory committee, divided into different information-gathering sections. After unsuccessfully approaching Farrington and Atherton to chair the committee, Judd followed the advice of Cooke and appointed George M. Collins, a trustee of the Bishop estate responsible for managing the Kamehameha Schools for Hawaiians. Collins and his executive committee, which included Cooke and Walter Dillingham, picked Dr. Charles A. Prosser, president of a small technical college in Minnesota and an apostle of vocational education, to make the survey.[84]

There was never any question how the report would turn out. The 1920 survey, done by outsiders, had forced an expansion of educational opportunities in Hawaii. The 1930 survey was intended to reverse that process. Special working committees, comprised primarily of teachers, were appointed by the Governor to submit reports to the advisory committee, but almost all of their important recommendations were ignored. The committee on kindergartens asked for forty-eight public kindergartens—there were none in the Territory at the time—but the advisory committee refused, arguing that there was no money for "frills." A special committee on high schools, which included Miles Cary, pushed for greater self-government in the high schools to help prepare the child "fully and richly as an adult." The advisory committee's report attacked this approach as "coddling."

Dr. Prosser made his survey for a fee of $100 per diem plus expenses, officially paid by the Bureau of Government Research, a private organization, but actually financed by the Chamber of Commerce. Prosser worker closely with Cooke, new president of the Hawaiian Sugar Planters' Association. Cooke told the Midwestern educator that if the New England school system was responsible for educating the immigrant laborer away from the textile mills and that if Hawaii's system was patterned after New England, "We had better change our educational system here as soon as possible." The problem, Cooke suggested,. was to convince "our worthy theorists and dour politicians" to change the system that encourages public-school teachers to keep "their students from working on the plantations" and being "opposed to vocational training." In a twenty-page memorandum, Cooke told Prosser confidentially, "I have heard that some schoolteachers contend that not only agricultural labor, but all manual labor is degrading and unworthy."[85]

Prosser, with the help of the executive committee, prepared a first-draft report that warned parents against the belief that children would improve their social and economic status merely by spending more years in school. The schools, it was charged, were cloistering the students and not recognizing differences in capacity. School officials criticized the draft, urging that Prosser consult parents of children in the public schools, not just Hawaii's industrial leaders. The officials resented the recommendation that teachers' salaries be fixed and refixed in each legislative session. The Curriculum Council of the Oahu Secondary Schools disagreed with the recommendation to cut high-school enrollment, arguing that every student could profit by secondary-school experience. The Council, which included the principal of the new English Standard Theodore Roosevelt High School, and Oren E. Long, a future governor of the Territory and later U.S. senator, did not agree that high schools should offer primarily vocational training. Rather, industry should make occupational opportunities more attractive to achieve their aims.

The final 1931 report contained recommendations for a five-year period, including a proposal to limit high-school enrollment at the 1931 level and to limit expenditures for senior high schools to the 1931 budget. It urged that prevocational and vocational training, particularly in elementary and junior high schools, be expanded, and that at the university, the enrollment of candidates for the B.A. degree be limited for five years to the present number and the construction of new buildings be curtailed.[86]

The Honolulu *Advertiser* applauded the Prosser report and consistently called for a drastic reduction in school expenditures, arguing, "A boy or girl is entitled to just the amount of education we can provide and no more."[87] Farrington's *Star Bulletin* agreed that vocational education should be stepped up, but did not like the hostility shown toward educators in the report. The *Hawaii Hochi* complained that the Prosser report would set up two educational systems, one for the "darker skinned peasants" and the other for the "fair skinned aristocrats."[88] Almost every recommendation, it pointed out, would cut opportunities for nonhaoles in Hawaii.

The Prosser report was bad politics; it went too far and backfired. It mobilized all the proeducation forces, including friendly industrialists and *kamaaina* missionary descendants and, especially, the women. It angered Hawaii's Orientals, who were increasingly influential at the polls. It infuriated many of Hawaii's teachers, who shared the view of Benjamin Wist, principal of the Teachers' College, that "the teaching profession in Hawaii is definitely opposed to sacrificing our objectives of good American citizenship to educational practices which are questionable. . . ."[89] The educational theorists and the dour politicians were not persuaded.

The Prosser report became a historical curiosity. The territorial legislature continued to authorize the building of new junior and senior high schools. Hawaii's children continued to exploit their educational opportunities with growing intensity. In 1933, faced with a deficit, the legislature authorized the collection of $10 tuition fees from high-school students. Among Hawaii's leading newspapers, only the *Advertiser,* which had earlier argued that high schools should be reserved for those capable of higher mental training, supported the new ruling.[90] The *Nippu Jiji* and the *Hawaii Hochi* called the law undemocratic and un-American, and as pressure built up in Japanese newspapers and in the Honolulu *Star Bulletin,* the law passed out of existence in 1937.[91]

In the meantime, plantation owners and managers, persuaded that it was impossible to stop the growth of high schools, began to accept the argument that public secondary education in rural areas near the plantations might feed trained workers back into Hawaii's agricultural industries. They saw hope in the *Star Bulletin*'s report that enrollment in agricultural courses in the public schools had increased from eighty-six in 1927 to 701 in the year ending June 30, 1932.[92] When the *Star Bulletin* pushed hard for senior high schools in rural areas in 1936, some plantation managers, including Jim Campsie on the Big Island, who had been extremely hostile to education, now agreed.[93] The *Advertiser,* which had earlier complained that junior high schools were "fads and frills," agreed that certain English Standard schools and other rural high schools might now be desirable.[94]

The big switch came in 1934. Working behind the scenes was Oren Long, a high Department of Public Instruction official and former schoolteacher who had once held a minor plantation post on the Big Island. Would it not be better, he asked, to build high schools near plantation communities rather than have the children run to secondary schools in the cities? A convert to this view was Frank Atherton, who worked ardently to convince others in the *kamaaina* oligarchy that it was correct. Long traveled to rural communities to help organize pressure in the legislature and in the Department for local high schools.[95] At Waialua, twenty-two local community agencies rallied to demand a high school. Arther Dean, appointed Department commission chairman in 1934, with the confidence of the Hawaiian Sugar Planters' Association, also argued for new high schools on Molokai, Lanai, and at Hana, Maui, three of the most remote areas in the Islands. In 1936, eleven schools were added to the list of rural institutions with junior-high-school curricula, making a total of twenty-six. Senior-high-school enrollments had increased 90 per cent five years after the Prosser report.[96] By 1938, secondary-school enrollment was up to 36,312, 39 per cent of all children in public schools, compared with 11 per cent in 1920. In the decade following the Prosser survey, the senior-high-school population rose from 5,176 in nine high schools to 16,105 students in twenty-three schools. At McKinley, which had been sharply criticized in the Prosser report, the student population soared to 3,736 by 1939. The junior-high-school population jumped from 9,834 in fifteen schools to 17,531 youngsters in thirty schools. The University expanded, too. The number of B.A. degrees granted increased from 142 in 1930 to 213 in 1939.[97] The Prosser report had been defeated in every major respect.

But the defeat of the Prosser report did not mean that Hawaii's public schools were supported as substantially as those in more-advanced mainland communities. Hawaii continued to adopt meager public-school budgets, and the complex system of public-school fees was different from anything known in the American states.

A major reason for the relative neglect of public schools was Hawaii's huge private-school establishment. The private-school tradition in Hawaii was stronger than anywhere else in the United States. At annexation, more than one third of all students were enrolled in private schools. During the 1930's and the decades that followed, the private schools of Hawaii grew at an even faster pace than the public schools. In the four decades after annexation, the number doubled, and there were 103 by 1941. Forty years after annexation, almost two of every ten youngsters attending school in the Islands still went to private institutions.[98]

Continuous pressure from a growing haole upper class and liberal support from Punahou alumni resulted in that school's expansion. The unwillingness of haole middle-class parents to send their children to polyglot schools, dominated by Orientals—on the island of Kauai, for example, there were only 110 haoles among the 7,314 students enrolled in public schools in 1943—resulted in the proliferation of middle-class private schools. The demand of part-Hawaiians and Hawaiians for entrance to the heavily subsidized Kamehameha Schools brought about their gradual expansion. The growing proportion of Catholics able to finance private education in Hawaii produced more and larger Catholic schools. Because the private schools were thought to be the prestige schools of Hawaii, and because college entrance might be facilitated by graduation from them, many Oriental families, especially the Chinese, scrimped and saved to send their children to private schools during the 1930's. At the time of the Japanese attack on Hawaii in 1941, two of every ten Chinese students were in private schools. Japanese children, as soon as their parents could afford it, enrolled in private institutions in increasing numbers, and the proportion in private schools rose from 7.4 per cent in 1927 to 17.5 per cent twenty years later. These combined pressures meant that by 1939, Hawaii had proportionately more non-Catholic students enrolled in private schools than any state in the union.[99]

One reason for the growth of private schools was that the public schools were far from free. Never soundly financed, and until 1942 dependent on appropriations made each legislative session and based upon revenues from unvaried tax rates, the schools leaned heavily upon a system of fees for books, library use, courses in homemaking, clothing and sewing, typing, music, and, after they were established in 1943, kindergartens. Tuition charges for high schools were abandoned in 1937, but the parents of youngsters still paid for schoolbooks. In some cases, charges were made that had not been authorized by law in order to pick up extra money needed for school services.[100]

Powerful private schools, inadequately supported public schools, and the English Standard system helped maintain social distance between Hawaii's races, but the democracy taught and experienced in many of Hawaii's schools, including some of the private schools, would one day effect every important aspect of Island life. The battle of McKinley High School had been fought and won for democracy.

In 1959, the year of statehood, more than half the classmates, many relatives and friends, and some faculty members of McKinley's class of 1924 met at the Hawaiian Village Hotel Long House for their thirty-fifth reunion. Among these sons and daughters of plantation laborers were medical doctors, dentists, lawyers, professors, and brilliantly successful businessmen. From Berkeley, California, came Dr. Rebecca Lee Proctor, who, thirty years before, had been a small Korean girl determined to go into medicine. Also present was Masaji Marumoto, then associate justice of the territorial Supreme Court and soon to be appointed associate justice of the Supreme Court of the fiftieth state. There, too, were Hung Wai Ching, son of an illiterate cook, now president of several corporations and member of the Board of Regents of the University of Hawaii; Chinn Ho, multimillionaire entrepreneur; Modesto Salve, a former plantation laborer and the first Filipino to graduate from a high school in Hawaii, now a successful businessman and civic leader; the former Kimiko Pearl Kawasaki, wife of Hawaii's most distinguished agricultural extension specialist, Baron Goto; and Stephen Kanda, one of the first nisei to be appointed principal of an Island high school. Perhaps the most illustrious of the 233 graduates of the class of 1924 was Hiram Fong, president of Finance Factors, former speaker of the House in the territorial legislature, and, within a year, to be elected to the U.S. Senate. A message of *aloha* was sent from the class of 1924 to Miles Cary, at the University of Virginia. Cary was to live only a few more months, just long enough to know that Hawaii had been accepted as a state by the U.S. Congress and, more importantly, that his boys and girls had learned their lessons well.

Chapter Twelve

HAWAII'S ORDEAL

The thunderous roar of Japanese bombers and the bombs that smashed the planes at Hickam Field and the battleships, destroyers, and dock installations at Pearl Harbor pierced the lives of every individual in the Islands. For businessmen still in their beds in Tantalus Heights, industrious university students poring over their texts in Manoa Valley, and Filipino farm laborers at Ewa, awake for Sunday mass, World War II upset decades of attitudes and habits. The war signified change to many cultures and many nations in the far corners of the globe, but nowhere in the Western World did it produce such drastic social changes as in the Islands of Hawaii.[1]

The *kamaaina* oligarchy of Hawaii, indestructible for over forty years, was replaced within twenty-four hours of the Pearl Harbor attack by military control. At 11:30 A.M. on December 7, 1941, only a few hours after the bombs had fallen, Lieutenant General Walter C. Short announced to the people of Hawaii, "I have this day assumed the position of military governor of Hawaii, and have taken charge of the government of the Territory. . . ." General Short warned that his ordinances must be obeyed and that offenders would be either punished severely by military tribunals or held in custody until the civil courts were able to function again. Governor Poindexter declared martial law at the request of the Army and acquiesced in General Short's proclamation. The Governor later admitted, "Of course, being a civilian I was not very keen about having martial law, you will understand," but, because of the attack and the large Japanese population in the Islands, he agreed with the Army that the situation "could be better handled through martial law than by civil authorities."[2]

Poindexter had hoped that martial law would be lifted within a reasonable time, but his expectation was not fulfilled. Despite the fact that the population remained orderly, that no acts of sabotage or subversion were uncovered, and that Hawaii's Japanese responded with as much patriotism as any of the Islands' racial groups, martial law and military government continued until October 24, 1944, when it was terminated by Presidential proclamation.

The rights of all citizens were assaulted by the actions of the military in Hawaii. The Army assumed the operation of civil and criminal courts, the regulation of labor, the licensing of the press, and the control of public health, hospitals, and other territorial and city functions. All prices, food production, and transportation were controlled by the Army. Almost every offense was tried before a provost court or military commission, where the judge or judges were often without legal training, no copies of charges were given the accused, and defendants sometimes were convicted of violating "the *spirit* of martial law." When Riley H. Allen wrote an editorial in the *Star Bulletin* criticizing the military administration, he was promptly told that such conduct would not be tolerated. Censorship was easily imposed through military control of shipping and newsprint. All wage rates were frozen and labor contracts suspended. Under one order, certain employees were frozen in their jobs. In addition, one decree imposed jail sentences for absenteeism. Under it, hundreds of workers were either fined or jailed during the war. Another order suspended all legal holidays and abolished premium pay for such days.[3] The military did not allow public criticism even of the Army's supervised system of prostitution, which led to a lucrative and widespread traffic in the oldest profession.

Civil libertarians, college professors, professional men, and some business leaders supported Governor Poindexter and the newly elected Delegate to Congress, Joseph R. Farrington, in their efforts to restore constitutional government to Hawaii. But many of the most important businessmen in Hawaii were content with military government. On December 27, 1942, the Honolulu Chamber of Commerce, through its president, wired President Roosevelt, protesting any effort to restore civil government. We ought not to hamper the Army and Navy, said the Chamber officials, while there are still grave dangers confronting us. Benjamin W. Thoron, director of the Division of Territorial and Island Possessions of the Department of the Interior, answered, "I was somewhat disturbed by the telegram from the Chamber of Commerce to the President which gave the impression that a large and responsible group of American businessmen had so far departed from normal American thinking as to prefer military control of all activities of civilian life . . . instead of the normal process of American government."[4]

The military governor used *kamaaina* haole leaders in top positions. Walter Dillingham was appointed director of food production, and Lorrin P. Thurston, the president and general manager of the Honolulu *Advertiser,* was given the position of public-relations adviser to the military governor, thus encouraging the *Advertiser*'s continued support of the military government. The U.S. Supreme Court later declared the imposition of military government in Hawaii unconstitutional, but the *Advertiser* and many key oligarchy representatives defended the military to the end. Dillingham told a Pearl Harbor investigation committee that only the legal fraternity protested about the rights of American citizens, "and all that sort of hooey that nobody cared a damn about."[5] In fact, Hawaiian businesses prospered under military government, which paid well for properties, materials, and services, while prices were permitted to rise and wage levels were frozen.

On the surface, it seemed that Hawaii would return to normal after the war, its ways of life intact, the *status quo* preserved. The changes the war and military government had wrought, however, evoked a chain of consequences that were to accelerate the spread of democracy in Hawaii. Many nisei college boys from Manoa were to become war heroes, attend mainland colleges under the G.I. Bill of Rights, and return to Hawaii as advocates of social reform. The leadership within the Japanese community was to pass from conservative issei fathers to their American-educated sons. Japanese customs and beliefs, so cherished by the older generation, were to be suppressed by anti-Japanese public opinion in Hawaii, where, to a large extent, the Japanese were judged on the basis of their ancestry rather than their actions.

Following the attack on Pearl Harbor, fear and even panic seized many Islanders. Some of Japanese ancestry were afraid that they would be blamed for the assault. Hysterical citizens, a small minority, were now certain that the Japanese had been untrustworthy. Their feelings of mistrust had been vindicated by Japanese treachery. But what was to be done now? Hawaii's defenses were down, and hundreds of saboteurs, spies, enemies—even the Japanese maid and yard boy—might attack.

Though not all Islanders felt the terror that gripped some, the latent

anti-Japanese feelings of many haoles, Hawaiians, Filipinos, and
Koreans burst forth and spread through the Islands like a brush
fire. Rumors of Japanese espionage were fed when it was learned that
the two persons of Japanese ancestry on the tiny island of Niihau had
given assistance to a Japanese pilot who had made a crash landing on
that island on the afternoon of December 7.[6] Self-appointed civic leaders listened to these rumors and concluded that the Japanese of Hawaii
should be interned on the mainland. Their views were opposed by
those who properly pointed out that it would be economic suicide for
Hawaii to deport 40 per cent of its population. They should, however,
be deported after the war, came the retort.[7]

The proposal for mass deportation never received wide support in
Hawaii, but many important haole leaders continued to urge the selective confinement of those Japanese—aliens or citizens—who appeared
to be untrustworthy. A leader of the prointernment forces, John A.
Balch, a major officer of the Hawaiian Telephone Company, wrote
Admiral Chester W. Nimitz in August 1942 that "at least 100,000
Japanese should be moved to inland mainland farming states . . . if such
a step as this was taken . . . not only the danger of internal trouble could
be avoided, but the future of Hawaii would be secured against the sure
political and economic domination by the Japanese within the next
decade."[8]

Most members of the oligarchy and probably a majority of haoles
opposed the near-hysterical demands for mass internment or deportation. The suggestion was impractical anyway, because there was an
obvious shortage of shipping space. Riley Allen, editor of the *Star Bulletin* and friend of many top *kamaaina* haoles, quietly told leaders in
the Japanese community that the chances of mass internment or deportation were practically nil. To destroy those chances completely, he
advised Japanese acquaintances to exercise utmost self-restraint in
politics and labor. To one man he wrote that it would be a mistake to
run for office while the war was on, since any Japanese attempt to enter
politics would adversely affect the entire A.J.A. community. To
another, he sent a memorandum on labor relations, warning the Japanese that their widespread activity in labor movements might lead to a
renewal of the proposal for mass deportation.[9]

Other important haoles rallied to the defense of the local Japanese.
Maui's Harold Rice complained to Ingram Stainback about the decision of an official from the Department of Agriculture to refuse loans

to nisei citizens. His son, Harold F. Rice, chairman of the local committee authorized to grant loans for the Farm Security Administration, would have a hard time telling citizens of Japanese ancestry that they no longer possessed the benefits of citizenship, Rice noted.[10]

In spite of these defenders, other rights of citizenship were summarily stripped from the local Japanese population. Between Pearl Harbor and the war's end, 534 citizens of Japanese ancestry (mostly *kibei*) were interned. Publication of twelve Japanese newspapers and three magazines was stopped within a few days after the attack, and the *Hawaii Hochi* and *Nippu Jiji* were allowed to continue only under the close supervision of Army officers. In an obvious attempt to crush the Japanese-language schools, the territorial legislature passed a foreign-language law that made it illegal to teach a foreign language to children under ten years of age or to those under fifteen whose public-school grades were below average.[11]

But in spite of these deprivations, the Japanese in Hawaii, aliens and citizens, were treated with far greater respect than on the mainland, where 110,000 of them were interned in relocation camps without due process of law. The total number of internees from Hawaii during the war reached only 1,444, more than 60 per cent of whom were aliens, and only 277 were held at the war's end. From February 1942 until April 1944, when Hawaii was no longer considered a combat zone, many internees were sent to the mainland, but federal authorities there refused to accept American citizens except those who came as the children of alien internees. In 1942 and 1943, slightly over 1,000 women and children left the Islands to join their husbands and fathers behind the confines of America's World War II relocation camps.[12]

It was not primarily the legal deprivations that demoralized the Japanese population of Hawaii. The fear and hostility of their neighbors hurt much more. Nisei, as well as their fathers and mothers, met discrimination in employment throughout the war. At first, nisei volunteers for the Army were turned away, and many Island politicians recklessly scorned the entire Japanese community. When Doc Hill said, "A Jap is a Jap even after a thousand years and can't became Americanized"—a statement he was to regret deeply in later years—he was voicing not just a common haole sentiment, but that of many representatives of Hawaii's multiethnic population.[13] Many of the 53,000 Filipinos in the Territory blamed the Japanese of Hawaii for the actions of Japanese conquerers in Manila, Bataan, and Corregidor. A large proportion of the 8,000 Koreans in the Islands had strongly disliked the Japanese since the annexation of their country by Japan in 1910, and now they gave vent to their feelings.[14]

The barrage of criticism against the local Japanese continued long after the Pearl Harbor attack, despite the fact that not one act of sabotage had been committed by anyone of Japanese ancestry in Hawaii, and such criticism served to intensify Japanese cultural characteristics of restraint, face, and obligation. Almost instinctively, the Japanese community realized what it must do for its self-preservation and enhancement. Before systematic curtailment of Japanese community life was imposed by outsiders, the Japanese themselves strenuously repressed manifestations of their own culture. The youngsters from college and high school told their mothers to put away their kimonos, stop eating Japanese food, throw away the small shrines and family swords, preserved for generations; and the old folks had to listen.[15]

Japanese leaders went from house to house urging their friends and neighbors to behave meekly and quietly, to stay out of the way, and not to take part in rituals and ceremonies that would offend the haoles. Women whispered to each other over fences and in markets that they would soon be rounded up and put in a camp. Husbands searched old closets and cellars for Japanese emblems, swords, and family heirlooms to be voluntarily turned over to Army authorities. The old folks, grandfathers and grandmothers, wept but obeyed when their children warned them not to speak Japanese. Twenty-two Japanese-language schools were abandoned, fourteen cultural and occupational associations and eight Buddhist and Shinto shrines and temples were dissolved.[16]

George Watase, popular politician on Kauai's Board of Supervisors, sadly told his haole friends that he would abandon his dreams of a political career. Regularly elected to the Board of Supervisors since 1936, Watase declined renomination, commenting that he did not want to prejudice the community against the Japanese. "What's already boiling should not boil some more," he observed sadly. Other Japanese candidates followed his lead, and only one ran for public office in 1942.[17]

Japanese restraint meant self-criticism, too. "We have to work toward acceptance if we are to get anywhere," a young leader told his friends and colleagues at a conference for Americans of Japanese ancestry. Perhaps even Japanese funeral rites should be abandoned if the haoles did not approve, suggested another conferee. Even the Japanese custom of exchanging gifts, the quintessential expression of *on,* was criticized.[18]

Nisei and sansei blamed their parents and grandparents for the hostility toward Americans of Japanese ancestry. The Japanese principle of filial respect came under heavy attack; many of the alien Japanese themselves, disillusioned with and indignant toward Japan for the Pearl Harbor bombing, looked to their children for leadership. A small minority of Japanese elders was fiercely nationalistic, believing that the Americans were responsible for the war and that the Emperor would ultimately triumph. Most of the old folks were bewildered, confused by advice from their children to be good Americans when their cultural habits and in some cases their political loyalties were Japanese. Others became ardent patriots, throwing away their Japanese clothes and prizing their Red Cross pins.[19]

Most of Hawaii's Japanese regardless of age wanted to make a good appearance, to win the approval of the haoles and others, and a deeply ingrained obligation to serve their country in time of need led them to volunteer in extraordinarily high proportions to be air-raid wardens, workers in medical units, and members of the regular armed forces. Indeed, A.J.A. warriors from Hawaii probably achieved the most distinguished war record of any group in the United States armed services.[20]

Although when war broke Americans of Japanese ancestry were removed from the National Guard and denied permission to serve their country in uniform, it soon became apparent to military leaders that these Americans were thoroughly trustworthy, and discharged National Guardsmen, after persistently requesting service, were turned over to the Army engineers as a labor force. Slowly the idea of a nisei combat group emerged, and on June 5, 1942, the 100th Battalion, comprised of nisei National Guardsmen and draftees from Hawaii, was organized. Finally, in 1943, the War Department, after rejecting spirited A.J.A. boys, agreed to accept them in small numbers. A call went out for 2,500 volunteers, and immediately five times that number responded, over one third of all the males of Japanese ancestry in the Territory who were of military age. Thus, Hawaii's famous volunteer 442nd Regimental Combat Team was born.

The 100th landed at Orno, North Africa, on September 2, 1943.

Twenty days later, the battalion made its second landing, at Salerno, Italy, and began the bitter fighting that marked its march northward. The 442nd sailed into the Mediterranean in May 1944, and within a month was locked in hand-to-hand combat on the bloody battlefield of Anzio. Tough German units, guarding key approaches in northern Italy, fell back as nisei American soldiers pressed forward, determined to expunge every aspersion cast on their loyalty. Before the men in the 442nd were relieved, they had liberated eleven towns and villages and had taken two major hills. Later, although the regiment was badly in need of rest, orders came for them to move to southern France to rescue the Lost Battalion, a group of the 141st Infantry, composed mostly of Texans, who with no food or supplies and very little ammunition were surrounded by the enemy. After repeated frontal attacks and heavy losses, the men of the 442nd charged up the slope leading toward the Texans, shouting at the enemy and firing from the hip, while the Germans shot point-blank into their ranks. The bayonet charge succeeded in liberating the Texans in what may have been the most heroic battle of the war.

Between them, the 442nd and the 100th furnished 60 per cent of Hawaii's fighting forces and 80 per cent of the casualties. Ten times the 442nd was cited by the War Department for outstanding accomplishments. Their slogan, "Go for broke," reflected the spirited determination of men anxious to vindicate themselves and their families. Of the 7,500 men on its rolls at one time or another, 5,000 were awarded medals, of which approximately 3,600 were for battle wounds. Seven hundred never came back; 700 were maimed; another 1,000 were seriously wounded.[21]

The nisei who fought and died on the battlefields of Europe to defend the honor of their people in Hawaii and to discharge their *on* to the country of their birth learned more about Hawaii and America on Army posts than in combat. Coming from the most insulated and perhaps most stratified society in the United States, they witnessed at firsthand the racial segregation of Southern towns and the inferior position of poor whites, who performed menial labor reserved only for nonhaoles in the Islands. They heard the dreams and ambitions of other soldiers who planned to go to college to become professional men after the war. They listened to the better-educated *kotonks*— their fellow nisei from the mainland who were also in the 442nd Regiment—tell of opportunities on the mainland. Most of all, they wondered quietly to themselves if they were fighting for mere acceptance or if, as warriors returning to Hawaii, they could assert their ambitions in politics and business.

The early years of war saw strict restraints imposed on the Japanese community from within and without. The bombs that echoed over Pearl Harbor halted the steady progress the Japanese had made toward full participation in Island civic life. But the education the nisei of the 100th and 442nd received in the Army camps of America and on the battlefields of Europe loosed forces of change that were to elevate the power and respect of the Japanese of Hawaii beyond what the community's most ambitious proponents had hoped prior to the war. The struggle that had begun with the battle of McKinley High School and that was fought again at Anzio was to be, within the next ten years, triumphantly continued in the economic and political life of Hawaii.

Chapter Thirteen

REVOLUTION AT THE POLLS

The heavy-set nisei stirred in his hospital bed as he thought of the past. He recalled his father's thwarted ambitions for education and respectability, and specific episodes, such as the brutality of the police in the 1924 strike at Hanapepe, and he wondered what it all meant. Sakae Takahashi turned on his side and looked into the face of the one-armed war hero in the next bed, Daniel K. Inouye. Takahashi wanted to share with his friend from Hawaii his thoughts of the past and his ambitions for himself and other nisei from the Islands.

The two men—Takahashi, a wounded veteran of the 100th Battalion, and Inouye of the 442nd Regiment, whose body was still filled with lead—talked until they were exhausted. Hawaii would have to change, maintained Takahashi, who, as territorial treasurer a few years later, became the first nisei to hold a high territorial office. The war veterans should study hard, enter politics, and right the wrongs that had been done the Japanese community of Hawaii. Inouye, who would one day become the first United States representative from the State of Hawaii, agreed to Takahashi's argument, but without passion. Takahashi, who later won a reputation as one of Hawaii's most temperate politicians, this day heatedly attacked the oligarchy. There would, he predicted, be a new Hawaii after the war, a democratic Hawaii, and he was determined to help bring it about.[1]

The changes wrought by war did not, however, immediately alter Republican domination of the strategic control points in Island politics. The G.O.P. remained in control of the legislature throughout the war and for eight years following; the Democrats stirred, rose from the doldrums, but could win neither the delegateship nor control of the territorial legislature. The major reasons for Democratic debility, despite the emergence of the labor movement and the party's control of gubernatorial appointments until 1952, were similar to those that had plagued the party in previous years: weak leadership and factionalism.

Secretary of the Interior Harold Ickes realized that Governor Poindexter had done little to build the Democratic party or further progressive goals in the Islands, and remarked to a White House aide in 1942 that the Governor had been nothing to cheer about. Ickes remained convinced that only a strong mainland appointment to the governorship could liberate the Islands from the clutches of the Big Five.[2] Instead, Roosevelt chose Ingram Stainback, then legal adviser to the military governor and long-time friend of politically powerful Tennesseans Secretary of State Cordell Hull and Senator Kenneth McKellar.

Stainback was born and educated through high school in Tennessee. After receiving a B.A. degree from Princeton University, he had taught school for a year in Tennessee and a year in New Orleans. He then earned a law degree from the University of Chicago, and left for Hawaii in 1912. Two years later, as one of the few Democrats in the Islands with important mainland friends, he had been appointed attorney general for the Territory by Governor Pinkham. After nearly twenty years of private law practice, he was appointed U.S. judge for the District of Hawaii in 1940, a position that meant little under the martial law following Pearl Harbor. President Roosevelt, deeply immersed in the military aspects of the war and knowing that the governor would have little power under military rule in Hawaii, chose Stainback for Hawaii's top appointive spot in 1942.

Once again, many of Hawaii's conservatives, including oligarchy leaders, were pleased with a Democratic appointment. For the fourth time, local Democratic party stalwarts were disappointed by the Democratic President's choice of governor. John Wilson held little hope that the Tennessean would do anything to build a multiracial party.[3] The new Governor, however, was not without progressive predilections. As a Southern lawyer in the constitutional tradition, he bitterly resented military rule. As a Woodrow Wilson Democrat, he thought it was un-American for so much land to be concentrated in so few hands while middle-class haoles and others found it extremely difficult to purchase even small lots for their homes. In short, Stainback was against martial law, for land reform, and mildly sympathetic to labor. Otherwise, he was generally conservative.

The new Governor made some appointments from the ranks of

organized labor during the war, but he consistently appointed more Republicans than Democrats to high posts.[4] He filled ten of the top thirteen positions with members of the G.O.P., and throughout his eight years in office, two thirds of his major appointments were Republicans. Among his Republican appointees were some of the most conservative men in the Islands: as police commissioners, he appointed George W. Sumner in Honolulu, Robert L. Hind on the Big Island, and Asa Baldwin on Maui. When Stainback designated a committee on employment in 1950 to present plans for relieving postwar unemployment, he chose Frank Midkiff, of the Bishop estate, as chairman and included on the committee Frederick D. Lowrey, Harold W. Rice, and George S. Waterhouse, all elite business representatives. It was not surprising that the committee failed to recommend a forty-hour week; of the fourteen committee members, only two came from organized labor, and one of these was hostile to the International Longshoremen's and Warehousemen's Union.[5]

Henry A. Baldwin continued to control appointments on Maui. Writing to the Democratic Governor on July 23, 1943, he said that he was happy with Stainback's acceptance of his recommendations. The Governor's close friend and Princeton classmate Harold Rice, although nominally a Democrat, was pleased that Stainback was sympathetic to the Baldwin interests with which Rice was identified. When Stainback visited Kauai, he naturally stayed at the home of Harold's brother, Charles, still the strong man of Kauai.

With strong Southern backing in Congress, Stainback was reappointed by President Harry S. Truman in 1946. Attempts to replace him were defeated by supporters from Missouri and Tennessee as well as by Senators Millard Tydings, of Maryland, and Claude Pepper, of Florida, both friends of the new President. President Truman's patronage co-ordinator, Gale Sullivan, reinforced Stainback's power in the Territory by clearing judicial and other appointments through the Governor rather than the Democratic Territorial Central Committee.[6]

With military law lifted, the Tennessean spoke frequently of the need for land reform, and might eventually have made some progress in this direction had not a new political issue—Communism—captured his attention. In 1947, the Commanding General of the Army in Hawaii and his chief intelligence officer paid a visit to Iolani Palace to lay before the newly reappointed Governor the Army's list of Communists in the Islands. Stainback later told congressional investigators that he was shocked. Heading the list was Jack Hall, "the man that I had put on the Police Commission in 1945," and powerful head of the I.L.W.U. Stainback had fired Hall in 1946 because the labor leader had accused Judge Philip L. Rice, brother of Charles and Harold, who had issued an injunction against striking workers of the Lihue Plantation Company, of having represented that company and other Big Five companies for many years as a corporation counsel. But, when shown the list of alleged Communists by the Army in 1947, Stainback said he had no knowledge of Communist activity in Hawaii by Hall or anyone else.[7] Also included in the Army's list were schoolteachers Dr. and Mrs. John Reinecke. The tall, slim, spectacled scholar and his Hawaiian-born nisei wife were discharged from the schools in 1948 following a seven-week-long hearing by the Board of Education ordered by the outraged Stainback.

The Governor embarked on a crusade to alert the population of Hawaii to the dangers of local Communists. In 1947, he made anti-Communism the theme of speeches on Army Day, the Fourth of July, and Labor Day. Partly because of his sledgehammer attack on Communist infiltration of the I.L.W.U. and as a result of decisions made before his activities, leading union officials, later repeatedly identified as Communists, decided in late 1947 to use every resource to capture the machinery, personnel, and policies of the weakened Democratic party. In 1948, the I.L.W.U., heady with success at the polls in the fall of 1946, when fourteen of the fifteen Democrats elected had been endorsed by the union, almost succeeded in taking over the the Democratic party. So amorphous and penetrable were the local Democrats that at precinct elections in the spring of 1948, five I.L.W.U. officials were chosen as candidates for the Democratic Territorial Central Committee. When the Democratic territorial convention met in the McKinley High School auditorium in Honolulu on May 2, 1948, battle lines were sharply drawn. Five persons frequently designated as Communists in testimony before congressional committees by former Communists were appointed members of convention committees. According to one count, forty-seven of the delegates were I.L.W.U. members. Former Communist Paul Crouch, whose reports over the years have not proved reliable, later testified that forty-one delegates were known members of the Communist party, but another former Communist, Jack Kawano, who was president of the Democratic Club in the twenty-sixth precinct of the fifth district of Honolulu and a delegate, was much closer to the local group and listed the number of Communists attending the convention as eight, probably an underestimate.[8] I.L.W.U. strength at the convention varied between one fourth and one fifth, since many delegates, unaware of or indifferent to the alleged Communist leanings of I.L.W.U. leaders, sympathized with the principles advocated by the I.L.W.U. faction.

Conservative Democrats, led by Stainback, Chief Justice James L. Coke, and William O. Heen, were infuriated when the convention seated delegates attacked as Communists and awarded key convention posts to members of the I.L.W.U. faction. Hopelessly outnumbered by the combined strength of the I.L.W.U. delegates and the several hundred delegates who, though not identified with the union, were anxious to break from the conservative past, these three oldtimers and their small following refused to take an active part in the convention. But even with the failure of the old guard to participate, the I.L.W.U. did not control the convention. Self-styled independents, including most of the future leaders of Hawaii's Democratic party, won a majority of crucial votes, in spite of the I.L.W.U.'s power in the party.

Years later, Hall admitted, "We made a grievous error in 1948 when we tied ourselves to the Democratic Party. . . . Some of our worst enemies have been Democrats, masking as liberals and friends of the workers."[9] But in 1948, Hall was satisfied that the Democrats would one day succumb to I.L.W.U. power. Independents formed their own minor factions, grouped around individuals, among them former police captain Jack Burns, lawyer O. Vincent Esposito, and Honolulu's amiable Mayor, John Wilson, who was sympathetic to the I.L.W.U. but very much his own boss.

Democrat fought Democrat in the 1948 campaign, enabling the Republicans to win another sweeping victory despite the fact that private Republican polls showed most voters now leaning to the Democratic party. Wilson wrote Truman's Secretary of the Interior, Oscar L. Chapman, that Stainback was more Republican than a Democrat, since he repudiated every recommendation made by the Democratic Territorial Central Committee.[10] Stainback's followers accused Wilson of succumbing to Communist influence, especially through his administrative assistant, W. K. Bassett, who was subsequently identified by Crouch in congressional investigations as a Communist sympathizer. Stainback wrote federal Attorney General J. Howard McGrath that leading Chinese Democrat Chuck Mau was friendly with the Communists and that Wilson was being run by them. To Chapman, he charged that the Communists had taken over the so-called Democratic party in Hawaii "lock, stock and barrel."[11] He accused Charles E. Kauhane, the new national committeeman, of being "completely subservient to Hall and his Communist gang." The Governor said that "practically no white men were elected to any position," and that the haole Democrats of Hawaii seemed to have no chance to win in intraparty struggles.[12]

In 1950, the three major factions again girded for war. The dynamic and volatile O. Vincent Esposito, friendly to the labor movement despite private quarrels with Jack Hall during a 1949 strike, delivered the keynote address at the convention. This time the most conservative delegates walked out and set up their own organization after the convention seated delegates who had refused to answer questions concerning their alleged Communist affiliations before the Un-American Activities Committee. Despite the walkout, the I.L.W.U. lost ground in the 1950 convention. Shocked by the revelations of Jack Kawano, such leaders as Jack Burns, Chuck Mau, and war hero nisei Daniel Inouye were determined to force a showdown with I.L.W.U. leaders for control of the party. Aware that the Democrats could not capture the delegateship or the legislature if the party was controlled by the union or was tainted with Communism, they fought and won control of the Democratic Territorial Central Committee, whose thirty newly elected members included only five I.L.W.U. representatives. Only three members of the committee were ever identified as Communists, and two of them denounced the party shortly after their election.[13] The multiracial committee, including twelve businessmen, five lawyers, and three doctors, was much more representative of Hawaii's growing middle class than the I.L.W.U.

Union leaders received another blow with the appointment of Hawaii's new governor. On May 8, 1951, President Truman designated Kansas-born Oren E. Long to succeed Stainback. I.L.W.U. leaders had hoped that John Wilson, then seventy-nine years old, would be designated. The jaunty Mayor, desperately clinging to his lifelong dream, wrote President Truman charging that Long had not been a member of a Democratic precinct club since 1922, and had not actively supported the Democratic party in any way.[14] But Secretary of the Interior Chapman was satisfied that Long was a bona fide Democrat, and he persuaded the President to appoint the former schoolteacher.

The new Governor, like other Democratic governors before him, was a mainland-born haole, personally acceptable to many key *kamaaina* oligarchy leaders. Never having been a grass-roots politician, he was not equipped by experience or temperament to build a broadly based, vigorous Democratic party. Nearly half of his key appointments were Republicans, and this quiet, friendly man from the plains, imbued with the Christian spirit of charity, never attempted a major assault on entrenched power in Hawaii.

But Long was no Pinkham. The son of a strong supporter of William Jennings Bryan, the slim haole with kindly eyes had first signed the Democratic rolls in Hilo during the tenure of Governor McCarthy and had been quietly making financial contributions to the party since 1928. He supported Roosevelt's New Deal and favored progressive legislation to improve the health, welfare, and education of Hawaii's people.

Nor was Long another Stainback. He neither patronized nor disparaged any of Hawaii's racial groups. Primarily an educator and social worker, the new Governor had been influenced by the work of Jane Addams' social settlement in Chicago and, when offered a position at the Waiakea Social Settlement in Hilo, he welcomed the opportunity to put the new social-work principles into practice. After serving in the personnel section of the North Kohala plantation, he returned to the mainland in 1920 to earn a degree at Teachers College, Columbia University. Called back to the Islands after two years of teaching at an Episcopal school in western Pennsylvania, he was chosen principal of Kauai City High School in Lihue. Conscientious and affable, he was designated as territorial deputy superintendent of public education in 1925, a position he held for nine years, until his appointment as superintendent of the Department of Public Instruction. As Hawaii's top educator from 1934 to 1946, he worked behind the scenes to further Hawaii's educational system, supporting such dynamic teachers as Miles Cary and visiting parent-teacher groups throughout the Islands. After a short spell as director of public welfare in 1946, President Truman designated him secretary of Hawaii, a position he filled until his appointment as governor. In the struggle to control the Democratic party, Long gave no comfort to the I.L.W.U., but in many of his appointments, especially that of Sakae Takahashi as territorial treasurer, and in his legislative proposals, he revealed his life-long interest in extending opportunity to the underdog.

One year after Long's appointment, a crucial showdown for control of the party developed at the 1952 territorial Democratic convention when anti-I.L.W.U. delegates elected the chairman and other officers of the convention. I.L.W.U. strength from the outer islands was not enough to prevail over the group of new Democratic leaders from Honolulu. When the I.L.W.U. faction sponsored the still-popular John Wilson for national committeeman, Jack Burns, who had built his own organization through nisei war veterans and who believed that Wilson would be under tremendous pressure from the I.L.W.U. if elected, backed Frank F. Fasi, a *malihini* former Marine, for the post. Persuading a delegate from the Big Island who carried eighty-five proxies to support Fasi, Burns won his first major personal victory within the Democratic party.[15]

In Honolulu, Burns had worked his way up and down the police force. Invariably in difficulty with his superiors, Burns had served during the war as liaison for the police with the F.B.I. on espionage matters and as captain of the vice squad. In the latter post, this devout Catholic was responsible for the regulation of houses of prostitution in Honolulu. Able to quote from Aristotle on achieving the good life or from papal encyclicals on the sanctity of labor, he had also learned to listen sympathetically to the problems of thugs, prostitutes, and other "social undesirables." Tough, shrewd, unsmiling, sometimes cold and ruthless, this Montana-born policeman favored the "outs," the downtrodden, and the oppressed. He passionately hated the "ins," the high and mighty hypocrites who, through no virtue of their own, were in a position to tell others how to vote, where to work, and what to think. During the war, as police representative to an unofficial organization called the Morale Contact Group, Burns had listened with sympathy to the growing resentment expressed by Hawaii's Japanese community. He had worked behind the scenes to distribute small favors to the demoralized Japanese, winning the lasting loyalty of the younger, more militant nisei and sansei. When Republican boss Roy Vitousek had asked him, as police captain, for a political favor, he had agreed on condition that Vitousek help the Japanese. Vitousek, prodded by Burns, changed a bill that was introduced in the legislature denying employment in any capacity in territorial government to Hawaii's Japanese people.

In his frequent contacts with the Japanese community, Burns had learned that many of the younger nisei viewed the world and Hawaii much as he did. The cumulative bitterness against the haole oligarchy could, he reasoned, be turned into votes. With militant leadership, the grip of the oligarchy could be smashed.

Passionately dedicated to rebuilding the Democratic party around these younger Japanese ex-servicemen, Burns argued incessantly that A.J.A. votes combined with Democratic votes of Hawaiians could swamp the oligarchy.

Dan Inouye, while completing his undergraduate studies at the University of Hawaii under the G.I. Bill of Rights in 1948, read of Burns's candidacy for the delegateship, telephoned him, and asked, "How would you like to have some help?" Over coffee and buns, they planned the future of the Democratic party. Inouye, who a year earlier had been one of a few Democrats in the 442nd Veterans' Club, spread the word among the "Go for Broke" gang. Here was a chance to change Hawaii, he argued. Burns, he said, wanted to help the boys achieve a better way of life than their fathers had known. They, in turn, should help Burns build the Democratic party. Many of the former warriors were not convinced. Burns lacked respectability—an ex-cop with no wealth or power, driving around town in an old car, wearing tattered clothes. The drive for respectability was still great for many in the A.J.A. community who considered an invitation to a cocktail or tea party by a member of Hawaii's *kamaaina* elite as the highest of honors. When Burns asked to be allowed to speak before the board of the 442nd Veterans' Club, he was given only three minutes, even though he was an honorary member because of his work with the Morale Contact Group, and was told that he could not discuss political subjects.[16]

Burns had to be sold to the 442nd, which at first thought of itself as a social club. Dan Aoki, its president, resisted entreaties to enlist the 442nd for the Democratic cause. Aoki, the son of a Protestant issei preacher on Maui, had no great interest in politics, but he was soon inspired by Burns's intrepid devotion to the young Japanese, and he succumbed to the pleas of Inouye and Burns to turn the energies of the 442nd Club members to political action while keeping the club officially nonpartisan. The 100th Battalion Club, made up of older boys who had been draftees in the war, refused to abandon the social-club concept, but 442nd membership was much larger, and Burns was delighted with the willingness of its key members to attend rallies, pass out handbills, raise money, and, in some cases, run for political office. Important additions to the closely knit Burns clique were Matsuo

Takabuki, Mike Tokunaga, and William Richardson. Takabuki, who grew up in a plantation community in Waialua and was active in the 442nd Club, first joined the Democratic party in Chicago, where he had attended the University of Chicago Law School under the G.I. Bill of Rights and had become acutely sensitive to discrimination against A.J.A.'s in Hawaii. Back home in 1950, he worked hard for Sakae Takahashi's election to the Board of Supervisors and responded eagerly to Burns's appeal to enter politics. As president of the 442nd in 1952, he vigorously supported Burns in his drive to right, as he saw it, the wrongs done the Japanese of Hawaii. His conservative father had hoped that young Matsuo would become a schoolteacher, and his mother repeatedly urged, "You should learn to be humble, Matsuo, you must learn to be humble." But Takabuki, like his friend Mike Tokunaga, was too bitter to be humble. Burns did not preach humility. He talked justice, and Takabuki listened and followed.

Tokunaga, who had been drafted from his job on a plantation in November 1941, was even more determined to eradicate every vestige of the past. He joined the Democratic party prior to its convention of 1950, soon after graduating from the University of Hawaii. He agreed with the simple arithmetic presented by Burns. Japanese and Hawaiian votes together could easily comprise a majority of the electorate. Tokunaga's father had been more aggressive than others of his generation. As a plantation supervisor, he had turned in his supervisor's badge in 1946 to join the I.L.W.U. Young Mike found in the haole Burns an astringent, remorseless antagonism toward the plantation bosses with which both his father and he could readily agree.

As a boy, Bill Richardson could not afford to go to Kamehameha School, even though his grandfather had been an aide to Queen Liliuokalani. His father, the son of this staunch royalist, was jailed by the Republic after the revolution, but carried on the legacy of protest against the haole oligarchy by joining actively in the weak Democratic party of Hawaii. Richardson, who grew up in the tough Palama section of Honolulu, recalled his grandmother's *aloha* for the Democrats, and when Burns asked him to help organize Hawaiian voters in alliance with the new Japanese electors, the part-Hawaiian Richardson responded warmly. He well remembered that Roosevelt High School would not admit his brother and sister, and etched even deeper was the memory of his paralyzed grandfather—a royalist until death—denouncing the oligarchy.[17]

The Burns faction could not take all the credit for the revival of the Democratic party. There were other haoles, in some cases distrustful of Burns and his organization, among them Thomas P. Gill, O. Vincent Esposito, and *malihini* Frank Fasi, who threw themselves in the Democratic cause. Gill, perhaps the most brilliant of the new Democratic leaders, had been born in Hawaii, the son of a newspaperwoman. He had passed up Punahou, preferring the public schools, and after graduation from the University of Hawaii and Stanford Law School, began his bid for political leadership. Esposito's father, Joseph S., was a doctor and lawyer from Connecticut who had associated regularly with John Wilson and other Island liberals. Vincent Esposito sought leadership within the party while rapidly building one of the best law practices in the Islands. Each of these haoles was sympathetic to the aspirations of Orientals—Esposito married a Korean girl, and Fasi a nisei—and each came from that group of rising small entrepreneurs and professional men who traditionally, finding little or no place in the major *kamaaina* companies, identified with the Democratic party. They were undoubtedly motivated in large part by a vision of a better Hawaii, but there were many other middle-class recruits from all races—lawyers, realtors, contractors, and others with jobs closely connected to politics—who saw the Democratic party as a potential vehicle for economic success. Others who helped to create a favorable climate for the rise of the Democratic party were *malihini* Democrats who openly maintained their political affiliation after coming to the Islands—men like Dr. Gregg Sinclair, Alan Saunders, and Thomas Murphy of the University of Hawaii, and former Governor Long, always available for help and advice to the younger politicians.

There was also the I.L.W.U., whose leaders, even after abandoning plans to infiltrate and capture the Democratic party, had stirred the union membership against the symbols of the past, including the Republican party. But Burns and his group, probably more than any other faction, were responsible for breathing life into the once moribund Democratic party of Hawaii. They indefatigably exploited the accumulated resentments of Japanese, Chinese, Hawaiians, and Filipinos against the injustices, real and imagined, of the past.

There had been other Democrats in recent decades who recognized the need to build a multiracial party. Using whatever influence he had over the distribution of patronage during the 1930's and '40's, John Wilson persistently argued for the appointment of Japanese, Chinese,

Portuguese, and Hawaiian postmasters. Delbert Metzger had written James Farley in 1935 that the Democratic party must appeal to all races and "have many friends among the Japanese and Portuguese as well as the Hawaiians, else it had as well close shop."[18] Martin Pence, running for city and county attorney on the Big Island in 1937, cultivated the Japanese vote through his young protégé, Tom Okino.[19] But weak Democratic leadership and chronic factionalism combined with the racial hostilities of some Democratic haole, Hawaiian, and Portuguese leaders frustrated these small and sporadic efforts. Confused nisei were ready for haole leadership, and, in the words of dentist Ernest Murai, "Jack Burns helped and encouraged us."[20]

Public-opinion surveys in Honolulu in 1948 showed that the days of one-party rule were over. When the voters were asked which party they thought could run the government best, a larger proportion designated Democratic than Republican. Of Hawaii's four largest voting racial groups, the biggest—the Japanese and part-Hawaiian—showed the strongest Democratic preference. When asked which they would choose if obliged to register as either a Democrat or a Republican, even the Chinese—by 1948, a distinctly middle-class group—showed a strong Democratic preference. The influence of the I.L.W.U. was important but far from paramount. Nonunion voters leaned to the Democrats only slightly less than did union members. One out of every four voters in the sample as a whole found the Democratic party either generally or extremely hostile, but only 8 per cent of the Japanese and 7 per cent of the Hawaiian electors agreed. When asked what they liked about the Democrats or why they tended to think of themselves as supporters of that party, the wife of a Japanese salesman said, "They take an interest in poor people. Republicans have only rich people's interest at heart"; the wife of a Japanese general manager remarked, "Democrats are poor, and poor people work harder for the good of others"; a Chinese mechanic observed that they were closer to the working people; the wife of a Hawaiian mechanic commented that the Republicans "don't help the poor, and they have all the money." Mayor John Wilson and the late President Roosevelt were repeatedly praised and the Big Five often scorned. There were critical comments made against the Democrats by voters from all racial groups, but, except among Caucasians, they were in a minority. Public opinion had clearly changed. No longer were Hawaii's nonhaole groups afraid to criticize the G.O.P. or praise the Democratic party, even to haole interviewers.[21]

This shifting climate of public opinion had not yet been translated into important electoral victories. It was one thing to identify with the Democrats; it was another to vote for them. When asked who they thought "is the best person we could elect in November as delegate to Congress," 70 per cent of the Japanese, 63 per cent of the Chinese, and 60 per cent of the Hawaiian voters mentioned Republican incumbent Joseph R. Farrington, who had been supported by the I.L.W.U. in 1946. Samuel Wilder King, another Republican, was mentioned most frequently after Farrington. It was no surprise to Republican party leaders who had seen the survey results that Farrington beat Burns for the delegateship by a three-to-one margin in 1948. In 1944, Republican control over the key post of delegate seemed as complete as during the war, and Farrington won handsome pluralities, actually running unopposed. In 1950, Burns could not afford to run, and the Democrats drafted an unknown, whom Farrington easily trounced. Two years later, the Democratic war horse Delbert Metzger, in a valiant showing, could win only slightly more than 40 per cent of the ballots cast against the seemingly unbeatable Farrington.

The Democrats fared somewhat better in their quest for control of the territorial legislature. When the Japanese attacked Pearl Harbor, Democrats held only one out of five seats in the territorial Senate and one out of ten in the House. In the 1946 election—the first postwar election in Hawaii—the party tied for control in the House and fell just one seat short of an even split in the upper chamber. During the next six years, Republican candidates for the legislature held off Democratic assaults. It would take time for returning war veterans to become established in businesses or professions and build local followings as Democratic candidates.

In local affairs, too, the G.O.P. was on the defensive. During the war, with many nisei and sansei voters away and the Japanese community demoralized, it had been relatively easy for Republicans to maintain control on the outer islands. Not a single Democrat was elected to the ten local offices on Maui in 1942, and only one was chosen in contests for nine positions on Kauai. The ratio of Republicans to Democrats in Honolulu and on Hawaii in the same years was eight to three. Four years later, with John Wilson leading the way, the Democrats won a slim majority on the Board of Supervisors of Oahu, improved their positions on the Big Island and Kauai, and, through a well-disciplined I.L.W.U. turnout, swamped the G.O.P. in the Republican stronghold of Maui for the first time in history.

A Democratic tide was coming in. Its high waves could be seen in the distance by discerning Republican politicians, who unsuccessfully urged key party leaders to recruit the up-and-coming young leaders of Hawaii's nonhaole groups. The deal that Kuhio had made with Merchant Street nearly fifty years before was off. The day when *lunas* and plantation bosses watched the pencil to control the votes of laborers had passed. The rising Democratic tide represented the ambitions of Hawaii's growing middle class, the rising resentments of Hawaii's nonhaole groups against the patterns of the past, and their increasing pride in the articulate and youthful leadership of Japanese and Hawaiian lawyers, Chinese businessmen, and Filipino union officials.

Although the Republican party continued to control the delegateship and the legislature, its strength steadily decreased after 1948.[22] During the war, not one single nisei sat in the territorial legislature. In 1946, five were elected to the House and one to the Senate. Six years later, there were seventeen haoles and the same number of A.J.A. representatives, and nearly all of the latter were Democrats. Although Japanese precincts like the fourth in Hawaii's first district and the tenth in the Big Island's second district went substantially Republican during the war, they shifted noticeably in 1948. In the race for the House in Oahu's fifth district, Republican nisei Joe Itagaki ran well, but behind Democrat James Murakami, a Japanese schoolteacher, now a businessman, Mitsuyuki Kido, a star pupil of Miles Cary and also a former schoolteacher, and even Hawaiian Charles Kauhane. In precinct nine of the same district, where six of ten voters were of Japanese descent, Kido, Murakami, and Steere Noda ran far ahead of the other candidates. Two years later, Kido, Murakami, Noda, and Esposito won handsome victories in the same Japanese districts. Democratic pluralities increased in most nonhaole precincts, and by 1952, only the preponderantly haole districts turned in large Republican pluralities.

The time of reckoning was at hand. Donald D. H. Ching, a product of Honolulu's slums whose poor Chinese father had died when he was very young, dialed the number of another young lawyer struggling to get established in his profession. On the other end of the line was Hawaii's first Filipino barrister, Alfred Laureta, the son of an Ilocano plantation laborer. Both men, handsome, alert, and representing

Hawaii's cosmopolitan tradition—Ching had married a Japanese girl—talked animatedly of politics. The year was 1954. The subject was familiar to many lawyers. Should we join a political party? they asked one another. Which would be best for business? "Do you want to join the Democrats?" queried Ching. "Let's go over and sign up." "Why not?" answered the Filipino. "Let's do it today."[23]

The tide was coming in now. Republican politicians threw up their arms to protect themselves from its inevitable onslaught. They ducked and dodged, and some became Democrats. The revolution of 1954 was on the way. When the ballots were counted, Democrats had captured more than two thirds of the House seats and won a comfortable nine-to-six margin in the Senate. On the Big Island, nisei newcomer Democrat Nelson K. Doi ran ahead of incumbent Senator William H. Hill. Also elected was another first-time winner, Stanley H. Hara. Nearly half of the seats in the territorial legislature were captured by Americans of Japanese ancestry. They included Daniel Inouye, Sakae Takahashi, Masato Doi, Harvard-educated Spark M. Matsunaga, each of whom was starred for leadership in the new Democratic party of Hawaii. Democratic landslides put the party in control of local affairs on Oahu, Kauai, and Maui. Mitsuyuki Kido and Matsuo Takabuki led two other nisei Democrats to election to the Honolulu Board of Supervisors. Only on the Big Island did the Board of Supervisors remain in Republican hands.

Republican Delegate Elizabeth P. Farrington, wife of the deceased Joseph and daughter-in-law of Hawaii's former governor Wallace Farrington, won re-election against Jack Burns by less than a thousand of the nearly 140,000 votes cast. Burns had run consistently ahead in Hawaiian and Japanese precincts with the exception of the A.J.A. eighth precinct in the fourth district on Oahu; it was only the large pluralities in the heavily haole districts that pulled Mrs. Farrington through. Personal victories still came hard for the tough ex-policeman, but Burns would return to the hustings two years hence to complete the revolution.

Chapter Fourteen

POLITICS OF DEMOCRACY

Paradoxically, Democratic victories in Hawaii came just as the Republican party, under the leadership of General Dwight David Eisenhower, recaptured the Presidency for the first time in twenty years. The Democrats were ascendant in Hawaii, but at least the G.O.P. could retain the governorship through the President's appointment power.

When old David ("Daddy") Bray, one of the last of Hawaii's authentic *kahunas,* wrote a message to the new President of the United States, he was putting on paper what many Hawaiians felt. Bray, who vividly remembered the overthrow of Queen Liliuokalani, told the President that under United States control not one of the Islands' governors had been of Hawaiian blood. He pleaded for the appointment, as the twelfth governor, of a one-eighth Hawaiian, Samuel Wilder King, whose father, ironically, had been a conspirator against Queen Liliuokalani and a minister in the cabinet of President Dole. Probably uppermost in Bray's mind was the fact that King was the only part-Hawaiian available for the governorship in 1953.[1]

Daddy Bray was not the only Hawaiian who pleaded and prayed for a part-Hawaiian governor. Judge Calvin MacGregor, whose Scotch sea captain grandfather married a Hawaiian, was a personal friend of his college classmate Richard Nixon and worked feverishly in Washington to put King across. But the odds against him were long. Secretary of the Interior Douglas McKay told MacGregor soon after he arrived in the capital that the President was determined to appoint territorial G.O.P. chairman Randolph Crossley. King wrote bitterly to Senator Robert Taft that it now appeared certain that Eisenhower would not appoint him.[2] The reason: King was a Taft man, and Crossley had supported Eisenhower before the Republican convention of 1952.

Crossley, a *malihini* haole on Kauai, became widely known in the 1930's after he reorganized the pineapple business of a group of Okinawans who had run out of money. In building it from a $60,000 to a $2,500,000 business, Crossley met strong opposition from the large pineapple companies, who at first refused to let him join the Pineapple Growers Association. After the war, Crossley branched into other businesses, was elected to the legislature from Kauai, and, with the help of King, became chairman of the territorial party organization. Crossley, whose personal and business counsel was Herbert Brownell, chief strategist in the Eisenhower camp, was promised the governorship shortly after the General's election. After four visits to the White House, the appointment was all but announced. Eisenhower assured Crossley that the gubernatorial commission was ready for signature, and all that remained was for Brownell and Crossley to work out the mechanics of the announcement. If Crossley preferred, the President assured the energetic Kauaian, the announcement could be made right from the White House. Crossley preferred to have Delegate Joseph Farrington tell the press of his appointment, since he had been feuding with Farrington, also a Taft man, and he hoped that the feud would end once the decision was made. Crossley sold his pineapple interests and waited for an announcement that never came.

Before the President could put his pen to the commission, the pro-King forces had gone frantically to work. Farrington and his wife were aided by Republican Senators Arthur V. Watkins, of Utah, Guy Corden, of Oregon, Hugh Butler, of Nebraska, and Taft. MacGregor and his delegation from Hawaii bombarded the White House with a fusillade of petitions and letters. The decisive pressure was probably applied by Taft and his friends. He wanted to reward Farrington and King for their devoted Republicanism and personal loyalty to him. After all, had not General Eisenhower promised Taft a fair share of patronage? Secretary of the Interior McKay, who had told MacGregor, only a few hours before, that the Crossley appointment was assured, now heard from Corden that Interior Department appropriations might be threatened unless the recommendation of Farrington and Taft was respected.

The Crossley drive had been stemmed. Crossley's friend industrialist-statesman Paul Hoffman, according to one eyewitness, warned the President on the phone that he could not go back on his word. "You simply cannot do this to a man," argued the automobile industrialist.

Eisenhower was firm; he would not reverse his decision again. Crossley could have an ambassadorship to one of the Asian countries, but the governorship would go to King. Crossley did not like it when Presidential Assistant Sherman Adams called him "Mr. Ambassador." He had wanted the governorship and, believing that he had been double crossed, preferred to drop out of politics entirely for a while.[3]

Republicans were glad to regain the governorship. Poindexter, Stainback, and Long had not been radicals, but they were Democrats, and Long had encouraged the growth of grass-roots Democratic activity. The three major Republican political leaders during the war years had been Farrington, King, and lawyer Roy Vitousek. A capable legislative leader, Vitousek usually spoke for the more conservative faction of the G.O.P. Farrington wanted to encourage friendlier relations with labor and identify the Republican party with the campaign for statehood. King was on good terms with both men, bridging the gap between the two camps.

Joseph Farrington and his *Star Bulletin* editor, Riley Allen, realized that political success in Hawaii would depend upon support from organized labor and the Islands' nonhaole groups. As delegate, Farrington kept in close touch with Japanese boys at the war front, expediting furloughs and obtaining other favors. He called for the repeal of all Chinese exclusion acts, although there was no demand for Chinese immigration from the sugar planters, and he favored legislation extending naturalization rights to Oriental aliens. The columns of his newspaper were friendly to the labor movement, and Farrington consistently received the support of Jack Hall in his campaigns for the delegateship. But his policies met opposition within the Republican party and from the *Star Bulletin*'s board of directors. At a board meeting, one director criticized the handling of a story and said that reporting the request of C.I.O. representatives for an upward revision in plantation wages played into the hands of labor unions.[4] The powerful president of C. Brewer, Alan Davis, also accused Farrington and Allen of not actively taking the side of management in its struggle against labor.[5]

As governor, King continued to try to placate both liberal and conservative factions within the Republican party. Recognizing that the Territory was no longer safe for the oligarchy-dominated G.O.P. of the past, he corresponded extensively with representatives of all groups and classes in an effort to put his administration in a favorable light. In 1953, he signed into law every appropriation for public-works construction passed by the legislature, and asked Congress to raise the limited bonded indebtedness of the Territory from $65,000,000 to $95,000,000 to make mortgage loans available to veterans for homes and farms and to implement Hawaii's postwar school-construction program. He directed the territorial Land Commission to examine all lands under his jurisdiction to develop additional areas to sell as house lots. He believed that lands held by large private landowners which were needed for public purposes should be obtained by condemnation proceedings or by purchase, and not by exchange, as had been done to the detriment of the public interest in the past.

But in practice, King's frequently expressed liberal sentiments were more than balanced by his conservative actions. He vetoed a large number of the tax and spend bills passed by the 1955 Democratic legislature. The Governor stopped the bill amending the Workmen's Compensation Act, arguing that it was too expensive. In addition, he vetoed a measure that would have abolished the fixed ceiling on the amount of money that could legally be raised by taxes on real property. Another bill would have enabled counties to classify land by best use rather than actual use as a basis for tax assessments, but this, too, received the Governor's negative vote. Realizing that Democratic and labor power was strong in the outer islands, King opposed decentralization of government authority, and vetoed a bill to transfer the power to appoint members to the Liquor Commission and Police Commission from the governor and territorial Senate to county executives. Eight home-rule bills were vetoed in all, and the Governor also opposed legislation to establish a foreign-affairs training center at the University of Hawaii as well as measures that would have resulted in higher taxes and deficit spending. Altogether, the Governor vetoed seventy-one Democratic bills, and only two of the vetoes were overridden by the legislature. Undoubtedly, some of his vetoes were correct on technical grounds; as in the past, some legislation was badly drafted. Other bills were clearly pork barrel, and one bold attempt to exempt the properties of the I.L.W.U. from property taxation, after passing the legislature, was stopped by King. But the over-all record confirmed the opinion of the majority of Hawaii's voters that the Republican party was tied to the conservatism of the past and had not yet caught up with the social and economic revolution that was sweeping postwar Hawaii.

The 1956 election gave the Democrats of Hawaii a decided victory at the very time of the Eisenhower landslide on the mainland. For Hawaii, 1956 was what 1936 had been in the states—endorsement of the New Deal and repudiation of the Old Guard policies. Despite its intraparty squabbles and legislative fumbles, the Democratic legislature put into law many of the aspirations and hopes of a majority of Hawaii's people. In education, it budgeted $1,250,000 more to the public-school system than recommended by Governor King; it lowered the University tuition rate from $200 to $170 and increased pay for teachers. In health and general welfare, it expanded Hawaii's slum-clearance program and doubled appropriations for general-welfare assistance. The state minimum wage was raised to seventy-five cents per hour on Oahu and sixty-five cents on the outer islands, unemployment benefits were increased, and workmen's compensation extended. A comprehensive net-income-tax law was passed, allowing exemption for dependents, and placing relatively heavier burdens on higher-income groups. Business taxes on banks and insurance and loan companies were passed, although they were later vetoed by Governor King. Another bill was passed to encourage mainland industrialist Henry Kaiser and other *malihinis* to invest in the Territory, and still another to provide comprehensive research on the development of new industries and agricultural products. These measures, private public-opinion surveys revealed, were generally well received and were identified with the Democratic party.[6]

Jack Burns, now soliciting the support of the I.L.W.U., achieved a landslide victory in 1956 over Delegate Elizabeth Farrington. Burns won in every county, but his largest pluralities came, not where the I.L.W.U. was strong, but from West Hawaii and Oahu. Twelve Democrats and only three Republicans were elected to the territorial Senate, and two thirds of the contests for the House were won by Democrats. To the Senate from Hawaii came vigorous nisei lawyer Tom Okino. Oahu contributed Mitsuyuki Kido, popular Chinese lawyer Herbert K. H. Lee, and former governor Oren Long. In the House, leadership fell to Spark Matsunaga, Daniel Inouye, the volatile Vincent Esposito, and Oahu's youthful Patsy Takemoto Mink, all from Oahu; Elmer F. Cravalho, of Portuguese descent, from Maui; and nisei Stanley Hara, from West Hawaii. Beaten in the Democratic landslide were such old-time Republican favorites as Hawaiians Flora Kaai Hayes, Mary K. Robinson, Richard Lyman, Jr., and a *malihini* lawyer from the mainland, William F. Quinn, who, while receiving strong support from both Merchant Street and the I.L.W.U., lost in his bid for election.

The plantation vote was obviously no longer controlled by managers. In some cases, union leaders had replaced *lunas* as political bosses. The two-to-one vote for Burns in Maui's third precinct and Kauai's twelfth and seventeenth precincts was ample testimony of the efficacy of the union machine on some plantations. But other plantation communities showed remarkable Republican strength, and it was in middle-class urban nonhaole districts that the Democrats ran strongest. In Honolulu's eleventh precinct (75 per cent Japanese), haole Democrat Oren Long ran well ahead of Republican nisei Joe Itagaki. In the city's eighth precinct (more than 70 per cent Japanese), Long ran far ahead of Itagaki, and Burns trounced Mrs. Farrington. In that well-to-do Japanese area, where rentals and incomes were above the medians for Honolulu, Republican strength, as measured in one study, fell from 57 per cent in 1944 to slightly better than 30 per cent eight years later.[7]

In the heavily Hawaiian twenty-ninth precinct on windward Oahu, Burns, Lee, Long, and Democratic candidates for the territorial House won smashing victories. Leading the ticket was Waiahole's own Hiram Kealiiahonui Kamaka, but not far behind were nisei Patsy Mink and George R. Ariyoshi in a district that was only 7 per cent Japanese. Only in the strongly haole precincts did the Republicans win substantial victories. In the 80 per cent haole ninth precinct in Honolulu, Mrs. Farrington and other haole Republican candidates won landslide victories. *Malihini* Quinn received 714 votes to 203 for Kido in the contest for the Senate seat. In the House race, Alexander & Baldwin corporation lawyer Hebden Porteus won 773 votes to 276 for Inouye. In Honolulu's upper-class twenty-ninth precinct (66 per çent haole), the Republican triumph was even greater. There, Mrs. Farrington won more than 80 per cent of the vote, and seven times as many ballots were cast for Porteus as Inouye.

The Democratic landslide in all but the most haole districts did not come as a great shock to Republican officials, who had hired Honolulu's leading opinion-survey organization to poll political opinions and party preferences in 1955. The results had showed that the percentage of declared Democrats had risen from 27 to 29 between 1948 and 1955 while the percentage of Republicans dropped from 19 to 14. Democratic party strength was distributed throughout the Territory, weakest on the Big Island and strongest on Kauai.[8]

When the voters were asked how they would declare if forced to register for one party or the other, nonhaoles, constituting the bulk of Hawaii's voting population, chose the Democratic party by a better than two-to-one margin. Of the 3,375 voters across the Islands in the sample, only the Chinese joined the haoles in leaning toward the Republican party. Almost five times as many Filipinos, more than twice as many Japanese, and nearly twice as many Hawaiians and part-Hawaiians thought of themselves as Democrats than as Republicans. Filipino and Hawaiian voters in every income category were decidedly Democratic, and only those Japanese voters whose incomes were over $7,000 moved substantially in the direction of the Republicans. Non-haole identification with the Democratic party cut cleanly across income levels. When the voters were asked which party they thought could run the territorial government better, nearly 60 per cent of the Japanese voters earning between $5,000 and $7,000 a year replied "Democrats" compared with less than 20 per cent of the haoles in the same income bracket. Although the Chinese appeared to lean in the Republican direction, G.O.P. strategists realized that the huge number of declared independents—65 per cent of the Chinese in the lowest two income groups refused to identify with either the Republican or Democratic party—were moving in a Democratic direction.

The Chinese were less willing to commit themselves to a party label than any other group, but the younger Chinese actively entering politics were predominantly Democratic. The Chinese constituted only 7 per cent of the population and probably less than 10 per cent of the voters anyway. The Japanese (37 per cent of Hawaii's people), Hawaiians and part-Hawaiians (nearly 20 per cent), and the Filipinos (12 per cent) were the big nonhaole voting groups of the present and future, and each inclined strongly toward the Democratic party.

The labor movement had been a factor in turning the nonhaoles against the G.O.P., but nonhaole identification with the Democrats transcended the union's influence. The proportion of nonunion Filipinos who called themselves Democrats was almost as high as the percentage of Filipino I.L.W.U. members choosing that party. Non-union Hawaiians and Japanese also leaned strongly toward the Democratic party. To most of them, the G.O.P. was identified with restrictions of the past, the Democratic symbols with aspirations for the future.

If the G.O.P. was in the doldrums, the Democratic legislature, only the second in Island history, was moving quickly ahead. It stepped up education appropriations, providing for free citizenship classes, salary advances for teachers, and more student scholarships. It extended Hawaii's unemployment-compensation law to include agricultural workers and passed a $1 minimum-hourly-wage law. It pushed economic development by creating an office to co-ordinate economic planning on a Territory-wide basis, authorizing the organization of business-development corporations to promote the economy of the Islands through loans and investments, and revising the real-property tax laws to encourage the productive use of land. The new Democratic tax system repealed the 2 per cent tax on salaries and wages, raised corporate income taxes and taxes on public utilities and insurance companies.

Republican officials had difficulty finding workers and candidates in 1958. A scheduled meeting of the Oahu Young Republican Club, called to elect a new president and to prepare for the 1958 elections, was adjourned when only seven persons convened.[9] Lifelong Republican Lawrence S. Goto, treasurer of the city and county of Honolulu, suddenly switched to the Democratic party to assure his re-election. Goto, elected three times on the G.O.P. ticket, told reporters, "I'm more basically a Democrat than a Republican." Adrian DeMello, another long-time Republican, filed his candidacy for the Honolulu Board of Supervisors as a Democrat. "If I run as a Republican," DeMello commented, "the voters might consider me a captive of industry."[10] To add to their woes, the Republicans failed to procure candidates for five contests in the territorial Senate.

The most serious G.O.P. problem was finding a Republican to run against Delegate Jack Burns. G.O.P. leaders received with dismay the results of a survey which showed that Burns would be extremely difficult to beat in 1958. When the voters of Oahu were asked if they approved of the way Delegate Burns was doing his job, almost four times as many approved as disapproved. A.J.A. voters were especially enthusiastic, giving Burns a five-to-one endorsement; and more than 70 per cent of the Chinese and 60 per cent of the haoles answering applauded Burns. In August 1957, territorial G.O.P. committeeman and sugar-industry official Arthur D. Woolaway earnestly pleaded with members of the Republican Territorial Committee, "We need a Delegate and we need him now." One year later, Woolaway and the Committee were still looking. Woolaway tried to recruit popular Representative Hebden Porteus; "Not this year thank you," replied the corporation lawyer. On the Big Island, Woolaway approached the extremely popular part-Hawaiian chairman of Hawaii's Board of Supervisors, James Kealoha; "I like it here," responded the easygoing Jimmy. To missionary descendant and telephone company president J. Ballard Atherton, Woolaway made an appeal for public service, but Atherton could honestly reply that he was untested in politics. Great pressure was put on Senator Wilfred C. Tsukiyama to oppose Burns. Haole businessmen promised a campaign chest to finance Tsukiyama's candidacy, but "Tsuki," with unfailing political instinct, went to Japan for a vacation when the pressure became unbearable.[11]

As the day for filing drew close, Woolaway joined party Chairman Ed Bryan and Hawaii's new Republican Governor, William Quinn, in an attempt to persuade territorial Secretary Farrant L. Turner to enter the race. Not a wealthy man, Turner, a loyal Taft Republican, was concerned that because he had to resign his territorial position to run, he would be out of a job after the election. Assured by the two party officials and the Governor that he would be taken care of in any event, the friendly white-haired man who had commanded the 100th Battalion overseas promised to try his best.[12]

Turner was motivated by the belief that the Japanese population could be won back to the Republican party. "We are going to have to go after the Japanese more and more," Turner warned. He deplored the inability of Republican officials to take advantage of the desire of returning nisei warriors to enter government service and politics. He told friends of the Central Union Congregational Church that his Shinto and Buddhist boys of the 100th could be converted if church members worked for them. But neither the officials at Central Union nor the Republican party followed his advice, lamented Turner.

The *aloha* that Turner felt for his boys in the 100th was often reciprocated, and his most ardent workers came from their ranks. But many of the men from the 100th had already gone over to the other party. Among them were such well-known Democrats as nisei Spark Matsunaga, Howard Miyake, and Sakae Takahashi. And if there was one haole in the Islands more popular among the Japanese than Farrant Turner, it was Jack Burns. Turner was a symbol of the benevolent and open-minded friendship occasionally found in haoles of a bygone era. Burns symbolized the militant repudiation of everything that era stood for.

Cheered by the response of many of his boys from the 100th, Turner was otherwise disillusioned. Governor Quinn appointed a *malihini* haole in his place as territorial secretary instead of the young nisei Republican Turner had recommended. To Turner, Quinn was another Eisenhower. Genial, able, undoubtedly popular, he was too much of a New Dealer and not interested in building the Republican organization. Quinn, it was often repeated in the corridors of Iolani Palace, acted more like a Democrat than a Republican, as did Honolulu's popular Republican mayor, part-Hawaiian former football coach Neal Blaisdell. Turner was known to ask of Blaisdell, "Is he a Republican or a Democrat?" Quinn, obliged to work with Democratic majorities in the legislature, and Blaisdell, forced to govern with a Democratic-controlled Board of Supervisors, maintained their individual popularity by disassociating themselves from the Republican party. To orthodox Republican Turner, that was treason. As he saw it, the patronage policies and legislative goals of both men frequently helped Democrats as much as Republicans. The money and help Turner had been promised for his campaign were not forthcoming, and he began to realize that, in his own words, he "had been thrown to the wolves."[13]

The pessimism that seized the Republican camp was matched by optimism on the other side. In the primary election held in October, the Democratic party's candidates for the territorial legislature received the highest proportion of votes ever cast for Democratic candidates in either a primary or a general election. The party's standard-bearer, Delegate Burns, amassed the highest primary vote ever polled by a Democratic candidate for Island office. Whereas Democratic legislative candidates had received only 39.7 per cent of the votes in the 1952 primary, their share soared to 58.5 per cent six years later.

Burns, by now the most controversial politician in the Islands, received support from I.L.W.U. officials as well as from the vast majority of the members of the 442nd Club. He attacked the Republican party for its defense of the past. "People born with silver spoons in their mouths really don't know that the people can think . . ." the Delegate told a rally in Moiliili, a Japanese neighborhood. The Republican party, he insisted, wanted to keep Hawaii "from an unruly mass of natives and Orientals." Turner accused Burns of raising the racial issue and argued that "there is no such thing as a Japanese, Chinese, haole or Portuguese community."[14] Burns was delighted to disagree and made much of the fact that he was the first delegate to choose a staff representative of all the people of Hawaii. His top administrative assistant was nisei Dan Aoki, one of his secretaries was of Japanese ancestry, the other a part-Hawaiian. He promised, if re-elected, to add a Filipino or Filipina to his staff. Burns intended to keep his coalition of nisei, Hawaiians, Filipinos, and militantly liberal haoles intact.

Turner, realizing that the haoles were identified with the Republican label, tried to dispel the cumulative frustrations and hostilities of Hawaii's nonhaole groups. He knew as well as anyone that the younger, more militant nisei tended strongly toward the Democratic side. Of the thirteen 442nd members running for office, nine were Democrats, and private Republican polls showed an A.J.A. preference for the Democrats of four to one. Of those respondents indicating their party preference, seven of every eight Filipinos and two of three Hawaiians chose the Democrats.[15]

While the support of nonhaole groups was far from monolithic, each one tended to identify Burns and the Democratic party with such popular causes as increased job opportunities and land reform, according to the results of a private poll of Oahu voters. The most startling and significant revelation of the study was the failure of the Orientals to substantially shift their allegiances to the G.O.P. as their incomes increased. The only hope for the Republican party to regain their position of pre-eminence was to win the loyalties of middle- and upper-income Orientals, but the new poll showed a surprisingly small amount of movement into the Republican party by Chinese and Japanese citizens climbing up the socioeconomic ladder. Among Japanese, the strongest Democratic attachments were held by those in the $4,000-to-$6,000 income category. Even in the next income group—$6,000 to $9,000—seven of ten Japanese respondents who identified with one party or the other chose the Democrats. The figures for the Chinese were even more remarkable. Between 1955 and 1958, there had been a marked shift in Chinese loyalties to the Democratic party. Only 2 per cent of the Chinese in the Oahu sample declared themselves as strong Republicans and 9 per cent as leaning toward the Republican party, while 4 per cent were identified as strong Democrats and 23 per cent as mainly Democratic. The Chinese in every income category preferred the Democrats. Eight of ten in the $6,000-to-$9,000 group and nearly six of ten in the $9,000-or-more category who chose one party or the other picked the Democrats. Whereas 53 per cent of the haoles in this latter income category called themselves Republicans, only 18 per cent of the Japanese and 20 per cent of the Chinese identified themselves with the G.O.P.

A great many middle-class or upper-middle-class Orientals obviously identified with the struggle to achieve social and economic equality in Hawaii and believed the Republican party to be associated with forces resisting that struggle. When a large sample of Oahu voters were asked if they identified either of the two political parties with racial prejudice, many more Chinese mentioned the G.O.P. than the Democrats. A much larger proportion of Chinese also believed the Democrats to be associated with increased job opportunities and land reform.

From the Republican point of view, the most discouraging aspect of the latest survey results were the responses of independent voters to a carefully designed word-association test. It was hoped that the so-called independents—49 per cent of the Oahu sample—would associate the Republican party with such favorable concepts as a strong civil service, balanced budgets, economic development, better schools, and good laws. Actually, the independents perceived little difference between Democrats and Republicans on these issues. The Democrats came out even on civil service and ahead on better schools. Fifty-three per cent thought of the Republicans when a balanced budget was mentioned, but 49 per cent also named Democrats. Republicans and Democrats were equally identified by the independents with the issuing of good laws. Fifty-six per cent associated Republicans with economic development, while 55 per cent listed the Democrats.

The survey surprisingly showed that a larger proportion of independents identified the G.O.P. with the spoils system and graft than they did the Democratic party; 49 per cent thought of the Republicans, while only one third mentioned the Democrats. But it was on the important issues of racial prejudice, taxes, job opportunities, and land reform that Democrats rated ahead of Republicans among independent voters. A majority of Republicans in the sample actually thought of the Democrats rather than their own party in connection with increased job opportunities.

The Democrats were unaware of the results of the poll, but their campaign nevertheless emphasized the party's strong points as indicated by the survey. The Democratic platform stressed increased job opportunities and tax revision as well as land reform, a popular issue with all racial groups and members of both political parties. When the voters of Oahu were asked if they favored breaking up the big estates, 56 per cent in the survey said yes, 13 per cent no, 25 per cent could not decide, and some gave no answer at all. The Chinese and Japanese showed greatest enthusiasm for land reform; middle-class haoles were not far behind. Only the Hawaiians, concerned for the future of the Bishop estate, showed less than 50 per cent willing to say positively that breaking up the big estates would be a good thing. Of those Hawaiians and part-Hawaiians who could make up their minds, twice as many were for the action as opposed it. The Democrats, primarily through haole leaders Thomas Gill, John J. Hulten, and Robert G. Dodge, called for a revision of Hawaii's tax-assessment procedures, which they alleged permitted estates to profit by keeping badly needed land idle. The Democratic program called for confiscatory legislation, if necessary, to require estates either to put land into productive use or to force its sale to private developers.

Republican candidates stressed their opposition to the 3.5 per cent retail sales tax on basic foodstuffs (meant by the Democrats to be a gross income tax on business). Surveys revealed that the tax was viewed as a sales tax by most of Hawaii's voters, regardless of race or party affiliation. Voters seemed to be less interested in real-property taxes than in getting relief from the gross income tax, which they correctly identified with the Democratic party. The Republican platform called for repeal of the tax and for the raising of personal net-income-tax exemption from $400 to $600. But Democrats stood behind their tax measures, claiming that Republican proposals would milk the territorial treasury of more than $10,000,000 in revenue and require deficit financing.

Avoiding the land issue, the G.O.P. stressed two other questions in addition to taxation: Communism and statehood. Jack Burns was repeatedly forced to deny Communist influence in the Democratic party. He argued that some labor organizers in Hawaii may have been Communists in the past in order to use the cells of the Communist party for labor purposes, but that the Communist apparatus in Hawaii was nonexistent now that there was a healthy two-party system. The success of the Democratic party, he claimed, had killed the Communist menace in Hawaii. He pointed to F.B.I. studies showing that although there were 160 Communists in the Islands in 1946, there were only thirty-six in 1952, and he maintained that now, in 1958, Communism in Hawaii was dead. But the G.O.P. charged that because Burns minimized Communist activities, he was jeopardizing Hawaii's case for statehood. And even if he was not a dupe of the Communists, he was, they argued, a prisoner of the I.L.W.U. and thus unable to make fair judgments between management and labor.[16]

It was on the statehood issue that Republicans hoped to make the strongest inroads on Burns's popularity. The Delegate had agreed to a deal in Congress separating the questions of Hawaiian and Alaskan statehood. Tying the two statehood bills together in the past united the opposition to each measure and meant defeat for both. Burns agreed to push Alaska first, while Hawaii waited its turn. True to plan, Congress passed the Alaskan statehood bill. But what about the Islands? Republican spokesmen wanted to know. Had not Burns sacrificed Hawaiian statehood? Did Alaska deserve priority? Burns countered by arguing that Hawaii's chances were better than ever and that he would never again run for public office if Hawaii was not accepted as a state in the next session of Congress.

Governor Quinn and Turner charged that Hawaii had been betrayed, but the voters did not agree with Burns's Republican adversaries. He was returned as delegate by a better than 14,000-vote margin over Turner. Democrats won sixteen of twenty-seven places in the Senate and thirty-three of fifty-one House seats in the newly reapportioned territorial legislature. Republican stalwart Wilfred Tsukiyama barely won re-election to the Senate. Running ahead of him in the fifth senatorial district contest were four popular young Democrats: Patsy Mink, Sakae Takahashi, George Ariyoshi, and Frank Fasi. In Oahu's fourth senatorial district, Daniel Inouye ran substantially ahead of Hebden Porteus, who just managed to beat Democratic newcomer John Hulten for the second Senate seat. Democrats swept most county offices on Oahu, Maui, and Kauai. Only on the Big Island did the G.O.P. win a majority of territorial Senate seats and county offices.

The 1958 Democratic victory proved that the long-time Republican grip on Island politics had been broken. The election results, however, along with findings from surveys and factionalism within the Democratic party, gave no assurances of continued Democratic hegemony in territorial politics. Although more voters identified with the Democrats than with the opposition, polls repeatedly revealed that 45 to 50 per cent of Hawaii's voters thought of themselves as independents, and election returns showed that many Democrats and independents were attracted to individual Republican candidates. New Republican faces, not associated with the memories of the past, did well in multiracial districts. Such liberal Republicans as haole Frank Judd, part-

Hawaiian Ambrose Rosehill, nisei Yasutaka Fukushima, all from Oahu, and Spanish-American Joseph R. Garcia of Hawaii and haole John Milligan, of Maui, won many votes from independents and Democrats. And Neal Blaisdell, Honolulu's Republican mayor, was swept back into office. Although Jack Burns carried the Big Island by nearly 2,000 votes, Republican Senators William H. Hill, Richard Lyman, Bernard J. Kinney, and Julian R. Yates ran well in heavily Oriental districts, despite the fact that the last three were part-Hawaiians and Hill a haole. Republican James Kealoha ran far ahead of his nisei opponent for chairman of Hawaii's Board of Supervisors, although the Japanese constituted the largest single voting group there.

Republicans could still win large pluralities if they wore the mantle of Republicanism loosely. On the Big Island, Doc Hill refused to work actively for other G.O.P. candidates and won handily, while his former business associate, orthodox Republican Gavien Bush, was badly defeated. On Oahu, Neal Blaisdell rose above party labels, claiming he could work better with a Democratic Board of Supervisors than his Democratic opponent for mayor, William C. Vanatta. Blaisdell knew that a private poll showed that Democratic voters gave him almost as much approval as Republican electors. His appeal, it revealed, was not unlike that of Jack Burns. While 33 per cent of the haoles in the sample approved of the way Blaisdell had done his job, 41 per cent disapproved. In the upper-income Republican groups especially, Blaisdell was frowned on. But Orientals and Hawaiians gave this part-Hawaiian Republican handsome endorsement. Since the hard-core Republicans did not approve of him, he ran on his own, seemingly unconcerned about the rest of the ticket.

The most popular Republican of all was not on the ticket. Had Democratic leaders been privileged to study the results of the latest private survey of Oahu voter preferences, their exultation at victory would have been tempered by the knowledge that *malihini* Governor William F. Quinn received more approval as governor than either Burns or Blaisdell had won for their respective jobs. The ebullient singing Irishman with the broad smile was endorsed by 71 per cent of Oahu's voters, and only 5 per cent disapproved of the job he was doing as governor. Approval was overwhelming in all ethnic groups, and even among strong Democrats, opinions were in his favor. Quinn, who had fared badly in a contest for the Senate two years earlier, had, in his short tenure as governor, impressed the Islands' population as a capable and liberal chief executive, despite his Republican affiliation.[17]

Problems other than the popularity of Quinn and Blaisdell plagued the Democrats. The factional disputes of past years had been replaced by complex cleavages no less bitter than those which worried the Democrats under Republican rule. The new Democratic party, now the majority party of Hawaii, was united in its opposition to the Republicans but bitterly divided by personality disputes, ethnic tensions, and conflicts on important issues. No one person or group could speak for the entire party. The factions were numerous: Burns and his devoted followers from the 442nd Club; I.L.W.U. officials and approximately half a dozen territorial legislators under strong I.L.W.U. influence; young Democrats inspired by the fiery Patsy Mink; so-called independents led by Honolulu-born Thomas Gill and Vincent Esposito; and representatives of Democratic conservatism from days gone by under former Governor Stainback, lawyer Garner Anthony, and William Heen.

These older conservatives were the least-influential faction. Stainback, now leading the fight against statehood, was considered anti-Oriental by many younger Democrats. Garner Anthony, a member of an important Merchant Street law firm and strong opponent of martial law during the war, had been passed over by Truman as a replacement for Stainback. Heen, once a towering figure in Island politics, did not run for re-election to the Senate in 1958.

In territorial politics, the young Democrats were represented by Patsy Mink, who had organized the group at the University of Hawaii, partly to keep the 442nd Club from taking over the Democratic party. At the 1954 convention, as chairman of the Rules Committee, her aggressive but pleasing manner won her a place in the party. A representative of neither the I.L.W.U. nor the 442nd, she shared the militant antioligarchy attitudes of both Burns and Hall and frequently found herself in agreement with their legislative positions.

The major factions fighting to control the party were the Burns-442nd group, the I.L.W.U., and the independents. Through 1954, Burns invariably fought the union. He won every crucial fight against it at the 1952 territorial convention. I.L.W.U. officials retaliated by opposing Burns' candidacy for the delegateship in 1954, and assisted young independent Tom Gill in his successful bid for the chairmanship of the Oahu Democratic County Committee against Burns' candidate, Tadao Beppu. Gradually, the ascending power of the independents, who liked neither the Burns group nor the I.L.W.U., forced these two factions to work together.

The antagonism of the independents toward Burns centered on what they called his "imperious personality" and his "racial approach to politics." In the 1954 battle to control the Oahu County Committee, Gill's backers charged that Burns was trying to pack the Democratic organization with too many nisei followers in key posts. When Spark Matsunaga, an independent nisei, decided to run for representative from the traditionally Republican fourth district in 1954, Burns attempted to discourage him. Anxious to elect Dan Inouye, Burns argued that it would be a mistake to run two nisei candidates at one time. The haoles would plunk for haole candidates, he maintained, and it would be better to center Democratic support around Inouye. Matsunaga disagreed, and both of the young war heroes were elected, but the independents did not forgive Burns for his attempt to dictate slates.

The independents did not challenge the legislative policies advanced by Burns and his nisei friends, Aoki, Inouye, Takabuki, and Tokunaga. But they did oppose what they thought was an autocratic effort to pack slates of candidates with Burns' followers. To them, he seemed cold, aloof, inflexible, and dictatorial. He appeared to mistrust any Democrat who had not been reared in the slums or on hard plantation labor.[18]

Whether they liked it or not, independents had to admit that Burns had helped to rebuild the Democratic party by appealing specifically to the two largest voting groups in Hawaii, the Japanese and the part-Hawaiians. He had not done away with widespread Hawaiian antipathy to the A.J.A.'s, but he had enlisted a large majority of both groups in behalf of the same candidates. He established Bill Richardson, a young part-Hawaiian lawyer, as territorial party chairman, and in 1955 worked behind the scenes to have Charles Kauhane elected speaker of the first Democratic House of Representatives in the history of the Territory.

The militant young nisei around Burns could not understand the personal attacks made against him by Democrats. To them, he was a self-effacing, self-sacrificing leader who correctly understood that the Japanese no longer had to apologize for what they were, no longer had to beg for acceptance. Burns sympathized with their rebelliousness, and he dedicated himself to their cause. He was ridiculed by others, lived on short rations, and worked tirelessly to build the party. How could the others accuse him of wanting to be a dictator of the party when Aoki, Inouye, Takabuki, and Tokunaga had to persuade him to run for delegate in 1956? But these nisei were sensitive to the charge that the Japanese were taking over the Democratic party; they supported Burns in his efforts to boost Richardson and Kauhane and increasingly tried to balance slates with Hawaiians, Filipinos, and haoles. When a group of Democrats, including many A.J.A.'s, attempted to depose Richardson in 1958, Burns and his closest nisei supporters fought to retain him.[19]

As the strength of the independents grew, their opposition to Burns intensified, and by 1955, Burns realized the necessity of establishing a working alliance with the I.L.W.U. Neither Burns nor his friends liked the dictatorial manner of Hall and I.L.W.U. public-relations chief Robert McElrath any better in 1955 than they had in 1950. But Burns had lost the delegateship three times in a row. In 1954, he had been opposed by the union and beaten despite the Democratic landslide. A majority of the independents were at least as strongly anti-I.L.W.U. as anti-Burns. The time had come, in his view, for a working alliance with the union.

By 1955, Hall was ready to make a deal with Burns, too. He realized that the union would be more effective working behind the scenes as a pressure group rather than putting union officials in key positions in the Democratic party. A public-opinion study done in 1955 showed that most voters did not think it proper for union officials to play an active role in political parties. Even I.L.W.U. members took a dim view of such activity. A majority of them in all racial groups agreed that union officers should not take an active role in the parties.[20]

To Hall, the philosophy, voting record, and party affiliation of the politicians were now irrelevant; what counted was their willingness to recognize I.L.W.U. power at the polls, to make deals based on that power, and to live up to them. At one time or another, Hall made deals with every variety of politician in Hawaii. His policy was simple. If the I.L.W.U. could not dominate, no other faction from either party should dominate either. In 1956, when Hall decided to back Burns for delegate, he also attempted to persuade Ben Dillingham to run for the legislature to cut down the power of the Democrats. It made no difference that Dillingham was consistently opposed to organized labor and against statehood.

On Maui and Kauai, where I.L.W.U. voting power could make or break the territorial legislature, Hall demanded strict obedience to union dictation. When a legislator became a little cocky, as did David Trask of Maui, during the 1955 session, the word was passed to cut him down at the next election. On the Big Island and on Oahu, I.L.W.U. support was given in only two situations: either a candidate was so popular that it would be impossible to oppose him successfully or a candidate was willing to deal on a straight power basis. Hall and his subordinates preferred conservative, even reactionary, candidates if they could be trusted to stand by their deals.

From Hall's point of view there were four kinds of legislators. The best were those half-dozen from Maui and Kauai who did not dare buck the union on any issue. Next were the political spokesmen for big capital who understood power and were desirable allies for two reasons: anxious for industrial peace, they wanted to avoid I.L.W.U. antagonism in labor-management relations; and they were symbols of the old regime, of a capitalism that could not be modified or ameliorated, but only destroyed, in the long run, and it was important from Hall's viewpoint to keep those symbols alive. The Burns faction and some of the young Democrats comprised the third group. Their own militant rejection of the past made them sympathetic to I.L.W.U. goals. More important to Hall, Burns and his group were tough. Their deals were based on self-interest, and in that sense, Burns could be trusted. The only group of politicians despised at union headquarters were the so-called independents in each major party, who, because of a liberal, prolabor record, believed they were entitled to union support without being obliged to take "advice" from the I.L.W.U. offices on Atkinson Drive. The Democratic independents, especially, came in for abuse. Who were they to masquerade as liberals when it was union power that had smashed the oligarchy in Hawaii? queried Hall, McElrath, and United Public Workers chief Henry Epstein. To the union officials, the independents were a collection of status-seeking lawyers, businessmen, and real-estate speculators. The union supported Tom Gill in 1954, and helped make him Democratic county chairman. But when Gill refused to bend to union direction, he was written off as a phony liberal. The I.L.W.U. had backed Sakae Takahashi in his first bid for the legislature. When Takahashi found the I.L.W.U. bill on unemployment compensation for agricultural workers financially deficient, he received a visit from union officials, including McElrath, who threatened to destroy him if he did not support the legislation. After Takahashi threw them out of his office, Hall made strenuous efforts to defeat him in subsequent elections. When Patsy Takemoto Mink, often wrongly accused by opponents of being "in the pocket of the I.L.W.U.," publicly criticized union leaders for attacking fellow senatorial candidates Takahashi and Ariyoshi, Mrs. Mink was immediately downgraded by the union, whose leaders passed the word in Hawaii's first state primary election to teach her a lesson. In Jack Hall's opinion, there was no room for independence or party loyalty if it interfered with I.L.W.U. aims.[21]

The marriage between the Burns and the I.L.W.U. factions was one of convenience as well as conviction. Burns knew that 80 per cent of the candidates endorsed by the I.L.W.U. in 1954 had been elected. Two years later, the union's record improved. Of the twenty-eight candidates formally endorsed by the I.L.W.U., only two were defeated. That year all four of the I.L.W.U.-endorsed-and-supported Republican candidates for the House from the outer islands were elected to the legislature, while unsupported Democrats met with defeat. In the 1957 legislature, most I.L.W.U.-supported legislation was passed, although the legislature stoutly refused to repeal the Territory's Dock Seizure Act, now a symbol in the union's struggle for power. Once again, in 1958, the I.L.W.U.'s Political Committee decided to back candidates from both parties. The union finally approved forty-seven candidates, at least a dozen of whom did not seek or even want such support. One political commentator observed, "With its strange list of 25 Oahu House endorsements, the union appears to be assuming the role of straight man in a political situation comedy."[22] The reason behind the union's endorsement of three Republicans in Oahu's fifth district Senate contest was easy to discern. The Democratic independents in the Senate had become too powerful. Such men as Kazuhisa Abe, Nelson K. Doi, Herbert K. H. Lee, Oren Long, Mitsuyuki Kido, and Sakae Takahashi opposed the labor faction of the Democratic party. Other endorsements seemed absurd, such as the approval given to outspokenly anti-I.L.W.U. Vincent Esposito and to Republican conservatives J. Howard Worrall, president of the Hawaiian Broadcasting System, and J. Ward Russell, who led the floor fight in 1957 against repeal of the Dock Seizure Act. Jack Hall, it was concluded, either had a good sense of humor or decided to endorse a few anti-I.L.W.U. men who were certain to win anyway.

Despite the ingenuity behind I.L.W.U. endorsements, the union received some sharp reversals on Election Day. Thirteen of forty-seven endorsed candidates were defeated. Independent Democrats led by

Esposito, Gill, and Howard Miyake, in the House, and Herbert Lee and Takahashi, in the Senate, won substantial victories. These Democrats, more disliked by union leaders than any other faction, comprised the largest voting bloc in both houses. Burns, elected delegate with I.L.W.U. support, gratefully acknowledged their help, but union officials felt no comfort from the growing power of Democratic independents in the legislature.

A coalition of I.L.W.U. and anti-I.L.W.U. Democrats organized the Senate, with independents in key positions. At first it appeared that the independents in the House, led by Esposito, would dominate that chamber. Hall wanted the Democrats' 1955 speaker, Charles Kauhane, to return to that powerful post. Delegate Burns's choice was Maui's Elmer Cravalho, Finance Committee chairman in 1957. But Esposito had the votes. New members of the House, not identified with either faction, sided with the Connecticut-born Italian-American rather than succumb to the arguments of I.L.W.U. officials and Burns representatives. So confident were the independents that they brought to the first Democratic caucus a list of committee chairmanships for ratification which failed to give either Cravalho or Kauhane an important post.

Fifteen members of the thirty-three-man Democratic House contingent walked out of the caucus, protesting the slates prepared by Esposito and Gill. Kauhane charged that he was double crossed by members of the Burns faction who agreed to support Esposito as speaker. The Burns group, headed by Matsuo Takabuki, city and county supervisor, was prepared to recognize Esposito's claim to the speakership, but insisted on the finance post for Cravalho and a shift in real power from the speaker to the floor leader, a post coveted for a Burns man.

The House organization fight was made to order for Kauhane, who called on talents developed in a lifetime of politics. His father, a pure Hawaiian, had been an active Republican precinct worker. Young Kauhane switched to the Democrats in 1937 and cultivated his political garden, planning one day to become speaker of the House. Strongly antihaole, Kauhane often used a racial approach in lining up support for himself or his ideas, maneuvering among Hawaiians and others as the spokesman for nonhaoles. But he was also hostile to the Japanese, who, from his point of view, had wantonly exploited the Hawaiians in recent years, as the haoles had in earlier times. In 1947, when the Democrats tied Republicans in House membership, this unpredictable Hawaiian was his party's choice for speaker. Among other antics,

Kauhane livened House proceedings by engaging in a fist fight with Representative Hiram Fong. Finally, Democrat George R. Aguiar, of Kauai, voted with the Republicans in order to proceed with legislative business. In 1954, after the Democrats captured the legislature for the first time in history, Kauhane fulfilled his dream of becoming House speaker. Supported by both the I.L.W.U. and the Burns groups, he won the post easily. But Kauhane unwisely flaunted his power, causing a Democratic revolt against his leadership. Burns's A.J.A. supporters were as unhappy with Kauhane as the independents, and in the organization of the House in 1957, they threw their support to Esposito for speaker on the second ballot at the request of Inouye. The deal gave key representation to each of the three major factions within the party. Esposito, for the independents, became speaker; Inouye, the most prominent of the Burns group after the Delegate himself, was designated majority leader; and Cravalho, representing I.L.W.U. power on Maui, was chosen finance chairman. Now, in 1959, Esposito wanted all important posts for the independents.

While Esposito's group comprised a majority of the Democrats, it was far short of a majority of the entire House. To control that chamber, twenty-six votes were necessary, and Esposito and Gill could count on only eighteen. Kauhane made a hurried visit to Hilo to confer with I.L.W.U. officials Jack Hall and George Martin. Hall encouraged Kauhane to form a coalition with the Republican minority, thereby wresting House control from Esposito. His overtures to the Republicans were successful. They would be delighted to work with Kauhane to embarrass the Democratic majority.

Democrats David Trask, of Maui, and Hiroshi Kato tried to forestall a Kauhane-Republican coalition. These two spoke for eight of the fifteen legislators who had originally voted against Esposito and for Cravalho as speaker. They received help from Burns, who telephoned his supporters urging them to work out an agreement with Esposito and Gill rather than join Kauhane in a bargain with the enemy. Only the solid I.L.W.U. group of six representatives was ready to follow Kauhane's plan. Esposito and Gill agreed to give better committee assignments to the rebel group but refused to make certain concessions deemed important by Trask and Kato. Confident that the eighteen would stick together and that eight of the fifteen would prefer to vote for Democrat Esposito than work with the I.L.W.U. and the G.O.P., the leaders of the independents were in no mood to compromise. Gill

taunted the Republicans and infuriated the dissidents in his own party
by insisting on the chairmanship of both the Judiciary and Land Reform committees. Certain they had the votes and determined to accomplish major land-reform legislation, Gill and Esposito refused to make
significant concessions until it was too late.

Republican leaders were unwilling to support Kauhane as speaker;
they did agree to oppose Esposito and the House rules submitted by
the independents. The eighteen Republicans and six I.L.W.U. Democrats needed two more votes for a majority, and received four from
David Trask, Ray Adams, Elmer Cravalho, all from Maui, and young
Walter Harada, from Oahu. When Cravalho was offered the speakership, it became extremely difficult for Trask and Adams, already under
considerable pressure from the I.L.W.U., to remain with Esposito,
who, up to the last minute, had refused to grant Maui an important
committee assignment. The independents were defeated. Cravalho was
made speaker, major committee assignments went to members of the
fifteen, and Republicans named their own committee representatives.

The struggle to control the territorial House of Representatives in
1959 revealed that the Democrats were as sharply divided by factionalism in victory as they had been during decades of defeat. Intensive interviews with legislators showed that the eighteen members of the
Esposito-Gill group were united primarily by common opposition to
what they perceived to be the autocratic tactics of the I.L.W.U. in
politics. The fifteen in the Democratic minority were actually divided
into three groups. Three legislators, including Kauhane, spoke mainly
for their own ambitions. Eight, whether out of conviction or political
necessity, were more or less willing to go along with the I.L.W.U. The
others—David McClung, an A.F. of L.-C.I.O. executive on Oahu and
official of the young Democrats, and 442nd veteran and lawyer Sidney
Hashimoto—believed it was a mistake for Democrats to make open war
on the union. Beppu and Kato, from the 442nd Club, agreed. To a man,
the fifteen thought that the independents tried too hard for respectability
to interpret correctly the militant aspirations of Hawaii's underprivi-
leged. When the showdown came, McClung, Beppu, Kato, and Hashimoto, as loyal Democrats, sided with Esposito rather than join the
Republicans and Kauhane; but they remained convinced that the Democratic eighteen were, in the words of one of them, "more concerned
about being smeared as friends of the I.L.W.U. or afraid of giving the
impression that the Democratic Party is a branch of the 442nd Club

than with building a militantly liberal program." "There are a great many people in the Territory who would like to destroy the labor movement," said another, "and no one in the Democratic Party should temporize with that point of view." "Why should the Esposito group be afraid to talk to representatives of the union? They are not afraid to deal with management spokesmen," lamented another of the fifteen.

To the eighteen, the dissident Democrats were more preoccupied with fighting such injustices of the past as racial prejudice than the real battles of the future, such as land reform. Another issue, as the independents saw it, was not whether they should contribute to redbaiting, but whether they should knuckle under to the arm-twisting tactics of the I.L.W.U. "The arrogance of union officials," as one A.J.A. put it, "is intolerable. They will not understand that a representative cannot take dictation from anyone." A part-Hawaiian from Oahu insisted that the union should not be allowed to dominate the Democratic party. Bernaldo Bicoy, the first Filipino to be elected to the legislature, wrote the I.L.W.U.'s political representatives that he could not commit himself in advance to support union-sponsored legislation because, as a representative of the people, he could not be accountable to just one group. Bicoy, coming from a district where the union was influential, fought pressure from all sources in an effort to remain an independent. A Chinese representative from Oahu and a Japanese legislator from a nearby district argued that the I.L.W.U. tail should not be allowed to wag the Democratic dog.

The I.L.W.U. was the major issue separating the independents from the Burns group. Esposito and Gill, both of whom had bargained with the union before, and their supporters wanted to relegate I.L.W.U. representatives to subordinate positions in the legislature. The Burns group wanted to fulfill and continue its working alliance with the union.

Underlying this split were conflicts on land reforms and ethnic tensions within the party. Of the eighteen independents, there were ten nisei, three haoles, two Chinese, two part-Hawaiians, and one Filipino. Among the fifteen, there were six nisei, three haoles, three part-Hawaiians, two Portuguese, and one Filipino. Superficially, it appeared that both groups were cosmopolitan. But the eighteen were actually more cosmopolitan in spirit than the dissidents. Heen and Kamaka, part-Hawaiians in the Esposito group, were much more willing to work things out with the haoles and Japanese than Kauhane. The nisei in the majority were far less hostile toward the haoles than the nisei contingent among the fifteen; the haoles among the dominant faction did not share the strong antihaole feelings carried by the three haoles among the rebels; the Filipino with Esposito did not seek retaliation against haoles and Japanese for the injustices done his people as did his counterpart in the minority; the two cosmopolitan Chinese in the Democratic delegation were in the Esposito faction, while the intensely antihaole, anti-Japanese representatives of Portuguese extraction were on the other side. In short, the fifteen appeared to be rejecting not only the past, but the present and future. They were rejecting a cosmopolitan Hawaii, in which the numerically largest ethnic groups—the A.J.A.'s and haoles—were predominant.

The issue of land reform also divided the factions, although not as sharply as the I.L.W.U. or ethnic tensions. Land reform, so desperately desired by middle-class groups, was frequently opposed by Hawaiian politicians who were concerned with the future of the Bishop estate, and by I.L.W.U. representatives, whose plantation workers would have little to gain by opening large land areas to middle-class housing. On this issue, Kauhane and the I.L.W.U. were natural allies of conservative Republican spokesmen. But the major point of division was the union itself. And underlying that division, with some modifications, were the different racial attitudes of the majority and the minority. The independents—favoring land reform and opposing union domination— also wanted to bury the hostilities and tensions of the past. The coalition of fifteen, with a few important exceptions, were often motivated by those same hostilities and tensions.[23]

It was inevitable that ethnic politics should be important in Hawaii, just as it is in large multiethnic cities on the mainland. One basic reason for the importance of ethnic factors in American politics is the absence of overriding national cleavages, dividing party loyalties along class or ideological lines. There is no set formula for predicting how ethnic factors will manifest themselves in American politics. At different points in different places, every major ethnic group in the nation has tended to identify its hopes and needs with a party, a faction within a party, a candidate or candidates, and even with policies and ideas. Participation in American politics is one of the most important parts of the acculturation process, but the nature and volume of participation will vary with each group and its peculiar historic circumstances through the first several generations. In Hawaii, where the tradition of racial *aloha* and actual widespread intermarriage often prevented overt expressions of racial prejudice, ethnic tensions frequently found their way into the voting booth.

Systematic interviews with more than three quarters of the defeated candidates in the 1958 primaries revealed that the overwhelming majority of these men and women attributed their loss to the racial prejudice or pride of other groups constituting a majority of voters in their districts. Defeated Chinese, haole, and Hawaiian Democrats often blamed Japanese voters for plunking for their own kind. A Chinese lawyer, Mr. X, complained, after closing the doors so that his Japanese secretary could not hear, that "the Japanese voted for their own kind." But a Korean loser, running in the same district, reported that the reason that he lost was that "lots of Chinese plunked for Mr. X, so I lost those Chinese votes." Exploring the intricacies of ethnic voting, it was his opinion that "I did poorly among the Japanese and some haoles, but the Filipinos and the Chinese will pick a Korean over a Japanese anytime." A constant complaint of Republican Japanese primary losers was that they could not win haole votes. One man, who claimed that he entered the race to prove to his Japanese friends that he could win as a Republican, reported with sadness that his friends were right; he was defeated badly in all haole precincts. Another nisei Republican, hoping for a career in a major haole bank, also anxious to prove that a Japanese-American could win in a haole district as a Republican, decried the plunking for haole candidates and the lack of support and encouragement received from G.O.P. party leaders, which he alleged defeated him in the primary. Another popular nisei, a small businessman introduced to the party through the influence of Joseph Farrington, was swamped by a relatively unknown haole in a predominantly haole district. Admitting that it was hard for Japanese Republicans to win substantial haole support except in rare cases—notably Tsukiyama's—he quickly pointed out that such haoles as Hebden Porteus were warmly endorsed by Japanese voters of both parties. Indeed, almost every nisei candidate believed that Japanese electors distributed their votes among the various ethnic groups more freely than did other citizens.

Many Republicans of Hawaiian ancestry also complained of haole domination in the party. The replacement of part-Hawaiian Samuel King with *malihini* haole William Quinn revived the historic tensions between the two groups. A well-known Hawaiian legislator complained that there is "still too much dictation from Merchant Street, from the haoles who want to run the party." A part-Hawaiian Republican lawyer, frequently a candidate for the legislature, complained that party leaders were affiliated with the pineapple and sugar interests. "They are wealthy men who do not understand the Hawaiian people," he asserted. Hawaiian Republicans who complained against haoles in their own party were often just as hostile toward Japanese politicians. One Hawaiian, a public servant for more than twenty years, reported, "I am sick and tired of kow-towing to the Japanese. Republicans should not seek their votes; we could win with all other groups." Repeatedly, Hawaiians assured interviewers that if the Hawaiian people could stick together like the Japanese, they would be more successful at the polls.[24]

Systematic study of key ethnic precincts and the results of voter surveys actually revealed that all major ethnic groups tended to favor their own kind, but that Japanese plunking was far less decisive than frequently claimed, and that other groups—the Chinese, haoles, Portuguese, and Hawaiians—plunked at least as extensively as the Japanese. A postelection survey of the fourteenth district on Oahu showed that Chinese candidates were strongly favored by Chinese voters regardless of party, the Portuguese candidate ran far ahead of the others among Portuguese electors regardless of party, and so on.[25]

Ethnic tensions could readily be inferred from election results in key precincts. In the Hana district of Maui, in the twenty-sixth precinct (more than 90 per cent Hawaiian), part-Hawaiian Democratic candidate David Trask received almost twice the number of votes given to haole Democrat Ray F. Adams, and more than three times the percentage awarded to nisei running mate Mamouru Yamasaki. The pattern was fairly consistent for other groups. For example, Portuguese candidates did unusually well in such heavily Portuguese districts as Maui's eighteenth and Kauai's eighth and thirteenth precincts. But there were exceptions, and in interviews victorious candidates often pointed with pride to the support that they received from other ethnic groups. Strong candidates often did well among all groups, but always best with their own. Weak candidates limped badly everywhere, but showed the least weakness among their own kind. The patterns were not much different from those observed in comparable elections on the mainland where vibrant political parties absorbed and accommodated the conflicting claims of ethnic groups. Ethnic claims in politics, far from being un-American, followed the typical American pattern, including Yankee, German, Scandinavian, and French as well as

Italian, Polish, Irish, and Jewish voters. Although there was no such thing as a bloc vote in the sense that all members of a group respond to parties, candidates, and issues in the same way, it was clear that ethnic factors played a significant role in the politics of democracy.

If democracy means anything, it means choice, and Hawaii's voters, whatever their ethnic background, increasingly exercised choice in the election of parties, candidates, and programs. But it did not mean that all pockets of local domination by autocratic union leaders, landlords, or politicians had been destroyed. On Kauai, union endorsement could mean more than party support. Charles Rice, now eighty-two years old, was no longer "boss," although he remained chairman of the Kauai Police Commission. As powerful as he had been, this veteran of thirty-three years in the legislature would not openly defy the I.L.W.U. in politics. Kauai's best vote-getters were Portuguese legislator Manuel Henriques and Portuguese county chairman Anthony C. Baptiste, Jr., both beneficiaries of unequivocal I.L.W.U. support and overwhelming Portuguese backing. The union replaced the Baldwins and their plantation managers on Maui as the most powerful single influence in that island's politics. So strong was its authority that two-term Democratic Representative Nadao Yoshinaga—known as a partisan Democrat—urged I.L.W.U. workers to support the entire union slate, including one of his own Republican opponents for the Senate in the 1958 election. Union officials hotly denied that voters were coerced to support their candidates, and the secrecy of the voting booth was unquestionably guaranteed. Workers were free to challenge union endorsements, and occasionally did, but hundreds of them accepted the union slate without question, much as their predecessors had taken the slate given them by plantation managers and *lunas*.

Visits to plantations on Maui and Kauai revealed that the dynamics of democracy had not yet completely dispelled the legacy of fear inherited by Hawaii's plantation workers. Behind drawn curtains in plantation shacks, laborers admitted that they were afraid to cross their union bosses but feared and disliked the plantation management even more. Caught between tough union leaders demanding conformity to the I.L.W.U. position and the unyielding opposition of plantation management, some of the workers on the great Baldwin plantation at Puunene on Maui, for example, were unwilling to talk about politics at all. Their tense voices, revealing fear of speaking truthfully to someone who could be a spy for either side, made it plain that freedom of speech had not yet become a reality for these workers.[26]

In East Hawaii, Doc Hill, exercising greater economic power than any individual ever possessed on the Big Island, wielded considerable political influence. With large real-estate investments, a chain of theaters, a laundry business, a big automobile dealership, and other extensive enterprises, he employed at least 600 persons. Hill, who savored the popularity he had won and the prestige accorded him when called "Senator," sustained his power by the same method used by successful political bosses elsewhere. He worked systematically to put key groups of voters in his debt. Although against unions, he opened his nonunionized theaters during the 1958 sugar strike for the pleasure of the strikers and sent donations of pigs, beef, and other foodstuffs to hard-hit families. He cultivated unit leaders in the union, rather than just the top men. One nisei mill foreman remembers that Hill loaned him money when he was in trouble and made large contributions to his church. Despite a famous anti-Japanese statement during the war, Hill quietly gave to Japanese and other charities, building good will on a personal level.

Hill's influence extended even into the Democratic party on the Big Island and several hundred miles away to Iolani Palace. There was at least one of his employees on every single major Big Island commission, appointed by a Republican governor and confirmed by Democratic legislators. His method was to persuade the governor to appoint men already acceptable to the Democrats. In the 1958 election, his influence was shown to have penetrated the Hilo *Tribune* when he seemed able to anticipate every major advertisement against him by placing an answer on the opposite page.

Like Charles Rice, of Kauai, Hill could just as easily be a Democrat as a Republican. He wanted to run his own *kuleana,* without interference from party officials, and despite the relative complexity of the Big Island's economic and political life, he was clearly the dominant force of East Hawaii on the eve of statehood. His influence did not reach most of the nearly 1,000 independent sugar growers on the Hamakua Coast or the thirty-five sugar planters in the volcano area; nor did it extend in great measure across the island to the coffee farmers on the Kona Coast. But in East Hawaii, he was as powerful as any man had ever been.[27]

The political life on the Kona Coast changed more slowly than anywhere else in the Territory, but even there the dynamics of democracy modified the power of Kona's landed aristocracy. Kona politics were still dominated by the instability of the coffee market and the scarcity of fee-simple land. When coffee prices went down, large numbers of farmers became almost totally dependent on the two large Honolulu-controlled millers in the area. These millers, owned by American Factors and the Dillinghams, were the largest bankers, insurance agents, and grocers in Kona, and by withholding credit from a small Japanese grower, they could easily destroy him. The economic squeeze resulted in greater political control by the Kona oligarchy, which, in partisan terms, resulted in Republican victories. Control over land also served as an instrument of political coercion. Many coffee farmers holding five- or ten-year leases on their small farms dared not challenge the millers or the major landlords—the Hinds, Ackermans, and Greenwells—who could always decide not to renew their leases.

Democratic precinct clubs were started secretly in Kona in 1946. The landlords and Republicans had first tried to buy incipient Democratic leaders, but, because of the new postwar militance of the Japanese, they were unsuccessful. In the old days, everyone was a Republican. People were afraid to think of being anything else. But after the political revolution of 1954, Kona Democrats increasingly came into the open. As one farmer replied when asked to describe the difference between prewar and postwar Kona politics, "In the old days we have to kiss the haoles' ass. Now we say to ourselves, let them kiss our ass." Another nisei, Harry Tanaka, a small coffee farmer who had grown up on a plantation where the *luna* told him how to vote, remembered his civics lessons from school. Called "Mr. Democrat" of Kona, he could be seen moving about from farm to farm, passing out handbills, putting up posters, and exhorting the citizenry to "go Democratic."

The continuing struggle for democracy in Kona was not without casualties. A stunning light Negro woman from Minnesota, Mrs. Helene Hale, and her husband moved to the island because she loved nature and sought racial *aloha*. They came to Kona to teach high school and were quickly confronted with a social system they had never dreamed existed in America. In their efforts to encourage the Japanese to express their own culture, to become friendly with the Hawaiians, and to promote knowledge of the requirements of democracy, the Hales met repeated rebuffs. When they participated in the Japanese bon dances, they were criticized. They were hurt to learn that Hawaii's vaunted racial *aloha* had not eliminated all aspects of racial prejudice. Mrs. Hale set up voting booths to teach the children in her social-studies class about secret voting, and her principal criticized her for being an agitator. Finally, the battle between the Hales and the "authorities" was drawn tight over the issue of teaching Communism in the school. Mr. William Hale argued with representatives of the Department of Public Instruction that to free young minds of prejudice, it was important to teach them about alien ways of thought and life. Downcast after losing his battle with the Department, he resigned from the school, as did his wife two years later. Hale was defeated when he ran for election as a delegate to the constitutional convention in Hawaii in 1950, but many voters in Kona, aroused by the activity of Tanaka, listened attentively to his discussions of land reform. In the meantime, Mrs. Hale, selling children's books from house to house, became a friend of hundreds of Japanese and Hawaiians along the coast. Local Democrats approached this remarkably energetic woman to run for the Board of Supervisors in 1954, and, as the only Democrat on the ticket, she was elected.

Tanaka and Helene Hale heralded the emergent democracy of Kona. They could not completely overcome its heritage of fear, nor could they eliminate the deep feelings of obligation that Japanese and Hawaiians felt toward the owners of wealth on the Kona Coast. They did, however, introduce the two-party system to that dry, but romantic, portion of the Hawaiian Islands discovered by Captain Cook less than 200 years before. On the eve of statehood, Kona stirred with a new activity which accelerated the process of democracy: coffee farmers organized their own co-operative mill; a farm bureau co-operative was established; and subdivisions were opened by enterprising realtors to make it possible for the people of Kona to own their homes. The dynamics of democracy were invading even the most remote reaches of the Islands.[28]

Chapter Fifteen

LABOR MILITANT

On a hot prewar morning in the fields of the Koloa plantation on Kauai, a nisei made a vow that he was to work to fulfill in the years after the war. He and his friends had been pulling weeds under a fierce sun, but despite the heat and a near-record performance, the assistant manager cut their wages. One of the boys slowed the pace of work in retaliation, and the angry field boss kicked him in the testicles and left him lying on the ground in pain. His friend swore to himself that day: "They will not treat us like mules any longer." He had learned at Kauai High School certain principles of justice; he would begin immediately to bring justice to his people. The next week, he led his friends back to the plantation and negotiated an agreement with the field boss to have workers paid by the yard rather than by the hour. In the decades to come, he was to struggle first to build a labor union in Hawaii and then to establish democracy within the union, against labor leaders almost as autocratic in their way as the field bosses of his youth.[1]

Unionism in Hawaii was halted by military government. Between December 7, 1941, and October 24, 1944, labor was ruthlessly suppressed under strict martial law. On the outer islands, it was necessary for a laborer to have a military permit to move from island to island, and plantation workers generally found it impossible to obtain such permits.[2] On Kauai, laborers were obliged to get a formal release from the plantation manager before receiving military approval to move. On Oahu, the laborers were not actually frozen in their jobs, but an informal agreement was made between the sugar and pineapple managers and the military not to hire plantation employees for federal and military jobs.[3] After March 10, 1943, plantation workers were no longer under military control, although most construction workers, stevedores, dock workers, and public-utility employees continued to be regulated by the Army and were virtually frozen in their jobs. In addition, a military order imposed jail sentences for absenteeism; under it, hundreds of workers were either fined or jailed during the war. Another order suspended all legal holidays and abolished premium holiday pay.

There were a few short strikes in Honolulu in 1943, and union organization on the plantations began toward the end of that year, but it was only after President Roosevelt terminated martial law in October 1944 that the repressed labor-union leaders could assert all their rights under the National Labor Relations Act without violating patriotic pledges. The war and its aftermath produced an overwhelming demand for labor, which virtually eliminated unemployment. It brought a vast inflow of federal funds constituting a massive economic break-through in the Islands. Labor organizers found the environment almost totally new, far more receptive to unionism than that which existed prior to the war.

The new money and the requirements of the military created new jobs. A large number of Filipinos moved into semiskilled and skilled jobs on various government projects and, at the huge naval installation at Pearl Harbor, many Americans of Japanese ancestry and some Chinese took positions with the public utilities theretofore reserved for haoles, Portuguese, and Hawaiians. In some cases, Chinese and Japanese girls and Filipino men replaced Japanese and Chinese men as truck drivers, leaving their old positions as waitresses and waiters to Filipino girls. The Hawaiian Pineapple Company reported 60 per cent fewer university students applying for summer work in 1944 than in previous years. Used-car companies showed an increase of 70 per cent in business among Orientals between January and April 1944. Retail sales rose, and banks showed sharp increases in savings.[4] Perhaps most important of all, the attitudes of laborers had changed. They became more receptive than ever to union organization. Although union membership during the war had declined sharply from the prewar peak in 1941, it began to pick up in 1943, and grew rapidly following the lifting of martial law.[5] When the war ended, according to the Islands' top economist, James H. Shoemaker, there was a "sudden release of forces which had accumulated before the war, and of the resentments which the military government controls had engendered."[6]

In late 1944 and early 1945, petition followed petition to the National Labor Relations Board requesting union recognition. In only a few cases was it granted without recourse to an N.L.R.B. election. Thirty-four elections in 1944 resulted in union certification. The following year, there were sixty-one successful elections. There could be no doubt that the union movement was in Hawaii to stay. Mill and plantation workers usually organized without the assistance of mainland haoles. Many plantation workers were now citizens, and they knew their rights. The proportion of citizens had already increased in the 1930's from 12 to 45 per cent. More self-assertive than their parents, they knew also that the agencies who ran the plantations did not want them to leave their jobs for work in the military or urban sectors of the Islands' changing economy.[7]

The passage of the National Labor Relations Act in 1935 had made trade-unionism a real possibility in Hawaii. It hopefully meant the end of "violence, intimidation, summary police action, blacklists and industrial spy systems," which had been used by the employers during the 1930's. But despite the help of N.L.R.B. representatives and the criticism of employers by congressional committees investigating statehood in 1937, it was not until the workers of Hawaii changed their own attitudes toward authority that the union movement was able to make substantial headway.[8]

Moving among the workers on the docks and on the plantations was the massive figure of Jack Hall. Hall, who was already said by friends and enemies alike to be a Communist or "close to it," believed strongly that laborers must exert political as well as economic pressure to establish the power of their unions.

To help Hall in 1944, the International Longshoremen's and Warehousemen's Union sent organizer Frank Thompson to Hawaii. In June of the same year, Hall left his job with the territorial Department of Labor to become regional director of the I.L.W.U. Already the union had claimed majorities at five plantations, and in October it received considerable help from an N.L.R.B. decision that classified 50 to 60 per cent of the employees on the plantations as industrial workers, rather than the 20 to 30 per cent requested by industry. In the nineteen plantation elections held in 1945, the I.L.W.U. won 5,568 favorable votes to 222 opposed, an indication of the drastic shift in attitude of plantation workers.

Actively entering the 1944 territorial elections, union leaders claimed credit for the election of several representatives and senators. In the 1945 legislative session, Hall conferred privately with outer island politicians, Democrat J. B. Fernandes, from Kauai, and the powerful William ("Doc") Hill, from Hawaii. Recognizing that their own political future might be at stake, Hill and Fernandes agreed to throw their support to territorial legislation to cover workers not under the National Labor Relations Act. The sugar agencies wanted Hall to leave agricultural workers alone, although they were willing to recognize, as they had to under federal law, the I.L.W.U.'s jurisdiction over industrial workers on the plantations. But the employers could no longer control the legislature with respect to labor, and when, under the leadership of Hall, the "Little Wagner Act"—the Hawaii Employment Relations Act of May 21, 1945—was passed, extending to agricultural workers the same rights given by the N.L.R.B. to industrial workers on the plantations, the union achieved a major victory. It had demonstrated its political power and now could legally organize all plantation workers.

Under the new law, fifteen elections were held in the following year, fourteen of them resulting in union certification. Under national legislation in the same year, ninety-five certifications were granted. By 1945, the I.L.W.U. had completed its organization of Hawaii's ports, and by mid-1946, had successfully moved into the pineapple industry and the plantation railroad system. In thirty-six months, it had organized workers in the Islands' two basic agricultural industries and on the docks of Hawaii. From a mere 900 members in 1944, I.L.W.U. membership rose to an estimated 30,000 by 1947.[9] For the first time, the major employers of Hawaii were on the defensive. They had been warned shortly before the beginning of the war by the president of the San Francisco Employers Council to prepare for inevitable unionization, but the war had given them a breather.

But the war would not last forever, and Hawaii's employers, patriotically hoping for its end, realistically recognized that the unions would be back. In the spring of 1943, industrialists and businessmen met frequently under the leadership of Leslie Hicks, president of the Hawaiian Electric Company. These meetings resulted in the formation of the Hawaii Employers Council in July 1943. Let the unions come; the employers would be ready. A high-priced staff, including Council President James P. Blaisdell, hired at a salary of $40,000 a year, reported for work in 1944. Blaisdell, experienced in dealing with unions, convinced local businessmen that stable labor relations required a recognition of legally certified unions. By 1946, Blaisdell's labor philosophy prevailed among the 253 members of the Hawaii Employers Council. The Hawaiian Pineapple Company, largest employer in Hawaii, instructed its foremen not to interfere with efforts to organize.[10]

Although the membership of the Hawaii Employers Council was diversified, including individual employers, corporations, and even individuals who did not employ labor, it was controlled by a relatively small group. In this respect, the Council reflected "the financial and industrial structure of the Territory as a whole."[11] The five factors still dominated a complex series of relationships between the sugar and pineapple industries, shipping and warehousing concerns, wholesale and retail enterprises, public utilities, banks and insurance companies, hotels, interisland air and water transport companies, and water and irrigation companies. As James Shoemaker reported in 1947, there remained in Hawaii an unusually large number of interlocking directorates in territorial corporations and a high degree of intermarriage between influential families in the Islands.

Under Blaisdell's guidance, the major agencies decided to work through the Employers Council to bargain with the unions, and between the inception of the new organization and June 1947, the number of effective labor contracts in Hawaii went from twelve to 156, covering thousands of workers in 116 separate business enterprises.[12]

Flexing their newly developed muscles, I.L.W.U. leaders called a strike of all plantation workers in the sugar industry in 1946. A wave of strikes had been successful on the mainland, and, encouraged by the shortage of labor in Hawaii, many union leaders believed that the I.L.W.U. needed to exercise its newly won power in Hawaii. The union asked for an eighteen-and-a-half-cent-an-hour general wage increase and a forty-hour work week. It also attacked the perquisite system, arguing that paternalism must come to an end. The total bill to management, including fringe benefits, would be $21,000,000. Industry offered fifteen cents an hour and other concessions, but the union was adamant.

The sugar agencies were divided in their reaction to union demands. Castle & Cooke, responsible for the Ewa plantation on Oahu, which depended on irrigation and was faced with a complete loss of crop, was prepared to deal more liberally with union leaders. The other factors disagreed. Before the seventy-nine-day strike ended, Ewa had

lost $6,000,000, and other plantations that lacked the necessary mois-
ture also suffered. After the government announced an increase in the
subsidy to domestic sugar producers, management agreed to a twenty-
cent-per-hour wage increase, slightly more than had been asked
for in the early negotiations. The perquisite system was substantially
abolished, and the union could realistically claim a major victory.[13]
Harry Bridges, I.L.W.U. chief, telegraphed from the West Coast triumphantly announcing that Hawaii "is no longer a feudal colony. . . ."[14]

The strike settlement, printed in English, Filipino, and Japanese,
established the I.L.W.U. as the bargaining agent for a large percentage
of Hawaii's laborers. It also brought an end to paternalism. Now
union officials would take the place of plantation owners in distributing
benefits and perquisites to the workers. In his annual report, Hawaiian
Sugar Planters' Association President Alexander Budge, the head of
Castle & Cooke, spoke of a new era in industrial relations, in which
labor unions must be recognized as permanent institutions in Hawaii.

The acknowledgement by Budge did not prevent a strike in the
pineapple industry in 1947. In this strike, picketing was unsuccessful
from the start, and such union tactics as intimidation, illegal picketing,
and trespassing evoked unsympathetic reactions from the public. During the strike, violence and police activity returned to Hawaii, resulting
in the arrest of forty-two strikers in less than a week. Arriving at a
settlement with the help of U.S. conciliation commissioners, the union
gained little or nothing by the strike, which was settled, for the most
part, on employer terms.[15]

In 1949, union leaders decided on another demonstration of strength,
and began one of the most traumatic episodes in Island history—the
178-day strike of 2,000 longshoremen. Sugar negotiations in 1948 had
been relatively amicable. Indeed, Hall agreed to accept a 5 per cent cut
on the distressed Olaa plantation following a sixty-seven-day strike—
the company wanted a cut of 17.2 per cent—and to ease the pressure
on three other distressed plantations in return for minor concessions.
But in 1949, the two sides were not so willing to make concessions.
The union pointed out that Hawaii's longshoremen had fallen thirty-
two cents behind West Coast longshoremen in postwar gains. Management proposed an eight-cent cost-of-living increase and refused to
accept arbitration, which the union was willing to do. The strike was
on.[16]

Almost completely dependent on shipping, Hawaii was devastated by the 1949 strike. Shipping was tied up. Small businesses went bankrupt because they could not get merchandise from the mainland. And the people of the Islands were bitterly divided once more. President Truman announced that he could do nothing to intervene in the strike, and the Honolulu *Advertiser,* in a front-page editorial, asked for a new law to prohibit aliens working in public utilities, shipping, transportation, and communications from participating in a strike vote: "Never again should nationals or aliens be allowed to cast deciding votes to crucify American citizens! There has been too much of that already."[17] As tension in the Islands mounted daily, Senator William Knowland of California introduced a bill in Congress at the request of management groups in Honolulu to stop the strike. By June, unemployment in the Islands had reached 20,000—most of which could not be attributed to the strike—and was continuing to increase by approximately 1,000 a week. About one fifth of the businesses in Honolulu were reducing wages, some by as much as 20 or 25 per cent, and more small businesses faced complete ruin.[18] Food shortages aroused the sentiments of Hawaii's growing nonunion population against the I.L.W.U. Hall and other strike leaders were repeatedly accused of being Communists inspired by political rather than economic motives in a brazen attempt to control the economy of Hawaii in behalf of a foreign power.

Public opinion mounted against the strikers after the union rejected a fourteen-cent raise recommended by Governor Stainback's fact-finding board. Although a new stevedoring company, Hawaii Stevedores, Ltd., succeeded in unloading considerable cargo, employers were not able to load ships bound for the West Coast, where ports were completely controlled by the I.L.W.U. On July 20, twenty-nine persons were injured when 2,000 pickets attempted to halt non-strikers at the gates of Hawaii Stevedores. One policeman, fifteen nonunion men, and three strikers were hospitalized. Other episodes of mass picketing brought about the arrests of more than 200 strikers. After failing to secure help from the federal government, the territorial legislature passed a dock-seizure law at a special session on August 6; it enabled the Governor to proclaim a state of emergency and subsequently to seize the two largest stevedoring companies, Castle & Cooke Terminals and McCabe Hamilton and Renny, and five other companies. But a court decision restrained the government from paying profits from these operations to the struck firms and prohibited further government suits against picketing in protest of the seizures. The strike continued until C. Brewer & Co., whose ready cash position had been weakened by the recent purchase of the Spreckels sugar interests, put pressure on the stevedoring companies to agree to a settlement following Harry Bridges's offer to reduce wage demands in return for arbitration. Castle & Cooke was also anxious for a quick settlement; they represented the Matson Navigation Company, whose entire fleet had been immobilized by the strike. Off-the-record negotiations in Honolulu resulted in an agreement on October 7 for a fourteen-cent-per-hour increase—of this, eight cents was retroactive from March 1 to June 29—plus a seven-cent hourly increase as of March 1, 1950, the previous contract expiration date. Although the union claimed victory, its workers had lost hundreds of thousands of dollars in wages and the I.L.W.U. had engendered considerable public disapproval.[19]

The vast majority of I.L.W.U. members remained faithful to the leadership of Hall and his efforts to raise their standard of living. As one of them remembers it, "Most of the boys did not know Communism from rheumatism, but they did hate the bosses, and they believed Jack Hall would help them." An elderly Filipino put it in pidgin English during the 1949 longshoremen's strike, "Befo' no Communista, befo' bus-àss, by 'n by little Communista, get mo' pay; if get plenty Communista, by 'n by mo' pay."[20] Every attack on Hall's alleged Communism seemed to reinforce the loyalty of most I.L.W.U. workers to him. To them, he was a dedicated man, willing and able to walk among them, to encourage them, and to fight for them.

As early as 1947, there had nevertheless been defections in the I.L.W.U. over the Communist issue. In May of that year, Robert K. Mookini, president of pineapple Local 152, was suspended by the union on the charge of "malfeasance of office." Mookini then joined the A.F. of L. Teamsters Union, claiming he was suspended because he refused to follow Communist orders. A much more important break came when Amos Ignacio and Ichiro Izuka, both of whom had been members of the I.L.W.U. for many years, left the union and set up the Union of Hawaiian Workers on the islands of Hawaii and Kauai, charging Communist domination of the I.L.W.U. The revolt frightened I.L.W.U. leaders. Izuka had been president of a Kauai local, and Ignacio, a territorial legislator, was a unit leader of the I.L.W.U. on the Big Island. The A.F. of L. tried to help the new union by granting it a charter in July 1948, when it was estimated to have 4,000 sugar workers, but the U.H.W. was unable to convince the vast majority of

I.L.W.U. members to switch, and, after a short but difficult battle, it passed from the local scene in 1949.

Another anti-Communist revolt was led in December 1952 by Bert Nakano, one of the heroes of the 1938 Inter-Island Steamship strike, who had testified in 1950 before the Un-American Activities Committee on Communist activities in Hawaii. He took 377 workers out of Local 155 in Hilo, forming the Federation of Hawaii Workers and the new group won an N.L.R.B. election at a Flintkote plant but lost the workers to the I.L.W.U. two years later. The workers at the Hilo Iron Works joined the new organization, as did laborers at other small plants. But the union was never a serious threat to the I.L.W.U., and its membership had dwindled to a few hundred by the year of statehood.

The various locals of the I.L.W.U. consolidated their strength in the early 1950's, and in January 1955, the locals for sugar, pineapple, longshore, and miscellaneous industries were merged into the new Local 142 for the Territory of Hawaii.

Although by 1955 the majority of the Islands' population approved of labor unions in Hawaii—at least according to surveys—the expansion of I.L.W.U. economic and political power following the 1949 longshoremen's strike caused alarm in many quarters.[21] To ever-growing numbers in the Islands not directly connected with the union movement, Hall and the I.L.W.U. loomed as a menace that could cripple the economy of the Islands and perhaps control its politics.

A high official of the International Longshoremen's and Warehousemen's Union, Local 142 in Honolulu, opened the door for a pair of F.B.I. men, who quickly came to the point. "What can you tell us about the Communist activities of Jack Hall, Harry Bridges, and other I.L.W.U. leaders?" they asked, but the union man, instead of answering, if indeed he could have, lectured his young visitors on the evils of the Big Five and the virtues of unionism in Hawaii. If Hall and Bridges thought Russia was paradise, that was their business. As far as he personally was concerned, they had never talked Communism to him; they had, however, improved the lot of the workingman in the Islands.[22]

The loyalty of the bulk of Hawaii's membership to Hall transcended his alleged Communist affiliations. The vast majority of Hawaii's workers went by results, and Hall, as no other union leader had, produced results. Hawaii's workers had heard strike leaders denounced

as subversive before. Under the Islands' antilabor laws, "labor agitators" had been imprisoned in 1909 and again in 1920, when many public officials, newspapers, and *kamaaina* leaders falsely branded the Oahu
strike as a Japanese conspiracy. By crying "subversion" or "Communism" at every major effort at unionization during the forty years
after annexation, oligarchy spokesmen had numbed the minds of
Hawaii's workingmen. To thousands, allegations against Hall were
no more substantial than those made in days gone by against Makino,
Soga, or Wright.

So successfully had Hawaii's oligarchy crushed indigenous labor
leaders, that Jack Hall and other sailors had walked into a virtual
vacuum of labor leadership in the 1930's. This hulking man with a
fondness for *aloha* shirts was a different kind of labor leader from those
Hawaii had known. Tough, ruthless, dedicated, he was prepared for
anything Hawaii could offer. A former Communist and close associate
later said of Hall and his friends, "It took their kind to put the union
over." By "their kind," he meant Communists. "These people had been
beaten up before and knew how to live on short rations. They believed
deeply in the idea of racial equality, and were prepared to sacrifice
for what they believed." He might have added that conservative management policies throughout the 1920's and '30's, as much as any other
factor, produced Jack Hall and other able, battle-scarred leaders.[23]

The evidence is overwhelming that Hall and other key I.L.W.U.
leaders were active Communist party members during the late 1930's.
Testimony has been given by several former Communists before numerous investigative committees affirming Hall's Communist affiliation
prior to the war. Before Hall's arrival in Hawaii, the party had made
little headway in the Islands. In 1922, a small Marxist-oriented Japanese newspaper appeared on Kauai, and seven years later, there
emerged a small Marxist study group on Maui. But as late as 1936,
according to a 1951 report of the Commission on Subversive Activities
in the Territory, there were no more than sixty Communist party
members on Hawaii's waterfront, most of whom were nonresident
seamen.

Hall, according to several accounts, dominated the plans of the
leaders of the Communist party in Hawaii during the years preceding
Pearl Harbor. The leaders of the important 1938 strike against the
Inter-Island Steamship Company—Hall, Jack Kawano, and Ed Berman, now a respectable lawyer in Honolulu—were alleged to have

frequented Communist meetings. Other key figures included Dr. John Reinecke, the scholarly and kindly man who was teaching at McKinley High in 1939 and at Kalakaua Intermediate School in the years following, Jack D. Kimoto, one of the original organizers of the party in Hawaii, and Robert McElrath, former seaman and delegate to the national convention of the Communist party held in New York City in 1940.[24]

With the outbreak of war, according to the testimony of former Communists, meetings of the local party stopped. Hall became a wages and hours inspector for the territorial Department of Labor and Industrial Relations, and was later appointed by Governor Stainback to the Police Commission for the city and county of Honolulu. Kimoto was given a job in the Office of War Information.[25]

The Honolulu cell was reactivated in the fall of 1945, when, according to former party member Ichiro Izuka, there were eleven branches on Oahu and four on the outer islands. To help them, the party sent full-time paid organizer Dwight James Freeman to Honolulu in October 1946. New leaders included Charles Fujimoto, who had been a chemist at the Agricultural Experimentation Station at the University of Hawaii, and who, with his wife, was chosen to attend the Communist party leadership school in San Francisco in September 1947. Also active was Ralph Vossbrink, who quit his job as a merchant seaman in 1946, married a local nisei girl, and became active in the National Union of Marine Cooks and Stewards as assistant to the port agent in Hawaii. Vossbrink, Hall, Reinecke, and McElrath all married local girls, the first three choosing nisei mates and the last marrying Ah Quon Leong, a former territorial Department of Public Welfare social worker who was alleged to have been an active Communist leader before the war.

Communist leaders organized newspapers and social and political clubs with non-Communists. The Honolulu *Record,* the major journalistic effort, which was begun in 1948, although seldom known to deviate in its foreign-policy opinions from the point of view approved by Moscow, published many excellent articles on the history of Hawaii and contemporary Island affairs. The Japanese-language paper *Hawaii Star* was also started in 1947; its pages consistently reflected the views of the international Communist movement. According to Kawano, the party instructed its members in 1948 to support the Honolulu *Record* and its editor, Koji Ariyoshi, a bright and able writer who had grown up in the land-poor economy of Kona.

It was Kawano's break with the party in 1950, even more than Izuka's defection two years before, that rocked high party officials in Honolulu. Kawano, because of his popularity on the waterfront and as president of the I.L.W.U. local in Honolulu, began organizing sugar workers in December 1943. He later served with Hall and Freeman on a committee planning the infiltration of the Democratic party. Although Kawano believed intensely in the labor movement, he was reportedly annoyed by the autocratic temperament of Hall. His own ambitions were thwarted by Hall, who was determined to remain boss. Kawano may also have been troubled by the political tactics of Hall. He found it difficult to follow the twists and turns of his day-to-day changes in policy. In 1946, he supported Farrington for delegate against a Democrat who was friendly to the labor movement. Support for the Republican was justified on the ground that the Honolulu *Star Bulletin* had and would continue to be "fair" to the I.L.W.U. Two years later, Farrington was dropped, and the I.L.W.U. leaders almost succeeded in taking over the Democratic party.

After Kawano broke with the party, he was, because of his important role in the I.L.W.U., courted by congressional investigators and the F.B.I. He was denounced as a traitor to the labor movement by Hall and by McElrath, who had become the public-relations chief of the I.L.W.U. He was influenced by new friends in the Democratic party, including Jack Burns, Chuck Mau, Mitsuyuki Kido, Dr. Ernest Murai, Dan Inouye, and, to a lesser degree, Sakae Takahashi. Kawano wrestled with his conscience, and finally he resolved to break with the Communist movement and some of his closest friends by telling his story to the F.B.I.[26] Fortified by a loan from his political friends, Kawano, who was a poor man, sensed that his days as a union leader were finished and met with federal officials in February 1951. He appeared five months later before the House Un-American Activities Committee to give a detailed recital of his associations and activities in the party, despite counterpressure from friends who sincerely believed that any criticism of the I.L.W.U. played into the hands of reactionaries. In fifty-three pages of testimony, the distraught nisei told how he joined the Communist party "because some individual Communists were willing to assist me in organizing the waterfront union," and the waterfront employers were totally intolerant of labor unions. The employers did all they could to smash attempts to organize the waterfront. No civic or community organization showed any signs of willingness to assist in the organizing efforts. ". . . the Communists were willing to assist me in bringing up living standards of the working man."²⁷ What repulsed Kawano, the longshoreman testified, was that the Communists intended to use the union for political purposes, rather than to help achieve better working conditions. He also hinted that Hall was no longer a Communist and had become fed up with taking dictation from the local Communist party, but no admissions were forthcoming from the union leader.

Federal officials now had considerable information, and probably some misinformation, on the Communist apparatus in Hawaii and the extent of its influence in the union movement. Co-operative former Communists, including Izuka, Kawano, Richard Kageyama, and Isaac Kauwe, filled the dossiers of more than a dozen I.L.W.U. officials and other persons in Hawaii. By 1956, the allegations of past Communist party membership of many I.L.W.U. officials had been made repeatedly before public committees. In some cases, as many as eight or ten persons testified to firsthand knowledge of the Communist affiliations of the accused. Among those labeled as sometime party members, in addition to Hall and McElrath, were Joseph K. Kealalaio, a member of the I.L.W.U. Executive Board; Levi Kealoha, another board member; Ernest Arenia, Local 142 business agent on Oahu; Tadashi Ogawa, Oahu division director of Local 142; and David E. Thompson, educational director of the union.

The majority of those identified were probably motivated primarily by a passion for justice, peace, racial equality, economic opportunity. Men such as Ariyoshi, Thompson, and Reinecke may have made a mistake in serving the Communist cause, but there is no evidence that they ever deviated from the ideals of the Declaration of Independence. In their view, drastic action was needed to right the wrongs in Hawaii. Impressed by the magnitude of the injustices of the past, they saw the vast dimensions of change needed for the future. There is little doubt that a majority of those actively associated with the Communist movement in the late 1930's and again in the late '40's soured on the Communist party for one reason or another and left it but refused to denounce it for fear of hurting the labor movement as a whole.

After the abortive attempt to capture the Democratic party in 1948 and the crippling longshoremen's strike the following year, strong sentiment against I.L.W.U. leadership developed in Hawaii and Washington, D.C. The strike had a traumatic effect on nonunion families in

Hawaii. Tourist business dropped, the pineapple industry faced ruin, many firms cut wages, child-care centers rationed milk, and small businesses failed. Irate mothers, calling themselves the "Broom Brigade," picketed I.L.W.U. headquarters, threatening to sweep the union leaders from Hawaii's shores. The legislature overwhelmingly endorsed Governor Stainback's request for a dock-seizure law and created the Subversive Activities Control Board, a commission of seven to investigate Communism in Hawaii. Edward M. Sylva, fresh from his victory in investigating the Reineckes, was appointed chairman. The Commission issued annual reports on alleged Communist activity in the Islands, but did not always exemplify careful scholarship in its work. It swung wildly, often making unsubstantiated accusations of Communist affiliation or sympathy against dedicated Americans, among them Louis Adamic, Stephen S. Wise, Langston Hughes, Mary McLeod Bethune, Robert Morse Lovett, and Adam Clayton Powell. The Commission sometimes made absurd statements, such as its charge that the I.L.W.U., merely by urging free trade, adopted a Communist position.[28]

Unofficial vigilante groups supported the Commission and even went beyond it in fighting Communism with reckless charges. Suspicion and fear resulted in wanton attacks on such liberals as P.T.A. worker Marion Saunders, who, because of her work in group dynamics, was accused of Communist sympathies, and the Reverend Adolph Meyer, Lutheran minister who publicly announced that the extreme anti-Communism of Mrs. Walter Dillingham and others would actually help Stalin.[29]

Mrs. Dillingham and other *kamaaina* leaders sponsored a new anti-Communist organization called Imua, the Hawaiian word for forward. Imua received the support of dozens of influential haole businessmen and military officers, but its strident, almost hysterical, anti-Communism alienated many of its supporters soon after it was established. Imua seemed to be playing into the hands of I.L.W.U. leaders by appearing to oppose the labor movement altogether. Some of the men and women most frequently identified with Imua were also so closely associated with the repressive policies of the past that attacks by Imua were welcomed by many union officials. A study of Imua radio broadcasts made in retaliation for I.L.W.U. newscasts by McElrath revealed that Imua broadcasters indulged in far more name-calling, glittering generalities, and other propaganda tricks than the notoriously propaganda-minded I.L.W.U. public-relations man.[30]

Union leaders quite understandably welcomed vigilante attacks which reinforced the loyalty of union members, and they were not much more upset by the denunciation and expulsion of the I.L.W.U. by the National Board of the C.I.O. in 1950. A thoroughly documented analysis of I.L.W.U. policies made in 1949 and 1950 revealed that its officials had unswervingly followed the Soviet Union's foreign-policy line. The C.I.O. report showed that Harry Bridges and other top I.L.W.U. officials sympathized with the Hitler-Stalin pact before World War II, opposed postwar loans to socialist England, and condemned the Marshall Plan through the I.L.W.U. Executive Board, which labeled it "a monstrous plot against freedom and living standards." The Soviet Union and its policies, regardless of turns and contradictions, were lavishly praised. The I.L.W.U. organ, the *Dispatcher,* launched vigorous attacks against Trotskyites and deviationists such as American Socialist Norman Thomas, using language similar to that found in avowed Communist publications throughout the world. The report was so devastating that it resulted in expulsion of the union from the C.I.O.[31]

The expulsion meant little to union members in Hawaii, who could not remember receiving much help from either the national C.I.O. or the A.F. of L. in their struggle to organize. The C.I.O. in Washington was remote. Jack Hall was in Honolulu doing a job for the workers. The I.L.W.U.'s 1951 contract represented the first major victory since 1946. Provisions were negotiated for a liberalization of sick-leave benefits, an eleven-cent-per-hour wage increase, and more consideration of seniority in promotions and layoffs. Out of such victories, loyalty to the local leaders was sustained.

Another factor bolstering the loyalty of the rank and file was congressional and F.B.I. "Red hunts." The proportion of persons in Hawaii visited by F.B.I. men during the early 1950's was probably greater than for any territory or state in the nation. Hawaii had always had its share of thought control and fear. Thousands of union and non-union families associated Communist probes with the intimidations of the past, and, unfortunately, there were too many instances when freedom of thought was curtailed. One outer island medical doctor and his wife recall a visit from an F.B.I. official who even advised them to cancel their subscription to the liberal British publication *New Statesman and Nation.*

Department of Justice investigations had far less public impact than congressional committee hearings and the famous Smith Act trial of 1953. The first major congressional investigation took place in Honolulu in April 1950, when a total of sixty-six residents of the Islands were called to testify before the House Un-American Activities Committee. Of those subpoenaed, thirty-nine refused to answer questions concerning their knowledge of Communist activities in the Islands. This group, subsequently known as the "reluctant 39," was cited by Congress for contempt and indicted in the U.S. District Court for the District of Hawaii, but they were later acquitted on the basis of Supreme Court decisions ruling against loose contempt citations by congressional committees. Ronald B. Jamieson, who served as Hawaii's attorney general from 1934 to 1947 and circuit court judge from 1952 to 1953, testified several years later that Jack Hall had admitted, after several drinks in the Young Hotel bar, that at least two thirds of the thirty-nine had been members of the Communist party.[32]

After Kawano's detailed testimony of party activities in 1951—he had been one of the "reluctant 39" a year earlier—the F.B.I. arrested seven of Hawaii's alleged Communist leaders, six men and one woman, on charges under the Smith Act of conspiring to teach the overthrow of the U.S. government by force and violence. Arrested on August 28 were Charles Fujimoto, self-announced chairman of the Communist party; Mrs. Eileen Kee Fujimoto; Dwight James (Jim) Freeman; Jack D. Kimoto, of the circulation department of the Honolulu *Record;* Reinecke, then a part-time worker with the *Record;* Koji Ariyoshi; and Hall. Of the seven, only Hall was affiliated with the I.L.W.U., and McElrath and David Thompson later produced a recording in which two F.B.I. agents were identified as telling Thompson that they would drop the indictment against Hall if he would co-operate with federal authorities in exposing the Communist movement in Hawaii.[33]

The trial was delayed by technical objections raised by the defense. One of these—that the Hawaii grand jury panel was not representative of the community as a whole, but was weighted excessively with Caucasians and persons in executive positions—was supported by a federal district judge. Finally, 435 days after the arrest of the Hawaii seven, the trial was begun under federal Judge Jon Wiig. Seven and a half months later, on June 19, 1953, the Hawaii seven were found guilty by an all-male jury which included representatives from each of Hawaii's major racial groups except the Filipinos. Pending a motion for a new trial, the defendants were freed on bail of $7,500 each.

Almost immediately, the bail was raised to $15,000, obliging six of the seven to spend a week in jail; but by keeping their appeal alive, the Hawaii seven avoided the five-year jail terms to which they were sentenced.

The Smith Act trial was another traumatic episode in the history of Hawaii. It made enemies of former friends, divided families, and reopened the scars of earlier battles. Character witnesses for Hall, among them Mayor John Wilson and Judge Delbert Metzger, were denounced as Communist tools. Those who testified against Hall or who refused to swear to his good reputation, such as Democratic national committeeman Frank Fasi, were labeled "black reactionaries" by union leaders. Following Hall's conviction, political strikes were called all over the Islands, further promoting the widely shared opinion that the I.L.W.U. was interested in power far more than in the establishment of good working conditions through collective bargaining.

For the most part, I.L.W.U. members were probably more loyal to Hall than ever. He had won slight gains for them in 1952, and the following year negotiated a two-year contract calling for a four-cent-per-hour increase in wages and a uniform medical plan. The Smith Act prosecution was viewed by them as just another attempt to "get Jack Hall." A former official of the union who had been asked to join the Communist party and pass its literature recalls that Imua, the congressional investigations, and the Smith Act trial made it more difficult for some union men who had flirted with Communism to repudiate their past involvements. For them, the purity, idealism, and comradeship of the golden years of the union movement were gone, but recognizing the support of the rank and file for Hall, distrustful but afraid of the union bosses, and unwilling to associate themselves with the extremist attacks of Imua and Senator James O. Eastland, of Mississippi, they kept their mouths shut.[34] Tensions over the Communist issue had come to a climax during the Smith Act trials. After the conviction of the Hawaii seven, anxiety and hysteria subsided.

Two important developments put the brakes on Imua's strident attempt to label the I.L.W.U. as Communist-led. The first was the growing desire of Hawaii's major business managers for stable labor relations. Recognizing that Hall maintained a strong grip on I.L.W.U. policies, they were obliged to deal with him, Communist background or not. They were encouraged by his responsible behavior in negotia-

tions in 1952 and 1953, when he agreed that distressed plantations could not afford to pay the general wage increase originally
requested of all plantations. The Communist issue also faded because
of strong prostatehood sentiment among the new managerial group and
the two major newspapers, the *Star Bulletin* and the *Advertiser*. It
would not do to persistently wash Hawaii's dirty linen in Washington.
Why help the opponents of statehood by advertising a condition that
probably no longer existed. Businessmen and newspaper editors were
not privileged to examine F.B.I. files, but they increasingly accepted the
view that neither Hall nor his friends were Communists any longer, and
it would be best to let this old divisive issue die.

But Senator Eastland, chairman of the Senate Judiciary Internal
Security Sub-Committee, Congressman John R. Pillion, of New York,
and their friends from Imua refused to let it expire entirely. One reason,
perhaps, was their opposition to statehood. Imua was not officially
opposed to statehood, but many of its key officials were, and representatives of the organization supplied congressional opponents with
literature and testimony to backstop their opposition. In December
1956, Eastland began hearings in Honolulu on Communism in Hawaii.
Some of the original "reluctant 39" paraded before the committee, once
more invoking the Fifth Amendment in response to questions regarding
Communist activities. Again, rank-and-file union members supported
Hall and West Coast leader Bridges, who cried "persecution." More
than 3,000 of the 24,000 I.L.W.U. members in Hawaii walked off their
jobs to hold protest meetings. The hearings and the walkouts revived
some bitterness, but soon after the Senator left Hawaii, the Communist
issue, except for Imua, faded substantially. The contract negotiated
for the sugar plantations was for two years and incorporated a six-
cent-per-hour wage raise, increased sick benefits, allowance for stop-
work meetings, better vacation benefits, and a severance-pay system.
Unemployment benefits were extended, and a special fund was established to finance the cost of the voluntary repatriation of Filipino
workers to their homeland. The union set up machinery to end illegal
walkouts, and assured the sugar factors of good faith in the administration of the seniority system to protect the companies' right to select the
best-qualified employees for promotion. The union and the industry
seemed to be willing to meet each other's survival needs, and both
sides wanted more than ever to bury the old Communist issue.

Imua was increasingly isolated in its attack on former Communists.

In January 1958, the conviction of the Hawaii seven was reversed on the basis of a previous Supreme Court ruling that conspiracy to advocate and teach the violent overthrow of the government cannot be made a crime. On its radio broadcasts and in its newsletter, *Spotlight,* Imua traced the activities of those who had been identified as former Communists. In May, it mobilized votes against Mrs. Robert McElrath in her bid for office in the Parent-Teacher Association. In the same month it implied that anti-Communist pacifist A. J. Muste was sympathetic to the Communist party. In June, it reported, with a sense of scandal, that Reinecke had been hired by the non-Communist Teamsters Union. Later in the year, it criticized Delegate Jack Burns for associating with identified former Communists. The most outrageous event of all, from its viewpoint, was the election to an advisory position with the Red Cross of Newton Miyagi, I.L.W.U. Local 142 secretary-treasurer, who had invoked the Fifth Amendment seventy-one times during the 1956 Senate hearings.[35]

Private public-opinion surveys showed that few people were listening to Imua. A 1958 poll revealed that it received the approval of only about one in five voters.[36] Some of the organization's major business supporters were reluctant to finance the $158,000 budget for 1959. Among Imua's 100 major supporters, there were not more than one or two nonhaoles or nonhaole firms. Some Imua leaders, according to one survey, were viewed by nonhaoles as being not just anti-statehood, but anti-Oriental, too.[37] But it was mainly the growing suspicion that Imua leaders and backers, among them Walter Dillingham and Dr. Lyle G. Phillips, were against statehood that engendered dissatisfaction on Merchant Street with the militant anti-Communist organization. When Dr. Phillips asserted that Hawaii did not qualify to be a state because of the allegedly Communist-inspired I.L.W.U. he met public opposition from Republican Governor William Quinn, Honolulu *Advertiser* publisher Lorrin P. Thurston, and University of Hawaii president Dr. Gregg Sinclair. Sinclair charged that Imua was "doing a terrifically bad service to the community."[38] The editor of one of Hawaii's major newspapers said privately, "Imua's major objective is to oppose statehood by helping Hawaii's major enemies in Congress."[39]

Perhaps the worst service performed by the organization was to obscure the real Communist record in the Islands. In all its attacks it did virtually nothing to explain why Americans should be opposed to totalitarian Communism. By lumping radicals, liberals, labor leaders, and Communists together, Imua's arguments, even more than confusing, became boring. Surveys showed that a large majority of Hawaii's voters were actually more indifferent than opposed to the organization. Through its redundant and extreme accusations, it inhibited rational discussion by Hawaii's people of Communist influence in the Islands or anywhere else.

On the mainland, President Harry Bridges, Vice-President J. R. Robinson, and powerful Secretary-Treasurer Louis Goldblatt remained in their respective I.L.W.U. offices during the decade that followed the expulsion of the union by the C.I.O. Bridges and Goldblatt had been repeatedly identified as members of the Communist party in testimony under oath, and persisted in private and public expressions of sympathy for the Soviet Union and opposition to all aspects of American foreign policy. Their union, of approximately 80,000 workers, representing almost all of the longshoremen and terminal workers on the West Coast, the sugar and pineapple workers and longshoremen in Hawaii, and the warehouse and processing workers in most of the mainland United States, used what influence it had—through publications, radio broadcasts, and lobbying—to direct public opinion against American economic and military efforts to stem Soviet imperialism.

But since Hall had almost certainly abandoned his strong Communist sympathies by 1950, the influence of the hammer and sickle in paradise was now remote. During the 1950's, the former Communist regional director of the nearly 25,000-member Local 142 spoke less of class warfare than Goldblatt and far less of the evils of American foreign policy than Bridges. Many antagonists of the labor leader now complained not that he was under Communist discipline, but that he recognized no discipline but his own. Hall sought power for himself and his union, regardless of the consequences, according to these opponents. He broadened his power by helping Henry Epstein, frequently identified as a former Communist, to organize 3,000 workers in the United Public Workers' Union. Beginning on the outer islands with road, hospital, and other unskilled laborers, the U.P.W. moved into other fields, organizing the guards at Oahu Prison, fire-department employees, and others. Epstein, a friendly but strong-minded former resident of Harlem in New York City, shared Hall's militant opposition to liberal prolabor politicians in Hawaii who would not take dictation from the union leaders. In this way, more than in any other, did Hall and Epstein resemble traditional Communist behavior. They believed in the absolute superiority of their own leadership and in tight discipline for those under them.

But it was one thing to believe in discipline and another to maintain it. When the Senate Sub-Committee on Internal Security reported, after its hearings in the winter of 1956, that the Communists "exercise an influence on the political life of the Islands that is significant," it overstated its case. After 1948, I.L.W.U. political power in territorial elections fell sharply. The union failed to elect most of the candidates that it endorsed for the territorial constitutional convention in 1950. I.L.W.U. leaders opposed ratification of the new state constitution, but Hawaii's people voted for it by a better than three-to-one margin. I.L.W.U. attempts to block the election of O. Vincent Esposito as speaker of the territorial House in the 1957 election were overwhelmed, and the union's efforts to repeal the Dock Seizure Act were defeated by a better than nine-to-one margin. In many individual contests, the union was successful in endorsing the winning candidate. Other times it failed; in 1956, it unsuccessfully supported William Quinn for the territorial Senate and missed endorsing important winning candidates including Inouye, Esposito, Heen, and Senate floor leader Herbert Lee. The I.L.W.U. leadership attacked the city-county charter for Honolulu, but it was approved by more than three quarters of the voters. In the 1958 elections, two candidates, union officials from Maui and Kauai, the islands where I.L.W.U. influence was strongest, were defeated by candidates the union opposed. Obviously, the picture of a monolithic Communist-led labor movement taking over the government in Hawaii had been grossly overdrawn.

The *ILWU Reporter,* Local 142's own newspaper, hardly resembled a party-line newspaper, as anyone who has read the Communist press would acknowledge. Articles eschewed Communist jargon, praised and criticized the achievements and failures of Congress, and read much less like the *Daily Worker* than did the West Coast *ILWU Dispatcher.* The local's paper and broadcasts concentrated almost entirely on domestic issues, and especially on local questions. By the mid-1950's, it appeared that Hawaii's union leadership had backed away from the aims of the Soviet Union and the world Communist movement and was no longer connected with the Communist apparatus in the United States.[40] If Hall, Epstein, McElrath, and others still believed in class struggle and in the destruction of the private-property system, they had, ironically, done more through successful collective bargaining to subvert their own beliefs than had any other group of men in Hawaii. In ten years, between 1948 and 1958, the wages of sugar-plantation workers increased from 44 to 74 per cent, and from 21 to 34 per cent for pineapple workers, making the sugar and pineapple workers of Hawaii not only the highest-paid agricultural workers in the world, which they had been for decades, but agricultural workers whose wages approached industrial wages rates on the mainland. In addition, they had won fringe benefits upward of $4 per day, benefits that the Hawaiian Sugar Planters' Association asserted were about equal to the entire minimum daily wage for eight hours of work for sugar workers in Puerto Rico.

A 1956 opinion survey of labor-management relations revealed that more union members believed that the companies in Hawaii wanted "to get along and work with the unions" than thought they wanted "to bust the unions."[41] The laborers surveyed also had a surprisingly limited view of the role the union should play in hiring policies. When asked whether the union or the company should have "a say about who a company hires," 70 per cent of the union members in the sample replied "the company," 6 per cent said "the union," and 18 per cent replied "both," compared with 86 per cent, 3 per cent, and 7 per cent for nonunion members in each category. Nor were union members dissatisfied with the way in which companies had lived up to their agreements. When asked "Which do you think have lived up to their agreements better—the unions or the companies?" only 30 per cent of the respondents, the vast majority of whom belonged to the I.L.W.U., answered "the union." Twenty per cent replied "companies"; others said "both" or had no opinion.

The views of union members on most labor-management questions were strikingly similar to those of nonunion workers and even to those of white-collar workers and professional men and women. When the citizens of Oahu, Hawaii, Maui, and Kauai were asked in 1956 whether or not they thought the larger companies were making "too much money," "just a fair amount," or "not so much," only 27 per cent of the union members said "too much," while 48 per cent replied "a fair amount" and 7 per cent responded "not so much," compared with 19, 49, and 12 per cent for nonunion members. Nor were there significant differences on this issue between income or racial groups. When asked "If in hard times prices go down, do you think Hawaiian business firms should lower wages or keep them up?" 62 per cent of the union members in the sample said "lower wages" while only 17 per cent would "keep them up," compared with 69 and 15 per cent for the non-union members polled.

The vast majority of Hawaii's laborers appear to have accepted the most crucial aspect of capitalist economics: the profit system. The very success of the labor movement in the Islands had destroyed the class struggle in Hawaii. It also limited the prospects for Communism by fighting racism and economic exploitation. On the eve of statehood, Jack Hall behaved like the tough and autocratic union boss that he was, but not like a Communist. Like the workers of his own union, who now enjoyed paid holidays, owned their own homes, and voted as they pleased, Hall, from all available evidence, had now joined the ranks of the bourgeoisie.

Chapter Sixteen

TOURISTS, WARRIORS, AND
ENTREPRENEURS

On the highway between the villages of Kaaawa and Waiahole, on the *mauka* side, there is a small grocery store and an unimpressive gasoline station with the remarkably impressive name "Chang's Enterprises." The proprietor, Lincoln Chang, who celebrated his thirtieth birthday in the year of statehood, sells a variety of products from motor oil to dried squid. Chang's Enterprises represents the unfolding of a dream which Lincoln Chang is certain will one day be completely fulfilled. That dream began in 1949, soon after his graduation from high school. Not yet out of his teens, Chang and his young wife moved from Honolulu to Kaaawa, where they began selling bananas from a roadside stand. Tourists circling the island observed the grinning Chinese boy, his almond-shaped eyes alive with hope. Chang and his wife virtually lived on bananas until they saved enough money to buy a parcel of fee-simple land from a Hawaiian who lived nearby. With the help of a loan, this daring entrepreneur transformed his banana stand into Chang's Enterprises.

Chang was not the first son of a Chinese immigrant to succeed in business in Hawaii, but his small victory on Kamehameha Highway was possible only because World War II and the airplane had revolutionized the Territory's economy from its prewar reliance on sugar and pineapple to a postwar emphasis on tourism and military expenditures. Lincoln Chang shared in the postwar prosperity as Hawaii evolved from an agricultural to a service economy. Chang sold his bananas and, later, gasoline and other products to an ever-increasing number of tourists, Marines, and suburbanites from Kaneohe, Kailua, and Lanikai as population and wealth moved over the Pali to the windward side of Oahu.

The 1950–59 boom was the result of the third important economic revolution in the history of the Islands. During the first half of the nineteenth century, a primitive subsistence economy gave way to one in which Hawaii served as an important provisioning and trading point for the clipper-ship commerce with China. In the middle of the century, there was a sharp rise and fall in the whaling industry, but there was no clear line of economic development until the American Reciprocity Treaty in 1872. The next sixty years saw a continuous expansion of the sugar industry and, after 1913, of the export of canned pineapple. By the mid-1930's, practically everyone in Hawaii assumed that the economy was almost totally dependent on sugar and pineapple. There was not much opportunity for enterprise, warned the *Star Bulletin* and the *Advertiser*. High-school graduates would be best advised to think of a career on the plantations. Only the Japanese newspapers and a few radical schoolteachers dissented. The *Hawaii Hochi* and *Nippu Jiji* argued that the tourist and fishing industries, for example, could be expanded, thus diversifying the Territory's economy and freeing its people from the rule of sugar.[1] Still, most objective observers disagreed with the Japanese editorials. In 1933, educator David L. Crawford argued that Hawaii's economic frontiers had been conquered. Corporation agriculture, Crawford maintained, was as natural to the Islands as were swaying hips and rolling surf. The industrial structure of the Islands would always require a large number of unskilled and low-cost workers, Crawford insisted, advising the schools to establish a closer relationship with agriculture.[2] Two years later, Frank E. Midkiff, then president of the Kamehameha Schools, wrote in his doctoral thesis that the Territory would inevitably remain an industrialized agricultural community.[3] Sociologist Romanzo Adams, sympathetic to the aspirations of non-haoles, reluctantly agreed. "Hawaii is approaching a condition of closed resources," he wrote, pessimistically concluding that social and economic mobility in Hawaii would decline.[4] Adams' able colleague from the University of Chicago, Andrew Lind, saw little prospect that the proportion of professional, proprietary, and clerical workers would increase. Writing in 1938, when the Islands' population was approximately half of what it would be twenty years later, Lind observed that there was no place for a surplus population in a contracting economy.[5]

These dark portraits of the Islands' economy seemed justified by the evidence. Sugar and pineapple production had leveled off. As far as anyone knew, Hawaii possessed no important natural resources. High transportation costs inhibited the development of markets on the mainland for Hawaii's other agricultural products. Without raw materials and easy access to markets, manufacturing was discouraged. Sugar and pineapple were the bulwarks of the Hawaiian economy, and no amount of wishful thinking could change that fact.

What wishful thinking could not accomplish, the war, the airplane, and automation did. The great need for agricultural labor predicted by economists and sociologists did not materialize because of the leveling of sugar and pineapple production and the introduction of labor-saving machinery during World War II. Plantations, hard pressed to compete for labor with defense industries, accelerated their efforts to substitute machines for men during the war years, and by 1957, there were 25,000 fewer permanent agricultural jobs than there had been on the eve of the Pearl Harbor attack. The decline in agricultural employment, the postwar reduction in defense activity, and the long waterfront strike in 1949 resulted in a temporary depression in the winter of 1949–50, again raising pessimism among students of the Islands' economy. But the cold war with the Soviet Union brought a renewed emphasis on military expenditures in the Islands, and amazing developments in commercial aviation ushered in a new era of tourism for Hawaii. Sugar and pineapple, long the kingpins of the Hawaiian economy, were significantly supplemented by the Pentagon and the tourist.

Between 1950 and 1959, defense expenditures in the Islands soared from $147,000,000 to $338,000,000. Whereas military spending in 1935 amounted to only about 9 per cent of Hawaii's earnings from its sugar and pineapple exports, such expenditures now exceeded the total value of all exports from the Islands. The magnitude of the change could be measured in people as well as in dollars and cents. Hawaii's military population had doubled since 1950, as the Territory became a central Pacific reserve of manpower for such outposts as Okinawa, Japan, and Guam. Even more startling was the fact that on the eve of statehood, roughly one sixth of Hawaii's population was made up of military personnel and their dependents; nearly one fourth of Hawaii's people depended directly on defense spending for a living. Pearl Harbor, the largest military center in the Islands, employed 6,000 persons, almost three times the number working for all of Hawaii's hotels and more than the total employment of all the Islands' public utilities.

Only tourism topped defense expenditures for spectacular growth during the 1950's. In the nine years before statehood, tourist spending increased from $24,000,000 to $109,000,000, a jump of more than 350 per cent. Tourism was now the fourth-largest producer of mainland dollars in Hawaii, exceeded only by the military and the sugar and pineapple industries, and economists predicted that within the next decade it would race far ahead of sugar and pineapple, perhaps bringing as much as $350,000,000 to the Islands annually.[6] Commercial flights to and through Honolulu—now only four and a half hours from the mainland—brought half a million air passengers to the Islands in 1959, compared with 520 only two decades before. The number of actual tourists—persons who remained in the Islands for two days or more—had grown from 34,000 to 243,000 since the war's end. The banyan trees, hula dancers, surf riders, and other Hawaiian delights celebrated by Mark Twain, Jack London, and Robert Louis Stevenson could now be sampled by millions. World-famous Waikiki, which before World War II was a quiet residential area beside a white sand crescent dotted with only three hotels, boomed into a bustling community where nearly every business establishment catered to thousands of visitors. The surf and sand of Waikiki, which had provided a playground for the chiefs of old Hawaii, were now within reach of persons of moderate means. After the war, multistory hotels rose in rapid succession—the Edgewater, SurfRider, Waikiki Biltmore, Reef, Waikikian, Hawaiian Village, and Princess Kaiulani. The number of hotel rooms quadrupled to 4,000. Property along Kalakaua Avenue—Waikiki's main street—sold at prices as high as $30 to $60 per square foot. Still more hotel construction was planned by the Sheraton Corporation of America after its purchase of four Waikiki hotels from the Matson Navigation Company. Henry J. Kaiser and the Hilton Hotel Corporation, successive owners of the big Hawaiian Village Hotel, also proposed vast expansion.

Among the major results of the economic changes brought about by increased defense expenditures and tourism was a significant shift in population and wealth from the outer islands to Oahu; a dramatic movement of capital and managerial personnel from the mainland to Hawaii; stepped-up diversification and competition in Hawaii's industries and agriculture; the emergence of sizable nonhaole businesses and millionaires; and a booster spirit second to none in the United States, rich in verve, imagination, and optimism.

The Island of Oahu became the postwar mecca of Hawaii. It was primarily to Oahu that the military and the mainland tourists came. In 1959, the year of statehood, ninety-two cents of every tourist dollar coming into the Islands was spent on Oahu. Ninety-eight per cent of Hawaii's defense activity was centered in sixteen major military installations on Oahu. Substantial increases in federal nonmilitary spending and state and county expenditures further pushed the migration of people and dollars to Hawaii's central island, especially to its capital city of Honolulu. The federal government practically doubled its nonmilitary expenditures in Hawaii between 1950 and 1959, bringing the Islands almost as much money as the entire tourist trade.

Because most military personnel and their dependents, tourists, mainland workers, and retired persons located on Oahu, a powerful economic magnet drew Islanders from the outer islands to serve them. The populations of Hawaii, Maui, and Kauai declined slowly but steadily during the 1950's, while Oahu absorbed more than 100,000 new residents during the five years preceding statehood. In 1930, the neighbor islands represented 45 per cent of the Territory's population, but by 1959, Oahu accounted for more than 78 per cent of Hawaii's 576,000 people. Following the national trend of urbanization and suburbanization, Honolulu's population had tripled between 1920 and 1950, revealing more rapid growth than any American city of comparable size with the exception of Miami, Florida.[7] By 1959, more than half the people in the state lived in Honolulu. But in the 1950's, the suburban areas surrounding Hawaii's major city grew even more rapidly. Although the civilian population of Oahu as a whole grew by one fourth during the 1950's, suburban and rural Oahu recorded gains of more than 40 per cent. The biggest jump in population, though not the largest percentage gain, was in the Kailua-Kaneohe-Waimanalo area, where the population roughly doubled. Windward Oahu was no longer considered country land. Workers from Honolulu clogged the famous Pali pass as they headed toward their homes on the other side of the island, necessitating the construction of two four-lane highways and two major tunnel complexes. The demands of Honolulu residents for less-expensive, more-suburban property brought forth at least eight new plans for home development on windward Oahu. It was predicted that within ten years, approximately 150,000 people would live along Oahu's east coast.

The population surge on Oahu produced a boom in retail trade and construction. Oahu, third largest in the island chain, accounted for nearly 90 per cent of its wholesale and more than 82 per cent of its retail trade. The five years preceding statehood recorded the most remarkable construction growth in the history of the Islands, values increasing from $97,000,000 to $216,000,000, owing to shortages in hotel capacity, housing, office buildings for new business firms, and shopping centers to serve growing suburban communities.[8] By 1959, some experts expected the rate of expansion to decline, but plans for highway construction, the building of a new East-West cultural and technical center at the University, continued demands for new housing, increasing tourist pressures, and the growing interest of mainland companies in establishing branch organizations in Hawaii foreshadowed the continuation of a sizable construction boom. In 1959, the educated guess of one of Hawaii's leading economists, Dr. Thomas K. Hitch, vice-president of the Bishop Bank (later The First National Bank of Hawaii), was that construction business might "top one billion dollars in the next five to seven years."[9] That same year saw the completion of the gigantic Ala Moana Shopping Center and the beginning of the biggest housing development ever planned for Hawaii, the $350,-000,000 building program organized by Henry Kaiser and the Bishop estate on 6,000 acres of land in the Koko Head section of Oahu. Work also began on the second entrance to Honolulu Harbor, the expansion of Honolulu's jet-age airport, and major industrial subdivisions on the outskirts of the city. One of the biggest construction projects could be attributed directly to Hawaii's role in America's military plans. Postwar housing for Army personnel, not included in armed forces expenditures on statistical tables, totalled 1,228 housing units costing $20,-000,000. Between 1959 and 1961, nearly 5,000 additional units were to be completed, bringing roughly $75,000,000 in payrolls and profits to the Islands.

While plans for windward Oahu focused on residential housing, leeward Oahu, west of Honolulu, seemed destined to become a major industrial center for the fiftieth state. In 1960, Standard Oil's $40,-000,000 refinery on Campbell estate land near Barbers Point went into operation. Construction also began on a $1,500,000 rolling steel mill by the Hawaiian Western Steel Company Ltd. The new corporation, backed by Island capital, planned to produce 25,000 steel reinforcing rods and other steel products by 1961, converting the Islands' supply of scrap steel into useful construction materials. Also begun at the Barbers Point Campbell property was a $12,000,000 cement plant for the Hawaiian Cement Corporation, an aggregate of mainland and local interests, which planned a capacity of over a million barrels a year, mostly to be used in local construction. The cement plant would meet competition from another new leeward firm, Henry Kaiser's Permanente Cement Company, to be built on a 208-acre lime-rich site in Maili, expected to produce 1,700,000 barrels a year.

More than any other individual, Kaiser symbolized the growing interest of mainland investors in Hawaii's burgeoning economy. By the year of statehood, according to newspaper accounts, Kaiser had invested $20,000,000 in the Islands and paid out $1,000,000 a year to more than 200 employees. Labeled a "genius" by his admirers and a "dictator" by his detractors, Kaiser joined Walter Dillingham and Jack Burns as one of the most controversial figures in the Islands.

Kaiser had come to Hawaii for a five-week vacation in 1950 and had stayed. Anticipating the vast expansion of tourism, he created a new luxury hotel—the Hawaiian Village—where slums and swamp had existed at the far end of Waikiki. From a suite at the Hawaiian Village where he lived and worked, he then expanded his operations to include a hospital, radio and television station, a new cement industry, and the creation of a city at Koko Head, to be called Hawaii Kai. The bustling mainland industrialist showed the Bishop estate how it could put to work a 6,000-acre tract which stretched from the top of Koko Head Peninsula as far inland as the ridge of the Koolau Mountain range and around the coast from Koko Head Park nearly to Makapuu Point. In 1959, work began on this vast resort city, which would house 50,000 persons. Built around a huge marina resort area and laced with peninsulas jutting into a lagoon like giant fingers, more than 14,000 homes would be constructed. Residents of apartments and homes on the hillsides and in valleys would be able to launch their boats from community piers. There would be two golf courses and a huge business and shopping area.

Kaiser's originality stirred the people of Hawaii. In bars, drugstores, and supermarkets, the local population talked about the unusual Mr. Kaiser. He was clearly bigger and busier than any haole industrialist the Islands had ever known. His organization, having assets of $1,700,-000,000 and sales of a billion a year, dwarfed the operations of the Big Five and Dillingham interests. More importantly, Kaiser's activities in Hawaii, while primarily designed for profit, obviously were also aimed at social betterment. When the seventy-seven-year-old *malihini* announced plans for his cement plant, he stressed lower costs for the construction of highways, schools, and other public works, and promised the people of Hawaii that all of his companies would co-operate in developing new industries and more local commerce in the Islands.[10] His $4,000,000 Kaiser Foundation Hospital on Ala Moana Boulevard, overlooking Ala Wai Yacht Harbor, was organized as a nonprofit institution and introduced dozens of innovations in hospital organization, designed for maximum comfort for its patients. Earlier, the Kaiser Foundation Health Plan introduced to the Islands the least-expensive, most-comprehensive health coverage yet available in Hawaii, and in the fabulous year of statehood, work had begun on the dream city, Hawaii Kai. *Kamaaina* citizens, whether thrilled or unhappy, shook their heads and muttered, "Only Kaiser could do it."

But if Kaiser was first, he was not alone among mainland investors. Between 1948 and 1958, investments of mainland companies increased from $17,000,000 to over $180,000,000. About one third of these investments were channeled into public utilities, one third in mortgages, and the remainder in industrials and Territory and city-county bonds. In addition to Kaiser and Standard Oil, Sears Roebuck and Woolworth had come to Hawaii. The large, for Hawaii, expansion plans of the Hawaiian Electric Company and the Hawaiian Telephone Company produced a stream of representatives from mainland investment firms to pass on the adequacy of Hawaii's economy. Through these contacts, expansion of both utilities was underwritten by mainland capital.

The Oahu boom of which Kaiser was a part was not shared by the outer islands. There, intense mechanization on the sugar and pineapple plantations replaced men with machines. Declining populations meant less purchasing power for plantation communities. In Lihue in 1959, a Japanese owner of three sundries stores confided his concern over the loss of business. He had written his will to leave one store to each of his three children, he said, but now he would change the will, to give them more flexibility in the management of the family property after his death.[11] When American Factors announced that its Hawaiian Canneries plantation on Kauai would shut down, 4,000 residents of the small city of Kapaa were stunned. Two hundred and eighty full-time and 1,500 part-time workers were on Hawaiian Canneries' payroll. Money became scarce, and frightened citizens wondered what would happen to them. Another pocket of depression existed on the Kona Coast of the Big Island, where, since 1957, the squeeze between rising costs and falling prices made it ever more difficult for the Kona coffee farmer to support his family. In dozens of small villages and hamlets throughout the Islands, citizens wondered what would become of their communities. At Hanapepe on Kauai, in 1959, the owner of a small gasoline station complained that bright youngsters were leaving for Oahu. The owner of a grocery-butcher store at Lahaina on Maui boasted of his three children on the mainland but, sadly shaking his head, doubted if they would ever come home.[12]

The great economic changes that were taking place had a profound effect on the sugar industry and the Big Five agencies. Although sugar executives agreed that profits were low, most of them asserted that the sugar industry would continue to play a major, if relatively less-significant, role in the Islands' economy. They pointed out that sugar had brought over $5,000,000 more to Hawaii in 1959 than it had nine years earlier, despite the fact that sugar acreage had been cut from 109,000 to 84,000 acres. Because of ingenious agricultural methods, production per acre had gone steadily up. The decline in employment on the sugar plantations was thus the result of automation and not of an absolute loss in sugar production. Under the provisions of the Federal Sugar Act, Hawaii's basic quota for mainland delivery was a little more than one million tons, or about 15 per cent of the American market. In addition, approximately 50,000 tons were consumed locally. Although Hawaii's quota rose as mainland consumption increased, the general consensus was that the Islands would come close to meeting their quota, at least for a while.

But nearly every sugar official interviewed was well aware of the cost-price squeeze that kept profits at a low level and the increasing threat of foreign sugar competition. Hawaii's vaunted efficiency had not yet been matched on the mainland or in foreign countries, but competitors were catching up. In addition, nowhere else were costs so high as in the Islands. Marketing expenses were important in pushing costs up, as were local taxes and the excise taxes that sugar refiners were required to pay to the United States government. Costs of labor, materials, and services went steadily up in the 1950's, while sugar's income was limited by the amount Hawaii could produce and sell in the highly competitive market at prices carefully controlled by the federal government through the quota system. Government permission to enter the domestic market with a certain number of tons of sugar was no guarantee of its sale. Even after production and refining, Hawaiian sugar faced intense competition from other cane and domestic beet producers. In 1959, for example, there were sixty-nine sugar beet factories in the fifteen states in which most of Hawaii's sugar was sold. In Hawaii's major market area—the eleven Western states—twice as much sugar was available as could be sold. Thus, in order to sell Hawaiian sugar, it was necessary to transport it hundreds of miles to other market areas, adding to the problem of price competition. One top Hawaiian Sugar Planters' Association official predicted that the pressure would eliminate those sugar plantations that consistently failed to show a profit, such as the Olaa Sugar Company (soon to be called Puna Sugar Company) on the Big Island. Perhaps, he added, the four plantations on Oahu would also be eliminated because of the demand for residential and industrial land. At a November 1959 meeting of the Hawaiian sugar technologists, Alexander G. Budge, president of the Association, stressed the need for improved profits.[13] Others pointed out that the industry's earnings were well below the national average of mainland industries. In 1957, for example, Hawaii's sugar plantations returned only 4.2 per cent on net assets, far lower than most comparable mainland investments.

The decline of sugar, combined with the introduction of capital and managerial know-how from the mainland, had a profound effect on Hawaii's Big Five sugar agencies. A growing number of Big Five stockholders recognized that to stand still in the face of mainland and local nonhaole competition would mean lagging profits. Sugar was no longer the lucrative investment it once was. Unleashed were the harsh competitive forces that pervade wholesaling, retailing, and factoring on the mainland. A former executive of one Big Five company explained that the sugar industry in Hawaii was doomed no matter how good the leadership.[14] There would be economic pressure to put land to other uses, he pointed out, while union pressures would force costs up and competition from other sugar-producing areas would squeeze Hawaii out of the mainland market.

These economic pressures and the slippage of sugar profits evoked a demand for new men with new outlooks to run the Big Five agencies and other haole firms. Commenting on the changed business atmosphere, a Chamber of Commerce official stressed that "nothing held Hawaii back as much as old-fashioned business leadership." During the late 1950's, almost every major *kamaaina* firm, responding to competition, changed its top personnel and policies.

Nowhere were the changes more profound than at Castle & Cooke. Because of the foresight of its president, Alexander Budge, one of the last of the managerial old guard, the firm had systematically imported mainland personnel and had begun a policy of diversified investments shortly after the war's end. Budge's policy was to procure "men who are different from myself in experience and temperament." For new blood, Budge, who had been with the firm for nearly forty years, picked John F. Murphy, a tough-fibered, erudite former social worker, to be in charge of Castle & Cooke's labor relations. To manage Castle & Cooke's public relations, he chose William Norwood, a former newspaperman known for his political liberalism, friendship with nonhaoles, and Democratic affiliations. For his own successor, Budge chose Malcolm MacNaughton, the son of Ernest Boyd MacNaughton, former president of the American Unitarian Association, the Urban League of Portland, and Reed College and chairman of the National Committee of the American Civil Liberties Union. The younger MacNaughton had been fully exposed to the major liberal intellectual currents of his generation. More important, from the point of view of the stockholders, the Castle & Cooke executive, who had been in the investment banking business in San Francisco, was thoroughly conversant with mainland business methods.

Under Budge's leadership, Castle & Cooke began its program of diversification in 1946 with the organization of the Hawaiian Equipment Company, distributor of industrial equipment. Three years later, the firm began development of the Islands' largest Macadamia nut orchard with the purchase of 1,000 acres of land near Hilo. Later, 2,000 acres were added, and nut production steadily increased, with sales through broker outlets in some twenty mainland cities. The tuna market attracted Castle & Cooke's attention in 1951, when the firm acquired controlling interest in Hawaiian Tuna Packers, Ltd., a firm which packed the Coral Hawaiian brand for local markets and Royal Hawaiian brand for sale on the mainland. A merger in 1956 of Hawaiian Tuna and a Pacific Northwest seafood-packing firm, Columbia River Packers, proved successful, and in 1958 and 1959, Castle & Cooke purchased additional stock, giving the company a 60 per cent interest in the Columbia River Packers. For the first time in its long history, Castle & Cooke had acquired a majority ownership in a mainland firm, a policy MacNaughton highly approved. "We're not interested in becoming just another stockholder," he asserted. The company purchased 35 per cent of Kentron Hawaii, Ltd., organized in 1956 as Hawaii's first electronics firm. In the same year, it acquired the 6,600-acre Blackhawk Ranch near San Francisco, later to be developed as residential land, but presently used primarily for walnut cultivation and cattle raising. The firm obtained controlling interest in a new warehouse and terminal on the Big Island, and for the first time became a substantial direct owner of land on Oahu with the acquisition of nearly 28,000 acres. It expanded its interest in Kentron (42 per cent), the Waialua Agricultural Company (47 per cent), the Home Insurance Company of Hawaii (40 per cent), Hawaiian Pineapple (52 per cent, from only 18 per cent following World War II), and guarded its interest (23 per cent) in the Matson Navigation Company. In addition, the firm, which had begun as a small store and expanded to sugar production and marketing, maintained its ownership of the Kohala Sugar Company and Castle & Cooke Terminals in Honolulu. Later, Castle & Cooke, Hawaiian Pineapple Corporation (whose name would be changed to Dole Corporation), and the Columbia River Packers Association would merge, creating Hawaii's largest company in total assets.

Budge stepped down as president in 1959, assuming chairmanship of the board of directors for the *kamaaina* organization. MacNaughton, who, as executive vice-president, had increasingly taken over Budge's responsibilities, now became president. He was determined to continue Budge's policy of diversification and to create a new public image for Castle & Cooke. Continually emphasizing the importance of service to the community, in 1958 he promulgated a staff bulletin encouraging all employees to take an active interest in political campaigns. Whether they were Republicans or Democrats made no difference, he said. Castle & Cooke would no longer be identified only with the G.O.P. "Any employee interested in running for office himself or who needs to take a reasonable amount of time from his job to work for a candidate of his choice is requested to make arrangements to do so," Mac-Naughton told the staff.

Budge and MacNaughton applied their policy of recruiting fresh personnel and ideas to the Hawaiian Pineapple Company. To keep pace with its two largest competitors, the mainland firms California Packing Corporation and Libby, McNeill and Libby, as well as competition throughout the world, Herbert C. Cornuelle was picked as president of the company. By 1940, the "king of fruits" accounted for plantings in 78,000 acres of land, and 35,000 Islanders were employed to grow, harvest, and seal the pineapples in tins. The industry far out-produced all other areas of the world combined in canned pineapple, and orders before the war were regular and profits steady. But after the war, the industry was threatened with some of the same pressures that beset sugar. Rising costs owing to unionization, new taxes, the pressure to put land to other uses, the competition of new food products, and the growth of pineapple production in far-flung sections of the world threatened profits in Hawaii. Pineapple production and the dollar volume of income from pineapple went up slightly during the 1950's, but profits were sporadic, and Hawaii's share of the world market steadily declined. At the war's end, the Islands supplied approximately 75 per cent of the world's demand for the fruit. In 1958, on the eve of statehood, Hawaii contributed only 57 per cent of the known world production. Pushing for a larger slice of the world's market were producers in Malaya, South Africa, Puerto Rico, the Philippines, and Formosa, each producing one million or more cases a year. Some executives at Castle & Cooke thought the pineapple industry in Hawaii had forgotten how to sell. Hawaii might boast that its pineapples were superior to those grown elsewhere—a claim challenged vigorously in Central America—but foreign pineapple was cheaper, and, unlike sugar, American pineapple was protected by only a token tariff against the Philippines and Cuba. Within a year after the signing of the statehood bill, Hawaiian Canneries, on Kauai, would announce liquidation of its operations; Grove Farm, a plantation company on Kauai, would also discontinue its pineapple plantings; and the loss of leased land at Waipio, on Oahu, would begin to force discontinuance of a Libby McNeill plantation.

Cornuelle, the man who was picked to meet these challenges for Hawaiian Pineapple, was strikingly different from the traditional *kamaaina* haole company president. The son of a Presbyterian minister, he had studied philosophy at the University of Denver, later shifted his interest to political science and planned to become a city manager. A chain of fortuitous circumstances led him to become assistant to the president of Hawaiian Pineapple in Honolulu, following which he was tapped by Budge and MacNaughton for the top job within a decade after joining the firm. Perhaps more than any other individual, Cornuelle represented the new managerial spirit in Hawaii. He had no old *kamaaina* relations, did not go to Central Union Congregational Church, had not attended a big Eastern school, and avoided *kamaaina* cocktail parties. Reflective, soft-spoken, able to quote and discuss Whitehead and Toynbee, Cornuelle also realized that he was in business to make a profit. He encouraged new methods of processing, new plans for marketing and selling pineapples, and new developments in plant breeding in an effort to produce more and better fruit.

The MacNaughton touch was also felt in Hawaii's oldest *kamaaina* firm, C. Brewer & Company. Its president, Alan Davis, who was, like Budge and others, the older managerial type, picked Boyd MacNaughton, Malcolm's older brother, to succeed him in the new economy of Hawaii. Boyd MacNaughton, only fifty-one years old at the time of statehood, inherited a company that was heavily invested in sugar. Founded in 1826, Brewer was unique among the factors in that it was the central office of its sugar companies' subsidiaries. Owning from 79 to 99.8 per cent of their stock, Brewer maintained central office, executive, staff, and service facilities to supplement the decentralized operating management of each of its ten sugar companies. Representing and servicing more sugar plantations than any of the other agencies, Brewer was second only to American Factors in tons of sugar produced under its supervision. Four of Brewer's plantations were on the sugar-rich Hamakua Coast of the Big Island, two in the Kau section of Hawaii, two on Maui, and two on Kauai.

Boyd MacNaughton was determined to expand Brewer's sugar interests in new and unusual ways. Among others, he talked of a new papermaking industry in Hawaii, using bagasse, the fibrous by-product of sugar cane remaining after the juice is extracted. Acting on the belief that, as a result of increased demand due to rising standards of living, the sugar industry could expand in many areas of the world, he helped organize the Hawaiian Agronomics Company to export sugar know-how and to manage sugar plantations throughout the world. The first contract for the C. Brewer subsidiary was given by the government of Iran to supervise a land development and agricultural operation of a sugar mill in the southern part of that country. In addition to these diversifications, MacNaughton pushed research on new crops, hedging against a more serious decline in the sugar industry than he anticipated.

Brewer also went into fields other than agriculture under MacNaughton's leadership. In 1959, it purchased nearly all the common stock of the Hawaiian Insurance and Guarantee Company, a small insurance underwriter organized in Hilo in 1914. MacNaughton told his stockholders in an annual report that C. Brewer should try "to share favorably in the expanding population and economic activity of Hawaii." To back his policies, MacNaughton sought new blood for his staff and board of directors. When three directors retired in 1959, they were replaced with three former mainlanders who had moved to top spots in Hawaii's business community and who did not hold substantial stock interest in the firm.

Diversification was nothing new to the smallest of Hawaii's Big Five agencies, Theo. H. Davies & Company. With branches in Hilo, New York, and San Francisco, this firm had been engaged in wholesale and retail merchandising, shipping, insurance, and other businesses for decades. Although it had once financed or assisted with the organization of twenty-two sugar plantations, by 1959 it remained as agent for only three, with a total production equaling a little more than a third of that of plantations run by Brewer. To run the company's far-flung enterprises in the late 1950's, the Davies board of directors picked Oklahoman James H. Tabor, who in the year of statehood was only forty-two years old. Youth was accented throughout the company's top management; the average age of its eight officers was forty-four years. Among them was former Marine Warren Titus, who persuaded the company to expand its shipping business and was placed in charge of the project. Titus, as different from old-line haole elite representatives as Dan Inouye was from Wilfred Tsukiyama, never went to college. Restless and ambitious, he represented for Davies the six passenger ships of the Orient & Pacific Lines and the ships of four freighter companies. But Titus soon left Davies for a bigger shipping job on the mainland. Although, for him, management in Hawaii was still too conservative, during the 1950's he represented at Davies the advance guard of the newer, dynamic management leadership of Hawaii.

The year of statehood, 1959, also saw major changes in Hawaii's largest company, American Factors. On January 1, C. Hutton Smith, an executive vice-president, took the administrative reins of the company from retiring President George W. Sumner. In Sumner's five years as president, American Factors had invested in excess of $4,000,000 in expansion. It built a suburban branch of the Liberty House in Waialai, doubled the size of its shops and drugstores in Waikiki, and built new warehouses. Sumner, even more representative of the old guard than Budge or Davis, also recognized that changes in management and policies were necessary. He decentralized operations, putting vice-presidents in charge of Amfac's four divisions—wholesaling, plantations, lands, and insurance. At the end of his tenure, the company had total investments of about $20,000,000 in wholesale operations, $10,000,000 in plantation securities, and $8,000,000 in its retail stores. Sumner, like others on his board of directors and in the Island business community, moved reluctantly into the new economy of Hawaii. He remained strongly opposed to labor unions, preferring the old paternalistic system. The missionaries, he believed, had been kind and fair to everyone and were responsible for Hawaii's good race relations. He opposed statehood, maintaining that Hawaii's peoples were not ready for it. A former submarine commander, Sumner had been in Hawaii for thirty-eight years. For twelve of those years he was an employee of the Bishop Trust Company; he joined American Factors in 1936. A *malihini,* he adopted the customs of the *kamaaina* elite and in 1959 was the last great representative of managerial paternalism. Even in the last year of his presidency, he kept a record of the birth dates of the company's 1,360 employees and personally telephoned birthday congratulations to each of them. He was proud that a nisei girl had been put in charge of cosmetics at the company's downtown Liberty House store and that Orientals were seated next to him at Amfac's annual dinner at the Oahu Country Club, since they were barred at other times. But Sumner regretted the changing of the guard in Hawaii, although—like Budge and Davis—he recognized its inevitability.

The racial and political attitudes of some American Factors executives had already come under public criticism, and recently stockholders had sharply criticized the company's wholesale, retail, and land policies. The wholesaling business in Hawaii had doubled since World War II. Whereas wholesaling was once practically monopolized by American Factors and Theo. H. Davies, now there was competition from the sales representatives of mainland manufacturers, local merchandise brokers working for commissions, and hundreds of jobbers. The growth of large supermarkets destroyed the control that American Factors had exercised for decades over grocery wholesaling. Some supermarkets owned by Americans of Chinese or Japanese descent became large enough to do their own purchasing directly from producers. Two co-operative wholesalers, Certified Grocers and Hawaiian Grocers, were formed to serve groups of grocery stores. Although American Factors remained one of the largest wholesale firms in the United States (listed twenty-sixth in 1959), it would now have to fight for its share of the wholesale business in Hawaii.

Liberty House, "Hawaii's first family store," and its three suburban branches no longer enjoyed a virtual monopoly over department-store retail trade. Sears, Woolworth, and other retail outlets had gradually reduced the percentage of the total volume of retail trade handled by American Factors outlets. Sears Roebuck, which had come to the Islands with opposition from *kamaaina* leaders, enjoyed a regular increase in business volume under the aggressive leadership of mainlander Morley Theaker. Sears policies were revolutionary in Hawaii. Theaker systematically purchased local merchandise, believing that dollars thus spent would be returned to the company. He staffed his store with Orientals, promoting many of them rapidly, and by 1959, approximately 60 per cent of his employees were Americans of Japanese ancestry. The Sears commission system encouraged individual initiative; its profit-sharing and pension plans won the loyalty of its employees. In 1959, Theaker proudly boasted that 72 per cent of the workers at the company owned their own homes. More importantly, there were no limits on initiative. Nonhaoles from his store would one day become managers of mainland outlets, the Sears boss predicted. To keep pace with Sears and other competitors, Liberty House needed aggressive new retailing policies.

American Factors' land-development policies—or lack of them— had also come under sharp criticism. In 1955, Harold W. Rice, a director of the Pioneer Mill Company on Maui, represented and substantially owned by American Factors, blasted Sumner in public for his failure to sell or develop Pioneer's beach property at Kaanapali, near Lahaina. He told of an offer, rejected by Sumner, from the Matson Navigation Company of $1,000,000 for 167 acres of Kaanapali property and a promise by Matson to put $4,000,000 into developing the property for tourism. Pioneer Mill had not paid a dividend to stockholders since 1944, although it had paid more than $1,300,000 to American Factors for the agency's services and another $1,000,000 to the Hawaiian Sugar Planters' Association in dues. The key to future financial success, argued Rice, lay in land development or sales.

Responding to new competitive pressures, C. Hutton Smith, upon his assumption of the presidency of American Factors, announced sweeping changes in policy and personnel. A public-and-employee-relations department was created to improve the public image of the *kamaaina* firm and to promote employer-employee relationships competitive with the most advanced companies in Hawaii. Smith announced plans for a new division dealing with land development and promised to push a ten-year, $36,000,000 resort-development project at Kaanapali, already approved by Sumner. One of Smith's chief lieutenants admitted that "certain individuals had to pass out of the picture, individuals who are addicted to the old ways of doing things," before aggressive new enterprises could be undertaken. Under Smith and his major assistant, Harold C. Eichelberger, Amfac's heir apparent, the company's land-development division made plans for the utilization of lands not planted in cane held by the Lihue Plantation Company on Kauai and by the Olaa Plantation Company on the Big Island. But the big project would be the resort for Kaanapali, which would eventually be divided into twelve hotel areas along the beach, a 210-acre eighteen-hole golf course, a boat club, and many private homes. American Factors, like everyone else, was betting on tourism.

Smith and Eichelberger also adopted the Brewer idea of exporting sugar know-how. In co-operation with its subsidiary, American Factors Associates, a San Francisco firm, and the Hawaiian Dredging and Construction Company, a new organization called Sugar International was formed to design, construct, and operate all or any part of the sugar industry in any country throughout the world's sugar belt. Hawaii had adopted the mainland aphorism "If you can't lick 'em, join 'em."

Pursuing other investment opportunities, American Factors Associates signed an agreement for the development of 1,300,000 acres in western Australia. The proposed development, covering an area three and a half times the size of Oahu, would be managed by the American Factors subsidiary for pasturing sheep and cattle and cultivating such crops as oats and barley. American Factors, like the rest of Hawaii, was on the move, and Smith and Eichelberger could boast at the end of 1959 —the first year under their management—that sales in its wholesale and retail divisions were at an all-time high. Total premiums in American Factors' insurance company had set a new record, and Amfac was ready to meet its competition throughout the world.

Changing least among Hawaii's Big Five agencies, perhaps, was Alexander & Baldwin, second largest of the sugar factors. But even this company, whose vice-president and general manager, J. W. Cameron, continued to hold the top spot throughout the 1950's, caught the diversification bug. Continuing to represent a total of eight affiliated companies in which it held interests ranging from 25 to 96 per cent, Cameron viewed the company's function as that of an old-fashioned private bank. "We lend these fellows money and cover their overdrafts. We try to give them the benefit of good management guidance." Among the clients were three sugar plantations and three pineapple companies, but A. & B. was not counting heavily on industrial agriculture. In addition to its one-third ownership of the Matson Navigation Company, obtained in late 1959, it held 25 per cent in the new Kentron Hawaii Electronics firm and smaller percentages in the Hawaiian Cement Corporation and Hawaiian Western Steel Company. It preferred to invest its money locally, but it was ready to support new and varied enterprises in Hawaii.

The Dillingham interests energetically pursued diversification throughout the world. Their Hawaiian Dredging and Construction Company, the main Dillingham operation, won important contracts in Japan, Hong Kong, Guam, California, Saudi Arabia, Kuwait, and Egypt. Two Dillingham ventures came into direct competition with other major Hawaii companies. After the Dillinghams had invested in the new Hawaiian Cement Corporation, they tried to block the rezoning application for Kaiser's Permanente Cement plant, projected for nearby Maili. At an open meeting before an overflow crowd of 600 at the Waianae High School, eighty-four-year-old Walter Dillingham, who, as the richest and probably the most powerful of Hawaii's *kamaaina* elite, symbolizing a rapidly fading era, argued that Kaiser's request should wait for the completion of the City Planning Commission's master plan for Oahu. Kaiser, in turn, charged the Dillinghams with an underhanded attempt "aimed directly at killing off the Permanente Plant at Maili. . . ." In what was probably the most dramatic public clash of personalities modern Hawaii had ever seen, Dillingham scorned Kaiser as a "visitor," an epithet that had significance only for a dwindling number of *kamaaina* citizens who resented the harsh competitive forces unleashed by Kaiser and other mainland entrepreneurs.

While Kaiser and Dillingham exchanged verbal blows, the *kamaaina* industrialist's son Benjamin Dillingham prepared for a battle over containerization with the Matson Navigation Company. Recognizing that loading and unloading freight is a major cost in sea transportation, several companies had experimented with various forms of containerization—the loading and unloading of the whole freight car and cargo onto and off of specially designed ships. Matson planned a $4,000,000 investment in a lift-on, lift-off, container system aimed at stabilizing the cost of moving Hawaii's annual cargo of 4,000,000 tons. Its aluminum container, with plywood-lined inside walls, could hold 42,000 pounds of cargo, and forty of these containers could be carried on each of the six freighters scheduled for conversion to containerization. At the Oahu Railroad and Land Company, run by young Dillingham, studies indicated that they were in a position to challenge Matson, which for years had been the only major carrier operating between the mainland and the Territory, by beginning a roll-on, roll-off containerization system. Ben Dillingham planned to make the company the western railroad and trucking terminal of the United States and spent over $2,000,000 in capital expansion for the company's yards and terminals on Oahu. Great Dillingham barges would unload containers at Pier 26 in Honolulu, where trains would transport the containers from the waterfront back to a terminal over land owned by the Dillinghams.

The Dillinghams' railroad company had been looking for additional transportation activities to replace the revenue lost from the decrease in railroad traffic after World War II. The Young Bros. Barge Line was acquired in 1952, but the company, owning a number of piers and strategic parcels of land in the harbor area as well as a tract of land granted by King Kalakaua for railroad operations, was ready for a major new venture. Additional incentive to go into the freight-carrying business through containerization came from a legal stipulation in the Kalakaua grant that the company use the King's land only for railroad purposes. From an economic point of view, some in the company were satisfied. Others on the board of directors were more skeptical and could not be persuaded by Dillingham that the roll-on, roll-off system could be made to work. Even if the engineering problems could be licked, government financing obtained, and Matson underpriced, there still might be formidable political problems. Even for the Dillinghams, competition with the Matson Navigation Company might prove more difficult than contending with Henry Kaiser. More than 40 per cent (it would be up to 73 per cent by 1961) of Matson was owned by local companies, primarily Alexander & Baldwin and Castle & Cooke. Matson, through its virtual monopoly of mainland freight shipping, influenced the policies of many Hawaiian companies. The strong political influence of Matson and the companies with which it was associated would make itself felt in Honolulu, San Francisco, and Washington.

The incipient Matson-Dillingham fight underscored the fact that even the oldest *kamaaina* firms were obliged to compete against each other in the new economy of Hawaii. Nowhere was that more clearly seen than in the bristling competition between Hawaii's two major banks. For decades, the Bishop Bank dominated Hawaii's banking scene. Steadily, under the aggressive leadership of mainland banker Rudolph Peterson, the Bank of Hawaii surpassed the Bishop organization. Sensitively interpreting the changes that were overtaking Hawaii, Peterson reorganized the personnel and policies of the Bank of Hawaii in the 1950's. He encouraged nonhaole employees and boasted, "We are determined to make our organization, our staff promotions and our relations with our customers truly representative of all groups on all islands." He energetically pursued mainland contacts until, in 1959, his firm outdistanced the Bishop Bank in dollar assets and came abreast of its sister institution in dollar deposits. Together, the two banks counted more than $525,000,000 of the $583,000,000 listed in total deposits in the Islands, but the friendly co-operation of bygone days had given way to sharp, if still friendly, competition. Three other banks, two under Chinese auspices and one sponsored by nisei businessmen, were pressing for an increasing share of Hawaii's banking business, each having between $22,000,000 and $28,000,000 in assets. Soon, a sixth bank, the City Bank of Honolulu, under Japanese leadership, would open its doors to Hawaii's increasing number of investors and depositors.[15]

Once the centralized economy of the Islands had been shattered by the war and the airplane, the fluid, relatively open economy of the new Hawaii spurred enterprising local nonhaole businessmen to success. Local fortunes were made in real estate, construction, wholesaling, retailing, insurance, and other businesses.

The first of Hawaii's new Chinese tycoons was Chinn Ho, who, with less than $200,000 in capital, organized the Capital Investment Company in 1945 in anticipation of the Oahu land boom and the proliferation of small businesses in the Islands. In 1947, the company purchased 9,000 acres of the Waianae plantation, and four years later it bought another 2,000 acres from the Hawaiian Avocado Company in Pupukea. Ho openly proclaimed his intention to break up large land areas and sell small lots on a fee-simple basis at a price ordinary homeowners or small farmers could afford. By July 1950, the company's assets totaled nearly $2,000,000, and it was showing handsome net profits. By 1959, Capital Investment had sold more than 1,500 fee-simple homes and farm lots, totaling some 4,200 acres in the two rural Oahu areas. Chinn Ho was also determined to provide financial leadership for small nonhaole businesses and individuals to enable them to compete with the larger *kamaaina* haole firms. Within a decade, Capital Investment had organized subsidiary firms to own and manage varied enterprises from apartment houses and an automobile distributorship to a Macadamia nut company. One of Chinn Ho's biggest investments, the development of 2,200 acres of ranch land in the San Francisco Bay area, was well under way in 1959.

The grandson of a Chinese rice planter who had migrated to Hawaii in 1855, Chinn Ho had graduated in the famous McKinley class of 1924 and become an office boy at the Bishop Bank. He had served in a minor capacity with a haole financial company until the war's end, when he foresaw and welcomed the rise of the labor movement, the increased pressure for land on Oahu, and the demands of nonhaoles for economic opportunity. Organizing his own company with an eye toward good public relations, he chose a cosmopolitan board of directors, representing each of Hawaii's major ethnic groups. He welcomed the new economic and political order and tried to accelerate change. Recognition of Chinn Ho's business acumen came with his appointment as managing trustee of the Mark Alexander Robinson estate, the first major break by one of the big landed estates from trust-company management. By the year of statehood, Chinn Ho's name was as familiar in Hawaii as Henry Kaiser's or Walter Dillingham's.

Postwar competition came to the insurance business through nisei insurance executive Larry Kagawa. This energetic salesman convinced A. P. Giannini, owner of Occidental Life Insurance Company of California, to open a branch in Hawaii. Between 1948 and 1958, Occidental Life did more business than any of the eighty other companies in the Islands. Other insurance companies had charged higher premiums to persons of Japanese, Chinese, and Filipino ancestry than to haoles, based on mortality statistics obtained from the Orient. Using proper statistics and only second-generation non-Caucasian salesmen, Kagawa ended the practice of including racial ancestry as a factor in setting premium rates and broke the hold of *kamaaina* companies on the insurance business of the Islands. Betting on Hawaii's economic future after World War II, the company became the first insurance firm in Hawaii to invest in other organizations. By 1959, Occidental had more than $18,000,000 loaned to Island homeowners or invested in local corporate securities and municipal bonds.

Following Chinn Ho's lead, popular Chinese politician Hiram L. Fong organized a new, locally owned company to take advantage of investment opportunities in real estate, business, and securities in 1952. Riding on the economic boom of the 1950's, Finance Factors soon owned a building on the corner of King and Alakea Streets, from which its directors organized the Finance Investment Company, Grand Pacific Life Insurance Company, and Finance Realty Company. Under Fong's aggressive leadership and limitless optimism, these organizations flourished. In the first four months of operation, Grand Pacific Life sold $10,000,000 worth of life insurance. In 1959, construction was completed on two major apartment-building complexes, Grand Pacific Towers and Diamond Head Gardens.

Most colorful of Hawaii's Chinese businessmen was Hung Wo Ching, president of Aloha Airlines. Before and during the war, inter-island air travel was exclusively controlled by Hawaiian Airlines, a subsidiary of the *kamaaina* haole firm, Inter-Island Steamship Company. Until 1946, Hawaiian Airlines employed no Orientals at their ticket counters or as stewardesses and pilots. Because of orders from military authorities during the war, Americans of Japanese ancestry were often refused passage on Hawaiian's planes, despite confirmed reservations. In 1946, Oriental businessmen under the leadership of Ruddy Tongg organized Trans-Pacific Airlines, predecessor of Aloha Airlines. The struggle for certification by the Civil Aeronautics Board as a scheduled airline was long and costly; by the time it received its permanent certificate in 1954, it had lost all of its capital of $1,000,000. Practically bankrupt in 1958, the board of directors offered the presidency to entrepreneur-philosopher Hung Wo Ching, who was given a free hand to attempt a merger with Hawaiian Airlines or to dispose of the company's assets.

After fruitless negotiation with its competitor, Trans-Pacific embarked upon a corporate reorganization, changing its name to Aloha Airlines, and bringing in $2,000,000 in new capital through two stock issues. Ching, a Ph.D. in agricultural economics from Cornell, who had once planned to establish a beet-sugar industry in China, worked eighteen and twenty hours a day to catch up with his competitor. To him, Aloha Airlines represented the biggest challenge yet cast at the established order in Hawaii. Aloha's stockholders, a majority of whom were of Oriental ancestry, supported Ching's ambitious policies in the face of unusual obstacles. Since the Bishop Bank was the principal lending institution for Hawaiian Airlines, Ching went to the mainland for insurance loans. Gradually, Aloha, through good public relations and personnel policies, flew into a competitive position with Hawaiian Airlines. "Hawaiian Airlines had it so good for so long," according to one Aloha official, "that it forgot how to compete." A major milestone in Aloha's young history was reached in 1959 when Hung Wo Ching negotiated a handsome mainland loan and $3,000,000 of insurance from a mainland insurance firm, thus enabling Aloha to purchase turboprop planes for its interisland business. For the first time, the younger line could boast faster equipment than its competitor. Hawaiian Airlines, hard pressed to stay ahead of Aloha in the number of passengers carried, procured energetic mainland management and sedulously cultivated nonhaole business. Although both companies were losing money, competition in interisland traffic was firmly established. For Hung Wo Ching, Aloha Airlines had an unusual personal meaning. His father had been a cook for the Inter-Island Steamship Company, the parent firm of Hawaiian Airlines. When it was announced in January 1959 that Hung Wo Ching had been elected to the board of directors of the Bank of Hawaii, everyone in the Islands knew that a new era had arrived.

Neither Hung Wo nor his elder brother, Hung Wai, limited their business interests to Aloha Airlines. Hung Wai started in the real-estate business in 1947, and after handling several profitable subdivisions on Oahu, he amassed enough capital to invest in an automobile distributorship, a large butcher shop specializing in steaks, and additional real property. His business leadership and interest in the cultural and educational life of the Islands won him a place on the University of Hawaii's Board of Regents.

All four Chinese businessmen had shared common experiences and revealed common attitudes, even though Chinn Ho and Hung Wo Ching were Democrats, while Fong and Hung Wai Ching were registered Republicans. Each man resented the injustices of the past; each was determined to speed Hawaii's postwar revolution; each had overcome the opposition of *kamaaina* firms; each manifested a relentless personal drive for success; and each, even in the late 1940's, when professional economists were dubious concerning Hawaii's economic future, was unswervingly optimistic. They had gambled their early winnings on Hawaii and won.[16]

Experts in Hawaii recognized that a continuance of the economic boom rested precariously on the expenditures of the federal government in Hawaii, primarily for defense activities, and the continued success of the sugar and pineapple industries in the face of increasing competition. If the $447,000,000 spent by the federal government in the Islands in 1959 were removed, Hawaii would lose nearly half of its total income in mainland dollars. More than any state in the union, Hawaii's economy rests on the continuation of the cold war, since more than three out of every four dollars spent by the federal government in the Islands could be directly attributed to defense expenditures.[17]

Unwilling to bet on either continued military payments or the viability of sugar and pineapple, business leaders gave considerable attention in 1959 to the further diversification of Hawaii's agriculture. At the University of Hawaii, an agricultural experimentation station undertook approximately 160 projects aimed at promoting the agricultural development of the Islands. Programs ranged from studies of mainland markets for Macadamia nuts to new methods of processing, packing, and shipping fresh papayas to the mainland. There was no doubt that almost anything grown in a tropical climate could be raised in Hawaii. At varying times, rice, tobacco, bananas, coffee, sisal, cotton, rubber, and honey had been tried, only to be abandoned because of high labor costs and marketing problems.[18] Rice, once an important product on Kauai and Oahu, could not meet price competition of imports from other areas. Production in 1910 totaled nearly 42,000,000 pounds, including a substantial export volume, but thirty-eight years later, Islanders imported 57,000,000 pounds and produced less than a third of a million. Only sugar, because of the high American tariff which protected the Islands, and pineapple, because of advances in processing and brilliant advertising techniques, could be profitably produced for large-scale export. Of the total value of agricultural products in the Islands in 1959, all but 14.4 per cent could be attributed to sugar and pineapple.

Much could be done to increase the Islands' share of the local market for vegetables (only 49.6 per cent in 1959), fruits (44 per cent), beef and veal (56.7 per cent), pork (55.8 per cent), chicken (37.9 per cent), and eggs (78.1 per cent); but increased dollar sales of these products locally depended upon continued extensive military expenditures and the co-operation of the military in using Hawaiian-grown products as well as the expected rise in the number of tourists visiting Hawaii. The Islands continually expanded their production of fresh milk, poultry, eggs, beef, and vegetables to feed an expanding population, although the percentage of beef, veal, vegetables, and melons imported actually rose in the 1950's. For Hawaii's long-run economic health, it seemed prudent to seek an expansion of mainland markets for coffee, tropical fruit, fruit products, and nuts.

The problems of marketing each of these products on the mainland were formidable, but Islanders were determined to solve them. In the case of coffee, determination might not be able to overcome the relentless economic forces which imperiled the coffee industry. The short-lived prosperity of the early 1950's, caused by the failure of the Brazilian coffee crop, had clearly ended. The overcapitalization of the Kona coffee industry led to high per-unit costs for processing and milling. Revival of the industry might require the organization of a centralized co-operative for marketing and processing, owned and controlled by the farmers; an aggressive and expensive information campaign on the mainland; political pressure from the Kona district to obtain state and federal legislation protecting the coffee farmer with special lowered minimum-wage rates for coffee pickers; tax relief; and perhaps federal price supports. Given the highly individualistic and competitive nature of the more than 1,100 producers of coffee and the fact that Kona coffee constituted less than 1 per cent of the world's supply, a revitalization of the industry and an expanded export crop seemed doubtful.[19]

The outlook for fresh fruits and nuts was better, although the volume of exports would continue to remain small for a long time. In the 1950's, Hawaii's fruit and nut industries had increased in value from $1,500,000 to $2,500,000. The dollar volume from the export of such products was still infinitesimal, but it was increasing every year. On the mainland, promotional campaigns pushed the sale of fresh papaya, papaya juice, guava nectar and juice, passion fruit (*lilikoi*) juice, Macadamia nuts, and coconut chips. Papaya production and export showed the greatest growth; if the shelf life of papayas could be increased four days, it would be possible to ship this delicate fruit as far as the eastern coast of the mainland, reaching a market 360 times larger than that in Hawaii. Macadamia nuts, which take eight years to cultivate, tripled in production during the 1950's, but it was still uncertain whether a large-enough market could be developed on the mainland for this delicious luxury nut to offset its high cost of production. There was virtually no limit to the amount of guava juice that could be frozen and shipped across the Pacific, but there was serious question as to whether mainland palates would support a market for guava products in competition with fruit juices produced on the mainland.[20]

The search went on for new products that would not only satisfy Island appetites, but that could be shipped economically to the mainland as well. A $300,000 plant was built to process the vitamin-rich ascerola cherry, sometimes called the West Indian or Barbados cherry. The sale of tropical flowers to the mainland increased slightly, but there was still a need for a central wholesale market in Honolulu where growers could bring products and retail merchants could pick out what suited their needs.

After the discovery of considerable amounts of bauxite on Kauai, reclamation studies showed that it was possible to cover bauxite-stripped lands to prevent erosion and to bring the mined area back to greater economic use. It was possible to obtain profitable crops on bauxite land that had been relatively unproductive of even native vegetation.

Hawaii's boosters reached for every straw in the wind, hoping to place Hawaii's economy on a sounder economic footing. But realism forced experts to concede that extraordinary economic and political problems would inhibit rapid agricultural diversification. Land values, taxes, and the cost of imported stock, feed, and materials meant Hawaii still could not afford to grow its essentials, to say nothing of surpluses for export. Territorial farmers complained that it was impossible to compete with mainland producers because of a tax pyramid that included a 1 per cent gross income tax and a 3.5 per cent general excise tax on everything purchased by the farmers—feed, fertilizer, and packaging materials. But even with more favorable taxes, the costs of land, labor, and marketing would sharply restrict exports to the mainland.[21]

Because of these difficulties, Hawaii's boosters talked increasingly of diversified manufacturing as a way to compensate for the absence of a solid economic base. The Economic Planning and Coordinating Authority created in 1955 by the Territory's first Democratic legislature investigated the possibilities of producing everything from cast-iron pipe to nylon hose. Its staff was assisted by the Stanford Research

Institute, which prepared evaluations of the industrial potential for each of the major islands. One of the first of these, prepared for the Hawaiian Electric Company and entitled "A Study of Industrial Development Opportunities on Oahu," became a bench mark for Oahu's industrial-diversification program. It was the Stanford report that first saw the Islands as the logical location for a small steel mill. The efforts of public and private agencies to displace imports wherever there was a sufficient local volume to justify the establishment of plants in the Islands resulted in nearly 100 national and regional manufacturers locating in Hawaii.

Most successful of these was the garment industry, which grew steadily by about 15 per cent yearly during the 1950's, as fashions designed and manufactured in the Islands found ready acceptance throughout the nation. By 1958, the industry's production had risen to approximately $12,000,000, and planning authorities predicted a bright future for it. It was hoped that Kentron Hawaii would be the first of a growing number of electronics producers, and that plywood, plastics, and processed-food manufacturers would also find Hawaii attractive. Actually, Kentron could not beat the volume sales competition of mainland firms, and the total volume of manufacturing, outside of food and beverage processing, was still small. Even Hawaii's steel mill and oil refinery were miniature by mainland standards. But who would have thought only ten years before that Hawaii would have even one steel mill or an oil refinery or sixty manufacturers of apparel and textile products? Boosterism swept the Islands, and sober-minded economists predicted the growth of plants utilizing the by-products of sugar and pineapple, lava for building purposes, and new products not yet thought of.

Behind the talk of new manufactures and expanded agricultural production lay the confident expectation of a continued tourist boom. "The boom has just begun" was the phrase repeated over and over by Island businessmen, economists, and promoters. In response to the crucial question "What will happen to Hawaii if peace breaks out?" came the answer that tourism would overtake defense expenditures in the 1960's anyway, and by 1980 it would produce a half a billion dollars in wealth for Hawaii, perhaps more than defense, sugar, and pineapple combined. But Islanders did not really expect peace to break out, and in the short run, the economy depended upon that assumption.

Nevertheless, plans were made for accommodating millions of tourists, large international conferences, and hordes of mainlanders who would retire to Hawaii in the decades ahead. In the boom fever that gripped Hawaii in the year of statehood, it was common to talk of two-hour jet flights from New York, of resorts on the outer islands rivaling Waikiki, and of Hawaii as the cultural and research center of the Pacific. Henry Kaiser had no doubt that the Islands would welcome more than a million visitors a year in the late 1960's, compared with 243,000 in 1959. The Hawaii Visitors Bureau prophesied 2,500,000 annually by 1975. Thousands of new rooms would be built on Oahu and the outer islands. For the neighbor islands, tourism could halt their steady economic decline. A study by the Stanford Research Institute found that the Big Island had more natural attractions for tourists than the other islands, and a master plan, drawn by Harland Bartholomew & Associates for the State Planning Office, projected a string of resorts along the Kona Coast. Vast improvements would be needed in Hawaii's roads and in preparing the Hilo airport for jet landings and take-offs, but tourist fever had already affected the Big Island. By the end of 1960, it was expected that Kauai would more than double the 237 hotel rooms that it had when the year began, making a small start toward the 3,000 hotel rooms and yearly $15,000,-000 of public improvements planned by 1970. Three major resort areas—one around Hanalei, one in the Lihue-Wailua area, and one in the Poipu–Port Allen region—were recommended by the State Planning Office, and private development plans were on the drawing board for each of the areas before 1959 was over. Maui, with not quite 750 hotel rooms, also planned 3,000 rooms by 1970. But the greatest growth would take place on Oahu, and population projections for the island, published by the Planning Office, indicated a continued drop for the neighbor islands through the 1960's and '70's, as the demand for services for the tourists on the core island accelerated. Sugar would continue to be the economic mainstay of the outer islands, at least in the immediate future, and mechanization would continue to reduce employment on the plantations and in the mills. The basic pattern of Hawaii's postwar economy, set by the cold war and the airplane, would continue. Wealth, talent, and labor would move to Oahu, where, in the offices of public officials, economic planners, and businessmen, dreams of economic miracles would unfold, and—if the determination of men could control—would be turned into reality.[22]

Chapter Seventeen

THE PROMISE OF HAWAII

Marine helicopters buzzed overhead, church bells rang, and little children raced barefoot along country roads, shouting, "Statehood! Statehood—it's come!" Approved by Congress in 1959, statehood arrived 106 years after pro-American King Kamehameha III first began discussions with the United States government about the annexation of Hawaii to the union as a new state. After the King died, negotiations lapsed, although the idea of statehood was never entirely abandoned. In his inaugural address as the first governor of the Territory of Hawaii, Sanford B. Dole prophesied eventual statehood, and in 1903, the territorial legislature petitioned Congress for an enabling act which would lead to statehood. The first bill calling for statehood was submitted in Congress sixteen years later by Jonah Kuhio. Dozens of congressional investigations, reports, and recommendations were produced in the years that followed, but Hawaiian statehood, a symbol of the right and ability of the peoples of the Islands to govern themselves, was always blocked.

Hawaii remained under the constitutional control of Congress, which could, at any time, abolish the territorial legislature and local government and place the Islands under a resident commissioner, as was done in the Philippines, or under a Navy commission, as had been done in Guam and Samoa. Hawaii had been threatened with the loss of self-government before. The President and Congress flirted with the idea of commission government following the Massie rape case in the early 1930's. During World War II, Hawaii became the first sizable territory in American history to be governed by the military. Throughout its history, the citizens of Hawaii had been unable to vote for President or for their own governor. With only one nonvoting delegate to represent them in Congress, the Territory did not get its share of federal money for roads, conservation, improvement of rivers and harbors, or land-grant colleges and vocational education. Hawaii, Congress said in repeated sessions following 1935, was not ready for statehood.

Delegates Jonah Kuhio and Victor Houston, after serving in Congress, believed that Hawaii could not achieve optimum economic and social benefits from participation in the American union unless the Territory was transformed into a state. Houston had warned the Hawaiian Sugar Planters' Association as early as May 1929 that the only sure way to prevent discrimination against the Islands' sugar industry was to obtain statehood.[1] Unless Hawaii carried more weight in Congress, the two major props of the industry—the high protective American tariff and the steady supply of cheap labor from the Philippines—might be destroyed. Congress could lump Hawaii with the Philippines as an offshore area and place the Islands outside the American tariff, or, responding to Hawaii's insistence on equal treatment short of statehood, might exclude Filipino labor from the Islands as they had from the mainland.

But not all of the citizens of Hawaii wanted statehood. Until 1935, the overwhelming majority of the *kamaaina* oligarchy of the Islands were steadfastly opposed. The trustees of the Hawaiian Sugar Planters' Association answered Houston by arguing that immediate statehood would be "premature and unwise," and were delighted when congressional sponsors of Filipino exclusion bills included an exemption for Hawaii. The plantations, over 60 per cent of whose laborers were Filipinos, could continue to draw their field workers from the giant archipelago in the western Pacific, and the tariff walls seemed as sturdy as ever.[2] When Houston complained to Henry A. Baldwin that as delegate he had to beg for benefits for Hawaii and that there was constant discrimination against the Territory, Baldwin replied that he understood Houston's feeling like a "book agent going around asking for *kokua* [help]." But territorial status was preferable to statehood, he advised, since the voters of the Islands were not mature enough to elect a safe-and-sane governor. "The bolsheviks and booze fighters seem to get the big vote, at least on Oahu, and Oahu would come pretty near controlling T. H. elections," predicted the missionary descendant. There was even a risk, suggested Baldwin, that Hawaii would elect a Japanese governor and a strongly Japanese state legislature.[3] Another missionary descendant, Clarence H. Cooke, opposed statehood in a

letter to a high-school debating team by asserting that "through appointment of officers by the President of the United States, such as the
governor, secretary of the Territory and judges, we have always had a
better class of men in these positions than states enjoyed through their
elective systems."[4] Until 1934, the other owners and managers of
Hawaii's sugar agencies and their subsidiaries agreed with Baldwin and
Cooke.

But following the Jones-Costigan Act of 1934, a fundamental re-
versal occurred in the attitude of many of Hawaii's leading *kamaaina*
citizens toward the issue of statehood. The Act classified Hawaii,
not as an integral part of the United States, but as a nondomestic producer of sugar, along with the Philippines and Puerto Rico. The practical effect was to increase the amount of sugar that might be marketed
by Colorado, Michigan, and other states by as much as 18 per cent,
while the Hawaiian quota was cut by 10 per cent. Despite protests from
the Hawaiian Sugar Planters' Association, federal courts supported the
right of Congress to discriminate against any territory in setting sugar
quotas. Association lobbyists failed to produce a change in congressional will, and suddenly the men who owned and controlled the great
agencies saw the wisdom of Houston's argument for statehood.

The sugar industry backed Delegate Samuel Wilder King when he
introduced a statehood bill to the House of Representatives in May
1935, and supported the Hawaii Equal Rights Commission, created by
the territorial legislature in the same year. The Commission was
charged with working to assure Hawaiian equality with the states in
federal legislation and to study the advisability of submitting the issue
of statehood to a plebiscite. The first act of the Commission was to
authorize Governor J. B. Poindexter, its ex officio chairman, to appear
before the congressional delegation then in the Territory to study the
question of statehood.[5]

This was the first of twenty congressional hearings on statehood
held between 1935 and 1958, hearings that saw more than 1,000
witnesses and that resulted in the passage of Hawaiian statehood bills
by the House of Representatives in 1947, 1950, and 1953, as well as
passage of a Senate bill to admit both Hawaii and Alaska in 1951.[6]
By 1940, the prostatehood forces in the Territory had persuaded the
territorial legislature to authorize a plebiscite on the question. The
sugar interests, recognizing that Hawaii's position in the domestic
market was in constant jeopardy, strongly supported statehood.

Joseph Farrington's Honolulu *Star Bulletin,* the *Nippu Jiji,* and
the *Hawaii Hochi* endorsed the plebiscite in editorials and news
columns. The Honolulu *Advertiser* opposed immediate statehood,
mainly on the ground that Americans of Japanese ancestry who held
dual citizenship were not yet trustworthy as Americans.[7]

The magazine *Fortune* helped prostatehood forces when it published
an Elmo Roper poll in January 1940 which showed that only 55 per
cent of the mainlanders questioned believed the United States should
go to the rescue of Hawaii if the Islands were attacked, while 74 per cent
favored the defense of Canada.[8] The *Advertiser* considered the poll
irrelevant, insisting that Hawaii should not become a state until its
citizens were Americanized. It pointed to the 37,000 alien-born Japanese in Hawaii who could not become citizens, the 174 Japanese-
language schools attended by more than 40,000 young nisei, and the
potential dangers of Japanese-language broadcasts. Disturbed by the
Advertiser's hard-hitting attacks, the *Star Bulletin* published an article
by University of Hawaii sociologist Romanzo Adams entitled "Getting
the Facts Straight About Statehood—A Myth About Japanese Dominance."[9] Although no group was more interested in the outcome of the
plebiscite than the Japanese, most of their leaders refrained from taking
a stand to avoid lending credence to the *Advertiser*'s allegations. In the
plebiscite, two of every three voters affirmed their support of statehood,
with the largest pluralities coming from the outer islands. On Oahu,
especially in the haole districts, statehood was more controversial,
since it was in such areas that fear of the "Japanese menace" had had
the greatest influence.

After the war, statehood efforts were vigorously renewed. In 1944,
the Hawaiian Equal Rights Commission recommended that its name be
changed to the Hawaii Statehood Commission, a proposal adopted by
the territorial legislature in January 1947. Later that year, the U.S.
House of Representatives for the first time passed a bill providing for
Hawaiian statehood, but the Senate defeated a move to remove the
statehood bill from its Interior and Insular Affairs Committee in the
following session. The citizens of Hawaii watched as statehood bills
were buried in one house or the other, and during the 1950's, they increasingly doubted that statehood would ever be approved by Congress.
Statehood commissioners for Hawaii collaborated with Delegate Jack
Burns in organizing testimony for congressional investigators. Proponents of statehood repeatedly argued that Hawaii should not pay

federal taxes without voting privileges, that Hawaii paid more federal taxes than nine other states, that the Islands had a larger population than any other territory at the time of admission to the union except Oklahoma, and that the per-capita income of its citizens was higher than that of thirty-five states. The peoples of Hawaii, they pleaded, were literate and patriotic, ready to assume the obligations of first-class citizenship.

Suddenly, in 1958, the statehood strategy of Delegate Burns diverged from that of certain statehood commissioners and Governor William Quinn in Honolulu. Following passage of the Alaskan statehood bill by the House of Representatives, Burns agreed with proponents of Alaskan statehood and Democratic leaders in the Senate that it would probably destroy the chances of statehood for either territory if Hawaii and Alaska were joined in the same bill. Burns agreed that it would be wise for Hawaii to wait its turn, even if it meant postponement of consideration of the Hawaiian bill until a new Congress met in 1959. Lorrin P. Thurston, chairman of the Hawaii Statehood Commission and publisher of the now ardently prostatehood *Advertiser,* did not agree that Hawaii's bill should be held up until the following year. Commissioner O. P. Soares said that it was "naïve" to believe that Hawaii would be better prepared in the next session "if Alaska goes through this time." Governor Quinn called for an immediate push and wondered why the Hawaii bill should be held up for Alaska.[10]

It became increasingly clear that Burns not only acquiesced in, but was one of the chief strategists of the plan to separate the two bills and push Alaska first. The theory was simple. Some congressmen opposed Hawaii, others were antagonistic toward Alaska. Why combine these minority oppositions to defeat an over-all bill? Also, Burns maintained, the momentum to accept Hawaii would be irreversible once Alaska achieved statehood. Not only would additional pro-Hawaiian statehood congressmen sit in both chambers, but it would be difficult to discriminate against Hawaii as the only remaining incorporated U.S. territory. Opponents of the Burns strategy in Hawaii did not agree that the alternatives were a combined bill or Alaska first and Hawaii second. Thurston pointed out that as long as Delegate Burns was committed to helping Alaska while keeping Hawaii off the House floor, the Hawaiian bill was doomed for 1958. Soares argued that Hawaii's willingness to follow Alaska provided statehood opponents with the argument that "we're going soft on statehood and don't really care any longer."[11]

When it was reported that Senate Majority Leader Lyndon B. Johnson and Democratic Speaker of the House Sam Rayburn, both from Texas, were working closely with Burns's two-step strategy, Republicans in Hawaii complained in the *Star Bulletin,* "It is increasingly clear that in a showdown, Hawaii will never get statehood while southern Democrats control key positions of leadership in Congress."[12]

Burns disagreed strongly. The Hawaii statehood bill was dead for 1958, but he had received private assurances from Johnson that it would receive early consideration in the Senate in 1959. Speaker Rayburn was not committed to support statehood, but he agreed not to stand in its way against the majority sentiment in his own chamber. To fortify that sentiment, Burns invited Representative Leo W. O'Brien, Democrat of New York and chairman of a special subcommittee of the House Committee on Interior and Insular Affairs, to visit Hawaii in late November. Strongly sympathetic to Hawaii's statehood request, O'Brien brought two like-minded members of the subcommittee with him to make what the committee called "an intensive inquiry" on the statehood issue.

In January, the three committee members submitted their report, signaling the opening thrust in the last congressional battle for statehood. The report systematically rebutted the major antistatehood arguments of the bill's two principal antagonists in Congress, Senator James Eastland, Democrat of Mississippi, and Representative John Pillion, Republican of New York.

Pillion's main argument was that the influence of the International Longshoremen's and Warehousemen's Union in Island politics and the extent of Communist control in the union were too great to admit Hawaii to statehood. We would be inviting "four Soviet agents to take seats in our Congress," charged the New York representative.[13] Eastland agreed. When informed on the Senate floor that the F.B.I. could identify only twenty-five known Communists in the Islands, Eastland maintained that "they control the economic life of the Islands."[14] A second, but less-important, argument advanced by opponents of statehood was that Hawaii's Oriental population would never be fully assimilated into American life. South Carolina Democratic Senator Strom Thurmond, while emphasizing that persons of Japanese ancestry were as moral in their way as any other group, added that they could not adapt to American political institutions.[15] Friends of statehood in the Senate and House pointed out privately that Senators Eastland and

Thurmond may have been less concerned about Communist influence in Hawaii or the cultural separatism of the Japanese than they were about the addition of two pro-civil-rights senators to the upper chamber. A persuasive friend of statehood from Louisiana, businessman George Lehleitner, stated that Southern opposition, as measured in votes, was even stronger against Alaska than Hawaii. Lehleitner, who lobbied privately for twelve years for both territories, told a group in Honolulu that Imua and supporters of its hysterical anti-Communist position had, more than any other factor, been responsible for blocking Hawaiian statehood.[16] Congressmen were genuinely concerned, insisted Lehleitner, when men of such stature and influence as former Governor Lawrence Judd and industrialist Walter Dillingham lent their support to the charge that Hawaii was dominated by the Communist leadership of the I.L.W.U.[17]

Another former governor, Ingram M. Stainback, also opposed statehood, insisting that a commonwealth arrangement comparable to that existing for Puerto Rico would be more advantageous for Hawaii than admission as a state.[18] The main advantage of commonwealth status, Stainback pointed out, would be exemption from federal taxation. A handful of citizens who agreed with Stainback formed the Commonwealth party, but all of its candidates were beaten badly in the 1958 election. Commonwealth did not ring a bell with the peoples of Hawaii, and economic and fiscal experts, while agreeing that Island taxes were high, pointed to a 1954–55 study which showed that, after taxation, the average citizen of Hawaii had $4 to every $1 left for the Puerto Rican citizen, indicating the ability of the Islands to support statehood economically.[19]

Internal opposition to statehood was not limited to Imua and the Commonwealthers. A comprehensive private public-opinion survey on all the islands in 1958 revealed that 23 per cent of the haoles and 27 per cent of the Hawaiians polled strongly opposed statehood. Congressional opponents of statehood would have rejoiced had they known of these results. Only 43 per cent of the sample favored immediate statehood; 24 per cent showed some degree of opposition, and the remainder were apathetic. Of the largest ethnic groups in the Islands, only the Japanese revealed a clear majority backing immediate statehood. Favoring immediate statehood were 62 per cent of the citizens of Japanese ancestry, 44 per cent of the Chinese, 39 per cent of the Filipinos, 33 per cent of the haoles, and only 30 per cent of the Hawaiians and part-Hawaiians.[20] An intensive 1959 survey of the fourteenth representative district on Oahu showed that respondents who had previously replied that they were "neither for nor against statehood" or that they were "opposed but would go along with it," would probably vote in favor of statehood in a referendum that put the issue squarely, yes or no. Still, 37 per cent of the Portuguese, 34 per cent of the haoles, and 32 per cent of the Hawaiians interviewed in the fourteenth district refused to endorse statehood.[21]

Antistatehood sentiment in the Islands correlated frequently with hostility toward Japanese. At a fall 1958 meeting with skilled and semiskilled workers in the thirteenth representative district, a Filipino cannery worker complained that there were too many Japanese in Hawaii for statehood to succeed. A part-Hawaiian stevedore said he was against statehood because he did not want a Japanese governor. A Filipino barber in Kaneohe complained that the Japanese politicians would take over Hawaii after statehood. "Who can tell what is behind those faces?" he questioned. A Chinese politician, explaining his loss in the primary election, confided that statehood would enhance the power of Hawaii's Japanese. A Portuguese contractor on windward Oahu claimed that statehood would bring an Oriental mayor, governor, and congressmen. "The Japs are taking over," he complained. Another Portuguese businessman, in Waikiki, was in favor of statehood until he realized the political strength of Americans of Japanese ancestry, who continued to be elected in large numbers in the Islands. Now, violently opposed to the admission of Hawaii as a state, he asked, "When will they learn to be Americans?"[22]

When the voters of the fourteenth representative district on Oahu were asked in early 1959 if they felt that any racial group or groups in the Islands had too much power, 60 per cent of the Hawaiians and 56 per cent of the Portuguese in the sample replied yes. Of those who answered affirmatively, nearly nine out of ten Hawaiians and Chinese, eight of ten Filipinos and haoles, and nearly seven of every ten respondents of Portuguese extraction specified the Japanese.

The survey revealed that tensions between the Hawaiians and Portuguese on one hand and the Japanese on the other were recognized explicitly by members of the first two groups. Latent hostilities between haoles and Japanese were also uncovered, although haoles were much less open than the Portuguese and Hawaiians about their feelings.

Filipino resentments toward the Japanese persisted, as was shown by intensive individual interviews.[23]

Despite opposition to Hawaiian statehood, the strategy of Delegate Jack Burns was validated in the second session of the 85th Congress when both houses voted overwhelmingly to admit Hawaii to statehood. All that remained was for the voters of the Territory to endorse the statehood bill in the June 1959 primary election. Every major group in the Islands, from the newspapers to the Hawaiian Sugar Planters' Association to the I.L.W.U., urged statehood. Not a single important political figure publicly disagreed. Statehood was no longer an academic question. The Congress of the United States had endorsed it. The voters on every major island in the Territory, despite the complex ethnic tensions intertwined with the statehood issue, overwhelmingly voted yes. The final count was seventeen to one, with prostatehood victories in every representative district, and significant antistatehood sentiment expressed only in small Portuguese and Hawaiian precincts. The only one of the Islands' 240 precincts to reject statehood was tiny Niihau, all of whose 107 registered voters were Hawaiian or part-Hawaiian. On that little island, invariably overwhelmingly Republican, Hawaiians, still trying to recapture the past, registered their protest to the final act in the absorption of Hawaii into the American Union. There, the seven out of nine voters who said no to statehood probably would have said yes to a restoration of the monarchy. But to the majority of Hawaii's citizens, justice in the Islands had finally been done.

Justice—what did it mean? For years, Hawaii's leaders had complained that it was unjust for Islanders to be excluded from first-class citizenship. Now, the peoples of Hawaii would be on an equal legal footing with their fellow citizens on the mainland. But justice within Hawaii was another issue. Statehood symbolized, but did not create, the vast changes that were taking place in the Islands' economic, political, and social systems, making it a "just" society.

There are tests of a just society: Is decision-making widely shared? Are goods and services widely distributed? Is creative talent rewarded without discrimination between sexes or among races and religions? To these questions, Hawaii could answer—with qualifications—in the affirmative, and could confidently prophesy a stronger, less-qualified yes for the future.

Was decision-making widely shared in the year of statehood in Hawaii? Within the past decade, the political system had been transformed from one-party domination to vigorous competition between two well-organized parties; the control of Hawaii's wealth had been widely dispersed; strong labor unions had been established, and competition among labor unions was increasing.

Poststatehood politics in Hawaii featured dozens of able politicians from all races actively seeking to serve the new state government. The proportion of college-educated and professionally trained candidates for state office in 1960 was probably higher than for any other state in the union. The variety of racial backgrounds of these candidates was incomparable. The Democrats, especially rich in talent, found it difficult to agree on a slate of state candidates before the June primary election. Daniel K. Inouye and others close to Jack Burns persuaded the Delegate to run for governor rather than for one of the seats in the U.S. Senate, although Burns, assured of a Senate victory, agreed reluctantly.[24] The new governor, under Hawaii's constitution, would be exceedingly powerful and would have hundreds of appointments to make. Against the popular Burns, whose statehood strategy had been vindicated, the Republicans could nominate only one man— the extremely popular appointed Governor, William F. Quinn. For lieutenant governor, Democratic primary voters chose territorial Senator Mitsuyuki Kido over Spark M. Matsunaga; for Representative, Inouye defeated Patsy Takemoto Mink; former Governor Oren E. Long and perennial mayoralty candidate Frank F. Fasi were nominated for election to the U.S. Senate. Republican strategists privately doubted that anyone could beat Inouye, but, hoping to win at least one Senate seat, they pitted Wilfred Tsukiyama against Long and former territorial Representative Hiram Fong, now a successful businessman, against Fasi. The big contest, of course, would be for the governorship. To help Quinn win among voters of Hawaiian extraction, the Big Island's county chairman and popular campaigner, James Kealoha, was matched against Kido.

The Republican Oahu county chairman, Benjamin Dillingham, worked tirelessly to regroup G.O.P. forces against the favored Democratic slate. He repeatedly criticized Burns as a captive of the I.L.W.U. and charged that his election would aid the cause of the Soviet Union and the Peiping government of China.[25] But Quinn, rather than Dillingham, sounded the major theme in the Republican campaign. Running on a liberal Republican platform, which he had helped to write, he spoke of eliminating taxes on basic foods, increasing net personal-income-tax exemptions, extending unemployment-compensation benefits, and distributing public lands on a fee-simple basis at rock-bottom prices to citizens of Hawaii. The last idea, introduced in the closing weeks of the campaign, captured the interest of hundreds of voters.[26] Quinn called it the "second mahele," after the Great Mahele of the nineteenth century, perhaps without realizing that the mid-nineteenth-century reform was viewed by Hawaiian voters as a fraud against their people. Nevertheless, Quinn and his scheme for land reform represented the desire of a growing number of Republican politicians to identify with the hopes and needs of the voters of various ethnic strains and to avoid positions and symbols that would associate them with the Republican party of the past. Among the new liberals was territorial Representative Frank Judd from Oahu's seventeenth district. Judd, whose famous great-grandfather had arrived in the Islands in 1828, bore a name that, as much as any in the Islands, was identified with the past. But he emphasized the need for the Republicans to establish a liberal record, to become the party of the people. Another missionary descendant, Ballard Atherton, president of the Hawaiian Telephone Company and former chairman of the City Charter Commission, was not a candidate for office, but he encouraged fellow Republicans to adopt a positive approach on the land question and to become sensitive to the special demands of Hawaii's ethnic groups. Hebden Porteus, popular senator from Oahu's fourth district, also decried what he called "110 percent Republicans who wanted to talk only about the devaluation of the dollar and high taxes." Porteus, an Alexander & Baldwin lawyer, helped write the liberal Republican platform planks on land and taxes, and encouraged large estates to open up more land to home owners. On Maui, plantation executive John E. Milligan joined the liberal Republican faction.[27]

When the votes were counted, these Republican liberals, including Quinn, were victorious, proving that the revolution of 1954 had far from destroyed the Republican party in Hawaii. There had never been so close an election in Hawaii's history. Individual Republicans, among them victorious Quinn, Kealoha, and Fong, showed amazing strength in Democratic districts. In addition to the governorship, lieutenant governorship, and one U.S. Senate seat, the Republicans also recaptured control of the territorial—now the state—Senate. The Democrats won a majority in the new state House of Representatives, Long defeated Tsukiyama, and Inouye won a magnificent landslide victory, to become the first American of Japanese ancestry named to the U.S. House of Representatives.

Although there is a serious question as to whether the ends of democracy are well served when power is so sharply split between the two political parties that it is difficult for the leaders of either party to be held responsible to the electorate, there could be no doubt that political power in the Islands was now fluid, that opportunities for advancement in politics were open to talent through two keenly competitive political parties.

The control of wealth and labor was still relatively concentrated compared with mainland standards, although in both sectors there was a marked tendency toward competition and a diffusion of power. The separation of ownership from control of Hawaii's major agencies actually began before the large-scale introduction of mainland capital and the rise of nonhaole entrepreneurs in the 1950's. In the twenty years between 1927 and 1946, the number of stockholders in Hawaii's ten largest corporations went up two and a half times. The tendency toward wider ownership was most marked in the Hawaiian Pineapple Company, the Hawaiian Electric Company, and in Castle & Cooke, where the number of stockholders leaped from twenty-four to 926. After the war, each of the Big Five agencies sought capital through the sale of stock to mainland and local investors, further diffusing the ownership of Hawaii's corporate wealth. But control through interlocking directorates remained a part of Hawaii's corporate structure. Despite the increased number of stockholders in Theo. H. Davies and Alexander & Baldwin, major Island businessmen agreed that only a few men holding a large proportion of outstanding stock in each firm still made the important decisions.[28] In other *kamaaina* firms, power was distributed more widely and was passing increasingly into the hands of nonowner managers from the mainland.

Labor, like industry, was highly centralized. The control of labor had passed from the oligarchy to the I.L.W.U., but automation and competition from the A.F.L.-C.I.O. were making inroads on I.L.W.U. power. Automation was driving hundreds of I.L.W.U. members from the plantations each year. The 35,000 workers in the sugar industry in 1940 had been reduced to 17,000 by 1957, and territorial Labor Department estimates indicated that there would be only 13,000 by 1961. Containerization now threatened to throw hundreds of the I.L.W.U.'s 1,600 longshoremen out of work. Regular pineapple-industry workers dropped from 16,500 workers in 1940 to a little more than 9,000 in 1957. But the number of service workers almost quadrupled during the same period, and by the year of statehood, almost 75 per cent of the jobs in the Islands were in service industries.

Those former I.L.W.U. members who remained in the Islands, Jack Hall believed, would continue to be loyal to the union. He pointed to the employees of the Honolulu Rapid Transit Company, many of whom were former longshoremen and who he believed looked to the I.L.W.U. for leadership. The future of the I.L.W.U. in Hawaii, maintained Hall, was in the service industries, particularly those connected with tourism. In the year of statehood, the 22,000-member I.L.W.U. set a goal of 3,000 new members a year for fifteen years (it fell far short of this goal in 1959–60), to be recruited from the ranks of service workers in tourism, the food industry, and the retail and garment industries. In 1959, only 738 of Local 142 members came from twelve units in the general trades outside of sugar, pineapple, and longshore activities. But Hall's organizers had already succeeded in winning ageements in such diversified businesses as the Snow White Laundry, Hawaiian Tuna Packers, Love's Bakery, Universal Motors, Simmons Mattress Company, and the Foodland Supermarket chain.[29]

The I.L.W.U.'s chief opposition until 1959 came from the federated labor group known as Unity House, under the leadership of Arthur A. Rutledge. Unity House, made up of the Teamsters Union and unions of hotel and restaurant employees and plasterers and bricklayers, was undermined by a mainland agreement between the national Teamsters and I.L.W.U. to help each other organize the Islands' service workers. In effect, this meant that the I.L.W.U. would move into areas traditionally outside its jurisdiction, but no invitations would be issued to the unions headed by Rutledge, then representing some 5,000 workers in Hawaii. Rutledge and his lieutenants could eye Hawaii's growing construction trades and hotel industry, but these preserves were now open to the I.L.W.U., with its advantages of more organizers, larger membership, and relatively stable working relationships with the Hawaii Employers Council. The national agreement limited Rutledge's power in Hawaii in a fundamental way. The Teamsters, largest of the Unity House unions, was a relatively small local in a great national union, while the I.L.W.U. in Hawaii constituted the most important local in that international union. National Teamster leadership could afford to

sacrifice Rutledge, but Hall was one of the two or three most powerful
men in the I.L.W.U.

Rutledge's position was also weakened by the fact that three of the
four Unity House unions were affiliated with the A.F.L.-C.I.O., and
their charters, like the Teamster charter, could theoretically be withdrawn from the control of the rotund, good-natured labor leader. The
A.F.L.-C.I.O. in Hawaii, embracing ninety locals and 15,000 members
in 1959, caused concern to Hall as well as to Rutledge. Both men met
the A.F.L.-C.I.O. in jurisdictional quarrels in 1958 and 1959. Rutledge
seemed to be losing his battle to organize independent building trades
against A.F.L.-C.I.O. competition. But the I.L.W.U. moved into
A.F.L.-C.I.O. territory in February 1959, becoming the largest union
among local retail-food-chain employees by winning the right to represent 235 clerks employed by the ten-store Foodland Supermarket
chain. Hall and other I.L.W.U. leaders watched warily as A.F.L.-C.I.O.
locals planned a state federation to achieve greater unity and direction
in 1960.

Even if the I.L.W.U. seemed to be holding its own in the battle to
organize the unorganized, considerable weaknesses in its vaunted political power were revealed by the 1959 and 1960 elections. Strenuously backing Burns for governor in 1959 and Richard M. Nixon for
President in 1960, Hall and his lieutenants were embarrassed when the
Islands voted for Quinn and John F. Kennedy. The Political Action
Committee of the A.F.L.-C.I.O. Central Labor Council enhanced its
prestige by actively supporting the winners in both campaigns. There
was no doubt of I.L.W.U. political power in certain outer island districts, where interviews in 1959 revealed the willingness of many in the
rank and file to accept political advice from higher-ups in the union.
"They say Kennedy does not have a good labor record," reported a
faithful union man when asked what he thought of the Massachusetts
Senator. But it was clear after these two elections that the I.L.W.U.
did not necessarily hold the balance of power in Island politics.[30]

Automation on the plantation would mean a further decline in the
I.L.W.U.'s political power. As workers moved into service industries in the cities, many would lose their identification with historic
I.L.W.U. causes. Public opinion turned against the union during its
1958 sugar strike, according to the results of a survey performed by
Robert S. Craig Associates, Honolulu's leading public-opinion organization.[31] Only a small minority of *every* ethnic group revealed pro-

union sympathies as the strike dragged on. Amazingly, a higher proportion of Filipinos and Japanese leaned toward the management view of the strike issues. By 1959, the union's demand for the abolition of the Dock Seizure Act was already a dead issue.

Hawaii's middle class continued to expand. The wealth of the Islands was shared increasingly among its citizens. Thanks to the I.L.W.U. and the new enlightenment of plantation executives, the real income of plantation laborers increased steadily throughout the 1950's. By 1957, the average daily earnings of field workers in Hawaii's sugar industry, including fringe benefits, totaled $15.63, more than twice that paid for similar work in Louisiana and more than four times the amount paid sugar workers in Puerto Rico. In 1958, Hawaiian sugar workers earned close to $17.00 per day, or more per hour than many workers in foreign sugar-producing areas earned in a day. Also extended were such benefits as vacations with pay, six paid holidays annually, sick leave, pensions for retired employees, medical and hospital care, and group life insurance.[32]

To keep pace with rising living costs, I.L.W.U. leaders called a strike of its 13,700 sugar workers on February 1, 1958. From that day until June 6, when the strike was settled, twenty-six sugar plantations throughout the Territory were crippled in what proved to be the industry's longest and most costly walkout. When the negotiations ended, the sugar industry had agreed to wage increases totaling from $5,000,-000 to $5,500,000 annually. Increases varied among the ten different grades of workers in Hawaii's sugar labor force. In the bottom grade, the increase would amount to twenty-three cents an hour by mid-1960, bringing the hourly rate to $1.35; in the top grade the boost would total thirty-five cents, to $2.13 an hour. Many workers privately acknowledged their disapproval of the strike, since the approved increases could not, in some instances, compensate for the loss of immediate pay until 1961 or 1962. And, indeed, in some respects the union had failed to achieve the objectives of the strike, since management was prepared to agree to the final terms long before the settlement was made. But plantation workers, pinched in the short run for hard cash, were guaranteed increased earnings to counter the chronic threat of inflation.

The following year, the I.L.W.U. and the pineapple industry negotiated without a strike. Although the I.L.W.U. did not achieve its goal of a union shop, substantial wage raises, ranging from thirteen cents an hour for workers in grade one to forty-one cents an hour for laborers in grade eleven over a two-year period, were won. Pineapple workers—traditionally paid more than sugar laborers—in the bottom grade would receive $1.43 an hour by February 1960.

Far more important than higher wages for Hawaii's plantation workers were the substantial improvements made in their standard of living and their increased economic independence. Whereas the cost of a minimum adequate diet for a family of four had gone up three times between 1939 and 1959, the average daily wage (not including fringe benefits) of an unskilled adult worker increased six times during the same period.[33] Impressive statistics could be mustered to show a dramatic improvement of plantation health conditions over the decades. In the early 1920's, three or four of every ten Filipino babies in the Islands died soon after birth. In 1958, fewer than twenty out of every thousand babies failed to survive their first year.[34] Most of the old plantation hospitals—only three remained—had been supplanted by community hospitals, with better facilities and an adequate number of doctors and nurses. Hawaii could probably boast the healthiest rural population of any area in the world. Gone were the inadequate, poorly staffed and equipped hospitals. Also gone were the plantation stores of old. Now, the wives of workers purchased goods from independent merchants competing freely with each other. The quality of housing varied greatly from plantation to plantation. At some camps, such as Puunene on Maui, many homes were little more than shacks; at others, like those in nearby Haliimaile, well-built plantation homes contained many modern appliances. On almost every plantation, regardless of the condition of the plantation homes, rents remained remarkably low. At one pineapple plantation on Molokai in 1959, rents were only $4.14 per month for a single man sharing a room with another worker, and $32.50 per month for a five-room house.[35] Gone, too, were the oppressive working conditions of the past. The eight-hour day had become universal both in the field and in the plantation factories. Work frequently began at six thirty in the morning and ended at three in the afternoon. At *pauhana* time, workers and their families enjoyed the recreational facilities of the plantation. In the evening, husband and wife could go to a plantation movie or visit the Filipino or Japanese clubhouse to socialize with friends.

The hierarchy of the plantation system still placed the haoles in the best jobs and in the homes on top of the hill, but nonhaole workers achieved a new self-respect and dignity in the 1950's. The arbitrary power of the *lunas* had been abolished. Grievances could now be negotiated on the basis of labor-management agreements, not personal factors.[36] The plantation manager, once the central authority on all matters of plantation life, had become a co-ordinator of activities, including welfare programs, and there were few plantation managers who did not covet a reputation as being concerned with the workers' welfare. Monthly publications of the Hawaiian Sugar Planters' Association encouraged such concern. A virtual deluge of printed matter told managers and supervisors to create confidence, rather than fear, among their workers, to think about group welfare as well as profits, and to provide psychological counseling for disturbed workers. One bulletin issued to *lunas* in the fall of 1958 urged the supervisors to do more listening and less talking to their workers.[37]

While many petty injustices still existed on the plantations, worker satisfaction, as the results of private polls revealed in 1955 and 1956, was remarkably high. In the 1955 survey, more than two thirds of the respondents believed that the plantations were trying to do everything that could reasonably be done for their workers. Especially noteworthy were the responses of union members, which varied only slightly from the nonunion responses. Among those expected to express the greatest dissatisfaction, the I.L.W.U. Filipinos, only one of every four in the sample gave a negative answer to the question "In general do you think most of the plantations are trying to do everything they reasonably can for their workers?"[38]

Even where bitterness toward and dissatisfaction with management existed, the workers proudly recognized their newly won rights. In 1959, the education service of Local 142 put into the hands of every one of its members an impressive codification of "Your Rights Under Labor Laws in Hawaii."[39] Hardly a week passed without discussion on some plantation by laborers of their "rights" to do this or that. But rights did not flow from union protection only. In 1953, a Filipino senior truck driver was discharged from his job by the Big Island's Olaa Sugar Company at the insistence of the I.L.W.U., which charged that he was "disrupting harmonious working relations." The worker appealed to the National Labor Relations Board, and four years later, the Board ruled that the man had been discharged unfairly and ordered that he be unconditionally reinstated and receive more than $11,000 in back pay. The N.L.R.B. charged that the company had been weak in submitting to pressure by the union, which desired to punish the worker for his charge that the union was discriminating against Filipinos in layoff plans owing to mechanization. In fairness to both the company and the union, they argued that the man was fired because he had stirred up Filipinos against Japanese on the plantation. Regardless of the issue, in the new Hawaii, the rights of the individual could be protected even against a combined power of union and plantation.[40]

The wages of skilled and unskilled laborers in Hawaii not employed by the plantations did not compare favorably with those on the mainland. Typists, carpenters, electricians, and truck drivers could earn more in most mainland communities, but the construction and tourist boom, which continued in Hawaii even during the mainland recession of 1960–61, narrowed the gap. At the height of the boom, annual median family incomes in Honolulu jumped substantially. The largest increase, $800, came in 1956 and 1957, and by 1960, more than half of all Honolulu's families had incomes of close to $6,000.[41] While wages lagged behind mainland standards, a majority of Hawaii's employers adopted various employee-benefit plans. A 1958 study revealed that health-insurance plans were available to 97 per cent of the employees in a large sample of firms. Pension plans were available to 67 per cent, life-insurance plans to 68 per cent, and deferred profit-sharing programs were offered to 15 per cent of the employees in these firms.[42] Four years earlier, the Craig survey on worker satisfaction showed that remarkably few of Hawaii's citizens (less than 10 per cent of the Orientals) said "no" when asked "Do you think most of the companies in Honolulu are doing everything they reasonably can for their workers?"

Despite the increase in employee-benefit plans among private companies, paternalism as Hawaii had known it was dead. The new managers of Hawaii's economy supported industrial and welfare legislation comparable to that adopted in the most advanced states on the mainland. In the year of statehood, the legislative committee of Honolulu's Chamber of Commerce, opposing an I.L.W.U. plan that would provide unemployment-compensation benefits for seasonal agricultural workers, made a counterproposal to raise the maximum benefits to two thirds of the average wage of all workers covered by the law, or approximately $45. The Chamber also suggested extending the duration of benefits from twenty to twenty-six weeks.

The distribution of wealth in a community results in part from its system of taxation. In Hawaii, tax problems dominated every legislative session between 1947 and 1957, until the issue of land reform replaced that of tax reform as the major political problem in the Islands.

A large proportion of the revenues needed to govern the Territory came from consumption taxes, which inevitably fell hardest on the less well to do. Hawaii's traditional income tax—persisting with modifications until 1955—was unusually regressive. It provided for a flat 2 per cent tax on gross income from salaries and dividends and a slightly graduated net income tax applied to earnings from self-employment, ranging from 3 per cent on taxable income under $5,000 to 6 per cent on all amounts over $100,000. Actually, no one paid more than 4.5 per cent, since deductible federal income taxes limited the amount taxable by the Territory for citizens in the upper bracket. Big business was also helped by the failure of the Territory to tax capital gains unless realized in the normal course of business. A general tax reform bill was passed by the Democratic legislature in 1955 providing for comprehensive graduated net income taxes and for amendments to other important territorial tax laws. Governor King's veto was sustained, preventing the measure from becoming law, and a ten-year cumulative deficit in the Territory's general funds reached $6,500,000 by the end of 1956.

Finally, in 1957, the legislature mustered enough votes to override a gubernatorial veto and passed a law providing for graduated income taxes on salaries and income from dividends, abolishing the flat 2 per cent levy which made no distinction between a $20,000 income from stock dividends and a $2,000 salary as a clerk. Other revenue-producing measures included an increase in two major insurance-tax rates, the adoption of a new income tax on savings-and-loan associations and banks, an advance on specific excises on tobacco, liquor, and public utilities, an upward revision of inheritance-tax rates, and an upward adjustment of ceilings on property taxes. Revision of the general excise or gross income tax, as it is called in Hawaii, was also passed. This unusual tax—nothing quite comparable existed on the mainland—continued to provide the largest source of revenue for the territorial government and its four counties. Under the new law, rates on production, manufacturing, and wholesaling were lowered, while the rates on retailing increased from 2.5 to 3.5 per cent, thereby giving Republican politicians their best single issue in the 1958 campaign. The Democrats, they could charge, had increased the gross income tax on retailers, who invariably passed the tax on to the consumers. Whatever name—general excise or gross income—was given to this tax, many voters viewed it as a sales tax that increased the cost of food and other basic commodities.

According to Professor Robert M. Kamins, tax expert and economics professor at the University of Hawaii, it was not always true that the general excise tax on wholesaling, processing, and retailing was shifted to the consumer. The processing tax on sugar, for example, probably was not passed on because of the relative weakness of Hawaii's sugar industry in the total world market. On the other hand, the tax on canning pineapple, whose markets are not controlled by the national government, and whose position in the world market was pre-eminent, probably did increase the price paid by the consumer. Large food chains undoubtedly increased prices to absorb the retail excise tax, while small stores and restaurants frequently did not. Many doctors, lawyers, and other professional men passed their gross-income-tax charge on to their clients, although others, probably a minority, scrupulously followed the spirit of the law.

The 1957 law also revised Hawaii's system of income taxes. The new system was patterned after federal income-tax legislation. Administered on a pay-as-you-go basis, it provided for taxation on income regardless of source from 3 per cent on the first $500 of taxable income to 9 per cent on amounts over $30,000. The new system hit the wealthier citizens of Hawaii harder than ever before by including capital gains and not providing for the deduction of federal taxes, as well as by increasing the rates along a more sharply graduated scale.

Hawaii's taxes were high, and Hawaii's Small Business Association complained that pyramiding excise taxes would discourage new industry; others pointed out that high income taxes would close the door to retired investors. Hawaii's Tax Foundation, looking at the fat surplus accumulated in the Territory's general funds by the end of 1959, called for a further reduction of the gross income tax on manufacturing, producing, and wholesaling.[43] There were undoubtedly inequities in Hawaii's tax system. Small retailers, unable to avoid payment of wholesale taxes by purchasing on the mainland, competed with larger retail establishments at a disadvantage. There were also sharp deficiencies in Hawaii's real-property tax. In the forty-nine mainland states in 1958, real-property taxes accounted for an average of 34 per cent of total tax revenue, while in Hawaii, comparable taxes amounted to only

14 per cent of the Territory's income from taxes. The state's tax structure would undoubtedly require revision in the 1960's, but the new individual and corporate income taxes of the '50's and other tax changes reflected Hawaii's adoption of the progressive mainland principal of ability to pay.

Increased agitation over Hawaii's property tax reflected the growing concern of thousands of Islanders for land reform, frequently called "the most important piece of unfinished business in Hawaii." Agitation for land reform, created primarily by Hawaii's growing middle class, was manifest in three related proposals: higher taxes on big landholders; forcing land into its most productive use; and opening land for homesites on a fee-simple basis.

The land problem in Hawaii stemmed from two basic sources, one physical and the other political. More than one third of the land in the Territory and more than one half of the land on Oahu has more than 10 per cent slope, making it extremely difficult to use for crops or communities. If geography made land precious, historical circumstances made it more so. Nowhere in the United States was the ownership of land so concentrated as in the Islands. In Hawaii, thousands of families owned houses on land leased from estates or trusts, and large investments made by businesses included buildings and equipment to be operated on leased land.

In 1959, the new state government owned 32 per cent of all the land in Hawaii; the federal government nearly 8 per cent; the Hawaiian Homes Commission 2.5 per cent; and twelve private landholders owned 30 per cent. Other smaller property owners could claim only 27 per cent of the land. The biggest private owner was a charitable trust, the Bishop estate, whose 363,000 acres was more than the area possessed by the next two largest owners combined, Richard S. Smart, owner of the huge Parker Ranch on the Big Island, and the Damon estate. In all, twelve large private landholders—actually only eleven, since the Robinson family owned two estates—controlled 52 per cent of all the private lands in Hawaii in the year of statehood.[44] The estate that Mrs. Bernice Pauahi Bishop left in 1884, then valued at $300,000, was worth $62,000,000 by 1959, and it alone accounted for nearly 16 per cent of all privately owned lands in the Territory. Its holdings were especially important on Oahu, where they constituted 22 per cent of all private land on the island, and where the pressure for homesites and land for industrial use was greatest. The Bishop and Campbell estates owned 40 per cent of the private land on Oahu, and over one fourth of the entire island.

Except for a short period under Governor McCarthy, territorial taxes on real property were virtually determined by the largest property owners. Prior to 1932, the legislature limited the amount that could be collected in any county within a given year by stipulating a maximum rate to be applied against assessed real and personal property. Both assessments and the maximum rate were remarkably low by mainland standards. In 1925, for example, property taxes in Honolulu could be imposed only up to 1.5 per cent of assessed values.[45] In 1932, the legislature changed the basis on which property taxes would be collected by placing a ceiling on the total amount of tax revenue that could be levied against property in any county. The effect of the ceiling, despite the fact that it was increased repeatedly by the legislature during the next twenty-five years, was to reduce revenues from property taxes. The pre-1932 level of revenues was not regained until 1948, despite the tremendous increase in land values. Theoretically, the tax base expanded, but because of dollar ceilings, revenues were kept low, and the rates actually went down. For example, the assessed valuation for the city and county of Honolulu between 1945 and 1956 rose from $147,-000,000 to almost $774,000,000, but because of dollar ceilings, the tax rate fell from $27.26 to $10.74 per thousand. Assessed valuation went up almost five times, the tax rate was more than cut in half, and revenue from property taxes merely doubled.

On the outer islands, these tax anomalies favoring large landholdings were even more striking. Because of dollar ceilings and rising land values, tax rates were sharply cut during the early 1950's. In many cases, the practical effect was to reduce the amount of money paid by large landholders and plantations despite the land boom. The value of the land held by the Ewa plantation on Oahu between 1948 and 1956 doubled, but the annual tax bill went from a little less than $79,000 to only a little over $52,000. The value of the 27,000 acres of the Wailuku Sugar Company on Maui almost doubled between 1951 and 1956, but property taxes were reduced by almost one fourth. On the Big Island, the value of the Hilo Sugar Company's lands increased approximately one and a half times between 1943 and 1956, but the amount of taxes paid was reduced by one half.

The Democratic legislature attempted to raise real-property taxes in 1955, but was stopped by Governor King's veto. In 1957, the legislature succeeded in abolishing the ceiling on revenues and went back to the old system of a fixed rate of $18 per thousand of assessed valuation. The change merely whetted the appetite of the exponents of land reform, who claimed that antiquated methods of assessment still favored the large landholders.

Primarily interested in increasing the tax base to secure new revenues to meet the increased costs of government, the Democratic Board of Supervisors and the Republican Mayor of Honolulu hired John J. Hulten, a professional appraiser, to investigate territorial assessment policies. Governor Quinn had already employed a Chicago firm, the Public Administration Service, to analyze territorial tax-assessment procedures for him. Both reports, published in 1958, helped the reformers. Hulten, whose analysis was tainted in the eyes of many by virtue of his own Democratic candidacy for the territorial legislature in 1958, analyzed 3,558 parcels of land on the island of Oahu with a market value of $77,600,000, which he found to be assessed at only 40.4 per cent instead of the 70 per cent required by territorial law. More significantly, perhaps, a check of all vacant-land sales in 1956 showed that parcels under one acre were assessed at 49 per cent of market value, while those of ten acres or more were at 30.9 per cent. The big owners, Hulten charged, were favored in every respect.[46] Hulten also maintained that up to 1956, the owners of large ranch, sugar, and pineapple lands virtually assessed their own property. The assessor's office sought advice from committees representing the industries with respect to the value of their land. Although the committee system was dropped after 1956, the assessors continued to rely on the income of individual sugar plantations as the principal criterion in making land assessments. Hulten said that often property taxes were not an actual expense to large property holders, since they were able to pass tax costs on to developers. He also found that the city was losing money because of the Territory's practice of licensing persons to use territorial land and exempting them from taxes, instead of leasing the land. Hardest hit by the Hulten report was the Territory's largest landowner, the Bishop estate. According to Hulten, the estate rejected a $2,740,000 offer for twenty-five acres of land in the Kapalama region, near downtown Honolulu, in 1957. Yet the property was only assessed at $765,619. Hulten also cited the Damon estate's sale of 1,000 acres in the Salt Lake area adjacent to Honolulu at $9,650 per acre, property that had been assessed at only $184 per acre.

According to Hulten, there was no fundamental dishonesty in the tax assessor's office, but the assessors, understaffed and badly organized, failed to keep up with changing values of property not up for sale. Property taxes in suburban areas and on other newly improved property were relatively high because assessors kept track of transactions and were able to estimate current market values with a greater degree of accuracy than for land or improved property kept off the market.

Quinn sharply criticized the Hulten report as politically motivated, but one month later, in October 1958, the report of the Public Administration Service confirmed some of Hulten's major findings. One of these, that the assessor's office had not been doing the job assigned to it by the 1957 law to assess property for tax purposes according to its market value and according to its highest and best use, was the major criticism of the report. The report found the assessment of "fee simple urban property of low or moderate value" to be efficient and equitable, but assessments on "urban vacant land, commercial property, sugar and pineapple plantations and . . . ranch properties" were frequently low. In those areas, the difference between assessment and market value "increases in a regular pattern," stated the Chicago firm.[47] The Public Administration Service urged territorial assessors to devise a comprehensive classification for judging the potential use of land. Already at work on the problem of classification was the University of Hawaii's Land Study Bureau, created by the territorial legislature to make basic land-classification and utilization studies for the entire Territory. Stressing that property assessments in Hawaii were better than in most mainland jurisdictions, the Chicago experts nonetheless backstopped Hulten's recommendation to bring the assessment of undeveloped and underdeveloped land up to the same level as that for property put to its highest and best use.

"Highest and best use" was a goal that politicians and landholders could agree on. The question was how to achieve it. From the point of view of large trusts and estates, the highest and best use of land during the Islands' land boom might be to withhold it from the market. Since assessment practices regarding such land were favorable to large owners and since the value of most land would continue to increase rapidly, there were good reasons not to sell. A major deterrent to land sales was the large federal tax on net income from such sales. A plank in the 1958 Republican platform called for amendment of federal tax laws or special dispensation for large landholders to, as Republican party

Chairman Ed Bryan put it, "help the big land owner help himself." Leading land-reform Democrats, adopting an approach that Republicans called "oppressive and confiscatory," called for new assessment procedures based on a thorough reclassification and rezoning of nonproductive property. Assessors would decide when unproductive land was ready for conversion to a higher use and subject landowners to a steeply graduated annual levy until the land was sold. Another forceful measure proposed by Democrats would limit the portion of an estate's assets that could be held in land, obliging it to sell holdings exceeding the legal limit. To achieve the first goal, a Democratic party bill was passed by the territorial House of Representatives in 1959 that would have transferred the functions of assessment from the Territory to the counties, giving each county power to set its own tax rate. Vigorously opposed by Hawaii's businessmen and Republican leaders, the bill was modified in the Senate through a resolution to permit individual counties—like any taxpayer—to appeal tax assessments through a resolution adopted by the Board of Supervisors. The bill also prohibited under any circumstances the use of the formulas of private owners in arriving at fair market values for real property, a blow at the system by which territorial assessors relied on special scales prepared by the sugar and pineapple industries and ranches.

The bill was vetoed by Governor Quinn, who argued that it would be a step backward to bring the counties into the tax assessments. But Quinn signed into law another proposal, which he had espoused early in the legislative session, creating a Hawaii Land Development Authority for Oahu, an agency empowered to declare a development area of not less than twenty-five acres for residential purposes, and to acquire property for that purpose through negotiations or eminent-domain proceedings.

Governor Stainback had proposed a Hawaii Home Development Authority in 1945 similar to the one created fourteen years later. Stainback, pointing out that the federal government and the 100 largest landowners in the Islands held 92.3 per cent of the Territory's land, wanted to endow the Authority with a $2,000,000 loan to force the sale of idle lands. The proposal, labeled "Communistic" by its opponents, including the Honolulu *Advertiser,* was defeated in the legislature.[48]

By 1959, the demand for homesites by Hawaii's growing middle class was far greater than it had been during Stainback's administration. The largest single user of land in the Islands continued to be the Territory's forest reserve. The next two largest users were the military and the sugar industry. The fourth-largest category of real estate in the Islands was unimproved land.[49] So little land was available for residential purposes that by 1950 the density of population on Oahu had reached 600 persons per square mile, making Oahu as crowded as Japan and Puerto Rico. In 1958, a land-use consultant for the territorial Planning Office predicted that 22,000 additional acres of Oahu land would be needed for urban, as opposed to agricultural, expansion in the next twenty years.[50]

The 1959 land-reform bill was aimed specifically at putting more fee-simple lots on the market for would-be homeowners. It was less extreme than the legislation sponsored by Democratic land-reform champion Thomas P. Gill, which would have required Hawaii's sixty landowners with 5,000 acres or more to declare every year, under oath, what they considered the fair value of their land, such declarations constituting an automatic offer to sell the land to the government at that value plus 25 per cent. Gill's proposal would have allowed the territorial Tax Office to use the declarations as the basis for assessing the land, thus combining both approaches to land reform, higher assessments, and the right of purchase by the government. Also eliminated from the law under Gill's proposal was an early provision that would have allowed the Development Authority to purchase or condemn private lands and use them for commercial or agricultural purposes.

The measure as passed empowered a group of five gubernatorially appointed commissioners plus four other state officials to contract with a private developer for financing the acquisition of lands, subdivisions, and developments, but limited the developer to a maximum 15 per cent profit. Disposal of acquired land to individual buyers could be on either a fee-simple or leasehold basis, the latter policy to be followed where land costs were high. The lessee would acquire an option to purchase at any time.

The creation of the Hawaii Land Development Authority and threats to pass more radical land-reform bills put Hawaii's large estates and trusts on the defensive. Damon estate spokesman Dudley C. Lewis asked that landowners be permitted to sell voluntarily without coercion.[51] The Bishop estate moved to extend leaseholds, opening land for residential development in rural and suburban Oahu. In 1959, a $10,000,000 fee-simple residential development in upper Manoa Valley was announced by American Factors. Several sugar plantations announced plans for major home-ownership programs. At Kohala on the Big Island, plantation management offered to give 200 lots of 15,000 square feet each free to employees who could arrange the financing.

The major Republican answer to Democratic land-reform agitation was Governor Quinn's 1959 campaign promise to sell territorial lands for homesites at $50 an acre. Despite Democratic charges that Quinn's offer was unrealistic because of the scarcity of usable territorial lands, the issue proved popular with land-hungry Islanders. Although Quinn's "second mahele" was bottled up in the 1960 state legislature, variations of the Quinn idea were under constant discussion and study.

Major landholders were not alone in opposing land-reform efforts that would force sales on a fee-simple basis. Twenty-two per cent of the Hawaiians and part-Hawaiians in a large 1958 sample of voters from all the major islands said it would be a bad thing to break up the large estates; another 25 per cent were undecided. Many Hawaiians were obviously concerned about the impact of land reform on the Bishop estate, whose proceeds were earmarked for the support of the Kamehameha Schools. Economists and politicians argued that the Bishop estate might profitably invest income from sales to produce greater revenue than that received from leaseholds, but a substantial proportion of Hawaiians were worried that the sale of land would jeopardize the schools. Small farmers and businessmen on Oahu frequently preferred to rent rather than to own land, and interviews revealed their concern over policies and programs that might ultimately force them to buy the expensive land under their feet in order to remain in business. Most farmers could not operate profitably if obliged to pay market prices for land, and many poultry, hog, and dairy farmers on Oahu would be forced to relocate on leased land rather than purchase the land they now worked. To meet these demands, territorial Land Commissioner Frank W. Hustace, Jr., unveiled in 1958 a plan to lease territorial lands to small farmers on a long-term basis.[52]

In 1958, almost one fourth of the houses in rural Oahu, as well as about one ninth in Honolulu proper, were on leased lands, and there were undoubtedly many homeowners who preferred to continue to lease the land under their homes rather than purchase it outright and add substantially to the cost of homeownership.

Homeownership as well as landownership would probably spread slowly in the 1960's, although the percentage of owner-occupied units of the total number of dwelling units actually dropped slightly in the year of statehood. But the pattern would break down as developments on leased land sprung up on former ranch lands, unimproved land, and farm areas. Now, too, the pressure to break up the large estates and redistribute the ownership of Hawaii's land was mounting. Wealth, in all forms—including land—was more widely shared in 1960 than ever before in Hawaii's modern history.

A just society, while distributing power and wealth widely, also rewards talent without discrimination against sex or race. Although opportunity for the development of talent in Hawaii for all peoples was far greater even under the oligarchy than in most other areas of the world, there were still, in the forty years prior to Pearl Harbor, special obstacles for nonhaoles. The one major exception had been the schools, where, despite the inferiority of rural schools, the English Standard system, and the great distinctions made between Hawaii's private and public schools, talent was nurtured and developed by devoted teachers and school administrators without distinction among ethnic groups. Now, in the year of statehood, educational opportunities for Hawaii's children were greater than ever before. Whereas only 40.1 per cent of the Islands' sixteen- and seventeen-year-olds were attending high school in 1920, 85.8 per cent of that age group were in school thirty years later.[53] Although attendance beyond the age of fifteen was not compulsory, 81.8 per cent of Filipino adolescents of sixteen and seventeen were in school in 1950, compared with only 17.6 per cent in 1920. Percentage increases were not as dramatic for other groups, but in the year of statehood, better than nine out of every ten Americans of Oriental ancestry in the Islands in the sixteen- to seventeen-year-old group went to high school. And the drive for education for many of these boys and girls did not stop at high school. Between 1954 and 1958, the proportion of Hawaii's high-school graduates planning higher education went from 46 to 59 per cent.[54] When National Science Foundation fellowships were awarded in 1959, six of them went to graduate students from Hawaii—four of Japanese descent, one of Chinese origin, and the sixth a haole. Three of every five students planning to continue their education hoped to attend universities, colleges, or junior colleges, the remainder to go to trade, technical, and other schools. The private high schools still sent proportionately more graduates to college than the public schools, but the gap was narrowing.

The public still believed that education in the private schools was superior to that in the public institutions, a reflection of the dual school system carried on in Hawaii even after the disintegration of the Islands' dual class system. A 1958 public-opinion survey found 57 per cent of the large sample of respondents agreeing that their children could get a better education in private than in public schools, while only 16 per cent chose public schools, and the others were unable to decide or asserted that it made no difference.[55]

Most of Hawaii's high-school graduates planned to continue their education in the Islands. For many, the transportation and living costs involved in a mainland education were prohibitive. By 1959, the University of Hawaii had 6,000 full-time students, and experts predicted that by 1975, student enrollment would increase twofold, creating the demand for a vast expansion of University facilities. The University of Hawaii regents had already gone on record as favoring branches of the University in more remote areas of the Islands, and one University branch at Hilo was well established by the year of statehood.

What did the new business leadership of Hawaii think of this drive for higher education? A governor's committee chaired by Malcolm MacNaughton, then executive vice-president of Castle & Cooke, and with James Shoemaker, then vice-president of the Bank of Hawaii, as vice-chairman highly approved.[56] The attitude of the MacNaughton committee, as revealed by its January 1959 report, was completely different from that advanced by the famous Prosser report in 1930. Rather than proposing a cut in opportunities for higher education, MacNaughton's group argued for the expansion of the University of Hawaii, the development of community colleges, and large-scale public expenditures to improve the quality and increase the size of public higher education in the Islands. In words completely contradicting the *kamaaina* business leadership of the 1930's, the MacNaughton committee argued for the advancement of knowledge for its own sake as well as to raise the material and cultural level of the community. Education should fire the imagination and ambition of students, maintained the committee, because "education . . . creates values that can never be measured in dollars and cents." Good education was costly, the study group warned, and called for the doubling of faculty salaries by 1968 as well as a substantial building program to accommodate increased enrollments.

Not all was well with Hawaii's schools, and the Department of Public Instruction came under constant criticism from study groups, the Parent-Teacher Association, and individual citizens. Behind most criticisms was the traditional failure of Hawaii's legislature to provide adequate funds for basic school services. A major study, filling five volumes, prepared by a Stanford University survey team in 1958 called for an additional appropriation for an enlarged school program, but Department of Public Instruction commissioners were given a much lower budget ceiling for the expansion of present services. Political leaders denounced the antiquated system of fees for special courses, student activities, library use, art supplies, and even hot showers, but were unwilling or unable to appropriate sufficient money to destroy this anachronistic fee system. To supplement inadequate budgets, local P.T.A.'s continued fund-raising programs on a scale not known on the mainland, where "free" public education meant just that. Hawaii's 5,000 teachers received relatively low salaries compared with good mainland standards, and high student-teacher ratios (32:1) resulted in crowded classrooms and heavy work loads.

Harried legislatures, even more concerned about the rapid increase of enrollments at all levels of Hawaii's public schools, would probably be unable to find the funds to improve existing conditions. In 1959, the Department of Public Instruction requested a six-year capital-improvement program which would cost the Territory more than $50,000,000 for the city and county of Honolulu alone. Public education in Hawaii was expensive, but there were few in the Islands who doubted its value, and although nonhaoles were the chief beneficiaries of the public system, 60 per cent of the haoles responding in a 1958 survey of opinion—more than any other group—believed that teachers' salaries were too low.[57]

Whatever the economic constraints on education in Hawaii, there was room for all of Hawaii's children in the public schools. But equality of opportunity in kindergarten did not necessarily mean there was room at the top. In June 1959, territorial official Jack Mizuha, speaking before a reunion of the 100th Battalion, charged that haole firms still placed rigid limits on opportunities for nonhaoles in the business community. In the beautiful conference rooms of the major factors, haole executives shook their heads in dismay. They admitted that they could not conceive of putting a nonhaole into the presidency or executive vice-presidency of one of the major firms in the near future. But this was not because of racial discrimination, they were quick to point out. The men at the very top must be good front men, articulate, knowledgeable about mainland business conditions, and rich in mainland financial and business contacts. Nonhaoles with such qualifications would be considered for the top posts, but even then there would be problems. Could a nonhaole fulfill the social obligations of a top executive? Visiting executives from the mainland expected to be entertained at exclusive social and athletic clubs; reciprocal entertainment on the mainland was also expected. At a group interview with the top staff officials of one of the major *kamaaina* sugar agencies, haole executives explained that they were trying to encourage nonhaole talent to move into important assignments, but that there were obstacles which were difficult to overcome. They pointed to nonhaoles who were promoted in *kamaaina* haole firms and then found it difficult to exercise discipline over haoles below them. In some cases, nonhaoles thus promoted were subjected to ridicule by friends in their own social group. The extreme sensitivity of nisei to criticism from Japanese friends who accused them of selling out to the haoles caused considerable psychological difficulty for at least one capable agency employee, according to a top company official. It was also pointed out that able young executives were recruited away from haole firms by Hiram Fong, Chinn Ho, and other enterprising nonhaole businessmen.[58]

Despite these limitations, many nonhaoles did move into positions of influence in the business community of postwar Hawaii. In addition to the appointments of Chinn Ho as a trustee to the Robinson estate and Hung Wo Ching to the board of directors of the Bank of Hawaii, other Americans of Oriental extraction were named to the boards of *kamaaina* haole firms. In the year of statehood, Robert Y. Sato, a graduate of McKinley High School and president of a local clothing firm, became the first non-Caucasian to serve on the board of Hawaii's biggest private employer, the Hawaiian Pineapple Company. Twenty-five years before statehood, the Honolulu Chamber of Commerce did not employ a single nonhaole, but by 1959, approximately half of the staff were nonhaoles. Nisei and sansei, in the Japanese pattern, were reluctant to put themselves forward, and it was sometimes extremely difficult to convince them to serve in posts traditionally reserved for haoles. A Chamber of Commerce official explained that seventeen Americans of Oriental extraction had refused positions on the board of the Chamber of Commerce in 1958. But positions were opening, although top Oriental businessmen sometimes called them "window dressing."[59]

Between kindergarten and top-policy positions in *kamaaina* firms, there was increasing mobility. While the 1950 census showed that there were proportionately more haoles in preferred positions than any other group, the gap between haoles and Orientals was closing. Indeed, the proportion of haoles classified as professionals had decreased between 1930 and 1950, while the proportion of Chinese had nearly tripled and that of the Filipinos and Japanese doubled.[60] Outside of the professions, job satisfaction among all of Hawaii's ethnic groups was generally high. A comprehensive 1955 public-opinion survey revealed that a majority in each group believed that "the average worker in Hawaii has a good chance to get ahead in his job." The majority agreed even in the lowest-income groups of Filipino and Japanese respondents.[61]

By mainland standards, the Chinese—next to the haoles—continued to be the most successful of Hawaii's immigrant groups. The median annual income of the Chinese surpassed that of the Caucasians by more than $100 a year by 1950. The Chinese desire to acquire and furnish homes provided much of the impetus behind land-reform proposals. When a territorial auction of nearly 500,000 square feet of land in upper Makiki Heights was held in February 1951, twenty-four of the thirty-four successful bidders of lots costing up to $16,500 were of Chinese descent.[62] The drive to own large expensive homes in the best sections of the city was matched by the interest of Chinese women in expensive clothes and jewelry. At a meeting of the United Chinese Society in September 1956, Hung Wo Ching chided his fellow Chinese for going soft.[63] He complained that conspicuous consumption had replaced the unleashing of creative talent as the primary goal of third- and fourth-generation Americans of Chinese ancestry. He warned against using education as a vehicle for accumulating status and wealth rather than for its own sake and for creative innovation. Whatever the motives behind the Chinese drive for education, it continued well into the third generation. According to the 1950 census, 8.8 per cent of the Chinese twenty-five years and over had completed a college education, compared with 3 per cent of the Japanese, 2.4 per cent of the Hawaiians and part Hawaiians, and .3 per cent of the Filipinos.[64] By 1950, one of every ten lawyers and one of every five medical doctors and dentists in the Territory were of Chinese descent, although the Chinese constituted only 7 per cent of the population of the Islands.[65]

Increased wealth and occupational status for the Chinese did not mean extensive social intermingling with haoles. A Chinese citizen might be chosen to the University of Hawaii's Board of Regents or as commander of the American Legion or governor of the Lions International of Hawaii, but the social life of the Chinese, even to the third and fourth generations, remained largely segregated. This was partly because the Chinese were not yet invited to join exclusive social organizations such as the Oahu Country Club, the Outrigger Canoe Club, and the famed Pacific Club, but it was also because many third- and fourth-generation Chinese enjoyed the company of their own group. At gala parties of the American-Chinese Club and the Hawaii Chinese Civic Association, young Chinese business and professional men and their wives found pleasure in recounting shared experiences which gave rise to special "Chinese-American humor" as well as cultural and economic interests. Indeed, at a deeper level, third- and fourth-generation Chinese, secure as Americans, were trying, as nearly all immigrant groups do, to recapture something of their ancestral culture, even as their parents, rushing to adapt to American ways, tried to forget elements of their background. Gone were the interminable conflicts between dialect and geographic groups. Gone, too, was the need of immigrant group organizations to strive for civil and economic rights. What remained was a romantic affection and sometimes intellectual interest in their Chinese heritage.

The Chinese Civic Association, organized in 1925, had fought against the English Standard schools and legislation directed against Chinese economic interests. Now, in the year of statehood, the Association sponsored the tenth annual Narcissus Coronation Ball, at which a Chinese maiden was crowned queen. The Association also participated in an international fashion show, sponsored the Mandarin Ball, and gave an annual Chinese dramatic production. There were serious objectives for the Association, too—providing scholarships for the University of Hawaii, encouraging naturalization for older Chinese, and assisting the Boy Scouts of America—but the days of struggle for recognition and protection had passed. What had not passed, and what was renewed and refreshed, was the desire of young Americans of Chinese descent to maintain their Chinese identification. Acculturation to the dominant social, political, and economic mores of America did not mean the obliteration of Chinese group cohesiveness for social and sometimes economic and political purposes. The late 1950's saw expanded activity on the part of major Chinese social and civic groups, including the first territory-wide Chinese convention, sponsored by the United Chinese Society. There was also new interest in Buddhism, as the two Chinese Buddhist temples in Honolulu enlarged their membership.

Of course, Chinese and Japanese Buddhist services in Hawaii resembled American Christian services much more than they did in the Orient. Choirs and lengthy sermons, not used in the East, were a part of Chinese Buddhist services in the Islands. Traditional Buddhism was compromised in other ways to interest segments of the younger Chinese population already curious about the ancient Eastern religion.[66]

Japanese group cohesiveness was not manifest in a return to Buddhism. Although approximately 70 per cent of the Japanese population in the Islands remained Buddhist, and efforts were made to make Buddhism increasingly attractive to younger Americans of Japanese ancestry through the creation of Young Buddhist Associations, the proportion of Japanese who were religiously unidentified or who converted to one of the Christian religions was increasing.[67] But many nisei and sansei, following the typical pattern of immigrant acculturation, showed a reawakened interest in things Japanese. "I am anxious to know more about my background," said one of Hawaii's best-known sansei.[68] This mainland-educated American of Japanese ancestry, bright, articulate, ambitious, and accepted by his haole friends, sent his children to Japanese-language schools and was pleased when Governor Quinn signed legislation repealing restrictions on those schools in 1959. A successful businessman whose customers were primarily haoles, he felt secure enough to examine his cultural heritage. A sansei friend who graduated from Punahou in the early 1940's and who was probably as comfortable with haole business associates as any American of Japanese ancestry in Hawaii, proudly described the revival and expansion of Japanese-language schools.[69] When it was proposed to abandon the Japanese Chamber of Commerce, he and his friends overwhelmingly rejected the implicit assumption that continuation of the Japanese Jaycee was incompatible with Americanism. In fact, young nisei steadily joined the Honolulu Japanese Chamber of Commerce during the 1950's, and an all-nisei slate was elected to lead the organization in the year of statehood.

Copying the Chinese pattern, representatives of fifty Japanese organizations met in June 1958 to launch the United Japanese Society of Hawaii. Additional groups, with a total membership of more than

30,000, were expected to join in promoting American-Japanese friendship, aiding aged Japanese, and protecting the rights and privileges of the Japanese community. The new society, born in part as a result of the dissatisfaction of many Japanese with the election results in the Chamber of Commerce, also symbolized the growing desire of hundreds of Americans of Japanese ancestry for an all-Japanese civic society which would cut across the interests of businessmen, veterans, and religious groups.

The organization of this new Island-wide Japanese society and Japanese participation in the political and economic life of the Islands through the formation of Japanese banks and businesses clearly indicated that acculturation to American ways did not mean the loss of group identity. The Japanese would undoubtedly follow the Chinese in becoming less militant concerning civil and political rights as the years passed, but group cohesiveness would express itself in different ways, even to the third, fourth, and fifth generations. Added to the list of major Island pageants in the 1950's was the Cherry Blossom Festival, a ten-day celebration reviving Japanese sports, formal tea ceremonies, and folk dancing as well as the traditional selection of a young queen and costumed court from among Honolulu's most attractive girls of Japanese ancestry.

The Japanese of Hawaii had already arrived, and, as one politician put it, "were feeling their oats." But for the Filipinos of Hawaii, the struggle to prevent economic discrimination and to achieve recognition in politics was just beginning. The nearly 70,000 Filipinos in Hawaii in 1959 were just emerging from the first phase of immigrant adjustment. Almost 24,000 of them remained aliens, and of these, approximately 500 to 600 a year were being repatriated to the Philippines. Although there were almost twice as many Filipinos as Chinese in Hawaii, the Filipinos, as the last major immigrant group to come to the Islands, controlled less of the wealth of Hawaii than any other important group. In spite of the fact that Filipinos constituted more than half of the laborers on the sugar and pineapple plantations of the Islands and held key posts in I.L.W.U. Local 142, there was undoubted discrimination against them on many plantations. At a plantation meeting on Molokai in 1959, several Filipino workmen asserted that haoles and Japanese in superior positions discriminated against the Filipinos. One haole student of another pineapple plantation wrote that in the promotion system "there is not the slightest doubt that the haole will be chosen" in competition with a Filipino.[70]

Discrimination against Filipinos in employment in Honolulu and other cities continued throughout the 1950's, although it was probably not nearly as widespread as claimed by Filipino respondents in interviews. Extremely proud and sensitive, Filipinos recoiled at every slight, real or imagined. But, in the tradition of other immigrant groups, they glorified every achievement of their more successful countrymen. By the year of statehood, there were five practicing lawyers, six medical doctors, three engineers, and many Filipino teachers in Hawaii, each a source of community pride. A Filipino column, reintroduced by the Honolulu *Star Bulletin* in 1959, reported the scholarships of Filipino college students, the prizes of those in high school, and the appointments of Filipino-Americans to positions in community and civic organizations.

Impending statehood undoubtedly quickened Filipino unity in Hawaii. Consul General Juan Dionisio used the excuse of statehood to organize Filipino community councils on every island for the purpose of furthering the political, economic, and social aims of Filipinos in Hawaii. Dionisio, mindful of divisions between Visayan, Tagalog, and Ilocano dialect groups, maintained, "The Filipinos here must first achieve unity through a common identification before they can be successfully integrated into the community." Leaders of the Filipino community movement—a police official, a lawyer, a labor leader, and a businessman—agreed. As one of them put it, discrimination against Filipinos in economic and political life would continue into the second generation unless the Filipinos were organized.[71] The internal tensions, bickering, and demoralization so characteristic of the first phase of immigrant adjustment were giving way to increasing group cohesiveness, forged through militant demands for protection of rights and recognition of claims.

There had been Filipino civic organizations before. In 1938, Francisco Varona, the Filipino representative in Hawaii, assisted a small group of leaders in organizing the first Filipino labor conference. Varona's movement was followed by Filipino conventions sponsored by the Hawaiian Sugar Planters' Association. Delegates from the outer islands had their way paid to the conventions in Honolulu, where they heard speakers from Hawaii's business community; but until Dionisio's effort in 1958, there had been no attempt on the part of the Filipinos themselves to organize and finance a territory-wide group. Now, Dionisio, who had come to the United States as an immigrant boy of sixteen and had worked wherever he could as a laborer on the West Coast, moved from plantation to plantation, helping organize local groups to represent the Filipinos in their communities and also to send delegates to an annual convention, the first to be held in 1959, to plan the role of the Filipinos in the new State of Hawaii.

Filipino leaders were keenly aware that in the politics of the new state they would be a force to contend with. Although two Filipino lawyers, Bernaldo Bicoy, a Democrat, and Peter Aduja, a Republican, were defeated in the 1959 elections, the Filipino community won a more important political victory with the firing of Oahu Liquor Commissioner Harry Kronick by Governor Quinn. In discussing a spring 1959 fatal stabbing at a Honolulu café, Kronick had blurted to the press that Filipino drinkers were troublemakers. Quinn had planned to reappoint the Democratic Oahu Liquor Commissioner, but promptly withdrew the nomination for reappointment and substituted Alfred Laureta, the first executive secretary of the Honolulu Filipino Chamber of Commerce, formed in 1954, and young law partner of Bernaldo Bicoy. Laureta, who had attended public schools on Maui before graduating from the University of Hawaii and receiving a law degree from Fordham in New York City, was the son of an Ilocano plantation laborer. Now, in the year of statehood, all Filipinos, whatever their dialect or local origin, took pride in his appointment. Later, in December, the Philippines Aloha Committee named Governor Quinn as "outstanding friend of the year to the Filipinos."[72]

If the Filipinos—the last of Hawaii's immigrant groups—had begun to shed inferiority feelings and to achieve political and economic recognition, what of the natives, the Hawaiians? In the year of statehood, there were only approximately 10,000 pure Hawaiians left in the Islands according to Bureau of Health statistics. The Hawaiians, it had long been noted, were a dying race. Shaken by disease and unable to adjust to the system of property and sex relationships imposed by the Caucasians, the natives of the Islands, it was often predicted, would be destroyed. Through intermarriage they would be absorbed by the rest of the population until there was not one full-blooded Hawaiian left.

In a literal sense, the prediction might someday come true. But, paradoxically, the intermingling of Hawaiians with the Islands' immigrant populations did not mean the extinction of the Hawaiian—

or, more properly, the part-Hawaiian. By 1959, approximately 18 per cent of the people in the Islands were part-Hawaiian, and so great was the identification of thousands of part-Hawaiians with their aboriginal heritage that they thought of themselves, not as cosmopolitan, but as Hawaiian. In interview after interview, part-Hawaiians with as little as one-fourth or even one-eighth Hawaiian blood explained that their primary identification was with the Hawaiian people.[73] The paradox was striking. As Hawaiians mixed with the rest of the community, they often maintained their feeling of "Hawaiian-ness" while adopting Caucasian and Oriental family and property values, and the feeling of "Hawaiian-ness" was intensified in many cases even though its character changed.

Hawaiians and part-Hawaiians still found it difficult to compete for status, wealth, and power on the terms imposed by the dominant haoles and Orientals. Far more than any other group, they thought of themselves as being treated unfairly.[74] Many of them still denounced the missionaries in private or scorned the Japanese as unfair and tricky. Family feuds and class divisions still hindered attempts at group action. But great changes were taking place in the Hawaiian community during the late 1950's. The coming of statehood, which may have crushed lingering hopes to restore the past, also stirred Hawaiians to look to the future. It was as if the Hawaiians were entering the second phase of immigrant adjustment along with the Filipinos. In that phase, immigrants give up the dream of returning home and plan for the future of their children in the land of their adoption. Internal bickering, carried over from the old country and intensified because of adversity in the first period of adjustment, gives way to growing unity. Feelings of despair, so common for generations among the Hawaiians, were invaded by glimmerings of hope that something might be done to enhance the prestige, power, and wealth of the group. These were the experiences of a growing number of part-Hawaiians as statehood approached.

At a faculty discussion at Kamehameha School for Boys, held in the spring of 1959, most of the instructors agreed that something which could be called "a psychological rebirth of the Hawaiian people" was taking place. While an increasing number of the growing student body at Kamehameha Schools were of mixed, rather than pure Hawaiian, ancestry, there was a continuing, even intensified, interest in things Hawaiian. More important, as one part-Hawaiian instructor put it,

"There is a developing opinion that something can be done to help the Hawaiian people." Later, a part-Hawaiian politician from Maui said, "We have got to get off our duffs and stop dreaming of past glories or whipping the Japanese for our troubles."[75] The Hawaiians, the politician counseled, should spend less time gossiping about the successes of the Japanese and more time examining their children's report cards. Although his father was a haole and his wife was three-quarters haole, he was determined to work for the betterment of his—the Hawaiian—people. Another politician of mixed ancestry—Hawaiian, Chinese, and Irish—complained that the Hawaiians had been overprotected, and it was time for them to compete on their own. Married to a Japanese girl, this young lawyer felt intensely his responsibilities toward the Hawaiian people and would join in any practical political or economic organization to fulfill them. Other part-Hawaiians, including legislators Hiram Kamaka, David Trask, and Walter Heen, spoke with feeling of their attachment to the Hawaiian people. The new Hawaiian politician was not the professional Hawaiian of old. He promoted group claims, but without sentimental demagoguery. He was bright, alert, ambitious, and "haolefied." But he hitched his haole skills, intelligence, and ambition to the hopes of the people to whom he was most strongly attached—the Hawaiians.

These hopes and the changes within the Hawaiian community that might transform them to reality were again expressed at the fifth annual meeting of the Council of Hawaiian Congregational Churches, where political and religious leaders representing sixty churches discussed the educational problems of Hawaiians. Part-Hawaiian Alvin Chang, employed by the Department of Public Instruction, warned his listeners against prevalent beliefs that Hawaiians were either too good or too inferior for education. Achievement levels for children past the fourth grade were low, he pointed out, because motivation was low, and not because of a lack of ability. A part-Hawaiian teacher, Mrs. Nellie Johnson, urged Hawaiians to put more money into education. She admitted that too many children quit school because of financial pressure, but instructed her audience to consult school counselors and principals before withdrawing children from school for any reason. Many speakers related the failure of Hawaiians to take advantage of educational opportunities to their relatively low economic achievements and high crime and divorce rates. It was pointed out that Hawaiians led in the number of desertions in divorce cases and that 80 per cent of the adolescents in juvenile detention homes were Hawaiians or part-Hawaiians, as were 40 per cent of the inmates of Oahu Prison. It was stressed that too often in the past Hawaiians had refused to help themselves. According to one speaker, 75 per cent of those in Salvation Army homes were Hawaiians or part-Hawaiians. The discussion did not probe the sociological causes of disintegration—the vast differences between the family and property relationships developed by Hawaiians over centuries and those imposed by the dominant outgroups. Religiously oriented, the discussants saw Hawaiian crimes, not as a product of culture conflict, but as a violation of Christian principles. We need a "sense of what is right and what is wrong," said Robert Naauao, the assistant deputy warden at Oahu Prison.

There was also considerable discussion of the need to protect Hawaiian lands through political action. Speakers warned Hawaiians to be on the alert against any further efforts to take land rightfully theirs. A part-Hawaiian land abstractor for the Territory insisted that "every person of Hawaiian blood is an heir to some land." He told Hawaiians to work on their genealogies to track down land that might be rightfully theirs. Another speaker reminded the audience that although Queen Emma's land had been left to support medical care for Hawaiians, her wishes had been disregarded. Now, it was important to protect Liliuokalani's small estate, which supported the educational and medical needs of poor Hawaiian children, and Lunalilo's estate, created to care for aged Hawaiians, and, most important of all, the Hawaiian Home Commission lands and the Bishop estate, which supported the Kamehameha Schools. Mrs. Flora Hayes, long-time legislator and spokesman for the Hawaiians, argued that the estates and Hawaiian Homes lands could be protected through politics. "It is through the Legislature that advantages are gained," she admonished, and complained that "not enough of us Hawaiians are active in politics." Others echoed her cry for leadership. Part-Hawaiian Marvin Thompson, of the Liliuokalani trust, insisted, "Nobody will care for us Hawaiians; we have to take care of ourselves." At the business meeting that followed the conference, a social-action committee was established in response to demands for leadership. The Hawaiian Congregational churches had not abandoned their heavenly apocalyptic vision of the future, nor had they entirely given up their attachment to the past. But they were also determined to face the wordly problems of the present.[76]

The precedent-setting meeting of the Council of Hawaiian Congregational Churches spurred another Hawaiian organization into action. The Hawaiian Civic Clubs, which until 1959 had been primarily social organizations, decided to hold their first territory-wide convention in April of the year of statehood. Under the prodding of the Reverend Abraham Akaka and others, a growing number of Civic Club leaders agreed that festivals, *luaus,* and fashion shows were not enough. At the convention, part-Hawaiian politician and main speaker William Heen continued to emphasize the need for self-help and advised Civic Club representatives to stress panel discussions and political action rather than mere socializing. He told his listeners to catch up with the other racial groups in Hawaii, who were sending their sons and daughters to college. "For us," he said, "it is not a matter of outstripping or outsmarting the others. It is a matter of keeping abreast of the times with them. After all, we are all American citizens. . . . I say, let us drive ahead."[77]

As a venerable Chinese-Hawaiian politician, Heen's words were respected. But it was probably Akaka, of the Kawaiahao Church, who, more than any other individual, symbolized and led the Hawaiian renaissance. One of the most sensitive and yet forceful personalities in the new Hawaii, Akaka believed that Hawaiians were better able to take advantage of opportunities because of their growing inter-mixture with others. Social and even biological intermixture would not dilute the psychological consciousness of Hawaiians and part-Hawaiians, he maintained. From their contacts with others, Hawaiians would learn to protect their own group. Hopeful for his people, devoid of hatred for the haoles or bitterness toward the Japanese, Akaka looked to the future and statehood with optimism. As president of the Council of Hawaiian Congregational Churches, he worked behind the scenes with future state legislators to protect Hawaiian interests. He also worked to enhance the Kamehameha Schools. He listened to criticisms that the regimented curriculum at the schools did not fit the graduates for the dynamic and creative leadership that would be needed in the new Hawaii.[78] Specific criticisms made by other Hawaiian and part-Hawaiian leaders called for the development of a Kamehameha Junior College, the abandonment of early grades, so that Hawaiian children would mix with others in the public schools before adolescence, and greater emphasis on liberal arts as opposed to voca-tional training.

When one-eighth Hawaiian Samuel Wilder King, trustee of the

Bishop estate, died in the spring of 1959, Akaka publicly announced his desire to have the Hawaii Supreme Court appoint him to fill the vacancy. The Honolulu *Advertiser,* without naming Akaka, supported the proposal to appoint a Hawaiian to the five-man board of trustees. Three of the other four trustees, as had been the tradition, were haoles identified with the *kamaaina* business community. Akaka followed the example of part-Hawaiian John Wilson, who in 1939 unsuccessfully offered himself for the position of trustee of the Bishop estate and criticized past Supreme Courts for not appointing "a Hawaiian or persons more familiar with the real intent of Mrs. Bishop's will and more sympathetic towards the Hawaiian." This time, a part-Hawaiian was appointed to the now $16,000-a-year post, but it was not Akaka. The new trustee was Richard Lyman, state legislator and extensive landholder in the Puna section of Hawaii. Lyman made no promises with respect to educational reform in the Kamehameha Schools, which were now training nearly 2,000 boys and girls, although Hawaiian religious and political leaders would be certain to press for change.

In the year of statehood, Akaka appeared at major public ceremonies to deliver blessings or prayers in behalf of the Hawaiian people. Deep-voiced, widely read, urbane, cultured, and youthful for his forty-two years, Akaka was himself a symbol of hope for the Hawaiians. Sensing the deep disappointment of many Hawaiians over the decision by Congress to grant statehood to the Islands, Akaka gave the principal address at a special statehood service at the ancient Kawaiahao Church on March 13, 1959. He told his parishoners and guests that "there are some of us to whom statehood brings silent fears." He then reminded his people of an old Hawaiian chant, which translated means: "There is a fire underground, but the firepit gives forth only smoke, smoke that bursts upward, touching the skies, and Hawaii is humbled beneath its darkness. . . . It is night over Hawaii, night from the smoke of my land . . . but there is salvation for the people, for now the land is being lit by a great flame." Akaka asked his people to view statehood as a lifting of the clouds of smoke and the releasing of opportunity for all the peoples of Hawaii. Opportunity, he stressed, was induced by the ancient spirit of *aloha,* and Hawaii's mission was to teach that spirit to the rest of the world.[79]

Even in Hawaii, *aloha* was, in some respects, more a symbol than a reality. An effort to change the rules of the Pacific Club to admit Oriental members was defeated in 1957, and at the Outrigger Canoe

Club it was still not permissible to bring Oriental guests for lunch. The symbol of *aloha* did not prevent Hawaiian children from taunting haole minorities in predominantly Hawaiian areas nor Japanese overseers from discriminating against Filipino workers on plantations; and ethnic tensions in the year of statehood were probably as numerous and certainly more complex than they had been ten years before. But the opening of opportunities for all of Hawaii's peoples inevitably meant greater intermingling among them.

Great changes were taking place in Hawaii, and the peoples of the Islands did have much to teach the world. A majority of the membership at the Pacific Club had favored admitting Orientals, but they were stopped by one veto on the club's board of governors.[80] The majority was realistic, not because Americans of Japanese, Chinese, Korean, and Filipino ancestry were beating at the doors of the club, but because Hawaii's people were already in the process of biological fusion. Decade by decade, the proportion of intermarriage increased, rising from just over 10 per cent of all marriages immediately prior to World War I to over 30 per cent in the 1950's. In the years immediately preceding statehood, well over one third of all male Caucasians in Hawaii married non-Caucasians.[81] But *aloha* in Hawaii could teach the world even more than the fact that racial intermixture did not mean a debasement of courage, intelligence, or creative initiative. *Aloha* set a standard of conduct in Hawaii which many people found difficult to live up to, but which nearly everyone openly approved.

On the eve of statehood, the principal of a Honolulu elementary school told how a Negro teacher in his school won the Parent-Teacher Association banner week after week because she was so popular with students and parents. One of the teacher's pupils was the little daughter in an Army family from Mississippi. When the principal met her Mississippi-born mother, he heard the parent praise the teacher as "the best my little girl has ever had." The nisei principal irreverently asked, "Isn't it too bad you can't use a person like that in an integrated school in Mississippi?" The Army wife was horrified and exclaimed, "Why no, we would not stand for such a thing in Mississippi!" When asked why she tolerated and even warmly endorsed the teacher in Honolulu, the mother shrugged her shoulders and said, "When you're in Hawaii, you do what you are supposed to do in Hawaii."

The Hawaiian aloha exemplified by this story was a product of many things—polynesian atttitudes, missionary conscience, and the patience and good will of immigrants from the Far East. But it was also the result of such democratic values as free public education and universal suffrage—values promoted by the Congress of the United States and educators from the mainland. Hawaii illustrates the nation's revolutionary message of equality of opportunity for all, regardless of background, color, or religion. This is the promise of Hawaii, a promise for the entire nation and, indeed, the world, that peoples of different races and creeds can live together, enriching each other, in harmony *and* democracy.

SOURCES
AND ACKNOWLEDGMENTS

This volume rests on a wide variety of sources. The Prologue, which depends almost entirely on secondary material, is not footnoted in detail. The remaining chapters are based on a searching examination of the published and available unpublished materials on modern Hawaii. Books, articles, government publications, and monographs have been supplemented by newspapers and journals, archival materials, numerous depth interviews, public-opinion surveys, and special research projects undertaken for this volume. The magnificent help of librarians, research assistants, and others will be acknowledged in the appropriate sections below.

1. Articles, Books, Documents, Monographs, Newspapers, and Periodicals

This bibliography is based mainly upon material from the Hawaiian collection in the Gregg M. Sinclair Library of the University of Hawaii. The Hawaiian collection includes some 15,000 references, but only those items were read which were judged to relate directly and significantly to the evolution of modern Hawaii. In making his selections, the author relied heavily on a bibliography on culture change in the Hawaiian Islands prepared by Margaret Mary Lavell Leeson during August and September 1958. Miss Leeson's bibliography, submitted in partial fulfillment of the requirements for the degree of Bachelor of Arts in the Department of Anthropology, Criminology and Sociology at the University of British Columbia in April 1959, is now the most comprehensive and useful of all bibliographies on Hawaii's ethnic groups.

My work at the Sinclair Library was made pleasant by the unfailing efficiency and patience of Miss Janet Bell, librarian of the Hawaiian collection, and her assistant, Miss Mary Muraoka.

Some of the sources listed below were procured at the library of the Legislative Reference Bureau at the University of Hawaii, whose facilities were placed at my disposal by the Bureau's Director, Dr. Robert Kamins, his assistant, Dr. Kenneth Lau, who is presently the Director, and the extremely efficient Bureau Librarian, Miss Margaret E. Holden.

Each of the items listed below was read and abstracted by the author or his research assistants, Mrs. Gay Fuchs (no relation), who worked primarily on economic and political history and English-language publications; Miss Catherine Pascual, responsible for Filipino materials; Miss Doris Okuhara, assistant on Japanese sources; and Mrs. H. S. Chung, who worked with Chinese and Korean materials.

Newspapers and periodicals were read selectively in the Sinclair Library, the Archives of Hawaii, and from special collections. Certain periods or episodes were explored in detail in newspaper or periodical files. A comprehensive content analysis of all issues was not attempted.

1. Adams, Romanzo Colfax, "Birth Rates of the Hawaiian Japanese," *Journal of Applied Sociology*, 8, 1924.
2. Adams, Romanzo Colfax, "Continuity and Change: Introductory," *Social Process in Hawaii*, 3, 1937.
3. Adams, Romanzo Colfax, "A Decade of Population Growth," *Social Process in Hawaii*, 6, 1940.
4. Adams, Romanzo Colfax, *The Education and the Economic Outlook for the Boys of Hawaii: A Study in the Field of Race Relationships*, Honolulu, Institute of Pacific Relations, 1927.
5. Adams, Romanzo Colfax, "Functions of the Language Schools in Hawaii," *Friend*, August–September 1925.
6. Adams, Romanzo Colfax, *Further Developments of Race Contacts in Hawaii*, Honolulu, Institute of Pacific Relations, 1929.
7. Adams, Romanzo Colfax, *Interracial Marriage in Hawaii: A Study of the Mutually Conditioned Processes of Acculturation and Amalgamation*, New York, The Macmillan Co., 1937.
8. Adams, Romanzo Colfax, *The Japanese in Hawaii: A Statistical Study Bearing on the Future Number and Voting Strength and on the Economic and Social Character of the Hawaiian Japanese*, New York, National Committee on American-Japanese Relations, 1924.
9. Adams, Romanzo Colfax, "Japanese Migration Statistics," *Sociology and Social Research*, 13, 1929.
10. Adams, Romanzo Colfax, "The Meaning of the Chinese Experiences in Hawaii," *Chinese of Hawaii*, 1, 1929.

11. Adams, Romanzo Colfax, *The Peoples of Hawaii*, Honolulu, Institute of Pacific Relations, 1933.
12. Adams, Romanzo Colfax, "The Population Movement in Hawaii," *Social Process in Hawaii*, 7, 1941.
13. Adams, Romanzo Colfax, *Race Contacts in Hawaii*, Honolulu, Institute of Pacific Relations, 1929.
14. Adams, Romanzo Colfax, "Race Relations in Hawaii: A Summary Statement," *Social Process in Hawaii*, 2, 1936.
15. Adams, Romanzo Colfax, "Some Statistics on the Japanese in Hawaii," *Foreign Affairs*, 2, 1923.
16. Adams, Romanzo Colfax, "Studies in the Trends of the Population of Hawaii," *Administration in Hawaii*, U.S. Congress, Senate, Committee on Territories and Insular Affairs, Washington, Government Printing Office, 1933.
17. Adams, Romanzo Colfax, T. M. Livesay, and E. H. Vanwinkle, "A Statistical Study of the Races in Hawaii," unpublished manuscript, 1925.
18. Agena, Masako, and Eiko Yoshinaga, " 'Daishi-Do'—A Form of Religious Movement," *Social Process in Hawaii*, 7, 1941.
19. Aiona, Darrow L., "Hawaiian Funeral," *Social Process in Hawaii*, 22, 1958.
20. Akinaka, Amy, "Types of Japanese Marriages in Hawaii," *Social Process in Hawaii*, 1, 1935.
21. Akiyoshi, Hayashida, "Japanese Moral Instruction as a Factor in the Americanization of Citizens of Japanese Ancestry," thesis for the degree of Master of Arts, University of Hawaii, 1933.
22. Alexander, Arthur C., *Koloa Plantation, 1835–1935: A History of the Oldest Hawaiian Sugar Plantation*, Honolulu, Honolulu Star Bulletin Press, 1937.
23. Alexander, Mary Charlotte, and Charlotte Peabody Dodge, *Punahou, 1841–1941*, Berkeley and Los Angeles, University of California Press, 1941.
24. Alexander, W. D., "History of Immigration to Hawaii," *Thrum's Hawaiian Annual*, Honolulu, 1896.
25. Allen, Gwenfread, *Hawaii's War Years, 1941–1945*, Honolulu, University of Hawaii Press, 1950.
26. Aller, Curtis, *Labor Relations in the Hawaiian Sugar Industry*, Berkeley, University of California Press, 1957.
27. Alverne, Macarriol, *Manual for the Progressive Laborer*, Honolulu, The Printship Co., 1930.
28. Anderson, Rufus, *History of the Sandwich Islands' Mission*, Boston, Congregational Publishing Society, 1870.

29. Andrade, Ernest, Jr., "The Hawaiian Revolution of 1887," thesis for the degree of Master of Arts, University of Hawaii, 1957.

30. Anthony, J. Garner, *Hawaii Under Army Rule*, Stanford, Stanford University Press, 1955.

31. Appeal, Chauncy, "American Labor and Annexation of Hawaii: A Study in Logic and Economic Interest," *Pacific Historical Review*, 23, 1954.

32. Araki, Makoto, *et al.*, "A Study of the Socio-cultural Factors in Casework Services for Individuals and Families Known to the Child and Family Service of Honolulu, 1954," thesis for the degree of Master of Social Work, University of Hawaii, 1956.

33. Ariyoshi, Koji, "My Thoughts for which I Stand Indicted," Honolulu *Record,* September 13, 1951.

34. Armstrong, Fred Eugene, "Aspects of Prejudice in the Territory of Hawaii," Hilo, Hawaii, Territorial conference of social work, 3rd annual regional conference, *Proceedings,* 1944.

35. Baker, Ray Stannard, "Human Nature in Hawaii: How the Few Want the Many to Work for Them Perpetually and at Low Wages," *The American Magazine*, 73, January 1912.

36. Balch, John Adrian, *Shall the Japanese be Allowed to Dominate Hawaii*, Honolulu, privately printed, 1942.

37. Bank of Hawaii, Monthly, semi-annual, and annual reports, Honolulu, 1960.

38. Bank of Hawaii, *Hawaii's Potentials and Programs for Island Growth*, August 1957.

39. Bartholomew, Harland, and Associates, *Land Use in Hawaii*, Economic Planning and Coordination Authority of the Territory of Hawaii, January 1957.

40. Beaglehole, Ernest, *Some Modern Hawaiians,* Honolulu, University of Hawaii Research Publications, 1937.

41. Bean, Robert, *Biennial Report of the Supervisor of Foreign Language Schools, 1923–5,* Honolulu, Hawaii (Ter.) Department of Public Instruction, 1925.

42. Benedict, Ruth, *The Chrysanthemum and the Sword,* Boston, Houghton Mifflin Co., 1946.

43. Blackey, Eileen, "Some Cultural Aspects of Social Case Work in Hawaii," *Cultural Problems in Social Case Work,* New York, Family Welfare Association of America, 1940.

44. Blumer, Herbert, "Paternalism in Industry," *Social Process in Hawaii*, 15, 1951.

45. Bock, Comfort Margaret, "The Church of Jesus Christ of Latter

Day Saints in the Hawaiian Islands," thesis for the degree of Master of Arts, University of Hawaii, 1941.

46. Bogardus, Emory S., "Native Hawaiians and Their Problems," *Sociology and Social Research*, 19, 1935.

47. Booth, Evie K., "One Navy Wife in Hawaii," *Social Process in Hawaii*, 21, 1957.

48. Bottomley, Allen W. T., *A Statement Concerning the Sugar Industry in Hawaii; Labor Conditions on Hawaiian Sugar Plantations; Filipino Laborers Thereon, and the Alleged Filipino "Strike" of 1924,* Honolulu, 1924.

49. Bradley, Harold W., *The American Frontier in Hawaii*, Stanford, Stanford University Press, 1942.

50. Brooks, Philip, "Multiple-Industry Unionism in Hawaii," thesis for degree of Doctor of Philosophy, Columbia University, 1952.

51. Brown, Roy E., "The Tax Structure of Puerto Rico," Hawaiian Tax Foundation, 1954.

52. Bryan, Edwin H., Jr., *Ancient Hawaiian Life*, Honolulu, Advertiser Publishing Co., reprint, 1950.

53. Bunker, Frank F., *Hawaii and the Philippines*, Philadelphia and Chicago, J. B. Lippincott Co., 1928.

54. Burroughs, Edgar R., "Our Japanese Problem," *Hawaii*, 5, June 30, 1944.

55. Burrows, Edwin Grant, *Chinese and Japanese in Hawaii during the Sino-Japanese Conflict*, Honolulu, Institute of Pacific Relations, 1939.

56. Burrows, Edwin Grant, *Hawaiian Americans, An Account of the Mingling of Japanese, Chinese, Polynesian and American Cultures*, New Haven, Yale University Press, 1947.

57. Cariaga, Roman R., *Filipinos at Ewa*, Honolulu, 1935.

58. Cariaga, Roman R., "The Filipinos in Hawaii: A Survey of Their Economic and Social Conditions," thesis for the degree of Master of Arts, University of Hawaii, 1936.

59. Cariaga, Roman R., "The Filipinos in Honolulu," *Social Science*, 10, January 1935.

60. Cary, Miles E., "A Vitalized Curriculum for McKinley High School," thesis for the degree of Master of Arts, University of Hawaii, 1930.

61. Castle, William R., *Hawaii, Past and Present*, New York, Dodd, Mead & Co., 1913.

62. Castro, A. D., "The Portuguese in Hawaii," *Mid-Pacific Magazine*, 8, July 1914.

63. Chamber of Commerce, *Report, Committee on Public Education and Vocational Training,* Honolulu, 1929.
64. Chambers, Henry E., *Constitutional History of Hawaii,* Baltimore, Johns Hopkins Press, 1896.
65. Chapman, Royal M., *Cooperation in the Hawaiian Pineapple Business,* New York, Institute of Pacific Relations, 1933.
66. Char, Tin-Yuke, *Immigrant Chinese Societies in Hawaii,* Hawaiian Historical Society, 1952.
67. Ch'en, Ta, *Chinese Migrations, with Special Reference to Labor Conditions . . . July 1923,* U.S. Bureau of Labor Statistics, Washington, Government Printing Office, 1923.
68. Cheng, Ch'en-K'un, "Assimilation in Hawaii and the Bid for Statehood," *Social Forces,* 30, October 1951.
69. Cheng, Ch'en-K'un, "A Study of Chinese Assimilation in Hawaii," *Social Forces,* 32, December 1953.
70. Cheng, Ch'en-K'un, and Douglas S. Yamamura, "Interracial Marriage and Divorce in Hawaii," *Social Forces,* 36, October 1957.
71. "A Chinese Family in Hawaii," *Social Process in Hawaii,* 3, 1937.
72. "The Chinese of Hawaii," *Overseas Penman Club,* 1, Honolulu, 1929.
73. "The Chinese Question in Hawaii," *Thrum's Hawaiian Annual,* Honolulu, 1890.
74. *The Chinese-Hawaii Journal.*
75. Ching, Hung Wo, "Economic Future of the Chinese in Hawaii," unpublished essay, September 22, 1956.
76. Chow, Richard, "The Chinese-Hawaiian Mixture," *Social Process in Hawaii,* 1, 1935.
77. Clopton, Robert W., "The Christianization of Hawaii Viewed as a Social Movement," unpublished manuscript, Honolulu, 1939.
78. Colket, G. Hamilton, "Suppressing Japanese Schools in Hawaii," *The Nation,* 115, November 22, 1922.
79. Coman, Katharine, *The History of Contract Labor in the Hawaiian Islands,* American Economic Association, New York, Macmillan Co., 1903.
80. Congdon, Charles Franklin, "Background and History of the 1946 Hawaiian Sugar Strike," thesis for degree of Master of Business Administration, Columbia University, 1951.
81. Connell, John Harden, "The History of Chinese in Hawaii," *Mid-Pacific Magazine,* 46, November 1933.
82. Conroy, Francis Hilary, *The Japanese Frontier in Hawaii, 1868–1898,* Berkeley, University of California Press, 1953.
83. Coulter, John Wesley, and Chee Kwon Chun, *Chinese Rice Farmers*

in Hawaii, Honolulu, University of Hawaii Research Publications, 1937.

84.   Council of Hawaiian Congregational Churches, *Report of 5th Annual Meeting,* 1958.

85.   Crawford, David, *Paradox in Hawaii: An Examination of Industry and Education and the Paradox They Present,* Boston, The Stratford Co., 1933.

86.   Crawford, Will Clark, "Characteristics of the Public and Alien Language Schools of Hawaii," *Administration in Hawaii,* Washington, Government Printing Office, 1933.

87.   Crowse, William W., "The Portuguese and Spanish in Hawaii: Their Racial Organization and Future," *Acta Americana,* April–June 1943.

88.   Culp, Daniel H., II, "Chinese Continuity," *Annals,* American Academy of Political and Social Science, November 1930.

89.   Davenport, William H., "The Religion of Pre-European Hawaii," *Social Process in Hawaii,* 16, 1952.

90.   Dean, Arthur L., *Alexander and Baldwin, Ltd. and Predecessor Partnerships,* Honolulu, 1950.

91.   Dean, Arthur L., *Cooperation in the Sugar Industry in Hawaii,* New York, Institute of Pacific Relations, 1933.

92.   Department of Labor and Industrial Relations, "1958 High School Graduates, Their Plans and Aspirations," October 1958.

93.   Department of Public Instruction, *Progressive Education and the Public Schools of Hawaii,* January 1, 1930.

94.   Department of Public Instruction, *Some Descriptions of Progressive Education in the Public Schools of Hawaii,* ed. Division of Research, Kawananakoa School, Hawaii, September 30, 1929.

95.   Digman, John N., "Ethnic Factors in Oahu's 1954 General Election," *Social Process in Hawaii,* 21, 1957.

96.   Director of Labor Relations, Department of Labor and Industrial Relations, Territory of Hawaii, revised report, March 1948.

97.   Dizon, Nicolas C., *The "Master" vs. Juan de la Cruz,* Honolulu, Mercantile Press, 1931.

98.   Dorita, Sister Mary, "Filipino Immigration to Hawaii," thesis for the degree of Master of Arts, University of Hawaii, 1954.

99.   Draper, Edgar M., and Alice Hayden, *Hawaiian Schools: A Curriculum Survey 1944–46,* Washington, American Council on Education, 1946.

100. Duckworth-Ford, R. A., *Report on Hawaiian Sugar Plantations and Filipino Labor,* privately printed, 1926.

101. Economic Planning and Coordinating Authority, "A Few Facts in Focus," April 1959.

102. Economic Planning and Coordinating Authority, *Major Land Holdings in Hawaii, Ownership Patterns and Leasing Policies,* Report #14, Territory of Hawaii, February 1957.

103. Economic Planning and Coordinating Authority, *The Problem of Farm Relocation on Oahu,* Report #12, Territory of Hawaii, November 1956.

104. Economic Planning and Coordinating Authority, *Public Land Lease Policies—31 States and Hawaii,* Report #10, Territory of Hawaii, August 1956.

105. *Education Beyond the High School in Hawaii, 1958–1968,* a report of the governor's committee on education beyond high school, January 1959.

106. Egan, E. J., *Report to Bertram Edises,* Twentieth Region National Labor Relations Board, 1937.

107. Elkin, W. B., "An Inquiry into the Cause of the Decrease of the Hawaiian People," *American Journal of Sociology,* 8, November 1902.

108. Ellis, William, *A Narrative of a Tour Through Hawaii,* Honolulu, Hawaiian Gazette Co., Ltd., 1917.

109. Embree, John Fee, *Acculturation Among the Japanese of Kona, Hawaii,* Menasha, Wisconsin, The American Anthropological Association, 1941.

110. Embree, John Fee, "New Local and Kin Groups Among the Japanese Farmers of Kona, Hawaii," *American Anthropologist,* 41, July–September 1939.

111. Eubank, Lauriel Elsabeth, "The Effects of the First Six Months of World War II on the Attitudes of Koreans and Filipinos Toward the Japanese in Hawaii," thesis for the degree of Master of Arts, University of Hawaii, 1943.

112. *The Evening Bulletin.*

113. Fate, W. A., "The Human Factor in Plantation Employment," *Friend,* October 1922.

114. Fei, Hsaias-T'ung, "Land as a Social Value," *Societies Around the World,* New York, Dryden Press, 1953.

115. *15th New Americans Conference, July 15–21, 1941,* Honolulu, New Americans Conference, 1941.

116. *The First Hundred Years, Report on the Operations of Castle & Cooke for the Years 1851–1951,* Honolulu, privately printed, 1951.

117. *14th New Americans Conference, July 15–21, 1940,* Honolulu, New Americans Conference, 1940.

118. Frear, Walter F., *Anti-Missionary Criticism with Reference to Hawaii,* Honolulu, Advertiser Publishing Co., 1935.

119. Fried, Jacob, "Forty Years of Change in a Hawaiian Homestead Community: Anahola," *Rural Sociology,* 20, March 1955.

120. *Friend.*

121. *The Future of the AJA's in This American Community,* Second Oahu Conference of Americans of Japanese Ancestry, Honolulu, 1945.

122. Gestep, G. A., "Portuguese Assimilation in Hawaii and California," *Sociology and Social Research,* 26, 1942.

123. Gibson, Warren, "A Study of the Number and Characteristics of Young Farmers on Hawaii, Oahu, Maui and Molokai," thesis for the degree of Master of Arts, University of Hawaii, 1941.

124. Glick, Clarence E., "The Relation Between Position and Status in the Assimilation of Chinese in Hawaii," *American Journal of Sociology,* 47, 1942.

125. Glick, Clarence E., "Residential Dispersion of Urban Chinese," *Social Process in Hawaii,* 2, 1936.

126. Glick, Clarence E., "Transition from Familism to Nationalism Among Chinese in Hawaii," *American Journal of Sociology,* 43, March 1938.

127. Glick, Doris Lorden, "The Chinese-Hawaiian Family," *American Journal of Sociology,* 40, January 1935.

128. Goo, Paul Kimm-Chow, "Chinese Economic Activities in Hawaii," *The Chinese in Hawaii,* 1929.

129. Gorospe, Otilio R., "Making Filipino History in Hawaii," *Mid-Pacific Magazine,* 45, March 1933.

130. Griffiths, Arthur Floyd, "The Japanese Race Question in Hawaii," *Journal of Race Development,* 6, April 1916.

131. Grip, A., "The Conditions of the Swedish and Norwegian Laborers on the Hawaiian Islands," *Honolulu Almanac and Directory of 1884,* Honolulu.

132. Grodzins, Morton, *Americans Betrayed: Politics and the Japanese Evacuations,* Chicago, University of Chicago Press, 1949.

133. Gulick, Sidney L., *Hawaii's American-Japanese Problem: A Description of the Conditions, A Statement of the Problems and Suggestions for Their Solution,* Honolulu, Honolulu *Star Bulletin,* 1915.

134. Gulick, Sidney L., "The Japanese in Hawaii," *Mid-Pacific Magazine,* 10, September 1915.

135. Halford, Francis John, *Nine Doctors and God,* Honolulu, University of Hawaii Press, 1954.

136. Hanaoka, Yoichi, "The Japanese Language School; Is It a Help or a Hindrance to the Americanization of Hawaii's Young People?" *Friend,* 97, April 1927.

137. Hanaoka, Yoichi, "We Must Understand American Ways," *Nippu Jiji,* June 1928.

138. Handley, Katharine Newkirk, *Four Case Studies in Hawaii: Intercultural Problems and the Practice of Social Work,* Honolulu, University of Hawaii Press, 1957.

139. Handy, E. S. C., *Polynesian Religion,* Bernice P. Bishop Museum Bulletin 34, Honolulu, 1927.

140. Handy, E. S. C., and M. K. Pukui, *Chana, the Dispersed Community of Kanaka,* Honolulu, Institute of Pacific Relations, 1935.

141. Harada, Koichi Glenn, "A Survey of the Japanese Language Schools in Hawaii," thesis for the degree of Master of Arts, University of Hawaii, 1934.

142. Hawaii (Ter.) Board of Immigration, *Third Report of the Board of Immigration to the Governor of the Territory of Hawaii: 1909–10,* Honolulu, Bulletin Publishing Co., Ltd., 1911.

143. Hawaii Chinese Civic Association, the President's Report, 1957.

144. *The Hawaii Educational Review.*

145. Hawaii Employer's Council, *Employee Benefit Plans in Hawaii,* March 1958.

146. *The Hawaii Hochi.*

147. *The Hawaii Shimpo.*

148. *The Hawaii Star.*

149. Hawaiian Economic Foundation, *A Study of Ownership of Corporations in Hawaii,* Honolulu, privately printed, 1948.

150. *Hawaiian Gazette.*

151. *The Hawaiian Reporter.*

152. Hawaiian Sugar Planters' Association, *Facts About Hawaii's Largest Industry, Sugar,* Honolulu, January 1959.

153. Hawaiian Sugar Planters' Association, "Monthly Sugar Facts and Features for Employee Publications," 1958–59.

154. Hawaiian Sugar Planters' Association, *Proceedings* of Annual Meetings, 1905–1941.

155. Hawaiian Sugar Planters' Association, *The Sugar Industry of Hawaii and the Labor Shortage: What It Means to the United States and Hawaii,* Honolulu, 1921.

156. Hawaiian Sugar Planters' Association, *Ten Dynamic Years: A Report on the Hawaiian Sugar Industry,* Honolulu, 1957.

157. *Hawaii's English Standard Schools,* Report #3, Legislative Reference Bureau, Honolulu, University of Hawaii Press, 1948.

158. Hayashida, Akiyoshi, "Japanese Moral Instruction as a Factor in the Americanization of Citizens of Japanese Ancestry," thesis for the degree of Master of Arts, University of Hawaii, 1933.

159. Hearn, Lafcadio, *Japan, An Attempt at Interpretation,* Tokyo, Charles E. Tuttle Co., 1955.

160. Heen, Elizabeth Lulu, "The Hawaiians of Papakolea: A Study in Social and Economic Realism," thesis for the degree of Master of Arts, University of Hawaii, 1936.

161. Henderson, C. J., "Labor—An Undercurrent of Hawaiian Social History," *Social Process in Hawaii,* 15, 1951.

162. Hilo, M., and Emma K. Himino, "Some Characteristics of American and Japanese Culture," *Social Process in Hawaii,* 21, 1957.

163. Hoag, E. B., "Delinquency in Hawaiian Schools," *Journal of Applied Sociology,* 7, 1923.

164. Hobbs, Jean, *Hawaii, A Pageant of the Soil,* Stanford, Stanford University Press, and London, H. Milford, Oxford University Press, 1935.

165. Honolulu *Advertiser.*

166. Honolulu *Record.*

167. Honolulu *Star Bulletin.*

168. Hormann, Bernhard Lothar, "The Caucasian Minority," *Social Process in Hawaii,* 14, 1950.

169. Hormann, Bernhard Lothar, "Certain Ecological Patterns of Honolulu," *Social Process in Hawaii,* 20, 1956.

170. Hormann, Bernhard Lothar, *Community Forces in Hawaii,* readings from volumes of *Social Process in Hawaii,* Sociology Club publication, Honolulu, University of Hawaii (Romanzo Adams Social Research Laboratory), 1956.

171. Hormann, Bernhard Lothar, "The English Standard School," *What People Have Been Saying and Doing in Hawaii,* 9, May 8, 1946.

172. Hormann, Bernhard Lothar, "Factors in Disorganization and Reorganization," *Social Process in Hawaii,* 6, July 1940.

173. Hormann, Bernhard Lothar, "The Germans in Hawaii," thesis for the degree of Master of Arts, University of Hawaii, 1931.

174. Hormann, Bernhard Lothar, "Hawaii's Industrial Revolution," *Social Process in Hawaii,* 15, 1951.

175. Hormann, Bernhard Lothar, "Integration in Hawaii's Schools," *Social Process in Hawaii,* 21, 1957.

176. Hormann, Bernhard Lothar, "Native Welfare in Hawaii," *What*

People Have Been Saying and Doing in Hawaii, 19, October 12, 1951.

177. Hormann, Bernhard Lothar, "A Note on Hawaii's Minorities Within Minorities," *Social Process in Hawaii,* 18, 1954.

178. Hormann, Bernhard Lothar, "The Problem of the Religion of Hawaii's Japanese," *Social Process in Hawaii,* 22, 1958.

179. Hormann, Bernhard Lothar, "Racial Complexion of Hawaii's Future Population," *Social Forces,* 27, October 1948.

180. Hormann, Bernhard Lothar, "A Report on the War Research Laboratory in Hawaii," *American Sociological Review,* 10, February 1945.

181. Hormann, Bernhard Lothar, "The Revival of Buddhism in Hawaii," *What People Have Been Saying and Doing in Hawaii,* 12, December 1, 1947.

182. Hormann, Bernhard Lothar, "Speech, Prejudice, and the School in Hawaii," *Social Process in Hawaii,* 11, May 1947.

183. Hsieh, T'ing-Yu, "The Chinese in Hawaii," *Chinese Social and Political Science Review,* 14, 1930.

184. Hsu, F. L. K., "The Chinese of Hawaii: Their Role in American Culture," New York Academy of Science, *Transactions,* 13, April 1951.

185. Hudson, Loring Gardner, "The History of the Kamehameha Schools," thesis for the degree of Master of Arts, University of Hawaii, 1935.

186. Hughes, Gladys F., "Folk Beliefs and Customs in an Hawaiian Community," *Journal of American Folklore,* 62, July–September 1949.

187. Hull, George Charles, "The Chinese in Hawaii," *Mid-Pacific Magazine,* 9, March 1915.

188. Hulten, John J., "Report of the Mayor and Board of Supervisors of the City and County of Honolulu," Territory of Hawaii, 1958.

189. Humphries, Grace, "Hawaiian Homesteading: A Chapter in the Economic Development of Hawaii," thesis for the degree of Master of Arts, University of Hawaii, 1937.

190. Hunter, Charles H., "The Sugar Act of 1934 Came as a Shock," Honolulu *Star Bulletin,* April 14, 1959.

191. Ige, Thomas H., "Working Conditions and Wages," *Labor in Hawaii,* Honolulu, Industrial Relations Council, University of Hawaii, 1956.

192. Ikeda, Kiyoshi, "Unionization and the Plantation," *Social Process in Hawaii,* 15, 1951.

193. *The ILWU Reporter.*

194. ILWU Education Service, *Your Rights Under the Law,* 1958–1959.
195. Imamura, Y., *History of the Hongwanji Mission in Hawaii,* Honolulu, Publishing Bureau of Hongwanji Mission, 1918.
196. Inagaki, John Y., "Economic Planning and Development in Hawaii, 1937–57," thesis for the degree of Master of Arts, University of Hawaii, 1957.
197. *The Independent.*
198. Iwasa, Henry K., Jr., "The Home Rule Party: Its Short Life and Decline," Honors thesis, University of Hawaii, 1958.
199. Izuka, Ichiro, *Truth About Communism in Hawaii,* Honolulu, 1947.
200. Jarrett, Lorna H., "A Source Book in Hawaiian Geography," thesis for the degree of Master of Arts, University of Hawaii, 1930.
201. Jarves, James Jackson, *History of the Hawaiian Islands,* Honolulu, H. M. Whitney, 1872.
202. Johannessen, Edward, *The Hawaiian Labor Movement: A Brief History,* Boston, Bruce Humphries, 1956.
203. Jones, Stella M., "Economic Adjustment of Hawaiians to European Culture," *Pacific Affairs,* 4, November 1931.
204. Jose, Dorothy, "A Portuguese Family in Hawaii," *Social Process in Hawaii,* 3, 1937.
205. Kai, Kanezo, "Foreign Language Schools in Hawaii," *Mid-Pacific Magazine,* 38, Pan-Pacific Union Bulletin, August 1929.
206. *Kaiser Industries Publications,* 1958–59.
207. Kamins, Robert M., *The Tax System of Hawaii,* Honolulu, University of Hawaii Press, 1952.
208. Kaneko, Richard, "Establish Contact with American Homes," *Nippu Jiji,* June 1928.
209. Kawachi, Kensuke, "How 'New Americans' May Survive in Hawaii," *Nippu Jiji,* June 1928.
210. Kawahara, Kimie, and Yuriko Hatanaka, "The Impact of War on an Immigrant Culture," *Social Process in Hawaii,* 8, 1943.
211. Keesing, Felix M., *Hawaiian Homesteading on Molokai,* Honolulu, University of Hawaii Research Publications, 1936.
212. Kelly, Marion, "Changes in Land Tenure in Hawaii, 1778–1850," thesis for the degree of Master of Arts, University of Hawaii, 1956.
213. Kim, Bernice Bong Hee, "The Koreans in Hawaii," thesis for the degree of Master of Arts, University of Hawaii, 1937.
214. Kimura, Evelyn Yama, and Margaret Zimmerman Freeman, "The Problem of Assimilation," *Social Process in Hawaii,* 19, 1955.

215. Kimura, Yukiko, "Psychological Aspects of Japanese Immigration," *Social Process in Hawaii,* 6, July 1940.
216. Kimura, Yukiko, "Rumor Among the Japanese," *Social Process in Hawaii,* 11, 1947.
217. Kimura, Yukiko, "Social Effects of Increased Income of Defense Workers of Oriental Ancestry in Hawaii," *Social Process in Hawaii,* 7, 1941.
218. Kimura, Yukiko, "A Sociological Analysis of Types of Social Readjustment of Alien Japanese in Hawaii Since the War," thesis for the degree of Master of Arts, University of Hawaii, 1947.
219. Kimura, Yukiko, "The Sociological Significance of the Japanese Language School Campaign in Hawaii," *Social Process in Hawaii,* 20, 1956.
220. Kimura, Yukiko, "Some Effects of the War Situation Upon the Alien Japanese in Hawaii," *Social Process in Hawaii,* 8, 1943.
221. Kinney, W. A., *Hawaii's Capacity for Self-Government All but Destroyed: The Assassination of Hawaii as an American Commonwealth Nearing Absolute and Complete Accomplishment at the Hands of Promoters and Exploiters of Asiatic Immigration,* Salt Lake City, Frank L. Jensen, 1927.
222. Kong, Hester, "Through the Peepsight of a Grocery Store," *Social Process in Hawaii,* 9–10, 1945.
223. Kosaki, Mildred (Doi), "The Culture Conflicts and Guidance Needs of Nisei Adolescents," thesis for the degree of Master of Education, University of Hawaii, 1949.
224. Koshizawa, Emi, "A Japanese Family in Rural Hawaii," *Social Process in Hawaii,* 3, 1937.
225. Kurita, Yayoi, "Employers' Organizations in Hawaii," *Labor Law Journal,* 4, April 1953.
226. Kurita, Yayoi, "Labor Movement Among Japanese Plantation Workers in Hawaii," unpublished paper written at the University of Hawaii, circa 1952.
227. Kuykendall, Ralph Simpson, *The Hawaiian Kingdom 1778–1854,* Honolulu, University of Hawaii Press, 1957.
228. Kuykendall, Ralph Simpson, *The Hawaiian Kingdom 1854–1874,* Honolulu, University of Hawaii Press, 1953.
229. Kuykendall, Ralph Simpson, and Lorin Tarr Gill, *Hawaii in the World War,* Honolulu, The Historical Commission, 1928.
230. *The Kwasan.*
231. Lai, Kum Pai, "Attitudes of the Chinese in Hawaii Toward Their Language Schools," *Sociology and Social Research,* 20, 1936.
232. Lai, Kum Pai, "The Natural History of the Chinese Language

School in Hawaii," thesis for the degree of Master of Arts, University of Hawaii, 1935.

233. Lai, Kum Pai, "Occupational and Educational Adjustments of the Chinese in Hawaii," *Chinese of Hawaii*, 2, 1936.

234. Lam, Fred K., "A Survey of the Chinese People in Hawaii," *Mid-Pacific Magazine*, 38, December 1929.

235. Lam, Fred K., *A Survey of the Chinese People in Hawaii, Historically, Educationally, Religiously and Socially*, Honolulu, Institute of Pacific Relations, 1929.

236. Lam, Margaret Mildred, "Racial Myth and Family Tradition-Worship Among the Part-Hawaiians," *Social Forces*, 14, 1936.

237. Lam, Margaret Mildred, "Six Generations of Race Mixture in Hawaii," thesis for the degree of Master of Arts, University of Hawaii, 1932.

238. Lane, Kimie Kawahara, and Caroline Ogata, "Change of Attitudes Among Plantation Workers," *Social Process in Hawaii*, 9–10, 1945.

239. Lasker, Bruno, *Filipino Immigration to Continental United States and to Hawaii*, Honolulu, Institute of Pacific Relations, 1931.

240. Lee, Bung Chong, "The Chinese Store as a Social Institution," *Social Process in Hawaii*, 2, 1936.

241. Lee, Clark, "They Left Her a Bible," unpublished manuscript, circa 1940.

242. Lee, Lloyd L., "A Brief Analysis of the Role and Status of the Negro in the Hawaiian Community," *American Sociological Review*, 13, August 1948.

243. Lee, Robert Man War, "Vertical Mobility Among the Chinese in Hawaii," thesis for the degree of Master of Arts, University of Hawaii, 1951.

244. *The Liberty News.*

245. Liebes, Richard A., "Labor Organization in Hawaii: A Study of the Efforts of Labor to Obtain Security Through Organization," thesis for the degree of Master of Arts, University of Hawaii, 1938.

246. Ligot, Cayetano, "Authoritative Statement Relative to Laborers in Hawaii," March 31, 1923–March 31, 1924. Printed by permission of the Governor General of the Philippines.

247. Ligot, Cayetano, "The Filipinos in the Territory of Hawaii," *Mid-Pacific Magazine*, 48, January–March 1936.

248. Lind, Andrew William, "The Changing Japanese In Hawaii," *Social Process in Hawaii*, 4, 1938.

249. Lind, Andrew William, "Changing Race Relations in Hawaii," *Social Process in Hawaii*, 18, 1954.

250. Lind, Andrew William, "Current Vital Statistics," *Social Process in Hawaii*, 1, 1935.
251. Lind, Andrew William, *Hawaii's Japanese: An Experiment in Democracy*, Princeton, Princeton University Press, 1946.
252. Lind, Andrew William, *Hawaii's People*, Honolulu, University of Hawaii Press, 1955.
253. Lind, Andrew William, *An Island Community: Ecological Succession in Hawaii*, Chicago, University of Chicago Press, 1938.
254. Lind, Andrew William, "Japanese Assimilation in Rural Hawaii," *American Journal of Sociology*, 45, September 1939.
255. Lind, Andrew William, "Japanese Language Schools, 1948," *What People Have Been Saying and Doing in Hawaii*, 15, December 7, 1948.
256. Lind, Andrew William, "Kona—Haven of Peoples," *Social Process in Hawaii*, 13, 1949.
257. Lind, Andrew William, "Mounting the Occupational Ladder in Hawaii," *What People Have Been Saying and Doing in Hawaii*, 24, January 1957.
258. Lind, Andrew William, "Occupational Attitudes of Orientals in Hawaii," mimeographed, Honolulu, University of Hawaii, circa 1928.
259. Lind, Andrew William, "Population Notes," *Social Process in Hawaii*, 3, 1937.
260. Lind, Andrew William, "Post War Attitudes Regarding Race Relations in Hawaii," *Social Process in Hawaii*, 11, 1947.
261. Lind, Andrew William, "Racial Bloc Voting in Hawaii," *Social Process in Hawaii*, 21, 1957.
262. Lind, Andrew William, "Types of Social Movements in Hawaii," *Social Process in Hawaii*, 7, 1941.
263. Lind, Andrew William, "Voting in Hawaii," *Administration in Hawaii*, U.S. Congress, Senate, Committee on Territories and Insular Affairs, Washington, Government Printing Office, January 16, 1933.
264. Lind, Andrew William, "Voting in Hawaii," *Social Process in Hawaii*, 1, 1935.
265. Littler, Robert M. C., *The Governance of Hawaii*, Stanford, Stanford University Press, 1929.
266. Littler, Robert M. C., "The Vote Cast by Various Races Living in Hawaii," Honolulu *Star Bulletin*, May 21–4, 1927.
267. Lorden, Doris M., "The Chinese-Hawaiian Family," *American Journal of Sociology*, 40, January 1935.

268. Luis, Anastacio, and Herman Sensano, "Some Aspects of the Filipino Family," *Social Process in Hawaii*, 3, 1937.
269. Lum, Henry, and M. Miyazawa, "An Abortive Religious Cult," *Social Process in Hawaii*, 7, 1941.
270. Lum, Kalfred Dip, "Education of the Chinese in Hawaii," *Chinese in Hawaii*, 1929.
271. Lum, Kalfred Dip, "The Evolution of Government in Hawaii," thesis for the degree of Doctor of Philosophy in Government and Public Law, New York University, 1926.
272. Lydecker, Robert C., *Roster of Legislatures of Hawaii, 1841–1918*, Honolulu, The Hawaiian Gazette Co., Ltd., 1918.
273. MacCaughey, Vaughan, "Education in Hawaii," *Mid-Pacific Magazine*, 22, December 1921.
274. McClatchy, Valentine Stuart, *Assimilation of Japanese: Can They Be Moulded into American Citizens?* Honolulu Rotary Club, October 27, 1921, Sacramento, California, J. McClatchy & Company, 1921.
275. McKinney, Albert, "A Study of the Treatment of Education in the Daily Newspapers of Honolulu," thesis for the degree of Master of Education, University of Hawaii, 1940.
276. Makishima, Fusako, "Citizens Should Serve One Country," *Nippu Jiji*, June 1928.
277. Malo, David, *Hawaiian Antiquities*, Honolulu, Bernice Pauahi Bishop Museum, 1903.
278. Manlapit, Pablo, *Filipinos Fight for Justice: Case of the Filipino Laborers in the Big Strike of 1924, Territory of Hawaii, 1924*, Honolulu, Kumalae Publishing Co., 1933.
279. *Manual of Hawaiian Securities*, Honolulu Stock Exchange, 1910–1959.
280. Marques, J. D., "The Portuguese in this Territory," *Pacific Commercial Advertiser*, 50th Anniversary number, July 2, 1906.
281. Masuda, Ruth N., "The Japanese 'Tanomoshi,' " *Social Process in Hawaii*, 3, 1937.
282. Masuoka, Jitsuichi, "The Changing Moral Basis of the Japanese Family in Hawaii," *Sociology and Social Research*, 21, November–December 1936.
283. Masuoka, Jitsuichi, "The Life Cycle of an Immigrant Institution in Hawaii: The Japanese Family," *Social Forces*, 23, 1944.
284. Masuoka, Jitsuichi, "Marriage in the Family: The Japanese Patriarch in Hawaii," *Social Forces*, 14, December 1938.
285. Masuoka, Jitsuichi, "Race Attitudes of the Japanese People in Ha-

waii: A Study in Social Distance," thesis for the degree of Master of Arts, University of Hawaii, 1931.

286. Masuoka, Jitsuichi, "The Structure of the Japanese Family in Hawaii," *American Journal of Sociology*, 46, 1940.

287. Mathison, Gilbert F., *Narrative of the Visit to Brazil, Chile, Peru and the Sandwich Islands During the Years 1821 and 1822*, Pall Mall East, London, Charles Knight, 1825.

288. Mead, Royal, "Sugar Interests in Hawaii," San Francisco *Chronicle*, July 18, 1910.

289. Meller, Norman, "Centralization in Hawaii: Retrospect and Prospect," *American Political Science Review*, 52, March 1958.

290. Meller, Norman, "Hawaii: A Study of Centralization," thesis for the degree of Doctor of Philosophy, University of Chicago, 1955.

291. Menor, Benjamin, "Filipino Plantation Adjustments," *Social Process in Hawaii*, 13, 1949.

292. Midkiff, Frank E., "The Economic Determinants of Education in Hawaii," thesis for the degree of Doctor of Philosophy, Yale University, 1935.

293. Mills, Arthur L., "Labor-Management Relations in Hawaii," thesis for the degree of Master of Arts, University of Hawaii, 1955.

294. Mitamura, Machiyo, "The Life on a Hawaiian Plantation," *Community Forces in Hawaii*, 1940.

295. Moncado, Hilario Camino, *Filipino Labor Conditions in the Territory of Hawaii, Report . . . to Honorable Manuel L. Quezon, President of the Philippines*, Honolulu, privately printed, 1936.

296. Morgan, Theodore, *Hawaii, A Century of Economic Change*, Cambridge, Harvard University Press, 1948.

297. Moroi, Consul-General, "Americanizing the Japanese in Hawaii," *Mid-Pacific Magazine*, 16, October 1918.

298. Mund, Vernon A., and Fred C. Hung, *Interlocking Relationships in Hawaii and Public Regulation of Ocean Transportation*, Honolulu Economic Research Center, University of Hawaii, 1961.

299. Murphy, Thomas Daniel, *Ambassadors in Arms: The Story of Hawaii's 100th Battalion*, Honolulu, University of Hawaii Press, 1954.

300. Nakahata, Yutaka, and Ralph Toyota, "Varsity Victory Volunteers: A Social Movement," *Social Process in Hawaii*, 8, 1943.

301. Nakasone, Henry I., "Propaganda Techniques Employed in Imua and ILWU Radio Broadcasts," thesis for the degree of Master of Arts, University of Hawaii, 1956.

302. *The Navy and the Massie-Kahahawai Case*, Honolulu, The Honolulu Record Publishing Co., Ltd., 1951.

303. *The New Freedom.*

304. *The Nippu Jiji.*

305. *Nippu Jiji,* "Golden Jubilee of the Japanese in Hawaii," Honolulu, 1935.

306. Norbeck, Edward, *Plantation Town, Hawaii,* Berkeley, University of California Press, 1959.

307. Ogura, Shiko I., *County Government in Hawaii,* Hilo, Hawaii News Print Shop, 1935.

308. Okamura, Takie, "Test of Japanese Assimilation," *Friend,* 110, March 1940.

309. Okamura, Takie, and Umetaro Okamura, "Expatriation—Back to the Soil: Remarks on the Occasion of the Fiftieth Anniversary of the First Japanese Immigration to Hawaii," Pan-Pacific Union, *Bulletin,* January–March 1935.

310. Okamura, Takie, and Umetaro Okamura, *Hawaii's American-Japanese Problem: A Campaign to Remove Causes of Friction Between,* Honolulu, 1921.

311. Onishi, Katsumi, "The Second Generation Japanese and the Hongwanji," *Social Process in Hawaii,* 3, 1937.

312. Onishi, Katsumi, "A Study of the Attitudes of the Japanese in Hawaii Toward the Japanese Language Schools," thesis for the degree of Master of Education, University of Hawaii, 1943.

313. Ozawa, A. K., "The Japanese Boy in Hawaii," *Mid-Pacific Magazine,* 15, March 1918.

314. The Pacific Club, "Report of Economic Planning Sub-Committee," 1958.

315. *The Pacific Commercial Advertiser.*

316. Pendleton, Edwin C., "Characteristics of the Labor Force," *Monthly Labor Review,* 78, December 1955.

317. Perlman, Mark, "Organized Labor in Hawaii," *Labor Law Journal,* 3, April 1952.

318. Philipp, Perry F., *Diversified Agriculture of Hawaii,* Honolulu, University of Hawaii Press, 1953.

319. Philippine Islands, Bureau of Labor, *Report . . . Covering Investigation of Labor Conditions and Employment of Filipinos in Hawaii,* Manila, Bureau of Printing, 1926.

320. Phillips, Lyle G., "The Communist Grip in Hawaii," speech given in Pittsburgh, November 16, 1957.

321. Pierson, Kathleen W., "The Development of Trade in Hawaii: A Statistical Analysis and Evaluation of Basic Trends," thesis for the degree of Master of Arts, University of Hawaii, 1948.

322. Piianaia, Abraham, "Statehood and the Native Hawaiian Homesteader," *Social Process in Hawaii,* 14, 1959.

323. *Plantation Health.*

324. *The Planters' Monthly.*

325. *The Polynesian.*

326. Porteus, Stanley D., *And Blow Not the Trumpet,* Palo Alto, California, Pacific Books, 1947.

327. Porteus, Stanley D., and Margery E. Babcock, *Temperament and Race,* Boston, R. D. Badger, 1926.

328. Pratt, Helen Gay, *Hawaii Off-Shore Territory,* New York, Charles Scribner's Sons, 1944.

329. Pratt, Helen Gay, "The Problem of the Filipino in Hawaii," *The Philippines in Hawaii,* 2, July 4, 1949.

330. Pratt, Julius, *The Expansionists of 1898,* Baltimore, Johns Hopkins Press, 1936.

331. Pratt, Julius, "The Hawaiian Revolution: A Reinterpretation," *The Pacific Historical Review,* 1, September 1932.

332. *Proceedings of Public Hearings Held Before the Secretary of Interior, Walter L. Fisher, On Conditions in the Territory of Hawaii,* Vol. 1–3, 1912.

333. Public Administration Service of Chicago, "Report to Governor William H. Quinn on Territorial Tax Assessment Procedures," 1958.

334. Quinto, Dolores, "Life Story of a Filipino Immigrant," *Social Process in Hawaii,* 4, 1938.

335. Rademaker, John Adrian, "Race Relations in Hawaii, 1946," *Social Process in Hawaii,* 11, 1947.

336. Rademaker, John Adrian, *These Are Americans: The Japanese Americans in Hawaii in World War II,* Palo Alto, California, Pacific Books, 1951.

337. Reinecke, John Ernest, "Language and Dialect in Hawaii," thesis for the degree of Master of Arts, University of Hawaii, 1935.

338. Reinecke, John Ernest, "The 1920 Strike," unpublished manuscript.

339. Reinecke, John Ernest, " 'Pidgin English' in Hawaii: A Local Study in the Sociology of Language," *American Journal of Sociology,* 43, March 1938.

340. Restarick, Henry B., "Americanizing Hawaii," *Mid-Pacific Magazine,* 7, March 1914.

341. Restarick, Henry B., *Tendency of Modern Education in Hawaii Leads Boys Away from all Forms of Manual Labor: Opinions of Employers of Labor Upon Education in Hawaii,* pamphlet, 1912.

342. Richards, Theodore, "The Future of the Japanese in Hawaii: Things

Problematic, Things Probable, Things Potential," *Japan and Japanese-American Relations,* New York, G. E. Stechert & Co., 1912.

343. Robinson, Clarence C., "Occupational Succession on the Plantation," *Social Process in Hawaii,* 1, 1935.

344. Robison, F. Everett, "Participation of Citizens of Chinese and Japanese Ancestry in the Political Life in Hawaii," *Social Process in Hawaii,* 4, 1938.

345. Roesch, Richard L., "The Hawaiian Statehood Plebiscite of 1940," thesis for the degree of Master of Arts, University of Hawaii, 1952.

346. Rowland, Donald, "Establishment of the Republic of Hawaii, 1893–1894," *The Pacific Historical Review,* 4, September 1935.

347. Russ, William Adam, "Hawaiian Labor and Immigration Problems Before Annexation," *Journal of Modern History,* 15, September 1943.

348. Russ, William Adam, "The Role of Sugar in Hawaiian Annexation," *The Pacific Historical Review,* 12, December 1943.

349. Sakamaki, Shunzo, "A History of the Japanese Press in Hawaii," thesis for the degree of Master of Arts, University of Hawaii, 1928.

350. Sakamaki, Shunzo, "Take the Best East and West Can Give," *Nippu Jiji,* June 1928.

351. Sanjume, Jisoo, "An Analysis of the 'New Americans Conference' from 1927 to 1938," thesis for the degree of Master of Education, University of Hawaii, 1939.

352. Sasaki, Hideko, "The Life History of a Portuguese Immigrant," *Social Process in Hawaii,* 1, 1935.

353. Second Oahu Conference of Americans of Japanese Ancestry, *A Report,* 1959.

354. Shapiro, Harry Lionel, *The Chinese Population in Hawaii,* New York, Institute of Pacific Relations, 1931.

355. Shirey, Orville C., *Americans: The Story of the 442nd Combat Team,* Washington, Infantry Journal Press, 1946.

356. Shoemaker, James H., "Economic and Labor Conditions in Hawaii," *Monthly Labor Review,* May 1948.

357. Shoemaker, James H., *Labor in the Territory of Hawaii,* Washington, Government Printing Office, 1938.

358. Shoemaker, James H., "Labor Trends in Hawaii," *Monthly Labor Review,* June 1948.

359. Slate, Daniel M., and Shelley M. Mark, *An Economic Study of*

the Kona Coffee Industry, Kona, Kona Community Federal Credit Union, March 1959.

360. Smith, Bradford, *Americans from Japan*, Philadelphia, J. B. Lippincott Co., 1948.

361. Smith, Bradford, *Yankees in Paradise: The New England Impact on Hawaii*, Philadelphia, J. B. Lippincott, 1956.

362. Smith, Jared G., *The Big Five*, Honolulu, Advertiser Publishing Co., Ltd., 1945.

363. Smith, William C., *The Second Generation Oriental in America*, Honolulu, Institute of Pacific Relations, 1927.

364. Soga, Y., "The Japanese Press in Hawaii," *Mid-Pacific Magazine*, 23, January 1922.

365. Soga, Y., *The Solution of the Labor Problem in Hawaii: Comprising Fifteen Articles, Pertaining Mainly to the Sugar Industry, Submitted in Competition and Printed in the* Pacific Commercial Advertiser *Beginning March 24, 1919*, Honolulu, Advertiser Publishing Co., Ltd., 1919.

366. Sousa, Esther L., "Walter Murray Gibson's Rise to Power in Hawaii," thesis for the degree of Master of Arts, University of Hawaii, 1942.

367. *Spotlight*, a monthly publication by Imua.

368. Stevens, Sylvester K., *American Expansion in Hawaii, 1842–1898*, Harrisburg, Archives Publishing Company of Pennsylvania Inc., 1945.

369. Strong, Edward K., *The Second-Generation Japanese Problem*, Stanford, Stanford University Press, 1934.

370. Stroupe, Conner B., "Significant Factors in the Influx to Private Schools on Oahu Since 1900," thesis for the degree of Master of Arts, University of Hawaii, 1955.

371. Sullivan, Josephine, *A History of C. Brewer & Co., Ltd.*, Boston, Walton Advertising and Printing Co., 1926.

372. Tajima, Paul Junichiro, "Japanese Buddhism in Hawaii: Its Background, Origin, and Adaptation to Local Conditions," thesis for the degree of Master of Arts, University of Hawaii, 1935, revised 1938.

373. Talbott, E. Guy, "Making Americans in Hawaii," *The American Review of Reviews*, March 1926.

374. Tanimura, Clinton T., and Robert M. Kamins, "A Study of Large Land Owners in Hawaii," Legislative Reference Bureau, Report #2, Honolulu, University of Hawaii, 1957.

375. Tax Foundation of Hawaii, "Our Tax Dollar," 1958–59.

376. Taylor, Ray, "Report on the Conditions at the Olawalu Plantation on Maui," June 1897.

377. Taylor, William H., "The Hawaiian Sugar Industry," thesis for the degree of Doctor of Philosophy in Economics in the Graduate Division, University of California, 1935.

378. Thompson, David, "The Filipino Federation of America, Incorporated: A Study in the Natural History of a Social Institution," *Social Process in Hawaii*, 7, 1941.

379. Thompson, David E., "The ILWU as a Force for Interracial Unity in Hawaii," *Social Process in Hawaii*, 15, 1951.

380. *Thrum's Hawaiian Annual and Standard Guide*, Honolulu, Honolulu *Star Bulletin*, 1875–1960.

381. Thurston, Lorrin A., *The Japanese Problem in Hawaii*, Citizenship Education Committee, Honolulu, Americanization Institute, 1919.

382. Toyama, Henry, and Kiyoshi Ikeda, "The Okinawan—Naichi Relationship," *Social Process in Hawaii*, 14, 1950.

383. Tsutsumi, Takashi, "History of Hawaii Laborers' Movement," translated from the Japanese by Umetaro Okumura, Honolulu, 1922.

384. Tuttle, Daniel, unpublished studies on ethnicity of precincts and electoral behavior, 1956.

385. *The United Chinese News.*

386. U.S. Bureau of Foreign and Domestic Commerce, *Hawaii: Its Resources and Trade*, by Emmett A. Chapman, Washington, Government Printing Office, 1927.

387. U.S. Bureau of Immigration and Naturalization, *Report on Industrial Conditions in the Hawaiian Islands*, 63rd Congress, 1st Session, Washington, Government Printing Office, 1922.

388. U.S. Bureau of Insular Affairs, *Filipino Immigration to Hawaii, 1906–1946*, Washington, National Archives, 1953.

389. U.S. Bureau of Labor, *Labor Conditions in Hawaii*, Washington, Government Printing Office, 1904.

390. U.S. Bureau of Labor, *Report of Labor Commissioner on Hawaii*, Washington, Government Printing Office, 1911.

391. U.S. Bureau of Labor, *Report of the Commissioner of Labor on Hawaii, 1901*, Washington, Government Printing Office, 1902.

392. U.S. Bureau of Labor, *Report of the Commissioner of Labor on Hawaii, 1902*, Washington, Government Printing Office, 1903.

393. U.S. Bureau of Labor, *Report of the Commissioner of Labor on Hawaii, 1905*, Washington, Government Printing Office, 1906.

394. U.S. Bureau of Labor, *Report of the Commissioner of Labor on Hawaii, 1911*, Washington, Government Printing Office, 1912.

395. U.S. Bureau of Labor, *Report of the Commissioner of Labor on Hawaii, 1915,* Washington, Government Printing Office, 1916.

396. U.S. Bureau of the Census, 11th through 17th census of the United States, Washington, Government Printing Office, 1900–1950.

397. U.S. Congress, House, Committee on Immigration and Naturalization, *Labor Problems in Hawaii,* Hearings, 67th Congress, 1st Session, Washington, Government Printing Office, 1921.

398. U.S. Congress, House, Committee on Public Lands, *Statehood for Hawaii,* Hearings, 80th Congress, 1st Session, Washington, Government Printing Office, 1947.

399. U.S. Congress, House, Committee on Territories, *Extension of a Franchise for Hawaii,* Hearings, 67th Congress, 1st Session, Washington, Government Printing Office, 1921.

400. U.S. Congress, House, Committee on Territories, *Nonassimilability of Japanese in Hawaii and the United States,* Hearings, 67th Congress, 2nd Session, Washington, Government Printing Office, 1922.

401. U.S. Congress, House, Committee on Territories, *Rehabilitation and Colonization of Hawaiians and Other Proposed Amendments to the Organic Act of the Territory of Hawaii,* Hearings, 67th Congress, 1st Session, Washington, Government Printing Office, 1921.

402. U.S. Congress, House, Committee on Un-American Activities, *Communism in Hawaii,* Hearings, 84th Congress, 2nd Session, Washington, Government Printing Office, 1956.

403. U.S. Congress, House, Committee on Un-American Activities, *Hearings Regarding Communist Activities in the Territory of Hawaii,* 81st Congress, 2nd Session, and 82nd Congress, 1st Session, Washington, Government Printing Office, 1950, 1951.

404. U.S. Congress, House, Committee on Un-American Activities, *Report on Hawaii Civil Liberties Committee (A Communist Front),* Washington, Government Printing Office, 1950.

405. U.S. Congress, House, Committee on Un-American Activities, *Report on the Honolulu Record,* Washington, Government Printing Office, 1950.

406. U.S. Congress, House, Report of Committee on Territories, *Leasing of Land in Hawaii,* 62nd Congress, 1st Session, Washington, Government Printing Office, 1912.

407. U.S. Congress, House, Report of Committee on Territories, *Rehabilitation of Native Hawaiians,* 66th Congress, 2nd Session, Washington, Government Printing Office, 1920.

408. U.S. Congress, House, *Report of Special Committee to Investigate* the *National Labor Relations Board,* Hearings, 76th Congress, 1st Session, Vol. V, Washington, Government Printing Office, 1940.

409. U.S. Congress, House, *Report on Industrial Conditions in Hawaiian Islands,* 63rd Congress, 1st Session, Washington, Government Printing Office, 1913.

410. U.S. Congress, House, *Report on Labor Problems in Hawaii,* 67th Congress, 4th Session, Washington, Government Printing Office, 1923.

411. U.S. Congress, House, *Report on Statehood for Hawaii,* 85th Congress, 2nd Session, Washington, Government Printing Office, August 23, 1958.

412. U.S. Congress, House, Subcommittee of the Committee on the Territories, *Statehood for Hawaii,* Hearings, 74th Congress, 1st Session, Washington, Government Printing Office, 1936.

413. U.S. Congress, House, Subcommittee of the Committee on the Territories, *Statehood for Hawaii,* Hearings, 79th Congress, 2nd Session, Washington, Government Printing Office, 1946.

414. U.S. Congress, Investigation, the Contested Election of Lincoln Loy McCandless vs. Samuel Wilder King, Territory of Hawaii, 74th Congress, Abstract of the Record and of Contestant's Testimony and Brief for Contestant, unpublished.

415. U.S. Congress, Joint Committee on Hawaii, *Statehood for Hawaii,* Hearings, 75th Congress, 2nd Session, Washington, Government Printing Office, 1938.

416. U.S. Congress, *Joint Committee on the Investigation of the Pearl Harbor Attack,* Hearings, 79th Congress, 1st and 2nd Sessions, 39 volumes, Washington, Government Printing Office, 1946.

417. U.S. Congress, *Report of Subcommittee on Pacific Islands and Puerto Rico on General Conditions in Hawaii,* Hawaiian Investigation, Vol. 3, Washington, Government Printing Office, 1903.

418. U.S. Congress, Senate, *Abstracts of the Report of the Immigration Commission,* 61st Congress, 3rd Session, Washington, Government Printing Office, 1911.

419. U.S. Congress, Senate, Committee on Immigration and Naturalization, *Immigration into Hawaii,* Hearings, 67th Congress, 1st Session, Washington, Government Printing Office, 1921.

420. U.S. Congress, Senate, Committee on Interior and Insular Affairs, *Report on Statehood for Hawaii,* 81st Congress, 2nd Session, Washington, Government Printing Office, June 29, 1950.

421. U.S. Congress, Senate, Committee on Interior and Insular Affairs, *Reports on Statehood for Hawaii, Communist Penetration of the*

Hawaiian Islands, 80th Congress, 2nd Session, Washington, Government Printing Office, 1949.

422. U.S. Congress, Senate, Committee on Interior and Insular Affairs, *Statehood for Hawaii,* Hearings, 83rd Congress, 1st and 2nd Sessions, Washington, Government Printing Office, 1953, 1954.

423. U.S. Congress, Senate, Committee on Interior and Insular Affairs, *Statehood for Hawaii,* Hearings, 85th Congress, 1st Session, Washington, Government Printing Office, 1957.

424. U.S. Congress, Senate, Committee on Labor and Public Welfare, *Hawaiian Labor Situation,* Hearings, 81st Congress, 1st Session, Washington, Government Printing Office, 1949.

425. U.S. Congress, Senate, *Report on Labor Conditions in Hawaii,* 64th Congress, 1st Session, Washington, Government Printing Office, 1916.

426. U.S. Congress, Senate, *Report on Law Enforcement in the Territory of Hawaii,* by Attorney-General S. W. Richardson, Washington, Government Printing Office, 1932.

427. U.S. Congress, Senate, Subcommittee of the Committee on Territories and Insular Affairs, *Statehood for Hawaii,* Hearings, 80th Congress, 2nd Session, Washington, Government Printing Office, 1948.

428. U.S. Congress, Senate, Subcommittee on Immigration, *Japanese in Hawaii,* Hearings, Washington, Government Printing Office, 1920.

429. *U.S. Congressional Record.*

430. U.S. Department of Labor, Bureau of Labor Statistics, *The Economy of Hawaii in 1947,* by James H. Shoemaker, Washington, Government Printing Office, 1948.

431. U.S. Department of Labor, Bureau of Labor Statistics, *Labor Conditions in the Territory of Hawaii, 1929–1930,* Washington, Government Printing Office, 1931.

432. U.S. Department of Labor, Bureau of Labor Statistics, *Labor in the Territory of Hawaii,* by James H. Shoemaker, Washington, Government Printing Office, 1939.

433. U.S. Department of the Interior, *Annual Report of the Governor of Hawaii to the Secretary of the Interior,* Washington, Government Printing Office, 1901–1959.

434. U.S. Department of the Interior, Bureau of Education, *A Survey of Education in Hawaii,* Washington, Government Printing Office, 1920.

435. U.S. Office of Education, *The Education of Native and Minority Groups: A Bibliography, 1923–32,* by Katharine M. Cook and

Florence E. Reynolds, Washington, Government Printing Office, 1933.

436.   Vinacke, W. Edgar, "Stereotyping Among National-Racial Groups in Hawaii: A Study in Ethnocentrism," *Journal of Social Psychology*, 30, 1949.

437.   *The Voice of Labor.*

438.   Wakukawa, Ernest K., *A History of the Japanese People in Hawaii*, Honolulu, The Toyo Shoin, 1938.

439.   Wakukawa, Ernest K., "Our Characteristics Are No Hindrance," *Nippu Jiji*, June 1928.

440.   Wentworth, Edna Clark, *Filipino Plantation Workers in Hawaii: A Study of Incomes, Expenditures and Living Standards of Filipino Families on an Hawaiian Sugar Plantation*, New York, Institute of Pacific Relations, 1941.

441.   Williams, R. D., "Dialogue Between Sugar Grower & Christian Educator," *Friend*, June 1917.

442.   Wist, Benjamin O., *A Century of Public Education in Hawaii, October 15, 1840, to October 15, 1940*, Honolulu, The Hawaii Educational Review, 1940.

443.   Wong, Elizabeth, "Leaves From the Life History of a Chinese Immigrant," *Social Process in Hawaii*, 2, 1936.

444.   Wong, Sau Chun, "Chinese Temples in Honolulu," *Social Process in Hawaii*, 3, 1937.

445.   Woods, Sister Francis Jerome, *Cultural Values of American Ethnic Groups*, New York, Harper & Bros., 1956.

446.   Yamamoto, George K., "Political Participation Among Orientals in Hawaii," *Sociology and Social Research*, May–June 1949.

447.   Yamamoto, Misako, "Cultural Conflicts and Accommodations of the First and Second Generation Japanese," *Social Process in Hawaii*, 4, 1938.

448.   Yamamura, Douglas S., and Raymond Sakumoto, "Residential Segregation in Honolulu," *Social Process in Hawaii*, 18, 1954.

449.   *The Yoen Jiho.*

450.   Young, Lucien, *Boston in Hawaii*, Washington, D.C., Gibson Bros., 1898.

2. Letters and Papers

The Archives of Hawaii, in a new building on the grounds of Iolani Palace, houses the most complete historical collection of Hawaiiana in the United States. Far from exhausting its contents, the author limited himself to systematic and thorough examination of several dozen cabinet files containing the papers of most of the principal political figures of modern Hawaii. Miss Agnes C. Conrad, chief archivist, and her staff went out of their way to expedite his work in the Archives.

451. The papers of Delegate Henry A. Baldwin.
452. The papers of Governors George R. Carter and Sanford B. Dole.
453. The papers of Delegate Joseph R. Farrington.
454. The papers of Governor Wallace R. Farrington.
455. The papers of Delegate Victor K. Houston.
456. The papers of Governor Lawrence M. Judd.
457. The papers of Delegate Jonah Kuhio Kalanianaole.
458. The papers of Governor and Delegate Samuel W. King.
459. The papers of Delegate Lincoln L. McCandless.
460. The papers of Governor Charles J. McCarthy.
461. The papers of Governor Lucius E. Pinkham.
462. The papers of Governor Joseph B. Poindexter.
463. The papers of Governor Ingram M. Stainback.
464. The papers of Mayor John H. Wilson.

3. Depth Interviews

The author conducted 155 interviews, lasting from one to four and a half hours, nearly all of which were with individuals who have held or now play significant roles in the political or economic life of Hawaii. In order to obtain reliable and important information from the respondents, certain rules were applied to these interviews. Each respondent was promised that no information revealed in the interview would be ascribed to him or her without permission as long as he or she were alive. Most respondents granted permission to use material from their interviews without attributing its source. The method of the author in interviewing was to ask the respondent to give his version or perception of important events in which he participated. The feelings and views of the interviewees were reflected until they were understood. They were never contradicted or threatened in any way. In many interviews the respondents were encouraged by this non-evaluative, empathic relationship to go into great detail concerning some of their deepest feelings and opinions.

During the interview, notes were jotted down which were used immediately following the interview by the author, who dictated his record of the interview at length. Information from interviews repeated in the text was checked and double checked against other sources, including other interviews, wherever possible. Where unusually significant information is repeated in the book but was not checked, special notice has been given to the reader.

Except in two cases, interviewees are not identified below. Each source is listed according to major category, rather than named, in keeping with the promise made to each respondent to protect his or her anonymity. For example, if the late former Governor and Delegate Samuel W. King or the late territorial Secretary Farrant C. Turner were presently alive, they would be identified below simply as part-Hawaiian and haole Republican politicians respectively.

Because individual depth interviews take a great deal of time, the author experimented with group interviews in depth. He conducted five of these, listed below, each with fundamentally different groups. The interview method employed was the same as used in individual interviews. The group interviews lasted from two to four hours. The interview at the Palama Settlement House was arranged through Robert S. Craig of Robert S. Craig Associates.

The author's interviews were conducted with the following:

OF CHINESE EXTRACTION:
465–467.   Business executives.
   468.   Civic leader.
   469.   Financier.
470–473.   Older politicians.
474–477.   Politicians.

OF FILIPINO EXTRACTION:
478–479.   Businessmen.
   480.   Government official.
481–482.   Labor leaders.
   483.   Lawyer.
484–486.   Politicians.

HAOLES:
   487.   Bank official.
488–500.   Business executives.
   501.   Businessman.
502–503.   Civic leaders.
   504.   Daughter of newspaper editor.
   505.   Democratic party official.
   506.   Former labor leader.
   507.   Former sugar plantation manager.
508–512.   Labor leaders.
   513.   Labor-relations executive.

514. Labor-union official.
515. Medical doctor.
516. Minister.
517. Missionary descendant.
518–519. Newspaper executives.
520. Newspaperman.
521–522. Older politicians.
523. Plantation owner.
524–540. Politicians.
541. The late Farrant L. Turner.
542–543. Republican party officials.
544. School administrator.
545–546. Schoolteachers.
547. Social worker.
548–551. Sugar agency executives.
552. Sugar plantation executive.

OF HAWAIIAN EXTRACTION:

553. Older nationalist leader.
554–555. Older politicians.
556. Older politician-civic leader.

OF PART-HAWAIIAN EXTRACTION:

557. City and county official.
558. Civic leader.
559. Labor leader.
560. Older leader.
561–563. Older politicians.
564–569. Politicians.
570. The late Samuel Wilder King.
571. Ranch owner.

ISSEI:

572. Business leader.
573. Labor leader.

OF KOREAN EXTRACTION:

574. Politician.

NISEI:

575–577. Businessmen.
578. Former labor official.
579. Insurance executive.
580. Labor leader.
581–582. Lawyers.
583–589. Older politicians.

590–607. Politicians.
   608. Psychologist.
609–610. Schoolteachers.

SANSEI:
   611. Bank official.

OF PORTUGUESE EXTRACTION:
   612. Businessman.
   613. Lawyer.
614–617. Older Politicians.
618–619. Politicians.

OF SPANISH EXTRACTION:
   620. Politician.

GROUP INTERVIEWS:
   621. Haole executives of major agency.
   622. Multiracial instructional staff of the Kamehameha School for Boys.
   623. Multiracial Lions Club members, rural Oahu.
   624. Plantation workers of Filipino extraction.
   625. Working-class voters, multiracial backgrounds, Palama Settlement House, Honolulu.

4. Public-Opinion Surveys

The results of the surveys listed below, with the exception of the 1959 Social Science Research Council survey done especially for this project, were made available through the courtesy of Robert S. Craig Associates of Honolulu, Hawaii. Because Mr. Craig is a valuable friend of research and scholarship, he enthusiastically placed the resources of his excellent organization at the disposal of the author. Two members of his staff, Mrs. Elva E. Kunihiro and Mrs. Lorraine Nambu, frequently assisted with tabulations.

Altogether, the surveys listed below comprised nearly 7,000 distinct interviews, based on carefully developed research designs, employing excellent sampling methodology. Mr. Robert Jones, the manager of the tabulating service department of the firm of Peat, Marwick, Mitchell and Company, was extraordinarily helpful in executing runs and reruns of IBM cards in order to yield useful information for the samples and subsamples interviewed.

The 1959 Social Science Research Council survey was conducted under the direction of the author. Assisting in the intensive interviewing of 457 respondents in Honolulu's fourteenth representative district were the following: Mr. Darrow Aiona, Mrs. Kathleen Bluett, Mr. Frank Brown, Mr.

Gordon W. Fullerton, Mr. James Helm, Mr. Henry Iwasa, Jr., Miss Nancy
Lindgren, Mr. Thomas B. Merrill, Miss Janice Nakamura, Mr. Osmund
Okazaki, Mr. Norman Okimoto, Miss Ednett Tam, Miss Joyce Tsunoda,
Mrs. Marilyn Vause, Mr. David Vokac, Mr. Harold Weaver, Miss Jean
Wedzel, a majority of whom were graduate or undergraduate concentrators
in political science or sociology at the University of Hawaii, and Mrs. M. F.
Heiser and Mrs. Norma Van't Woudt, wives of faculty members at the
University of Hawaii.

626. A Political Study, 1948, Territorial Surveys (now Robert S. Craig
Associates), Honolulu, Hawaii, 1948.

The survey sample consisted of two parts. The major sample
of 1,200 interviews with men and women twenty-one years
of age or older was apportioned through the city of Honolulu. The second sample, also adult men and women, consisted of 400 respondents restricted to voting precincts two,
four, and thirty in voting district four, an area known as
Kaimuki. An areal type sample was utilized, insuring adequate geographic coverage of the city and controlling appropriate proportions of major population characteristics. Interviewing took place during the second and third weeks of
August.

627. The Hawaii Poll of Labor-Management Relations, the Hawaiian
Economic Service (now Robert S. Craig Associates), Honolulu,
Hawaii, Fall–Winter 1955.

A detailed questionnaire was administered to a carefully
selected cross section of Hawaii's population on the islands
of Oahu, Hawaii, Maui, and Kauai. Separate samples were
created for the city of Honolulu, for rural Oahu, and for
each neighbor island. An areal survey method was employed, areas selected by random means and interviews
made at intervals beginning from a random point in a community. The sample of 3,377 respondents conformed in
important respects with the 1950 census. Mathematical
computations were made to yield the possible percentage
error for the total sample and subsamples within it.

628. The Hawaii Poll of Public Opinion and Party Preference, the Hawaiian Economic Service (now Robert S. Craig Associates),
Honolulu, Hawaii, 1955.

Methodology and sample same as above.

629.   The Hawaii Poll of Social and Economic Opinion, the Hawaiian Economic Service (now Robert S. Craig Associates), Honolulu, Hawaii, 1955.

Methodology and sample same as above.

630.   Political Opinion and Party Preference, the Hawaii Poll of Public Opinion, research devision of Robert S. Craig Associates, Honolulu, Hawaii, 1958–1959.

The sample for this survey of voter opinion on the island of Oahu was developed by the area probability method. The number of interviews conducted in each representative district was in proportion to the number of voters in that district with a total of 1,321 respondents interviewed in the winter of 1958–59.

631.   Survey of Political, Social, Economic, Ethnic Opinions and Attitudes in the 14th Representative District of Oahu, conducted under the auspices of the Social Science Research Council, 1959.

An intensive and detailed survey of 457 voters comprising a sample drawn by an accepted random method of selecting every nth name from voters lists was conducted in the spring of 1959. The fourteenth district was chosen because of its cosmopolitan ethnic and socioeconomic characteristics.

5. *Other Special Projects*

A number of special research projects were designed and implemented for this study in addition to the 1959 survey. The most important of these was an exhaustive analysis of election returns for all primary and general elections in the Territory of Hawaii between 1900 and 1958 for all contests for delegate and the territorial legislature by precincts and ethnic groups. This extremely difficult undertaking was made possible through the co-operation of election officials working in the Office of the Secretary of the Territory in Iolani Palace. Thousands of computations had to be made for those precincts selected for analysis having distinctive ethnic characteristics. Statistics on the ethnic composition of voters in any precinct were kept by election officials until 1948. For subsequent elections, the ethnic characteristics of selected precincts were determined through an analysis of voters lists, checked against the judgments of working politicians and the results of public-opinion surveys. In no case can the statistics on the ethnic composition of the voters in a precinct be said to be completely accurate, but they are definitely reliable for purposes of this study. Mr. Henry Iwasa, Jr., was of great help in assisting the author in making computations.

Two other complex projects, which did not yield as significant information as the analysis of election returns, were the intensive monitoring of all political broadcasts on radio and television, in English and foreign languages, during the 1958 territorial election campaign and the assignment of research assistants to the attendance of rallies, coffee hours, and other public meetings during that campaign. Participants in these projects included the following: Miss Kathleen Bluett, Mr. Frank Brown, Mrs. Bruce Cooil, Mrs. Leonard Diamond, Mr. Gordon W. Fullerton, Mrs. M. F. Heiser, Mr. Henry Iwasa, Miss Adrienne Kaeppler, Mrs. Barbara Kalish, Mr. Kenneth Kanda, Mr. Rudy Largosa, Mr. Harold Masumoto, Mr. Thomas Merrill, Miss Doris Okuhara, Mrs. Jean Polhemus, Miss Marlene Sneiker, Miss Ednett Tam, Mr. Oliver Thurman, Mrs. Norma Van't Woudt, Mr. David R. Vokac, Mr. Harold Weaver, and Miss Jean Wetzel.

The special studies by Mrs. Chung and Mrs. Vause were undertaken to obtain information needed for this book.

632. Analysis of election returns for territorial contests by precincts, 1900–1958.

633. Analysis of 1958 election campaign through content analysis of speeches and other public utterances by selected candidates on television, radio, and at public meetings.

634. Mrs. H. S. Chung, "Buddhist Services in Contemporary Hawaii," an unpublished essay.

635. Mrs. H. S. Chung, "Chinese Civic, Patriotic, and Economic Organizations in Hawaii, 1900–1960," an unpublished study.

636. Mrs. Marilyn Vause, "English Standard Schools in Hawaii," unpublished notes and statistics based on information received from the Department of Public Instruction.

6. *Additional Acknowledgments*

Throughout the preparation of this study I have had the assistance of three wonderful secretaries, Mrs. Jean Polhemus, in Hawaii, and Mrs. Jean Haskell and Mrs. Ruth Talley, on the mainland. Mrs. Talley's duties went far beyond the usual secretarial chores. Trained as a sociologist and capable of remarkable precision in expression, Mrs. Talley rendered invaluable editorial assistance in the preparation of the manuscript.

The hospitality of the officials of the government and the University of Hawaii lived up to the Islands' reputation for *aloha*. From Governor William Quinn and University President Lawrence Snyder down, every facility and resource was placed at my disposal. Members of the Departments of Government and of Sociology and Anthropology at the University provided especially helpful advice. Professor Andrew Lind generously shared his vast experience and knowledge.

Portions of this manuscript were read and checked for accuracy of fact and interpretation by the following: Rev. Abraham Akaka, Mr. Bernaldo Bicoy, Dr. Richard Blaisdell, Mr. Juan Dionisio, Mrs. Elizabeth Easley, Professor John Easley, U.S. Senator Hiram Fong, Professor Clarence Glick, Mrs. Thelma Hadley, Prof. Bernhard Hormann, Mr. John E. Hulten, U.S. Representative Daniel Inouye, Prof. Robert Kamins, Mrs. Marian Kelly, Mrs. Mildred Kosaki, Prof. Richard Kosaki, Dr. Kenneth Lau, Mr. William Lederer, U.S. Senator Oren E. Long, Mr. Malcolm MacNaughton, Prof. Shelley M. Mark, Mrs. Patsy T. Mink, Mr. Donald K. Mitchell, Mr. John Murphy, Mr. William Norwood, Governor William Quinn, Dr. John Reinecke, Dr. Richard Takasaki, Mr. Hung Wai Ching, Mr. Hung Wo Ching, and Prof. George Yamamoto. Those errors that remain are, of course, my own.

NOTES

Sources for the numbers in boldface can be found on pages 451 to 483.

PROLOGUE

The material for this chapter on ancient Hawaii is derived primarily from: **28, 52, 89, 139, 200, 227, 277.**
On the transition of ancient society following the impact of foreign influences, see: **40, 77, 108, 201, 203, 212, 227, 287, 296, 361.**
Concerning political and constitutional developments in Hawaii prior to the Great Mahele, see: **64, 212, 227, 228, 368.**
For economic developments, see: **40, 116, 212, 218, 228, 296, 347, 362, 371.**
On annexation and the events preceding it, see: **29, 82, 198, 330, 331, 346, 348, 366, 450.**

CHAPTER 1

1. **23, 61, 164, 494, 517, 523, 571**   2. **523, 530**   3. **118, 434**   4. **120**, March 1891
5. **391**, p. 92   6. **390**, p. 696   7. **393**   8. **507, 523**   9. **120** from 1900 through 1920
10. **106**, pp. 8–9   11. **91**   12. **491, 517, 518**   13. **288**   14. **297**   15. **328**, p. 63, **438,**
pp. 114–117   16. **327**, p. 327   17. **24, 280**   18. **131**   19. **197**, Nov. 15, 16, Dec. 1, 1898,
315, Nov. 10, 17, Dec. 19, 1898   20. **173** for this and other material on the Germans
21. **391**, p. 57   22. **393**, pp. 31, 99   23. **394**   24. **394**, p. 16   25. **393**, p. 98   26. **514**
27. **507**   28. **395**   29. **391**, p. 137   30. **393**, pp. 111, 112, **328**, p. 47   31. **87**, pp. 250,
260, **62**   32. **393**, p. 70   33. **280**, p. 47, **122, 204, 352**   34. **419**, p. 213   35. **391**, p. 222
36. **395**, pp. 78–118   37. **615**   38. **43**, p. 106   39. **34**, speech by Dr. Ruby Norris, p. 22
40. **612**   41. **7**, pp. 139, 140   42. **292**, pp. 53, 54   43. **507, 551**   44. **504**   45. **306,**
pp. 127–128, **609, 610**   46. **507**   47. **306**, p. 126   48. **523, 504**   49. **507, 547**   50. **610**
51. **478, 547**   52. **547**   53. **168**, p. 49   54. **253**, p. 16   55. **302**   56. **253**, pp. 11, 12
57. **7**, pp. 127, 128   58. **7**, p. 131

CHAPTER 2

1. **252**, p. 48, **40, 107, 119, 172, 203**   2. **160**, pp. 13, 22, 33, 39, 72, **189**, pp. 13, 14   3. **253,**
pp. 322–324   4. **253**, pp. 102–103, **122, 186**   5. **7**, p. 262   6. **189**   7. **160**, pp. 68–70,
211   8. **7**, pp. 261, 287, **243**, p. 4   9. **7**, pp. 64, 244   10. **40**, pp. 62–69, **43**, pp. 48–54,
140, pp. 7, 8   11. **553, 554, 544**   12. **557**   13. **562**, 326   14. **557**   15. **558**   16. **185**
17. **45**, pp. 88, 89   18. **570, 555, 556**   19. **563, 40**, pp. 45–47   20. **563**   21. **569**
22. **397**, p. 55   23. **397**, p. 455   24. **555**   25. **56**, p. 144   26. **556**   27. **457**, unpublished speech   28. **554**   29. **397**, p. 457   30. **252**, p. 48   31. **553**   32. **76, 126, 267**

CHAPTER 3

1. **183**, p. 38   2. **243**, pp. 74–75   3. **253**, p. 250   4. **79**, p. 25   5. **253**, pp. 215–216
6. **391**, p. 18   7. **67, 376**   8. **391**, pp. 40–41   9. **453**, petition dated Feb. 26, 1902
10. **315**, Sept. 7, 1891   11. **315**, April and May issues, 1897   12. **315**, Jan. 10, 1899, **197,**
Jan. 10, 1899   13. **315**, Nov. 2, 3, 1899   14. **114**, p. 52   15. **83, 128**   16. **243**, p. 36
17. **252**, p. 48   18. **7**, p. 116   19. **243**, pp. 64–65, **66, 232, 444**   20. **126, 177, 7**, pp. 145–
147, **232**, pp. 29–43, **443**   21. **83**   22. **235**, p. 2   23. **23**   24. **243**, p. 65   25. **635**
26. **635, 232**, pp. 77–79   27. **7**, p. 151, **231**   28. **232, 270**   29. **6**, pp. 8–9   30. **635**
31. **252**, p. 104   32. **143, 468**   33. **472, 271**, pp. 206–209, **344**   34. **125**   35. **81, 143**
36. **7**, p. 242   37. **184**   38. **253**, p. 258   39. **124**   40. **467**   41. **43, 71, 240, 445**, p. 232
42. **124, 233**   43. **243**, pp. 20–23   44. **187**   45. **7**, p. 261   46. **128**, p. 13   47. **128,**
p. 13   48. **88**, p. 27, **184**, p. 135   49. **270**   50. **7**, p. 268, **10**, p. 11   51. **253**, p. 263
52. **243**, p. 85   53. **445**, pp. 85, 345–346, **184**   54. **471, 472, 473**   55. **55**, p. 44

CHAPTER 4

1. **42, 109, 162**   2. **109**, pp. 8–9, **282, 283**, pp. 60–69, **284**, pp. 240–248, **224**   3. **159**, p. 71
4. **43**   5. **42**, pp. 152–154   6. **141**   7. **141, 158**   8. **55**   9. **7**, pp. 163–164   10. **469**

11. **218, 150**   12. **515**   13. **382**   14. **608**   15. **177**, p. 52   16. **360**, p. 49   17. **226**
18. **253**, p. 224   19. **315**, Jan. 19, 1894   20. **315**, June 27, 29, 1893   21. **315**, Jan. 5,
1895   22. **315**, Aug. 17, 1896   23. **315**, Nov. 19. 1897, **197**, Nov. 19, 1897   24. **315**, Dec.
30, 1893   25. **315**, March 15, 29, 1897   26. **315**, April 26, 1890   27. **573**   28. **393**, p.
498   29. **393**, p. 97   30. **253**, pp. 230–231   31. **390**, pp. 683–684   32. **393**, p. 57, **133**,
pp. 8–9   33. **393**, p. 98   34. **390**, p. 690   35. **390**, p. 688   36. **393**, p. 97   37. **390**,
p. 732   38. **393**, pp. 43–44, 126–127   39. **393**, pp. 136–137   40. **393**, pp. 137–138
41. **390**, pp. 720–730, **8**, p, 16   42. **390**, pp. 740–742   43. **390**, p. 740   44. **390**, p. 748
45. **390**   46. **395**, p. 30   47. **390**, pp. 684–685   48. **215**, p. 125   49. **395**, p. 14
50. **395**, p. 39   51. **306**, pp. 87, 93   52. **431**   53. **26, 343**   54. **253**, pp. 322–324
55. **357**, p. 99   56. **593**   57. **294**, p. 145   58. **252**, p. 55   59. **292**, p. 424   60. **253**,
pp. 322–324, 327, **257**   61. **292**, p. 50   62. **575, 576, 611**   63. **572, 575**   64. **608, 585**,
123   65. **109**, pp. 19–21, 33, 52–53, 69, 135–136   66. **218**   67. **584, 587, 588, 589**
68. **602**   69. **445**, pp. 78–79   70. **349**, p. 37, **5**   71. **304**, Oct. 6, 1926, Jan. 30, 1927
72. **282**, pp. 167–169, **223**   73. **17**, p. 31   74. **349**, pp. 94–95   75. **146**, July 22, 1926
76. **349**, pp. 100–101   77. **428**, p. 22   78. **167**, p. 37   79. **419**, p. 11   80. **274**   81. **151**,
May 12, 1960   82. **419**, p. 100   83. **419**, p. 300   84. **146**, July 21, 1930   85. **327**,
pp. 321, 322   86. **308**, March 1940, pp. 45–47, **276, 309, 310**   87. **439**   88. **137**   89. **209**
90. **151**, May 12, 1960   91. **632**   92. **55**   93. **326**, pp. 71–77

CHAPTER 5

1. **624**   2. **11**   3. **98**, pp. 14–20, **239**   4. **440**, p. 17   5. **53**, pp. 114 ff   6. **7**, p. 176
7. **27**, pp. 25–26   8. **253**, p. 206   9. **147**, p. 145, **146**, May 6, April 14, 1930, 304, May 5,
1929   10. **58**, p. 48   11. **306**, pp. 56–58, **440**, p. 27   12. **177**, pp. 49 ff, **58**, p. 43, **306**,
pp. 57–58, **440**, p. 48   13. **334**, p. 94   14. **480, 481, 484**   15. **378**, pp. 176–177, **97, 269**
16. **482, 57, 291**   17. **113**, Oct. 1922, pp. 220–222   18. **431**   19. **253**, p. 240, **154**, for
1922–26   20. **262**, p. 101, **292**, p. 184   21. **243**, p. 88, **59**   22. **292**, pp. 194–196, **253**,
pp. 28, 263, **478**   23. **58**, p. 3, **306**, p. 64, **292**, p. 64, **620**   24. **252**, p. 104   25. **100**, p. 6
26. **58**, pp. 151–157

CHAPTER 6

1. **397**, p. 301   2. **265**, p. 14   3. **35, 292, 426**   4. **290**   5. **292**, p. 133   6. **380**
7. **315**, April 9, 1900   8. **150**, April 17, 1900   9. **150**, April 29, 1900   10. **112**, April 25,
1900; also April 20, 28   11. **150**, April 29, 1900   12. **452**, letters from Commissioner
Edmund S. Boyd to Sanford B. Dole, Feb. 1, 1902, Feb. 10, 1902   13. **198**   14. **315**, Jan.
15, 1901   15. **120**, March 1903, p. 4   16. **570**, this anecdote has not been confirmed by
any other source   17. **632**   18. **266**   19. **456**, unpublished study in memorandum of
Governor Lawrence M. Judd from anonymous assistant   20. **266**, May 23, 1927   21. **292**,
p. 82   22. **457**, letter from George R. Carter to Jonah Kuhio, Aug. 15, 1904; letters from
Kuhio to Presidents of the Merchants Association and Chamber of Commerce, Sept. 2, 1904
23. **457**, letter from Jonah Kuhio to Mr. E. D. Tenney, President of Chamber of Commerce
24. **457**, correspondence connected with Kapiolani Estate; letter to Jonah Kuhio from Paris
Hotel, Nov. 21, 1913; letter from Jonah Kuhio to New York Life Insurance Co., Dec. 20, 1914
25. **303**, Oct. 21, 1913   26. **457**   27. **399**, pp. 7–8   28. **457**, letter from Jonah Kuhio to
the President of the Hawaiian Sugar Planters' Association, Jan. 4, 1904   29. **457**, unpublished notes describing the exchange of letters   30. **519, 530**   31. **457**, letter from Jonah
Kuhio to Jack Atkinson, Secretary of Hawaii, Dec. 28, 1903   32. **457**, letter from Stephen
Desha to Jonah Kuhio, undated; letter from an unknown Hawaiian to Jonah Kuhio, Jan. 4,
1904   33. **457**, letter from Curtis P. Iaukea to Jonah Kuhio, Jan. 16, 1903   34. **457**,
letter from Curtis P. Iaukea to Jonah Kuhio, Jan. 17, 1904   35. **457**, letter from Curtis
P. Iaukea to Jonah Kuhio, Jan. 16, 1903   36. **530, 561**   37. **457**, letter from A. N.
Kepoikai to Jonah Kuhio, Jan. 6, 1904   38. **457**, letter from Curtis P. Iaukea to Jonah
Kuhio, Jan. 6, 1904   39. **457**, letter from Jonah Kuhio to John Lane, April 6, 1906   40. **457**,
letter from John Lane to Jonah Kuhio, Feb. 2, 1906   41. **457**, letter from John Lane to
Jonah Kuhio, Feb. 2, 1906   42. **457**, letter from Jonah Kuhio to John Lane, April 6, 1906
43. **457**, letter from H. L. Holstein to Jonah Kuhio, May 7, 1908   44. **457**, letter from
W. J. Coelho to Jonah Kuhio, March 5, 1910   45. **332**, Vol. 1, p. 4, **457**, letter from
Jonah Kuhio to Walter L. Fisher, Secretary of the Interior, April 2, 1912   46. **457**, letter
from W. K. Kinney to Jonah Kuhio, undated   47. **457**, letter from W. K. Kinney to Jonah
Kuhio, Nov. 1911   48. **457**, letter from W. K. Kinney to Jonah Kuhio, April 2, 1912
49. **457**, letter from John Lane to Jonah Kuhio, Feb. 21, 1911   50. **457**, letter from
Edward Henriques to Jonah Kuhio, April 18, 1921   51. **457**, letter from W. K. Kinney to
Jonah Kuhio, July 1912   52. **457**, letter from John Lane to Jonah Kuhio, Feb. 18, 1913
53. **457**, letter from Jonah Kuhio to Lucius E. Pinkham, Aug. 28, 1913   54. **457**, exchange
of letters between W. K. Kinney and Jonah Kuhio, July 1912   55. **457**, letter from H. L.

Holstein to John Desha, June 27, 1914   56. **454,** speech by Lincoln L. McCandless at Wailuku, undated   57. **457,** letter from H. L. Holstein to Jonah Kuhio, July 29, 1914   58. **457,** letter from H. L. Holstein to John Desha, Aug. 12, 1914   59. **530**   60. **455,** letter from Charles B. Dwight to Victor K. Houston, Nov. 8, 1927   61. **322,** p. 38   62. **563**   63. **455,** see exchange of telegrams with Hawaiian Sugar Planters' Association executive, Jack K. Butler, in the late '20's   64. **455,** letter from Riley Allen to Victor K. Houston, Jan. 10, 1930   65. **455,** letter from Walter F. Dillingham to Victor K. Houston, July 25, 1930   66. **632**   67. **632**   68. **419,** p. 92   69. **397,** p. 9   70. **464,** letter from Louis Cain to John H. Wilson, Nov. 25, 1933   71. **397,** p. 349   72. **428,** p. 34   73. **428,** p. 40   74. **565**   75. **473, 507, 586, 593**   76. **632**   77. **428,** p. 16   78. **146,** Jan. 9, 1928   79. **146,** Feb. 1928. Also Feb. 4, 1928 of the *Hawaii Asahi*   80. **146,** Nov. 1, 1930, and Nov. 31, 1930, for examples   81. **230,** June 14, 1929, **449,** June 18, 1929   82. **445,** letter from Jack K. Butler to Victor K. Houston, undated   83. **464,** letters from John H. Wilson to James A. Farley, April 6, 9, 1935   84. **446**   85. **55,** pp. 58–59   86. **632**

CHAPTER 7

1. **632, 522**   2. **459, 464,** various letters and memoranda   3. **464,** letter from John H. Wilson to Lincoln L. McCandless, March 20, 1913   4. **464,** letter dated April 4, 1913   5. **464,** letter from John H. Wilson to Franklin K. Lane, Secretary of the Interior, Feb. 7, 1918   6. **461,** letter from Lucius E. Pinkham to Miki Saito, Japanese Consul-General, Oct. 1, 1907   7. **461,** letter from Lucius E. Pinkham to Royal P. Mead, Nov. 13, 1914   8. **461,** letters from Henry A. Baldwin to Lucius E. Pinkham, Jan. 28, 1914, and from Pinkham to Baldwin, March 18, 1916, and June 18, 1917   9. **461,** letter from Lucius E. Pinkham to Charles Rice, May 13, 1915   10. **461,** letter from Charles Rice to Lucius E. Pinkham, May 28, 1915   11. **461,** letters from John M. Ross to Lucius E. Pinkham, Jan. 30, 1914, and June 8, 1914   12. **464,** memorandum from John H. Wilson to President Woodrow Wilson, July 16, 1914; memorandum from M. C. Pachecho to John H. Wilson, April 30, 1914   13. **464,** memorandum from John H. Wilson to President Woodrow Wilson, July 16, 1914   14. **303,** Oct. 1, 1914, Nov. 2, 1914   15. **303,** Nov. 2, 1914   16. **522**   17. **460,** letter from Charles J. McCarthy to Henry A. Baldwin, May 1920   18. **460,** letter from Walter F. Dillingham to Charles J. McCarthy, June 13, 1921   19. **464**   20. **456,** July 5, 1929   21. **455**   22. **456,** telegram from Victor K. Houston to Lawrence M. Judd, Jan. 13, 1932   23. **426**   24. **146,** May 20, 1932   25. **455,** letter from Henry A. Baldwin to Victor K. Houston, Dec. 11, 1932   26. **459,** letter from Delbert E. Metzger to Lincoln L. McCandless, March 25, 1933   27. **464,** letter from John H. Wilson to J. Walter Doyle, Sept. 19, 1933   28. **459,** letter from Lincoln L. McCandless to Manuel DeMello, May 30, 1934   29. **459,** letter from Lincoln L. McCandless to President Franklin D. Roosevelt, March 20, 1933   30. **464,** letter from James A. Farley to John H. Wilson, April 12, 1932; letter from John H. Wilson to President Franklin D. Roosevelt, April 5, 1932   31. **459,** letters from James McCandless to Lincoln L. McCandless, March 7, 1933, April 4, 12, 1933; letter from Lincoln L. McCandless to James McCandless, April 28, 1933   32. **459,** letter from Lincoln L. McCandless to James A. Farley, May 24, 1933   33. **459,** letter from Lincoln L. McCandless to James A. Farley, July 13, 1933   34. **459,** letter from Rufus H. Hagood to Lincoln L. McCandless, May 3, 1933   35. **459,** letter from Rufus H. Hagood to Lincoln L. McCandless, May 20, 1933   36. **459,** letter from Delbert E. Metzger to Lincoln L. McCandless, March 25, 1933   37. **459,** letter from Lincoln L. McCandless to Louis Howe, Jan. 13, 1933   38. **464,** letter from Jerome J. Marshal to John H. Wilson, Aug. 2, 1933   39. **464,** letter from John H. Wilson to Jerome J. Marshal, July 26, 1933   40. **464,** letter from John H. Wilson to Claus Roberts, July 27, 1933   41. **464,** letter from Jerome J. Marshal to John H. Wilson, undated   42. **464,** memorandum written by John H. Wilson on conference with Secretary of Interior Harold Ickes, Jan. 8, 1934; also letter from John H. Wilson to Louis Cain, Jan. 8, 1934   43. **462**   44. **462,** memoranda and records concerning the visit of Franklin D. Roosevelt to Hawaii   45. **462,** letter from the Waipahu Civic Club to Joseph B. Poindexter, July 24, 1934   46. **462,** memoranda and records concerning the visit of Franklin D. Roosevelt to Hawaii   47. **464,** letter from John H. Wilson to James A. Farley, March 22, 1937   48. **464,** letter from Delbert E. Metzger to James A. Farley, April 13, 1935   49. **464,** letter from Walter F. Sanborn to James A. Farley, April 18, 1935   50. **464,** letter from George Watase to John H. Wilson, undated   51. **464,** letter from William C. Achi to John H. Wilson, Oct. 12, 1938   52. **459,** letter from Manuel DeMello to Lincoln L. McCandless, March 13, 1933   53. **459,** letter from Lincoln L. McCandless to James McCandless, April 28, 1933   54. **459,** letter from James McCandless to Lincoln L. McCandless, April 12, 1933   55. **464,** letter from E. Colvillen to John H. Wilson, Aug. 30, 1934, **459,** letter from James McCandless to Lincoln L. McCandless, April 4, 1933   56. **464,** letter from John H. Wilson to an unidentified person, Dec. 1, 1934; letter from William C. Achi to U.S. Senator William H. King, Oct. 12, 1934   57. **464,** letter from John H. Wilson to James A. Farley, Jan. 14, 1935   58. **303,** Sept. 8, 1934, for example   59. **414**   60. **452,**

letter from George R. Carter to Henry P. Baldwin, Dec. 12, 1904   61. **452,** letters from Henry P. Baldwin to George R. Carter, Feb. 22, March 12, Oct. 7, 1904   62. **452,** letter from Henry P. Baldwin to George R. Carter, undated   63. **454,** letter from Lorrin Andrews to Wallace R. Farrington, Oct. 5, 1921   64. **459,** letter from Leslie Burr to U.S. Senator William H. King, Dec. 30, 1933   65. **454,** letter from Henry A. Baldwin to Wallace R. Farrington, July 27, 1923; letter from Wallace R. Farrington to Henry A. Baldwin, July 30, 1923   66. **454,** letters from Henry A. Baldwin to Wallace R. Farrington, Jan. 12, 1926, Jan. 26, 1926, March 9, 1926, **456,** letter from Henry A. Baldwin to Lawrence M. Judd, Jan. 9, 1932   67. **561, 586, 617**   68. **452,** letter from George R. Carter to William H. Rice, Jr., Feb. 10, 1906   69. **452,** letter from Walter Frear to Charles Rice, Sept. 26, 1910   70. **452,** letter from Charles Rice to Walter Frear, June 20, 1913   71. **464,** letter from John H. Wilson to James A. Farley, April 6, 1935   72. **530, 616, 617**   73. **325,** Jan. 8, 1853   74. **33,** Sept. 13, 1951   75. **464,** letter from Charles Otani to John H. Wilson, April 26, 1935   76. **521, 533, 601**   77. **464,** letter from Louis Cain to U.S. Senator Arthur H. Vandenberg, Nov. 14, 1933

CHAPTER 8

1. **368,** p. 144   2. **79**   3. **253,** p. 214   4. **79,** p. 51   5. **348,** pp. 345–346   6. **315,** March 15, 1894   7. **293,** pp. 14–15   8. **315,** July 3, 1900   9. **315,** July 26, 1904   10. **391,** p. 18   11. **453,** letter from Henry E. Cooper to William O. Smith, May 17, 1903   12. **453,** letter from Sheriff Andrews to High Sheriff Arthur M. Brown, June 27, 1902   13. **452,** report from Sheriff Arthur M. Brown to Governor George R. Carter, 1905   14. **393,** pp. 33–34, 41   15. **393,** p. 109   16. **438,** p. 136   17. **457,** letter from George R. Carter to Jonah Kuhio, Jan. 18, 1904   18. **98,** pp. 7–10   19. **338,** letter from George F. Fairchild to the Labor Commission of Hawaii, 1895   20. **315,** Jan. 16–22, 1906   21. **393,** p. 59   22. **393,** p. 48   23. **393,** p. 61   24. **393,** pp. 46, 47   25. **31**   26. **161,** p. 50   27. **317**   28. **393,** p. 134   29. **390,** p. 726   30. **390,** p. 726, **253,** p. 234   31. **390,** p. 751   32. **428,** p. 30   33. **390,** p. 727, **425**   34. **35,** pp. 331–333   35. **394,** p. 66   36. **166,** Oct. 6, 1949   37. **245,** p. 59   38. **383, 304,** Oct. and Nov. issues, 1919   39. **338**   40. **315,** Jan. 15, 1920   41. **304,** Jan 3, 1920   42. **338,** Jan. 20, 1920   43. **146,** Jan. 21, 1920   44. **315,** Jan. 27, 1920   45. **304,** Jan. 28, 1920   46. **315,** Feb. 3, 1920   47. **315,** Feb. 5, 1920   48. **315,** Feb. 8, 1920   49. **315,** Feb. 11, 1920   50. **383**   51. **338**   52. **146,** Feb. 17, 1920   53. **167,** July 12, 1920   54. **167,** Feb. 4, 1920   55. **315,** Feb. 12, 1920   56. **146,** Feb. 10, 1920   57. **304,** Feb. 21, 1920   58. **428**   59. **167,** Feb. 23, 1920   60. **315,** Feb. 24, 1920   61. **315,** Feb. 25, 1920   62. **315,** Feb. 27, 28, 1920   63. **304,** March 18, 1920   64. **304,** March 24, 1920   65. **167,** March 27, 1920   66. **304,** March 27, 1920   67. **315,** March 6, 12, 1920   68. **315,** April 7, 1920   69. **167,** April 26, 1920   70. **304,** April 21, 1920   71. **304,** April 22, 1920   72. **304,** April 23, 1920   73. **315,** Nov. 30, 1920   74. **338**   75. **338**

CHAPTER 9

1. **460,** notes and memoranda   2. **397,** pp. 230, 402, 403   3. **397,** pp. 215, 256   4. **397,** p. 355   5. **397,** p. 390   6. **397,** p. 477   7. **397,** p. 502   8. **397,** p. 506   9. **419,** p. 5   10. **419,** p. 15   11. **460**   12. **397,** p. 393   13. **397,** p. 659   14. **397,** pp. 374, 687   15. **397,** p. 744   16. **454,** letter from Walter F. Dillingham to Wallace R. Farrington, Feb. 17, 1922   17. **454,** letters from Walter F. Dillingham to Wallace R. Farrington, April 28, June 2, 1922   18. **419,** p. 75   19. **419,** pp. 85, 91   20. **454,** cables from Walter F. Dillingham to Wallace R. Farrington, March 7, June 19, 1922   21. **165,** Jan. 30, 1922   22. **165,** Jan. 4, 1922   23. **454,** letter from Wallace R. Farrington to Walter F. Dillingham, Feb. 17, 1922   24. **165,** March 8, 1922   25. **245**   26. **245,** pp. 39, 44   27. **246,** pp. 15, 16   28. **278**   29. **454**   30. **454,** letter from Sheriff William H. Rice to Wallace R. Farrington, Sept. 20, 1924   31. **478**   32. **202,** p. 70   33. **202,** p. 71, **478,** this anecdote has not been verified by another source   34. **278,** p. 99   35. **165,** Jan. 8, 1922   36. **98,** pp. 66, 70   37. **454,** exchange of telegrams and letters between Victor K. Houston and Wallace R. Farrington, 1931–32   38. **454,** letter from Victor K. Houston to Wallace R. Farrington, Jan. 8, 1932   39. **146,** March 17, 1932   40. **98,** p. 99   41. **26,** p. 48   42. **245,** p. 100   43. **26,** p. 51   44. **245,** p. 100   45. **437,** Nov. 11, 1935, Oct. 21, 1937   46. **202,** p. 88, **338**   47. **514**   48. **431**   49. **202,** p. 89

CHAPTER 10

1. **507, 550**   2. **91**   3. **390,** p. 81   4. **377,** Ch. 3, **523**   5. **377,** Ch. 2   6. **395,** pp. 11–13   7. **390,** p. 81   8. **26,** p. 23, **377,** Ch. 3, **393,** p. 9   9. **328,** pp. 171, 172   10. **253,** p. 183   11. **457,** p. 29   12. **521**   13. **303,** May 12, 1923   14. **572, 395,** p. 38   15. **479**

16. **253**, p. 183   17. **575**   18. **321**, May 12, 1923   19. **488**   20. **395**, p. 61   21. **321**, p. 76   22. **65**   23. **357**, pp. 84, 85   24. **253**, pp. 170, 171   25. **292**, **357**   26. **39**   27. **368**, p. 144   28. **393**, p. 83   29. **393**, pp. 83, 84   30. **406**, p. 73   31. **406**, p. 34   32. **406**, report of Governor Walter F. Frear on conservation, p. 36   33. **406**, p. 40   34. **456**, summary of land laws and land policies of the Territory of Hawaii in the form of memoranda   35. **456, 406**, p. 59   36. **329**, p. 139   37. **434**   38. **406**, p. 61, **457**   39. **332**   40. **434**, p. 31   41. **331**   42. **401, 407**   43. **253**, p. 86   44. **455**, letter from Charles B. Dwight to Victor K. Houston, Nov. 8, 1927   45. **456**, memorandum from C. T. Bailey, Commissioner of Public Land, to Joseph R. Farrington   46. **279**

CHAPTER 11

1. **545**   2. **442, 292**   3. **393**, pp. 123, 124   4. **442**   5. **370**   6. **370**, p. 34   7. **393**, pp. 123–124   8. **452**   9. **35**, p. 38   10. **587, 588, 589**   11. **433**, report of the Governor for 1911   12. **514**, this anecdote was not verified by another source   13. **452**, letter from the Superintendent of Schools, Mr. W. H. Babbit, to A. L. C. Atkinson, Secretary of the Territory, Aug. 6, 1907   14. **315**, Jan. 22, 23, 1912, **425**   15. **544**, this anecdote has not been verified by another source   16. **434**, pp. 52, 53   17. **461**, statement by Governor Walter F. Frear, June 5, 1913   18. **441**, pp. 130, 131   19. **434**, pp. 5, 31   20. **434**, pp. 68, 74, 105–106, 186–187   21. **434**, pp. 219, 223, 234, 250, 251   22. **434**, p. 307   23. **434**, p. 280, **442**, p. 181, **370**, p. 36   24. **454, 99**   25. **434**, pp. 113, 247   26. **434**, pp. 112, 113   27. **428**, pp. 29–33   28. **78**, pp. 588, 589   29. **86**, p. 112, **41**   30. **85**, p. 196, **157, 171, 182, 339**   31. **393**, p. 58   32. **547**   33. **17**   34. **544**   35. **454**, minutes of meetings of the Commissioners of Public Instruction, 1926–28. For example, see April 26–28, 1926   36. **60**, pp. 20–21   37. **545, 596**   38. **157**   39. **636**   40. **609, 610**   41. **454**, letter from Wallace R. Farrington to Vaughn MacCaughey, May 20, 1922   42. **454**   43. **454**, letter from Wallace R. Farrington to Vaughn MacCaughey, Feb. 14, 1923   44. **454**, letter from Wallace R. Farrington to Will C. Crawford, Dec. 3, 1925   45. **454**   46. **146**, Aug. 7, 1928, **304**, Aug. 8, 1928   47. **154**, Nov. 16, 1925   48. **563**   49. **154**, Nov. 16, 1926   50. **63**, p. 4   51. **303**, March 19, 1922, **146, 304**   52. **434**   53. **144**, Oct. 1, 1921, and other issues in 1921–23   54. **454**, unclassified material on education in Hawaii   55. **243**, p. 33   56. **546, 610**   57. **144**, Jan. 1927   58. **243**, p. 63   59. **94**, pp. 6, 12   60. **94**, pp. 205–227   61. **94**, p. 22   62. **93**, p. 5   63. **454**, letter from Miles E. Cary to Wallace R. Farrington, May 18, 1926   64. **60**, pp. 347, 119   65. **60**, pp. 70 ff, 91   66. **454**, letter from Will C. Crawford to Wallace R. Farrington, March 5, 1929   67. **60**, pp. 142–147   68. **463**, memorandum from the Department of Public Instruction   69. **60**, p. 178   70. **456**   71. **4**, for this and the material that follows   72. **4**, p. 30   73. **4**   74. **434**, pp. 263, 264   75. **275**   76. **60**, p. 28   77. **60**, p. 22   78. **481, 545**   79. **442**, p. 181   80. **60**, p. 29   81. **456**, letter from Frank E. Midkiff to Frank C. Atherton, June 16, 1928   82. **456**, letter from Frank E. Midkiff to Frank C. Atherton, Dec. 8, 1929   83. **456**, letter from Lawrence M. Judd to Richard A. Cooke, Sept. 23, 1929   84. **456**, memoranda and letters on educational survey for this and material that follows   85. **456**   86. **456**   87. **165**, March 9, 1933   88. **146**, Feb. 9, 1931   89. **442**, p. 165   90. **165**, Feb. 9, 1931   91. **146**, Jan. 4, 1936, April 10, 1936, Dec. 20, 1936, **165**, Oct. 18, 1936, **167**, Jan. 11, 15, 1936   92. **275**, p. 67   93. **167**, Sept. 8, 1936, **544**   94. **165**, Aug. 3, 1933, Feb. 6, 1936   95. **544**   96. **442**, p. 168   97. **99**   98. **442**, p. 143   99. **370**, pp. 73, 74, 25   100. **462**, records of the Department of Public Instruction

CHAPTER 12

1. **416, 25, 30.**   2. **30**, p. 9   3. **202**, pp. 94, 95, **30**, pp. 41–45   4. **30**, pp. 29–30   5. **30**, p. 107   6. **25**, Ch. 3, **216**   7. **54**, pp. 7–13, **222**   8. **36**   9. **453**, memorandum from Riley Allen, Sept. 27, 1943   10. **463**, letter from Harold Rice to Ingram M. Stainback, Feb. 4, 1944   11. **360**, pp. 181–185, **219**, p. 47   12. **25**, pp. 138–139   13. **166**, Dec. 7, 1950. The statement was made on Sept. 11, 1944   14. **111**   15. **210**, pp. 191–192   16. **575, 220, 251, 218, 353**   17. **586**   18. **353**   19. **218**   20. **251**, pp. 121, 122, **229, 299, 300, 336, 355**   21. **299**

CHAPTER 13

1. **596**   2. **453, 448**, letter from Harold Ickes to Marvin McIntyre, Nov. 28, 1941   3. **464**, letter from John H. Wilson to James L. Coke, April 23, 1939   4. **463, 464**   5. **463**, letter from Ingram M. Stainback to J. P. C. Cooke, Oct. 31, 1944   6. **463**, letters and memoranda   7. **422**, p. 15   8. **422**, pp. 307, 380   9. **167**, Nov. 7, 1956   10. **464**, letter from John H. Wilson to Oscar L. Chapman, Aug. 14, 1950   11. **463**, letter from Ingram M. Stainback to Oscar L. Chapman, May 14, 1948   12. **463**, letter from Ingram M. Stainback to Oscar L.

Chapman, May 14, 1948   13. **402,** pp. 2725–2728   14. **464,** letter from John H. Wilson to President Harry S. Truman, undated   15. **590, 591**   16. **518, 520, 536, 569, 590, 591, 597, 600**   17. **590, 591, 600**   18. **464,** letter from Delbert E. Metzger to James A. Farley, April 13, 1935   19. **526, 601**   20. **151,** May 12, 1950   21. **626**   22. **632**   23. **475**

CHAPTER 14

1. **453,** letter from David Bray to President Dwight D. Eisenhower, Jan. 7, 1953   2. **453,** letter from Samuel Wilder King to Senator Robert Taft, Jan. 2, 1953   3. **538, 565**   4. **453,** letter from Riley Allen to Joseph R. Farrington, Oct. 6, 1943   5. **453,** letter from Riley Allen to Joseph R. Farrington, July 11, 1948   6. **628**   7. **632, 95, 384**   8. **628**   9. **167,** Sept. 10, 1958   10. **167,** Sept. 5, 1958, **165,** May 19, 1958   11. **167,** Charles Parmiter, Aug. 7, 1958   12. **541**   13. **541**   14. **167,** Oct. 22, 1958   15. **630**   16. **165, 167,** Sept.–Oct. 1958   17. **630**   18. **472, 534, 535, 536, 590, 598, 603**   19. **590, 591**   20. **627**   21. **499, 512, 591, 593**   22. **167,** Charles Parmiter, Oct. 14, 1958   23. **402, 411, 423, 436, 474, 475, 477, 485, 486, 525, 531, 564, 566, 567, 568, 569, 581, 582, 590, 591, 592, 593, 594, 595, 596, 597, 598, 599, 600, 601, 602, 603**   24. **554, 555, 556**   25. **631**   26. **624**   27. **521, 526, 601**   28. **585**

CHAPTER 15

1. **578**   2. **202,** p. 96, **430**   3. **430,** p. 21   4. **217**   5. **317,** p. 273   6. **430,** p. 184   7. **26,** pp. 43–45   8. **26,** p. 48   9. **430,** pp. 184 ff, **202,** pp. 107–110   10. **26,** p. 57   11. **430,** p. 177   12. **225, 430,** p. 178   13. **26,** pp. 82–86   14. **80, 202,** p. 122   15. **202,** p. 124   16. **26,** p. 189, **50,** p. 264, **202,** pp. 125–132   17. **165,** July 15, 1949   18. **386**   19. **202,** pp. 125–132   20. **482, 580**   21. **627**   22. **481**   23. **508, 510**   24. **199, 402, 403, 404, 405, 422**   25. **199**   26. **514, 536**   27. **402,** p. 2811, **422,** p. 384   28. **402,** pp. 2698, 2813   29. **502,** this allegation has not been verified by a second source   30. **301**   31. **402,** pp. 2568–2581   32. **402,** p. 2367   33. **402,** p. 2757   34. **578**   35. **367,** Vol. 8, 1958, 320   36. **630**   37. **465, 466, 467, 479, 576, 577, 579**   38. **167,** Sept. 19, 1958   39. **519**   40. **193,** 1956–58, for example see Sept. 19, 1958, **508, 509, 510, 512, 513, 514, 536**   41. **627**

CHAPTER 16

1. **304,** Aug. 14, 1928   2. **85,** pp. 225, 258   3. **292,** p. 46   4. **7,** pp. 41–42   5. **253,** p. 282   6. **37,** reports for 1957–60   7. **252,** p. 241   8. **37,** report for midyear, 1960   9. **165,** Jan. 1, 1959   10. **206,** release for June 17, 1959   11. **575**   12. **624**   13. **167,** Nov. 17, 1959   14. **550**   15. **165,** June 19, 1960, **487, 488, 492, 493, 495, 496, 498, 499, 500, 513, 548, 549, 550, 551, 552**   16. **465, 469, 491**   17. **37,** report for 1960   18. **321,** p. 122   19. **359**   20. **318**   21. **37,** *Monthly Review of Business and Economic Conditions,* Jan.–Dec. 1959   22. **196**

CHAPTER 17

1. **455,** letter from Victor K. Houston to Henry A. Baldwin, May 21, 1959   2. **190**   3. **455,** letter from Henry A. Baldwin to Victor K. Houston, undated   4. **455,** letter from Clarence H. Cooke to Victor K. Houston, April 1933   5. **458**   6. **398, 411, 412, 413, 415, 420, 421, 422, 423, 427**   7. **411, 422, 423**   8. **345,** pp. 75, 76   9. **167,** Oct. 31, 1940   10. **165,** March 3, 1958   11. **167,** June 3, 1958   12. **167,** June 20, 1958   13. **165,** May 4, 1958   14. *Congressional Record,* 85th Congress, 2nd Session, March 11, 1956, p. 3454   15. *Congressional Record,* 85th Congress, 2nd Session, March 11, 1956, p. 3464   16. **167,** Sept. 19, 1958   17. **422,** p. 76   18. **167,** Aug. 26, 1958   19. **51,** p. 16   20. **630**   21. **631**   22. **476, 615, 618, 625**   23. **631**   24. **590, 591**   25. **167,** April 29, 1959   26. **165, 167**   27. **527, 528, 529**   28. **149, 495**   29. **96**   30. **580**   31. **630**   32. **152**   33. **323,** April 1959, p. 16   34. **323,** Jan. 1959, p. 25   35. **306,** p. 48   36. **26, 191, 192**   37. **153**   38. **627**   39. **195**   40. **167,** Dec. 1, 1958   41. **101**   42. **145**   43. **375**   44. **102, 104, 374**   45. **207,** p. 21   46. **188**   47. **333**   48. **165,** Feb. 25, 1945   49. **39**   50. **167,** Aug. 29, 1958   51. **165,** May 11, 1959   52. **167,** Dec. 30, 1958, **103**   53. **252,** p. 87   54. **92**   55. **630**   56. **105**   57. **630**   58. **621, 496, 548**   59. **466, 469, 489**   60. **252,** p. 76   61. **627**   62. **243**   63. **75**   64. **69,** p. 164   65. **243,** p. 81, **69**   66. **634**   67. **178,** Jan. 27, 1959   68. **577**   69. **606**   70. **306,** p. 123   71. **484**   72. **624**   73. **631**   74. **631**   75. **564**   76. **84, 555, 564**   77. **165,** April 1959   78. **314**   79. Special statehood pamphlet, Kawaiahao Church   80. **489**   81. **314**

INDEX

491